MAKING IT UP AS YOU GO ALONG
NOTES FROM A BASS IMPOSTOR

OR

A SHORT SOCIAL & POLITICAL HISTORY OF ROCK 'N' ROLL IN SOUTH LONDON
1966 -1980

BILL MacCORMICK

IONA BOOKS

British Library Cataloguing In Publication Data
A Record of this Publication is available
from the British Library

ISBN 978-0-9558119-7-5

Published 2024 by Iona Books
and printed by Lightning Source, Milton Keynes

Cover design by Nigel Soper
(http://www.nigelsoper.com/)

Also by Bill MacCormick writing as Alan MacDonald:

Pro Patria Mori
The 56th (1st London) Division at Gommecourt, 1st July 1916

A Lack of Offensive Spirit?
The 46th (North Midland) Division at Gommecourt, 1st July 1916

Z Day, 1st July 1916
The Attack of the VIII Corps at Beaumont Hamel and Serre, 1st July 1916

The Affair at Lagarde
10th-11th August 1914

Episodes on the Long Road to the Somme
Britain and France, 1870-1915

The Long Road to the Somme
Planning the Big Push

Liberating Elsaβ
The French Invasions of Alsace, August 1914

Profits Without Honour
The British Arms Trade and the Great War
(with annotated versions of: *The War Traders* by G H Perris &
Le Patriotisme des Plaques Blindées: L'affaire Poutiloff
by F Delaisi)

CONTENTS

PHOTOGRAPHS

THIS BOOK IS DEDICATED TO:
PHIL MILLER
HUGH HOPPER
GARY WINDO
LLOYD WATSON
FRANCIS MONKMAN
DAVID FERGUSON
&
IAN MACDONALD MACCORMICK

AND, LASTLY, A NOTE TO ANYONE
DAFT ENOUGH TO READ THIS

BE WARNED:
I either have a fantastic memory
or a very vivid imagination.
Or possibly both.
Maybe neither.
Buggered if I know which, if any, is true.
Or I could just be barking

READER DISCRETION ADVISED

ACKNOWLEDGEMENTS

WE SHALL TRY TO BE BRIEF HERE. Obviously I need to thank all of the proper musicians I played with between 1970 and 1980 and apologise to them for my many musical inadequacies. Thank you for putting up with me for more than a decade. Well above and beyond the call of duty.

Two names stand out: Phil Manzanera – old school friend, musical collaborator and, of course, psychedelic guitarist *par excellence*. We have known one another for over sixty years, meeting at Dulwich College in 1962, and have been involved in one project or another in every decade since. His autobiographical version of some of the events described within, *Revolucion to Roxy*, comes out in 2024. Let's hope there aren't too many discrepancies between his book and mine. The sight of two old men arguing about who has the best memory would not be an edifying one.

And Robert Wyatt, who I first met in 1966 and who was a key person in my musical 'journey' over the next ten years. We keep in touch and the last time we met, after he was awarded a Gold Badge by the *British Academy of Songwriters, Composers and Authors*, it was as if we were simply resuming a conversation interrupted a few minutes earlier when one or other of us went off to make a new pot of tea. One of the great British musicians and composers of the last sixty years and just a wonderful person to know.

Next, I need to recognise the sterling work of the two main published 'historians' of parts of this period: the late Mike King whose *Wrong Movements* (SAF Publishing Ltd., 1994) charts the history of Robert Wyatt through to 1993; and Marcus O'Dair who, in *Different Every Time* (Serpent's Tail, 2014), produced a detailed and moving biography of Robert. I was happy to have helped with some of the detail for each book.

I must also fulsomely thank Phil Howitt who has been of immense help both as a Canterbury archivist, through his fanzine and *Facebook* page *Facelift*, but also as a proofreader, suggester of good ideas – in the main :-) – and corrector of errors. His reflections and comments on earlier drafts have been invaluable and helped immensely in getting the project finished. And, all the while, he was working on his own biography of the late and much-lamented Hugh Hopper. So, go seek that out when it emerges. Check with the publishers *Jazz in Britain* for when it's due.

No references to the details of the Canterbury Scene would be possible without acknowledging the research and writing of Aymeric Leroy, the archivist of all things Canterbury (and other bands too, i.e. *Yes* and *King Crimson*). His web site – *http://www.calyx-canterbury.fr* – is an essential resource for anyone interested in any of the bands linked, however tenuously, to what has become known, rather loosely IMO, as the

Canterbury Scene. He is also the author of a book about the Canterbury Scene even weightier than the tome you currently hold in your hands. His 726-page *L'École de Canterbury*, first published in April 2016, is currently only available in the French edition. Hopefully it is being published in the USA/UK in 2024/5.

A lot of the facts herein have pretty much been stolen from the four people mentioned above. Everything else, dates, times, places... memories (whether right or wrong), are entirely down to me. So, sue me, if necessary.

No book is much use without a cover and I must thank Nigel Soper for discreetly clothing this little item. Nigel also produced the striking cover of the *Quiet Sun Mainstream* album back in 1975. So there's a certain symmetry to him closing out my musical 'career' in 2024.

Lastly, two people even closer to home.

My late brother, Ian MacDonald MacCormick, music writer and critic, assistant editor of the *New Musical Express*, and author of, amongst others, *Revolution in the Head*, a book about *The Beatles* still recognised as one of the best ever written about the Fab Four. In about 2000, frustrated by what he saw as my tendency to collect vast amounts of information about a particular subject with no end product he told me, in no uncertain terms, 'to do something useful with it. Write a book!'. The subject, in this case, was the 1916 Battle of the Somme in which our grandfather won the Military Cross and was nearly killed and a cousin of my mother disappeared on the awful first day, 1st July 1916, It had never occurred to me that I *could* write a book. It was not something idiots like me attempted. But I did. Sadly, he did not live to see the results published in 2006. Two more military history books have emerged since and four more will be published in 2024. I doubt I would have ever contemplated writing this volume without that initial, if metaphorical, kick up the back side. So blame him.

Finally, my wife, Helen, who has put up with more than enough nonsense from me over the last fifty years and will be delighted when I stop bunnying on at inordinate length about music, politics, and life in general. Ever patient and supportive, none of this would have been possible without her.

So you can blame her too.

Bill MacCormick
West Wickham, 2024

INTRODUCTION

OVER THE PAST FEW YEARS I have written a number of short pieces on *Facebook* recounting various episodes in my brief time as a professional bass player with a variety of obscure and mostly unsuccessful bands. Well, unsuccessful in commercial terms at least. I will leave it to those who have, or might yet, listen to the output of the various projects in which I was involved to determine whether they have any musical merit.

Sadly, over the years, several of the musicians I played with have departed to the great gig in the sky and I thought that, in some way, writing about them, and what we did together back in the 1970s, might be some small memorial to them.

Of course, the '70s are a long, long time ago and people seem to forget that time. This was brought home to me when I recently attended a memorial for the late Francis Monkman. Part of the day was spent listening to his friends and relatives talking about Francis and his work. It seemed not one of them either remembered his early career or, indeed, knew him back in those times. That period went unmentioned. *Curved Air* was one band strangely ignored. Perhaps less surprising was the absence of any reference to the rather more obscure *801* project of 1976. That this highlighted his brilliance as both a soloist and accompanist is sadly forgotten. I regret, now, not speaking up and talking about those times when Francis seemed a happier and more contented man than sadly seems to have been the case in in later years.

So, in a way, the things I write about here, either more or less irreverently, are intended, in part, to refresh others' memories about some of the great but lesser-known musicians this country has produced but who have since left us.

Six musicians come to mind:

PHIL MILLER, a guitar virtuoso and unique instrumental voice with whom I worked in *Matching Mole* and who sadly died on 18th October 2017. You should visit the *Phil Miller Legacy* website to get a full picture of Phil's career (*https://philmillerthelegacy.com*);

HUGH HOPPER who died on 7th June 2009. I never really worked with Hugh (though we did play together on a few bits of Gary Windo's *Steam Radio Tapes* in 1976) but knew him from 1969. He very generously helped me with some very useful bass exercises whilst *Mole* and the *Softs* briefly toured together in September 1972. His style (and his use of a fuzz box!) influenced me greatly. His official website is here: *http://www.hugh-hopper.com*;

The raucous, joyful sax player GARY WINDO who was to be a member of *Matching Mole Mk. II* but for Robert Wyatt's accident, and with whom I both gigged and worked alongside in the studio. He died way too early on 25th July 1992 at the tragically young age of 51. You can find out more about Gary's career here: *http://www.calyx-canterbury.fr/mus/windo_gary.html*;

LLOYD WATSON, slide guitarist extraordinaire whose singing and playing adorned the *801 Live* album of 1976 and who, it seems, almost single-handedly put Peterborough on the musical map of Great Britain until his untimely death on 19th November 2019. Lloyd's official web site is at: *http://www.lloydwatsonmusic.co.uk*;

The aforementioned and brilliant FRANCIS MONKMAN who passed on 12th May 2023 and who I first met, and became friends with, in 1972, and who worked on Phil Manzanera's *Listen Now* album and, of course, on the *801 Live* project. For an extended interview with Francis covering his whole career please visit the rather wonderful *Uzbekistan Progressive Rock Pages* at: *http://www.progressor.net/interview/francis_monkman.html*;

and finally…

DAVID FERGUSON, one of the founders of *Random Hold* who went on to be a leading composer of TV and film scores and a hugely successful Chairman of the *British Academy of Songwriters, Composers and Authors* (then *BASCA* and now the *Ivor's Academy*) and who died, again way too early, on 5th July 2009, aged 56.

There are others mentioned here I knew less well but who should also be recognised and remembered, amongst them PIP PYLE, DAEVID ALLEN, KEVIN AYERS and, so recently, the great CARLA BLEY.

And then there is my late brother, better known as the writer IAN MACDONALD, who will feature hereabouts from time to time.

THE MENTION OF DAVID FERGUSON brings to the fore another consistent connection I experienced during my ten years in 'the business', i.e. my school, Dulwich College. Not only did I enter the main part of the school at the same time as Phil Targett-Adams, *aka* Phil Manzanera, with whom I have worked and collaborated pretty much ever since, but it was there I met Charles Hayward. It was because Robert Wyatt's mum's house was on the way home from school that I was able to take advantage of his open invitation to drink tea and listen to music after we first met in 1966. Simon Ainley, who sang on the *Listen Now* album, and was a member of the *801* line-up which toured the UK in 1977, was also an Old Alleynian, an old boy of the school. And both David Ferguson and David Rhodes of *Random Hold* went to the school, though two and five years later than me.

For good or ill it was influential and, in many ways, the story starts there…

POOH & THE OSTRICH FEATHER

BEFORE WE GET DOWN TO THE NITTY-GRITTY, as apparently people used to say back in the day (though just how people 'back in the day' described the recent past I really don't know. The recent past, perhaps), a history lesson.

Public schools. Or, rather more precisely, British public schools, of which Dulwich College is but one. In typically opaque British fashion, for 'public' one should read 'private', as they are all increasingly expensive fee-paying schools catering for the wealthy. Or the not-so-wealthy parent who aspires to something better for the education and advancement of the darling fruit of their loins than the literally crumbling state school system.

Public schools are one of the deep foundations underpinning the still sadly robust British class system. They provide access, exclusivity, a sense of smug superiority, excellent contacts in the business and academic world, privilege and, quite often, very good sports facilities, especially if you fancy starting down the path to early-onset dementia by playing rugby, the winter sport of choice for most of these establishments.

In the case of Dulwich College, in the late 1960s it also provided multiple potential venues for a bunch of rock musician wannabees. But more on that later.

One of the great ironies of the now private and exclusive British public school is that none of them started in this fashion. Quite the opposite. The older ones, the ones with status and history, and architecture inappropriate to the education of anyone in the 21st Century, all started as charities to educate 'poor (but male) scholars'.

The term 'Public School' comes from the *Public Schools Act 1868* which sought to reform and to regulate the activities of, initially, nine ancient private schools. The Act gave these schools complete independence from the Crown, State or Church. Two of the schools, St Paul's (founded 1509 to serve children of 'all nacions (*sic*) and countries indifferently') and Merchant Taylor's (founded 1561), successfully argued they should be excluded from the provisions of the Act as they were already, in legal terms, private. That left seven schools for the Act to impact. They were all male, boarding schools:

Winchester College (founded 1382 for 70 poor scholars);
Eton College (founded by Henry VI as the *Kynge's College of Our Ladye of Eton besyde Windesore* in 1440 to provide free education to 70 poor boys);
Shrewsbury School (founded 1552 as a free grammar school);
Westminster School (previously a charitable school, re-founded in 1560);

Rugby School (founded 1567 as a free grammar school for the boys of Rugby and Brownsover);

Harrow School (founded 1572 as a free school for local boys); and

Charterhouse School (founded 1611 to educate 40 boys, and which we must thank for the existence of *Genesis* as Tony Banks, Mike Rutherford, Peter Gabriel, and Ant Phillips all went there)

The City of London School (founded 1834 though a school existed in 1442) was added to the list on appeal in 1887.

Perversely, as mentioned, many of these schools were founded for the benefit of 'poor scholars' but, by the mid to late-Victorian period, they became the fee-paying educational home for the sons (and only the 'sons') of the upper and the wealthier middle classes.

Nowadays, a place at Eton, for example, will set you back over £46,000 a year, or £322,000 over the lifetime of the average pupil (plus annual inflationary increases which, courtesy of the economic policies of several Tory so-called governments are running at rather a high level). Time for a second, or third, mortgage! But, hey, who knows, your over-privileged little oik with a deeply engrained sense of entitlement might yet become the tenth Prime Minister produced by this élite institution. He might follow in the august footsteps of such luminaries as the serial philanderer and laughably incompetent Boris Johnson, or David Cameron who cravenly handed the country over to the dangerously right-wing Brexiteers Cummings and Farage. Or maybe he might be a future Chancellor of the Exchequer, like the ever-so-briefly-in-post economy wrecker Kwasi Kwarteng. Alternatively, however unlikely, he might go on to achieve something useful and productive.

I digress. Back to a history of education for the privileged few.

Later, 782 endowed grammar schools were examined by the *Taunton Commission* after the 1868 Act. The result was the *Endowed Schools Act 1869*, passed by Gladstone's first administration, which produced the basis for a national network of secondary schools. To counter this process of improving state education, Edward Thring, the Head at Uppingham School (founded 1584), convened annual meetings to consider and counter the impact of the *Endowed Schools Act* on the private school sector, meetings which became the basis of the *Headmasters' Conference* representing now some 296 independent schools. It is but another bastion of privilege.

In the midst of all this Victorian reorganisation, Dulwich College sailed serenely onwards, safe in the knowledge that the deity was behind their every move.

The school was founded as the College of God's Gift on 21st June 1619 by the actor and landowner Edward Alleyn. Alleyn was, perhaps, the leading actor of the Elizabethan era with, it is said, Christopher Marlowe writing three roles for him: *Doctor Faustus, Tamburlaine,* and Barabas in *The Jew of Malta.* His wealth, however, came from less salubrious activities. Alleyn was the *Chief Maister, Ruler and Overseer of the King's (i.e. James I) games of Beares, Bulls, Mastiff Dogs and Mastiff Bitches.* In other words, he not only managed the *Rose Theatre,* built in 1587 by Philip Henslowe, the stepfather of Alleyn's first wife, Joan Woodward, he also managed the grounds of the old manor house belonging to Robert de Paris[i]. This was then known as the Paris Gardens and he oversaw the pits where took place bearbaiting, dog and cock fighting and other savage pastimes of which Elizabeth I, our Virgin Queen, was a keen adherent. And, all the while, the male customers, young and old, were 'serviced' in the highways, by-ways and hedgerows by the hundreds of probably pox-ridden prostitutes known as the *Winchester Geese,* all officially licensed by no less than the Bishop of Winchester. Religion? Hypocrisy? Never!

Alleyn reputedly earned £500 a year from the Paris Gardens, the equivalent nowadays of a minimum of £3 million and quite probably an awful lot more. He thus owned large tracts of what are now the southern parts of the London Boroughs of Southwark and Lambeth, and, in particular, the manor of Dulwich, which he bought in 1605. He started building a chapel and schoolhouse (both still in existence) on the green there in 1613, establishing a charity which would see twelve poor orphans (note the 'poor' and giggle):

> "...taught in good and sound learning... that they might be prepared
> for university or for good and sweet trades and occupations."[1]

Suffice to say, the education provided did not live up to expectations for nearly 250 years until, in 1857, the *Dulwich College Act* was passed by Parliament which allowed the place to ditch the rather restrictive conditions imposed by the original foundation. Under the new headmaster (or, simply, The Master as they became known), the Rev. Alfred Carver, the place became effectively what we see now, occupying its huge swathe of prime south London real estate. The three main buildings, excitingly called the North, Middle and South blocks, were designed by Charles Barry, the son of Sir Charles Barry, the man responsible, amongst too many other projects to mention, for the building of the Palace of Westminster between 1837 and 1852, when the House of Commons was completed. Thus Dulwich College, re-formed and re-built by the time Carver retired in 1883, became one of the leading public schools in the country.

---

[i] It lay between Southwark and Blackfriars Bridges.

The previous year, the foundation was carved up into three separate entities: Dulwich College, Alleyn's School and James Allen's Girls School, all within a mile of one another. This, it would turn out, was good news for our budding rock stars as these establishments, plus the nearby but since defunct Mary Datchelor's Girls' School[i], provided the audience which progressively began to fill the aforementioned venues which became their equivalent of a Stateside Tour in 1968 and 1969.

In the 1940s the school fell on hard times and was rescued by an innovative social experiment instigated by the then head, Christopher Gilkes (Master 1941-53). This 'experiment' changed the social make-up of the place beyond measure as the fees of boys who might otherwise not be able to attend because their parents didn't earn enough were, instead, paid by their local council.

Now, at long last, you will see the relevance of all this historical tosh.

Two of the beneficiaries of this scheme were the author of this long-winded nonsense, and his older brother, Ian MacCormick, later better known as the music writer and journalist Ian MacDonald. In 1959, Ian was the first ever entrant to a Public School from our little London County Council school at the top of Brixton Hill, a stone's throw from the ill-reputed prison of the same name. In 1962, I was the second lucky sod (or third, as a mate, Ronald Johannes, got in at the same time) to access a place then with an excellent educational reputation, something I would do my level best to undermine over the next seven years.

Back then, if you passed an exam called the 11+, passed the entrance exam, passed the intimidating interview with The Master (a diminutive figure, Ronald Groves, who struck fear into all who trod the hallowed grounds), your parents' reward was that they got to spend a relative fortune buying an expensive uniform, horrible shirts with detached starched collars and cuffs necessitating studs and cufflinks, a blue and black striped tie, a stupid little black cap with blue stripes you wore on the back of your head[ii], rugby kit (both blue and white shirts, blue shorts), house socks (I was in Raleigh, so blue with red and white tops), a fucking straw boater in the summer should you choose (I did not), and a blue blazer with a white DC badge (summer use only).

---

[i] A Grammar School for Girls established in Camberwell in 1877. It closed in 1981. It had an excellent reputation for music. In 1985, one of its pupils, Kitty Lux, was co-founder of the *Ukulele Orchestra of Great Britain*, an organisation deemed responsible for the resurgence of interest in the ukulele. We forgive her.
[ii] One of the, since removed, requirements when wearing this cap was that, should you pass a teacher within a few hundred metres of the school grounds, you had to cover the cap badge with your right hand until acknowledged. On such traditions was the greatest Empire the world has ever seen based. Or probably not.

4

You then entered an establishment where you went to school on Saturdays up to 1 pm., where you attended every home school 1st XV Rugby match played on a Saturday afternoon or face punishment of the equivalent duration, where fagging in the boarding houses (of which there were four) was still prevalent, and where there was a school song, warbled in Latin, the meaning of which I have only just discovered sixty years after I first sang it. Composed by the then Master, J E C Welldon (he followed on from Carver and lasted two years) its snappy lyric reads:

Pueri Alleynienses, quotquot annos quotquot menses
Fertur principum memoria, Fertur principum memoria,
Vivit Fundatoris nomen, unicae virtutis omen
Detur soli Deo Gloria.

Which, in translation reads… you at the back, staring out of the window, yes, MacCormick… translate! OK, here goes:

Boys of Alleyn, may our forefathers' memory
Endure through as many years and as many months as there may be,
The Founder's name lives on, a promise of unparalleled virtue to come,
Glory be given to God alone.

I mean, really, what twaddle. 'Unparalleled virtue'? Give us a break. This was a school which, for example, held to is corporate bosom for seven years that political viper Nigel Farage[i], one of the handful of people (mainly men) for whom I would gladly forego my lifelong vow of peaceful co-existence to smash in the face and kick in the goolies (if they possess them). Others on this short list include Donald Trump, Vladimir Putin, Alexander Lukashenko, Victor Orbán, Xi Jinping, Kim Jong Un, Narendra Modi, anyone in the Myanmar government, several Saudi Princes, Boris Johnson, Liz Truss and most of the current Tory Party, Recep Tayyip Erdoğan, Ali Khamenei, any member of the Republican Party… Hmmm. The list is sadly rather longer than I thought.

So, this place of 'unparalleled virtue' was one where, in the early 60s, Prefects could still beat boys, or hand out arbitrary punishments such as

---

[i] See *Channel 4.com*, 19th September 2013: *Nigel Farage schooldays letter reveals concerns over fascism* by Michael Crick. It opens: "In the late 1970s and early eighties the Ukip leader was a pupil at Dulwich College in south London, one of Britain's most prestigious schools. Channel 4 News has uncovered strong evidence that teachers at Dulwich thought Nigel Farage was "racist", and "fascist" or "neo-fascist"."
(*https://www.channel4.com/news/nigel-farage-ukip-letter-school-concerns-racism-fascism*).
See also: *The Independent*, 13th May 2019: *'Dear Nigel… I wish your teenage fascist views had been dealt with. History could have been very different'*
(*https://www.independent.co.uk/news/uk/politics/nigel-farage-open-letter-schoolfriend-brexit-poster-nazi-song-dulwich-college-gas-them-all-a7185336.html*)

Prefect's Half Hour (a misnomer as, amongst the more psychopathic prefects, this usually extended to two hours or more), or, and this was the worst, Prefect's Special Detention. Special Detention kept you in on Saturday afternoons at the whim of the Punishment Prefect in charge. One only got out of Special Detention if one achieved 100% in a test the subject of which was the more arcane and obscure elements of the school's history and its grounds. A favourite question was: 'how many trees are there in The Clump?' Naming places around Dulwich was never especially imaginative and The Clump was exactly as it sounds, a group of trees on a low mound between what was then the 1st XV Rugby Pitch (hallowed turf in them there days) and the 2nd XV Pitch. The answer was something like 18½ (a tree had partially blown down in a gale), but the more unpleasant prefects often varied this to ¼ or ⅛ or ⅝ or whatever fraction was *not* the one the unfortunate detainee provided in their answer.

How do I know all this? Because on several occasions I fell victim to a Prefect who noted I was running in the Cloisters (yes, there were cloisters between the three main blocks), or wore the wrong-coloured socks (dark grey only), or simply looked at him the wrong way. Or 'askance' as they called it in those days.

You will, undoubtedly, be pleased to hear that the Prefects got their comeuppance in the most spectacular fashion in the winter of 1966. A day I look back on with great fondness, revenge, as we know, being a dish best served cold. And the snow lay deep on the ground when we surrounded a group of them on the 1st XV pitch one December lunch time and pelted them with snowballs, some of which may have contained something rather harder than snow.

How did this drastic breakdown in discipline come to pass, you may ask. Go on then, ask away.

Well, in July 1966, Ronald Groves, the tiny terror of Dulwich, retired. In charge for twelve years, he apparently knew the face, the academic record, the family background, and disciplinary record, perhaps even the shoe size, of every one of the 1,400 pupils. It was disconcerting, therefore, to be stopped by someone no taller than you, but with infinitely greater gravitas, whilst you were hurrying across the South Gravel towards lunch in the Great Hall (The South Gravel: another example of the exciting names given to areas of Dulwich, this being the area of pink-painted tarmac, i.e. not gravel at all, which lay in front of the South Block. You will, undoubtedly, be shocked to hear that a similar area was to be found in front of the North Block. It was called.... The North Gravel). But back to one's encounter with The Master. As one's stomach grumbled in anticipation of dried out gammon, watery mashed potato and over-cooked cabbage followed by a solid semolina pudding or some other culinary delight, he would look you in the eye and pronounce:

"MacCormick, have your Latin test results improved? And why was your brother absent from the match against Bedford on Saturday?"

The truthful answer to the first question was 'no/you must be joking', but that was replaced by an obsequious and clearly optimistic 'I think so, sir'. And in answer to the second question, where one wished to say 'fuck alone knows, but he sensibly hates rugby thinking it an uncivilised and barbaric sport. That, and he hates getting his knees dirty', instead one was forced to shrug and shake one's head in false dismay at such an appalling lapse of school decorum and loyalty displayed by one's older sibling.

But then Groves left, and by early September 1966 it became clear no-one with any authority was currently in charge, his replacement not being available until the following year (they'd stolen the head from Alleyn's. Geezer by the name of Lloyd. Was not a fan). This against a radicalising political and social back drop which saw Labour winning only their third outright majority, but with their highest ever share of the popular vote (48%), in the March General Election; increasing grumblings about a vicious colonial war being fought by the US in Vietnam; and the rumours of something weird going down in a rundown part of San Francisco called Haight-Ashbury. That, and *The Beatles* released *Revolver* on 5th August. If there is such a thing as a cusp, we were most certainly on it.

In the quiet form rooms (not classrooms, this was a public school after all) and gloomy hallways of Dulwich College something was afoot. It was a morning School Assembly in the Great Hall that was the harbinger of things to come. First up, an unknown hero decided he didn't want to be in the direct line of sight of the interim Master in charge, *aka* the Head of Physics, one George Way. So, said pupil shuffled to the right to hide behind the boy in front. Then another lad took the same view and hid behind the first. And then another, and another, some moving left, some to the right, until, after a few minutes, some 700+ giggling pupils were pressed up against one another and the walls of the cavernous hall, leaving its centre entirely vacant. When no reaction was forthcoming, the following day, teachers were ironically applauded onto the stage at the western end of the Great Hall. Then, when the unfortunate Mr Way tripped up the stairs one morning, the entire assembly shrieked with laughter and cheered the furious staff members off the dais and back in full retreat to their common room.

Then came the incident with the prefects. It snowed that December and, for a lark, some of the more boisterous or, perhaps, loutish students decided to throw snowballs at the windows of the Prefects' Common Room on the ground floor of the South Block. After a while, as the glass disappeared behind a covering of ice and slush, one of the more senior, less sensible Prefects dedicated to the idea of hierarchy and discipline, the virtues that put the 'Great' in Great Britain don't you know, decided that it was time to sally forth to teach those fellows a lesson they would never forget. To teach them respect for their elders and betters. To give them a damned good thrashing, indeed. Big mistake. In the fine traditions of the British Victorian military, they advanced convinced of their superiority, were drawn into an obvious trap, were surrounded by superior forces, and utterly and humiliatingly defeated. Think in terms of General Elphinstone's catastrophic advance to, and retreat from, Kabul in 1842, from which one man survived; the annihilation of the British column by the Zulus at Isandlwana in 1879; or the shambles of Majuba Hill in 1881 where Boer farmers wiped out a force of British regulars (there are plenty more embarrassing disasters to choose from, but these will do for now).

The power of the Prefects was broken.

The place was never the same. A bit later, *Ban the Bomb* signs and *Hammer and Sickle* emblems were painted on the North and South Blocks. Some prat stole a disabled Bren Gun from the Cadet Corps stores which event briefly excited the interest of *Special Branch*. The sightscreens on the 1st XI Cricket Pitch were adorned with red-painted revolutionary slogans. And, sacrilege, weedkiller poured on the 1st XI square.

Hair, previously millimetres short at the back and well above the ears to the side, began to creep dangerously towards the collar. Turn-up trousers, *de rigueur* ever since given the regal seal of approval by Edward VII, were abandoned. Lace-up black shoes were replaced by slip-ons, with some even favouring the Chelsea boot. Ties were either narrow and knitted or kipper wide. Scarves, multiply woven together, were suddenly ten-feet-long fashion items, not something to wear whilst shivering on a Saturday afternoon as the 1st XV slugged it out with Christ's Hospital or King's, Canterbury.

The swinging sixties had, at long last, landed in SE 21.

BUT FOR SOME, THE SIXTIES HAD SWUNG for rather longer. The family MacCormick lived in a small semi-detached house in Uffington Road, West Norwood, SE27. A house unremarkable except for some extraordinary wallpaper in the dining room made up of large blocks of shiny black, orange, red and gold. It must have seemed to our parents a good idea at the time.

Those parents, Ewen and Olwen, were both born in the early 1920s. My dad went to Alleyn's where he excelled at cricket. Academic subjects, not so much. In 1940 he joined the *Royal Air Force* and was trained to fly Hurricanes and Spitfires which he did in North Africa and Italy. What he actually got up to in action we never knew. Like his father, winner of the Military Cross on the Somme on 15th September 1916 and nearly killed by machine gun fire ten days later, he never, ever, talked about it. Our mum joined the *Women's Royal Air Force* pretty much straight from school at Haberdashers' Askes some time later, serving at air bases in Dorset and Oxfordshire. She and some fellow *WRAFs* were once given a lift back to quarters from a pub outside Oxford by Princess Victoria Mary Augusta Louise Olga Pauline Claudine Agnes of Teck, better known at that time as Queen Mary, the widow of the late King-Emperor George V. She happened to be passing in her chauffeur driven Rolls Royce and, more than a bit awe-struck, the young ladies squeezed in next to her and were driven back to *RAF Benson*. A Royal doing something useful. Who knew? Less happy was her experience in September 1944 when she witnessed wounded Paratroopers returning from the shambles at Arnhem. Ever after she could not bear to see people with their heads swathed in bandages because too many of the young men brought back in that condition died over the coming days.

But for her, being something of a 'looker', boyfriends abounded, until our dad took a fancy. Exploiting his position in charge of ferrying aircraft across Africa and on to India in the final months of the campaign against Japan, he despatched the current pilot boyfriend to central Africa – and kept him there on rotation betwixt Bamako and Ouagadougou or some such faraway places. All is fair in love and war. They married in 1946.

They went through the war tapping their feet to the beat of big band leaders like Glen Miller, Duke Ellington and Count Basie. Since then, they subsisted on a diet of Frank Sinatra and Ella Fitzgerald (excellent) and Ray Conniff and his fucking singers (awful). Meanwhile, my mother's cousin, Derek (who will feature again later in this tale), introduced us to the joys of classical music, mainly the 19th Century romantics: Beethoven, Brahms, Tchaikovsky, Mendelssohn, etc. etc. Also, a personal favourite: Benjamin Britten's *A Young Persons Guide to the Orchestra*. We were taken off to the Proms. Culture vultures. All good. If mainstream.

Meanwhile, the likes of Elvis Presley, Chuck Berry, Little Richard *et al* passed us by (I never 'got' Presley). But then came *The Shadows* – Hank Marvin, Bruce Welch, Brian Bennett, Jet Harris. Oh yeah. Still have *Apache*, *Kon-Tiki* and *Dance On!* in a box in the attic. The next 45 I bought was Andy Williams' *Can't Get Used to Losing You* in spring 1963. Great song and arrangement. But next to them on the *Dansette's* turntable were EPs of Tchaikovsky's *1812*, Sibelius's *Karelia Suite* and more.

Then, of course, came *The Beatles*, *The Stones*... and black American music: *The Supremes*, *The Crystals*, *The Chiffons* and *Martha and the Vandellas*, but also James Brown, Junior Walker, Sam & Dave, Wilson Pickett... the list goes on. We listened. We sang along. We waited with keen anticipation for the next single, then the next LP. We watched *Ready, Steady Go!* on Friday nights for, as we all knew, the weekend started there! We were part of the audience, happy just to hear the music. The big change came in '66.

THROUGH THE LATE 50S AND EARLY 60S our mum worked in a big department store in Oxford Street: *D H Evans*. But, fed up with the commute[i], and looking for something different to do, she took up a position as a teaching assistant at Dulwich College Preparatory School. DCPS is not actually a part of the Dulwich College foundation but is a few hundred metres from the college's grounds. It was full of polite, well brought up kids aged up to eleven, all from well-heeled households who presumably assumed attendance paved the way unerringly to a place at the College. Great, if misleading, marketing on the prep school's part!

A lovely, if somewhat eccentric, lady by the name of Honor Wyatt also worked there as a teaching assistant. She lived in Dalmore Road in West Dulwich, a fifteen-minute walk from the school. In passing, knowing her sons were interested in music she told my mother that her son, Robert, was in a 'pop group'. Then she said: why didn't we all come round for dinner one day and the 'youngsters' could meet up.

It proved the thinnest of thin ends to an extremely slippery downhill metaphor. Nothing would ever be the same.

Come that day in the summer of 1966, we troop *en famille*, down the hill towards Dalmore Road. No. 48 is a standard, Edwardian semi-detached in a highly desirable area near West Dulwich Station. In 2019, it sold for a snip under £1.4 million. Prices have gone up about 10% since then. Such houses tend to be long and relatively thin: two reception rooms, then a small kitchen/breakfast area a couple of steps down at the rear. A large front bedroom on the first floor, with two smaller ones and a cramped bathroom at the back. On the second floor another couple of rooms under the roof. It is now a smart, clean, nicely decorated and slightly extended family home for a smart, clean, nicely dressed, middle class family.

In July 1966 not so much. The outside of the house is painted in various bright psychedelic colours. What must the neighbours think? What do my parents think? Then the front door opens. A shortish, young man, with long blonde hair and a ready smile greets us. And so, Ian and Bill MacCormick and their non-plussed parents meet Robert Wyatt and wife Pam and very young son Sam, and Kevin Ayers, and Mike Ratledge, who drifts past mysteriously (Daevid Allen was elsewhere, on another astral plane)… and then, revelation, Ian and Bill see a drum kit in the front room and an electric organ, a big bass guitar and amplifiers and speaker cabinets as tall as them. But, jeez, that's a lot of fucking amplifiers!! Really, what *must* the neighbours think???

---

[i] The 137 Bus via Streatham, Clapham, Battersea, Chelsea, Sloane Square, Knightsbridge, Hyde Park, Marble Arch, Oxford Street. Probably on a *Routemaster* in the later years. Yeah, I was briefly a bus spotter.

My dad was a *Daily Telegraph* reader (for the sports pages, you understand). Innately conservative, he maintained a bemused smile throughout, talked when spoken to, and observed everything under a slightly arched eyebrow. My mum, wide-eyed, perhaps wondered where this all might lead. We just had fun. And when, as we left, Robert issued an open invitation to pop round whenever we liked for tea, a chat and some music, Ian and I both readily said yes. I, especially, would be limpet-like, impossible to shake off. Even when the band left for the States to support Hendrix on a seemingly year-long tour in 1968 I'd still go round from time to time, have a chat with Honor and sometimes Pam. Their door was always open, even to a short-haired public schoolboy like me.

To quote myself being quoted:

"If you have an idealistic view of the mid-to-late 1960s this was it. You knocked on the door, and instead of somebody going, 'Oh, not really, we haven't got time', they'd go: 'Come in! We haven't seen you since... yesterday! Drink lots of tea!'"[2]

Within a few days of the visit came a second invitation, again courtesy of Honor. Robert's 'pop group' were to play at an 'event' over in Kingston. We were all invited. To my surprise my parents said 'yes'.

The 'event' was to take place at a place called Coombe Springs in Kingston Vale. Coombe Springs was a seven-acre estate from which operated the *Institute for the Comparative Study of History, Philosophy and the Sciences*. The driving force behind the institute was the extraordinary multi-lingual polymath John Godolphin Bennett. Bennett was an officer in the Royal Engineers in Great War and was seriously wounded in 1918. Comatose for six days, he underwent what we now call an 'out of body experience' which convinced him there was something beyond death. He embarked on a life-long investigation into religion, philosophy and the occult. He was a seriously interesting bloke. Look him up on *Wikipedia*.

Anyway, he bought Coombe Springs back in 1946. By August 1966 it contained a large house, including what one might describe as an Orangery, and extensive gardens with paths, grottos, pools and lawns. In early 66 Bennett handed the place over to the Sufi teacher Idries Shah who then promptly sold it for housing thereby pocketing a tidy sum[i]. Clearly, however much they might despise it, even religious philosophers live in the material world. Anyway, the mis-named *Midsummer Revels* (it was late August), was one of the last events to take place there before the bulldozers moved in.

---

[i] All that appears to remain is Coombe Springs Lodge on Coombe Lane West. The rest is housing on a private estate and a Junior School.

The band occupied one side of the, not very large, Orangery. As I recall, Mike was on the left looking across the rest of the band. Robert central, Daevid and Kevin somewhere in-between. Everyone, including the audience, was somewhat cramped for space. Now, there is a dispute whether this was *Mister Head's*[i] last gig or *Soft Machine's* first or, even, something in between[ii]. I subscribe to it being *Soft Machine's* first if only so I can boast 'I was there!'. They played, loudly, but don't ask me what.

I get excited and think 'I want to do that'. But what 'that' is, is not entirely clear as I don't play an instrument. Hmmm. But I once sang a solo version of *Once in Royal David's City*[iii] in front of my entire junior school. Problem solved. I will be the lead singer. All I need is a band to, err... lead.

Though our parents leave early, we hang out into the early hours (which, given I was 15, was extremely relaxed of the aged Ps) and then we wander home, on foot (which is a hell of a walk[iv]), in something of a daze.

Now, dear reader, this is not to be a history of the *Soft Machine*. There are plenty of other books out there, written by far better writers, if you want that sort of thing. Nor is it a biography of Robert Wyatt. Marcus O'Dair's excellent *Different Every Time* does that job very well. If you haven't got a copy, go out and buy one. Now. But their influence and, in particular, that of Robert on both Ian and me was profound. A cup (or cups) of tea with Robert in his and Pam's bedroom at the front on the first floor of 48, Dalmore Road, inevitably was accompanied by jazz. And, on a few occasions, fried eggs on toast slathered with *Marmite*, a combination beloved of Robert and to which I, still, am more than partial.

But back to the jazz. Sure, we'd heard Dave Brubeck's *Take Five*, *Blue Rondo à la Turk* and *Unsquare Dance*[v] and, of course, our dad was still partial

---

[i] *Mister Head*: a short-lived band formed in June 1966 comprising Kevin Ayers, Daevid Allen, Robert Wyatt and American guitarist Larry Nowlin met whilst having fun in Mallorca. Nowlin soon left to be replaced by Mike Ratledge.

[ii] Phil Howitt kindly tells me that Canterbury archivist Aymeric Leroy thinks they may even have performed under the moniker *The Bishops of Canterbury*. (*https://canterburyscene.wordpress.com/2016/11/10/larry-nowlin-3-and-the-birth-of-soft-machine/*). I'm sticking with *Soft Machine*.

[iii] Lyrics: Cecil Frances Alexander. Music: Henry Gauntlett. Just so you know.

[iv] Somewhere in the region of 8½ miles. It took us over three hours, time not including being stopped in Balham High Road by the police who, 'hello, hello', wanted to know what two young 'gentlemen' were doing out and about at 4 a.m. in the morning.

[v] Notable for their use of 'odd' time signatures, i.e. 5/4, 9/8 and 7/4 respectively. *Blue Rondo à la Turk* was adapted by Keith Emerson and the *Nice* and transformed into the rather more mundane 4/4 *Rondo* recorded for their first album *The Thoughts of Emerlist Davjack*.

to a bit of Ellington, but what we heard in Robert's bedroom was eye opening. And brain widening. John Coltrane, Charlie Parker, Charlie Mingus, Pharoah Sanders, Eric Dolphy, Miles Davis, Cecil Taylor… To be fair, I once returned the compliment rushing round to play him Hendrix's *Wind Cries Mary* which I still think one of the best songs he ever wrote/recorded. I strongly believe all budding lead guitarists should be forced to listen to the solo, learn it, and then repeat to themselves whilst playing it, 'less is more, less is more'.

Now, I must admit that, prior to this, I struggled with some of the new music being introduced *chez* MacCormick by my sadly late bro'. It took me some time, for example, to get next to *The Rite of Spring*. At first a jumble of rhythms and noises but now, one of my favourite pieces. In such things he led, I followed (but I was better at sport than him which must count for something, eh? I mean, I played for the School 1st XI at cricket and still have the blazer to prove it. I won the Fielding Cup FFS! I was even watched by Phil the Greek, *aka* HRH The Duke of Edinburgh!).

Then, one day, he brought home *Mingus, Mingus, Mingus, Mingus, Mingus*. I am sure you all know it. Charlie Mingus's 1963 classic. To my young ears most of it was great. Truly great. I'm listening to it as I write. For fuck's sake, *Theme for Lester Young (Goodbye Pork Pie Hat)* alone. Oh boy. But then came Eric Dolphy's solo on *Hora Decubitus*. Like, what the fuck was that? Sounded like a series of squeaks and grunts. An animal in pain. It made me angry. Surely anyone can do that. But the more I listened, the more I came round. Just as the brain can be trained in one way of thinking it can be untrained if the person so desires. I began to see that music wasn't just pretty melodies to sing along with. It could be anger, pain, regret, joy, love, chaos, despair. And the music I then heard round at Robert's was the icing on the cake. Blinkers fell away. Shackles were removed. Ears were opened. The great shame was that I didn't pay enough attention to Mingus's bass lines. Now, there was (is) a rich education for any aspiring member of a rhythm section.

To add to the cultural mix a new library[i] opened in West Norwood to replace the tiny, tired, little thing opposite the railway station. The new library included an extensive record section run by an enthusiast for modern music. Soon, things like Olivier Messiaen's *Turangalîla-Symphonie* were spinning on the *Dansette's* turntable along with Ives, Britten, Bartók, Alban Berg (especially his utterly sublime Violin Concerto, dedicated 'to the memory of an Angel', the 18-year-old Manon Gropius, the daughter of Walter Gropius and Alma Mahler *née* Schindler, the widow of Gustav

---

[i] Now the *West Norwood Library and Picture House*. It backs on to the extensive West Norwood cemetery and crematorium, the grim walls of which I passed every day on the way to school.

Mahler), Stravinsky, and Shostakovich, an especial favourite of Ian's and which led to his book *The New Shostakovich* about which the composer's second son, Maxim Shostakovich, wrote:

"One of the best biographies of Dmitri Shostakovich I have read."

Fair enough.

Then, in April 1967, I turned sixteen. Taking advantage of my parents' surprisingly liberal attitude to the activities of their offspring, I attended another seminal musical/cultural event: *The 14-Hour Technicolour Dream* at Alexandra Palace on 29th April 1967. The *Softs, Pink Floyd, The Move, Pretty Things* and, first up, *The Social Deviants*, the late Mick Farren's statement making, if not actually very good, band. Being naïve, I stood front left. Right in front of what turned out to be a 4 x 12-inch *WEM PA* speaker column. I swear my left ear has never recovered from the opening notes Pete Munro, bass, Clive Muldoon, guitar, and Mike Robinson, guitar, strangled out of their instruments. Deaf in one ear, I wandered from stage to stage, watched the films projected on to the walls, wondered what that strange smell was, and regarded John Lennon from a distance, as he and his entourage cut a swathe through the crowd in the early hours. And, as I strolled onto the terrace overlooking the park with the centre of London laid out before me in the early morning sun, I thought again: I want to do that. But now it was a case of finding someone to do 'that' with. It took a bit of time. About a year, it turned out.

THUS, DEAR AND PATIENT READER, we eventually come to a short history of that rockin' high school combo, yes, the very great *Pooh and the Ostrich Feather*, rightly famed in its own lunchtime. The little bear's first steps, however, were extremely tentative. He was yet but a cub.

A fellow student at Dulwich was the son of an acquaintance of my dad. My dad worked in the airline business for a company called *Canadian Pacific* (also known for its transcontinental railway and enormous hotels in one of which I have stayed, the gigantic *Hotel Vancouver*. There, in its restaurant, my then young family was introduced to the concept of gammon baked in *Coca Cola*. Weird people, Canadians).

So, the other dad worked for *BOAC*, the *British Overseas Airways Corporation* (now subsumed into *British Airways*) and they met on one of my dad's frequent trips abroad. Somewhere in South America I believe. His son was now a boarder at Dulwich College. Blew House. Big gaff, opposite the swimming pool (of significance later). He was taller than me but wore glasses which made up for the difference in height (*Editor: what?*). His name was Philip Geoffrey Targett-Adams – yes, Manzanera to you lot – but PGTA to us. Phil was known to own an electric guitar and to harbour hopes of doing something in music. Circa 1967, Phil and Bill were in the College's Colts Rugby XV. Mr Targett-Adams was, as I recall, a mobile No. 8 with a cunning dummy pass on him, whilst I played centre, wing or fullback or, in other words, got as far away from those nasty, large forwards as possible. The photo below thus includes half of *Quiet Sun*, a *Mole* and a *Roxy*, and 40% of the *801*. Spot those scoundrels! Or simply read the caption. (Photo courtesy of Señor P Manzanera)

1 The Dulwich College Colts Rugby XV 1967.
From left to right and back to front (as far as I can remember them): Thorne, Pilarczyk, no idea, Chapman, Looker (we didn't get on), McMullen, MacCormick, Dick Rhodes (older brother of Random Hold and Peter Gabriel guitarist Dave Rhodes), Clayton, Targett-Adams, Stapleton, Cryer, Jones (who once deliberately knocked me out in a 7-a-sides match. I bear no grudge), Howell and Telford.

One day, flushed with knowledge of PGTA's guitar ownership, Bill sidled up to him, probably somewhere on the North Gravel, or it could have been the Buttery, where BMac was known, on occasion, to consume a cheese roll and an apple turnover at first break with which to keep up his blood sugar levels until lunch (then more at 4.15 p.m. when school finished, possibly a cream bun, and topped off with a ¼lb bag of wine gums for the walk home. He was a growing boy and needed such sustenance to see him through to dinner).

"Pssst. Wanna form a rock and roll band?" he may have whispered through the turnover's crisp yet flaky pastry. To which PGTA, looking down his nose and through his glasses, may well have replied: "Why not? Nothing better to do." And thus is a music dynasty created… Or not.

First attempts were barely fruitful. Recruiting a third prospective band member, one Jon Copeland from Cheam, a few not very productive 'rehearsals', one uses the term very loosely, took place. Phil and Jon on guitars, *moi* on bongos and vocals. So, not quite the 100-watt *Marshall* stacks with all the trimmings as in our collective dreams.

Things stuttered along until someone, no idea who, asked: do you know Charles Hayward? Utterly baffled, the reply was: who? You have to understand that at Dulwich knowledge of pupils outside one's year group was minimal bordering on non-existent. Charles was two years younger than Phil and me. Therefore, as far as we were concerned, he might as well not have existed. Until it was mentioned that he owned a very large *Premier* drum kit, with two bass drums in a garishly bright red glitter and, what is more, knew how to play them. He'd even had lessons FFS!

Charles was in the band before he knew it. Invited round to Phil's mum's house in West Road, Clapham, he arrived with his dad in what I believe was a 1966 *Morris Minor 1000 Traveller*. This was a wonderfully British sort of vehicle. An adaptation of the hugely popular, and cheap, *Morris Minor*, it was an estate, with two large doors at the back and a wooden frame reminiscent of a Tudor house. It looked, therefore, as though it might have been designed in the first Elizabethan era and not the second. Its main virtue was that it just about took all of Charles's drum cases. These were hurriedly unloaded, transported upstairs, and set up in the front bedroom. The bongos were consigned to the dustbin of musical history. The band had a drummer. With Phil and his red and white *Hofner Galaxie* electric guitar, there was a lead guitarist. And a poseur who thought he was a singer. A bass player was next on our shopping list. We also needed a name.

Both were vaguely urgent as we'd submitted to the school's 'Powers That Be' a request to perform at the *Summer Miscellany*, an annual summer-time event which took place in the Great Hall and was supposed to highlight the elevated cultural atmosphere of the school: string quartets, poetry recitals, choral outings, that sort of thing. It was attended by proud parents, teachers, and students, and was regarded as a highlight of the artistic calendar. Foolishly, the PTB agreed. We then panicked.

My brother solved one problem: *Pooh and the Ostrich Feather* was the moniker selected. It might have been *Wing Commander Nixon and his Wheat Eating Bees*, but *PatOF* was already printed on the programme before my late bro' also came up with *WCNahWEB*. Looking back, as the lead singer I think I'd rather have been a Wing Commander than a small talking (or singing in this case) bear. But there you go. Can't have everything.

Back to bass players. Step forward one Dave Buckley. We knew Dave a bit. Nice guy. Friend of another friend, Dave Price. Dave Buckley was one of those annoying folk: perfect pitch, could make almost any instrument sound good. Played the trumpet. And the violin. And, it turned out, immediately made sense of the rudimentary bass parts for the material we planned to play. He was in, feet not touching the ground.

16

By now, we were more aware of goings on in the Frisco Bay, especially the *Avalon Ballroom* and *Fillmore Auditorium*. Bands played and they were accompanied by light shows. Light shows with pulsating colours projected behind the musicians. And, if the *Jefferson Airplane* and the *Grateful Dead* sported a light show, then so must we! Thus, friend Tim Seaman teamed up with another mate, Dave Price, and duly obliged. Tim, it turned out, saw the *Pink Floyd* play at an *Oxfam* charity gig at the Albert Hall on 12th December 1966 and was inspired. An inspiration reinforced by *The Doors* and *Jefferson Airplane Roundhouse* gig on 6th September 1968. With them came one of the premier Bay-area lightshows, *Glen MacKay's Headlights*[i], so us Brits got the full West Coast psychedelic experience. Without the LSD in my case. Now, Tim and Dave raided the Science Block for overhead projectors, and, I may be wrong, experimented with cooking oil and food colouring, to provide a pulsing, squirming, amoeba-like liquid light show. Throw in a few Moiré patterns and slides and it was a go. They became a fixture at all *Pooh* performances, getting bigger and better as we went on.

Indeed, much bigger, and much better. Unbeknownst to me all these years, Tim, now with a new partner Richard Callan, went on to form the *Ultramarine Lightshow* (Ultramarine = Super Seaman, as you sensed). They appeared all over London and Southern England until 1972 when Tim left college with a BSc in electrical engineering and lighting and needed to get a day job (or, alternatively, until bands started to travel with their own dedicated lighting rigs).

But they certainly appeared with some bands. 'Not 'alf', as the late Alan Freeman was fond of saying. And here's an abbreviated list of them:

Aardvark, Atomic Rooster, Blonde on Blonde, Brinsley Schwarz, Caravan, Curved Air, David Bowie, East of Eden, Fanny, Groundhogs, High Tide, John Hiseman's Colosseum, Juicy Lucy, Matthews Southern Comfort, Mott the Hoople, Pink Floyd, Steamhammer, Stoneground, Swinging Blue Jeans, T Rex, Uriah Heap, Van Der Graf Generator and Yes.[3]

So, far more successful than we were at any point. Hmmmm.

Moving on, come the night, our 'set' was strictly limited timewise. Three songs as I recall, one of which I cannot for the life of me remember. First up, a raucous version of *Love's '7 and 7 is'* culled from their album *Da Capo* released at the end of 66[ii]. Pre the internet and lyric websites it was, of course, almost impossible to make out what words people were actually singing (e.g. Jimi Hendrix, *Purple Haze*: 'Excuse me while I kiss the sky' or, as some would have it, 'Excuse me while I kiss this

---

[i] Initially formed in 1966 with Jerry Abrams, who later went his own way, they did the lights at the famous Monterey Festival in June 1967.

[ii] Some excellent stuff on that one: *Stephanie knows who, Orange Skies, ¡Que Vida!, The Castle, She Comes in Colours.* Rather ruined by the interminable *Revelation.*

guy'). This applied here so I just mostly made shit up but did so with confidence or, perhaps, *brio*, this being a musical reference. For example, the actual lyrics start:

'When I was a boy, I thought about the times I'd be a man.
I'd sit inside a bottle and pretend that I was in the can.'

OK, so I heard the second line as:

'I'd sit inside a bottle and pretend I was in a jam.'

Which, I would venture, makes a tad more sense lyrically than Arthur Lee's nonsense. Not a lot more. But some.

2 *An historic document:*
The Summer Miscellany Programme, June 1968

Phil, meanwhile, sporting a large black hat, played the entire thing with his back to the audience. Charles drummed with his customary exuberance, whilst Dave quietly and efficiently got on with things. Too quietly and too efficiently as it turned out. It was his one performance. The final song was an original ditty composed by Phil and Charles, *Marcel my Dada*, a reference to Charles's much-beloved Dadaist artist Marcel Duchamps. And that was that. The audience seemed astonished, bored, or appalled. We, meanwhile, started to plan for inevitable stardom.

18

Now, you will note from the programme above, that I am credited with 'vocals/bass'. Fuck alone knows what that was about, though I have a dim memory that Dave Buckley played violin on one piece (bugger me but we were avant-garde) and I may have plunked along with a one or two-note bass part, but at least I can pretend I started playing the bass three years earlier than I did. PGTA is also already credited as Phil Manzanera (it being his Colombian mum's maiden name). A man clearly already with an eye to the future as a guitar god with an appropriately god-like name.

Flushed with success we moved forward. Dave Buckley departed, others joined: Bob Lubran on a home-made bass, and the soon-to-be-expelled Dick Hearn on second guitar. Rehearsals took place at Charles's parents' house opposite *Camberwell College of Art*. The walls of a small corner room were covered with egg boxes. Whether it helped reduce sound leakage I could not say. The neighbours might have taken a view but then Peckham Road, *aka* the A202, was a busy one, and the house was on a corner. The boxes were painted orange, which bright colour helped keep us awake. It was a small room for five people, a very large drum kit, and various amps, but we squeezed in and went through our expanding repertoire. To add to '7 and 7 is' (proving we could add up) came Nick Gravenites' *Born in Chicago* (lifted off the *Paul Butterfield Blues Band's* eponymous album, and proving white public schoolboys could play the Blues. My late brother played harmonica on this number. He was pretty good, god bless him), a slowed-down, extended version of the *Jefferson Airplane's Somebody to Love* (proving we had imbibed the current psychedelic atmosphere if not anything actually psychedelic), and an even more extended version of *Cream's Spoonful* (proving we could be self-indulgent). There was other stuff, but I'm buggered if I can remember what (except *Crossroads*. We did a version of *Crossroads*. No, not the theme from TV show about the eponymous motel. The classic by *Cream* off *Wheels of Fire*. Not sure I ever got the lyrics for that completely right either).

Afterwards we retired to the front room to listen to whatever exotic and exciting albums were to hand: Joseph Byrd and Dorothy Moskowitz's *The United States of America*, *Captain Beefheart*, a particular favourite of Charles, and *The Mothers of Invention*.

Charles's mum fed us royally (I was particularly fond of *Mr Kipling's Fruit Cake* and could consume an entire one if no-one intervened. I was a growing boy, etc., etc.). His dad would pass through from time to time beaming quietly. His younger brother, Tony, might entertain us with some new artistic creation. And their Boxer dog, Tarzan, would try to eat any of us caught between the two rooms. Once, he almost devoured Bob Lubran, a shoe suffering significant damage before he, and it, were rescued by Charles. Bad doggy!

OF COURSE, 1968 WAS SIGNIFICANT IN OTHER WAYS.

First, *Soft Machine*. They were now a three-piece after Daevid was refused re-entry into the UK with an out-of-date visa on 24th August 1967, after the band spent most of the summer in the South of France. No matter, they carried on with Kevin on bass and, on 30th January 1968, they flew out to New York to support Jimi Hendrix on a two-month, nearly 50 city, tour Stateside. First date was the *Fillmore Auditorium* on 1st February. In mid-April they found enough time to record an album's worth of material at the *Record Plant*, NYC.

Robert briefly returned in May, and I happened to invite myself for tea on the day that the band's new guitarist was there. He seemed a nice guy. Quiet. Confident. Andy Summers lasted six shows on the second US Hendrix tour before leaving at the end of June. Musical differences between him and Kevin apparently. Their loss was undoubtedly Andy's gain as he went on to earn more money in a week or two when *The Police* were at their peak than the *Softs* did in the entire time Robert was a member. The tour finished in September. Kevin went to Spain, didn't come back and effectively left the band. Robert stayed in NYC.

Apart from that time in May, I didn't see Robert again in 1968. But that's not to say we weren't in touch. Robert likes a good postcard, though following his not very tidy handwriting and somewhat eccentric layout can be a tad challenging. One often needed to rotate the card through 360° to read everything written. But he would send through updates from time to time on what, in his terms, was musically hot. And hot were: *The Mothers of Invention*, *Spirit* (see page 222), and what was then called *The Chicago Transit Authority* (later, simply *Chicago*. First album only for them. Some great brass arrangements. Then they went soft and soppy).

We, mainly I, rushed off to buy their albums. The shop of choice was *One Stop Records* in Dean Street, Soho[i]. Imports were an eye-watering 39 shillings and 6 pence which, remarkably, translates into £36 in today's dosh. No wonder I bought so few of them. The *Mother's Freak Out* was already available (though only in the single vinyl edition. Didn't get the double album until later) but I bought the gatefold *Absolutely Free* and *We're Only in it for the Money*. We'd already got word of wild happenings in NYC so the gatefold import *Velvet Underground & Nico*, complete, with peelable banana, already adorned my shelves. I guess they were paid for out of the princely £7 a week I was paid for a six-day week stacking shelves in the Streatham Hill *Sainsbury's* over the summer[ii]. Ee, but times was 'ard.

---

[i] Now a restaurant: *Pizza Pilgrims*.

[ii] About £219 now as it is based on a different form of economic index. Still below the current national minimum wage for someone under 18, £5.28/hour in 2023)

Then the first *Soft Machine* album was released in November. Again, serendipitously, I happened to be round at Dalmore Road enjoying a cup of tea with Honor and Pam when in rushed Julian Glover. Julian was Robert's senior by ten years and his half-brother, the product of Honor's first marriage with Claude Glover, a BBC radio producer. A graduate of RADA, he was a regular on British television, appearing in series such as *The Avengers*, *The Saint*, *Strange Report*, *Doctor Who* and *Blake's 7*. Whereas Robert was on the short side, Julian was tall. But they shared their mum's nose (not literally, you understand). The reason for his sudden and rather excitable appearance was that he was clutching in his hands what looked suspiciously like an LP. And so it was. A US copy of the first *Soft Machine* album in its gatefold cover with rotating front sent post-haste from New York by Robert. All conversation ceased as it was placed carefully on the record player.

Their only previous vinyl output was the single *Love Makes Sweet Music*. So, what to expect? Not what I heard, I must admit.

Kevin later said he was disappointed with the album, that it was badly produced and could have been a lot better. I beg to differ. I had never heard anything quite like it. It was quite extraordinary. I felt exhausted by the end. In those days I was prone to a little nervous tension at moments of stress, like watching Scotland lose to England at rugby each spring. It showed itself by an uncontrollable quivering of my right leg. I am somewhat embarrassed to admit, this transmitted itself to my entire body the first time I made love to my first girlfriend. She professed to finding it endearing, which was kind of her. Listening to the *Soft's* album wasn't exactly stressful but my entire body was so wound up by what I heard, and as adrenaline flushed through my veins, everything seemed staggeringly clear. It was not simply an aural experience but a physical one. It changed the way I thought about music.

I can't say how hearing the album impacted Phil and Charles, but on one thing I think we were all agreed. When we were, at last, out of the clutches of Dulwich, there were directions and rhythms and sounds we needed to explore in ways never previously considered.

But I mentioned two significant events. The previous academic year Mark Hancock, a very tall American lad, turned up at the College. He came from Palo Alto, California, home of Stanford University and just down the peninsula from San Francisco. He his family were over in the UK as his dad took a sabbatical from teaching. Before he flew back, he offered an open invitation to anyone who could get there to spend Christmas 68 with them. Two of us took up the offer: one of our intrepid lighting crew, Dave Price, sadly no longer with us, and me. My dad still worked for *Canadian Pacific Airlines* and one of the perks was a free trip once a year for any of the immediate family anywhere on the network.

They didn't fly out of the UK, *Air Canada* had that franchise, but flew Amsterdam to Vancouver. So, never once having flown before, I set off from Heathrow to Amsterdam staying with one of my dad's colleagues overnight, before heading west across the North Atlantic. Customs and immigration were at Edmonton, so running from the aircraft in a Canadian Great Plains blizzard was – yeah, cold. Vancouver was wet and windswept and another *CP* colleague put me up for the night before I flew *United* to SF (also free, as *CP* had a reciprocal deal with *United* on such flights). I enjoyed a proper cooked breakfast on the plane: poached eggs and bacon, juice, the works. When did you last see that in Economy Class?

Mark was, and still is, an excellent host and we met with his friends, visited his High School, where I was asked if I knew the Queen, Britain being such a small place we must know everyone surely. We watched TV with the family as we waited for *Apollo 8* to re-appear from behind the dark side of the moon, and whooped and hollered along with them when contact was made. And we went to gigs.

On December 26th we saw all sorts of bands at the huge *Cow Palace*, previously the *California State Livestock Pavilion*, a vast place in Daly City on the southern fringes of SF proper. It was big enough to stage raucous and chaotic indoor rodeos, as well as the 1956 and 1964 Republican National Conventions which, when they nominated for President Barry 'In your heart you know he's nuts' Goldwater in the latter year, amounted to about the same thing. When the *San Francisco* (now *Golden State*) *Warriors* basketball team used to play there in the '60s and '70s it had a capacity of 15,000. It was big enough to host indoor soccer and teams from the *National Hockey League* such as the *San Jose Sharks*. Yup, it was big.

On the bill for that all-nighter were:

Steppenwolf fresh off the back of two hit singles: *Born to be Wild* (No. 2 in the US Singles Charts) and *Magic Carpet Ride* (No. 3). To my mind they were far more interesting as the psychedelic group *The Sparrow* (not *The Sparrows* as per *Wikipedia*). Check out the 1966 single *Tomorrow's Ship* and, most especially, the B-Side *Isn't it Strange*;

Canned Heat, then enjoying success with *Going up the Country* (No. 11 in the US charts) which I wasn't keen on and, earlier that year, *On the Road Again* (No. 16, though No. 8 in the UK) which I was;

Buffalo Springfield, technically *The New Buffalo Springfield* as the important ones, Stephen Stills and Neil Young, had both departed. Not much else to be said;

The Spencer Davis Group, but minus Steve Winwood who left in April 1967. On the other hand, their string of hit singles from 65 to 67 are up there in the pantheon of rock greats: *Keep on Running, Somebody Help Me, Gimme Some Lovin'* and *I'm a Man*. Yes, please;

Blue Cheer, the trio which laid claim to being 'the loudest band in the world!', and whose version of Eddie Cochran's *Summertime Blues* reached No. 11 on the Billboard chart earlier in the year. I can confirm they were loud. Very;

Three Dog Night (for information: a reference to how many huskies an Eskimo cuddled up with depending on how cold it was). This band, with three lead singers, specialised in close harmonies at which they were very good indeed. The had a big hit (Billboard No. 5) with the very good single *One* in early 69, but what was startling live was the rendition of the short song *It's For You* (a mere 1 minute 42 seconds) with its complex vocal arrangement and sparse instrumental backing. Extraordinary. Their big success was to come in the early 70s with three No. 1 singles: *Mama Told me not to Come*, *Joy to the World*, and *Black and White*.

The Electric Prunes, a LA psych-garage band whose best days were gone. They had two unexpected hits: *I Had Too Much to Dream (Last Night)* (1966) and *Get Me to the World on Time* (1967), and late 68 was the dregs of their career. Interesting to note, however, that their two hits were written by women: Annette May Tucker wrote the music to both songs and the lyrics were by, respectively, Nancie Mantz and Jill Jones. Well done, ladies;

The Flamin' Groovies, about whom I can say little despite being on the bill with them with *Mole* at the *Roundhouse* in July 1972. Formed in Frisco, they'd been around since '65 but done little since. They later recorded nine studio albums and nine live ones. Who knew? Not me, clearly.

Santana. Ah, the great guitarist Carlos Santana and his band which had just signed to *Columbia*. They were in the process of moving away from their original Blues base towards the Latin percussion-based sound which became their trademark. They were yet to record their first album (May 1969) but were one of the 'hot' acts around town and the musical highlight of the night.

But the real star was *Jerry Abrams and his Headlights*. By a very long way, the best light show I ever saw. Sorry, Tim.

On New Year's Eve 1968 we were fortunate enough to attend the All-nighter at the *Winterland* in SF. On the bill were *Santana*, *It's a Beautiful Day*,[i] *The Grateful Dead* and *Quicksilver Messenger Service*. The absolute stars were *QMS*. In particular, John Cipollina, in my view the best SF guitarist of the 60s. Dave, Mark and I got in early and were right in front of the stage so saw everything clearly. And we weren't stoned so I can remember it too!

---

[i] *It's a Beautiful Day* was notable for three things: a husband and wife in the band, David LaFlamme and his wife Linda LaFlamme (keyboards), a female singer, Pattie Santos, and the fact David LaFlamme played an amplified violin. Their first album was released in 1969 and their signature piece was called *White Bird*. It was in the middle of this song the interloper gained the stage.

Cipollina's rig was amazing enough, but his technique and originality something else completely. The guitar solo which starts at 5 minutes in their 13-minute-long song, *The Fool*, on their first album still makes me smile. The growls, the plectrum flicks on the pick-ups, the drama and lyricism. Sublime. Being in front of the stage we also nearly got trampled on by some aggressively wired stoner who leapt on stage during *It's a Beautiful Day's* set, grabbed a microphone stand, then put a boot through the bass drum before being wrestled off stage. Not by Bill Graham's security, who were probably too stoned to notice, but by the *IaBD's* road crew. Shades of Altamont.

After *Winterland* we just managed to fit in *The Grateful Dead*, the most wonderful *Spirit*, and *Blood Sweat and Tears* at the *Fillmore West* before we flew back home. I picked up the poster for the next week's shows as I went out. It featured the first west coast appearance of a band called *Led Zeppelin*. It still hangs on my wall and no, you cannot buy it.

My flight out was delayed by fog, and I nearly missed my connection in Vancouver, but the incoming flight from Japan was delayed too. Phew.

So back to Dulwich, head full of ideas, and with *Spirit's* second album, *The Family that Plays Together* released in the US in December, tucked under my arm for the lads to hear. Though there were eighteen months to go at Dulwich, in my head there was now little stopping us on the way to a laughably bad recording contract, and from being ripped off by some shark-like manager. Well, apart from A-Levels (due 1969) and parental expectations of me trotting off to university somewhere. Preferably Oxbridge. I was, after all, still at school.

Bizarrely, some time earlier (spring 67) I did unaccountably well in my geography mock O-Level. Now, I spent most of my time at Dulwich avoiding as much work as possible. I even went as far as actually using the justly-famed 'the dog ate my homework' excuse at some point in the 2nd year (we never owned a dog) and, on another occasion, randomly threw the contents of my desk around the form room so as to be found by a French teacher shaking my head forlornly and muttering 'it was there earlier', in reference to never started, let alone finished, homework. Mind, I was not alone in my reprehensible behaviour. Knowing one Religious Education teacher to be especially useless, we once all draped our raincoats over our heads whilst at our desks, and, when asked what was going on, chorused: 'it was like this when we came in, sir.' On another occasion, a certain Danny Madigan (subsequently expelled) hid in the large cupboard where the bibles were stored. It was right next to the master's desk, and he stayed concealed for the entire 45 minute lesson. A competition to see who might be thrown out of the room quickest was easily won by Mick Telford. Less than a minute! An Olympic record performance! He was made School Captain, so no-one held it against him.

OK, ok. So, back to geography mock O-Level. Somehow, I came first in the year. Go figure. Suddenly, I was the geography side's star pupil. Stick with us, kid, the head of geography, Mr P R Thomas, burbled one day and we'll see you right. He was promising easy access to a particular Oxford College, though not in those actual words, of course. This was one of the perks of the public school system in those days. A word in the ear of the right chap at the right college and you were in. Result: I was persuaded to do Geography A-Level rather than stay on the history side as I'd planned. The history side was where PGTA was headed. Bugger.

Suffice to say I gave up geography A-Level after a year, switching to art. Suffice, further, to say, I did as much work at Art A-Level as I did at History and English. That is to say: nothing. Somehow, I was allowed to get away with writing not a single essay in two years. I never read the set English texts. Or the relevant History books. As it turned out, I passed History (grade C) on my general knowledge. I turned up at the first English exam and sat there for an hour until invited to leave by a master, as my inaction was persuading increasingly panic-stricken examinees that the clocks on the wall must be wrong as how else had MacCormick already finished the fucking paper!?! I spent the next exam drinking tea on the lawn of the house of the Head of English, Lawrie Jagger (lovely bloke), until he realised I was supposed to be doing an English exam, at which point he invited me to evacuate the premises pronto as it might not appear a 'good look'. I simply didn't turn up to the Art exams. Made life simpler for all concerned.

I thus comprehensively screwed any chance of going to university (which was the point). As added, if unnecessary, insurance I buggered up my one interview, at Sussex University. During this, the two professors interviewing me argued amongst themselves who should ask the questions. When, at last, one was forthcoming, I provided a laughably stupid reply which left them shaking their heads in dismay. All that tertiary education nonsense out of the way, I was now focussed on music.

In the meantime, *Pooh* conducted a tour of almost every conceivable potential venue Dulwich College offered. Supported by our intrepid light show artistes, Tim Seaman and Dave Price (every band should have a light show), we had already played the Great Hall (a Great Hall, something every school should have). Then we did lunchtime in a science lab (something every school should have, except those in GOP-run states in the USA. They can make do with a copy of the Bible and much good will it do them), turning it into a mid-day version of *UFO/Middle Earth*. Minus the drugs. For the most part. And Room 31 (something every school with enough pupils should have. Bottom of the North Block) and the Bath's Hall – twice (something every school with rich enough parents probably possessed but, in this case, preferably emptied of water).

3 Charles playing at a Pooh gig at Dulwich.
Note cool light show courtesy of Tim and Dave

This latter performance (and *Pooh's* last at the school) was attended by a few hundred somewhat hysterical lads and lasses from Dulwich and several neighbouring schools, i.e. the aforementioned Alleyn's, JAGS and Datchelors. By now, an area of the school grounds, far away in the corner of the extensive playing fields by the railway line and Hunts Slip Road, was where you went to get stoned. No doubt some of the audience had just returned from that location. Where their heads were at was another question altogether. People were turning on. Some, even, were tuning in. Not too many yet had dropped out.

We later even managed a couple of (very badly) paid gigs outside the school. The evidence of this is attached below. For those of you too young to remember, 5 shillings is now 25p, a sum with which you can buy absolutely nothing nowadays, but was several bags of *Maynard's Wine Gums* or multiple cheese rolls in those days. That's inflation for you.

YOUNG SHELTER

DANCE

The Crypt, All Saints Church Rosendale Road S.E.21

Pooh and The Ostrich Feathers

SATURDAY MAY 3

Entrance 5 shillings   8 to 11

In late July 1969 my time at Dulwich came to an end. Prior to that, I spent the summer rock and rollin' and playing cricket for the 1st XI. I was, briefly, threatened with being dropped because my hair was too long, but a great show of solidarity from the rest of the team, who threatened to 'withdraw their labour', resulted in my reinstatement. Pupil power! Basically, though, I made up the numbers. Batted No. 9, second change medium pace bowler. But I could catch – thus the *Fielding Cup*! The upside was that, being awarded School 1st XI colours, gave me the chance to buy an expensive blue and black striped blazer, a fancy gold braid badge (I still have the blazer. It now sports a 'Have a nice day' badge. I'm wearing it in various *Matching Mole* publicity shots) and, more importantly, allowed me to fool the ladies who served in the Buttery that I was a prefect (I never was) which allowed me to jump the queue for much-needed, pre-lunch, carb-heavy, sustenance.

My last match was a two-day game against some Dutch school team. I have rarely been so bored. How people play five-day Test Matches is beyond me. Although, quick name drop, two of my relatives did: Mick Stewart and his son, Alec, both of Surrey and England fame. Large parts of the Oval Cricket Ground are named after them. I shall briefly bask in some very dim reflected glory.

On my final day I wandered the school grounds thinking: what the fuck happens now? I was technically an adult but, at heart, still sixteenish and not at all ready for the real world. I would have to get a job. Bloody hell. And, with Phil staying on for another term, there'd not be much action on the music front either. And, as for Charles, he would not be free for another twelve months. What was one to do?

So, that was it for *Pooh and the Ostrich Feather* and our first step to rock stardom.

Instead, I joined the Civil Service.

MCC v Dulwich College (350th Anniversary)

Played at Dulwich College, 12th June, 1969: Duke of Edinburgh in attendance

MCC

AH Brown	b Mitchell	89	Mitchell	9	0	44	1
CJ Payne	run out	127	W Sheeran	9	3	21	0
ML Carr	b J Sheeran	7	Wright	2	0	11	0
EA Clark	not out	5	McCormick	4	0	19	0
JP Fellows-Smith	not out	11	J Sheeran	19	0	95	1
P Lush			Edwards	3	0	16	0
ML Wood			Marchant	4	0	33	0
J Cosgrove				50	3	239	2
GN Thornton							
CB Howland (Capt. & Wkt.)							
RG Musson							
Extras	(b3, lb3)	6					
	3 wickets (declared)	245					

FoW: 1-169, 2-229, 3-229

Dulwich College

TR Wright	b Musson	0	Musson	10	3	29	2
BA O'Connor	b Cosgrove	47	Fellows-Smith	19	4	60	2
RG Edwards	c Musson b Lush	38	Cosgrove	19	8	33	3
PI Marchant (Capt.)	b Cosgrove	1	Lush	11	4	35	2
DJ Mitchell	c Brown b Lush	6	Thornton	6	3	10	0
JT Sheeran	c Wood b Cosgrove	14	Clark	4	2	7	0
R Bonnet	b Fellows-Smith	25		69	24	174	9
SH Cole	b Fellows-Smith	2					
WAG McCormick	b Musson	13					
WAP Sheeran	not out	20					
MJ Hunsworth (Wkt.)	not out	8					
Extras	(b5, lb1)	6					
	9 wickets	180					

FoW: 1-0, 2-89, 3-89, 4-96, 5-96, 6-132, 7-36, 8-138, 9-152

Match Drawn

4 Proof I really did play for the Dulwich College 1st XI.
Just not very well.
The 350th Anniversary bit celebrated the founding of the College in 1619.

5 Charles and me in the North Cloisters, 1969.
The hair almost got me thrown out of the School 1ˢᵗ XI. The length not the style.

6 Dulwich College

RANDOM ENDNOTES FOR YOUR EDIFICATION AND DELIGHT:
The cricket pitch in the foreground was where I played for the school 1st XI back in the summer of 69.

Behind the big clump of trees on the left (known to all as The Clump. Who says public schools have no imagination?) was the 2nd XV rugby pitch where I did my best to avoid physical contact in the autumn of 68. Almost certainly the fifteenth name on the team sheet. I did score two tries in one game, though. How 'bout dat?

But, far more importantly, behind the big window in the central building (you guessed it, known as the Middle Block) lies The Great Hall where Manzanera/Targett-Adams, Hayward and I first strutted our stuff.

Behind the sight screens and the low building on the right (not there in my day) was/is the Science Block. Was/is because, since 68/9 it has been demolished and re-built. Ironically, it being a science block, some bright spark thought to put the radiators on the ceilings of the original building thus ignoring some science even I knew, i.e. heat rises[i]. In winter, the top floor sweltered and the ground floor froze. Clever stuff.

Even further to the right (so you can't see it) was the also since demolished Baths Hall (are the authorities trying to tell us something?). In the summer term it housed the swimming pool but, in the winter, it was boarded over and a stage put in so that pupils and parents alike could

---

[i] Science, not my strongpoint. Grade 9 in both Physics and Chemistry O-Levels. Grade 6 was a minimal pass. You got a Grade 9 if you remembered to put your name on the top of the paper and could, therefore, be identified as a dunce.

enjoy the annual production of the school play and the House drama competition (competitive plays? WTF?).

I once featured (I use the term very loosely) in the former. The play was *The Royal Hunt of the Sun* written in 1964 by Peter Shaffer about the destruction of the Incas by the obnoxious conquistador Francisco Pizarro (was there an unobnoxious conquistador? I think not. Appalling bastards the lot of them. Mind, the colonists of North America were no better and almost certainly killed a whole lot more native Americans than even the Spanish and Portuguese managed).

I 'played' an Inca messenger (or chaspi?) by the name, if memory serves, of Manco. I was, in Shakespearean terms, a voice 'off'. I would sit in the little echo chamber of the swimming pool's emptied foot bath (when filled with some disinfectant or other, it was designed to prevent the transmission of the plantar wart, or verruca as we knew it). My contributions all started with: 'Manco your Chaspi speaks....'. Because no-one saw me, I didn't bother to learn my lines, I just read them. I think we did three performances and, bored rigid by the end, I won a major argument with myself not to substitute the 'M' of Manco with a 'W'. Thankfully, my better instincts prevailed over silly, smutty, teenage irreverence. Shame.

My one appearance on stage was when we were all massacred by the Spanish towards the end. It was done under a strobe light for added dramatic effect, a piece of equipment we later 'borrowed' for the *Pooh* light show and put to far better use.

PatOF played the Bath's Hall twice and generally had a jolly good time, light show and all.

It made up for all the Latin lessons, the algebra and quadratic equations, the unpleasant dissecting of worms in biology, the arbitrary punishments of the prefects, and all the other educational indignities heaped upon us.

We just wanted to rock'n'roll.

ENDNOTES:

[1] Hodges, S, *God's Gift: A Living History of Dulwich College*, 1981, Heinemann, p. 9.
[2] O'Dair, M, *Different Every Time*, Serpent's Tail, 2014, p. 60.
[3] *http://pooterland.com/lightshows_ultramarine.html*

QUIET SUN

1970 – NOT THE GREATEST OF YEARS. In the *Estadio Nou Camp*, León, Mexico, on 14th June, England gave up the World Cup so famously won in 1966, losing 3-2 to, of all people, the old foe West Germany. Labour then unexpectedly lost the General Election held on 18th June, with some blaming the result on England's loss four days earlier. So, if you were one of those idiots who changed their vote from Labour to Ted Heath's Tories just because England lost a football match, I hope you will also take responsibility for Margaret Thatcher's election in 1979, cos the two events are inextricably linked. Pillocks.

Phil eventually left Dulwich in December 1969 on the completion of his French A-Level. Did he pass? I have not a clue. Let's assume so. He got a job in a rather pokey little travel agents in the City, as every aspiring guitar god should. Reason? He was saving for a new guitar because, if you wanted to be taken seriously, your axe absolutely *must* be either a *Fender* or a *Gibson*. *Hofner* simply did not cut it.

I was working for the *National Economic Development Council*, known as *Neddy*, in the Millbank Tower, south of the Houses of Parliament. The only exciting thing that happened there was when the staff of the Rt. Hon. Anthony Neil Wedgwood Benn, MP, previously Viscount Stansgate but now simply Tony Benn, the Minister of Technology whose offices were above ours, would commandeer the lift and send it straight to the ground floor for him to be rushed by ministerial car to the House of Commons 845 metres away, as the Division bells were ringing and he needed to vote. He was always most apologetic about inconveniencing people who, say, wanted to go from the 16th Floor to the 14th Floor but ended up, instead, in reception. But, hey, what's a Minister of the Crown going to do? A 3-line whip is a 3-line whip, as the actress said the bishop.

Bored, I then got a job as an assistant at a small library, the since demolished *Jeffreys Library*, Jeffreys Road, Stockwell, in the middle of a council estate. This was even more tedious, even if closer to home and thus quicker to get to, and away, from. Each day's 'highpoint' was lunch as it got me out of the building. Though a limp cheese sandwich in what was *The Swan*, opposite Stockwell Tube Station[i] and now an Irish pub adorned by the Republic's tricolour flag, hardly amounted to much. The most exciting moment came when some local kids dismantled a small, if

---

[i] The scene, for those of you who care to remember, of the murder of the completely innocent Jean Charles da Silva e de Menezes by armed officers of the Metropolitan Police Force commanded by the unutterably incompetent Cressida Dick, later promoted Commissioner as her reward for her abject failure on 22nd July 2005.

absurdly inappropriate, exhibition about angling. Not a lot of that goes on in a council estate in Stockwell as you might imagine. Initially we thought they had stolen all the rods, reels, nets, hooks, and flies and were now catching plastic bottles and discarded prophylactics somewhere along the detritus-strewn Thames embankment. They certainly wouldn't catch any fish, as the river was perfectly dead at that time. As it turned out, rather more creatively, they cunningly concealed everything on the library's shelves, as we progressively discovered over the coming weeks. All hidden in plain sight.

The money earned was needed as a deposit on musical equipment.

First up, you must understand that I really wanted to be a drummer. In *Pooh et al* we had a drummer, in fact, THE drummer in the personage of Charles Hayward. So, I was reduced to leaping about and screaming at the front of the stage like a demented person, *aka* a wanker. But I slipped behind Charles's drum kit whenever he wasn't looking and gave it a good pounding. We'd even done a drum 'duet' at school one lunchtime as part of an arts society called *Muse* founded by my brother in 1967, and we played at a couple of parties, one in Blew House. When I left school, I was determined to rectify the absence of a drum kit in my bedroom and, taking on board the behaviour of Governments before and since, I bought one (*Olympic*, I couldn't afford *Premier*), with money I didn't have (Governments don't buy drum kits, by the way. It's paying for things with money they don't have that's the issue).

I got a bank loan which, in those days, involved a personal interview with the bank manager at the Victoria branch of the newly formed *National Westminster Bank*[i]. Nowadays, you'd just shove it on the credit card without bothering to work out whether you could afford it. A change for the better? Not sure. Anyway, the rather fetchingly blue coloured set of drums was transported to Uffington Road, set up in my bedroom from where I entertained the neighbours at a variety of unsuitable times of day.

What to do next? Obvious really, Phil and I put an advert in the back pages of the *Melody Maker* for a bass player. One joker replied and we held a fairly embarrassing 'audition' in a room somewhere off Streatham High Road (not quite halfway between me in West Norwood and Phil near Clapham Common). Amazingly, Phil and I failed our own audition and the bass player walked out in a huff. Can't blame him. We, well, I was crap. Drummer? You must be joking.

---

[i] Formed in 1968 from a merger of the *District Bank* (founded 1829), *National Provincial Bank* (founded 1833) and *Westminster Bank* (founded 1834). It started trading under the new name on 1st January 1970. Just in time to lend me some money. You see, you are getting a swift course in British banking history at the same time as the torrid story of *Quiet Sun*. All for the same money. What a deal.

Then to everyone's relief, Charles left Dulwich in the summer of 1970 and so we swooped, like a swoopy thing, and dragged him away kicking and screaming to be our new, old, drummer.

A quick note about Charles. Ideas burst out of him in a more, or often less, controlled fashion. He possesses a creative mind determined to enthusiastically explore... everything, and for as far and as long as possible. For fifty years Charles has restlessly delved into the outer reaches of melody, rhythm, and sound. The results are uncompromising adventures not for the faint-hearted. He shows no signs of stopping anytime soon, which is good for you as you may still have a chance of catching him performing somewhere. He, and his often far younger collaborators, pop up all over the place. Keep an eye/ear/brain open. It will be worth it.

But, back in South London in 1970, we were determined to be adventurous, nay ground-breaking. Thus, we planned to have two drummers, a bit like the *Grateful Dead*, but rather more like we'd seen the *Mothers of Invention* deploy at the Royal Albert Hall on 6th July 1969. And what an awesome gig that was.

OK, so now we needed a keyboard player. Ideally, one who could play a very large number of seemingly unconnected notes in a very short period *à la* Mike Ratledge (sorry there, Mike, only joking). To our astonishment, just such a person replied to another *MM* "Musicians Wanted' advert in the small, and very long haired, shape of David Jarrett. David was considerably older than Phil and me but had his own organ. (At this point, can I quiet the muffled titters of amusement from the oiks at the back by stating this was an electric organ, a *Farfisa* no less. with white notes and black notes and a plug and shit. I do not know what else you might have been thinking of). Secondly, and this made it feel just *so right*, he too was an Old Alleynian (NOTE: an Old Alleynian is not some secret flagellant branch of the Roman Catholic Church but an old boy of Dulwich College though, in certain quarters, it might have proved difficult to tell the difference).

It is only right to state here unequivocally that Dave was a 'proper' musician. Just how 'proper' is, perhaps, best explained in his own words (and I hope he forgives me from quoting from an email at some length):

"I was useless at all sports, hated rugby, and was relieved that my hay fever gave me a medical certificate to get out of cricket for the whole of the summer term. I coped adequately but not brilliantly in my first four years, but I very much enjoyed my last three (Maths Form Remove, 6th and upper 6th) where two thirds of my time was studying maths, and I did well in my A-Levels.

My musical memories include singing in the choir in my first couple of years, with the Christmas concert in the boarded-over swimming pool and the summer concert at the Festival Hall; I loved some of the music we did, especially Bach's *Christmas Oratorio*. I had private piano lessons from the age of 7 or 8; I was much better at the theory exams than the piano ones and gave up. A year or two later I became interested in orchestral music, had oboe lessons at school and soon played in the school orchestra. A bit later I returned to the piano and played in the house music competitions – we (*Drake*) had a quartet consisting of violin, flute, bassoon and piano and I got to play the 9-foot *Bluthner* grand in the Great Hall. I also played the piano for the twice weekly house prayers in the room called the Old Cinema (in the old music block[ii]); the house master always let me choose the hymn, so I could make myself popular with the rugby players in the back row by giving them *Bread of Heaven* or *Jerusalem* at the end of term. I had some piano lessons at the school in my final year (after my A-Levels) and played Bartók's *From the Diary of a Fly* at a lunchtime concert. This piece, from *Mikrokosmos* Vol 6 is bitonal, with one hand playing the white keys and the other playing the black keys immediately above – a technique used by Cecil Taylor. Other pieces in Vol. 6 include the *Six Dances in Bulgarian Rhythm* which taught me about 'exotic' time signatures like 7/8 and (3 + 2 + 3)/8. Bartók must also have shown me how to compose music that was chromatic but tonal (e.g. *Bargain Classics* for *Quiet Sun*). I was also fascinated by Bach's *Musical Offering*, with its fugues and 'puzzle' canons. I learnt the 3-part ricercar (fugue) in my piano lessons, and arranged some of the canons for our quartet, with me also playing oboe. I can't remember how I thought we were going to play the 6-part ricercar with only 4 players; my notes suggest there may also have been a viola player, but we were lacking a cello. We had a few rehearsals, but the project never came to fruition, because I had gained a university place so left school at Easter 1964, a month before my 18th birthday, and spent 6 months working at Peckham tax office.

---

[i] One of the six 'day houses' of which every boy was a member. I was in *Raleigh*. The others were *Spencer, Sidney, Grenville, Drake,* and *Marlowe,* i.e. all famous Elizabethans. What baffled me is that the houses played one another at rugby, cricket, hockey, etc. Some of these were knock-out competitions. Having eight houses might have been more sensible. You do the arithmetic. This was belatedly realised, and *Jonson* and *Howard* added in 1982. At the end of the year the top 'house' was awarded a prize and title *Cock House*. Seems fabulously appropriate.
[ii] Demolished in the mid-60s.

So, music for me at school was all classical (including modern classical)... I... didn't really understand how jazz worked. I was ignorant of pop music until I was about 16 and it didn't interest me at all until it became more blues-influenced (e.g. *The Rolling Stones*) and less guitar-dominated (e.g. *The Animals* or *Manfred Mann*). I vaguely remember playing in a short-lived group... in the summer of 1964. I think we played one gig in (of course) Herne Hill Methodist Church Hall. There was a vocalist and I can't remember who else. I think we played endless jams on *Green Onions*, *House of the Rising Sun*, and 12-bar blues."

Suffice to say, Dave's arrival on the scene transformed what the band was capable of though, perhaps, this did not become clear until we recorded *Mainstream* in 1975.

This left us with two musicians still to find: a bass player and a sax player. From where did the need for a sax player arise you may ask? Well, in autumn 1969, those bastards in *Soft Machine* added a four-man brass section[i]. This was then eventually whittled down to just the one (thank god) saxman, Elton Dean. Whatever the *Softs* did then so would we.

Our saxist and flautist *extraordinaire* came in the form of ex-Army bandsman Dave Monaghan. Dave was a really nice guy, if somewhat diffident, and a good musician who wanted to branch out into some musical experiences beyond playing *The British Grenadiers*, etc., on some dusty parade ground. He also needed to earn some money, something we could not then, indeed, never could offer. So, apart from playing on our first demos, Dave exited stage left somewhat quickly. A sad loss.

In the meantime, something with serious repercussions for the future of British, nay World, music occurred. Frustrated by our inability to find Hugh Hopper Mk 2, the ex-*Soft Machine* roadie, member of the *Wilde Flowers*, and now the extremely tall, thin bass player and composer of complex compositions with the *Softs*, yours truly idly suggested that, in order to be able to rehearse, he should learn the various bass parts. After all, I thought, with only 4 strings, the instrument couldn't be *that* difficult

---

[i] First heard by yours truly at the *Regent's Street Polytechnic* on the 8th November 1969. Absolutely amazing. I preferred the septet, Nick Evans (trombone), Mark Charig (trumpet), Lyn Dobson (sax/flute), Elton Dean (saxes), to the quintet (Lyn and Elton) and, certainly, to the quartet (Elton). A brass section demands a different type of arrangement to a solo sax player. The movement towards jazz-rock (which the Wyatt/Ratledge/Hooper trio most certainly was not) accelerated once it was whittled down to Elton Dean. Nothing personal against Elton, who was a great player, but I preferred what went before, and was never a great fan of jazz-rock played by anyone much.

to play. Call it what you will – stupidity, arrogance – it kept the band going for a year and me vaguely gainfully employed for the next ten years.

And so it proved. Within minutes I located bottom E and within half an hour, A, D and G. Impressed, or simply desperate, the rest of the band agreed to the plan and a legend was born (*Ed.* who dat?).

Now there was a band, that band needed a name. Someone, probably my brother, noticed an article in the science section of a newspaper about something called '*The International Years of the Quiet Sun*'.[i] It was a eureka moment of which Archimedes himself would have been proud.

I, having sold the drum kit (for a good deal less than I paid for it), really needed an instrument appropriate to my new standing. Phil, after all, owned a sunburst *Gibson 335* (but only because the jerks at *Macari's* sold the *Gibson SG* on which he had put down a deposit and, indeed, set his heart, to someone with a more immediate source of cash). I, however, was stoney broke, penniless, brassic and generally bereft of funds. Step forward my generous, and greatly lamented, late uncle Derek, or 'drunk, punk, unc' as my brother and I used to call him. Out of the goodness of his heart, he gave me the £110 (no small sum and well north of £2,000 nowadays) required to buy the battered *Fender Precision* of my dreams.

Derek King was my mother's cousin and a senior civil servant who had worked in the UK, Malaysia, and India. He liked to play tennis and golf even if he was tall, somewhat overweight, left-handed, and not especially athletic. Back in the late 50s he owned a large stereo record player. Most of my late brother's and my grounding in classical music came from listening to LPs and EPs (remember them?) in his home in Dulwich. But he liked popular music too and came to love *The Beatles* and some other 60s artists. He was liberal and broad-minded. It was in his home, and on his now updated stereo, that my parents and he were utterly, if politely, bewildered on hearing the first *Matching Mole* album in 1972.

Derek was a widower and childless. His wife of a few brief months died almost immediately they arrived in India on a diplomatic posting in the early 50s and, on his return, we became something of a replacement family for him. Always generous, he gave my wife and me most of the furniture with which we filled our first house in 1977. He died suddenly and, worse, on his own from a massive stroke over 30 years ago. I owe him an awful lot. Almost certainly, I never thanked him adequately. Never too late, though. So, cheers, Derek, hope I made you proud.

---

[i] An international research programme in 1964/5. According to *Oxford Reference*, it was a period when 'solar and geophysical phenomena were studied by observatories around the world and by spacecraft to improve our understanding of solar–terrestrial relations'.

Back to the new, old, bass guitar. It takes a special kind of idiot to buy an expensive, if battered, mid-60s, dark blue *Precision* which, with no experience whatsoever, he dismantles, sands down, varnishes, and re-assembles in his father's garage. And an especially lucky idiot who ends up with a lovely natural wood *Precision* which, miraculously, still plays beautifully, and with a gloss finish so sharp he could comb his ever-lengthening hair in the reflection (this was the bass some bastard stole from Robert's house in Notting Hill just before the sessions for *Mole* 1. Never forgave the thief. We think we knew who it was, someone we turned down as a roadie, but couldn't prove it. I loved that guitar).

7 Quiet Sun, autumn 1970, wrapped up warmly against the cold.
L-R: MacCormick, Manzanera, Hayward, Jarrett.
I have my hands up as a foreign dog appeared to be about to piss on my trousers.

More to the point, and we are talking early autumn 1970 here, we now had a vaguely functioning line-up. Before Dave Monaghan's departure, and after several weeks' writing and rehearsal, we recorded some tracks at a demo studio, an environment totally new to all of us and something we probably did not make the best use of (OK, ungrammatical, 'something of which we did not make the best use'. Better? Nitpickers).

One track was *Trot*, Phils' tribute to Terry Riley, which resurfaced on *Mainstream*. The main piece, coming in at 10 minutes 30 seconds, was written by Ian and appropriately entitled *Years of the Quiet Sun*.[i] Live, the final part featured some less than thrilling singing by yours truly, but here they were replaced by Dave Monaghan playing the theme on sax. Be grateful for small mercies. The sub-Wyatt style lyrics were also by Ian. In the hope its deeply felt emotional content might promote meaningful

---

[i] If you *really* need to hear it, try *The Manzanera Archives: Rare One*, EXPCD21. Best not, however.

discussion, world peace, and a year's free tea from some, indeed any, supplier I include them here:

I can see you and I know that you can see me
If you're polite I might invite you home for tea
But if you're rude or I think that you're in a mood
When the tea's brewed I will let it stand til it's stewed

All of which begs several questions: was it Assam or Darjeeling? Or even Rooibos, the green version currently popular in the MacCormick household? If proper tea, was it white, green or black? Earl Grey even? Perhaps Herbal. Who knows? Who even cares?

But back to the music. We were attempting to be serious musos. Charles and Dave could read music, Phil and I could not. So, an intense period of musical self-education took place. People did not just turn up with a new piece and strum a few chords and sing a top line. Everything was written down properly, lead and bass parts, chords sequences, etc. Again, neither Phil nor I could sight read but, given a bit of time, we were able to make sense of whatever was presented to us. Yes, there was a certain amount of doing things 'by ear' but not a lot. Suddenly, we were all finding out about Ionian, Dorian, Phrygian, Lydian, Mixolydian and Aeolian modes and other what seemed like arcane shit like Pentatonic, Diatonic and Chromatic scales. Ian and I used to take scores out from West Norwood Library alongside the recording of whatever it might be, and we'd read them whilst listening to the music.

Thus, Ian's piece *Years of the Quiet Sun* came to us as a complete score with parts written for all instruments and even 'composer's notes' on the mood to be created. We were nothing if not pretentious. So, part one of this epic, *Years of the Quiet Sun*, was to be played 'Fairly fast' in 12/8 and evoke a 'warm, tranquil and exotic' mood. This then segued into Part Two, *Apogalacticon* by name. It was, I now see, partly written by me (who knew?). It was, apparently, meant to be 'cold, desolate, tragic' as it slipped through various time signatures, 12/8, 13/8, 7/8, before moving seamlessly into section three, *Star Drift* by name and 'mystical, unearthly' by nature, so it says here. It was to have a 'vague *Pink Floyd* feeling' (but without the resulting recording contract). The three soloists over the piece, Phil, Dave Monaghan, and Dave Jarrett, were also given 'notes' to inform their improvisations:

Guitarist: Imagine you are on a warm beach beside a pink sea on a tropical planet. The planet is inhabited by chuckling bubbles.
Sax: Imagine you are a dark planet roaming the universe between star systems. Your temperature is absolute zero.
Organ: Imagine you are alone in a spacecraft approaching the limit of the known universe.

Ok, then. Noting there were no instructions to the so-called bass player (which might have read: 'try to stay in tune and in time. Keep your fingers away from the upper reaches of the fretboard') let us place this in context. This was 1970, so very nearly the sixties. Some pretty silly stuff still went on. I must ask Phil sometime what he might do now if faced with such advisory notes on guitar solos. Never one to play as many notes as possible in the time made available, he might be one of the few who might make sense of it all.

8 The score for Years of the Quiet Sun
(page 1 of 4)

Interestingly, one forgets these things after 50 years or so, *Apogalacticon*, too, had lyrics which, on the tape were thankfully replaced by sax parts taking the lead. Anything to avoid the sound of my feeble warbling. You, dear reader, are thus one of the first people in the known universe to read said lyric, one heavily influenced, it seems, by sci-fi fi authors such as Philip K Dick (who will be blamed for other weird shit in about six years' time) and Alfred Bester, with a splash of *1984*. After studying them you will, I suspect, be none the wise but far better informed. They read:

London, ten thirty five
We're more dead than alive
It's like an iceberg
We heard they landed down the road

People running around
Just ignore them and they'll fuck off
Heading for higher ground
There's a suitcaseful of this stuff
She turned her eyes and
Her face flew open
Oh no, it wasn't me…

Turn that radio down
There's an order coming over
Charles is wearing a frown
And there's plenty more where that came
From, when your sleep dies
Dreams splash in your eyes
Oh no, it wasn't me
Killed the Chairman of the Party with a fart
And started World War Three

To be honest, the resulting tracks were a bit like my earlier description of Dave Monaghan:, i.e. nice but diffident. It didn't reach out and grab you by the wotsits. It was not truly radical, dangerous, assertive… out there. It was, in truth, a bit limp. Everything would, no doubt, have benefited from being played live, tested in front of an audience, kicked around in rehearsal, shaken up. It was all too polite.

So, looking back, it is no real surprise it generated little interest. Nevertheless, in October, the resulting tapes, accompanied by a somewhat OTT publicity handout penned by big brother (see page 323), were sent to a variety of record labels, and Richard Williams at the *Melody Maker*. It was accompanied by a promo photo, as every serious band needed a pic of them badly dressed and standing/sitting around looking gormless or grinning optimistically into the lens. We duly obliged. In spades.

So, back to the tapes and our dreams of stardom. Well, to quote Frank Zappa: 'It's such a drag when you're rejected'.

The responses from the record companies were uniformly negative. The one from Muff Winwood at *Island Records* seemed particularly, even aggressively, brutal, which makes the fact that *Mainstream* was released through *Island* in 1975 all the more pleasing. Really, up yours Winwood! Or, as my mum used to say, 'if you can't say something nice, don't say anything at all'. Bastard didn't even sign it himself. Had he known Ian would soon be Assistant Editor of the *NME* and in a position to be just as, but publicly, judgemental on the output of *Island Records* one wonders whether his unnecessarily acerbic little aside might have been moderated. We will never know. Ooh, feels better having written that.

He was, to be fair, absolutely correct in his summation of our musical efforts. Judge for yourselves:

Dear Mr Manzanera,

Thanks for dropping in your tape. Unfortunately I didn't think any of your music is this suitable for our label at the moment. Actually I am not too knocked out with it, it seems to lack a bit of bite. Perhaps the guy who wrote the superb literate hand out should stick to hand outs. Nevertheless I am sorry I can't help but it just didn't happen.

Yours sincerely,

pp Muff Winwood

On 11th November, *Liberty/United Artists* advised us there were 'no plans to use it at the moment' but invited us 'to try again in the future' when they would 'be only too happy to have another listen'.

And a week later the unknown representative of the *CBS* A&R[i] Department was pleasantly polite if equally dismissive. The tape was 'listened to carefully' but was not 'a commercial proposition for us at the present time'. He (almost certainly 'he' from my experience of testosterone-fuelled 70s A&R Departments) thanked us for our 'kindness in submitting it to us'. How sweet. Of course, *Matching Mole* ended up on *CBS*, so I snuck in their back door somehow.

Richard Williams at least wrote a short article about us in the *MM*, but the headline was hardly the sort of encouragement we sought:

"Richard Williams, *Melody Maker*

Outlook Cloudy for *Quiet Sun*

THE FIRST THING which attracted me to *Quiet Sun* was the carefully typed handout they included with their little tape. The prose mentioned such names as Ornette Coleman, Bartók,

---

[i] Artist and Repertoire as if you needed telling.

Messiaen, Randy California, Lou Reed, Jack Casady, Erik Satie, Andrew Cyrille, Marcel Duchamp and Cecil Taylor, and contained some interesting theories on the state of modern music.

The tape, too, was interesting, although initially it sounded derivative and emotionally rather cold. It contained passages in 10/8 and 13/8, and while that's no guarantee of any excellence it is an indication that something may be going on. Well, something is going on, in the heads of David Jarrett (keyboards) Philip Manzanera (guitar), Dave Monaghan (alto, flute, piccolo), Bill MacCormick (bass, vocals), and Charles Hayward (drums, percussion).

Quiet Sun has existed in one form or another since 1966, when Bill, Charles and Philip first got together. In fact, the only member of the group who wasn't educated at Dulwich College is Dave Monaghan who spent almost a decade as a musician in the Army, God bless him. The drawback which they'll inevitably suffer in the beginning of their career is an unfavourable comparison with the *Soft Machine*. The instrumentation is similar the sound bears a passing resemblance and their use of unusual time-signatures and the balance between written and improvised passages are not dissimilar. They are at pains, though, to disclaim true likeness and influence, despite their friendship with *Softs* drummer Robert Wyatt. 'We want to concentrate on more melodic things, writing tunes which aren't controlled by bass riffs. The trouble with odd metres is that people think you have to define the time by writing riffs, but we're trying to get away from that. It's difficult, because when you do that you stop signalling the beginning and end of each bar.' They are, however, fond of the *Softs*, as they are of a surprisingly catholic collection of 'heavies'.

From talking to them and from listening to their tape, I'm sure they'll have something to say for the future. If the present looks a little grim, then perhaps that's the price all young musicians of value have to pay."

So, not quite *all* bad, then.

THE REJECTIONS SIGNALLED THE DEPARTURE of Dave Monaghan who needed to earn. No idea what happened to him, but good things, I hope. He was a lovely guy.

With Dave gone, the four of us (well, five really, as Ian hung around to make useful comments, write the promo material and compose one of our first pieces. Versatile little git) rehearsed, initially in the egg-carton lined room at Charles' house in Camberwell. We then moved to a church hall in East Dulwich (now something called the *Deeper Life Bible Church*, linked to some weird organisation in Nigeria). There we would warm up with a *Quiet Sun homage* to the *Grateful Dead's Dark Star*. In other words, 20 minutes or so of inconsequential noodling minus the awful vocals (sorry Mr Weir and Mr Lesh, etc., but they weren't your strong point). Finally, we moved to a large room near Waterloo Station somewhere behind the old Fire Station (now a gastro pub), as seen in the photo above.

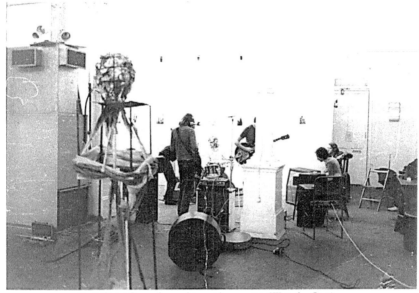

9 A Quiet Sun rehearsal in a place next to Waterloo Station.
L-R Someone's backside, my back, Charles's front, Phil's right shoulder, and the torso of Dave Jarrett. Might be the left arm of Charles's younger brother, Tony, behind Dave.

Nothing now could hold us back from world domination. Except a lack of cash, gigs and any interest from record companies.

Somehow, an agent was persuaded to put us on the bill supporting *Steamhammer* at the *Pavilion Theatre*, Worthing. Worthing is, for those of you who like such irrelevant detail, the town with the oldest age profile in the country. It was, therefore, the perfect place for our first gig.

Steamhammer, a local band had, by this time, recorded three albums, the first two for *CBS*. They enjoyed moderate success in Europe until they split in 1973. Lead guitarist Martin Pugh played on Rod Stewart's first solo album and a former guitarist, Martin Quittenton, co-wrote with Stewart his international hit singles *Maggie May* and *You Wear It Well*.

Sadly, the band and its successors were twice hit by tragedy. First, 25-year-old drummer Mick Bradley died from undiagnosed leukaemia in February 1972. Then, Pugh joined up with ex-*Yardbirds* and *Renaissance* lead singer Keith Relf in 1974 in a band called *Armageddon* (signed to *A&M*

Records). Relf sadly died on 12th May 1976 when he electrocuted himself whilst playing the guitar at home. I must admit to not knowing this fact. *The Yardbirds*, of course, was the seminal 60s band which moved music forward monumentally with their three lead guitarists – Clapton, Page and Beck – and their series of singles between 1965 and 66: *For your Love* (I mean, combining bongos and harpsichord – played by Brian Auger – in 1965. Get out of here!), *Heart Full of Soul, Evil Hearted You/Still I'm Sad, Shapes of Things*, and *Over Under Sideways Down*. Loved them all though, to be honest, *Shapes of Things* was the favourite. That Beck guitar solo! Wummph!

10 The Pavilion Theatre, Worthing
Located on the landward end of Worthing Pier. I don't suppose it looked quite so good back in 1971.

On a more positive note, Martin Pugh reformed *Steamhammer* in 2020 and they released a new album, *Wailing Again*, in 2022. Good luck to them.

Anyway, back to Worthing Pier. We turned up in two vehicles. Most of us and the equipment in a small van and Charles with his dad and the drums in the *Morris Traveller*. The stage was large, the hall was bare, and the rather sparse audience greeted our appearance with something between indifference, boredom and hostility. If I been in that audience I might well have agreed. We seemed to have taken the 'poo' out of *Pooh and the Ostrich Feather* and applied it to *Quiet Sun's* live performance. I soon found out that playing bass and singing at the same time was a good deal easier when there was no-one around to notice either errors or going out of tune. We pretty much became an instrumental band after that.

To sum up, we were, I think it fair to say, a bit 'limp'.

Things could only get better, and eventually they did. New compositions were forthcoming such as Phil's very extended *Corazon y*

Alma which would feature in various guises on his first solo album *Diamond Head* (divided up into *Frontera, East of Echo, Same Time next Week* and *Alma*. The original was *very* long), and *Sol Caliente*. Dave Jarrett brought his classical background to bear with two pieces: *Bargain Classics* (originally called *A young person's guide to the Bargain Classics*) and *RFD* (which, in a nod to the *Softs* and Mike's *Outbloodyrageous* was more properly called *Re-fucking-diculous*). I contributed a little something which, after several titles (first *Dog*, which was expanded to *Mummy was a Maoist, Daddy was a running dog capitalist lackey of the bourgeoisie*), was eventually given the title *Mummy was an asteroid, Daddy was a small non-stick kitchen utensil* some time in the middle of recording the *Mainstream* album. Please do not ask why. I haven't got a fucking clue. It just sort of came to me, man, like out of nowhere, know what I mean? And the only drug I was imbibing was caffeine. But lots of it.

As I had nothing else to fall back on, my compositions were riff rather than chord based. And linear rather than circular in the tradition of the western pop song. I would knit together various ideas which emerged from messing about on the bass whereas everyone else wrote songs on guitar or keyboards which involved chord progressions. With me there was no great sophistication at work and some pieces needed a better ear and greater imagination to turn them into something worthwhile. Robert Wyatt and *Gloria Gloom* for example. With a little help from Brian Eno. *Mummy* was one such piece and was later variously recycled by the *801* and a bit even incorporated into the 1977 version of *Out of the Blue* of which that's year's version of the band played a rousing version.

Then there were pieces that, for one reason or another never, or very belatedly, saw the light of day. Ian wrote a rollicking instrumental called *A Parking Ticket* which we ran out of time to learn. I used to have the score and Phil and I both remember it fondly. I wrote a short piece, *Fortunately I Had One With Me*, which was eventually recorded at Phil's Kilburn studio for his 2008 album *Firebird VII*, being played by Phil, with Charles, the hugely talented Polish keyboard player Leszek Możdżer, and fabulous Israeli bass player Yaron Stavi. It was based on a thing written back in 1971 and 'liberated' by Phil at the time.

Belated was the extraordinary *Rongwrong*. Towards the end of the band's very brief life, Charles sat us down in front of the piano at his house and performed the entire thing. I think we were all stunned. Looking back, it could, in a way, have been the band's *Moon in June*. Great melodies, interesting rhythmic ideas, changes of mood and pace. It was all there. Plus, the opportunity for me to play an extended bass solo. What's not to like? It is my favourite *Quiet Sun* piece. But *Quiet Sun* simply ran out of gas, and me out of money, before we had the time to learn or play it. By now, I was walking the four miles, 90-minute, trip to Charles's house for rehearsals as I could not afford the bus fare. It could not last.

But, before then, in early '71, *Quiet Sun* was spluttering along quietly, barely creating a ripple on the placid surface of the UK music biz. But, foolishly, one label did not reject us out of hand and these idiots were *WEA*. They owned an old Georgian country house down in Dorset and there installed a small, and not very sophisticated, recording studio for demos. It was a place they sent bands every now and then to see what they might come up with. Nice house but barely a recording studio – the vocal 'booth' was the stone-floored corridor from the front door. A lonely place (and cold) when you are trying to sing in tune (barely). We were there for two or three days and several tracks, including the ever-so-long *Corazon y Alma* (with some pretty dodgy singing by yours truly), and the rather briefer, *RFD*, were recorded, the results being of variable quality. Thankfully for *WEA's* shareholders, the A&R Department saw the light before it was too late and we were again rejected.

LIVE PERFORMANCES WERE FEW AND FAR BETWEEN.
12th February 1971 was the date of one of the few *Quiet Sun* gigs we did didn't organise ourselves (have I told you how huge we were in West Norwood and Dulwich? Trump-like hooooge! I was constantly swatting away fans. Or was that fanning away flies? Can't remember). Anyway, someone at the Students' Union at what was then *Portsmouth Polytechnic* (since 1992 the *University of Portsmouth*), booked *Symbiosis* for one of the eight gigs they played in the first two months of the year. For whatever reason, *QS* was booked in as support (coincidentally we later played support to more Canterburians in the shape of *Caravan*, as we shall see).

Symbiosis[i] was but one of the steps taken by Robert down the path of growing disillusion with the *Softs*, and a reflection of the widening musical and social gulf between him and Mike and Hugh (and Elton Dean).

Stepping back a bit, early 1970 was a hectic time for the *Softs*: touring Germany, Belgium, Holland and France between January and April; a six-night residency at *Ronnie Scott's Jazz Club* in Frith Street, Soho, between the 20th and 25th April; then most of May recording *Third* for their new label *CBS* at *IBC Recording Studios* in Portland Place; and culminating in their ground-breaking appearance on 13th August at the Royal Albert Hall as part of the programme of the *Henry Wood Promenade Concerts*.

---

[i] Not to be confused with the band of the same name formed in 1987 by John Hackett, brother of ex-*Genesis* guitarist Steve, or, indeed, any of the other bands of the same name which have existed variously in Florence, Melbourne, Frostburg in Maryland, or Slovakia.

Hectic but, for Robert, deeply unhappy. And, back then, when Robert was unhappy, he tended to drink, a tendency which did not endear itself to either Mike or Hugh.

The sad thing was that, according to Robert, he really liked what the other two wrote for *Third* and did his level best to enhance the music with his drumming.[1] But Mike and Hugh's feelings about Robert's music were not mutual. According to Robert:

"They hated *Moon in June* and refused to play on it."[2]

Now, I have never met an early *Soft Machine* fan who does not love *Moon in June*. Indeed, one of my greatest disappointments with *Matching Mole* was that Robert didn't want us to perform it. Beautifully melodic, warm, playful, *MiJ* possessed the one factor sometimes missing from other *Softs'* output (and missing altogether once Robert left): humanity in all its facets, warts and all.

Now, Robert has always been one to jam with musicians of almost any type. In the States with Hendrix he did it all the time and, increasingly so in 1970. Recording with Kevin Ayers, playing with the improv jazz group, *Amazing Band*, gigging in Europe with *The Whole World* in the summer. And then came the Royal Albert Hall. *Soft Machine*, the first electric band to ever play the Proms. Could've, should've been great. It was good to listen to, to be at, as we all were, but not good at all for Robert.

Whilst digging around for some additional material for Adele Schmidt and José Zegarra Holder's 2015 *Romantic Warriors III: Canterbury Tales* film documentary, I came across a letter from Robert to brother Ian. It was dated from some time before the Albert Hall Proms performance, June maybe. It reveals the true depth and breadth of Robert's utter disillusion with the band. The relevant section reads:

"Risking sounding sordid (or whatever word comes to mind) I take little responsibility for the general direction of our live sets and none at all for ¾ of *Third*. Frankly, trying to inject honest creative life into the *Soft Machine* these days is flogging a dead horse, by which I mean, more or less: 'don't ask me mate, I just work here'. Like the phoenix, me and a few mates hope to rise from the ashes of our various current groups with life and vigour anew (new group tentatively called *The Inevitable Split*) at our mutual convenience. Meanwhile I shall go on the road with David Bedford and the *Whole World* sometime after *SM's* absurd Albert Hall exposure in August."

So, there you go then. Thankfully (for me, at least) *The Inevitable Split* was delayed until after Robert saw *Quiet Sun* supporting *Symbiosis* at Portsmouth Poly, as the memory of this clearly lodged in his brain and I was no longer just the public school boy who constantly turned up uninvited to drink his tea at Dalmore Road.

symbiosis

11 Promo for the Symbiosis gig

Anyway, *Symbiosis…* post Proms, Robert got involved with Keith Tippett, as *SM* gigs and the recording of *Fourth* allowed (an album notable as the third composer in the group was now Elton Dean). On a trip to Bordeaux with *Centipede* he got friendly with exuberant tenor sax player Gary Windo and out of this was born a band: Gary, Robert, Steve Florence (guitar), Mongezi Feza (trumpet), Nick Evans (trombone and previously part of the *SM* septet), and Roy Babbington (bass, who would replace Hugh in the *Softs* in the not-too-distant future). Gary christened it *Symbiosis*. In fact, membership was never fixed, as the promo piece for the Portsmouth Poly gig below confirms.

Starting at *Bedford College*[i], part of *London University*, on 5th December, the combo played at irregular intervals, even recording a session for the BBC's *Top Gear* on 11th January 1971. Now, on 12th February they were about to play *Portsmouth Poly*.

And so was *Quiet Sun*.

Off we toddled down the A3 with our random collection of gear, Charles's humungous drum kit and my beautifully restored *Fender Precision*.

We turned up. Set up. Think: boy, this stage is a bit small for *Symbiosis*. And play. By now, we have abandoned any thoughts of having vocals. I was having enough trouble standing up straight and playing bass without having to warble waywardly. So, it was 50 minutes or so of pure

---

[i] Created in 1849 at 47, Bedford Square, by Elizabeth Jesser Reid, it was, as the Ladies College in Bedford Square, the first higher education college for women in the UK. Degree courses became possible in 1878. In 1900 it became part of London University. It merged with *Royal Holloway College* in 1985 to form *Royal Holloway and Bedford New College* but, in a rather bad move, Bedford was subsequently removed from the college's name which seems rather an insult to all the highly educated and extremely talented ladies who attended the college over its 136-year history.

instrumentals. Seemed to go OK. Robert watched. *Symbiosis* took over and, after a brief withdrawal to the Students' Union bar for 'refreshment', we go back and watch. Lovely stuff. *Symbiosis* finish. Crowd applauds (as do we). Robert thanks audience and announces there is some spare time. OK then, he suggests, why don't the members of *Quiet Sun* get back on stage and we will jam together. Cue stunned silence from us (Charles may have screamed. He was like that back then), if not from the audience who seemed to think it a passable idea.

As our gear is still on stage we slink on at the back, turn on, tune in and bugger about. I can remember very little except it was great fun. Robert's recollection is somewhat more detailed (as you will see in the very sadly late Mike King's *Wrong Movements*, whose copyright I do not wish to infringe too much, so go and find/buy a copy and read it for yourselves, you lazy buggers). Broadly speaking, Robert laid down a solid, soul beat and the rest of us looned about. Fabulous. And, for me, rather useful, even if I did not know it at the time.

12 'Promo' posters for two of our self-promoted gigs, Spring 1971

Thereafter, we toured extensively… West Norwood, Dulwich, Catford. We often organised our own gigs and a group of complete numbskulls (sorry, dedicated followers) followed us to most of them. We were supported by the band of Dave Jarrett's younger brother, Chris. They rejoiced in the name *Zurgo Grotte*, which moniker makes *Quiet Sun* seem to be the absolute epitome of all known band names.

Then, on 15th July came the highlight and, as it turned out, the end. We were booked to be third on the bill to *Caravan* at a *Shelter* fundraising benefit at *St Dunstan's College* in Catford. *Caravan* was promoting their third album, *In the Land of Grey and Pink*, released in April. *Caravan* is, of course, the band most closely intertwined with *Soft Machine* with pretty much all of the original members coming from East Kent – Canterbury, Herne Bay and Whitstable mainly – and most of them having played, though not at the same time, in the *Wilde Flowers* which, in numerous incarnations, existed between 1964 and 1967. *Caravan*, made up of David Sinclair, Richard Sinclair, Pye Hastings and Richard Coughlan[i], was formed in 1968. Richard Sinclair was, and is, a great bass player who has adorned many an album down the years: Robert's *Rock Bottom*, *Hatfield and the North's* albums and *Camel* to name but a very few. Dave Sinclair, with his *Hammond* organ put through a fuzz box, was, perhaps, their most recognisable instrumental sound and, of course, an excellent composer. His *Nine Feet Underground* from *Grey and Pink* was briefly on the list of 'things to try out' when Robert invited Dave, Phil Miller and me to the house in St Luke's Mews in Notting Hill, and which invite led to the formation of *Matching Mole* late in 1971.

13 The last QS gig.
I'd like to know who described us 'Jazz based rock'. Never.

---

[i] Richard Coughlan stayed with *Caravan* until he sadly died on 1st December 2013. After fifteen studio albums and 19 live albums *Caravan* are going strong with original member Pye Hastings at the helm. Richard Sinclair lives in southern Italy and Dave Sinclair in Japan. They are both still very active musically.

52

But we get ahead of ourselves. The gig went OK. The members of *Caravan* were a great bunch, though Dave and I had no inkling we would be meeting up again in a few weeks' time.

Life was, however, getting tricky. No money, no prospects. A bit like the average working-class teenager in Tory Britain since 2010. As economic realities dawned it was clear I needed to earn some money. I got another job in the civil service working in the registry (i.e. filing department) of the *Overseas Development Administration* in the since demolished Eland House in Stag Place, Victoria. It would later be renamed the *Ministry for Overseas Development*, which did nothing to change its role, but necessitated an expensive replacement of all its signage and stationery. Another excellent example of the UK government's careful husbandry of hard-pressed taxpayers' money.

Having to work during the week put a bit of dampener on our rehearsals and, by the middle of 1971 we were all more or less ready to call it a day. Then two things happened. Phil replied to an advert in the *Melody Maker* for 'The Perfect Guitarist' for a new band about which there was already something of a buzz. *Roxy* something or other. He didn't immediately get the gig as Ferry apparently wanted ex-*Nice* guitarist David O'List, a case of be careful what you wish for, perhaps. Said guitarist was found but Phil hung around as a roadie and then made out he knew something about sound-mixing. All the while, with a sixth sense all was not as it seemed, he was learning the guitar parts. So, when O'List and the new drummer, soon-to-be The Great Paul Thompson, fell out, Phil stepped in and the rest, as they say, is history.

And second, Robert phoned the idiot bass player and asked whether he fancied messing about musically alongside Dave Sinclair, who he'd heard of, and Phil Miller, who he had not. Bored rigid punching holes in bits of paper and stringing them together in buff-coloured folders which would then never again see the light of day, he readily agreed. Who wouldn't?

But *Quiet Sun*, it seemed, had disappeared without trace.

Bugger.

ENDNOTES:
[1] King, M, *Wrong Movements*, SAF Publishing Ltd., 1994, no page numbers but comment below 13th August 1970.
[2] Ibid.

MATCHING MOLE

S O, MOVE FORWARD A COUPLE OF MONTHS to late summer 1971. Robert has left, been kicked out of, *Soft Machine* (announced in the first week of September) and, to be blunt, is not in great shape. As we have seen, *Quiet Sun* has disintegrated in the face of an (eminently reasonable) lack of interest from anyone very much. I have been working for the civil service. Phil has just answered, or is about to, a certain advert in the *Melody Maker* for a guitarist and a drummer for some arty bunch who modestly want to change the face of British music.

And Robert, in a moment of weakness/madness, picks up the phone and calls me...

He was no longer living in Dalmore Road. Now, after moving unhappily between several addresses, he resided at 35, St Luke's Mews, Notting Hill. Though most of the mews has since been re-built, No. 35 survives. It now sports a new, narrow balcony, an alarm system, whitewashed walls and woodwork and doors in a discreet grey. What also remain are the garage doors to what was, effectively, the entire ground floor in 1971. The living accommodation – small kitchen, smaller bathroom, a living room, and a bedroom – was all on the first floor. To be honest, it wasn't in the best of shape in those days. One suspects a lot of people had passed through in its lifetime, one which probably extended back to the Victorian era, and more than a few left their mark. It was rather cold, gloomy, and very sparsely furnished. Not that I cared.

Having handed in my notice, I started a new commute from West Norwood via Victoria and the Circle Line to Notting Hill and then the mile long walk to the house. In all, a journey of some 90 minutes. So, sod that, most days when we were rehearsing, I stayed the night, sleeping on a thin mattress on the living room floor.

At this time, Robert was co-habiting with a red-haired, and sometimes fiery, French lady called Cyrille. She was tall, model thin, and seemed to live on her nerves. Their relationship was, from time to time, tempestuous. Teacups were occasionally thrown, but not by Robert. Then there would be calms between storms. Calms when tea was served, eggs were fried, toast smeared with Marmite and all was smiles. But then sudden, unexpected squalls, when it was best to leave Cyrille to it and retreat downstairs to make loud noises in the garage.

Cyrille, you see, was the ex-wife of Kevin Ayers and the mother of their daughter, Rachel. For a while she lived at Dalmore Road, not that I ever talked to her there. She then contributed some percussion to *End of an Ear* and, as is the case, with such things, sooner or later, one thing inevitably led to another. Such relationship rotations were not unusual in this *milieu*. Pam, Robert's ex, was now the partner of drummer Pip Pyle (who will feature again later) after an extended affair to which Robert was, for a time, oblivious. Alfreda Benge, Alfie, soon to become Robert's lifelong partner, was once the girlfriend of drummer Laurie Allan (who will also feature again later) and also Pip Pyle. It was all circuits and bumps, if you get the flying analogy.

Let us now pop back a bit in history. A year earlier, in August 1970, Robert recorded his first solo album which was not, as *CBS* expected, more sweetly melodic *Moon in June*-type material, but an album of mainly improvised jazz. Sandwiched between versions of Gil Evans' *Las Vegas Tango*, the various pieces were dedicated to people who were influential in his life at the time:

To Mark Everywhere, dedicated to his half-brother Mark Ellidge who played piano on the album;
To Saintly Bridget, the British folksinger Bridget St John[i] on whose album, *Thank you For*, Robert had added some uncredited percussion;
To Oz Alien Daevyd and Gilly, Daevid Allen and his partner Gilly (*sic* Gilli) 'the space whisperer' Smyth;
To Nick Everyone, Nick Evans, the trombonist who, alongside trumpeter Mark Charig, who is on the album, had been half of the *Soft's* original brass section back in 1969;
To Caravan and Brother Jim, i.e. *Caravan* and wind player Jimmy Hastings;
To the Old World (Thank You for the Use of Your Body, Goodbye), Kevin Ayers and his band *The Whole World* with which Robert played from time to time; and
To Carla, Marsha and Caroline (For Making Everything Beautifuller), the late and greatly lamented Carla Bley, the outstanding jazz composer and pianist whom I came to know later through Gary Windo's *Steam Radio Tapes*, Marsha Hunt, the singer and actress, and, from 1967, Mike Ratledge's long distance wife (they barely lived together but are still married), and Caroline Coon.

Caroline Coon, therefore, features twice in the titles of songs written by Robert, the second being *Matching Mole's* best-known piece, *O Caroline* (and, of course, *To Carla, etc.* is recycled as *Instant Pussy* on the album). In between the recording of these tracks, they enjoyed a deep if non-exclusive relationship. I remember seeing them soon after it started. She

---

[i] Bridget St John was born Bridget Anne Hobbs in 1946. A singer, guitarist, and composer, she produced three albums for John Peel's *Dandelion* label: *Ask Me No Questions* (1969), *Songs for the Gentle Man* (1971) and *Thank you For* (1972). She was a friend of, and had worked with, Kevin Ayers, appearing on *Shooting at the Moon*. She produced a fourth album, *Jumblqueen* (*Chrysalis*, 1975). She then moved to New York where she now lives and works.

had him on a macrobiotic diet, he'd cut down on the drinking and smoking, and he'd never looked better. His long blonde hair gleamed, he was cheerful, neatly dressed, and next to him, Caroline, who was several inches taller, was a stunning looking lady, fiercely intelligent, and equally fiercely independent.

His happiness did not last. Marcus O'Dair in *Different Every Time* describes their relationship in detail. Go read it. It becomes painfully sad.

Life in *Soft Machine* was going from bad to worse. Beneath it all, Robert was desperately depressed. People, friends, he had known most of his life seemed intent on squeezing him out the band he helped form and of which he was the most recognised and popular member. It would be enough to upset anyone, but Robert was particularly fragile at this time.

I will now do something I try to avoid, infringing somebody's copyright by quoting from their book but, as they are my words I am quoting, I don't feel quite so bad about it. I was at a party in someone's house in central London. I think Phil was there too. Robert arrived:

> "We all turned up fairly jolly, but Robert sat in a corner and within half an hour, nobody wanted to talk any more. He was just oozing depression, it was terribly, terribly sad. We just didn't know what to do. I was really worried about him. He came across almost as suicidal. He just sat and didn't say a word and slumped. I thought, 'Shit, what is going on here?' Because it's so unlike him, he's usually so exuberant and bouncy and positive. And he really was in a very bad state."[1]

I have only ever known one other person who could do this to a room of people. That was my late brother Ian in the time before he committed suicide in 2003. Sometime after, Robert and Caroline came back from a brief *Soft Machine* tour of the USA in July, Robert tried to end it all. Thankfully he failed, but the relationship with Caroline Coon was over, even if that fact was not yet totally accepted.

But, in September 1971, with the umbilical cord to *Soft Machine* at long last severed, Robert needed to take some sort of control, and getting David Sinclair, Phil Miller, me, and from time to time, Dave MacRae, into the garage at St Luke's Mews to play music was, I believe, part of that process.

I remember David Sinclair as a quiet, studious, precise personality. But a man with a twinkle in his eye. Often compared to Mike Ratledge, they were two completely different musicians. Not simply because David played the rather more commonplace *Hammond* Organ whilst Mike played a rarer *Lowry* (though both employed a fuzz box when playing lead parts) but also because of their approach. I have always thought *Caravan* to be more 'mainstream' than *Soft Machine*, more part of what might now be termed the progressive rock scene which developed as from c. 1969. But their music seemed typically 'English', whimsical, bucolic, sardonic, witty, with none of the bombast which affected certain bands (Name them! *Ed.* OK, *ELP* for one). It seemed, however, that, whilst David enjoyed improvising within a defined structure, he became less comfortable, or, perhaps, simply less interested, in blowing in a much freer musical environment. There was a period within *Mole* when, on stage, the latter environment held true. Perversely, after David left and Dave MacRae started to contribute more material, more structure crept into the live performances but, by that time, David had determined *Mole* was not for him. A shame, as I enjoyed playing with him and knew him to be a fine composer who might have contributed significantly had the circumstances been different.

Phil Miller was not your standard guitar player. Not for him repeated rapid arpeggios, sweeping flourishes and attendant dramatic poses. With Phil, each element of his work, be it playing in support of others or as the lead voice, was approached with care and thought. It was not about how many semi-quavers could be fitted into a bar but what was the right note or chord to place just *there*. With Phil, less was, more often than not, more.

One sometimes felt that he had discovered a whole new world of tonality of which he was the lone explorer. His solos were extended explorations of a theme, sometimes tortuous and extreme, but played with a focus so total he seemed in a world of his own. One in which he was clearly oblivious to the grimacing facial expressions and tendency to go cross-eyed when embedded deep in the music. Though we would discuss with enthusiasm the guitar work of John McLaughlin on Tony William *Lifetime's Emergency!* album, Phil was not intent on copying the great guitarist. Instead, he was carving out his own path to becoming a unique voice, later writing and playing pieces of such complexity and dexterity they sometimes defied belief – and the efforts of others to play along.

Tall and thin, Phil seemed to exist on a diet of fresh air. Quiet, with a dry sense of humour, his apparent favourite item of clothing was a very tight, short-sleeved jumper in several horizontal pastel bands. On occasion, he would wear a boiler suit on stage. Rock 'n' roll he was not. But, as the band developed, he came forward with a series of compositions which became the bedrock of the live set, and his playing a key part of the 'sound'.

Phil sometimes relaxed with a joint or two. Once, it was almost his undoing. We had travelled back from France to land at Folkestone where Customs was in the railway station. As usual, Phil carried his guitar case (he was rarely without it. Mine was in the truck) which contained his *Gibson SG*, strap and, under a little flap, his spare guitar strings… and a small bit of dope. As Robert, Dave and I were empty-handed, we three long hairs were grudgingly waved through by the suspicious customs officials. Not so Phil. We hurried through with a 'nothing to do with us, boss' shrugging of the corporate shoulders, leaving Phil to his fate. Hovering a hundred metres or so along the road outside we were, after about five very long minutes, relieved to see an ashen faced Mr Miller emerge, a sickly grin on his face. They had looked everywhere in the case except under the packet of guitar strings which concealed the offending item wrapped carefully in some foil.

Just as well. The band needed Phil. He had become essential.

Dave MacRae was not to become a full-time member of the band until the spring but, as his session playing allowed, he rehearsed, recorded, and played with us intermittently until David Sinclair left. Then he became a full-time, and essential, playing and composing *Mole*. Dave was the oldest member of the unit, having been born in Auckland, New Zealand, in 1940. He was, therefore, eleven years my senior, but so far ahead of me in musical terms – skill, technique, experience, sheer musicality – we might have existed in different universes. Not that Dave would have ever hinted at such. He smiled at my eccentricities, OK, interminable solos, and, perhaps, put them down to youthful exuberance. He worked with whoever was there and did not judge.

Dave was trained at the *New South Wales Conservatorium of Music* before he moved to the States in the late 60s. In 1969 he joined the Buddy Rich Band, a hugely prestigious gig reflective of his immense skill and musical abilities. He arrived in London in 1971 and was immediately in huge demand as a session player. But what he loved was to play live, to improvises, to compose – to have no limits. In a sense, *Mole* gave him that platform.

Personally, Dave is a lovely man, warm, funny with no sense of self-importance or ego. We met up to have afternoon tea in the grand surroundings of the *Grosvenor Hotel*, Victoria, a few years ago when he and his wife Joy, a professional singer, visited London. Though we hadn't seen one another for more than forty years, it was like a continuation of a post-rehearsal chat over a mug of builder's tea back in the day. Despite my very limited abilities, I was hugely fortunate to have played with two of the very best keyboard players in British music of the past fifty years: Dave MacRae and Francis Monkman. I can confidently assert they do not get any better than those two. Giants.

Back in St Luke's Mews the garage was soon full of equipment. Phil set up by the door. Then came Robert's drums, Dave's *Hammond*, and me, tucked away in the corner. Introductions were made, sheepish grins exchanged, first impressions formed. Then, turn on, plug in and tune up. But, where to start?

---

[i] Now *The Clermont*.

Moon in June would have done for me, but it was not to be, or not, at least, for very long. We toyed with elements of Dave's *Nine Feet Underground*, but Robert's mind was elsewhere. So, from *End of an Ear*, we played around with Gil Evans' *Las Vegas Tango*. The original *Las Vegas Tango* is gloriously chaotic yet melancholy, in the mood of much of the earlier *Sketches of Spain*. It seemed to fit the general vibe.

Do you know about Gil Evans? If not, go find out. The album from which *Las Vegas Tango* was drawn, *The Individualism of Gil Evans*, was recorded in 1964, by which time Evans was 52 years old. Think about that for a moment. He was born in Canada two years *before* the First World War broke out. Think about the scale of musical changes over the intervening decades. His stepfather, whose surname he assumed, was a peripatetic miner, journeying wherever work took him and his family. Gil, born in Toronto, ended up in Stockton, California, all the while listening to big band jazz on the way. A pianist and arranger, he worked with many of the jazz greats throughout the 1940s and 50s. A true high point was a trio of albums recorded with Miles Davis: *Miles Ahead* (1957), *Porgy and Bess* (1958), and *Sketches of Spain* (1960), the latter album being a personal all-time favourite. His arrangements could veer from lush to austere, with the standard jazz brass section often augmented by French Horns and Tubas. Rhythmically complex, these were challenging scores to perform, even for the best of musicians. A list of the people Evans later worked with, or whose music he then played, gives a vivid impression of man of unlimited creative interests: he recorded pieces by Jimi Hendrix, played with Jaco Pastorius (has there been a better bass player?), Don Preston of the *Mothers of Invention*, and Gordon Matthew Thomas Sumner, better known as *The Police's* Sting, to name but a few. Evans sadly died after an operation in 1988.

Other random stuff was thrown into the mix. George Harrison's *Beware of Darkness* from *All Things Must Pass*. It fitted the generally downbeat mood. The doleful lyrics, especially of verse II, certainly did:

Watch out now, take care
Beware of the thoughts that linger
Winding up inside your head
The hopelessness around you
In the dead of night
Beware of sadness
© *George Harrison, BMG Rights Management, Warner Chappell Music, Inc.*

A lot of the time we simply jammed. On occasions, I would re-live my ambition to be a drummer, getting behind Robert's kit whilst he improvised on the *Hammond*. But mainly material was narrowed down to stuff which appeared on the first *Mole* album, or which was recorded and not used: *Instant Pussy*, *Instant Kitten*, *Dedicated to Hugh*, Phil's *Part of the Dance*, an extended jam based around Hugh's song *Memories* and an adaptation of the instrumental riff from the *Caravan* piece *Waterloo Lily*, here renamed *Horse*. When sessions and gigs allowed, New Zealand keyboard ace Dave MacRae would swing by, *Fender Rhodes* in tow, and show us why he was in such demand.

In the meantime, our manager, one Sean Murphy, about whom the less said the better, was dealing with *CBS* to which company Robert was still contracted. Negotiations didn't appear to involve any upfront money, except for the purchase of some equipment which would remain the property of the record company. That, and studio time.

Unfortunately, one call on what limited funds the band possessed came as a result of theft. The garage at St Luke's Mews was not exactly secure and, I suspect, was not necessarily properly locked up overnight. Anyway, one morning I turned up from an overnight south of the river to discover my lovingly restored *Precision* was not where I left it. Phil, sensibly, took his guitar with him wherever he went, but I left mine in full view of anyone coming through the door. More fool me. The *Precision* was gone. Stolen. At that time Tony Wigens, our tour manager, was recruiting a road crew. Tony interviewed some prospective roadies and one seemed especially pissed off when turned down. He had been to the garage and seen the equipment. Tony reckoned he'd stolen my bass in retaliation for being sent on his way.

With recording imminent the rush was on to find a decent replacement, but another *Fender Precision* was not to be affordably found in any music shops in Charing Cross Road, where most of such businesses lurked. Eventually, and reluctantly, the only option was an unusual short-scale *Gibson EB3* built the year before and purchased from one *Maurice Plaquet* in the Uxbridge Road, Shepherd's Bush. I still have it. It's hiding in the corner of the office. The neck warped a long time ago and it was never played outside *Matching Mole*.

MOLE'S FIRST ALBUM was mainly recorded in the elderly (and freezing) *CBS Studios* in New Bond Street. Their new studio complex was being built in Whitfield Street (where *Mole II* was recorded) and the level of maintenance, etc., in the old studio was poor. It was also very cold and keeping instruments in tune was something of a problem (well, that's my excuse). Add to that the soon-to-start national miners' strike, which would lead to the Three-Day Week and regular power cuts throughout February, and it is no surprise that recording ran somewhat erratically from 29th December 1971 into the first week of March 1972.

Work started on Thursday, 29th December when it was found that the studio piano was out of tune. The same applied the following day. Thus began an interminable wrangle with *CBS* over studio costs. We argued that we shouldn't have to pay the full rate for a studio where basics like pianos were out of tune, headphones didn't work, tape machines ran erratically, and key bits of kit like *Dolbys*[i] malfunctioned. Some of this was not sorted out for ten months but the compromise was, eventually, that out-of-tune pianos, *Dolbys* and problems with the desk were a *CBS* problem, but wonky headphones didn't count, so full rate,

There were then three, eight-hour sessions (4 p.m. to midnight) from 3rd to 5th January. On each day the headphones did not work properly. On Sunday 9th mains interference prevented us from working for five hours and the next day the *Dolbys* kept dropping out leading to two hours' engineering maintenance. Amazingly, the two days' work on the 13th and 14th January were trouble free. We were back in the studio on 25th January for three days. On the first day the *Dolbys* failed after two hours. The next day they failed completely, and the tape machine refused to run at 30 IPS. Instead, we spent four hours in *Command Studios* (where *Roxy's* first album would soon be recorded).

Back at *CBS* on the third day, 27th January, work was abandoned at 5.30 p.m. when the *Dolbys* failed again. To celebrate this catalogue of failures we, earlier in the day, did the only reasonable thing in the circumstances, *Matching Mole*, corporately and individually, signed a contract with *CBS*. It pinned us down to producing 'two 33⅓ r.p.m. Long Play records' within a two-year term as from 1st January 1972. They would spend up to £5,000 on any 'musical equipment you require' (which, and fuck me, is £70,000 today. Where did it all go?). Other than that, it was the usual seven pages of catch-all goobledegook. Derisory royalty rates, rights over your first born, that sort of thing. And, of course, no reversion clause, which meant they owned the rights in perpetuity. None of us read it. None of us consulted a lawyer. We had a manager. We were safe in his hands. Not.

Having spent most of the week watching *Dolbys* dropout at *CBS Studios*, Bond Street – which resulted in one studio move and one abandoned session – 28th January 1972 was one of the happier days. The *Acoustic 360* bass rig I ordered arrived. When *CBS* said they would buy (but retain ownership of) some equipment my eyes lit up. I had fallen in love with *Acoustic* kit the moment I saw it piled high on stage at the *Roundhouse* behind *The Doors* back in 1968. I had no idea what it might sound like 'cos *The Doors* had no bass guitarist and I had never used one. But it was American, super big, pale blue and black – and preposterously expensive. So, when the man at *CBS* 'he say: yes', I was more than happy.

---

[i] A noise reduction system invented by Ray Dolby (1933-2103). The *Dolby A* was used in recording studios. An American, he gained a PhD at Pembroke College, Cambridge. He formed *Dolby Laboratories* in London in 1965.

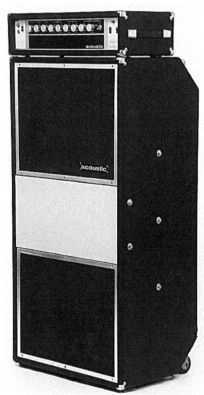

Backed up by 200 watts of solid-state power and an 18-inch reflex mounted speaker, I was never put through the band's PA system irrespective of the size of the venue. If the place was large, I would just crank the volume control up towards 10. Sadly, not being *Spinal Tap*, it could go no further. But that was more than loud enough. Even when chief roadie and soundman *extraordinaire* Benjamin Lefevre somehow liberated two enormous horns from the 1971 Reading Festival speaker system the good old *Acoustic* was still more than powerful enough to defeat those *WEM* monsters and severely irritate Benj into the bargain. Happy days.

14 The Acoustic Bass 360 rig.
Gets me hot just looking at it.

Rather oddly, one of the controls was a five-octave tuner. I never did work out what the point of it was, but I did play a solo on it once, at our last ever gig in Groningen. I was in a bad mood so apologies to everyone at the *Stadschowbourg* that night (22nd September 1972). The statute of limitations on any ear damage caused has long since passed so don't even think about consulting some ambulance chasing lawyer.

I was mortified when CBS took my baby back. They offered to sell it to me, but I was broke. The story of *Matching Mole's* life.

On the 30th January, we moved to a small studio called *Nova* near Marble Arch where we managed two trouble free days mixing. We were back on the 14th (OK) and 15th (power cut for three hours, so blame Ted Heath's Tory government). Returning from a quick trip around Holland and Belgium, there was another power cut on the 29th and we managed a full day on the 3rd March. The final day's mixing, Sunday, 5th March, was fun: supposed to be at *CBS* from 7.30 p.m. to 3 a.m., the 16-track failed for two hours, so we popped over to *Nova* instead to finish up.

So, that anything came out of the sessions was something of a miracle. The album was finally released (or, perhaps, escaped) on Friday, 14th April (I think). We, meanwhile, were intermittently gigging (or should that be giggling), on which more later. Negotiations with *CBS* to ensure we weren't charged for times the studio didn't work properly were prolonged and not agreed until after the band broke up. But, before any discounts, the album cost us the princely sum of £4,811 to make, which, amazingly, is the equivalent of c. £70,000+ in today's dosh. Who'd have thunk it? I'll go to the foot of our stairs, etc., etc.

IN BETWEEN ALL THIS was *Mole's* first 'performance' outside of a studio or the garage at St Luke's Mews. Thanks to people like John Peel we spent many happy hours either recording sessions or playing live concerts in one of the various BBC studios littered around London. Our first was recorded for Peel's show *Top Gear* at the *Playhouse Theatre* in Northumberland Avenue near Trafalgar Square[i]. It was recorded on Monday, 17th January, and we were joined by Dave MacRae to play Phil's *Part of the Dance* and Robert's *Instant Kitten* and *Instant Pussy*. On this you can hear the unmistakable tones of Dave Sinclair taking the lead. I think it was a great shame he left when he did a few weeks later after some gigs in Europe. As the band broadened its musical base, and all of us started to contribute compositions, I feel he might have felt more at home. But there you go, he soon left and that was that.

Our first gig would not be until the following Saturday, 22nd January. It was played at a venue called *Hydraspace*, otherwise known as the *Kingham Hall* at the junction of St John's Road and St Alban's Road, in Watford. The place is now a car park for a *Fiat* dealership. *Sic transit gloria mundi*, as they say. Also on the bill was Carol Grimes' *Uncle Dog*. Carol, as the more astute amongst you will already know, was loosely connected to *Mole*. In 1969, she, and bassist Roy Babbington, joined Pip Pyle and Phil Miller in Phil's big brother's band *Steve Miller's Delivery* with which she recorded an album, *Fools Meeting,* in 1970[ii]. Small world.

Other than it being a tiny venue with an even smaller stage, I can remember bugger all about it except that my legs gave way when we came off stage, the expenditure of nervous energy being considerable.

---

[i] Opened 1882 as the *Royal Avenue Theatre* and rebuilt when part of Charing Cross Station inconveniently fell through the roof in 1905, killing six people. Re-opened as the *Playhouse* in 1907. The BBC took over in 1951 to record things like the wonderful *Goon Show*. In the 60s/70s it was a venue for live rock bands, e.g. *Led Zeppelin, The Who, The Beatles, The Rolling Stones* and us. Threatened with demolition in 1976 it was, in 1987, restored. Post-Covid, it was renamed the *Kit Kat Club* and has hosted a long-running version of the musical *Cabaret*.

[ii] Coincidentally, when Pip joined *Gong* he was replaced by Laurie Allan, later to join *Gong*. Carol Grimes still sings and performs. I never knew her but, from what I have read, she is 'good people'. Check out her website: *https://carolgrimes.com*.

15 The bill for the UCS Benefit.
Solidarity – not enough of that around any more

The following night *Mole* played at the *Roundhouse* in Camden with the Mike Gibbs Band[i], the *Third Ear Band* and others (see the poster) as part of a fundraising benefit for the workers involved in the 'work-in' at *Upper Clyde Shipbuilders* (*UCS*) in Glasgow. *UCS* was a consortium of Clyde shipbuilders created in 1968 under the Wilson Labour government. By 1971, despite a full order book and forecasts of an operating profit in 1972, the Heath Conservative government[ii], having recently nationalised *Rolls Royce*, refused to cover the short-term losses of *UCS*. Investors lost confidence which led to a severe cash flow problem. Rather than strike, the men conducted a 'work-in' which attracted massive public support and a large fundraising effort to help the men and their families. The Tory government then gave in and restructured the business. Two of the four companies involved in the consortium survive to this day.

As to the gig, again I can recall bugger all about it except that it was good to have helped the men of the shipyards, even if in a very small way.

---

[i] In which played: Jack Bruce, John Marshall, and Chris Spedding. Oh yeah.

[ii] The Tories don't like Scotland because they have not won a majority of seats there in a General Election since May 1955. In May 1997 they didn't win a single seat. Laugh! Being 50% Scottish I approve of such results wholeheartedly.

When I say 'bugger all' I am, however, talking about the music as, off-stage, something rather momentous took place. The show went on from mid-afternoon through to just before the last buses ran on a Sunday night. So, if you were going to do a soundcheck, it was done just after lunch, which left c. 8 hours of down time to fill. You couldn't just pop outside and do a run around Camden Market, mainly because it didn't yet exist. In fact, where it eventually ended up was supposed to be disappearing under a part of what was to be called the *Northern Cross Route* (*NCR*), a six-lane motorway which the *Greater London Council* wanted to build from Hackney in the east to Harlesden in the west. The *NCR* would have demolished thousands of homes and blighted many others and gone straight through Camden. The project was cancelled the following year (Sounds of cheering, off). The other reason why shopping was not a goer was that the archaic Sunday Trading Laws were still in operation. Shops were closed. Sunday was the Lord's Day, apparently, and people should be free to attend churches and all their numerous Sunday services. Or, alternatively, they could get pissed and/or smashed at the *Roundhouse* for 7½ hours. No guesses which I would have chosen.

OK, getting back to 'momentous' events. Before we went on stage, Robert saw a lady called Alfreda Benge dancing in the audience and, I am truly happy to say, the rest is history. Soulmates is a much mis-used and abused term. But, looking back, no other word better describes the depth, the breadth, and the intensity of their relationship/partnership. Yes, there would be ups and downs, not least after Robert's terrible accident in 1973. But these two people were made for one another, and it makes me happy just to think they have been together for so long and so joyfully entwined.

After their fortuitous chance meeting, though they passed like ships in the night on more than one occasion, it was not long before Robert abandoned the cold and dreary St Luke's Mews and moved into Alfie's flat on the 21st Floor of *Hermes Point*, a towering edifice built in the early 60s and part of the huge *Elgin Estate* which sits astride the Harrow Road. It was not a large flat. Nor was it especially tidy. But, at that vertiginous height, it was a good place to talk to passing sparrows and to stare out across the vast panorama of West London spread before you.

Robert's morale, thus everyone's morale, improved. We became better equipped to withstand the rigours of the British winter when Alfie knitted us all woolly hats. I still have mine. She made us all *Matching Mole* badges which we sported proudly in various PR shots done around the time of the release of the new album. And then, as it turned out, having worked in the film industry, she had a good friend who, when her name was mentioned, made me go weak at the knees. But more on that anon.

What further helped raise morale was a short but nonetheless welcome positive review from Steve Peacock in *Sounds*:

"It's very rare to see four musicians working together as closely and unassumingly as *Matching Mole* did. All four of them contributed more or less equally to what was going on, but they managed to do it without making a big deal out of people taking solos.

But the main thing I noticed about them was the way they'd take an idea – be it rhythmic, melodic or whatever – and work around it, not distorting it exactly but giving it extra little twists, developing it in unexpected directions. This is particularly true of Phil Miller (guitar), but it applies equally to the other three – Robert Wyatt (drums and vocals), Bill MacCormick (bass) and Dave Sinclair (organ).

Their set was quite short, and the effect quite understated; I enjoyed it very much."

16 Hermes Point front (Chantry Point to the rear).
Alfie's flat was about five from the top on the corner nearest to the viewer. The block was demolished in 1994.

Backing up a bit, it was not, technically, the first time we'd played at the *Roundhouse* as we rehearsed there the previous Wednesday, but it was a place I was somewhat in awe of, having seen some major gigs there over the previous few years. The most notable was probably the appearance of the *Jefferson Airplane* and *The Doors* on 6th-7th September 1968. I was there for the first night having queued, without a ticket, for hours. The entrance was at the top of some wooden stairs and, by the time the doors opened, the stairs were blocked solidly from top to bottom. When I explained I had the money but no ticket the guy on the door looked at the crowd, shrugged, took my fiver and let me in. So, front row seating (there were no actual seats) for the two sets each band played. *The Airplane* (who I saw a few days before at a free concert on Hampstead Heath with *Fairport Convention*) thought they were playing to two different crowds, but when Grace Slick examined the people sitting at the front, she realised it was the same bunch, so the band changed the set. Nice of them. Having been star struck by watching Grace and Jim Morrison strut their stuff, being on the same stage, even if over three years later, felt a bit weird.

Last time I was there was for a *Classic Rock* magazine awards ceremony when Señor Manzanera was given some thoroughly deserved award or other. The old place has changed a bit and, the mind playing tricks no doubt, seemed to have got smaller. Chatted happily with Arthur Brown (of the *Crazy World*....) beforehand. We'd never met before but that didn't stop us getting on like the on-fire crown he used to wear in his wilder, and pre-Health & Safety, days. Lovely man.

I then renewed acquaintances with *Genesis's* Tony Banks, and the band's manager, Tony Smith, at half-time. Ok, diversion, so how did I know them? Well, leap forward to page 135 and you can find out. Just don't forget to come back here afterwards.

Back on subject, rather excitingly, the day after the *Roundhouse* Tony Wigens asked for the details of my passport (issued in 1968 to enable me to go on a geography A-Level field trip to Holland, which adventure immediately preceded my decision to give up geography. My parents, who coughed up for the trip, were moderately dis-chuffed). In three weeks we would be off on our travels. Holland again, as it turned out.

In between the previously described fun and games in, or out, of the *CBS Studios*, we rehearsed intensively, but this time not at St Luke's Mews. Instead, we repaired to a place called *Jubilee Studios* in Covent Garden where we added several toons to the repertoire. At the time, the 1904-era *Jubilee Hall* and the heart of old Covent Garden, including five theatres, were under threat from a typically mindless re-development plan proposed by the Tory-controlled *Greater London Council*. They apparently fancied a large number of tower blocks and a four-lane road through the middle of it. That it all survived, even after a Public Inquiry found in favour of the *GLC's* plans, is testimony to the activism and enthusiasm of dozens of local people. Well done, ladies and gentlemen.

None of the above, of course, was anything to do with us.

AT THE UNGODLY HOUR OF 9.00 A.M. on Friday, 18th February 1972, a yawning and disgruntled if surprisingly sober but long-haired and strangely garbed quintet of young men came together on the concourse of Liverpool Street Station. One was very tall, one was quite tall, two were of average height and one was on the petite side. Doing it by hair length, the longest (and curliest) hair belonged to the tallest, the shortest the second longest, the most handsome one (*Ed*. who he?) the third longest, the one with the beard and glasses the next longest, and the one with the moustache the (relatively) shortest. There is an exam question in there somewhere (as well as several useful police profiles).

At some point, the five of them boarded a train which rattled towards the somewhat drab East Anglian port of Harwich, there to board a ferry of some sort on which to sail to the Hoek van Holland (Hook of Holland to you illiterates). It being mid-February the North Sea was on the skittish side. Having a cast-iron stomach, the handsome one (medium height, medium hair length) managed not to reveal the ingredients of his somewhat paltry breakfast during the crossing. He cannot confirm the same for the others.

On arrival in Holland (or the Netherlands, take your pick) and having managed to pass the scrutiny of Dutch passport and immigration control (this all being pre-EU. I cannot tell how much I have enjoyed the post-Brexit return of these petty restrictions on my movement. Thank you, Boris, you destructive buffoon) we then boarded another train, almost certainly cleaner, quicker and cheaper than anything previously provided by the Eastern Region of British Rail and set off for Amsterdam. Disembarking at Amsterdam's *Centraal Station*, we hefted our bags manfully over our shoulders and headed south towards what was then known as the *Hotel de Haas*. Apparently, it no longer exists, or has been renamed since we (or because we) stayed in it. It over-looked a bridge over a canal. Not far away on the other side of the canal was a small bar (of which more later). And not very far away was an old church now behaving badly as a rock music venue called *The Paradiso*. *Matching Mole* (for it is they!) would be playing there the following night.

Our road crew – Tony Wigens, tour manager, Benjamin Lefevre, roadie and sound engineer, and Mouse, roadie and drum technician – crossed by a more direct route and laboured their way through several comprehensive customs checks during which every guitar string and drumstick was checked against the *Carnet* (*The Carnet*: the detailed list of freight items shipped across foreign borders, the reintroduction of such petty red tape to British exporters and artists being another 'benefit' of Brexit). Now they, and multiple empty and some still full, bottles of alcohol, were contentedly established in the top floor suite to which we were consigned. It was accessed via a lift, a spiral staircase and was some 4-5 storeys above the road. There was a balcony. Irrelevant detail, you may say, but patience and all will be revealed.

I should take the opportunity of saying something about the 'crew' who made everything possible and, at least two of whom, who went on to far bigger and better things than slumming it with the likes of us. The one I can tell you least about was Mouse. I don't know his actual name, sadly.

He was tall, spare and quiet... perhaps as a mouse. Who knows? He just got on with things, assembling and dismantling Robert's *Ludwig* drum kit every night and dealing with whatever life on the road threw at him.

17 Benjamin 'Benj' Lefevre nowadays

If there was anyone who might do the throwing it was Benjamin Lefevre. Benj was a larger than life figure, hugely strong but equally hugely talented at what he did, i.e. the sound. And being a brilliant sound engineer would take him a long way: *Led Zeppelin*, where he was Robert Plant's vocal engineer, *The Rolling Stones*, Elton John, Peter Gabriel, George Michael and *INXS* to name but a few. You will find Benj's name on the credits to the *Zep* film *The Song Remains the Same* and as producer on various Plant solo albums. It was Benj who discovered John Bonham dead in bed in 1980. In '72 it was he who thought it a grand idea to get me stoned (see below). This must remain one of his few failures in life.

Benj lived life large, as they say. His favourite tipple was *Remy Martin* cognac. So, not just any old stuff. He found a restaurant, down the Fulham end of the King's Road as I remember, where, if you ate a huge bowl of pasta, they gave you a bottle of the stuff. One night I watched him work his way steadily through a pasta mountain, an Everest of durum wheat. There was never a doubt he would succeed. And the bottle of *Remy* didn't last long. It was because of his dedication to this amber liquid that a song on *Little Red Record* was named *Brandy as in Benj*. Initially it was *Brandy for Benj* but it disappeared so fast the second title seemed more apt.

It was Benj who gave me my first driving lesson. Sort of. After *Mole's* final gig in Groningen, feeling (temporarily) less than well-disposed to Robert, I went with Benj in the truck back to the Hook of Holland to get the ferry. There are various routes available for the 270 km trip but he took the A7 then A4. This meant crossing the 32 km long *Afsluitdijk*. This is a dam which now divides the huge freshwater lake of the *Ijseelmeer* to the south and the *Waddensee*, the area of the North Sea inside the West Frisian Islands. It was built between 1927 and 1932 across what used to be known as the *Zuiderzee*, the area of salt water which allowed ships access to the port of Amsterdam on its southern edge. Since then, large tracts of land have been reclaimed along the south-eastern and eastern shore. These are the *Flevopolder*, which now contains the cities of Almere (pop: 203,000), and Lelystad (pop: 80,000), and the *Noordoostpolder*, largest town Emmeloord (pop: 27,000). I've been there on a school geography field trip in 1968. It is *very* flat. And *very* damp.

But back to the *Afsluitdijk*. Benj was driving something like a 3-ton truck. I guess the speed limit on this dead straight piece of motorway was 120 kph (75 mph) and I feel sure Benj was doing his level best to achieve this speed. About halfway across, he decided to do something, light a cigarette, eat a sandwich, I don't recall but it certainly involved taking both hands off the steering wheel. And he didn't want to stop. He got me to slide across the seat until I was in reach of the steering wheel and told me to take over. I did not pass my driving test until 1977. I had never in my life been behind the wheel of car, let alone a high speed 3-ton truck. I tried to explain this but Benj was having none of it. His response was: 'Don't be a pillock', or something rather more fruity. I was too nervous to notice. 'Just keep it straight', he muttered and took both hands off the wheel. To my right, separated by a flimsy crash barrier, were the murky waters of the *Waddensee*. To my left, the central reservation, two lanes of traffic travelling north, and then the equally murky waters of the *Ijseelmeer*. Not precisely between 'the devil and the deep blue sea' but you get the picture. For what seemed like an eternity, but was probably only a minute at most, the truck veered gently from lane to lane whilst Benj did what Benj had to do. He then resumed control. It would be five years before I was prepared to drive another vehicle.

But Benj was, is, such a good guy. He never lost contact with people like Phil Miller and elements of the Canterbury crowd however exalted were the artists who were his main source of income. He helped them out whenever he could. I last met him, 45 years later, at the wake after Phil Miller's funeral in 2017. His hair was shorter and grey, his beard was stubble, but the man was the same: larger than life, generous, and a good laugh.

18 Tony Wigens nowadays

Tony Wigens also went on to far bigger and better things. He was the calm one, the unflappable presence, the man who got us there on time, and dealt with stroppy promoters in a diplomatic yet firm fashion.

He lived in a flat at 7, Hansard Mews, overlooking the railway line coming up from Earl's Court near Shepherd's Bush. I visited him there one day. Back in the day it was not the most salubrious of places (it has since been gentrified). Tony lived upstairs and, as we climbed the stairs, we passed several apparently stoned, very long-haired gentlemen stretched out, fixed glazed grins on their faces. 'Who are that bunch?' I asked Tony as we entered his small flat. '*Hawkwind*', he replied succinctly. Happy daze.

Anyway, Tony is a really good guy who, as I say, went on to work with a roster of the best in the business: Paul McCartney, Michael Jackson, Eric Clapton, Annie Lennox, Mark Knopfler, Herbie Hancock, *Aerosmith*, *Iron Maiden*, *Dire Straits*, the *Steve Miller Band*, the *Spice Girls*, and the *Eurythmics*. He has since worked for *CBS* as their *Manager of Tour Administration* and was involved in setting up the live performances for the TV hit show *American Idol*. He now lives in Georgia. A step up from Shepherd's Bush, I might venture.

BACK IN AMSTERDAM, we ate that night in the hotel whilst attracting hostile and/or bewildered looks from our fellow diners. And, as you know is the normal behaviour of all rock musicians, we were off for an early night, a dreamless sleep, ready to be up and at 'em the next day. No, really.

The next morning, we were interviewed for a Dutch music mag, *Muziekkrant OOR* (still in existence but just *OOR* now), a publication which first hit the streets on 1st April 1971. I feel sure we were excellent value though, with the arrogance of youth, I was prone to the odd indiscreet comment about bands I really did not like. Their names shall not pass my lips.

That afternoon we headed over to the *Paradiso*.

19 The Paradiso, as it is now not as it was then

The *Paradiso*, built as a nineteenth century church, is at *8, Weteringschans* and backs on to the *Singelgracht*, one of the main canals circling the centre of the city. Originally the home of a religious group, *De Vrije Gemeente*, (*Free Congregation*), which words are still engraved over the entrance, it became a concert venue after being briefly occupied by hippies in 1967. It was a place to hear music and get stoned, as soft drugs were tolerated within its portals.

Even in those days there was a certain aura about the place. And a certain smell. Being totally innocent in this department (alcohol, when I could afford it, was my only vice) this passed me by, but there were others with knowing looks and a conspiratorial gleam in their eye. The *Paradiso* is not large and nor is the stage. Intimate might be the word, but for the vaulted ceiling to which churches are prone. We sound-checked and retired to what is now known as the 'green room'. Here, it was a large place with several armchairs which appeared a through route from one place to another for everyone involved in putting on the show.

I have never smoked, which was good for me but not for the fellowship of conspirators *aka* the road crew. Despite my flowing locks and youthful good looks (Ed: WTF?) I was regarded as Mr Straight, after all, I still played cricket for the school Old Boys team whenever I got the chance in the summer and was known by the rugby team as Hiawatha because of my headband. The crew, therefore, decided that I needed to get high, if only for their own amusement. A joint being out of the question, someone realised their victim was both sweet-toothed and permanently hungry (at two months short of 21 I was still a growing boy. Sadly, the horizontal 'growing' seems not to have stopped). Some rather nice, if oddly flavoured, cookies were produced, offered, and eaten. I was then carefully watched for some time for any signs of eccentric behaviour. Garrulousness is an apparent sign of being somewhat stoned. They, of course, forgot that, once going, I can talk the hind leg off the proverbial donkey, as my ever-patient wife reminds me from time to time. Me being stoned was, therefore, rather difficult to detect. Bored, they went off and did whatever roadies do in their down-time (best not to ask). I sat there, thumbs a-twiddle, contemplating the fact that I was to play the first solo of the set. And that it didn't include a fuzz box. So, I was nervous, but little else.

At some point we were called to the stage to perform. The reason for my nervousness was this: the set opened with a version of two *Soft Machine* pieces which always ran together: *Noisette* and *Backwards*. I played the themes of both and then soloed over the *Backwards* chord sequence. Ha! All unknowing, as I was yet to meet Brian Eno, he of the *Oblique Strategies*, I had somehow already taken to heart one of his better known *bon mots*, to wit: 'Honour thine error as a hidden intention'.

And, boy, did this twit honour that bum note he played halfway through the solo. Calculating hopefully that, at some point, this mis-placed semi-tone must appear in an appropriate scale over the chord sequence, I decided to keep playing it whilst smiling in a knowing, and yet avant-garde, fashion at the front row of the audience. They smiled back happily, but then they were all totally out of their gourds and I could have dropped my fetchingly tight blue velvet bell bottoms and sung a rousing chorus of 'God save the Queen' and I doubt it would have raised them from their drug-induced torpor. Robert, however, noticed, and congratulated me afterwards for my musical *chutzpah*. He was laughing at the time, though.

Otherwise, I think it all went quite well for our first ever continental gig. It would, however, go seriously downhill in the next 48 hours for at least one of us….

20 De Doelen, again as it is now.
The photograph gives a feel for the concrete jungle which was central Rotterdam back in 1972

Anyways, we should now move on to Sunday, 20th February 1972 and the days beyond. An odd day that Sunday as, believe it or not, we played two gigs, in two different theatres, in two different cities. It is, perhaps, just as well that The Netherlands is the size of a small, if heavily populated, shoe box, otherwise we would have never been able to drive from Amsterdam to Rotterdam (36 miles/58 kms), do a show at *De Doelen* just after lunch, before jumping in a car to head off to Eindhoven (54 miles/87 kms) to play at what was then called the *Globa Theatre* (now the *Parktheater* I believe). Quite how the crew did it I have no idea.

Sadly, in 1972, the centre of Rotterdam looked like how one might imagine Milton Keynes would have appeared if Hitler's personal architect, Albert Speer, was involved in its design: cold, monolithic, soulless (thinking about it, perhaps he was an adviser when MK was dreamed up). Of course, in a way, *Herr* Speer was indirectly implicated in the unwanted re-design of Rotterdam because he supported the Nazis whose *Heinkels* and *Dorniers* ripped the centre of the old port to shreds in 1940 after their previous dry runs at Guernica and Warsaw proved so successful.

De Doelen is part of that modern centre and lies in the *Schouwburgplein*. We didn't play in the main hall (the size of the *Festival Hall*) for the afternoon show (though we did later). Such daytime gigs possibly don't happen nowadays. But we played a couple (the other in rather-closer-to-home Ealing), and, as mentioned previously, I happily remember going to see the very wonderful *Blossom Toes* play one afternoon in a lecture theatre at the *LSE*, sometime in 1969. So, these things happened.

54 miles to the south-east of *De Doelen*, the *Global Parktheater* lies, as the name suggests, in a park in the capital of *Phillips* corporate land, *aka* Eindhoven. It goes by the rather wonderful name of the *Stadswandelpark* which apparently translates as City walk park. I remember nothing of this but am indebted to *Google Earth* for all of this material. I remember as little about the two gigs. We turned up, we played brilliantly/moderately/awfully (delete as appropriate), and we left. All the genuinely hard work was done by our devoted crew: Benj, Mouse and Tony. Cheers, guys.

We then returned to the *Hotel de Haas* (68 miles/110 kms) who were about as delighted to see us late Sunday night as they were on Friday, i.e. not much. I have no recollection what time the crew returned. I was probably fast asleep. Or hiding in case they were in a foul mood.

Monday was the first of two unsupervised days off in Amsterdam. This is not something I would recommend to young and inexperienced persons yet to be seriously inebriated. We wandered around the shops, were somewhat embarrassed by the displays in the red-light district and avoided anything cultural like the *Rijksmuseum*. Some of us, however, ended up in the little bar on the other side of the canal from the hotel.

In those days the Dutch still used guilders. No idea how many we spent that night, but I have a recollection we parted with something like 30 quid's worth. Context is all, however, so it should be pointed out that this is the modern equivalent of at least £420. It was also, at the time, the equivalent of two weeks' wages for us members of the band, so where it came from I have no idea. I suspect there were no more than five of us in that bar. We started with *Oranjeboom* on draught. Then the array of brightly coloured bottles on the shelves behind the barman caught our eye. Some were a vivid blue, others a pretty pink or of a golden hue or deepest red but, after working our way along the shelves with each liqueur followed by an *Oranjeboom* chaser, we no longer cared. Either that, or we had gone blind with alcohol poisoning. Eventually, the barman, having doubled the bar's weekly profits in one night, suggested we should leave. Not that we were rowdy or violent. No, nothing like that. The problem was that we could barely stand. We were bordering on the comatose.

The *Hotel de Haas* was probably no more than 200 metres away. Being almost literally legless I probably walked the best part of a kilometre getting there. The journey was accomplished in a series of small circles punctuated with sidesteps the average All Black wing three-quarter would kill for. Fortunately, it was very late and there were few cars on the roads which might have wiped me out as I staggered from one side of the road to the other. Equally fortunately, the balustrade along the bridge over the canal was of sufficient height to prevent me toppling into the dark, cold waters below. Gradually, I was left behind by the more experienced tipplers and was forced to find my way to, and through, the hotel door on my own. Somehow, I found the lift. Somehow, I got the door to open. Slumping to the floor I managed to press the nearest button. I then spent approaching half an hour in the basement wondering why the lift was so fucking slow. Having eventually realised that the top rather than the bottom button was more likely to send me towards our 4th floor room, I was eventually decanted from the lift to be greeted by the spiral staircase (you see, I told you all this info was crucial to the history of rock and roll music). These stairs now became a challenge equivalent to the first ascent of Everest. I cannot say how many times I tried, and failed, to mount each of those daunting steps. Thankfully, I was so 'relaxed' I did myself no obvious damage each time I fell down them. Eventually, like some long-haired, wasted Edmund Hillary, I realised I needed to approach this fearful task in stages. I set up base camp by propping myself up by a convenient chair. Then, heroically, I pulled myself up stair by stair, all with no crampons, ice-picks, or oxygen, until, at last, I reached solid ground and the door to our suite. Unsurprisingly, this was wide open. Inside, general hilarity ensued when I crawled in. For the road crew this was even better than trying to get me stoned.

The windows to the balcony were open (why? It was bloody February!) so I dragged myself out into the somewhat fresher air. But now, bladder grossly over full, I needed to take a 'comfort break'. Let me admit here and now I have no head for heights. None whatsoever. I go weak at the knees looking out of a first-floor window. So, to clamber onto the edge of the balcony, unzip the trousers and train Terry at the tarmac below was more than out of character. What happened at ground level I don't know. Perhaps a young, future President of the USA was walking below and this is where he first experienced the joys of an unexpected 'golden shower'. If so, I have an awful lot for which to answer and I apologise to the American nation and the world. Some higher power was on my side, however, and, instead of following my organically processed beer and spirits over the edge, I fell backwards.

I awoke, many hours later tucked up in bed. It was early afternoon. The hotel staff sensibly decided to leave tidying the rooms until we left, so the debris of the night before still littered the landscape. Everyone else was out enjoying themselves. I stayed in that darkened room for the rest of the day with an Everest-sized hangover. Silently, I vowed never to get drunk again. A vow which must have lasted at least four months (but then, in my defence, after a gig attended by c. 8 people, what else is there to do in Redruth but get royally pissed?).

Apparently, that is rock and roll.

On Wednesday, 23rd February, we left Amsterdam heading for Brussels. No doubt the road crew spent a happy few hours being checked over by Belgian customs officers who, probably being Flemish, might have been called *douanebeambtes*. Please feel free to correct. Please also feel free to explain why these ridiculous restrictions now again apply to all and any British freight travelling around Europe. Fucking escapes me.

Where was I? Oh yeah, we were to be interviewed by *RTB Radio* which, surprisingly, was neither *Radio Television Brunei* nor *Radio Télévision du Burkina* (though we were *huuuge* in both countries but sadly never toured either place. Strange). *RTB* was, in fact, more correctly *RTBF* or *Radio Télévision Belge Francophone*. I doubt I contributed much to the ensuing discussions except, perhaps, in the form of a low moaning sound emanating from a prone position on the floor and out of the way. Amsterdam still had an awful lot to answer for.

Where we stayed that night I am really not sure. In a cardboard box under a flyover for all I knew but, somewhat revived by numerous glasses of water, I joined our happy team on our way east to Verviers, a small town east of Liège and on the northern edge of the Ardennes. Here we stayed in a place called the *Grande Hotel* which, like the *Hotel de Haas*, and this must be more than coincidental, no longer exists, or has been renamed since we descended on it on Thursday, 24th February 1972. We were due to play the *Maison de la Culture* which is now, but was not then, a nice modern building on the *Boulevard des Gérardchamps*. This is another of those gigs about which one remembers nothing. Personally, I blame this memory lapse on the *Oranjeboom*, and/or the *Curaçao*, and/or the red/orange/yellow/green stuff, whatever they were.

Things, however, were about to improve.

On Friday we headed back to Brussels, or Bruxelles as those bloody foreigners insist on calling it. Talking of which (bloody foreigners, that is) I see at long last our brave and patriotic supermarket chains have removed the word 'Brussels' from in front of sprouts on their packaging. Now, that really is taking back control! British sprouts for British idiots!!

We checked into a hotel called the *Hotel Duc du Brabant*. Tragically, on 21st May 1977, this hotel would catch fire and 19 people were killed, twelve of them British tourists. Which sad fact exposes the rest of this material for the self-indulgent twaddle it is.

To be blunt, in 1972 at least, this hotel was a dump. I shared a room with Mouse as I recall. The windows of the shabby room simply faced other windows of the hotel a few yards away. Directly underneath was the kitchen. In those days I believe the national dishes of Belgium were: chips, horse meat, chips, mussels (if you were lucky enough to be close to the sea and they were fresh, otherwise they were lethal) and chips. All were served with either (or both) mayonnaise and ketchup. I suspect the same foetid vat of fat (I rather like that phrase) was used to fry *les pommes de terres* over a very extended period. A grimy slime of air-borne grease covered our room's walls and windows, and the stink was appalling. On the other hand, the hotel was cheap, so that was alright then, and the surroundings at least encouraged us to get out and about.

21 The intimate interior of Theatre 140.
You cannot see this but the seats here are blue. Feel certain they were red 'back in the day'.

I was last in Brussels in November 2019. It has improved beyond all recognition since 1972. Clearly, the EU has been very good for some member countries. Odd how we managed to fuck up so badly at the same time (*Ed.* Focus!). Oh right. We were due to play two nights at the small and yet perfectly formed *Theatre 140* so named because it lurked behind a block of flats the address of which was *Avenue Eugene Plasky 140*. The theatre was in the neighbourhood of Schaerbeek in eastern Brussels/Bruxelles.

The theatre opened its doors in 1963 and, over the years, it staged shows by numerous artists none of whom, except for Serge Gainsbourg, I have ever heard of. But then, they probably had never heard of *Matching Mole* and they undoubtedly got the better part of that deal. More recently, though, a variety of rock combos had (or would) perform there. Amongst them, and get this: *Pink Floyd, Zappa, Yes, Soft Machine, Talking Heads,* Johnny Rotten and *Public Image ltd*. Even Thelonious Monk played there!

It was a lovely little venue. Intimate, comfortable, decent sound… and had a bar. Now, OK, after my recent exploits you'd think this was bad news. And, yes, I did drink a lot in that bar. But it was mainly water. And there was another reason for my repeated visits. Serving there was a young, beautiful, blonde lady with sparkling eyes, a magical way with the beer taps and absolutely no English. My French was a grade 5 O-Level (6 was the lowest grade) taken in those good old days when it was thought writing a foreign language and knowing its grammar intimately was of more use than being able to hold a sensible conversation. Spoken French, at that time, represented something like 20% of the total marks of O-Level French. And you could, it seemed to me anyway, fuck up the oral exam as long as you passed the written one, which, somehow, I did. I failed Latin btw so have never been able to visit Latin America (which is a blatant but convenient lie[i]). That's what they talk down there isn't it? I mean, otherwise, what was the point of all that amo, amas, amating?

Undismayed by my inability to converse properly (though I might have been able to conjugate a variety of verbs in the pluperfect tense) we resorted to writing stuff down. In my little green Civil Service diary. I have it here in front of me. It really is rather charming in its way and no, no-one is getting to read what we wrote. Suffice to say we parted good friends, even if my declarations of undying love were politely, if smilingly, deflected. I did get a kiss though. She was, to be honest, sweet and gorgeous and I left Brussels/Bruxelles the following day with more than a few regrets and a huge pheromone deficit.

What? None of this interests you? What about the music, you cry? Who gives a flying something or other. My heart is breaking and I'm trying to be sensitive and meaningful here. Yeah, we played OK. Actually, as I recall, we did more than that. I think we were bloody good. Must have been the endorphin overload or something.

What else do you want to know? On Sunday 27th we got the ferry back from Oostende to Dover and I went home. The next day we went into *Nova Studios* in an attempt to finish mixing the album. There was a bloody power cut and I didn't give a toss. I had left my heart in Schaerbeek (and parts of my liver in Amsterdam). If anyone finds the ticker, please pop it in the mail. 2nd class postage will do. It would be good to connect it up to the pacemaker some sawbones stuck in my chest a few months ago. You can have the liver, with some fava beans and a nice chianti, perhaps.

Lastly, and sadly, these were the six and only gigs which *Mole* played as a five-piece with both Dave Sinclair and Dave MacRae on board. For purely musical reasons Dave Sinclair decided *Mole* in its current rather frantic and unstructured form was not really for him.

---

[i] My wonderfully athletic son played Junior World Cup rugby for Scotland in 2001 (and again in 2003). The 2001 matches were played in Santiago de Chile. I went to watch courtesy of Mr Manzanera's connections with *Colombian Airlines* with which I flew Business Class for nowt. Result.

The next week was spent in the final mixing of the first *Mole* album which was completed, in spite of a breakdown of the 16-track at *CBS*, at 3 a.m. on the morning of Monday, 6th March, appropriately in *Nova Studios* where the kit worked (when there weren't any power cuts). We would be back on stage later that day....

In the early evening of Monday, 6th March 1972, we did our second Peel session, this time at the studio in Kensington House in Richmond Way (now the *KWest Hotel*). We played two pieces: *No 'Alf Measures*, an Ayers/Wyatt collaboration, and Phil Miller's *Lything and Gracing* which was still part of the set when the band collapsed in September. Perplexingly I cannot find these pieces on *YouTube* though they were on an album (*Matching Mole – On the Radio*). The session was broadcast on Friday, 24th March, though we didn't hear it, we were in Amsterdam again.

We maintained the Kevin connection on Wednesday, 8th March, when, as part of a massive tour of West and South-West London, we played with him in support at *Kingston Polytechnic* in Penrhyn Road (I'd earlier seen *Yes Album*-era *Yes* play there and jolly good they were too. Later stuff leaves me totally cold though). Apparently, Robert went on stage at the end with Kevin and bass player, Archie Leggett, for an impromptu jam. I say 'apparently' as I have no recollection of it, probably because I met up with my late brother's lovely ex-girlfriend Diana (hi, Diana, hope you and yours are thriving), an art student at the college. We went for a late-night curry.

Odd things happened in them there days. I have previously mentioned the afternoon gig in Rotterdam and the *Blossom Toes* lunch-time gig at the *LSE*. Well, we did the same on Friday, 10th March at *Ealing College of Higher Education* (now part of the *University of West London*). We kicked off at 1 p.m. in a not especially large room on the first floor. I have a vague recollection of band and audience indifference. Maybe too early in the day for 'over-tired' students.

Continuing our swing through the suburbs, Saturday night was *Merton College*. No, this was not the historic and august Oxford college founded in 1260 by Walter de Merton, chancellor to Henry III and later to Edward I. T'was the rather more prosaic establishment based in Morden in the London Borough of Merton and established in 1890 and now part of *South Thames College*. There, we were supported by *Dando Shaft*. They did at least pay us £100 which is, cor blimey, about £1,700 in modern dosh. As we were being paid the princely sum of £15 a week (or c. £210 nowadays, so not even close to the current minimum wage) this was quite a lot. So impecunious were we that for a short time, I helped out, using money

---

i A band formed in Coventry in 1968 with connections to the British folk-rock revival. They recorded *An Evening with Dando Shaft* and *Dando Shaft*, without significant success. When the third album, *Lantaloon*, failed they broke up in 1973.

saved from the previous summer's Civil Service job. So, I paid for things like Phil's rent. The amount eventually paid back amounted to £200 or the best part of £3,500 at current prices.

Gigs, however, were few and far between at this point, and fewer and further between when two the following week (Windsor and Greenford) were both cancelled at short notice. We did have two other places to play before returning to Holland: *Chelmsford Civic Hall* (about which I can tell you nothing, not even the name of whoever shared the bill) and *Guildford Civic Hall* where we supported *Barclay James Harvest* who, minus a couple of original members, appear to be still going. Good luck to them.

Small colleges and civic halls seemed about the limit of our ambitions at this point, though there was talk of a tour supporting 'a major artist' but which, to be part of, meant we supply and truck the PA system. Must have seemed like a good idea at the time.

But, before all of that, on Thursday, 23rd March, we were off to Amsterdam again, via our favourite Liverpool Street-Harwich-Hoek van Holland route. You can never get too much of the North Sea during Spring gales so I am told.

Yeah, right. Once you've experienced such a weather system in the North Sea you're always keenly anticipating the next opportunity to enjoy the rolling seas, the rolling chairs and the rolling stomachs to be endured on the 120-mile crossing. Not to mention the toilets. So I won't.

Yes, we were heading once more for our favourite ex-place of worship – the *Paradiso* in old Amsterdam. This time we played two nights (Friday and Saturday, 24th/25th 1972) with *Plainsong* in support. For those of you who don't know them, this band was formed in early '72 by Ian Matthews, late of *Fairport Convention*, and Andy Roberts from *The Liverpool Scene*.

To add to the fun, both nights were recorded by Dutch radio in the shape of *VPRO*, Hilversum. As you all know, *VPRO* stands for *Vrijzinnig Protestantse Radio Omroep*. I am sure there is no need to translate this for such an erudite multi-lingual bunch as you lot. Oh, except, it seems, some wastrel at the back wearing a tie-dyed t-shirt and bell bottoms who did not pay proper attention during Dutch lessons at infants' school. '*Liberal Protestant Radio Broadcasting Corporation*', you numbskull! (sorry about this guys. I know you're keen to move on to something more important). *VPRO*, founded in 1926 (as if you needed telling. This is for the idiot with the glazed expression at the back) was originally a religious radio station which became somewhat more liberal after the war (please don't ask which one. I mean, really). There was also a TV station which screened (albeit briefly) shows like *Hoepla* which, and I am sure you really need to know this, on 9th October 1967, featured the first ever completely naked lady on Dutch TV in the comely form of one Phil Bloom (there are photos. The perverts amongst you can find them for themselves). One notes that there does not seem to be a similarly recorded date for the appearance of the first completely naked man on Dutch TV. Who'd have thunk it?

Anyway, I digress (again). *VPRO* recorded the performances and, for many years, I tried to persuade them to allow someone to release the tapes. They repeatedly rejected my advances (or, as they say in Hilversum, '*ze wezen herhaaldelijk mijn voorschotten af*', as you all know). Then, the late and much-lamented Mike King persuaded some idiot at *VPRO* to let him have a tape 'just to listen to', as he was writing *Wrong Movements* and listening to tapes was, like, crucial. The tape may have found its way to a small, independent record company (no names to protect the guilty) and may have been released in 2002. Result!

Whilst in Amsterdam we stayed in yet another hotel which has since disappeared (making us something like 3 for 4 in this respect. Nothing to do with us, guv). This rejoiced in the name of the *Hotel de Herberg* (not to be confused with the *Hotel Herbergh* near Schiphol Airport nor the *Hotel Eetcafé De Herberg* near Maastricht. Fine establishments both, I am sure). No. This one was slap in the middle of the red-light district. I got a pain in my neck every time I left the building and returned to the hotel as I looked everywhere but at the brightly lit and very large windows of the establishments which crowded those streets and canals east of the Dam Square. I mean, who wants to see numerous young ladies flaunting their underwear at 11 o'clock in the morning? And before breakfast too! Those of you that would are probably the ones who have just googled Phil Bloom for whatever reason. Shame on you!

Our hotel was tall but very thin. A bit like Phil Miller but without the hair. It contained numerous tiny rooms strangely equipped with just a bed. Nowt else. It was, however, cheap. And cheerful too, if you were an overweight businessman on expenses and sufficiently far enough from the wife not to care. Yes, dear reader, this establishment was what is known in the trade as a 'knocking shop'. Though my room was right at the top of the building, which meant climbing numerous sets of stairs, it did at least mean there were no rooms on the other side of the paper-thin walls. Not everyone was so lucky, and at least one member of the band was kept awake one night by the sounds of continuous rutting involving what sounded like a rather large man and an extremely enthusiastic 'lady of the night' who, apparently, enjoyed more orgasms in about eight hours than the average female might experience in a lifetime at the hands, etc., of the typical selfish male. Faking it? Surely not.

We had the Sunday off in Amsterdam which, my liver is relieved to report, was far less adventurous than the previous sojourn in the city. On Monday 27th March, we drove south to Brussels, where we checked into the *ABC Hotel*, yet another hotel which has disappeared since we graced it with our presence (spooky or what?).

The following lunchtime we were off to the Heysel area of Brussels. Here we recorded a TV performance at a place called the *Amerikaans Theater* for *VMT* (*Vlaamse Radio en Televisieomroeporganisatie* – Flemish, you understand). I have a recollection of playing in a very large and very empty studio of some type. It is, however, one video recording which has never re-surfaced as far as I know so, all you super-sleuths out there, set to work and locate a copy. We also did an interview for some Belgian radio station (presumably *VMT*). No trace of that either.

That night we returned to good old Blighty. Possibly from Oostende. Perhaps Dover. Folkestone even. Who knows? Who cares? We would now have a few days off before we started a tour proper. How exciting.

And, on Thursday, my parents moved house from West Norwood to Beckenham. I went with them. It was either that or live in the proverbial cardboard box under a flyover somewhere. But I got a free breakfast in Beckenham so that settled any debate.

VEERING SOME WAY OFF PISTE, how many of you remember the *Letters* page of the *Melody Maker* where, every now and then, some stamp-collecting anorak (sorry, a dedicated fan) would write in to ask what equipment a band used, preferably down to the drumstick type and, even, the bass guitar strings?

Our dedicated fan was one Nick Utteridge from Cheltenham (if you're reading this, hi, Nick. How are the stamps? Sorry, cheap shot. Hope things are well with you and yours. And, of course, thanks for the *MM* letter as I would otherwise not have been able to compose this drivel 'cos I had no idea what amps/speakers/etc., everyone else used)[i].

You have already been regaled with stories of the awesomeness of my *Acoustic 360* bass rig and will be relieved to read I do not propose going down that path again (but what a fucking noise it made! Pretty too).

For some unpatriotic reason our back line eschewed the use of standard British amplification, e.g. *Marshall*, *Hiwatt*, etc. (bring back *Vox* and *Selmer* I say!). No, we were mainly American equipped. Both Phil and I used *Gibson* guitars, his a *Gibson SG Special*. To power his unique sound and style Phil used a *Fender Dual Showman* amp (100 watts) plus two *Dual Showman* cabinets each with two 15 in. *J B Lansing* speakers. Now, I fondly remember the days when I would swap details of power output, speaker size and type, effects pedals, etc., etc., with fellow musos with comments like 'Look at the *Altecs* on that'. I have since grown up.

---

i Phil Howitt tells me Nick is now the *Soft Machine's* tour manager and even played percussion on a 2018 album entitled *Hidden Details*. Awesome. You have to truly admire that level of dedication to the cause even if, like me, you don't think the name of *Soft Machine* should still be in use.

22 Dave MacRae
Exploring the inner-most workings of the Fender Rhodes

To more important matters. Dave MacRae played a mysteriously 'specially modified' *Fender Rhodes* piano. As far as I could see this 'special mod' involved taking the top off so he could run his fingers up and down the tines which produced the sound (Interesting fact: did you know the *Rhodes* was invented by Harold Burroughs Rhodes [along with the *Army Air Corps Piano* and the *Pre-piano*. Don't ask, no idea] under a strict budget to produce pianos to teach recovering soldiers during World War II. No? Me neither). Dave, too, employed twin *Fender Dual Showman* speakers but driven by two, what must have been very early, *H/H 100-watt* slave amps.

Robert's *Ludwig* kit was given to him by Mitch Mitchell at the end of the *Hendrix/Soft Machine* 1968 USA tour: 24-in. bass drum, 14/16/18-in. toms, *Gretsch* 14-in. snare, a combination of *Avedis Zildjian* and *Super Zyn* 16/20-in. cymbals, 14-in. *Avedis Zildjian* hi-hat and, yes!, *Ludwig 3S Sticks*.

Strings! I forgot the strings! I suspect Phil's were *Ernie Ball Super Slinky*. Weren't everyone's in those days? As I recall, I started using *Rotosound* roundwound but then moved to *La Bella*. You have not properly lived until you've found out about this shit, have you?

We now come to the *pièce de résistance*, the PA system somehow put together by soundman/roadie extraordinaire Benjamin Lefevre. Are you sitting comfortably? It consisted of:

Two *WEM Reading Festival* horns, 400 watts per horn;

Two *JB Lansing C55* bass bins with dispersal lens and super tweeters powered by three *H/H 100-watt amps*;

An *Allen and Heath* 12-channel mixer;

On stage monitoring: 300 watts of *WEM B* columns (One of Benji's party tricks was to run up and down stairs with one on each shoulder);

Four *AKG* mikes for the drums and one *AKG D1000* for the vocals (plus Robert's *WEM Copycat* tape echo);

Guitar and piano direct-inject into the board; BUT

The *Acoustic*, loud and proud, uncontrollably ruining the sound balance all on its ownsome (but I didn't care).

You all now, of course, feel so much better for knowing all of this essential detail. And I am reminded why I suffer from tinnitus. The sacrifices we musicians make to keep you people entertained.

ON MONDAY 3ᴿᴰ APRIL 1972 *Mole* played two shows supporting veteran bluesman John Mayall and his band of black jazz musicians. They were the first of twelve gigs spread across Britain and France in April and May. We were due to go to Germany too but, due to the machinations of our manager, we were dropped for this section of the tour.

As mentioned, to get on the tour, and to play to an audience in the main not particularly interested in our brand of musical anarchy, we supplied and shipped the PA system. Step forward Mr Lefevre and his recently liberated *Reading Festival* horns.

I cannot tell you much about Mr Mayall. I don't think one word passed between us. But let me thank him publicly for his 60s *Bluesbreakers* and for introducing me musically to people like Eric Clapton, Peter Green and Mick Taylor. His 1972 backing band, however, was a different matter altogether. Though considerably older than us, they were lovely, cheerful, brilliant players who seemed genuinely interested in the strange stuff we churned out. We drank and chatted and admired their great musicianship.

The two Monday performances (two, no idea why) were at the *Royal Festival Hall*. Being a place more accustomed to classical concerts, there were seats behind the stage (for an orchestral chorus/choir). It was in these seats my parents sat to watch their second born play in a modern music combo for the first time. As a result, they only got to see the back of my head and my undoubtedly pert buttocks, but at least they were not deafened and left with tinnitus for the rest of their lives. Only I enjoy that constant mosquito-like whine and ringing in the ears. Nice.

What they made of *Matching Mole* they were too polite to say. Instead, they probably pondered what had gone wrong with their children. From a junior school just up the road from Brixton Prison, they both attended the elite Dulwich College. It all seemed to be going so well. Oxbridge loomed. Glittering careers beckoned. And then the late 60s happened.

ROYAL FESTIVAL HALL
DIRECTOR: JOHN DENISON. C.B.E.

JOHN MAYALL and
SUPPORTING MUSICIANS
PLUS MATCHING MOLE
MONDAY, 3 APRIL, 1972
9 p.m.

Management: John Smith Entertainments Agency Ltd.

GREEN SIDE

Please enter the auditorium by

DOOR 5

LEVEL 5

TERRACE

GANGWAY 10

ROW   SEAT

65p   T   18

23 RFH and Mayall: two shows in one night.
Nobody could have played for very long. Weird.

So, three years after leaving school here we are. Me on stage ruining people's hearing with interminable fuzz bass solos and, in the audience ready to write a laughably complimentary review of his little brother's band, Ian (now known as MacDonald and soon to be Assistant Editor of the radically transformed *New Musical Express*). It is fair to say that Donald Trump learnt everything he knows about nepotism from us. Sorry USA.

The next night it was staid Bournemouth and their elderly *Winter Gardens* and Friday the rather more modern Brighton *Dome*. I have since been to political conferences at both. With the Lib Dems (Bournemouth), and the Tories (Brighton) where I stole all their fundraising ideas.

Supported by a band called *Gringo*[i], we ended the week playing in Canterbury, for the first and only time, at a venue which previously hosted the *Wilde Flowers* and *Soft Machine*. I have a distinct recollection this was not one of our finest performances.

St Thomas Hall, unfortunately, was not as historic as the name suggests, and as the photo below confirms. But then you can't have everything, it was the brutalist '70s after all. I believe this building has since been demolished in the fine tradition of many premises touched, in one way or another, by *Matching Mole*. In this case, no great loss to Canterbury in particular, and the world of modern architecture in general.

---

[i] This took a bit of finding. *Gringo* emerged out of a band called *Toast* formed in 1968. One suspects the name change was driven partly by a desire to stop people saying to them threateningly, if accurately, 'You're Toast'. *Gringo* signed a recording deal with MCA in 1971. Their bass player, who left in November 1971, was one John G Perry, later a member of *Caravan*. They broke up later in 1972.

24 The ugliness that was St Thomas Hall, Canterbury.
What must the ghost of Thomas à Becket think of such a monstrosity erected in his name?

ACCORDING TO *WIKIPEDIA*, the first *Matching Mole* album was released on 8th April 1972. As this was a Saturday, I think we can happily ignore this date. No-one released albums on a Saturday. They didn't even escape on a Saturday. Not even ones as weird as *Matching Mole's* first vinyl offering.

The confusion about dates, however, does not stop there. I have two diaries in which I recorded events in '72. The one that went everywhere was the little green *Civil and Public Services Association* pocket diary which I picked up whilst working for the *Ministry of Overseas Development* in Eland House, Stag Place, SW1. Rather like many of the hotels *Mole* stayed in, Eland House no longer exists. Just how long one can accept this as coincidence I really don't know. It's as if someone powerful is trying to eradicate all evidence of *Mole's* existence. Spooky or what? I am trying to interest David Duchovny and Gillian Anderson in a TV mini-series but, oddly, they won't return my calls. Their loss.

OK, enough of the paranoia and the paranormal. Back to the diaries. The other diary was a desktop job, big and glossy blue, purchased from that well-known high street emporium of stationery, paper clips, etc., *Ryman*. It spent its life on the desk in my bedroom in West Norwood before moving to Beckenham (a 60s flat in Copers Cope Road for the completists amongst you). Now comes the strange part (other than that both properties are still standing. An oversight by the 'authorities' I think you'll agree). The big blue diary says 'Album released' Friday, 14th April. The little green diary says Friday, 21st April *and* Friday, 7th April. What can I say to clear up the confusion? Nothing. I have no clue which is correct, though there are hints suggesting 'later' more likely correct than 'earlier'.

25 Alan Cracknell's lovely artwork for Matching Mole I
(or should that read: Robert Wyatt II?)

OK, record companies like it when you help promote 'product'. Interviews. We did some bloody interviews. On Tuesday 18th we nattered to Steve Peacock from *Sounds* for an article due for publication on the 29th April. Steve was always a good bloke and wrote and reported on several of the musical ventures in which I was involved in the '70s. So, hello Steve!

The following day it was the turn of that doyen of the British musical press and all-round great guy (and tall. Very tall) – Richard Williams of the *Melody Maker.* Yes, the man who wrote the prophetic *'Outlook cloudy for Quiet Sun'* piece a couple of years earlier and who was now championing the imminent release of the first *Roxy Music* album (of which I gained a sneak preview, wandering into *Command Studios* during the mixing of *Chance Meeting,* if I recall correctly, and meeting Eno for the first time).

The next Monday we would be chatting to my late bro' masquerading as Ian MacDonald for *Cream* magazine's June issue. You can read what Richard, Steve and Ian wrote in *Appendix 5.* Just like in a real history book.

26 The new Mole, early spring on a walking tour of Notting Hill.

27 Mole in the swing.
Alfie's influence: my knitted hat and Mole badge, and whatever it is sprouting out of Robert's chest. The inspiration for Alien seven years later?

There were album reviews too but they were last seen somewhere in the attic. And no, I have no immediate plans to retrieve them. It's dusty up there.

Instead, I will give you my thoughts, for what little they are worth.

In the light of the travails and heartbreak of Robert's recent life I find it hard not to cry when I listen to *Mole's* first album. It is essentially a very sad album in the saddest of minor keys, from the deep melancholy of *Signed Curtain* to one of the most beautiful, if most desolate, pieces of music I know: *Immediate Curtain*, recorded alone by Robert, the heart-rending *Mellotron* coda not heard by the rest of us until mixed.

But, let me absolutely clear about something. Except in name, this was *not* a *Matching Mole* album. Don't be fooled by the presence of Phil's *Part of the Dance*. You could argue this played a similar role to *Las Vegas Tango* on *End of an Ear*, a nice instrumental in which to stretch out. *Matching Mole*, the album, was Robert's second solo album, part two in the line running from *End of an Ear* through to *Rock Bottom* and on to *Ruth is Stranger than Richard*. This particular one a catharsis, maybe. A jettisoning of two years' worth of personal baggage. Perhaps the title of the sixth track tells you all you need to know about his unhappy departure from *Soft Machine*: *Dedicated to Hugh, but You Weren't Listening*.

Five months after the recording of *Dedicated* and *O Caroline*, Robert, in an interview with *Time Out's* Al Clark, put these pieces into perspective rather more bluntly. After a rehearsal at Dave MacRae's house in Park Walk, Chelsea, on 11th May, Robert sat down with Al and reviewed the later period of his time with *Soft Machine* and the genesis and development of *Matching Mole* (for the part of the interview relating to *Mole* see page 355). When asked whether there might be more introspective, backward-looking songs like the two mentioned he replied:

"Those things are like cutting off malignant parts of a diseased body. I really don't need them anymore."

This was a change in mindset more than adequately reflected in the lyrics Robert then wrote for *Little Red Record* where, in the main, bigger and external issues were addressed: e.g. religion, and capitalism v. socialism. And his approach was no longer that of a solo artist plus backing musicians. When asked whether any part of the first *Mole* album best represented where the band, and he, was at now Robert replied:

"Hopefully I'm now becoming a quarter of whatever gets said or played. So for me *Part of the Dance* is the most useful pointer to the group because it was written by Phil and I'm just doing my quarter on it, like I'm doing now and like I hope to be doing on the next album".

But large sections of the first album were recorded by no-one other than Robert. The rest of us, in a way, were (unpaid) hired hands. Session musicians in all but name. With the exception of *O Caroline*, which clearly involved Dave Sinclair, the rest of us did not hear pieces like *Signed Curtain* and *Immediate Curtain* until the final album was being put together.

I have no problem whatsoever with this. I was just pleased, amazed, to be in the same studio with Robert and these other superb musicians. Yes, there were several 'band' pieces we recorded which *might* have made it onto the album. I am glad they did not. They would have diluted the power and emotion, the pain, of what Robert revealed through the music. I should quote something my late brother wrote in a two-article retrospective of the career of *Soft Machine* from 1966 to 1975:

> "It's doubly significant, thereby, that Wyatt's first move away from the *Softs*, the *Matching Mole* LP of early '72, is an album primarily about misery. Musically shakey, it devastates anything by the corporate cool smoothie *The Soft Machine* has become in the last two years sheerly in terms of emotional engagement."[2]

Looking back at what Robert recorded between 1970 and 1975, *Little Red Record* was the outlier, the only '*Matching Mole*' album. Maybe that's why Robert broke up the band. With all our compositions getting in the way, perhaps we'd interrupted his musical train of thought. The one which then led to his master work: *Rock Bottom*. Who knows?

Well, Robert.

OUTSIDE OF THE STUDIO, we were keeping very vaguely busy though, to be frank, with no gigs between Canterbury (8th April) and the *Manchester Free Trade Hall* (26th April) the only musical activity, aside from desultory rehearsals, was a BBC *Top Gear* recording at Kensington House. We played three pieces – *March Ides, Instant Pussy* and *Smoke Signal* – which later appeared on CD as *Matching Mole on the Radio* along with two other Peel sessions and an *In Concert* recording. The choice of material showed the way the band was changing – two pieces by Dave MacRae – and would be reflected in the balance of material as the band wandered its way towards a second album.

But now we were gearing up for a remarkable sequence of five gigs in five nights. Just like a real rock 'n roll band. Yes, the John Mayall tour was resuming. And we were heading north.

My father was born in Scotland, in the schoolteacher's house[i] on the tiny but important island of Iona (off the larger island of Mull, off the coast of Argyll). I first went north of the border, on holiday, in 1967. To a place on the River Spey called Grantown on Spey, a place surrounded by golf courses and distilleries. A peculiarly Scottish version of heaven. I next returned on Friday, 28th April, 1972, to a place then called *Green's Playhouse* in Renfield Street in central Glasgow. It was the third gig on the resumed

---

[i] It's now the visitor centre. The lady on the desk seemed genuinely enthusiastic when I told her my dad was born somewhere in the house in September 1921. BTW, Iona has the most incredible white beach on its west, i.e. Atlantic, coast.

Mayall tour. We played Manchester and *Newcastle City Hall* on the two previous nights and arrived in Glasgow from the direction of Edinburgh, coming in on the A89 I would guess, driving through the east end of the city through Parkhead and near to *Glasgow Celtic's* famous football stadium.

In 1972 Glasgow was not a pretty place. Rows of dowdy rundown multi-storey tenements were interspersed with fields of brick dust where entire blocks were being raised to the ground. Every now and then, what passed for a pub could be seen, with iron frames over the windows, doors heavily barred and few optimistic tipplers waiting hopefully by the doors for the all-too-brief opening hours to start.

In fact, Glasgow was, in its working-class areas, bloody grim. Nowadays, at least in its centre, it is a city transformed. Then, it was a relic of the faded British Empire's industrial and mercantile collapse with the shipyards closing or under threat, industrial relations at best febrile and at worst violent, and living standards amongst the poor appalling.

28 Green's Playhouse.
As ugly inside as out.

Green's Playhouse was opened as a cinema in 1927. All told, the building could hold some 10,000 patrons and the cinema, by now a concert venue, some 4,000. Arguably, it was the biggest cinema in Europe. Now, as the picture above reveals, it was an ugly, vast monolith with an enormous auditorium, a very high stage, tiny and squalid dressing rooms, all connected by a network of incomprehensible corridors.

We checked into our hotel before heading off to the gig. At reception, the young man on duty asked why we were in Glasgow. 'Supporting John

Mayall at *Green's* we explained. He laughed. 'Best of luck,' he muttered, 'they fucking hate support bands there. They'll fucking kill you'.

Thus fortified, we got into the car, wrote our wills and last letters home, and gave vague instructions as to what should happen to anything remaining of us found by the authorities. Even then I wanted to be composted under a tree. Fucking hippy.

Our dressing room was tiny, dirty, and perhaps somewhere underground. Or on the top floor. It was impossible to tell. In front of the stage was a long drop into what presumably was an orchestra pit. Nowadays, it kept the audience members off the stage, which might have been helpful, but we were warned the more robust members of the crowd would be waiting for us outside the stage door. There could be no escape for a bunch of up themselves middle-class southerners with artistic pretensions, even those armed with a *Shaftesbury Duo-Fuzz*. These people still remembered the Battle of Flodden (9th September 1513, as I am sure you all know) and harboured a historic grudge. They didn't much like people from Edinburgh but London....! Even the 50% of me distinctly Scottish courtesy of my Dad would not be granted mercy. I lived in London, spoke 'proper' and was, therefore, fair game.

At some point in the early evening, we were told to get our asses on stage. Feeling somewhat like a Christian about to be introduced to a 'cruel but fair' Roman crowd and their pet lions at the *Colosseum* I trudged off, guitar in hand, in what I thought was the direction of the stage. Becoming separated from the rest of the band in the rabbit warren of dingy cob-webbed passages, I wandered about, randomly opening doors, going up and down flights of stairs, turning corners and acting the completely useless waste of space I am still today.

Eventually, I opened a door and dimly recognised the outline of one of our enormous *WEM Reading* PA horns. They being the only real reason we were there I cursed their existence as they seemed imminently about to lead us to our corporate demise at the hands and feet of various inebriated Glaswegian hardcore Blues fans. Finding no way round the back of the PA I gingerly edged my way around the front of the large, flared speaker cabinet, holding onto it with one hand and onto the trusty *Gibson* with the other. Suddenly, various large spotlights went on and I was revealed to the several thousand-strong crowd, hanging by one hand over the orchestra pit some 20 feet below. Impressed (or aghast) the rest of the band stared in awe at my desperate attempt to divert the audience's attention away from what we were about to perform.

Expecting to be splattered with beer or hit by other flying objects, I was surprised when I was, instead, greeted by widespread laughter and even a smattering of applause as reward for the unique manner in which I arrived on stage. Grinning sheepishly, I plugged in and off we went.

I have always found that the less I remembered of a gig the better it usually was. I remember nothing of our performance at *Green's* that night. Except the rather decent reaction of the crowd. Finding myself back in the dressing room, I realised we were all laughing, relieved, and alive. We had, it seemed, survived to play *Lancaster University* the next night and the *Colston Hall*, Bristol, on Sunday. Result! Thankfully, my salvaged organs and limbs were not required to act as fertiliser to an Oak tree, or any other species of decent sized plant for that matter. Pathetic final letters to loved ones were retrieved and destroyed. Wills were amended (by those of us with anything worth passing on to our nearest and dearest. Basically, just musical instruments).

To celebrate the fact I might now see my 22nd birthday (the 21st having taken place a couple of weeks earlier), I met up with a friend who was working nearby at Greenock and who came in for the show. The friend was no less than Jon Copeland who, cast your minds back, was an original member of *Pooh and the Ostrich Feather* five years' earlier. He took me to a typical Glaswegian pub. It rejoiced in the name of the *Muscular Arms*, a moniker too little used by the publican fraternity in my humble opinion.

In those days, opening hours in Scotland were scandalously brief. Imagining somehow that reducing the time during which one could purchase alcoholic beverages would thereby reduce the amount consumed, the authorities determined that 10 p.m. was plenty late enough for public bars to stay open (unless, like us, you were in a hotel). As a result, they thought, everyone should be safely home and tucked up in bed by no later than 10.30 p.m. ready for a hard day's industrial action rousting scabs the next day. Instead, what happened was that, on the call of 'Last orders', every single customer in the bar rushed to the counter and ordered multiple pints of 'Heavy' with several whisky chasers which were then consumed at high and relentless speed. Leaving that fine establishment to return to the rather more salubrious surroundings of the hotel bar, we literally stepped over the prone bodies of numerous comatose patrons of the *Muscular Arms* whose bed that night was either the gutter, a nearby alley, or a police cell if they were sufficiently 'with it' to cause some small disturbance on the streets. It would be more than five years before I returned to Glasgow and, by then the belated transformation of this fine metropolis was, at last, underway.

The next day we headed south via the Lake District towards Lancaster (via the M74, A74(M) and M6 for those needing directions).

McMole thus survived both *Green's* and Glasgow.

Oh, and by the way, *Green's* is sadly no more. It closed on 30th June 1973 and was demolished in 1987. So, unlike all those disappeared hotels, nothing to do with us then.

After Mole played the *Colston Hall* supporting John Mayall on 30th April we were supposed to set off supporting him in Germany and Austria, with the first gig in Frankfurt on Tuesday 2nd May. Other cities to be visited were: Saarbrucken, Ludwigshafen, Stuttgart, Zofingen (Switzerland), Nuremberg, Munich, Vienna, Linz, Graz and finishing in Berlin on Friday 12th May. That we didn't go to any of these places Aymeric Leroy puts down to *Soft Machine* taking our PA system on a tour of Italy, though it has to be said, we did play at least one gig when they were out there. Anyways, we didn't go, which is a shame as I still haven't been to any of those cities and, if do it now, I will have to pay for the privilege. Twice, as her indoors will insist on accompanying me.

Instead, on Wednesday 3rd May, we turned up at one of those ubiquitous Victorian school buildings which litter what used to be called the *Inner London Education Authority* area. I went to two such Victorian-era schools, the second being at the top of Brixton Hill (and quite close to Brixton Prison, as you will know if you have been paying attention). Sturdily brick built to a defined look. None of that Reinforced autoclaved aerated concrete in them. That's why they are still standing.

But now, as a long-term political nerd, I will give you a quick overview of London politics in the 1970s and 80s. Are you sitting comfortably? No? Who cares?

ILEA, as it was known, covered, in the case of South London, the boroughs of Wandsworth, Lambeth, Southwark, Lewisham and Greenwich. It was one of two authorities formed on the abolition of the *London County Council* (the *LCC*) in 1965, the other being the *Greater London Council* (*GLC*). At the same time (or actually the year before) 32 London boroughs were formed out of the numerous smaller councils which existed under the *LCC*, things like *Beckenham Urban District Council* which became part of the *London Borough of Bromley*.

The *GLC* was directly elected (and I stood as the Liberal Party candidate for the *GLC* in 1981 in Beckenham and fucking good I was too. Too good, as it turns out, as the fine people of the area elected some Tory prat which allowed me to go on working in a previously hopeless Labour-held ward we won the following year in the Borough Council elections). *ILEA*, however, was technically a committee of the *GLC* made up of representatives of the twelve inner London boroughs. Thus, it was possible for the *GLC* to have a Conservative administration and *ILEA* to be run by Labour. Something which happened twice and, indeed, was actually the case in 1972.

Both the *GLC* and *ILEA* did some good shit until they fell victim to the 1980s war between the Thatcher government and the increasingly left-wing *GLC/ILEA* administration featuring such Labour lefty luminaries as Ken Livingstone and John McDonnell who ran London until 1990 when

Thatcher abolished both bodies. When you can't beat them, abolish them. Seems fair.

One of the fun things *ILEA* did was to form its own educational TV service which, apparently, may have been the largest closed-circuit TV service in the world at the time. Now, you can see why right-wing nutters might develop a problem with the idea of a left-wing political body directing TV shows of its own creation into schools across twelve London boroughs. I mean, perish the thought that a public service broadcaster might fall into the hands of those with a political axe to grind. Oh, you say, the *BBC* already has. OK, never mind.

29 Mole on ILEA ETV.
Phil examining his fingernails, me looking pensive (or bored).
Note: Dulwich College 2nd XV Rugby shirt and, left, the lovely Acoustic PA killer.

Anyway, *ILEA's Educational Television Service* was based in the buildings of the *Tennyson Secondary School* in Thackeray Road, Battersea, SW8 (now converted to apartments I believe, as the Tory-controlled borough of Wandsworth has no secondary schools of its own anymore. Instead, it lets neighbouring boroughs pay for the costs of the education of local children. Nice one, guys!). We were due to be filmed playing, and we duly did this. As proof, above, a photo extracted from the session.

What happened to the video I hear you ask. Damned good question. The service closed down in 1977 'cos the Post Office, whose cables were used, wanted to get out of the contract. Such recordings were transferred to VHS tape and stored god knows where. I long hoped the tape was lost permanently but, sadly, I was wrong. It can be seen on *YouTube* in all its ever-extended, self-indulgent glory. It is the one *Mole* artefact I cannot bring myself to watch. But, hey, feel free if there are 15 minutes and 40 seconds of your life you don't mind never getting back.

So that was Wednesday (when we should have been in Saarbrucken). The following Monday (8ᵗʰ May. Should have been Munich and lots of excellent Bavarian beer), we trotted off to *CBS Studios* for three hours to hear a single being edited. Three of us knew nothing about this as it was recorded by Robert and Dave Sinclair who snuck into *CBS Studios* to put this gem on tape. This would be *O Caroline*.

That finished at 3 p.m. and I then wandered off south towards the *Woodstock Public House* in Sutton, South London. Somewhere along the line the late, great, sax giant Gary Windo and I met and, for reasons known only to himself, the publican at the *Woodstock* agreed to let Gary and a few of his mates play that night. The mates were a couple of *Pattos*[i] – Ollie Halsall and John Halsey – *et moi*. Somehow my gear got there, we set up (me wondering if the fine patrons of this particular South London watering hole were quite ready for what was about to be unleashed) and, around mid-evening and with a detailed briefing from our band leader that whatever we did was to be approximately in C (or D or E, who knows? What difference did it make?) and 4, 6 or even 7, we let loose.

We bemused, or drove people out, for about ten minutes until the pub owner concluded that Sutton was not yet ready for our particular brand of free-form jazz rock. We were summarily dismissed. Audition failed. And we didn't even get a drink.

Before our time yet again. But it was fun while it lasted.

ON THE MORNING OF MONDAY, 15ᵀᴴ MAY, your intrepid *Molers* trekked westwards from Notting Hill to Heathrow Airport there to board a flight to Orly, an airport to the south of Paris. They were to embark on the final and extremely brief element of the John Mayall tour: an organisationally rather confused trip around France. At one point, gigs in Paris, Toulouse, Bordeaux, Metz, and even Barcelona, were mooted but for reasons far beyond my knowledge this minor tour was reduced to just Paris, Metz, and Bordeaux.

---

[i] *Patto*, formed 1970 by singer Mike Patto, guitarist Ollie Halsall, drummer John Halsey and bass player Clive Griffiths. Signed by *Vertigo*, the first album was produced by our favourite A&R man, Muff Winwood. Dropped after their second album, Winwood signed them to *Island*. A third album, *Roll 'em Smoke 'em Put Another Line Out*, did moderate business. A fourth, recorded in 1973, didn't see the light of day until 2017 maybe because of its title: *Monkey's Bum*. Halsall and Halsey later played with *The Rutles*. Great musicians both.

30 A normal day in the life of a Mole.
Dave with my bass, Phil with his guitar, Robert with part of a toilet cistern, me with a toy
saxophone. Notting Hill, spring 1972.

After landing at Orly, we were whisked off to our hotel in the centre of Paris. Remarkably, this one still exists and appears to be thriving. I believe it was one previously visited by Robert when in the *Soft Machine* but there does not appear to be a plaque on the wall commemorating either their or our visit. Questions should be asked of the authorities.

Those of you of a literary bent will, perhaps, be able to locate the hotel from its name: the *Hotel Esmeralda*. It is in the *Rue St Julien-le-Pauvre* and faces the *Quai de Montebello. Bien sûr!* It is on the Left Bank (or *Rive Gauche* for you sophisticates out there) of the Seine, opposite the great façade of the cathedral of *Notre-Dame de Paris*. Esmeralda, as you undoubtedly all now remember, is the tragic heroine of Victor Hugo's *The Hunchback of Notre Dame*. But, of course, there is no need for me to tell you this, you being such a well-read bunch.

On the other hand, this you probably don't know. Opposite the hotel is a little park and an isolated statue. The statue is of one René Viviani, the unfortunate Prime Minister of France during the first year of World War One, a period in which the best part of 2 million Frenchmen became casualties in the various disastrous campaigns which stretched across northern France in 1914 and 1915. Not so *bien*. You will be able to read all about this in one of my next books[i]. How exciting for you.

So that's it for the educational bit (almost).

We were due to play *L'Olympia*, located in the *9th arrondissement* at 28, *Boulevard des Capucines*, and on the other side of the river. Built in the late 1880s by the people who also started the *Moulin Rouge*, it became a concert venue in the 1950s and saw numerous performances by Edith Piaf, amongst many others. *The Beatles*, apparently, played there for 18 consecutive nights in 1964 and, a few days before we appeared, the *Grateful Dead* did two nights in the 2,000 plus auditorium.

What appeared to irritate the main act was that the French media seemed rather more interested in us than him. Our performance was filmed for the French TV show, *Pop Deux*, and, after we came off stage, we were interviewed (or, rather, Robert was interviewed while we sat around looking lovely) in the dressing room for the same programme. We were also interviewed by French radio for a show called *Pop Club*. Pop? Us? *Sacre bleu!*

I must admit I forgot all about the filming of the gig. Then, in 2006, having just published the first edition of a book on the subject[ii], I was in northern France staying at a hotel in Arras as part of a visit to the battlefields of the Somme. Having eaten, and unable to sleep, I was idly flicking through the TV channels late at night when I came across a programme showing grainy black and white TV footage of some dim, distant rock combo abusing the ears of numerous poor and unsuspecting punters. Looking more closely, and turning up the volume, I realised I recognised the long-haired figure torturing an innocent *Gibson EB3* (Note:

---

[i] To be published in 2024. Written under the *nom de plume*: Alan MacDonald

[ii] *Pro Patria Mori: The 56th (1st London) Division at Gommecourt, 1st July 1916*, if you really need to know. Published under the pseudonym of Alan MacDonald.

if Gina Haspel/the CIA needs any advice on enhanced interrogation techniques I'm her man[i]). For yes, dear reader, it was me and, bloody hell, someone should either have shot me or confiscated my fuzz box. I was inflicting cruel and unusual punishment, as you too can hear should you look said video up on *YouTube*. I expect to be prosecuted for historic human ear abuse at the International Court at the Hague at any moment.

An aside. Back in Arras, the following morning, which was 1st July, I got up early and drove south to an isolated military cemetery called *Gommecourt British Cemetery No. 2*. I wanted to be there at 7.30 a.m., the time British troops went 'over the top' on the opening day of the Battle of the Somme, a day on which over 59,000 British and Newfoundland men became casualties, of whom over 19,000 died. One of those young men who disappeared into a thick smoke screen that day was 4540 Rifleman Charles Robert Tompson from Watford. He was a member of the *1/9th London Regiment, Queen Victoria's Rifles*, and he would have been my mother's cousin had he survived the war. He disappeared that day and his remains were never identified. He is listed amongst the 72,246 names carved into the limestone panels of the *Thiepval Memorial to the Missing of the Somme*. Thus, my presence in an otherwise empty French field on the 90th anniversary of this tragic event.

At 7.30 a.m. I sat on the wall of the cemetery which is set astride the ground over which young Charles advanced. The sky was blue – as in 1916. There was a light mist – as in 1916. But, unlike, 1st July 1916, there was no 'monstrous anger of the guns'. Instead, there was a perfect silence, broken only by the dawn chorus of the songbirds in the trees standing guard amongst the ghostly ranks of gravestones.

I was about to leave when a car drove down the narrow sunken lane, stopped and reversed. A middle-aged Frenchman jumped out, came over, shook me by the hand, and gave me a little metal badge before returning to his car and driving off. The badge commemorated the thousands of French soldiers killed and wounded a few hundred yards to the south in the early summer of 1915. Not a word was spoken between us but there was definitely an *Entente Cordiale* which spanned the years.

So, OK. Enough of that. Back to 1972.

---

[i] OK, something of an obscure reference but Gina Cheri Walker Haspel was the director of the *Central Intelligence Agency* between 2018 and 2021 and its deputy director for twelve months before that. She was in charge of the CIA's Thailand Detention Site GREEN in 2002 which specialised in 'enhanced interrogation techniques' such as waterboarding when having a chat with *Al-Qaeda* suspects. She later went on to destroy video evidence of these 'chats'. Donald Trump believed this made her eminently suitable to head up the CIA. Even some Republican senators objected. She retired the day before Joe Biden became president.

AFTER THE SHOW AT *L'OLYMPIA* we were entertained by the promoter. This involved being taken to a club he owned, a place with several attractions if one was young and red-blooded (or, indeed, were old with high blood pressure). On a small stage, various statuesque young ladies disrobed in an elegant if bored fashion for the entertainment of several dozen well-lubricated, overweight and, I presume, for the night at least 'unmarried' middle-aged businessmen. As the only other people in the club under the age of 30, we were regarded by the performers as slightly odd, if unthreatening, interlopers. We sat in an area *en route* to the ladies' dressing rooms and, I was told, some of them bestowed the odd smile on us as they returned backstage to put on some much-needed clothing. I was told this, as I suspect my eyes might have been otherwise engaged.

Also 'working' in the club were several glamorous and attractive hostesses whose job, sadly, was not to entertain rock musicians but to improve the cash flow of the establishment by persuading some of these drunk, fat, pervs (let's call a spade a spade here) to pay *Roederer Cristal* prices for some cheap and sweet *crémant* from the South-West of France in the forlorn hopes they might eventually get their leg over. I was seated next to one of these entrepreneurial young ladies who pretended to drink large quantities of this muck whilst pouring it on the floor. Or sometimes down my leg and into my shoe. Her client, befuddled by cheap fizz and overwhelmed by a rush of hormones probably not experienced since his wedding night, tried unsuccessfully to engage manually with parts of her anatomy but, somehow, he always missed. Every now and then she would look at me, smile sweetly, shrug, pour more 'bubbles' over my feet and return to the fray. It was like watching a Sunday morning park football team play Manchester City. You knew for certain neither he, nor they, would ever score.

The following day we were interviewed by two magazines, *Rock & Folk* and *Actuel*. Then, as you do when close to the *Boulevard Saint-Germain*, Phil and I went shopping. For reasons still not entirely clear, we both bought suits. Both were the colour of an anaemic *café au lait* (being polite). Why suits? I haven't a clue. Where did the money come from? Equally clueless.

And then we were off to Metz. There, we stayed in the *Hotel le Royal* on (and keeping the First World War references going) the *Avenue Foch* (Ferdinand Foch, supreme Allied commander on the Western Front in 1918, did his Army entrance exams in Metz before it became part of a Greater Germany after the Franco-Prussian War 1870-1. You learn some interesting shit hereabouts, don't you?). The hotel is now, I believe, part of the *Ibis* chain which must mean it is still standing. We played a large, modern, rather soulless building called the *Palais de Sport* which lay across the other side of the *Gare de Metz* and its numerous rail tracks. It did, at least, have a stage, unlike Bordeaux.

Below you will see a photo of Robert and me onstage at said venue. It is in black and white and therefore you cannot see my new milky coffee-coloured trousers in all their glory. Be grateful for small mercies.

31 Robert and me at Metz.
Me undoubtedly in the middle of one of my lovely extended fuzz bass solos, as why else was my left hand so far up the fretboard? A location no self-respecting regular bass player would ever contemplate

Now, what baffles me is how the hell the road crew got from Metz to Bordeaux in time to set up and be ready for the show the following night, Thursday, 18th May. It is a 900+ km drive even on today's autoroutes, or a 10-hour or more non-stop slog in a large and heavily laden truck. Well, I suppose that's what they were paid the not very big bucks for.

We were slightly more fortunate, getting the train from the previously mentioned *Gare de Metz* to the *Gare de l'Est* in Paris (c. 1.5 hours), a taxi to Orly (30 minutes on a very good day), a plane to Bordeaux-Mérignac (just over the hour) and a taxi to the hotel (30 minutes). So, about half the travelling time of the road crew, barring waiting times. And, of course, someone else drove and there were no heavy-duty weight-lifting exercises at journey's end.

We stayed at a place called the *Hotel Etche-Ona* and, oh happy day, it too has not joined the growing list of establishments blighted by the visit of *Machine Molle*. It is now a *Best Western Premier* hotel and still located on the *Rue Martignac*, some 500 metres from the left bank of the River Garonne.

In Bordeaux we played at the, then, perfectly hideous *Palais de Sports*. Built in 1966, it was, as it is now it seems, mainly designed to host basketball. There was no stage. We set up on the (as I remember) concrete floor of this cavernous mess with the huge *Reading* PA horns wedged and angled upwards in order to reach the audience arrayed in the seats the length of the court away. The sound was awful. The audience physically and emotionally remote. We were knackered and we played accordingly.

It was with some relief that we boarded the plane back to Heathrow the following day. We said farewell to Mr Mayall's lovely and hugely talented Black American sidemen with whom it was a joy to drink and chat.

We now faced a rather quiet month. I celebrated by getting glandular fever, perhaps better known to our American friends as mononucleosis or even 'the kissing disease'. Unkissed for several months, I think we can be assured that was not how I caught it. But, given our financial position (parlous in the extreme) I needed to work through it.

UNIT was a rehearsal room based at 265, Pentonville Road, immediately to the west of the *Scala*. As is only too typical of places frequented by the *Mole* it is no more, the area now being part of the King's Cross *Thameslink* station. So, it would now be a lot easier to get to – if it still existed.

We would spend many happy hours there permanently damaging our ear drums and learning the new material which would effectively change *Matching Mole* from Robert's backing band to a fully functioning co-op.

In the early days we performed a mix of Robert's material off *End of an Ear*, the first *Mole* album, a couple of *Soft Machine* pieces (*Noisette/Backwards*), part of Dave Sinclair's *Waterloo Lily*, Phil's very first offering, *Part of the Dance*, and Kevin Ayers' *No 'Alf Measures* but, with Dave MacRae onboard, a far greater range of music became available. His *March Ides* and *Smoke Signal* were the first to be incorporated alongside Phil's *Lything and Gracing*, with other pieces still to come in the early summer.

I was fiddling about with two pieces, both of which would eventually appear on *Little Red Record* and both of which we played live. One was slow, spare and atmospheric (well, that was the intention). The other quick, nervy and energetic. I would steal their titles. The former piece was called *Gloria Gloom* and was the extremely lovely Julie Christie's nickname for her best friend Alfie, and the latter was entitled *Flora Fidgit*, which moniker Alfie applied to her mate Julie. Robert, at least, took a minor fancy to *Gloria Gloom* (in more ways than one) and wrote a top line and lyrics to the initial bass riff and final theme. Poor *Flora* was left to fend for herself which, perhaps, was not such a good idea (again, in more ways than one).

In the time off between the rather sparse number of gigs (one in two weeks at the end of May) we either rehearsed, wrote or, in my case, enjoyed the effects of glandular fever. These symptoms first became apparent during a rehearsal at the aforementioned *UNIT* on Wednesday, 24th May, 1972 (it takes a real nerd/hypochondriac to know the starting dates of his illnesses!). Headache, stiff neck, tiredness, etc., etc., all became so debilitating that we abandoned work and I was given a lift across London to Brixton railway station so I might get the train back home to Beckenham. By the time I got onto the platform my neck was so solid I couldn't turn my head. At all. In order to read the destination information I stood and directed my gaze at the train as it came into the station. Once home I went straight to bed.

Next morning was bright and sunny (unfortunately) and I walked to the doctor's surgery, head down, eyes nearly closed, wearing dark glasses because the light was enough to make the pain in my head excruciating. A cursory examination resulted in a diagnosis of glandular fever and the advice was to take plenty of paracetamol and to rest. Nice idea sunshine! Sod's Law meant our only gig until 3rd June was Saturday, 27th May, i.e. in two days' time. We could not afford to cancel. So we didn't.

Playing very loud music whilst affected by glandular fever is not something I would inflict on my worst enemy (Donald Trump and Boris Johnson are amongst a few exceptions).

We were due to play at *Essex University* near Colchester. This was a modern (first students in 1964) and radical establishment and became a hotbed of student activism in reaction to, amongst other things, the Vietnam War. Amongst the 'other things' were visits by the appalling Enoch 'Rivers of Blood' Powell and a so-called scientist from Porton Down, there, no doubt, to encourage science students to come and help develop weapons of mass destruction in the verdant British countryside near medieval Salisbury. Neither visit went well, I am pleased to say..

The radical roots of the university can be seen from names of the various tower blocks built to accommodate the fast-growing number of students (see above). First up were *Tawney* and *William Morris* towers, followed in the '70s by *Bertrand Russell* and *Eddington* towers. Two more followed (*Keynes* and *Rayleigh*). Putting students in 12-storey tower blocks must have seemed like a good idea at the time. Unfortunately, what it did provide was a grand vantage point from which to drop heavy items during the frequent bouts of student unrest.

I gather things have calmed down since, something I regret given the current state of the world. If students cannot find a reason to be out on the streets in today's political climate they deserve everything they get in the future (if there is one). On the other hand, if you weigh young people down with large student debts then there will be a tendency to tie them to a rather narrower and financially self-interested path to survival. The state of the bank balance rather than of the world becomes the rather more pressing priority. Which, after the dangerous radicalism of the 60s and 70s, was part of the purpose of student debt in the first place, wasn't it?

32 Essex University,

Once a hotbed of student radicalism. Now just a politically correct university We were to perform in a hall lurking somewhere deep amongst the nasty, brutalist architecture which was so fashionable in the '60s. We would share the stage with Dave Stewart, Mont Campbell and Clive Brooks, *aka Egg*. They were a few short weeks away from breaking up (they played their last gig at the *Roundhouse* on 9th July). I would like to say I watched their set but, not feeling too bright, I retired to trudge the long hallways in search of a toilet. Finding something which seemed suitable I went in, said hello to Alfie who, for some reason, was there brushing her hair, and disappeared into one of the cubicles. Having flushed with pride, I wandered out to wash my hands (being a well brought up young man) where Alfie politely informed me I was in the Ladies. "And very nice they are too," was the response from someone clearly not in a fit state to appreciate the point being made. We played. I was put in a car and driven home. I remember nothing else.

Despite this we were back rehearsing the following Tuesday. This time at a pub called the *Pied Bull* which was at *1, Liverpool Road* near The Angel, Islington. Sadly anonymous, it is now a branch of the *Halifax*. We were there from Tuesday to Friday, sometimes in the afternoons, sometimes at night. Getting there involved a train journey to Victoria and then two different lines on the Tube. I cannot tell you how much fun that was with a thumping headache. But there were gigs to play over the weekend of the 3rd/4th June and we needed the dosh.

And I had an appointment with several bottles of *Carlsberg Special Brew* and a large pile of towels. In Redruth. In deepest Cornwall. Ah, the lengths I went to to get legless.

On the morning of Saturday, 3rd June, 1972, I was dragged out of my sick bed, bundled into a car against my will and spirited away westwards towards Cardiff. As we drove, I usefully researched elements of the writer's soon-to-be-released and much anticipated tome: *A Complete History of British Motorways and A Roads, Volume 4, The M4 and other Western Trunk Roads, Minor A Roads and By-Passes*. We travelled down the M4, the last 50 miles of which, between Maidenhead and Swindon, was only opened in December 1971. Given that plans for this motorway were first published in 1956 this must be viewed as something less than a triumph for the *Ministry of Transport* under the auspices of which the road was constructed. Thankfully, the Severn Bridge was completed six years earlier so there was no need for the previous lengthy detour upstream along the Severn to Gloucester in order cross said river (via the A419 from Swindon to Cirencester, the A417 to Gloucester and the A48 via Chepstow and Newport. As if you needed telling).

33 The Bristol Hotel, Cardiff.
Since demolished. Another hostelry which never recovered from our visit

We were booked into an elderly hotel called the *Bristol* located somewhere on the Penarth Road (*aka* A4160) between the River Taff and the Docks. You will now not be remotely surprised to hear this hotel is no more. It has long since gone to meet the great architect in the sky (where it hosts the *Cardiff Celestial Freemasons Lodge* every third Friday of the month. Ladies not allowed. Smoking encouraged. Getting royally pissed mandatory. Handshakes silly).

We were due to play what was then called the *University College*, Cardiff (Cardiff University not being officially formed until 2005, just so you know). I have no idea where in its many historic buildings we played. I have no idea how many people turned up. I have no idea how we were received. I was far more interested in returning to the *Bristol Hotel*, taking several paracetamol, and going back to bed. Painkillers and sleep – that rock 'n roll lifestyle, don't you know?

The following day we drove south-west, well eventually. Pedantically, we first went east, then south, then south-west via, amongst others, the M5, A38 and A30. Obviously.

We were driving the 210 miles or so into deepest, darkest Cornwall and the old mining community of Redruth. It was a 4 to 5-hour journey with by far the slowest part being the laborious trek across eastern and central Cornwall because, well, the roads were (and are still) shit. There are still no motorways in Cornwall. It is as if central government has entirely forgotten about the place. Well, that's what happens when you continually elect Tory MPs, you get take for granted, you stupid buggers! Sorry, I digress. Fundamentally, Cornwall is a bastard to drive across (if extremely and, in places, wildly beautiful). Great beaches, mind, if you ever get there. Except for the surfers. Stupid sods. Barring the *Beach Boys*, of course. I mean, *Pet Sounds*. What an album!

The *Flamingo Ballroom*, was located on the *Agar Road* (the A3047, as you all know) in the village of Illogan Highway between Redruth and Camborne. It was built on the site of a spoil tip created by the nearby *East Pool and Agar tin mine*, that is until the bottom fell out of the global tin market and it closed. In the nearby churchyard is buried one Thomas Merritt, a Methodist who wrote numerous Christmas carols involving lots of 'Harking' and 'Loing', words I have never yet found a home for in any of my lyrics. Can't say I'm working too hard to rectify this omission.

The *Flamingo* opened in 1957 as a multi-purpose sports and entertainment venue with a capacity, I read now (and chuckle), of 1,300. As you can see from the photo below it was not the most prepossessing of places and the vague similarity to a car showroom is accurate, as this was part of its original purpose. It was demolished at some time in the 1980s and is now a *Morrison's* supermarket. This is marginally less ugly.

Nonetheless, in spite of its remote location and not very good looks, over the years it hosted bands/artists of all shapes and sizes (and degrees of popularity): amongst them Tom Jones, Gene Vincent, *Canned Heat*, *Chicken Shack*, *the Small Faces* and the Barrett-era *Floyd* to name but a very few. And the *Mole*.

I can confidently state we hold the record, in perpetuity, for the smallest audience ever to be seen at the *Flamingo*. There were four of us on stage and there were three road crew. We came very close to equalling the number of customers present. It was humorously suggested by someone in charge that we might, perhaps, delay our appearance in case there was 'a late rush'. There was no late rush. It just got later.

We wandered around the cavernous venue and chatted with the faithful few huddled around the very large stage (it could hold 300 performers so I hear). I recall sitting on the edge of this quite low platform talking to the entire membership of the *West & Central Cornwall Matching Mole Appreciation Society*. There were fewer members than words in its title. But then I was ill, and the *WACCMMAS* was later revealed to be a figment of my (glandular) fevered imagination. If anyone cares to form (re-form) it, you have my blessing.

We treated the gig as an extension of our rehearsals at the *Pied Bull*, except we didn't stop in the middle of things and start again when we fucked up. Nor did we pause halfway through to have a cup of tea. We certainly did not call on the audience for requests, as no-one knew any of our music and, anyway, the 'request' might have been to 'bugger off back to London'.

34 The Flamingo, Redruth, being demolished.
Nothing to do with us, honest

What we did play was: *Part of the Dance, Lything and Gracing, March Ides, Instant Pussy* and *Smoke Signal*, which relatively brief set list suggests that, in spite of my parlous health, I was still capable of boring people to tears, and filling up infinite amounts of time, with my trademark, and interminable, fuzz bass solos. Now, it turns out, the Cornish bear a grudge big time. Indeed, after this transgression, I was only allowed to return to the county about five years ago and on the understanding that I was not accompanied by any musical equipment or amplification. Seemed fair, but the armed checkpoint at the Devon-Cornwall border on the Tamar Bridge seemed a tad excessive. As was confiscating my CD player until they were sure I departed the county. Some people's memories are far too long.

Back to what we will loosely term 'the gig'. To blatantly steal a joke from the late and much-lamented Ronnie Scott (he of the Jazz Club in Soho's Frith Street): 'There were more people in the gents' toilets and they were having more fun' during this particular *Mole* appearance. BTW, if you never heard Mr Scott in full spate in one of his humorous monologues between performances at his club then you have not lived. Rib hurting stuff. And he played the tenor saxophone pretty damn well too.

After the gig, and having said a heartfelt and personal goodbye to every single attendee, we retired to the modest hotel (another which no longer exists) called the *Carlton*, about which there was nothing *Ritzy* whatsoever. The landlady (it was really a bed and breakfast) asked if we wanted anything from the bar before she closed up. Foolishly, I ordered something I had never drunk before, i.e. several bottles of *Carlsberg Special Brew*. This concoction was first brewed on the occasion of Winston Churchill's 1950 visit to Copenhagen. It was supposed to have brandy-like flavours, as Winnie was known to be partial to the odd cognac, and was of 'super-strength' when compared to the average lager (to wit, a robust 9% ABV against about 5% for wimpish 'normal' lagers). Even though now reduced to a mere 7.5% ABV it is, today, unkindly nicknamed 'Tramp Juice' for the mind-numbing impact it has on those unfortunates outside mainstream society forced to sleep rough and for whom, sadly, this, and various illegal if potent drugs, are a temporary relief and oblivion from the pain and emptiness of their everyday and marginal existence. Knowing none of this I supped deeply. Perhaps not a good idea for someone suffering from my particular medical condition.

Apparently, at some point during the night, I stood up, said not a word, lurched out of the door and staggered upstairs. I woke several hours later, fully clothed and face down across the bed. The lights were on. The door was flung wide. Both taps in the wash basin in the corner were running and, somehow or other, I had accumulated a large collection of towels from my room and other locations in the hotel. These were now piled in the centre of the floor. I have no idea how or why.

I avoided breakfast, which was probably just as well as I was violently ill on the side of the A30 just north of Redruth as we drove home. I have not touched a drop of *Special Brew* ever since. It joins a short list of alcoholic drinks I will never indulge in again, the other items being *Southern Comfort* (after the imbibing of which aged 17 I nose-dived down the stairs the following morning), the unutterably feeble *Blue Nun* so-called *Liebfraumilch*, and *Limoncello*, simply because it is bloody disgusting.

Having returned to *UNIT* to rehearse on Friday, we adjourned next door the following night for a gig in what was then the *King's Cross Theatre*, an old pre-First World War cinema (later the *Scala*), which had seen better days some long time before. Apparently, it was briefly used as an 'adult cinema' the previous year. It didn't look as though much had changed since. Seedy is putting it politely. Clean it certainly was not.

Our manager was a gent (and I use the term very loosely) called Sean Murphy. Sean was middle class, cleaned up, tidy 'hip'. And a shark. He was also the manager of *Soft Machine*. Sadly, the *Softs* had never been too good at selecting their managers. Previously they had suffered in the hands of Chas Chandler (previously bass player with *The Animals*) and Mike Jeffrey, manager of a certain Jimi Hendrix. It is my understanding that, between them, they managed to put together contracts for the *SM* which resulted in no-one seeing a penny from the first two albums. Ever. The trend was continued with current manager and royalties both 'disappearing' some time in the 70s. I am led to understand bankruptcy followed at some point in the 80s with which event went any chance of recouping any of the *SM/Mole* dosh generated post-1972. Ho hum, just another day in the life of the average musician.

Anyway, Mr Murphy, having already sent the *Softs* to Italy in April with at least part of our PA system (which meant withdrawal from the Mayall tour of Germany/Austria/Switzerland), now concluded that some rationalising of his artists roster was in order and that it would save everyone time and money if we appeared on the same bill on a pretty regular basis.

The first two such dates were to be: *King's Cross Theatre* on Saturday, 17th June, and the *New Theatre*, Oxford, the next day (though put back to 9th July as John Marshall suddenly went down with hepatitis). It would not just be the *Softs* and the *Mole* appearing together. Elton Dean's *Just Us* was on the bill at both venues whilst, at *King's Cross*, the evening would also feature the *Brotherhood of Breath* and *Stud* (two ex-members of *Taste* [McCracken and Wilson], one ex-member of *Family* [Weider] and one future member of *Family* and previous member of the wonderful *Blossom Toes* [Cregan]. They broke up a few months later. Seems like 1972 was a good year for breakups).

Also playing was a band made of three ex-members of *King Crimson*: Mel Collins, the late Boz Burrell and Ian Wallace plus two people I have down simply as 'Brown' and 'Bond'. Thoughts, anyone?

Moving on, I really disliked the *King's Cross Theatre* (which we would play again with pretty much the same line up on 7th July). It was dark, soulless, dirty, cold (even in summer) and generally fucking miserable. I, at least, played accordingly.

35 The King's Cross Theatre since reincarnated as the Scala

And, talking of miserable, we must move on to what I reckon was the true downside to Mr Murphy's decision to try to get his stable of 'artistes' playing together. This 'downside' was the effect I believe it had on Robert.

I was young, barely 21, and typically up myself (or basically just bloody arrogant), self-absorbed and, barring the glandular fever, having too much unexpected fun to notice what else was going on (except, later, when Julie Christie was present. I became very observant at such moments). Robert, however, was metaphorically but not deliberately, having his nose rubbed in it by having to be the support act to the band he formed and named six years before. His contribution to that band, both in terms of composition and performance, had been integral and essential to the band's success, image and sound. Now his old childhood friends were off messing about with other musicians who technically may have been better (define 'better' though) but who lacked the heart and soul which drove the *Soft Machine* through its various previous incarnations.

I was not sufficiently aware to realise what this might mean. Even if I had been, what could I have done?

I did, however, instinctively loathe (OK, too strong, 'was left totally cold by' is a better description) the new version of the band. My baseline was the Wyatt/Ratledge/Hopper trio (though I also loved the Wyatt/Ratledge/Ayers version). At no point did this new, noodling, jazz-rock version of the band come remotely close to the urgency, drama, humanity, and innovation of that line-up. So, as far as I was (and am) concerned, *Soft Machine* ceased to exist the day Robert left. The name should have died at the same time (and certainly after Mike departed).

Do not try to argue with me. I am not listening. Nah, nah, nah, nah…..

On Tuesday 20th June we all dutifully turned up at a new rehearsal venue: i.e. *St Andrew's Church Hall* at 106, Bethune Road, in Stoke Newington. Robert was concealing a little surprise up his sleeve. At some point, a slight, bespectacled figure with a bit of a west country accent turned up. This gent, Robert explained, was to produce the next *Matching Mole* album which, given the last one only escaped about two months earlier, was nothing short of bizarre. Anyway, Mr Robert Fripp, because it was he, was taking time off from working with his hot, rocking combo, *aka King Crimson*, to produce the *Mole*. We chatted. He was very nice and amusing. We played a bit. He nodded sagely whilst, no doubt, wondering: WTF?! We agreed to meet later. In *CBS's* brand-new recording studios in Whitfield Street in what, in polite circles, is known as Fitzrovia.

The next day we headed off to W9, better known to its friends as Maida Vale, and the *BBC Studios* in Delaware Road. It is a long, low, cream coloured building still currently occupied by the *Beeb*, though they are moving out in 2025 and the place has been bought by a consortium of film makers and composers including Hans Zimmer.

The place was built in 1909 and was, interestingly, the *Maida Vale Roller Skating Palace and Club*. Didn't know roller skating was a 'thing' in Edwardian Britain. You learn something new….

Next to its rather fancy entrance is a Blue Plaque which reads:

Maida Vale Studios
Home of the BBC Symphony Orchestra and the Radiophonic Workshop
1934

The BBC took the place over in 1934 and the *Symphony Orchestra* was based there. They were joined by the *Radiophonic Workshop* in 1958. The building is now Grade II listed.

Anyway, it contains seven studios, one of them, *Studio 1*, being large enough to accommodate 150 musicians and a 200 strong audience. Not the one we used. We were in *Studio 4*, if my handwriting is to be believed, and we were there to record a session for Pete Drummond's *Sounds of the 70s* radio show. Three songs were to be played, all new: Phils' *Nan True's Hole*, Dave's *Brandy for Benj* (later retitled *Brandy as in Benj* – Benj being the aforementioned Benjamin Lefevre, sound man extraordinaire and partaker of ample quantities of *Remy Martin*), and *Gloria Gloom*, based on an idea by yours truly and brought to life by R Wyatt, esq. Oddly, at the moment, I cannot remember if this session has since seen the light of day as I can find no record of *GG* appearing on anything other than *LRR*. Please advise if wrong.

On Sunday, 25th June, we played in the somewhat incongruous surroundings of *Barbarella's* in Birmingham. According to one web site:

> "*Barbarella's* is one of Birmingham's legendary venues. It stood on the site of what is now the *RBS Bank* in Brindley Place. If memory serves me right, the address was 37, Cumbernauld St."

Who am I to argue? I have a memory of a somewhat tacky, mainly red, low-ceilinged establishment in which a band like *Mole* seemed singularly ill-placed. Mind you, this could have been the gig in Swindon a short time after. They all blur into one after a while. It wouldn't surprise me if one or more glitter balls were suspended from the ceiling. From the back of one of the sofa-like seats, one could have probably headed them football-style (were one seriously inebriated or drugged up to the eyeballs. I was never the latter and, after Amsterdam and Cornwall, rarely the former nowadays). Apparently, Ike and Tina Turner played there later that year. God alone knows how they got the band and backing singers in along with an audience.

Life drifted by, with our next gig on Thursday, 29th June, at *Liverpool University*. We were one of nine bands playing that day. Yes, day, as this was a two stage 'concert special' starting at 11 a.m. and finishing at 10.30 p.m. We were the headliners, due to hit the Stage B at 9.15 p.m. Whoever wrote the promo stuff at the university was a fan, declaring the first *Mole* album 'the best of the year'. 'I could go on writing about them for pages and pages', he gushed. Hmmm. Perhaps I wrote those notes in another guise[3].

On immediately before us was a bunch of exotically dressed poseurs *aka* the UK's 'next big thing'. Yes! We were playing alongside *Roxy Music*. Robert meets Eno (in full feathered and made-up regalia) for the first time, and I meet them for the second having previously popped into

113

Command Studios to hear them mixing the first album (*Chance Meeting* I believe). Mr Manzanera briefly wears his silly diamante specs through which he cannot see a bloody thing. It is very clear from the outset who is going to sell the most records. We all smile through gritted teeth.

On finishing, the *Mole* shoots off south because, in a triumph of organisation, the next night we are playing a small pub 250 miles away called *The Falcon* in Eltham in south-east London (it's now a *Harvester*. Yikes). Brilliant. Or not. I have no idea.

And the next day we go even further. To Paris, France, would you believe? First Heathrow to Orly… and then back again the same day.

I was, perhaps like some others on the flight out, more than a bit nervous. Thirteen days earlier, *BEA Flight 548*, with a crew of six and 112 passengers, took off from Heathrow on the way to Brussels. The aircraft was an eleven-year-old *Hawker Siddeley Trident 1C*, call sign *G-ARPI* or *Papa India*. It took off at just after 4.08 p.m., stalled and, 150 seconds later, crashed into a field near Staines. All 118 passengers and crew died. The first few minutes of our flight were, therefore, a time of extreme buttock clenching for yours truly.

36 Robert in his balaclava. Drumming between bank heists

Anyway, the quick 'in and out' nature of this trip to France was the reason why we only take our guitars, and end up using Pete Brown's band's drums, amps and *Hammond*. We do *Gloria Gloom* and *Part of the Dance* for the TV show *Rockenstock*. Robert wears a balaclava for reasons known only to him. I sport my two-tone green and white stars and stripes trousers bought in the King's Road a few days earlier because I am a prat with absolutely no fashion sense. Things have not improved down the years. Sadly, the show is in black and white so one does not get the full visual impact of these splendid items of clothing. We are surrounded by several young French ladies who have perfected that look of glacial Gallic indifference to their surroundings, as well as to any long-haired gits lurking in the vicinity. They are unmoved by my trews.

We play. We finish. We get a taxi back to Orly. We fly back to Heathrow. We disperse to our various homes. We have nothing more to do until the following Friday. It seemed exciting at the time. For your delectation and delight this video has also found its way on to *YouTube*.

On Thursday, 6th July, Pete Drummond's aforementioned *Sounds of the 70s* session was broadcast. I used to have a link to it somewhere on the jolly, old Interweb but it seems to have disappeared into the ether. Never mind. If you *could* hear it, you would note that the versions of *Gloria Gloom* featured on Mr Drummond's show and on the *Rockenstock* video do not include the lyrics Robert sings on *Little Red Record*. The explanation is simple. At this moment they did not exist. Those heartfelt phrases emerged between the recording of backing track on Tuesday, 15th August and the adding of the vocal overdubs which were done two weeks later. Pretty straight forward.

37 Melody Maker advert for the first Soft/Mole/Us gig

The following night we did our second show at the dreary and gloomy *King's Cross Theatre*. We were sandwiched between *Just Us* and *Soft Machine*, as we would be on Sunday when we all played the *New Theatre*, Oxford.

I dunno but, looking back, such a show smacks of 'too much of a good(ish) thing'. I used to like gigs when there was a bit of variety, like the shows at the *Lyceum Ballroom* in the Strand when the old (and best!!!) version of *Soft Machine* played alongside *Procul Harum* or *Van der Graaf*

Generator. Or shows briefer and to the point, like *Soft Machine tout seul* at the intimate little *Country Club* in Hampstead. I mean, would you voluntarily sit down for several hours to be hit over the head by a bunch of extremely serious people lecturing you musically about 'real music'? Well, not if sober.

Of course, this is where silly trousers play a vital role. They reminded people these buggers on stage were *trying* to entertain you. A bit of rock showmanship, and extremely bad sartorial taste you could laugh at. I was trying to lighten the mood. Well, that's my story and I'm sticking to it.

38 The infamous trousers.
Phil more discreetly attired at the back. For the nerds out there, note the unusual Spanish guitar-style head on the Gibson. Only made 70-71.

On these nights we played the following toons: *Gloria Gloom, Part of the Dance, Lything and Gracing, March Ides, Instant Pussy* and *Smoke Signal*. We even did an encore: *Brandy for* (or soon, *as in*) *Benj*. I sense from this distance plenty of opportunities there to strangle the upper reaches of the *EB3's* fretboard to the sound of the *Shaftesbury Duo-Fuzz*. Oh happy day!

Amongst the crowd that night, and, no doubt, wishing he was elsewhere, was long-time friend and musical accomplice Señor Felipe Manzanera who was given special dispensation by Mr Byriani Ferret to explore musical pastures new. And then, and sensibly, ignore them.

My sadly late brother Ian was there too, furtively representing the *New Musical Express* under the guise of a cunning pseudonym. The following night we both tootled off to the *Royal Festival Hall* there to see the also sadly late David Bowie and his *Spiders from Mars*. Lovely. What an alchemist and chameleon that Bowie was.

And that, broadly, was that for the first half of July.

On Thursday, 13th July we wandered down to Dorset where a student with a finely tuned sense of humour booked us for the end of year dance at *Weymouth Grammar School*. I admire his style. He either held a severe grudge against his fellow pupils or was a true nerd. Or perhaps both.

We were supported by a band called *Snake Eye*. Apparently previously called *Red Dirt* (I think their management was right when they changed the name) they went on to support a number of significant acts: *Free, Marc Bolan, Status Quo, the Kinks* and *the J Geils Band*. Manfred Mann thought highly of them I read. They did one album and folded. I know the feeling.

And that, for the next fortnight, was it.

MID-JULY 1972, OTHER THAN OUR BRIEF TRIP TO WEYMOUTH, was a quiet time for the London branch of the Talpidae family in the order Eulipotyphla (*aka* Moles, OK?). But things were about to hot up.

Before all that nonsense, we were laying plans for the recording of the second *Mole* album. You see, things were different in those days. You churned out albums on an industrial scale. First *Mole* album out in April, then why not record the second album in August. I mean, the first one was such a rip-roaring success, why the hell not?

So, we were contemplating what songs we might record and in what order they might appear. In my little green Civil Service diary (which went everywhere. Except the shower or bath) I compiled, like the Lord High Executioner in the *Mikado*, a little list. Not of people who might have their heads removed (I have a very long and current list of them) but of songs which might appear on said *Mole* long player v. II. The list reads:

Side One
March Ides
June Brides (wtf? I have no idea) linked to

Nan True's Hole
Phil's Song (aka God Song)
Lything and Gracing
Brandy for (as in) Benj (these last two to be continuous)
Side Two
Gloria Gloom
Waltz aka No 'Alf Measures (the one written by Kevin Ayers)
Flora Fidgit
Smoke Signal

Anyway, on Thursday, 20th July, we might (or might not) have rehearsed at *UNIT* (one diary [the little green one] has it crossed through, the other [the big blue one] does not).

On Friday we foregathered at Victoria Station around 1.30 p.m. to get the train to Dover. We then boarded a ferry to Oostende (OK, Ostend if you insist) where we retired to a small hotel somewhere in the middle of the town (I must apologise for not knowing this hotel's name. Remiss of me). There we found the road crew who had beaten us to it.

The owners of this establishment looked somewhat askance at this bunch of long-haired, scruffy Brits devoting much time to drinking various beers in their small bar. Things, however, rapidly went downhill.

Unfortunately, a school party from somewhere in the south of England was also staying there that night. Normally, a bunch of twelve-year olds tearing around pursued by harassed teachers would not have been a problem. But this was not a bunch of twelve-year olds. Rather it was a collection of 17-year-old young ladies who found the presence of some (even if unknown) rock musicians more than a bit exciting. Whilst the musicians amongst us ate and drank before retiring to bed at a modest hour, the road crew, so it was later suggested, had other things on their minds. Certainly, the sounds of creaking floorboards, knocks on doors and girlish giggles, suggested something was up (read that as you may).

Unhappily, the teachers in charge took the task of protecting their charges' vital interests seriously and, before you knew it, there was a loud rapping on our various bedroom doors which, when opened, revealed an irate Flemish landlady demanding we (innocent as lambs, m'lud) depart her fine hostelry forthwith. Extending the hill farming analogy, with the road crew looking somewhat sheepish, we packed and vacated pronto while someone (I assume Tony, our tour manager) was despatched to find room at another inn. Or, failing that, a barn, perhaps containing a tableau of the first ever artificially inseminated virgin, along with wise men and cribs whilst, all the while, shepherds washed their socks. Or something.

But why were we in bloody Oostende only to be thrown out of a hotel you ask? Well, my fine feathered friends, we were there to play a thing called the *Europop Festival 1972* (I do not believe there was *Europop* '71 or, indeed, '73. Except, perhaps, in the promoter's imagination). Quite who organised the bands due to play at this fine event (in what I believe was called the *Media Center*) it is impossible to say. The decision-making process which led to what they thought constituted a balanced line-up is difficult, if not impossible, to fathom. The bands invited to play were:

Brainbox (no idea)
Dizzy Man's Band (ditto)
If (know them)
Jericho (vaguely heard of them)
MC5 (well alright!)
Matching Mole (who?)
Mungo Jerry (OK)
The Pebbles (back to no idea)
The Sweet (putting the sugar into pop)

It is a long way from the serene shores of the sublime to the rocky crags of the ridiculous, but this line-up spans that great void effortlessly.

The venue was a huge, hangar-like space with a large stage at one end. Behind it was an even larger area where the various road crews set-up their band's equipment. Each band's performance was, therefore, separated by a longer or shorter delay depending on the relative efficiency/sobriety of the relevant crew. The delays got longer as bored crew members got stuck into the pallets of bottled beers stacked behind the stage.

The audience seemed not to care. Stretched out in serried ranks, they were either stoned out of their minds or drunk as lords. Or both.

We watched the various bands from the side of the hall. Robert and I liked *The Sweet*, who also lived up to their names when we chatted to them. They performed robust versions of their various hits, though the really big ones – *Blockbuster* and *Hell Raiser* – came out in 1973. I cannot remember any of the others.

I was also keeping a beady eye on the promoter who was in a small office counting money. And shaking his head. I suggested Tony put him under surveillance. He did more than that. He went in and demanded our dosh (the princely sum of £525 or c. £7½ grand in today's money). After some negotiations we were paid £200, with a cheque for the remainder. Ho, ho. All jokes about bouncing Czechs/cheques are now appropriate.

Whilst Benj and Mouse assembled our gear on stage, certain members of the *MC5* became bored and, therefore, busy. One of them left the venue to visit a nearby grocer's shop. There they bought a large number of tomatoes. Thus, when we were introduced to the snoring crowd of young Flemings, we found these tomatoes everywhere. Lined up along the tops of amps. Gaffer-taped to mike stands. Adorning cymbal stands. The guys from the *MC5* grinned hugely. We smiled and plotted our revenge.

We played. The audience slept. We left the stage, as did our somewhat tomato-stained kit. The *MC5's* people started to set up.

Who threw the first tomato I cannot say. Probably one of us. As it splattered the stage, a full-scale tomato war broke out as both musos and crew gleefully flung the soft fruit (they are fruit you know, and genius is knowing *not* to put them in a fruit salad) in all directions. Only the belated intervention of a peas keeping force (geddit?) led by the promoter put an end to this brief break down of the Special Relationship.

As it turned out, this skirmish cemented (or tomatoed) relationships with our transatlantic friends. On Monday night, we met up with them to see *Weather Report* play at Ronnie Scott's[i]. Those boys adored their jazz. We shared drinks, laughed, and loved the music. I mean, how good is that?

Sadly, of course, the *Motor City Five* were on their last legs. Though still including the hard core of the band – vocalist Rob Tyner, guitarists Wayne Kramer and Fred *Sonic* Smith, and drummer Dennis Thompson (the bass player at this time was one Derek Hughes) – they would break up at the end of the year in rather sad and sorry circumstances when only a few dozen people turned up to see them play at the *Grande Ballroom*, Detroit, near their home town of Lincoln Park[ii].

But you cannot deny their pedigree, their history, and their politics. I mean, these guys played for eight hours straight outside the 1968 *Democratic National Convention* whilst Mayor Richard J Daley's thuggish Chicago police rioted and, aided and abetted by the Illinois National Guard, brutally and unmercifully beat and tear-gassed previously predominantly peaceful anti-Vietnam war demonstrators in front of the Democrat HQ in the *Conrad Hilton Hotel* in downtown Chicago.

Filmed by numerous TV crews, the demonstrators set to chanting 'The whole world's watching' which refrain found its way on to the *Chicago Transit Authorities'* first album in the form of *Prologue*, which then morphs into *Someday*, August 29th 1968 (the whole album is great. Give it a listen)

The *MC5* in Grant Park, 1968, now that is *real* history. Kick out the jams, motherfuckers! Or words to that effect.

SO, AFTER OUR BRIEF DIVERSION INTO US POLITICAL HISTORY, we left our *Moles* sitting alongside members of a rockin' Stateside combo, the *MC5*, in the gloom of Ronnie Scott's intimate jazz establishment downstairs at 47, Frith Street, Soho, listening to *Weather Report*.

---

[i] Formed by Joe Zawinul and Wayne Shorter in 1970 after they played together on Miles Davis's ground-breaking *In a Silent Way* (1969) and *Bitches Brew* (1970). They featured the great Czech bass player Miroslav Ladislav Vitouš, and just released their second album: *I Sing the Body Electric*.

[ii] Kramer and Thompson survive and still active. Rob Tyner died of a heart attack in 1991, and Fred Smith from the same cause in 1994. They were both aged 46.

The next night (Tuesday, 25th July 1972) the band reconvened in the *Greyhound Public House* at 175-7, Fulham Palace Road[i], there to entertain the unsuspecting punters out for a quiet pint and a game of darts. Actually, of course, the *Greyhound* was a well-established music venue. Coincidentally, the *MC5* had played there only a few weeks earlier on 28th June. The stage was small, the front row seats barely a few feet away. One could easily see the faces of everyone in the room.

So, we hit the stage and, oh look, there's Alfie sitting at the front, smiling conspiratorially. She is talking to a beautiful blonde lady sitting next to her who turns her head, looks up, and smiles radiantly. Cue the bass player's disintegration.

39 The Greyhound, Fulham Palace Road.

Let us go back a few years to when the writer was a callow, undoubtedly pimply, teenager with raging hormones. Around 1965, he saw a photograph of an actress and was, to be blunt, instantly smitten. The object of his very remote affections had just won an Oscar for two films; *Darling* and *Doctor Zhivago*. Her name was Julie Christie and the 14-year-old BMac was in lurve. Utterly besotted. He would trawl newspapers and magazines for all, and any, photographs of this vision of loveliness. He even went as far as tracking down copies of a *recherché* little French publication called *Cahiers du Cinema* when he discovered there was an extensive article about her participation in François Truffaut's 1966 film

---

[i] Music ceased there in the 1990s and it later became the *Southern Belle* restaurant. Since closed, the building is now sadly derelict.

Fahrenheit 451. He got a strange look from the staff at *W H Smith's* in Streatham High Street when he bought a copy of the French fashion magazine *Elle*. But she was on the cover, and he did not care. Each photograph and article was lovingly clipped and pasted into a large notebook (which, sadly, he still possesses). If the piece spread over both sides of the page, then, of course, two copies of said publication were essential for completeness sake. Whilst the intensity of his devotion reduced somewhat over the years, he was still pretty much first in the queue whenever a new film opened in London: *Far from the Madding Crowd* in 1967, *Petulia* (1968), *In Search of Gregory* (1969), *The Go-Between* and *McCabe & Mrs. Miller* (1971, two films, making it an especially good year).

Thus, you may imagine the young bass player's complete discombobulation when he realised the lady seemingly smiling at him from about six feet away was, yes!, his teenage heart throb.

Not much else piqued his attention that night. He may have played several extended (*Ed*: interminable) fuzz bass solos for all he can remember. All he does recall is having to slap his tongue out of the way when attempting to reach certain parts of his little *Gibson's* fretboard. It was probably an interesting night. Who knows? Did he speak to her afterwards? Don't ask me? I could barely move, let alone talk.

Let me just say, however, how lovely it was to find someone to be just as beautiful on the inside and as on the outside. As we shall soon see.

It was probably just as well we rehearsed the next day as who knows what the bass player might have got up to left to his own devices.

On Thursday, 27th July, we headed down to the *Paris Theatre* in Lower Regent Street there to record a live performance for the BBC's *Sounds of the 70s*. This 'live' performance apparently took 7½ hours to complete. Given that we only played *Instant Pussy/Lything and Gracing/March Ides/Part of the Dance/Brandy for Benj* this is weird. The bass solos must have been rather longer than normal. (All tracks to be found on the absolutely splendid *Matching Mole – On The Radio*, Hux Records – *HUX 083*, released 2006[i]. Or you can cut out the middleman and just send me a donation to the pension fund by bank transfer).

Two more days of rehearsal later and we were back at the *Roundhouse*, scene of our second ever gig six months earlier. Sunday night at the *Roundhouse* was '*Implosion*' night when young men in tie-dyed t-shirts, bell bottoms and greatcoats tried painfully to impress the young ladies there foregathered but who really wished to be entertained by musicians of different types (can I say 'genres'? *Ed*: OK, but just this once) which *genres* were represented that night by a band called *Biggles* (about which I can tell

---

[i] And still currently available at https://www.huxrecords.com/cdsales83.htm!

you nothing), great British jazzer Keith Tippett, from across the pond, the *Flamin' Groovies*, and us. It was probably wonderful. I cannot remember.

We then spend the next two weeks rehearsing. A couple of times we were in a room over in leafy Richmond by the Thames. Several others were at the premises of the *Jazz Centre Society*. I can only find one reference to an address for said place which is the *Seven Dials Community Centre* on Shelton Street, Covent Garden (which still exists) but whether this was where we were I cannot for certain say.

We were rehearsing for two events.

The first was on Sunday, 13th August, the final day of the *11th National Jazz, Blues & Rock Festival, aka The Reading Festival,* held at Richfield Avenue, Reading, between the 11th and 13th August 1972. We played sometime during the afternoon in what was, according to accounts, a somewhat lacklustre event all round.

40 The complete bill for the Reading Festival, 1972. Four bands in three hours.

We certainly increased the 'lack' of the diminishing 'lustre'. I mean, put yourself in the position of the average audient, i.e. pissed, stoned out of your mind, probably suffering from a bout of diarrhoea caused by inadequate toilet facilities, sweaty, smelly, and generally not nice to be around after three days in a field on the flood plain of the nearby River Thames. Now, the last thing you need is for some twerp, possibly sporting two-tone green and white stars and stripes trousers, to regale you with a 30-minute fuzz bass solo. I mean, talk about cruel and unusual punishment!

Anyway, there were other, more mainstream, bands to entertain the soggy and somewhat somnolent assemblage: *Ten Years After, Quintessence, Wizard, Status Quo, Stray, Vinegar Joe, Sutherland Bros.* (not yet including *Quiver.* They got together the following year), *Stackridge*, and *Brewer's Droop* (possibly one of the worst-named rock groups in the history of the *genre* [*Ed*: once I said! Don't go taking liberties]).

To be perfectly blunt, I would not have paid good money to see any of this lot (apologies to those offended) but then, after the rain and mud and wind, the execrable food and swamp-like toilets, the horrendous delays, the traffic congestion and general all-round shitness of the *Bath Festival of Blues and Progressive Music* held at Shepton Mallet over the weekend of the 27th-29th June 1970, I decided that I would never attend another festival unless I was on stage.[i] A promise I have kept ever since. Well that's a lie. I've attended two festivals in recent years as a guest of Mr Manzanera and *Roxy*. I can tell you, therefore, backstage at modern festivals is a whole new ball game relative to sitting in the mud in the middle of several thousand music fans who have paid good money to see some band or other only then to talk through their entire set. That, and you are miles from some of the most disgusting toilets it will ever be your misfortune to need. So, Brussels 2001 and the Isle of Wight (whenever) with a Triple A pass. Yes, please. Free drink, very good food, and the chance to watch from the side of the stage. Plus, very important, easy access to relatively clean toilet facilities. *That* makes *all* the difference.

There was, however, life after Reading for, on Monday, 14th August, 1972, at 1.00 p.m., the band members, a certain Robert Fripp, and engineer Mike Fitzhenry assembled at *CBS's* brand spanking, new recording studios at Whitfield Street, W1. We would be in the smaller *Studio 2* until midnight and, during that time, laid down the basic tracks for *March Ides*, *Nan True's Hole*, *Lything and Gracing* (later, and after the addition of lyrics 'spoken' by Robert and Alfie, re-named *Righteous Rhumba*) and *Brandy for/ as in Benj*. Not bad for a day's work.

The following day we knocked out the elements of *Gloria Gloom* and *Smoke Signal* and, on Wednesday 16th August, in a somewhat abbreviated session between 7 and 12 p.m., *God Song*. By this time, we had racked up studio costs of a princely £723 (north of £10 grand nowadays, as I am sure you are keen to know). Don't ask where the £3 came from.

---

[i] Apparently, the inspiration for the Glastonbury Festival. The line-up was phenomenal, but the weather prevented some bands from performing. Amongst those who did, or should have, appeared, were: *Santana*, *The Flock*, *Led Zeppelin*, *Hot Tuna*, *Country Joe McDonald*, *Colosseum*, *Jefferson Airplane* (rain-affected), *The Byrds*, *The Moody Blues* (rained-off), *Dr. John*, *Frank Zappa & The Mothers of Invention*, *Canned Heat*, *It's a Beautiful Day*, *Steppenwolf*, *Johnny Winter*, *John Mayall with Peter Green*, *Pink Floyd*, *Pentangle*, *Fairport Convention*, *Keef Hartley*, and the *Maynard Ferguson Big Band*.

On Thursday we headed off for Belgium, there to play on Friday, 18th August, the *Bilzen Jazz Festival*. For some reason I ended up playing a long-scale *Fender Jazz* rather than my short-scale *Gibson EB3*. I robustly deny any suggestions I played the entire set in several different keys.

Clearly, though, *Mole* and Festivals didn't mix (The only good one I ever played was with the *801* at *Reading* in 1976), as a critic recording the events of the festival concluded that:

> "Despite some progress since its appearances at the *Theatre 140*, the *Matching Mole* performance did not leave an unforgettable memory on the plain of Bilzen."

Can't really argue with that. Somewhere on *YouTube* there is an audience recording of the performance. Do yourself a favour. Avoid it.

Also entertaining the youth of Belgium that night was *Curved Air*, *Lindisfarne*, *Edgar Broughton*, *the Holy Modal Rounders*, *Michael Chapman* and some other more local bands. What fun.

41 Bilzen with the Fender Jazz of unknown provenance.
And another glimpse of the special trousers

We were supposed to dash off to northern Holland to play another festival at Groningen but came home instead. We would make Groningen's acquaintance in just over a month in less than happy circumstances.

On Monday, 21st August, having first done an interview for the *NME* with my bro, we moved into the symphony orchestra-sized *Studio 1* in Whitfield Street in an attempt to record *Flora Fidgit* and *No 'Alf Measures* (a

Robert/Kevin piece we sometimes played live). There were some problems with the former piece. The next day, we tried to get *Flora* sorted but it was only ever partly finished. We also started a mix of *Smoke Signal*.

A two-day gap intervened after some sessions were cancelled by *CBS* before we were back in *Studio 1* mixing/overdubbing again. *Smoke Signal* again loomed large on the horizon, as did *Starting the Middle of the Day*. Issues with *Flora Fidgit* remained unresolved. We also met up with Bob Norrington who was designing the album cover based on a Chinese postcard about the 'liberation' of Taiwan which Robert provided.

All of which bring us up to date.

Certain items have been skated over, e.g. the 'issues' surrounding *Flora* and my drunken protestations of undying devotion to Ms Christie to an embarrassed Robert in a hotel in Belgium. The less said about all that the better... though, perhaps, too much has been said already. Cringe.

一定要解放台湾！

42 *'We are determined to liberate Taiwan'.*
I'd rather they left the place alone and used the resources to help solve global warming.

From Tuesday, 29th August, various wonderful people started to turn up at the *Mole's* recording sessions. Step forward that day Mr Brain One (*aka* Brian Eno), and on Wednesday, Ruby Crystal (*aka* Ms Julie Christie), the Little Honest Injun (*aka* Gloria Gloom *aka* Ms Alfreda Benge), and David Gale (erm, *aka* Mr David Gale. Hmmm).

Your intrepid reporter first met Brian Eno at *Command Studios* during the recording of the first *Roxy Music* album earlier in the year. Then the two bands played on the same bill at *Liverpool University*. They remained in touch and, when it came to the recording of *Mole's* new album, the bass player asked Mr Eno to attend in order to sprinkle some star dust over elements of his *oeuvre*. As anyone who knew Brian well in those days, he was into that sort of thing. And music too.

Thus, Mr Fuzz Solo, freshly returned from Corellia in his brother's YT-1300 light freighter, called Mr Eno at his flat in Maida Vale (286 2663 if you need to know. I hope he's changed it since) and invited him to attend Whitfield Street studios at 2.30 p.m. on Tuesday, 29th August 1972.

Mr Eno duly arrived with his *VCS3* in tow, his long blondish hair dyed in several fetching pastel shades. He set up in the control room to the right of the door and the fun began. I hoped he might provide a suitably robust noise with which to fill out the rather thin-sounding *Flora Fidgit*, instead, he provided the ominous, threatening and atmospheric intro and outro to *Gloria Gloom* by overlaying several pre-set synth sounds. Mr Fripp, who I do not believe had seen Mr Eno at work before, sat at the desk wreathed in a benign smile whilst his children played. What fun!

The following day was, for this person at least, as near to heaven as one could get except by believing such a ludicrous place existed in the first place. It was the day *Der Mütter Korus* came to town!

For reasons not entirely clear to some of us, I suspect Robert (for a larf) and me (lust, pure and simple), determined that what the album really needed was a few people talking over various parts of the music. In particular, Phil's *Nan True's Hole*. As you do. But which few people? Well Alfie for one. Then her mate Dave. And, finally, their mate Ruby. What can I tell you? The chance of spending seven hours in a recording studio with Julie Christie swept all and any musical considerations clean out of my head. I will admit to getting somewhat giddy.

Microphone stands were set up in three corners of *Studio 2* and Alfie, David and Julie invited to say whatever came into their heads for as long as they wanted. Indeed, from my point of view, the longer the better. For reasons you would not find it difficult to ascertain, I spent the entire session in the recording studio and not in the control room as one would normally expect.

David ("I rarely work naked for this reason") Gale, one of the nicest and funniest people you will ever meet, kept us in stitches most of the time. Alfie commented with her usual tongue in cheek gravity on the insanity surrounding her, whilst Ms Christie tantalised this writer with her sound effects at the end of her tale about an inexperienced middle-aged man losing his virginity to a 'lady of the night'. The results were now deemed essential to the general vibe of Phil's piece. So entranced was I, however, that I suggested we do it all over again as an enhancement to

---

i Nan True's Hole was the name of the home of the late John Peel.

Gloria Gloom. Thus was Ms Christie kept gainfully employed, and me in a state of testosterone-sodden incapacity for another hour or so.

What's not to like?

And so passed probably the two best days in a recording studio one could wish for. And, yes, I could have illustrated this with a photo of Mr Eno or Mr Fripp but really... Eno/Fripp/Julie?, Julie/Fripp/Eno?

Sorry guys, *nolo contendere*.

43 Julie in Venice during the making of Don't Look Now

The next day we worked on vocals and other details for *Side II*. These included Robert's vocal parts to *Gloria Gloom* and *God Song*. Gone were the days when Robert wrote about broken relationships. Politics was the order of the day alongside striking dystopian imagery, as *Gloria* made clear:

Like so many of you
I've got my doubts about
How much to contribute to the already rich
How long can I pretend that music's more important
Than fighting for a socialist world

Someone watching us knows I'm bad
Plastic along blue black wall
Small square (for faces)
Where dead men can look through.
Run along and see the prison bath;
Throw a stone along an empty road;
You and your friend will be found.
Outside the daydream, I've woken up to watch you sleep

God Song's lyric was an acerbic assault on the hypocrisy and irrelevance of religion, well Christianity at least, as the middle section makes clear:

And next time you send your boy down here
Give him a wife and a sexy daughter
Someone we can understand
Who's got some ideas we can use, really relate to
We've all read your rules, tried them
Learnt them in school, then tried them
They're impossible rules, and you've made us look fools

I don't think anyone in the band had any argument with the content of the lyrics though, rather absurdly, Robert (on one side) and Phil and me (on the other) spent an inordinate amount of time debating whether the first millisecond of Phil's guitar part had been cut off. Robert, yes/Phil and me, no. We might have solved the problem by splicing the edited piece of tape into an otherwise blank section and listened to the results. But we didn't, and Robert lost the argument.

On Sunday, 3rd September, we started mixing *Side I*. On Monday we did a late mixing session (11 p.m. to 3 a.m.). Rather than find our way back home, Julie offered Robert and me the use of her small house in Selwood Terrace, Fulham, whilst she was away for a few days. Her *Oscar* for *Darling* was hidden away on top of her fridge in the kitchen. There was no sign of the other ten awards from 1965 (a *Golden Globe* and *BAFTA* amongst others).

The next morning, we wended our way north-west to the environs of *Shepherd's Bush Cricket Club* in East Acton Lane where we were to rehearse for the next two days. The final mixing session was thrown in late on Tuesday night (so another excuse to snooze *chez* Christie).

BTW I stayed in touch with Julie a bit after *Mole* broke up. And, of course, in a typically generous gesture she bought Robert and Alfie the flat in Lebanon Park, Twickenham, which was their home for several years after Robert's dreadful, immobilising accident in May 1973.

In 1974 I interviewed her for the *NME* on the subject of nuclear power (we were both opposed on the grounds of safety, waste disposal, and civil liberties, in particular, the draconian powers afforded to the armed *Atomic Energy Authority Constabulary*, *aka* the Nuclear Police, and the *Civil Nuclear Constabulary* since 2005, who then could go practically anywhere and arrest practically anyone).

I previously wrote another piece for the paper (nothing like exploiting one's brotherly contacts) on the infiltration of football crowds by the *National Front*. I got a death threat from some nutter in Manchester for my trouble, bomb under the car sort of thing. I didn't have a car. Couldn't even drive. Instead, I was visited by a very nice, and grossly underpaid, detective sergeant from *Special Branch*. We know this prat, he told me. All mouth and trousers. Local coppers will have a stern word.

That done, I gave him a cup of tea and we chatted more generally. Apparently, at that time, police pay was so bad many rural constables were on what was called *Supplementary Benefit*, i.e. a government hand-out made to those whose wages failed to make ends meet. So, lots of experienced officers were leaving. Even as a detective sergeant he couldn't afford to own a car, so he'd walked the four miles from his home in Hayes to interview me. I suspect with organisations like the police you get what you pay for, and, therefore, what the public deserves. Mind you, they are far better paid now and just look at the state of the *Metropolitan Police*. Hopeless and riddled with sexism, racism, misogyny and corruption.

But back to Ms. Christie. In November 1975, I was helping Charles Hayward and *This Heat* record some demos on a *Teac* 4-track I had somehow managed to purchase. We were at Charles's parents' place in Camberwell, though no longer in the room with the egg-boxed walls. As I recall, we were working on a lengthy piece entitled *The Fall of Saigon* which eventually saw the light day on their 1979 album. It was a song which started with the light-hearted lyric:

> *We ate Soda, the embassy cat*
> *Poor Soda's coda*
> *No more da capo, she's decapitated*
> *Running round the room, half-baked*
> *The other half is bacon and sizzling in the frying pan*[4]

Interrupting the laying down of this sweet ditty, somehow, I got a phone call asking me to call a certain number. It was Julie who wanted to know whether I would be interested in interviewing actor and ex-boyfriend Warren Beatty who was in London with the intention of inveigling her to go back to LA with him. She told him she would meet only if he gave me an interview. Agreeing to talk only about US politics (ladies and films strictly off-limits), I met him in his enormous suite in *Claridges*. A 15-minute chat turned into an hour and that chat into an article in the sadly short-lived British alternative to *Rolling Stone*, the magazine *Street Life*. Mr Beatty was charming, witty, hugely intelligent, and clearly desperate to get Julie back if he was prepared to talk to the likes of me. On this latter issue, I understood his point of view completely.

The Beatty interview was published on 7th January, 1976. As a follow-up I wrote an enormous piece for *Street Life* on the state of the US Presidential Primaries which was in *Street Life* in the 18th February edition.

On the back of this, I persuaded the editor to take at least one more article before I headed off to the US in early April 1976, courtesy of another free flight through my dad. I started in LA talking to the campaign manager of Jane Fonda's then husband, the late Tom Hayden, previously a *Freedom Rider* in the extraordinarily racist south in the early 60s, and a leader of the radical *Students for Democratic Society*[i]. He was, along with the *MC5*, in Chicago in August 1968 and was one of the *Chicago Seven* charged by the Federal Government for conspiracy and incitement to riot. If you've not seen Aaron Sorkin's film *The Trial of the Chicago 7* go find it. It is brilliant.

Now he was running for the Democratic nomination for a US Senate seat in California. I went to a couple of Hayden rallies, pretty small, intimate affairs where people discussed issues rather than ram rhetoric down people's throats. Jane Fonda would be there too. Although an Oscar winner with *Klute* in 1971, she was a divisive figure still in the US after her much-publicised trip to North Vietnam in 1972. 'Hanoi Jane' as she was dubbed, having been what she described as 'grey-listed' by film bosses, had plenty of time to campaign, which she did with gusto. Trouble was, Hayden was running against an incumbent Democrat, U.S. Senator John V. Tunney. In spite of that, he did pretty well, coming in second with 1.2 million votes (37%) to Tunney's 1.78 million (54%). Tunney, however, would lose to a Republican in November[ii].

Happily for me, Julie was also in LA, preparing to work on a new movie, the sadly less than wonderful *Demon Seed*. It pretty much bombed at the box office. Currently, she was staying at *Darling* director John Schlesinger's house in the hills above the Strip. We lunched. She ordered steak tartare which she didn't really like. N.B. this is the only dish ordered by anyone at any time in a restaurant which I can precisely remember. Meanwhile, fellow customers wondered who the hell her long-haired companion was and, probably, why wasn't she with Warren!?

She was looking for a house to stay in during filming, so we visited a number of extraordinary and vast properties in the Canyons suggested by the production team, none of which seemed to suit. She was not one for grandiose, as her small, terraced house in Fulham underlined. Again, I didn't care, I got to be driven around LA by her in a not very large American car, again courtesy of the production team, while nattering away with her a nervous nineteen to the dozen. When she realised I was getting taxis around the metropolitan sprawl of Greater Los Angeles in pursuit of interviews and meetings, she offered me the use of the vehicle, which kind

[i] They married in 1973 and divorced in 1990. Tom Hayden died from a heart condition on 23rd October 2016.

[ii] Hayden served in the California State Assembly (1982–1992) and the State Senate (1992–2000). He contested the Democratic Primary for the California Governorship in 1994 and ran as Mayor of Los Angeles in 1997, losing both times. A good guy.

offer I had to refuse as I still hadn't got round to learning to drive. No matter, before flying out east, I spent the day hanging out with her at Schlesinger's place where I interrupted her learning the script.

Eventually, and reluctantly, I left for DC (a long talk with Sen. George McGovern being a highlight. What a lovely and decent man he was too) and then NYC, where I met up with Brian Eno and Carla Bley who I met during the Gary Windo *Steam Radio* sessions. Carla let me stay in her NY office for the few days I was there. Another wonderful person and great artist and a tragic recent loss to the world. Whilst there I visited the HQ of the Communist Party of the USA to see how they were reacting to life and the world in general. The visit served two useful purposes. It proved to me that extremism on either flank was as absurd as I imagined it to be. Eventually, the two extremes meet and shakes hands on the dark side. And second, it probably put me on an FBI watch list for the foreseeable future.

During the summer of '76 Julie and I exchanged postcards (there's a song in there somewhere) and we last met up in '77.

She is even lovelier in person than on the screen. Truly beautiful in every conceivable way.

I still have the postcards...

On my return to London, I set to writing the article *Street Life* had undertaken to publish. When it started up, the magazine was given a time period within which it was to break even. Its main investors were significant people, with friends in high places, the odd Governor General and their ilk. Its distributor was *Condé Nast*, the large American publisher which produced, amongst other things, *Vogue*. Its first edition hit the streets on 1st November 1975 and featured Pete Townsend on the front cover. The Beatty interview appeared in Issue 6 (7th January 1976. front cover: David Bowie from *The Man who fell to Earth*). All seemed set fair, but *Street Life* wanted to be more than just a coverer of popular culture, it wanted to be investigative, cutting edge and fearless. Thus, this edition also featured an article about the goings on in Ulster which, in early 1976, were going downhill fast. The six-day siege of the violent *Provisional IRA* Balcombe Street Gang had only ended with their surrender on 12th December 1975 and then, in January, the so-called Provo 'ceasefire' was ended. There was, therefore, a degree of sensitivity in 'official circles' when *Street Life* started to dig into the murky goings on of the security forces in Belfast and elsewhere. The follow-up article on the US Primaries appeared in the 21st February edition but the front page was dominated by a photograph of a professional assassin. The cover photograph of issue No. 11 on 20th March was of a man in shades using a tiny camera with the headline: *Where the Spies are*. Top left it shouted: '*Spies! CIA, MI6, KGB*'. They followed this on 3rd April with two articles: *SAS: Killer Elite* and another about MI5 and which identified several of their London bases. The article about the SAS was rather histrionically trailed with:

"… the army's killer elite whose antics have appalled even the hard-bitten Green Berets and (which) chronicles the army's seven bitter years in Northern Ireland."

Neither article was the sort of thing destined to endear the magazine to the authorities. Their last piece to stir things up came on 1st May when the cover story – *The Big Fix* – was trailed as an *exposé* of the international heroin trade and its connections with politicians and governments.

This became apparent when, some weeks before, it became clear 'the authorities' were taking a hands-on interest in the goings-on at the magazine. One of the staff went to make a telephone call when they realised they were hearing their previous call being played back. With MI5 on their backs *Street Life's* days were numbered.

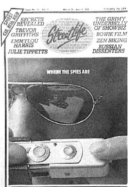

44 Street Life, Warren Beatty interview.
Issue 6

45 Street Life, US Presidential Primaries.
Issue 9

46 Street Life, Where the Spies are.
Issue 11

The last edition, Issue 17, appeared on 12th June and featured footballer Stan Bowles on the front page and nothing controversial at all. Too late. I got back from the States in mid-May and when, in early June, I found I couldn't get through by phone I rolled up to the *Street Life* offices to find chaos and confusion. The last edition had gone to print before a representative of 'the backers' called to say the money was being pulled. Technically, the magazine folded on Monday 7th June. Surprisingly, 'the backers' agreed to pay off any creditors in the unheard amount of £1 to every £1 owed. So, I got paid as did everyone else, having all agreed not to take matters any further. An NDA of a sort.

It was against this backdrop the lyrics of Phil Manzanera's second solo album *Listen Now* were written in 1976-7.

AFTER THAT MEANDER down memory lane, back to September 1972.

What was to become *Little Red Record* was now complete. Mr Norrington's artwork approved. Next, we would play on the South Bank for the second time, but this time the *Queen Elizabeth Hall*, rather than the *Festival Hall*, and as the headline not the support. Then the band would embark on an intense tour of France, Belgium and Holland, the latter two countries in the company of *Soft Machine*.

The band members would return. *Matching Mole* would not.

47 The Queen Elizabeth Hall,
Scene of two great gigs, Mole/801

Thursday, 7th September 1972 was possibly the high point of the *Mole's* brief existence. That night we played at a full *Queen Elizabeth Hall* on the South Bank in London. There are just over 900 seats in the *QEH* so, to fill it was for us rather surprising. But then the *QEH* has proved a lucky place for me at least. Just four days under four years later it was the venue for the third and final *801* gig in 1976 and it was then the *Basing Street Mobile* and Rhett Davies did some of their finest work.

Sadly, no similar recording exists of the *Mole's* night at the *QEH* which is a shame as:

1. I think we played rather well; and
2. We played three songs we did not then play live again: *God Song, Starting in the Middle of the Day* and *Flora Fidgit*.

As it was our gig, and we were in control, I suggested to Robert, and he agreed, that we get in a support act. The 'act' was a friend of my late brother. They met when he spent a year getting stoned at King's College, Cambridge, before coming down to work at the *NME*. The friend's name was Paul Wheeler, and a lovely talented guy he was/is. He (connections, connections) was a friend of another singer/songwriter with whom my brother became quite obsessed, writing about him often – Nick Drake.

We had known Paul for a couple of years and, I believe, Señor Manzanera, played on a demo of one of Paul's songs. That song was later recorded, again as a demo, by the second incarnation of the *801* (i.e. the 1977 *Listen Now* version). It is called *Blue Gray Uniform* and you can hear it on *YouTube*. TGPT is on drums. I rather like it. In fact, I will listen to it again.

Anyway, back to 1972.

Paul was well received. Which was good and very well deserved.

This left us.

There were plenty of friends both back and front of house and this included all three of *Der Mutter Korus*. I do not normally get nervous going on stage. Well, not much. No throwing up in the toilets for me. So, there I was wandering around the fairly large 'green' room, waiting to go on stage when someone took, and held, my left hand (though not for some time, I have washed it since).

"Just wanted to see whether you were nervous," whispered a radiant Julie Christie.

Ye gods! Nervous? *Moi?* I think I just wet myself.

Totally undermined, I wandered on stage.

I hoped to be able to be able to use Eno's wonderful *Gloria Gloom* synth tapes to set the scene but for one reason or another this proved impossible. Instead, the lights went down, and we started up.

God Song came first. Phil's lovely music and Robert's biting lyrics. Then came Dave MacRae's *Drinking Song* (later *Starting in the middle of the day…*) followed by *Flora Fidgit* (named for the lady with the wandering hands). I'm not sure we ever played these pieces again. Afterwards *Smoke Signal*, *Gloria Gloom* and *Nan True's Hole*, all drawn from the new album before the first reference back to *Mole* No. 1 with *Instant Pussy*. *Lything and Gracing*, *March Ides* and *Part of the Dance* completed the evening. Oh, bar an encore of *Brandy as in Benj* (as it was now officially called).

I don't think we played better. Reviews were positive.

Things were looking up. Ish.

Early next day we were up and about and on our way to Paris there to overnight again at the *Hotel Esmeralda* near Notre Dame. Next day we plodded south-east for over five hours on the nearly 500 km drive to Montbéliard down near the French-Swiss border. There, we were to play at the *Franche-Comté Pop Festival 1972* in the *Halle Polyvalente* (subsequently burnt down and re-built, so I believe). The festival ran over two days, the 9th and 10th September, and featured friends of ours, *Caravan*, plus *Arthur Brown's Kingdom Come*, *Nektar* from Germany, and various other bands about which I know nothing. Oh, and *Genesis* on their *Foxtrot* tour.

I disliked *Genesis* considerably. Peter prancing about in a fox head seemed somewhat laughable to me. Surprising, then, that I ended up with *Random Hold* being managed by Peter's manager, published by *Genesis's* manager's company and, funnier still when, in 2001 I took over the official

Genesis web site, followed soon after by the Phil Collins' site too. Strange thing life. And, of course, *Random Hold* toured with Peter Gabriel in the UK and North America. A lovelier, more generous man you cannot imagine. His solo work I have always enjoyed.

Anyway, we played, the crew dismantled our equipment and loaded up the large lorry ready to drive overnight to Rotterdam where, a few days later, we were to meet up with *Soft Machine* to play gigs in Holland and Belgium. Offered the chance of staying to watch *Genesis* (on next) and then enjoying a peaceful night's sleep in the *Hôtel de la Balance* (which still exists! *Mon dieu!*), a decent breakfast, even if continental, and a pleasant drive across north-eastern France the following day, I decided, instead, to go overnight to Rotterdam. Anything to avoid *Genesis*. I told Phil Collins, Tony Banks and Mike Rutherford this story over breakfast one morning some 20 years ago just before they asked me to run their web site. Phil, in particular, seemed particularly tickled.

48 The Hôtel de la Balance.
One of the few hotels still standing after a Mole visit. In 1972 it looked a bit better than this, even after our visit.

And so off we set on our 650 km drive through Épinal, Nancy, Metz, passing the flaring steelworks of Longwy, and off into the Ardennes. But not before we enjoyed the attentions of the *douaniers* of both France and Belgium anxious to check our *carnet* and inspect every last guitar string, plectrum and drumstick before allowing us out of one country and into another. I am glad we can now share this lengthy and tedious exercise with anyone who voted for Brexit and fancies a trip to the continent. They deserve it.

Deep in the densely wooded Ardennes we drove up and down hills in the Stygian gloom (nothing like a good Public School education for a background in the classics). Then, taking a sharp left-hand turn with all due care, we spotted a vehicle whose driver was either not so careful or not particularly lucky. A car was off the road, nose buried deep in the thick undergrowth. We 'ummed' and 'aahed' (or something) and then did the decent thing and stopped. I trotted back to the car just to check no-one was still in it and got something of a shock when a gentleman's face peered back at me. Thankfully, he was not badly injured and, even better, someone had alerted the authorities (but not then stopped to help. Strange behaviour). The police turned up soon after, allowing us to go on our way once it was established the accident was nothing to do with us.

We arrived at the *Hotel Henegouwen* (another place which no longer exists) at some ungodly hour there to crash out. We now had four days off in Rotterdam which, given the state of the place in 1972, was not the greatest of news. We did find a café in the Kruisplein just outside the *Centraal Station* which did a great breakfast though. And, after my previous escapade in Amsterdam I stayed sober (well, relatively).

The next day the rest of the band joined us. We set to, waiting for the *Mole's* final showdown. Though three of us never saw it coming.

By Sunday, 17th September, 1972, *Mole* was three gigs into its final tour of Holland and Belgium supporting *Soft Machine*. We spent several days off in Rotterdam and Amsterdam whilst the *Softs* played three other gigs in Holland (9th September the *Sporthall* in Alphen an der Rijn, 10th at the *Duinvermak* in Bergen, and on the 14th the *Stadsschouwburg* in Tilburg). The plan was that we play with them on several gigs in France, but these gigs were, for some reason, cancelled and replaced by the *SM* solo dates.

Anyway, on Friday 15th September we returned to *De Doelen* in Rotterdam. It's a bit like the *Festival Hall*, all concrete and carpets, and, as we set up, one or two of us remarked on the young men who, smiling and nodding, were setting up a series of microphones on stage, duplicating the ones the crews were putting in place. Eventually, as we did not know of any radio broadcast or recording, someone asked the authorities who they were. Bootleggers it turned out, there to make an illegal recording of the concert. How they got in no-one knew, though one guesses at an inside job. They were escorted from the premises and their equipment, at least temporarily, confiscated.

We played, we waited for the *SM* to play. We got into our joint transit bus and returned to the *Regina Hotel* in Amsterdam (yet another which has since ceased to exist).

The next day we drove to Den Haag (The Hague, OK!) where we played a place called the *Circus*. No recollection of it at all.

On Sunday, we were at the *Concertgebouw* in Amsterdam, the splendid concert hall which opened in 1888. To get to the stage we walked down the long, red-carpeted stairs either side of the enormous pipe organ which is quite a way to appreciate the venue and the crowd. Generally, Amsterdam audiences were good to us and, as I recall, the same applied that night. We returned now to the *Hotel de Herberg* (since defunct) with none of the high jinks which so characterised previous visits to the city. No trips to little bars with multi-coloured liqueurs for me this time.

I have no idea how Robert felt about these gigs supporting a band he helped start and which he named. I found the experience progressively somewhat depressing. I cannot recall saying word one to either Karl Jenkins or John Marshall throughout the eight days we were together. Mike was quiet and reserved. Hugh was happy to chat and, as posted some long time ago, wrote out some exercises and scales for me to help me on my musical way (see *Appendix 18*. As you can see, I love a good appendix and here you have plenty to choose from).

49 The Concertgebouw, Amsterdam

We sometimes played cards in the back of the bus. The game of choice was *Hearts*, also known then as *Hunt the C*nt* as the Queen of Spades was the worst card to end up with. Basically you tried to lose as many hands as possible. If you were ambitious or, like me, simply a bit of a twit, you'd declare 'misère'. This meant losing all thirteen tricks. I think I pissed off Mike a tad by going for broke rather too often. But most of the time we just stared out of the windows as we rushed up and down the motorways of first Holland and then Belgium.

I watched the new version of *Soft Machine* for two or three nights, having seen them before at King's Cross and in Oxford. Nothing they did changed my mind. No drama. No hairs rising on the back of the neck. I can remember earlier gigs, one at the Hampstead *Country Club* in particular, where I was in tears so powerful was the emotional impact of the Ratledge/Hopper/Wyatt trio. Then, the band was experimental, creative, technical, emotional and, to that, Robert added the vulnerable, erratic humanity which took their music into a different sphere. Lose that emotion and humanity and the *SM* became just another very good jazz-rock fusion band. Technically excellent, emotionally empty. *Nucleus* with fuzz boxes. I stopped watching and sat in the bar, slept in the dressing room, or chatted, most often with Phil.

50 The Kinema Roma.
In all its Art-Deco glory

On Monday, 18th September, we drove into Belgium there to book into the imaginatively named *Tourist Hotel* in Antwerp which was about exciting as its name. That night we played the *Kinema Roma*, on the *Turnhoutsebaan* in Borgerhout. It was a cinema with a stage. What can I say? No idea how that went. The theatre, though, was another matter. Built in 1928 in the Art Deco-style, it was a 2,000-seat auditorium which put on music shows through the 70s, closing in 1982. It then fell into disrepair being sadly neglected for twenty years. In 2002 it was rescued. A team of volunteers renovated the building, restoring it to something of its old glories. They did such a good job it won a prize in 2016. Good for them.

Tuesday was Brussels and the *Salle de la Madeleine* and accommodation at the *Hotel Windsor*. Brussels was a strange place in those days. Slightly down at heel, though the *Windsor* was a distinct improvement on previous hotels. The *Salle de la Madeleine*, however, did not have the lovely barmaid at the *Theatre 140* with whom I was briefly besotted back in the spring so, frankly, who cares what it was like.

Whatever else took place in Belgium, we were adopted by a young local guy whose name sadly escapes me. He tagged along with the road crew and was funny and entertaining, something this brief tour was in need of.

On Wednesday we were due to play the *Conservatoire royal de Liège* and we duly booked into the elderly *Hotel d'Angleterre* (yet another hotel alas no more). Expecting to get into the venue for the sound check, we were somewhat bemused to find the stage occupied by the *Liège Conservatoire Orchestra* who were apathetically rehearsing something or other. It turned out our manager, Sean whose name must never be mentioned, switched promoters for this gig. The previous promoter, feeling somewhat pissed off, and being a bit of a hard case, retaliated by booking the orchestra for most of the afternoon, thereby preventing us from getting in for a decent sound check. Belgian ex-promoter 3, stupid English manager 0.

51 The rather impressive stage of the Liège Conservatoire.
Once known to have hosted a dancing pig

All was not lost, however, as, whilst the orchestra played some waltz or other, our young Belgian chum invited me to trip the light fantastic across the stage in 3/4 time. *Strictly come dancing/Dancing with the stars* material I certainly am not. At Dulwich College they organised dancing classes in the Great Hall to which young ladies from our associate school, James Allen's Girls School (JAGS to its friends) were bussed in to provide partners to certain senior members of the sixth form. Occasionally, some of my more irreverent friends and I would foregather at the doors to the Great Hall to titter and giggle at the clumsier efforts of the less-well co-ordinated within. My smugness now came back to haunt me as, after wheeling across the stage in full view of the assembled *Liège Conservatoire Orchestra*, my partner advised me loudly that I danced *'comme un cochon'*, i.e. like a pig. So, no points there then, eh Mr. Revel Horwood?

Liège was played and we returned westwards towards Ghent (or Gent as they say in Vlaanderen. Flanders, you dig?). Whilst all of this was happening, other events were transpiring back in good old Blighty. Having not been paid for our appearance at the music festival in Oostende, where we made the tomato-splattered acquaintance of the *MC5*, the promoter was being pursued for at least some of our fee. Reminders were sent and, at long last, a cheque for £325 was posted. It bounced. A week or so later we were offered, and accepted, 75% of the promised monies. On 26th September we would eventually settle for £194 (4? Wtf?) in full and final payment for services rendered.

52 The Ciné Capitole, Ghent.
A bit before we got there.

In Ghent we played the *Ciné Capitole* on the *Graaf van Vlaanderenplein*, another Art Deco cinema with a stage built in the 1930s. The difference was this stage sloped towards what used to be an orchestra pit. One of the few joys for the road crew of my super-powerful *Acoustic* bass rig was its wheels at the back. Combine wheels with the enormous vibration caused by an idiot playing through an 18-inch reflex-mounted speaker and you get movement. Movement down the stage towards the orchestra pit. With me in-between. Our devoted, very tall, and very thin roadie Mouse spent the evening clinging on to the back of the *Acoustic* in a, thankfully, successful effort at preventing me from being crushed as it rolled inexorably forward to the edge of the stage, over the lip and into the orchestra pit with me beneath it. Thank you, Mouse.

53 The Stadschouwbourg, Groningen.
Where Moles go to die

On the morning of Friday, 22nd September, 1972, we drove from one end of the Netherlands to the other (or near enough), ending up, 370 kms later, at the then modern *Hotel Helvetia* in Groningen. We were due to play the *Stadschouwbourg*, another pretty and elderly Dutch venue.

There, for reasons which escape me, I decided to employ the five-octave tone generator on the *Acoustic* broadly 'because it was there'. As there was no indicator what note was being played and as it glissed up and down in microtones it served, to me at least, no useful purpose. Except that night. Bored with boring people with boring fuzz bass solos, that night I played a solo on the *Acoustic*. Quite what the audience made of the resulting high-pitched whining noise I have no idea, but it amused me.

We played. We finished. We went back to the hotel. We got up the following morning. We met for breakfast.

Robert told us he was breaking up the band.

We were gobsmacked. I was angry. I punched a wall.

We went home, me with Benj in the truck via the Hoek van Holland and Harwich as I didn't want to talk to anyone in the band.

The *Acoustic* went back to *CBS* as they owned most of the gear. They let me keep the *Gibson*.

That was that.

OK THEN. BUT WHAT HAPPENED NEXT?

A dozen or so gigs in the UK and Holland were cancelled.

Our somewhat flimsy financial affairs were finalised. I was repaid the money I either loaned other band members or which went towards expenses. The best part of £3,000 in today's money.

Then, before he joined up with what became *Hatfield and the North*, Phil and I mounted a half-hearted effort to see whether something might arise out of the *Molean* ashes. We got together for a chat and met with 'the manager whose name we will not mention' to see how the land lay. Rather barren was the reply. I mentioned Charles Hayward as a drummer and, according to the diaries, we met up, but the tide was fast running out to sea leaving me somewhat stranded on the foreshore. Phil joined *Hatfield*.

I must say I was angered and perplexed by Robert's decision. It came out of the blue and after we recorded what we thought was a pretty decent album. We were also playing live better than before. Gigs, and better paid ones, were coming in, both in the UK and in Europe. Reviews were good. We sold out the *QEH*. What was not to like?

On the other hand, *LRR* was a band album not a Robert album with sidemen as was the first album. Did this make a difference? Who knows? Robert blamed the pressure of feeling responsible for other people's livelihoods, and his drinking – though, as I recall, at this time, this was not much of an issue. Certainly, it was one pre-*Mole* and it re-surfaced every now and then, disastrously in 1973, but he was, to my mind, in far better physical and mental shape than when he left *Soft Machine*. A condition for which Alfie should take a significant part of the credit.

What I cannot judge is the impact on him of playing as the support act to a band central to his life for five years. Humiliating? Who knows?

On the other hand, I was angry and out of work.

Funnily enough, it seems I cannot sustain grudges – unless, of course, you are a Conservative (or GOP) voter/supporter in which case I loathe you all deeply, and always will.

For example, in 1980, within weeks of being sacked from *Random Hold*, I was helping produce some demos for David Rhodes and was managing Dave Ferguson's new version of the band. We remained friends.

Same in 1972.

Shortly after the yet-to-be-described brief sojourn in France, I was again socialising with Robert and his new musical friend Francis Monkman, recently departed from *Curved Air*. In early December, Robert and Francis recorded a session for *Top Gear* and, according to singer Sonja Kristina, Francis was looking for a new musical freedom because:

> "his… obsession is/was jamming… real 'out there' cosmic rock jamming."

That, and playing classical harpsichord concerts. A complicated man.

BUT I GET AHEAD OF MYSELF.

Before all of that, on the 18th October 1972, I was invited to phone a strange Australian I first met a few times six years earlier – Daevid Allen. He was in the UK looking for a new rhythm section for *Gong* and he asked if I'd be interested in taking a trip to *Virgin's* new *Manor Studio* near Oxford in order to audition. Perhaps Robert suggested me. I know not. The auditions were held on Saturday, 21st October (when *Mole* would otherwise have been playing the *Paradiso*). Amongst those present were luminaries such as Rob Tait from *Battered Ornaments*, *Piblokto* and *Vinegar Joe*, the late Roger Bunn. who too was in *Piblokto* and in one of *Roxy Music's* very early line-ups, and several others I recognised but could not now name. Embarrassingly, we all sat around watching as we were, one by one, called into action.

By this date I'd played bass for approximately 2½ years. I knew no 60s standards. I learnt the bass parts for *Quiet Sun* because we couldn't find anyone to play them properly. Afterwards, *Mole* did not require me to play like the James Brown rhythm section. Basically, I spent the previous twelve months making things up as I went along and so I did again at the *Manor*. You could say I didn't have any bass *clichés* to fall back on. I guess in a band like *Matching Mole* this sometimes helped. With others, sometimes it didn't.

Imagine my shock when Daevid called and asked me to go to France.

On Thursday, 26th October, I flew to Paris Orly where I was picked up and driven the 120 kms to a hunting lodge in the countryside between the town of Sens and the village of Voisines. It was called the *Pavillon du Hay*. I carried with me my *EB3*, a change of clothes, and French O-Level, grade 6. Grade 7 was a fail.

Apart from Daevid and Gilli Smyth, amongst others living in the *Pavillon* were Christian Tritsch, Didier Malherbe, Rob Tait (who briefly got the drummer's seat) and various girlfriends. French was the common language. I could barely speak it. Well, no, I could not speak it.

I got on well with Didier, with whom I'd like to think I struck something of a rapport. I last met him at the *Royal Festival Hall* a few years ago when a concert of Robert's music was performed. Wonderful musician, lovely man. Otherwise, though people were friendly, I felt at a distance from them all.

54 The Pavillon du Hay.
Gong's home near Voisines, département de l'Yonne.
I slept, and/or shivered, in the room front left with lots of windows.

I slept on the floor of a sort of conservatory at one end of the lodge. It was built before the concepts of double glazing and underfloor heating became *de rigueur* in modern housing. In other words, in late October and prior to the joys of global warming, it was fucking freezing.

Rehearsals took place in a long narrow room off the main living room. I found a home about half-way up on the right side next to the drums. Daevid stood opposite and, it seemed to me, examined me minutely. Everything we played was recorded (thus a version of a riff I started for a jam ended up on *Flying Teapot*) and there were some enjoyable moments. However, after a few days, when my one set of clothes started to smell, when my teeth could not stop chattering because of the cold, and when I got fed up not talking to anyone outside rehearsals and mealtimes, I decided this was not for me. After nine days I said I was going home. I have long since assumed the scheduled gigs, at Angers and Rennes, due five days later, were cancelled/postponed but apparently not. Francis Moze, *Magma's* bass player, stepped in at short notice and the dates, and others, were played.[5]

So that was France. Here today and *Gong* tomorrow. Sorry.

LITTLE RED RECORD WAS RELEASED on 27th October 1972 whilst I was in France. It got generally good reviews (not *all* of them written by my bro'). Richard Williams in the *Melody Maker* seemed somehow, and mistakenly, to have picked up some scuttlebutt suggesting all was not well within the band during the sessions and that line-up changes were imminent (not counting breaking up the band, of course). There was nothing in this, the only tension coming from the issue between Fripp and Phil Miller when it came to recording *Flora Fidgit*. Other than that, however, his review was excellent – a *Mahavishnu Orchestra* with wit no less! – if too late to keep the band afloat.

MATCHING MOLE'S
LITTLE RED RECORD

55 The artwork for Little Red Record.
Personally, not been keen to be associated in any way with Mao or the modern Chinese Government for rather a long time.

Extended versions of both albums were re-released forty years later and we eventually saw some money but, sadly, too late for Phil. Like the *Soft Machine's* early royalties, the rest 'disappeared' into someone else's pocket in the meantime. But, with the music still selling 50 years after the event someone must have quite liked us. People are strange.

When I returned to London from my brief sojourn with *Gong* in France, the sadly late Francis Monkman and I met up. (I really am getting fed up having to describe so many of my friends as 'sadly late'. Please stop dying). We hit it off. I visited him several times in his flat in Belsize Square where we drank tea, talked music and played chess. Chess, it turned out, was one of Francis's passions and he was mortified when, the first time we played, I beat him. Pure accident, of course, but it ensured I was invited back to the flat so he could get his revenge. Several times.

56 Daevid Allen, Karl Jenkins, John Marshall, BM, Mike Ratledge, Robert, Elton Dean, Francis Monkman.
The photo's venue is given as the Wyndham Theatre but I can find no reason why any of us should have been there. The Soft Machine did play the London Coliseum on 22ⁿᵈ October 1972. Could be there. It is certainly NOT Paris as Mike King and Marcus O'Dair suggest.

Another passion was good Chinese food. On 23ʳᵈ November 1972, he took me to still-going *Lee Ho Fuk* in Gerrard Street where we gorged on dumplings and other goodies not yet seen in the average Chinese high street restaurant. It became a regular haunt. Another favourite venue was the *Ceylon Tea Centre* (as it was) off Leicester Square. Francis enjoyed a decent cuppa and that place, too, became a venue at which to enjoy a malty brew and natter about music.

One of the topics was: what was Robert going to do when he returned from Venice. There, Alfie, having previously worked with director Nick Roeg and now employed as 2ⁿᵈ Assistant Editor, was working on Julie's next film, *Don't Look Now?* Robert, initially reluctant, was persuaded to go and, just after Christmas 1972, they flew out to share a house with Julie for the duration. To keep him occupied, Alfie bought a small 3-octave *Riviera* organ. The material he wrote formed the nucleus of *Rock Bottom*.

I was pestering Robert long distance to reform *Mole*, suggesting we reform with any line-up (as long as I was in it). In January, I wrote him a long letter setting out a number of scenarios with different possible line-ups. Looking back, I was being amazingly pushy. But, desperate people...

Names mentioned were: Francis Monkman, Fred Frith, Gary Windo, Didier Malherbe, who I'd really enjoyed playing with during my brief stay in France, even a certain John Michael 'Poli' Palmer who played vibraphone, flute, piano, synthesizers with the very excellent *Family*.

Robert replied on 31st January. The main theme of the card, written in felt tip in Robert's typically large scrawl, was to ask whether I knew *Let the Wind Carry Me* and *Ludwig's Tune* (*aka Judgement of the Moon and Stars*) off Joni Mitchell's *For the Roses* album released in November, the spare arrangements enhanced by Tom Scott's sax parts which he seemed to like.

Then crammed in at the top and, at right angles in the middle, he wrote in neat blue biro. He was 'touched and impressed' by my letter, he expressed an interest in playing with Didier, but was not especially keen on Poli Palmer (though we did later meet him at his flat. Would never have worked). Instead, he said he:

"... rather liked the idea of a MIGHTY TRIUMVIRATE + HIRELINGS FOR A WHILE AT LEAST."

Triumvirate? Robert, hopefully me, and...?

He finished with some comments about his own music:

"My own ideas are extremely sparse and slow and dreamish at the moment. I only write while I'm fast asleep these days, *Sleep around the Clock, Bored Walk, Do the Snoozaloo,* etc. What d'y say t'that?"

Ten days later things moved on:

"I've got an expandable/contractable but relatively finished 10/15 minutes we could get down pretty quick I reckon, as they say..."

As with most of Robert's cards, something intervened. In this case, it was a brief 'word from my sponsor', i.e. Alfie. Unlike Robert's expansive scrawl, Alfie's writing is neat, runs in straight lines, and is punctuated rather more than Robert bothers with. Alfie inserted a brief poem:

There was a young drummer who ponged
Which made him believe he'd been wronged
When he entered a room
He cast such a gloom
(For the shit house was where he belonged)

There was an old girl called Alfreda
Who was born a natural leader
She led fifteen men
Three dogs and a hen
I know, I was there, and I see'd her.

To which there really is no answer.

But this was not all. Robert wrote:

"Well I must say really I don't know. I should/will/shall be back during next week or indeed this week or indeed weeks, before this card arrives I'll be bound. I was thinking if we could work out a song or two at say Florians (?), put them on tape at say Nick Mason's (he's got a few instruments) and have a listen, what do you reckon?"

I will say here that, what was written here doesn't quite square with the uncertainty of Robert's thoughts in the account in Marcus O'Dair's biography *Different Every Time*.

Feelers were put out to *Henry Cow's* Fred Frith, and he and I met, as it happens, in the *Ceylon Tea Centre*. Francis, too, was to be involved and we carried on having tea, eating dumplings, chatting on the phone. Then, when Robert came back, he gave in to my entreaties. The late Gary Windo was the fifth recruit to *Mole* Mk. II and, on Tuesday, 29th May, 1973, we got together at Alfie's 21st floor flat in the since demolished *Hermes Point* on the Edgware Road. There, Robert played us the material written to pass the time in Venice and which later formed the nucleus of *Rock Bottom*. In the meantime, with Robert now free of the shackles of his *CBS* contract, we spoke to Richard Branson who was very keen to sign the band to *Virgin*.

That Saturday there was an open invitation to a birthday party for Gilli Smyth at Lady June's[i]. Robert and Alfie went. I did not – and have regretted it ever since. Chaos theory… butterflies in the Amazon… hurricanes in the Caribbean… if I been there…?

On Sunday, 3rd June, Gary phoned me to tell me Robert had fallen from a window. Forgetting the party, I immediately assumed it was from Alfie's 21st floor flat and that he was dead. But no, somehow, he had survived, possibly because he was ridiculously drunk, having fallen four floors (plus a bit, as he fell into the basement, avoiding spiked railings).

---

[i] June Campbell Cramer, artist and poet who met Daevid Allen and Kein Ayers in Palma, Majorca, in the early 60s. For a time, she lived in Deià on Majorca and associated with Robert Graves. She later lived in a flat at Vale Court, Maida Vale, where the accident happened. A constant on the fringes of the Canterbury Scene, I first met her at Dalmore Road. Later in 1973 she released an album – *Lady June's Linguistic Leprosy* – recorded with the help of Kevin Ayers, Brian Eno, Pip Pyle and others. She returned to Deià in 1975 where she pursued her artistic interests. Another album was released in 1996 – *Lady June's Hit and Myth*. She was working on a third when she suffered a fatal heart attack on 7th June 1999. Her obituary in *The Independent* described her 'a great British eccentric and cosmic prankster'.

He was in *Ward IX* at *Stoke Mandeville Hospital*, his back broken. My body reacted to the news with a bout of acute appendicitis and by 6 a.m. on Monday I was in *St Thomas's Hospital* about to have it removed. Stress can do that to you, apparently. But, at least, I was thoroughly enjoying the pre-op morphine jab.

My diary entry for 1st June 1973 simply reads:

"Robert falls out of window.
Stoke Mandeville Hospital.
Ward IX"

I was in hospital for a week. Robert, having fractured his twelfth vertebrae and lost the use of his legs, for over seven months.

I was discharged on Monday, 11th June. Or, put it another way, they told me to go home without warning. I donned the smelly and somewhat vomit covered clothes I arrived in and, more or less bent double, shuffled across Lambeth Palace Road to get a bus to Victoria. There was just about enough loose change in my pockets to cover this expense and a rail ticket to Beckenham. NHS after-care seemed somewhat lacking in those days.

I arrived home to find a postcard – from Alfie sent a week after the accident. Drawing herself sitting on her own in the *League of Hospital Friends* canteen, a bubble said: 'Hello Bill'. Overleaf she wrote:

Dear Bill,
Get better soon we need you.
Robert sends his love and so do I.
Alfie XXX

Not sure what this uncommon display of thoughtfulness and care under extreme pressure does to you, but it's got me in a bit of a state reading it again.

On 2nd July I was given the all-clear and on Thursday, 5th July, I went to see Robert and Alfie as she was basically living in at the hospital. From Beckenham to Aylesbury by train, tube and train was a 2½ hour journey. *Stoke Mandeville Hospital* was then a 40-minute walk away. It was a warm day.

The hospital was originally built in 1830 to deal with patients affected by cholera. An isolation hospital was built there in the 1890s and it developed into a 'fever' hospital treating a wide range of infectious diseases. Another isolation hospital was added in 1933. In 1939, the site was purchased by the War Office, and when war broke out a large number of wooden hutted wards[i] were built in expectation of huge numbers of civilian casualties from the expected German bombing campaign. When this did not immediately materialise, the Blitz did not start for another

---

[i] They had a 21-year life expectancy. They were still in use in 1973 and beyond.

year, the wards were used for wounded soldiers. In 1944, it was turned into the *National Spinal Injuries Centre* (*NSIC*) under the guidance, ironically, of a German doctor, Ludwig Guttman. A Jew, he was kicked out of his position at Breslau Hospital in 1933 and he and his family fled Germany in 1939. After five years at the *Radcliffe Infirmary* in Oxford, he created the *NSIC* to deal with servicemen with spinal cord injuries. The *NSIC* is now one the largest such centres in the world.[6]

57 Alfie's postcard sent 9th June: 'Hello Bill'

Having first opened in 1944, by 1973 the place was in desperate need of an overhaul. Indeed, it was only a flood caused by a storm in 1979 which led to the essential improvements required, though they were not all financed by the newly elected Thatcher government. Public donations as well as government funding led to a re-built hospital opening in 1983. Of historic interest, but no use to Robert in 1973.

He, as I recall, was in the last bed on the right in *Ward IX*, one of the draughty wooden wards. Brings a lump to the throat just remembering the long walk down the ward to the two figures at the far end. For someone with such a serious injury Robert was surprisingly chipper. He ended up cheering me up, not the other way round.

Thereafter, I got up as often as possible but, money always a problem, not as often as I would have liked. Soon, though, helped by his well-developed upper body musculature, Robert was doing wheelies down the corridors in his wheelchair. Apparently, he found a piano in the visitor's room and used it to develop the Venice material.

On occasions we talked about the future. The idea was briefly broached of *Mole* Mk. II adding a drummer, with Robert turning to keyboards and vocals. Francis Monkman was still on the scene and keen to be involved should anything evolve. In November, I met Pip Pyle a couple of times to explore such avenues. But it was not to be, and I now needed to get a day job.

On the upside, I had a new girlfriend who, in a fit of madness, would become Mrs Helen MacCormick in a few years' time. Every cloud...

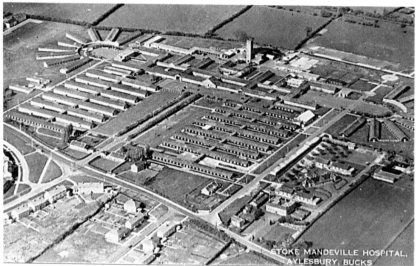

58 Stoke Mandeville Hospital pretty much as it was in 1973.

ENDNOTES:

[1] O'Dair, M, *Different Every Time*, op. cit., pages 140-1.

[2] MacDonald, I, *Lookin' Back: The Soft Machine Pt. 2, New Musial Express*, 1st February 1975.

[3] Cutting courtesy of Phil Howitt.

[4] Lyrics Charles John Hayward / Gareth John Williams / Charles Bullen, © Blackhill Music Ltd.

[5] *https://www.calyx-canterbury.fr/gong/chrono.html*

[6] Silver, J R, *A History of Stoke Mandeville Hospital and the National Spinal Injuries Centre, Journal of The Royal College of Physicians of Edinburgh*, Vol. 49, Issue 4, December 2019, page 328 onwards.

DIAMOND HEAD & QUIET SUN REVISITED

ATHER LIKE THE NORWEGIAN BLUE in the justly famed *Monty Python Dead Parrott* sketch (7th December 1969), it turned out *Quiet Sun* was not dead, it was merely lightly 'stunned'. The result of its resuscitation was that Muff Winwood was forced to release an album by a band he rejected in no uncertain terms four years earlier. Ho, ho.

But the question remains, after the pathetic fiasco of *Quiet Sun's* first life, how on earth did this bunch of losers (excluding, of course, the extremely talented and rather better remunerated Mr Manzanera) get to record a real long-playing record in a proper studio for an international label?

Beats me. The end. Or not....

Right. As you now all know, *Matching Mole* failed in September 1972 and the new version collapsed, admittedly rather slowly, in June 1973 after Robert's accident. Always in need of cash, yet another soul-destroying job in the civil service ensued at the, now renamed *Ministry of Overseas Development*. It was soul-destroying because it was pointless. The job involved putting forward 'experts' to work for various UN-linked organisations around the world. It soon became clear that these *Non-Governmental Organisations* or *NGOs* I guess we call them nowadays, knew exactly who they wanted before the 'job description' even left their offices. We were being invited to put names forward merely for the sake of 'form'. My suggestion that we abandon that part of our work to concentrate on recruiting more 'experts' thereby widening the pool available to the *NGOs* went down like a cup of cold sick, the senior civil servant in charge being terrified of losing his little fiefdom so it seemed.

So, apart from playing a lot of cricket and rugby for the Dulwich College old boys' team, the Old Alleynians, I did little. At least I was fit.

The only highlight was being asked to play on two tracks of Eno's *Here Come the Warm Jets*. The session was at *Majestic Studios* next to Clapham Common and took place on Monday, 17th September. The songs were *Needle in the Camel's Eye* and *Blank Frank* and the whole thing was the most enormous laugh. On *Frank* for the first time ever, I was asked to play a Bo Diddly-like bass part. Simple yet effective. Then there's that Fripp guitar solo – pure aggression. And the keyboard part you can hear after that, and through to the end, performed by what Eno apparently dubbed *Nick Kool & the Koolaids*, was not, in fact, cunning overdubs but Brian, drummer Simon King and me leaning over one another's shoulders and playing repeated random phrases on a *Hammond* organ.

Here Come the Warm Jets – what a fucking great album that is. If I was to abandon pretensions to musical stardom what a great way to finish.

1973 crept into 1974 and I decided to pursue my other interest: politics. But of course. By now a member of the Liberal Party (an organisation which, on occasions, had as little to do with real politics as possible. This might have been one of its attractions), I worked locally throughout the February General Election and stood for election to my local council in May. Result: a campaign about as successful as *Quiet Sun's* attempt to get a recording contract (I came fifth out of six[i]). Nevertheless, I was hyperactively involved in campaigning throughout 1974, as the uncertainty surrounding the Harold Wilson-led minority government's future meant another General Election was always just around the corner. This duly took place on 10th October. Labour won a wafer-thin majority of three seats and the next five years of economic chaos, culminating in the 1978-9 Winter of Discontent when the now Prime Minister Jim Callaghan managed to fall out with the Labour Party's major benefactors, the Trades Unions, prepared the way for the doleful reign of Margaret Thatcher from which this country has never recovered.

In a roundabout pursuit of my political ambitions, in September, I went to a place called *Walbrook College* near Old Street in Shoreditch to do some extra A-Levels – Government and Politics and Economic History (which subject I would not now recommend to anyone. It plumbs depths of dull you cannot imagine). *Walbrook* was what one might term nowadays a crammer, i.e. a place kids went to after either failing or underperforming in earlier exams or left school before taking them. At 23, I was five years older than almost every other student. I probably found it as depressing as the lecturer when, in the first Government and Politics lesson, it turned out I was the only one who knew the name of the current Prime Minster. (sigh). Anyway, I applied to read politics at numerous universities and was later offered a place at the *London School of Economics*[ii] which I accepted. So far, so good.

---

[i] 2nd May 1974, Bromley Council, Lawrie Park and Kent House ward: Tories 1,060 and 1,055 (elected), Labour 779 and 723, MacCormick W A M (Liberal) 319, running mate who I have never ever met, 305. Bit disappointed only to get 14 more votes than she did for, as far as I know, she never set foot in the ward. Mind, I had hair down to my shoulders and a wispy moustache and, barring sandals, was everyone's preconception of the hairy, feckless liberal. Knocking on doors and introducing myself to voters probably cost me votes, but it seemed the right thing to do. I got a lot better at fighting elections later in life, running campaigns for the national party throughout the 1980s, and doing their opinion polling in the 90s. I even got myself elected to Bromley Council in 1990, held the seat twice, before retiring in 2002.

[ii] A place I had only ever been to once, and that was to see the wonderful *Blossom Toes* play a lunch-time gig. If you don't know them, might I recommend their excellent second album, *If Only for a Moment*, released on *Marmalade* in 1969.

Life for Felipe was somewhat different. The first *Roxy Music* album was a great, and deserved, success and the single, *Virginia Plain*, reached No. 4 in the singles charts. Album number two, *For Your Pleasure* released on 23rd March 1973, went six places higher than the first album, reaching No. 4 in the UK charts. *Stranded*, recorded barely eight months later and released in November 1973, topped the album charts. *Country Life*, recorded over the summer of 1974, peaked at No. 3. It was a stellar career. And, with Phil contributing three songs to the last two albums: *Amazona* on *Stranded* and *Out of the Blue* and *Prairie Rose* on *Country Life*, his stock rose beyond being simply the original and creative lead guitarist of the band. Thus, when, in autumn '74, Phil suggested he should record a solo album, both *EG Management* and *Island Records* readily agreed.

Before all that, *Roxy's Country Life* promotional tour needed to be completed. This started on 21st September 1974 in Cardiff, five days after I started at *Walbrook*. Nine days later, on a day off somewhere between Birmingham and Leicester, Phil phoned me and set out his thinking about his recording sessions. It was a cunning plan. Between *Roxy's* last 1974 gig in the aptly named Roxy Theatre in Atlanta, Georgia, on 29th November, and the resumption of the *Country Life* tour in London, Ontario, on 8th February, he was going to record two albums, his own and that of *Quiet Sun*. He booked *Island Studios* in Basing Street, Notting Hill, all day and all night through all of January 1975, with December devoted to rehearsals of the various musos set to participate. These principally revolved around a trio of Phil, John Wetton and Paul Thompson with Brian Eno adding what only The Refreshing Experience[i] could add.

As Phil was somewhat tied up touring, he asked me to call Charles Hayward and Dave Jarrett to sound them out. It seemed like a good idea to the two of them and vague plans were laid for some sort of rehearsals when the first leg of the *Roxy* tour finished at the end of November. On Saturday, 5th October, I toddled along to the *Rainbow Theatre* where *Roxy* was playing for three nights. And jolly good they were too (especially with the great John Wetton on bass).

There was a week's gap between the end of the British dates on 28th October and isolated gigs in Berlin on 5th November and Stockholm on the 8th, during which phone calls flew between us. We even managed a quick get together at Phil's place in Acton on Wednesday 6th November.

---

[i] A slogan used to promote *Eno*, an effervescent antacid drink first marketed in 1852 as a *Fruit Salt* by its inventor James Crossley Eno (no relation). Early claims apparently included it was a cure for cholera. Sadly not, as the disease is currently in the midst of its seventh pandemic in 200 years. It is reputed to have killed 38 million people in India alone between 1817 and 1917. Ironically, in spite of having no effect whatsoever on the disease, *Eno's Salts'* main market is in India.

On the day I was interviewed for a place at the *LSE*, 19th November, Phil was off again to Europe to play dates in Germany, Holland, Belgium and France before the rather odd one-off date in Atlanta. Whilst he was away, Charles, Dave and I got together a few times to start re-familiarising ourselves with the *Quiet Sun oeuvre* (*Ed.: Oeuvre?* Pretentious git)

In between me writing or, more likely, failing to write essays on economic history, *Quiet Sun* rehearsed a couple of times. I dined with Robert, Alfie and their enthusiastic pooch Flossie, in Twickenham and the following day, Friday the 13th as it turned out, term ended at *Walbrook*. I never went back (except to do the Government and Politics exam in a test of my general political knowledge. Grade B. Hotcha! Didn't bother with economic history. Blank pages don't get graded).

Phil had decided to break up the lengthy *Corazon y Alma* into its component parts and invited various people to add top lines, lyrics and vocals: i.e. Robert Wyatt on *Frontera*,[i] John Wetton on *Same Time next Week*, and me on *Alma*. *East of Echo* featured cameos by *Quiet Sun*, i.e. Charles Hayward – percussion, Dave Jarrett – 'keyboard themes', and Bill MacCormick – 'fuzz bass themes'. An Ian MacDonald also featured on bagpipes. This was *not*, as *Wikipedia* has it, my late brother. *Lagrima*, previously the intro to *QS's Sol Caliente*, would feature on both albums but with different arrangements.

As mentioned, Phil asked Robert to sing and play percussion on one of the elements of *Corazon y Alma*. This part, like its final section, *Alma*, was not a solo composition. I wrote the top line and lyrics for *Alma* whilst the bit Robert sang over, *Frontera*, was a Manzanera chord sequence to which Ian and I added various sections of the top line back in 1970. Sensibly, Phil jettisoned the lyrics I wrote back then, and invited Robert to 'sing something in Spanish'. Randomly selected words and phrases from a Spanish dictionary produced a lyric which has perplexed and confused the large number of Spanish-speaking Manzanera fans the world over ever since. One feels such a lyric should be reproduced in translation for all to enjoy:

> *It's important that we make it to the border before nightfall.*
> *We must find whatever is hiding.*
> *It's doubtful that this actor is capable of such an important role.*
> *I'll end up believing that you don't want to help us.*
> *Do you think we could convince him?*
> *I will tell my employer soon to go to the aviation office.*
> *Do you deny that the accused has perjured the plaintiff in the most unforgivable way?*

---

[i] Which, of course, took on yet another life as *Team Spirit* on Robert's 1975 album *Ruth is Stranger than Richard.*

We are sorry that it is impossible for you to assist the theatrical production.
I was happy to note that the theatre was completely full of people.
I'll do whatever is possible to see you again.
I was amazed at what has happened.[1]

Don't know what the problem is. Makes perfect sense to me.

Robert's singing, lifted by the Wetton/Thompson rhythm section, turned the song into a whole new beast, and one to which Robert then became somewhat attached.

The only other track in which I was deeply involved was the final song, *Alma*. When *Quiet Sun* used to play this live it was the set's finale, its soaring Manzanera guitar solo over the final chord sequence an attempt to overwhelm the meagre audiences who ever watched us. The little instrumental link section between the vocal section and the dramatic, echo-laden guitar solo underpinned by John Wetton's regal bass line was, in the full-blown version of *Corazon y Alma*, a much lengthier introduction to the entire piece. My contribution to the final track was the lyrics and some dubious lead vocals.

With *Corazon* now otherwise engaged, us *Quiet Sunners* focused on the remaining *QS* pieces, two of Phil's, one of mine and two by Dave Jarrett, plus the never-before rehearsed, let alone played, *Rongwrong*. Well, when I say we, when it came to *Rongwrong* I mean Charles and me as most of the recording was Charles on piano, overdubbed drums and vocals and me on overdubbed bass. Our final rehearsal was on Tuesday, 30th December 1974. The recording sessions for both albums started on Thursday, 2nd January 1975.

Island Studios, Basing Street Studios as from 1975, was established by Chris Blackwell, the founder of *Island Records*, in 1969. It occupied a deconsecrated chapel and was about 60 metres from Robert's old place in St Luke's Mews. There were two studios. *Studio One* on the ground floor was the main body of the old chapel with an elevated control room at one end. It could accommodate an orchestra. *Studio Two*, was in the basement (or crypt) and was half the size and fairly intimate. *Mainstream* was mainly recorded in *Studio Two*.[i]

We would sneak in towards the end of the real musicians' sessions, drink excessive amounts of coffee and run riot, sometimes not vacating the premises until three in the morning. Assisting with the rioting were a certain Mr Eno and big bro' Ian. The engineer was the rather wonderful Rhett Davies assisted by Robert Ash. Something seemed to click. It wasn't the same bunch of diffident, callow musicians from 1970/1. Confidence had grown and it showed (can I say all this bollocks? Yes? OK).

---

[i] The building was turned into luxury flats in 2018. Shame.

59 The control room. L-R: Robert Ash, Rhett Davis, BM.
(Photo by Richard Wallis)

Before embarking on one's vague reminiscences of these sessions, a
word about Rhett Davies, above. His is a name inextricably linked to Phil,
Eno and *Roxy's* careers in the 1970s and '80s. He came from a musical
background, his dad, the late Ray Davies, being a trumpeter and band
leader who was closely associated with the *BBC Radio Orchestra[i]*. Rhett had
just finished working with Brian Eno on *Taking Tiger Mountain by Strategy* in
September 1974 and on which Phil played. He seamlessly continued on
through the *Diamond Head* and *Mainstream* sessions, making a major
contribution to both the studio experience but also the resulting sonic
quality of the recordings. He became a constant on albums involving Phil,
Brian and *Roxy* over the next decade and more, working on five *Roxy*
albums, four Manzanera albums, six Eno albums, and eight Bryan Ferry
albums. In between, he fitted in work with *King Crimson, Split Enz, Talking
Heads, Dire Straits,* Robert Palmer to name but a very few. Rhett was a great
engineer/producer, always ready to embrace the most 'out there' ideas
which, especially with Eno in the studio, was a major requirement. A truly
good guy.

Sessions for *Diamond Head*, of course, took priority, though Charles
and I would usually infiltrate them to see what was going on. When it
came to our turn, the album was the most enormous fun, and I was
helped enormously by John Wetton generously lending me one of his

---

[i] Ray Davies died in 2017.

basses. I played what I regard as the best thing I ever did – the bass solo on *Rongwrong*, recorded in one take. I would love to have played both the song and the bass solo live. So, thank you, John, a lovely and generous man, and one of *the* best bass players ever to have graced the British music scene. That John died so relatively young, on 31ˢᵗ January 2017, aged 67 is both a personal tragedy, but also a huge loss to the British music scene. For me, his work with *Family* and *King Crimson* is up there with the best of British bass playing. As a young man he was given a grounding in the bass parts of J S Bach, something which would benefit any bass player who wishes to add more than just propulsion to their music. It would have benefited me had I the sense to study them properly. Again, thank you John.

And thank you Charles for composing such a great piece of music.

60 John Wetton's white Fender Precision used on Mainstream
(Photo by Richard Wallis)

The group performances were all recorded as a piece, i.e. not edited but not necessarily first, or even second takes. *Rongwrong* was recorded in various layers: the entire piano track played by Charles, the rhythm section minus the bass solo, then the bass solo, Charles's vocals, Phil's guitars, and the MacCormick brothers as a vocal chorus last. There were, on other tracks, some overdubs, for example twin bass guitar tracks in places, but not a huge number as time was against us. One bit of heavy multi-tracking, however, was Phils' riff at the end of *Mummy* which Allan Jones in his *Melody Maker* review described as a sound 'which could literally melt a sensitive record player'.

61 Eno amusing BM whilst assisting DJ with a VCS3.
Charles lurking. Bongos in the back. No fuzzy dice, however
(Photo by Richard Wallis)

The mixing and final overdubs for the album were compressed into a hectic six-day sequence of relatively brief sessions between Monday, 27th January and Saturday, 1st February. We recorded nine pieces:

Lagrima (Phil solo)
Sol Caliente
Trumpets with Motherhood (Charles solo)
Bargain Classics
RFD version I (Band)
RFD version II (Dave solo)
Mummy Was an Asteroid, Daddy was a Small Non-Stick Kitchen Utensil
Trot
Rongwrong

The following reprobates were later credited with appearing on the album at one time or another:

Charles Hayward: Drums, Voice, Percussion, Keyboards;
Dave Jarrett: *Fender Rhodes, Steinway Grand, Farfisa* & *Hammond* Organs, *VCS 3*
Bill MacCormick: Electric & Treated Bass, Back-up Voices;

Phil Manzanera: Electric, 6 & 12-String Guitars, Treated Guitars, *Fender Rhodes*;

Brian Eno: Synths, Effects, Treatments & *Oblique Strategies*;

Ian MacCormick: Back-up Voices.

62 Dave temporarily perplexed by the eccentricities of a synth.
(Photos by Richard Wallis)

63 BM with sandwich.
Might be lunch. Could be dinner.
(Photo by Richard Wallis)

A few days later, Phil flew out to Canada on an eighteen-city *Roxy Music* tour of North America which started on the 8th February, followed by an eight-date tour of Australia and New Zealand. He returned on 1st May, by which time, and against all my expectations of the previous autumn, I had another album under my belt.

EG and *Island* were gobsmacked when Phil presented them with two albums. *Diamond Head* came out in spring '75 and *Mainstream* mid-summer. My brother suggested calling *QS* album *Mainstream*, simply because it wasn't. The striking album cover was designed by a friend of Ian's who he'd met at Cambridge, the hugely talented designer Nigel Soper (thanks again Nige).

The whole thing seemed to go down OK. Quite pleased really.

We then went our separate ways. I haven't seen Dave Jarrett since, which is a downside. The upside was that Robert was in the studio for the *Diamond Head* sessions and heard the *Quiet Sun* album. On the basis of that I was asked to do Robert's next album, *Ruth is Stranger than Richard*. The place at *LSE* was abandoned, though I feel sure I never told them, and I did another five years as a bass player.

What a hoot.

So, *Mainstream,* eh? It was all Manzanera's fault. No, really.

64 El Supremo guiding the ship of state
(Photo by Richard Wallis)

ENDNOTES:
[1] King, M, *Wrong Movements*, SAF Publishing, 1994, no page number but first entry for 1975.

RUTH IS STRANGER THAN RICHARD

OR ME, THE SIMULTANEOUS RECORDING of *Diamond Head* and *Mainstream* was just as significant as *Quiet Sun* playing alongside *Symbiosis* back in February 1971 as it again brought me to the attention of Robert.

Of course, with Robert being in the studio so was I. I was a fairly regular visitor over at Lebanon Park – tea, chat, jazz, laughs, the usual – and was keen to hear just how Robert would treat the old *Quiet Sun* piece now *Frontera*. However, at some point, he heard some of the tracks from *Mainstream*, a reminder, perhaps, that I was still playing and vaguely competent.

I spent February and early March tidying up some political stuff from the October General Election (our candidate, Graham Mitchell, was tragically killed in an air crash in Scotland and I was involved in selecting a replacement). I was also still vaguely pursuing the idea of university in September. In between, I fitted in a couple of trips over to Twickenham. During one of them Robert mentioned he was due to record a follow-up to the magnificent *Rock Bottom* and might I be interested in helping out?

'Is the pope catholic?', as the saying goes.

Some material already existed if incomplete. A track called *Sonia*, recorded in October 1974, had a bass part by *Henry Cow's* John Greaves and a trumpet part by its composer Mongezi Feza, with Robert on piano and percussion. I never met Mongezi but knew a bit about his playing, not least because he was on *Rock Bottom* and appeared at the *Theatre Royal* fundraiser for Robert on 8th September 1974.

He was born on 11th May 1945 in the Mlungisi township, one of several townships for the black and coloured communities living around Queenstown (Komani since 2016), in the Eastern Cape, South Africa. Having learnt to play the trumpet, he joined a jazz sextet, *The Blue Notes*, which featured, amongst others, Chris McGregor on piano, Dudu Pukwana saxophone, and Louis Moholo on drums. This being apartheid-era South Africa, such a mixed-race unit was not simply frowned upon, the band was actively harassed by the authorities. In 1964 they left South Africa and fled to Europe, eventually congregating in London.

Fabulous musicians all, McGregor would go on to form the *Brotherhood of Breath* in 1969. Dudu Pukwana played with bands such as *Assagai*, with Louis Moholo and Mongezi, and *Spear*, and with *Centipede* and reggae greats *Toots and the Maytals*. Louis Moholo has played with an impressive roll call of some of the greats of British and American jazz amongst them Derek Bailey, Evan Parker, Roswell Rudd, Cecil Taylor, Archie Shepp and Keith Tippett.

Sadly, Louis Moholo (now correctly called Moholo-Moholo) is the only survivor of those mentioned above. Mongezi died from untreated pneumonia in London on 14th December 1975, aged 30[i]. Chris McGregor died from lung cancer on 26th May 1990, aged 53. Dudu Pukwana died five weeks later from liver failure on 30th June 1990. He was just 52. Vital musical voices all stilled far too early. Mongezi's death hit Robert very hard. He believed it avoidable and, perhaps, that the poor treatment he received might well have been to do with the colour of his skin.

Though Mongezi was not in the studio when *Ruth/Richard* was recorded, he had been there in the weeks previous, contributing to *Henry Cow's In Praise of Learning*, an album brother Ian would review extensively in the *NME*. Good, bordering on great, in parts. Less so in others, was his conclusion. Of course, one of the members of *Cow* was Fred Frith, nearly a member of *Mole II* back in 1973. He was working on a large-scale piece, with Robert supplying the lyrics, but only Fred's piano backing track, recorded at the *CBS Studios* in Whitfield Street of happy memory, existed. This would become the beautiful and wistful three-part *Muddy Mouse* which appears on *Side Richard* of the album.

So what were we to play? There was no fund of songs by Robert to draw upon. To some extent, therefore, things would happen as we went along. What would be, would be.

Virgin's Manor Studio was booked for two weeks starting on Saturday 16th March 1975. I was, of course, driven up there in Richard Branson's Rolls Royce. No, me neither.

The Manor lies on the south side of the tiny village of Shipton-on-Cherwell, which itself is 1 km north-east of Oxford Airport's runway. The River Cherwell runs to the east and, in places, has been canalised and is well-used by pleasure craft. There is a small bridge across the Cherwell to the east but the track on the far side leads nowhere. You therefore enter the grounds from the west. Access is up the road from Kidlington and then east towards the village. Where the road turns north towards the village centre some gates on the right mark the entrance to *The Manor*.

The earliest buildings date from the 17th century and, through the large main door, one accesses this part of the building: bedrooms, the kitchen, pantry, and cellars. The buildings on the northern flank (which contained the studio) were built in the 18th century, and the southern flank in the next century. It is thus a mixture of styles and materials, but none-the-less charming for that. Richard Branson bought the estate in 1971, dammed a small stream which ran into the Cherwell to create a lake, and then converted the northern range into a recording studio.

---

[i] He was commemorated by a recording made by the remains of *The Blue Notes*. *Blue Notes for Mongezi* was released in 1976.

65 The Manor.
The entrance is off to the right. The kitchen ground floor left. Studios out of shot to the left.

66 The Manor Studio to the left behind the trees.
16th century part, central. 19th century part, right of the main door.

The first recordings there, in November 1971, were part of a *Bonzo Dog Band* reunion album, *Let's Make Up and Be Friendly*, and it was then used by a variety of artists amongst them Sandy Denny, John Cale, *Magma* (who recorded *Mekanïk Destruktïw Kommandöh*. Never could get next to *Magma*) and *Gong* (*Flying Teapot* – recorded January 1973. Could have been me on bass!). The recording that put the place on the map, however, was Mike Oldfield's *Tubular Bells* recorded in 1972 and '73.

Advertised as a residential studio, it originally sported a 16-track *Ampex* recorder and a 20-channel desk and came with cooks/housekeeper, resident engineers and, because of its isolated position, no restrictions on what hours of the day or night one might work. At some point, c. 1974-5, major changes were made to the studio involving *Westlake Audio* from LA, and Phil Newell who was technical head of *Virgin Studios* and responsible for the design and kitting out of the *Manor Mobile*, the first mobile 24-track recording facility. I really could not say whether *Ruth/Richard* was recorded before or after these changes, but the layout suggested by some photos hints at after.

Arriving at *The Manor* we found Robert and Alfie in residence and met our other partners in crime, one of whom I knew – tenor/alto sax player Gary Windo – and two I did not: drummer Laurie Allan and tenor/baritone sax player George Khan. Brian Eno turned up for a while during both recording and mixing. The presence of Eno and the two jazzers was sure to create some 'dynamic tension'. Brian really did not like improvised jazz and Gary and George were sure to provide some.

A word about these three. Gary[1] was born in Brighton on 7th November 1941, the son of Edgar and Audrey Windo. Edgar, like my father, had flown fighters in the Second World War but there the similarity ended. The Windo household was highly musical, with Edgar leading a 20-piece accordion band, if you can get your head around such a concept. Audrey accompanied on the piano. Inevitably, Gary was drawn to music, learning the drums and, you guessed it, the accordion. Thankfully, in his teens he discovered the saxophone and, by 1960, and after a stint in the Merchant Navy, he was in New York learning and playing the tenor sax. He played in various bands including, briefly, the *Paul Butterfield Blues Band*, and married in 1967. All was not well, however, His wife died, drugs were involved, and he spent a term in the infamous Rykers Island prison in New York. Finally he was deported back to the UK.

Back in England he hooked up with his childhood friend, the recently divorced mother of two, Pamela Ayton (see page 179). Gary, never bashful, dived straight back into the London music scene with the likes of *Brotherhood of Breath*, *Centipede*, then *Symbiosis* with Robert. This, led to the 'near miss' of *Matching Mole II*, then on to *Rock Bottom* and the Drury Lane concert. And finally, here he was, in deepest, leafy, somnolent, rural Oxfordshire ready to make lots of noise and wake everybody up. Sometimes, that noise involved playing his sax!

George Khan was born Nisar Ahmad Khan in London in 1938, his parents were an exotic mix of a Punjabi father and a mother of mixed English/Swiss/Italian descent. Aged thirteen, the family moved to Pakistan where, somewhat surprisingly, school friends introduced him to jazz. There he started to learn to play the alto sax. Returning to the UK, he attended Art College and continued with his music education. His wife, Gudula, was also an art student the *Royal College of Art*. His first recording was in 1966 when he appeared on pianist Pete Lemer's album *Local Colour*. He then later played with Mike Westbrook and Pete Brown's *Battered Ornaments* whilst also playing with a unit called *The People Band* until 1972. George was a long-term stalwart of the British free jazz scene. He was an exuberant and engaging personality whose work is, sadly, known only to a limited few. Get onto the internet and add to those numbers.

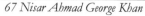

67 Nisar Ahmad George Khan   *68 Laurie Allan*

Laurie Allan, too, was a long-term member of the British avant-garde jazz community. Born in 1943, he started to play drums in his early teens and through the '60s played with some of the greatest names in British jazz: John McLaughlin, Chris McGregor, Dudu Pukwana and others. His first close connection came when he replaced Pip Pyle in Steve Miller's *Delivery* (Pip joining *Gong*) which band, of course, was also home to Phil Miller at the time. Laurie then followed Pip across the Channel, replacing him in *Gong* in 1972. Returning in the expectation of re-joining a newly reformed *Delivery*, when this project collapsed, he found himself instead recording with Miller and Lol Coxhill and with Robert on *Rock Bottom* before joining us at *The Manor* for *Ruth/Richard*.

I was fortunate to play with Laurie live as well as on this album (see page 176). He was a fabulous inventive, subtle drummer, understated yet with incredible attention to detail. Sadly, towards the end of the 1970s he faded out of the music scene entirely. As far as I know he has not played since. An immense loss to the British music scene.

EVERYTHING ABOUT *THE MANOR* WAS LARGE. The bedrooms, the kitchen, the hallways, the lawns, the lake. Large, but comfortable and relaxed. Days went down the route of: rise mid-morning, take a substantial breakfast at leisure, walk the calories off round the grounds... and try not to get flattened by the Irish wolfhounds.

Beatrice and Bootleg were the Irish wolfhounds, grey, shaggy, with huge jaws, and a doleful look in their eyes. I mean, who wants to be chasing wolves all their lives, even if the last one in Great Britain had been killed in 1680[i] and which fact makes you rather redundant? Ah, but you say, these are 'Irish' wolfhounds. OK, but the last known Irish wolf was killed near Mount Leinster in County Carlow in 1786. So... Beatrice and Bootleg were not just unemployed but unemployable. Instead, they focused on being domestic doggies, just very, very big ones.

Bootleg was the older of the two... and the biggest hound I have ever come across. And one of the friendliest. If he spotted you, say down by the lake contemplating nature and digesting a large fry-up with all the trimmings, HP Sauce, the lot, he would run at you. Well, charge, really. The key thing was to stand still. Leg it, and he thought you needed chasing, and bringing down – a wolf in jeans and a t-shirt. In a slobbery, doggy, playful sort of way, of course. Stand still and he'd gallop towards you before putting on the brakes and then, just as you thought, fuck it I'm in trouble here, he'd shudder to a stop, put his paws on your shoulders, look down on you (he was that fucking big) and slap his tongue across your face in a canine 'hello, mate, ain't life great' moment.

Now go back through the big front door and turn left along the wide and stone-flagged hall towards kitchen. Halls wide enough, you'd think, to get out of the kitchen and then left into the studio. Easy, you'd think. But just outside the kitchen, within easy reach of food piled high in a huge bowl (and nearby gullible humans who'd slip you a tasty bit of dinner, or lunch, or breakfast), was the best place for an Irish wolfhound to lay down his huge head to get a bit of kip. And where Bootleg went, there was

---

[i] Officially, the last wolf in mainland Britain was killed by Sir Ewen Cameron of Lochiel in 1680 at Killiecrankie in Perthshire. An official policy of extermination was pursued for some seven centuries before that.

Beatrice – enormous and growing still – stretched out alongside, across, or wherever. And, to add to the furry roadblock and tucked in between their giant paws, an Afghan hound whose name I sadly forget. Impossible to pass, except very carefully. Don't disturb a mass of wolfhound when they are asleep. When they stretch, they can knock you sideways. And a huge dog-breath yawn. Nice.

But the kitchen was where we were royally fed and watered by the staff for two weeks. Now, Bootleg could only get into the kitchen if the door was pulled wide open. He was so long his 'turning circle' was considerable. You'd be sitting with your back to the door scoffing breakfast and, next thing you knew, an enormous head was resting on your shoulder, the big brown eyes staring down longingly at the toast, fried eggs, and marmite about to be eaten. And, perhaps, a nicely browned sausage, or the odd rasher of crispy bacon (or two). Always wise to stay on-side with an Irish wolfhound. So, a bit of sausage here, a slice of toast there, and you were friends for life. Or until the next muso with a soft spot for enormous, friendly dogs turned up.

So, anyway, that was Bootleg and Beatrice at *The Manor*.

Woof!

WHAT OF THE RECORDING SESSIONS?
Recording essentially occupied the first week and mixing much of the second. Halfway through, even though I had now decided to abandon thoughts of university in favour of trying to eke out a livelihood as an itinerant bass player, I got trains from Oxford to Paddington to King's Cross to York and back in one day. And not just for the hell of it. I had an interview at York University. When asked by a young lecturer, 'why do you want to come here?', I replied: 'I don't, I've just never been to York before'. We then chatted for half an hour about music before the next interviewee was due and I got the bus back to York Station. Seemed like a good idea for a day out at the time.

Either side of this little jaunt, the 'band', for want of a better term, recorded four pieces:

Soup Song, a version of a *The Wilde Flowers* song written by Brian Hopper, Hugh's older brother, and originally called *Slow Walkin' Talk*.[i] The track is somewhat slowed down from the original. Main reason for this is that I wasn't sure what the bass part should be and suggested I replicate Robert's left-hand piano fingering with a few ornamentations. In fact, this

---

[i] As Phil Howitt kindly reminds me, a version of this song, with no less a bass player than Jimi Hendrix, appears on a limited edition release of demos, entitled *68*, recorded by Robert in New York in 1968 and released in 2013. Yes, Jimi does a rather a better job. I can live with that.
(Go here: *https://www.youtube.com/watch?v=agO_R0h1V84*).

had the happy result of liberating Robert to play a far freer version of the keyboard part. Well, that's my story and I'm sticking to it.

Robert contributed a new lyric… about bacon being turned into soup (oh, no!) rather than a bacon sarnie (yes, please!):

There was a time when bacon sandwiches
Were everyone's favourite snack
I'm delicious when I'm crunchy
Even when I'm almost black
So why you make a soup with me
I just can't understand
It seems so bloody tasteless
Not to mention underhand
© EMI Music Publishing Ltd

Aided and abetted by some raucous high-speed grunts and squeaks by the sax section, as well as some jaunty ensemble playing, and a loping drum part by Laurie, the song has an extended fade over which Robert expresses the hope that the resulting concoction will provoke 'a tummy ache' to 'bring you to your knees'. OK then.

Song for Che was taken from Charlie Haden's remarkable *Liberation Music Orchestra* album released in January 1970 to which the late Carla Bley contributed three pieces and a series of fantastic arrangements. Don't know it? Go listen.

Since *Mainstream* I had equipped myself with a brand, spanking new sunburst, maple-necked *Precision*. And an *MXR Phaser*. I don't think I turned it off throughout the entire week's recording. You can hear it most clearly on the solo bass intro to this song. I listen back to it from time to time and hope Mr Haden wasn't too embarrassed by my effort. I shall never know, as Charlie Haden sadly passed on 11th July 2014.

The piece is notable for being just the five of us: Robert, Gary, George, Laurie and me. It was Eno-free. I especially like Laurie's drumming on this. On the second rendering of the theme, he acts like the snare drum in Carl Nielsen's extraordinary 5th Symphony which tries, and fails, to create chaos out of order by playing *ad lib* across the orchestra. The best recordings of the symphony are always the ones where the drummer gets *really* extreme. It usually starts about 15 minutes in and builds to the most shattering of climaxes before the orchestra overwhelms the attempt at anarchy and the first movement is peacefully resolved, but with the snare now a military drum roll in the distance. It was composed just after the First World War between 1921 and 1922 and is replete with sadness and drama.

Also very fond of the 11-second snare drum roll and the bass drum thud with which Laurie ends it all. Little things…

Five Black Notes and One White Note is a riff on Jacques Offenbach's *Barcarolle* from *The Tales of Hoffmann* first performed in 1881. In its original form it is a bouncy, cheerful little thing. Not after we dealt with it. Over a mournful, minor key, fugue-like Eno synth sequence, the saxes and Brian's overlaid fuzz guitar repeat the simple theme whilst Robert and I play descending phrases in an effort to enhance the general air of melancholy thus created. Maybe not what Offenbach intended, but I am rather fond of the result.

Which brings us to *Team Spirit*, aka *Frontera*, aka the opening part of *Corazon y Alma*. Robert seemed to have rather taken *Frontera* to heart back in January and now it re-appeared, slowed down, with new lyrics, a searing Tenor sax solo from Geoge, and a rhythm section which jogs along underneath and works quite well, I think. One of my favourite bass outings, indeed. And Laurie is superbly inventive. He had a funny little drum kit of almost random bits and pieces which he made sound fantastic. Behind the scenes Eno is doing Eno-ish things with multiple delays and treatments which sweep and soar across the landscape in the near distance. I've always thought the eight minutes the track lasts pass quite quickly. There is always something going on to grab the attention.

Then there are Robert's lyrics. When you are in the studio, especially when mixing, one tends to focus not on the content of the vocal but the sound quality, pitching, intonation, timing, etc. I will admit to not having appreciated the frustration and sometimes anger at his situation which the words suggest:

"... you can hardly miss me
I'm the one face down in the mud on the ground
I'll be stuck here forever, unless you come over
And kick me Hardy"[2]

Marcus O'Dair vividly sets out the nature of these frustrations, the incidents including several involving his wheelchair, all bound up with his ongoing capacity to drink, all of which made 1975 a hugely difficult year. One made worse by the sudden, harrowing, and avoidable death of Mongezi Feza. Again, this is not a biography of Robert so, if you haven't read Marcus's book, I strongly suggest you go on Amazon (other retailers are also available) and get yourself a copy. The relevant pages are 226 to 235. So, there you go. You don't even have to look it up in the index.

Moving on.

Solar Flares was a case of over-dubbing bass onto a cowbell, percussion, and piano track already laid down by Robert. Adding that five note bass part demanded the utmost concentration. Yes, you can easily drop in and out to correct mistakes, but getting this right was a matter of honour: 5:36, metronomic, no errors. For some reason this seemed an achievement for someone for whom the strictest musical discipline was somewhat foreign. Possibly the same for Gary, who replicated it on the bass clarinet. But no Wyatt/MacCormick collaboration can be complete without at least a little fuzz bass, even if it is the scraping, almost atonal, stuff swirling around the stereo mix. I really love *Solar Flares*. It is relentless and Robert's voice and piano over the top extraordinary.

My recollection is that recording was a mainly trouble-free process. I enjoyed playing with Laurie even if, in the studio, we were placed in diagonally opposite corners with Robert and the grand piano and Gary and George in between. Being able to record whenever Robert felt like it, which sometimes meant him going into the studio on his own for things like *Muddy Mouse*, made it stress free for most of us though, of course, we weren't paying the recording costs, unlike Robert.

Mixing, however, was something else. The control room was upstairs in a gallery overlooking the studio and everyone crowded into it when the ensemble pieces were being mixed. Both George and Gary were, one might say, ebullient personalities. Somewhat larger than life and sometimes with opinions voiced… *fortissimo*! To be honest, things might have been better if we'd all gone home after the recording and left Robert to it, but Robert was way too nice to suggest such a thing. So, everyone chipped in with their thoughts on this song, or that solo until, on one song (I'm not sure which one), the dominant voices became those of George and Gary.

Not long before, Brian had given me copy Number 407 of a little box full of cards called *Oblique Strategies* which I have in front of me now. Described as 'Over one hundred worthwhile dilemmas', it was something used in earlier recordings when there was an impasse of some sort, a disagreement, uncertainty, confusion. One drew a card, interpreted, and tried to apply what was on it. Often, they were just a means of making one think in a different way. One which might help cut through the mental clutter which can build up over a long day of caffeine-fuelled attention to musical detail. Sometimes they are of direct help. For example, I have just drawn a card. It says:

"Look closely at the most embarrassing details and amplify them."

This, funnily enough, is precisely what I am doing throughout this entire book.

In the control room at the *Manor* on this day, affairs became somewhat fraught. George and Gary were dominating an increasingly circular conversation, Robert was becoming frustrated, and Alfie fretful. Eno had long since decided not to get involved in an argument between two jazz men. So, I suggested we resort to consulting *Oblique Strategies*. I might as well have been recommending casting yarrow stalks to access the wisdom of the *I Ching* for all Gary and George knew about *Oblique Strategies* but I explained its purpose as best I could, knowing that, sitting in the corner, interest newly piqued, was the author of said *Strategies*. Whether or not my interpretation of their use was up to scratch I don't know, but Brian sensibly kept his counsel on that one. So, my copy was produced. I drew a card. Looked at it. Probably laughed, and then read out:

"Tape your mouths."

Silence, stunned or otherwise, ensued. Apart from, I suspect, some muffled laughter from Alfie. The mixing session resumed and, as far as I can remember, was quietly productive.

A few days later we all bade farewell to *The Manor*, to Beatrice and Bootleg, and the lovely staff. I had enjoyed myself and, in the process, seemed to have forged a bit of a relationship with Gary Windo which would develop over the next twelve months.

From a purely mercenary perspective, one of the key things for me was that, between session fees on *Diamond Head* and *Ruth/Richard*, I was paid c.£1,000, which doesn't sound much but is the equivalent of £12,000 nowadays. Not exactly a princely sum but enough to enable me to contemplate hanging on in music and, with Phil already planning his next solo album, there would soon be things to keep me occupied.

DIAMOND HEAD WAS RELEASED on 9th May and *Ruth/Richard* three weeks later. It is fair to say that Robert's albums garnered mixed reviews.

In many ways, this was inevitable after the huge and justifiable critical acclaim which greeted *Rock Bottom* in 1974. But several critics also picked up on what they heard as a sense of 'helplessness' as Robert's physical condition manifested itself in greater or smaller frustrations with his restricted mobility and his lack of independence.

Pete Erskine at the *NME* didn't know what to make of it:

"So I called Al up and asked him why I was finding it impossible to review *Ruth Is Stranger Than Richard* and he drew my attention to the lyrics of *Team Spirit* and furnished me with a brief but detailed dossier of background information."

The 'Al' involved was Al Clark, late of *Time Out* and now *Virgin's* head of PR. The 'dossier' suggested Robert had 'issues', both personal and professional, and some of them created by his own record label.

Virgin had decided against releasing a new single – *Yesterday Man* – as a follow up to the unexpected success story that was *I'm a Believer*. *Yesterday Man* was a Top Ten hit in 1965 for singer/songwriter Chris Andrews who had previously written two hit singles for Adam Faith and four for Sandie Shaw. His first solo single got to No. 3 in the British charts. In spite of its lyric about being unlucky in love (with, typically, the woman to blame), the song was a bouncy ditty with a Bluebeat/Ska rhythm. Typically, Robert inverted a cheeky upbeat number into a melancholy, minor-keyed melody replete with a doleful brass section containing Gary Windo and Mongezi Feza. Listening to it again it is brilliant, if wistful/mournful, and fades over some typical Windo-esque sax wails.

It was all too much for the big boss at *Virgin*. Richard Branson described it as 'a bit too gloomy'.[3] Robert's perspective was, of course, different. According to an article by Mac Randall in *Musician Magazine*:

"I did *Yesterday Man*, a major-key, upbeat, jolly pseudo-reggae thing. I bent all the chords out of shape and did the whole thing kind of sideways. And I was so happy with that. They said, 'We're not putting this out. It's too lugubrious'. I thought, 'That must be good', but I got a dictionary, and it's not."[4]

So, *Yesterday Man* didn't see the light of day until included on a *Virgin* sampler, *V*, in 1977.

Erskine then went onto recount the story that Robin Nash, the producer of *Top of the Pops*, had objected to Robert appearing in his wheelchair when performing *I'm a Believer*. 'Distasteful', was the word used by the arrogant, insensitive prick, but that didn't stop the BBC later promoting him *Head of Variety* and then *Head of Television Comedy*. Apparently, everyone at the *Beeb* loved him. Itself absolutely no recommendation.

In spite of his reservations, Erskine still went on to describe the album as 'essential' (see page 362).

Allan Jones at the *Melody Maker* was, initially, even more dismayed by *Ruth/Richard* (see page 369):

"It is a most disturbing record. There are moments here which appear to be the product of a vision so bleak that even the more optimistic perceptions persist as terminal daydreams streaked with the most profound depression."

He then expounded on his thesis:

"*Ruth* explores a reality which is as harrowing in its reflection of helplessness as (Samuel Beckett's) *How It Is*, but the experience is made tolerable because even at his most desperate (*Team Spirit*, which alludes most forcefully to Beckett's strange landscapes) Robert is not given to emotional firework displays and hangs tenaciously to a facade of humour."

But, like Erskine, as Jones further explored and became immersed in the album, he, too, realised its significance:

"*Ruth Is Stranger Than Richard* is an album which sabotages any conventional approach. One has to be drawn into it slowly, picking out familiar points of reference at first, then with growing confidence begin to assimilate some of the finer details in its design. It's an important and essential album."

But still too difficult to digest for many.

FOR ALL THAT, ROBERT AND ALFIE were active that summer. As I spent the weekends playing cricket, as all good bass players should, they were away for the odd week here or there in May and June and, in between, I would pop across for yet more tea and chats. *Quiet Sun's Mainstream* was released in early August and the odd day was spent chatting to journalists. Then, in early September, Alfie asked if I'd like to join them in a holiday on Minorca, partly to be there and have a laugh, and partly to help out if required. We were joined by Brian and his then girlfriend, the lovely Ritva Saarikko (she took the photographs on the back of *Another Green World*) and we enjoyed a sun-soaked two weeks at a little place called Binibeca on the south-east corner of the island. The small villa was on a volcanic outcrop a few yards from the perfectly clear waters of a rocky inlet. Thankfully, everywhere was fairly flat, allowing Robert to get out and about a bit. I made friends with a local octopus when I went for the occasional swim. He/she took to wrapping his/her tentacles very gently around my hands as I descended some metal steps into the tepid, crystalline waters. All rather idyllic.

On my return I was given a call by Gary who asked if I would be interested in working up some material which his wife Pam had written. This would later, on Friday 28th November, turn into a one-off gig at *Maidstone College of Art* with a band comprising Pam, vocals and piano, Gary, saxes, Richard Brunton, guitar, Laurie Allan[i] and *The Floyd's* Nick Mason on drums, and me.

Nick was, perhaps, the surprise element in the band. Obviously, far better known for his role under-pinning the *Pink Floyd's* music from the Syd Barrett[ii] days all the way up his recent *Saucerful of Secrets* tour, Nick is a delightful guy always keen to get involved in something new. He was very supportive of Robert after the accident, with the *Floyd* performing two fundraisers for him at the *Rainbow* on 4th November 1974. He went on to produce *Rock Bottom* and Robert's unlikely hit single *I'm a Believer*.

Nick is also keen on cars, he later drove the 24-Hour Race at Le Mans every year between 1979 and 1984, and, for the drive down to Maidstone, he loaned Gary one of his big *BMW's*. It was a wet evening, and we

---

[i] The drum kit used by Laurie at the gig was the same one used on *Ruth/Richard*.
[ii] My preferred era. *See Emily Play* was one of the great psychedelic songs. I didn't go for the post-Barrett anthemic *Floyd* output too much. Nevertheless, Nick kindly gave me some tickets for their 'inflatables' show promoting the *Animals* album on 17th March 1977 at the Empire Pool, Wembley. Impressive stuff.

travelled down the A2, never the nicest of roads and heavily used by foreign freight vehicles. We were overtaking a large Belgian trailer lorry when it suddenly pulled out without warning, forcing Gary to drive the car into the central crash barrier. We then overtook the lorry, with Gary steering the car into the barrier, leaving the wing mirror and several bits of trim scattered along the road. I remember watching the very large wheels of the trailer a few inches away from my side of the car and hoping they wouldn't get any closer. Thankfully, due to Gary's skill and some good Bavarian engineering, we survived. I doubt the lorry driver even knew we were there. He just didn't see us in his mirrors. If nothing else, it got the adrenaline flowing for the gig. Later, Nick dismissed the damage. He was just pleased to see us.

We appeared as *Gary Windo and Friends* playing some of Pam's material. It was lively. It was loud. It was fun. It was Gary.

69 Maidstone College of Art, 28th November 1975.
L to R: Laurie Allan (behind the cymbal), Nick Mason, Gary, BM
[Photo Richard Wallis]

*70 Maidstone College of Art, 28th November 1975.
L-R: Richard Brunton, Laurie Allan, Gary Windo
[Photo Richard Wallis]*

71 Pam Windo

72 Nick Mason

73 Special Guest: Hugh Hopper
[All photos: Richard Wallis]

Pam was, and still is, a lady of many parts who came somewhat late to the role of lead singer/composer in a rock and roll band. She was born in Brighton in 1942, a few months after Gary was born in the same town. They became friends but, in the late '50s, and after leaving school at 16, Pam's wanderlust took her far and wide across Europe and North Africa. When she came back to England she married and had two sons, but divorce followed. Gary, meanwhile, had been living in the USA, honing his skills as a saxophonist, but, on his enforced return in 1969, the two childhood Brightonians got together to form an intense and productive relationship tragically cut short by Gary's untimely death in New York on 25th July 1992.

Encouraged by Gary, Pam learnt to play the piano and, one thing leading to another, she was soon composing her own material and it was these songs we played that night in Maidstone. The relationships formed continued into the sessions at *Britannia Row*.

When, later, the couple emigrated to the USA, they took up residence in Woodstock (yes, where the festival was in 1969). There Gary formed the *Gary Windo Quartet* and went on to work with most of the leading jazz musicians in the States, whilst Pam went her own way, forming *Pam Windo and the Shades*, a 5-piece band which recorded an album for *Warner Bros/Bearsville* in 1980. She was an ever youthful 38.

In 1987, deciding enough was enough, she turned to writing and, after Gary's death, travelling, returning to North Africa where she immersed herself in the culture and landscape of Morocco, a place she fell in love with. Several books emerged from this including: *Zohra's Ladder: And Other Moroccan Tales* and *Escape to Morocco* (the Fodor's Guide to the country). In

2014 she published *Him through Me: making love and music in the Sixties and Seventies*, her account of her time with Gary and their path through the music scene. The introduction was written by Nick Mason. Go get a copy. She now lives in Santa Fe, New Mexico. We are still in touch from time to time.

Sadly, most of Pam and Gary's joint work was released after his death. *The Steam Radio Tapes* and two other albums *Anglo-American* (2004) and *Avant Gardeners* (2008), all emerged at the beginning of the century, thirty years or so after their initial recording.

Guitarist Richard Brunton had been on the music scene for half a dozen years when he first played in a band with Gary and Mongezi Feza called *I Dougou* in 1974, backing up a singer called Norma Green on a tour in Europe. The partnership continued beyond Maidstone into the *Britannia Row* sessions. Richard later went on to work with Rab Noakes, Gerry Rafferty, and Barbara Dickson and appears on three of Gary's posthumously released albums *His Master's Bones* (1997), *Anglo-American* and *The Steam Radio Tapes*. Very nice player.[5]

The following spring, Nick Mason produced Gary's solo album, *The Steam Radio Tapes*, at the Floyd's *Britannia Row* studios[i]. There, for the only time, I played alongside Hugh Hopper and also met Carla Bley. These sessions were the first to take place in the *Floyd's* new studios in Islington and were, in a way, a means of testing the capabilities of the studio as well as recording the results. They not only introduced me to several new faces but, I believe, did the same for Nick Mason, and the connections made led to his involvement in Mike Mantler's *Hapless Child* in 1977, and the recording of his *Fictitious Sports* album in 1981, an album recorded at Willow near Woodstock, New York State, and featuring Robert, Carla Bley, Mike Mantler and Gary Windo, amongst others.

IN THE MEANTIME, and for some time, Phil, Ian and I had been kicking around ideas for Mr Manzanera's second solo album and, from which, other things would flow.

---

[i] *The Pink Floyd* recorded the album *Animals* at *Britannia Row* and part of *The Wall*. Other artists to use the studio included Björk, Kate Bush, *Joy Division*, Kylie Minogue, *Pulp* and, hey ho, *Westlife*.

HISTORICAL NOTE:
The Manor closed as a studio in 1995 after *EMI* took over *Virgin*. In 2010 *The Manor* was sold with a guide price of £6.5 million. It was advertised as having eight bedrooms, five bathrooms, four reception rooms, a tennis court, swimming pool, lake and 26 acres. The tennis court and swimming pool were not there when I stayed.

ENDNOTES:
[1] Much of is drawn from a contribution to an on-line forum by someone signing themselves gypsy-tail-wind: *http://forum.rollingstone.de/foren/topic/reel-recordings-2007-2012/*. On a similar subject, there is a lengthy piece which contains a commentary on Gary's recorded output by Clifford Allen on the *All About Jazz* website. The 2008 article is entitled: *Reel Recordings: Progressive Leanings With An Archivist's Care* and can be found here: *https://www.allaboutjazz.com/reel-recordings-progressive-leanings-with-an-archivists-care-by-clifford-allen#.UZsnmL2MmSo*
[2] © BMG Rights Management, Universal Music Publishing Group, Kobalt Music Publishing Ltd., Reservoir Media Management Inc.
[3] Aston, Martin, *Robert Wyatt, Q Magazine*, October 1991.
[4] Randall, Mac, *Robert Wyatt & Bill Nelson: Tough Guys Don"t Dance, Musician*, August 1992).
[5] Source: *http://musiciansolympus.blogspot.com/2016/02/richardbrunton-guitar.html*

801 Mᴋ I

1976 WAS A FUNNY KIND OF YEAR. It started early, and I mean *early* – Friday, 2ⁿᵈ January to be exact, with sessions for the album that would, in 1977, become *Listen Now*. *Listen Now* was a project with a gestation period that would put an elephant to shame and, on the tortuous path to its conclusion, it encompassed many musicians, many revisions and the odd laugh or two. There were, however, two – or three – or four (depending on how you viewed things) – constants throughout the inordinate passage of time that creating *Listen Now* spanned. The first 'constant' was, of course, Phil. It was, after all, his album, his studio time, his budget, and his reputation on the line. There were others, though, whom he found impossible to shift from the project. People who, whenever he wandered upstairs to work on some new musical idea, seemed to have taken up residence, ready to wreck his best laid plans, hijack the album, and send it down some crazy, gloom-filled path in order to reflect their especially pessimistic world view.

The brothers MacCormick were clinging grimly to the as yet un-named *Listen Now*. Songs were being slowly beaten into shape on Phil's *Teac* 4-track and then, every now and then, there would be a foray into Notting Hill for an 8-10 hour recording session at *Basing Street Studios*. But things were grinding slowly, not least, perhaps, because the right drummer for the songs was yet to be unearthed. But it was at *Basing Street* that the fourth 'constant' was often to be found – making tea, draping tape loops inconveniently around the control room, and sometimes making the 24 tracks run backwards. Brian Eno seemed always to be there or thereabouts. If Phil wasn't playing on one of his albums, then Brian was doing something strange in one of Phil's sessions. It made life interesting at least.

But there were other delays. Phil was constantly leaving the country – if it was January it must be Sweden – and my attention was also being drawn to non-musical issues. After the Beatty interview appeared, I decided to write an extravagantly long article about the still numerous candidates lining themselves up to be Nixon/Ford's successors. So, some time was spent researching, often in the library at the US Embassy, and writing and, by the time it was done, Phil was otherwise engaged, off to the States on *Roxy* business throughout February and March. *Listen Now* sessions consequently stalled and, by the time Phil returned from North America at the end of March, I had something else on my plate which caused further delays. The sessions at *Britannia Row* for Gary Windo's album meant any *Listen Now* recording had to be fitted in between days with Mr Windo.

And so we struggled on through April. By now, however, the drumming issue had come to a head. A number of backing tracks had been recorded with Bill Bruford, e.g. *Flight 19*, but, for whatever reason, the end result was not quite 'it'. Dave Mattacks, the very excellent drummer from *Fairport Convention* (amongst many other bands), was successfully employed on three tracks (*Listen Now*, *Law and Order* and *City of Light*) but he then became unavailable. What to do? Rhett Davies, producer/engineer/golfer/really nice bloke, came to the rescue. He suggested we try a young drummer of his acquaintance, one Simon Phillips. Simon was barely 19 years old but had an impressive pedigree, playing professionally with his father, Sid Phillips and his *Dixieland Jazz Band*, since he was 12 (and getting time off school to do so!). His most recent project had been the short-lived band *Chopyn* with singer Anne Odell but, with their demise, he had returned to the session circuit where he was fast building a reputation as Britain's best young drummer. Nothing ventured, nothing gained, was the general consensus so Simon was asked to 'come on down'. And so he did, with his enormous double bass drummed kit, lots of curly blond hair, fantastic enthusiasm and mind-boggling technique. It was immediately apparent that Simon was the man for the job. Not only could he play everyone else's socks off, he was a listening drummer who wanted to work with and around the other musicians. Sympathy, empathy – and a huge drum kit. Who could ask for more? And in one so young! *Extraordinaire!*

The prospects for the *Listen Now* sessions seemed set fair. Well fairish. Overwhelmed at seeing my name in print – twice – in *Street Life*, I decided to 'follow my dream'. I was off to the States to write about the US Presidential Primary Campaigns. Being a stupid bastard, I had already written off the prospects of a little-known peanut farmer from a small town called Plains in Georgia. Now I jetted off to LA to see at first hand Jimmy Carter's campaign crash and burn (or, as happened, he won both the nomination and the Presidential election which may explain why I am not currently the *BBC's* US political reporter). So, while I swanned around the City of Angels, was taken out for dinner by Julie Christie, got pretty damned close to Jane Fonda and, after a flight to NYC on the 'red eye', fell asleep in an apartment in Manhattan whilst – extraordinary coincidence! – Eno expounded on cybernetics[i] to an otherwise attentive audience, Phil twiddled his thumbs and conceived 'grand plans'.

---

[i] I am not about to explain cybernetics. One reason I fell asleep was I hadn't a clue what Brian was on about. Therefore, a brief explanation courtesy of the *Norwegian University of Science and Technology* (or *NTNU*). I could provide it from *Wikipedia* but when else does one get the chance to quote from an organisation with the acronym *NTNU*? They say: 'The word Cybernetics was first defined by Norbert

By mid-May I was back in the country, *Street Life* went bust, thus savagely cutting short my budding literary career, and attention was firmly re-focussed on 'the album'. Only now we needed a keyboard player and, ideally, one with the same technical prowess and feel of the new drummer. Enter Francis Monkman, ex-*Curved Air* keyboarder, who I had briefly known around the time of *Matching Mole Part Deux*. Again, as with Simon, things clicked, and May and June were spent in some intermittent recording. Though I'd heard Francis with *Curved Air* and on other stuff, it was not until you played alongside him you realised what a phenomenal musician he was. Technically supreme but with a fantastic ear for the sounds and notes which complimented the work of the band.

But Phil was about to spring a surprise on us all. In the middle of June, before slipping off on a short break somewhere exotic, he called the 'Big Four' together and announced his plan. He would form a temporary group, inviting Simon and Francis to participate, and then shoot around the continent in August and September cleaning up at some of the many Rock festivals being held at places like Orange, Perpignan, and Dusseldorf. With Phil and Eno heading up the band, he had been assured that the festival organisers were prepared to cough up some pretty silly money to have the band prance around for an hour or so. It seemed like a plan and so everyone agreed to meet up at the beginning of July and head out west, i.e. towards Wales not California, to get our 'heads together in the country' in classic '70s style.

'Out west' turned out to be a rather draughty cottage just outside Ludlow where Phil, Eno, Ian and I congregated on Friday, 9th July and proceeded to eat, drink, sleep, chat, worry sheep, and think about what we might do with this new band. A list of potential songs from Phil's and Brian's solo albums was considered. *Diamond Head*, for sure. *Baby's on Fire*, yes. *Miss Shapiro*, undoubtedly. Songs were added then rejected then, sometimes, put back on the list. Thought was also given to whether we should attempt any music by other bands. Something by *Creedence Clearwater Revival* for example, or *In A Gadda da Vida* by *Iron Butterfly* (the extended version) but, in moments of sobriety and clarity these ideas – all utter nonsense, as you know – were firmly put to one side. Or, even, never, ever considered.

Then, out of the blue I came rushing in: *"Tomorrow Never Knows"*, I suggested tentatively. People looked at the floor, shuffled their feet and looked away. Someone, perhaps Brian, coughed politely. The air seemed

---

Wiener, in his book from 1948 of that title, as the study of control and communication in the animal and the machine. The term cybernetics stems from the Greek κυβερνήτης (kybernētēs, steersman, governor, pilot, or rudder — the same root as government)'. That, apparently, was what Eno was baffling us with.

heavy with embarrassment, or so it seemed. It was in fact, the moment when three other people were saying to themselves: "Bugger, why didn't I think of that". (Well, that's what I reckon and I'm writing this rubbish). The suggestion was greeted with acclaim and, in a spontaneous expression of gratitude and enthusiasm, I was chaired around the room before being knocked stone cold by one of the very low door frames in the rather elderly and cramped building which had been built several centuries before for short-arsed agricultural workers and not somewhat taller and rather effete ex-Public School boys.

Rehearsals were programmed to start the following Friday, 16th July, and *Island Records*, no doubt hoping they might profit from this venture, kindly allowed the band to use the studio in the basement of their offices in St Peter's Square, Hammersmith. In the meantime, Phil, thinking that we might need some extra vocal and guitar support (as well as a rather more outgoing on-stage personality than anyone else possessed) contacted his old chum, singer, and slide guitarist, and *Melody Maker Best Newcomer 1972*, Lloyd Watson, who had performed as the warm-up act to several of *EG Management's* roster including *Roxy Music* and *King Crimson*. Thus was the band complete and now came the task of learning some tunes!

74 The obligatory PR shot: 801 mean and moody

Rehearsals were scheduled to last four weeks before the first Continental outing was due to place. In addition to the European festival circuit, an appearance on the Saturday night of the *Reading Festival* was added, as well as a rather more discreet event at the *Queen Elizabeth Hall* booked in for Friday, 3rd September.

One of the first pieces to be tried was *Rongwrong* off the *Quiet Sun* album and that seemed to go OK. So, we all thought, onwards and upwards. With the equipment arranged in a circle so that members could all easily communicate, we went over and over the material identified in Ludlow as 'suitable' and, in the main, the time spent was enjoyable and productive. I suspect the inclusion of *You Really Got Me* in the middle of *Miss Shapiro* was probably my fault. Having never felt the need to learn any standard bass parts, this one was one of the few not beyond my limited capabilities. So, those of you out there who regret the song's inclusion: sod off. Go and organise your own concert at the *QEH* and then *you* can play whatever you want.

Only once, from memory, did relations get a bit strained and this centred on the 'muso' tendencies of some of those present. Having decided to include a section from my *Quiet Sun* epic *Mummy was an asteroid*, it was necessary for Brian to learn to count music in something other than 4/4. For the technically skilled amongst us, i.e. Simon and Francis, and for those with pretensions in that direction, 13/8 wasn't much of a problem. You counted "1, 2, 3, 4, 5, 6 and..." or some other mathematical combinations of 2 or 4 or even 6 with a one on the end. This was, initially, somewhat foreign territory to Brian, whose frustrations were compounded by the likes of me saying helpful, if condescending, things like, "It's really simple, Brian, you just count....." But such problems were few and far between. The only other real issue was that Simon and Francis were having to rehearse with the rest of the band two or three times a week when they'd got the whole thing down in about one session.

Rehearsals were reaching a fine pitch when the French Government dropped a bomb. There was a riot at a festival at Orange, probably a few *flics* were beaten over the head with a stale *baguette* or some such, anyway this was sufficient justification for every festival to be banned immediately by Valery Giscard d'Estaing, the Prime Minister. Suddenly, the entire financial *raison d'etre* of the project was in ruins. No European festivals, no large pay day, no large pay day meant everyone had been working their socks off over the summer for nowt. Not big and not clever.

Phil's solution was canny. The final gig would be recorded by the *Island Mobile* under the tender care of the ubiquitous Rhett Davies. An ever so cheap and cheerful live album would be released. Everyone would just have to wait a bit for their dosh. On the 'better than nothing' principle, our little sextet morosely agreed and, on 16th August, shifted rehearsal venues to a place in Acton for the last run through. In the hope of generating a bit of interest, Angus MacKinnon from *Sounds* was invited along for a listen and then we were off to the rather grander surroundings of *Studio L* at the *Shepperton Film Studios* for the final production rehearsals. For two days, Sunday, 22nd and Monday, 23rd August, the vast hangar-like space echoed to the sounds of the band as the road crew came to grips with the stage gear and Chris Michie, who was sound engineer, the competing elements of the front of house sound. It was here, also, that final decisions were made about which songs were to be included and *Mother Whale Eyeless* sadly drew the short straw. For no other reason than I thought I should, I recorded the final two 'dress rehearsals' (which, edited, now make up the second CD of an *801 Live* complete edition boxed set) and then, as satisfied as we could be, we readied themselves for the first of only three gigs the band was to perform.

But first, reluctantly and under pressure from *maestro* Manzanera, the flowing locks, uncut since 1969, were partially shorn by a very nice gent called Keith at *Smile*, his high-end gaff in Knightsbridge. Keith was the *coiffeur* to the stars, well *Roxy Music* at least, and, if the hair had to be cut, this was an excellent way of doing it. Lovely man. Excellent coffee, too.

At 11.00 a.m. on Thursday, 26th August, the band, with several wives and girlfriends in tow, congregated at *EG Management's* offices at 63a King's Road. At short notice, an extra 'warm-up' gig had been organised and, today, we were to descend upon the small and sleepy seaside town of Cromer up on the north Norfolk coast. It was thought to be far enough away to deter any music critics from following us up there, but not so far away as to be an utter pain in the neck to get back from. The first part of the thinking was, at least, correct. Sometimes gigs go past in a blur and there is little anyone can recall of them afterwards. The *801* at Cromer was one such performance. The only evidence, another tape recorded by me but notable mainly for the 'okay yahs' of some upper-class twits on a day out from Cambridge, has been lost but, overall, it was thought to have been fun. Sort of. Later that night we all went our own separate ways, most back to London but Francis Monkman to visit his dad somewhere in Yorkshire. "See you on Saturday," he said cheerily before disappearing in the general direction of King's Lynn and all points north.

Saturday, 28th August, the day of gig two – the *Reading Festival* – was uncomfortably hot and sticky. The threat of rain was never far away. The band was due to play at 7.25 p.m. and, again, we met up at the offices in the King's Road. As the day drew on the humidity levels soared and the clouds grew thicker, heavier, and more threatening. Our little convoy headed off down the M4 and then the inevitable happened – a veritable cloud burst. The motorway was awash, traffic was reduced to a crawl and, inwardly at least, we all groaned – the stage would be soaked and, as for the crowd, they'd be like drowned rats. Arriving at the *Reading Festival* site it resembled a sodden World War One battlefield: mud, mud, and more mud. But, as they say, the show must go on and so we headed for the warm-up caravan where were laid out stage clothes and instruments.

75 *The Reading Festival '76.*
For some reason Francis doesn't get a mention.

76 *The sodden Reading Festival crowd.*
This is why I never went to festivals unless on stage

Phil had generously lent me a rather fetching pair of ex-*Roxy* trousers which showed me off to advantage even if being a tad tense across the rear. I could move, but only carefully. Bending down was out. But this was the least of our problems. As we sat in the caravan someone had the foresight to count numbers. We were five. One man was down! Francis was absent without leave. There was still half an hour to go so, as best we could, we relaxed and told one another he would arrive. Perhaps a slight traffic problem caused by the inclement weather. He wouldn't let us down! With ten minutes to go, and still only a quintet, anxiety was turning to panic. Desperate re-arrangements were being planned. Who would take over the Monkman solo in that song? Who would start that one? Notes were frantically scrawled by all and sundry. Keyboard players were cursed for being generally unreliable, expletives were not deleted. "Five minutes", came the call at the door. Grim faced we stood ready to face shame and embarrassment when, wonder of wonders, the door flew open and in fell Francis. "Trouble on the M1. Sorry guys", he muttered breathlessly. The relief was palpable and, generously, no one thought to enquire why he had not come back from Yorkshire the previous day. But the cry was now, "You're on!" and so we were. Enthusiasm got the better of my sartorial concerns and I leapt up the runway to the stage, at the same time splitting asunder Phil's expensive trousers beneath either cheek (which explains why I didn't turn my back on the audience throughout the performance and why I reversed off stage at the end).

77 *On stage at the Reading Festival.*
L-R: Eno, PM, Simon, BM, Lloyd, Francis

78 801 Live at Reading: Francis, Lloyd, BM, Simon, Phil and Eno
There is a clock on the far side of the stage just to the left of Phil's head.
The time reads 8:01 (or thereabouts, ish, close enough…)

And then, as we arrived on the stage to face a vast crowd made almost invisible by the steam gently rising off these soaked souls, the sun came out behind them in the west. Whether the crowd cheered the warmth of the sun or the band's appearance was never clear, but it made for a fine start to the evening's entertainment. The release of tension, the resulting high good humour, the generous reaction to our arrival on stage, all made the set flash past. The *801* came off to rousing cheers and we would later be greeted with a series of excellent reviews, most them remarking how untypical the performance had been. Expectations had been of a jamming band, under rehearsed (if rehearsed at all) and depending on on-stage 'magic' to generate anything of interest. No one seemed to realise we had been rehearsing for six weeks but, with musicians of the quality of Simon and Francis, it was difficult to go wrong anyway.

1 × BASS DRUM L
2 × BASS DRUM R
3 × OH L
4 × OH R
5 × DRUM MACHINE
6 BASS DI
7 × KEYBOARDS DI
8 × CASSETTE L
9 CASSETTE R
10 ENO AMP
11 GUITAR
12 GUITAR
13 LES Hi L
14 LES Hi R
15 LES Lo
16 × YAMAHA
17 × VOC ENO
18 × VOC
19 × VOC
20
21
22
23
24

4 MORE DRUM Mic STANDS including
6 MICS including 2 × D12

X = MONITORS

79 The 801 stage set-up for the recording at the QEH

The following Friday saw the last of the *801's* performances. We had the entire afternoon at the *QEH* to rehearse and sound check and, indeed, to record the whole set at least once – just in case. Rhett was there and, instead of previous live recording practice where everything was miked up, all instruments were sent direct to the recording desk in the mobile as well as to the amps on stage. Only drums and vocals depended on mikes and, by reducing the number of variables in the recording equation, Rhett was able to focus on the quality of these elements to the benefit of all. The concert was another enjoyable success, well received by both audience and critics alike.

And then the band went our separate ways.

The *801* was the best I ever played because I was playing with the best: Francis, Simon, Lloyd, Brian and Phil. A bit more time and 'we could've been contenders!'.

I was out of the music biz four years later and, very sadly, I never saw either Lloyd Watson or Francis Monkman again.

Lloyd died on 19th November 2019. Phil and I went to his funeral in the huge Peterborough Cathedral, an event which recognised both his talent, and his great significance to the music scene in that city. His slide guitar work and vocals were an essential element of what we produced in those few short weeks in August and September 1976. In addition, he was a lovely and funny man of great skill which, sadly, went unrecognised by too many. He is gone way too soon.

Francis died from cancer on 12th May 2023. I attended a memorial get together in his old house near Leighton Buzzard with his family and friends which I was pleased to do. It was a sad affair in rather too many ways. I was to have picked up *Curved Air* singer, Sonja Kristina, on the way north but, unfortunately, she was not well and was unable to travel. On arrival, we first congregated around a tree in some nearby woods where various people stepped up to reminisce about their friendship with Francis. Their memories of him were all of his later years. No-one mentioned *Curved Air* (though the band's third bass player, Mike Wedgwood, was there). Obviously, no-one mentioned the *801*. Even *Sky* was barely referred to. Afterwards, I felt I should have stepped forward and said something about those earlier days, but then I knew none of the people there and thought it might be deemed presumptuous. Those who talked seemed keener to chat about his later fascination with German church organs and the music of J S Bach. The sub-text never mentioned was his increasing interest in conspiracy theories, and his own personal isolation following relationship breakdowns.

Then, the house looked barely cared for, almost as if his spirt had moved on before his body was ready to go. In one room were his keyboards, one a large, pale blue harpsichord. He studied both organ and harpsichord at the *Royal Academy of Music* and, in the 1980s performed several solo harpsichord concerts. He was an incredible technician and a great musician if a complicated man. His last years were not especially happy though he later found comfort in a partnership with Christine Pilkington-Miksa, the widow of *Curved Air's* drummer, Florian, who died from complications relating to pneumonia on 20th May 2021.

I look back with great fondness to my time as a friend of Francis Monkman. To some great meals, to some enjoyable chats, to some pretty good music, and to the look of incredulity on his face when I beat him at chess that once and only time. He never let that happen again, but he grinned as he beat me like a gong thereafter. Happy days. Then, later, my abiding image of Francis is on stage in full flow with the *801* in 1976. That is how I will remember him.

Looking back, I was amazingly fortunate to play with two of the best keyboard players in the world: Francis and Dave MacRae. Both utterly brilliant in their different ways. Both lovely people. Neither of them flaunted their amazing ability, they worked with, and for, the music but, boy, could they turn it on when needed.

THE FOLLOWING WEEK, Phil, Brian and I returned to the subterranean joys of *Basing Street No. 2 studio*. There was some tweaking, editing and lots of mixing. And, yes, the odd vocal overdub. For reasons to do with tuning one song was dropped, *Fat Lady of Limbourg*, and for reasons of time, this being vinyl with its limitations of c. 20 minute a side, another was excised, *Golden Hours*, but as this had been recorded during the sound check and not played during the gig (no idea why) this didn't seem like too big an issue.

After just seven days in the studio the album was ready to be cut, and so it was, at *IBC* on Monday 20th September. Amazingly, the *801 Live* album was released on Friday, 29th October. There's productivity for you.

There is no point on commenting on the reviews as you can read them all from page 393 onwards. Suffice to say the band was gratified by the critics' response. Four days later Jimmy Carter was elected 39th President of the United States of America which, again, proves conclusively I know zilch about American politics.

801 Live showed briefly in the UK album charts, reaching the dizzy heights of No. 28 in the *Melody Maker* and 52 in *Sounds* in the third week of November. It was beaten to No. 1 by *Songs in the Key of Life* by Stevie Wonder, so that's alright. Other countries seemed to take it to their hearts. It was one of the top imports in the USA for nearly six months and was the top import in Australia for several months before eventually getting an official release there. The album was re-released in 1999 with the two tracks which had been left out in 1976 re-inserted into the running order.

Then, in 2009, thirty-three years after their brief flirtation with the 'big time', the *801* made their final stand with a new double CD edition of the full *Queen Elizabeth Hall* concert of the 3rd September 1976, and the final dress rehearsal CD from *Studio L* at Shepperton recorded on the 23rd and 24th August 1976. Does it stand the test of time? We'll leave that to you to decide.

Soon after its release I received a call from Richrd Williams, now involved in A&R at *Island Records*. Richard Thompson, ex-*Fairport Convention*, a musician for whom I have the greatest admiration, needed a new bass player. Was I interested? Though flattered, I politely declined. Thompson was Premier League. I was, at best, Conference League South. I knew my limitations.

THE FOCUS NOW WAS ON COMPLETING the *Listen Now* album.
Over the previous 15 months Phil had accumulated a lot of backing tracks. Ian and I had then gone off and added top lines and lyrics, though there was still more to write. The only issue was who was to sing them?

The obvious answer was yet another ex-pupil from Dulwich College.

Simon Ainley left Dulwich to pursue an architecture degree course at Manchester University. He took with him a guitar, an amplifier, and a half-formed desire to be something in rock 'n' roll. Performing with a variety of more or less (usually more) inebriated student bands, he honed his heavy guitar licks and wrote a bunch of songs. On his return to London, he ended up inhabiting a house in Upper Norwood which he shared with various other student and Dulwich friends. They, too, took to drinking at a pub called the *Railway Bell* in Gipsy Hill. There we met up. Letting no opportunity pass him by, he conned me into listening to his song tape.

Listening to Simon's material, I was struck by his vocal style and took the tape off to Chertsey, where Mr. Manzanera now lived in a large white circular house that resembled a wedding cake. This was St Ann's Hill Court, designed and built by the Australian-born architect Raymond McGrath in 1936[i]. When Phil took the place over it was not in the greatest of condition. Built mainly out of poured concrete, quite a radical building material in 1936, it had several flat roofs many of which leaked, as flat roofs tend to do. But, with more rooms than Phil, his then wife Sharon, and two Alsatians, Gibson and Layla, knew what do with, one was taken

---

[i] The main building, the Round House, and the studio, the Coach House, were up for sale for some years. So, if you had a spare £9 million lying around you too could have owned the Grade II-listed house, a recording studio in the Coach House, 8 acres of landscaped and wooded gardens, all set in the grounds of a house originally owned by Elizabeth Armistead, the wife the 18th century radical Whig, Charles James Fox. Alternatively, it could have been rented at a mere £270,000 a year. A bargain.

over as a makeshift music room. It was there, Phil, Ian and I congregated from time to time to kick songs ideas into shape.

Basically, the writing process was this:

- Phil would come up with chord sequences, or riffs, or pretty much formed ideas;
- We would play around with them, guitar, bass, rhythm box (thank god for *Roland!*) and record outlines on a *Revox* or a *Teac*;
- Copies on tape (for me, as I had two flash tape machines by this time) or cassette (for Ian. Who didn't) were then made and we disappeared back to our respective homes, Ian in a flat in north London and me back to my parents' place (Cringe. But it was free, and they fed me well);
- Each of us would try to come up with top lines for the tracks which, for some reason, were given the names of various football teams. One was provisionally entitled *Sunderland*, another, which became the instrumental *Island*, was christened *Queen of the South*;
- Lyrics was slow in coming and, in many cases, were finalised a long afterwards and, in some cases, not until well into 1977 and in time to be influenced events yet to be described.

At some point post-*801*, I played Phil Simon's tape. He liked what he heard and, within a matter of weeks, Simon was working at *Basing Street* studios, crooning the MacCormick/MacCormick lyrics in his own inimitable style. Recording, including some new backing tracks, continued throughout the autumn and into the new year.

Recording sessions at Basing Street went on throughout January but were somewhat disrupted by Phil's involvement with the presentation of Japanese percussionist Stomu Yamash'ta's band *Go*[i] at the Albert Hall which ran over three nights in early February.

On 16th March, I played on a couple of Eno tracks which appeared on *Before and After Science* (*Through Hollow Lands* with Robert and Fred Frith) and *Music for Films* (*Two Rapid Formations* with Dave Mattacks and Fred Frith). Then, on Tuesday, 22nd March I was asked by Brian Eno to be at *Basing Street No. 2 studio* at noon. There I was introduced to two German musicians: Holger Czukay and Jaki Liebezeit, the rhythm section from *Can*. Two bass players? Well, as I recall, Holger played other things. Also there was Paul Rudolph, but this time playing guitar not bass. According to my diary, the session went on for eight hours in which time we basically

---

[i] Truly a 'super group' made up of Yamash'ta, Steve Winwood (*Traffic*), Mike Shrieve (*Santana*), Al Di Meola (*Return to Forever*) and Klaus Schulze (*Tangerine Dream*). They recorded three albums: *Go*, *Go Live from Paris*, and *Go Too*, between 1976 and 77.

jammed. Whatever happened to the results I have no idea, but I can at least say I played with two of the most notable German musicians from the 70s from, perhaps, the most influential band of that time (with apologies to *Faust* who produced some extraordinary stuff, not least *Meadow Meal* and *It's a Rainy Day (Sunshine Girl)*. Not heard them? Rectify this omission now!).

Gradually, however, *Listen Now* was completed. It had taken the best part of two years.

80 St Ann's Hill Court in 1936.
The L-shaped building behind the Round House is the Coach House and in the longer wing is the recording studio used by numerous artists, including Roxy Music and Robert Wyatt. In the lower right-hand corner is the semi-circular and bridged swimming pool. I do not know how I have lived without one.

LISTEN NOW AND THE 801 MK. II TOUR

THE LYRICS, AND GENERAL MOOD, of *Listen Now* were very much a product of the politics of the time and of the preoccupations of brother Ian and myself.

People jokingly say that 'if you can remember the 60s, you weren't there' such was the proliferation of mind-altering drugs. Drugs were different in the 70s. They weren't designed to expand your mind, but to help get you through a dull, grey, mundane, sometimes desperate, existence, or simply get you 'up' for whatever you were about to do. And, increasingly, the drugs of choice were physically and psychologically destructive: coke, heroin – a brief high and a long death rattle.

The 70s were not cool. They were wretched and forlorn, and the further down the 'Food chain' you were, the worse they became. As a sticking plaster, first, they gave us glamour in the shape of Bowie, *Roxy*, Bolan, etc., in an effort to break out of the gloom and despondency. Then, when that failed, and was shown to the masses to be unreal and insubstantial, the 70s brought us punk: the anger, nihilism, and associated violence of the likes of the *Sex Pistols* and *Sham 69*. And, finally, they brought us Margaret 'There is no such thing as society' Thatcher[1], rampant selfishness, 'trickle down', petty nationalism and everything else that has since gone wrong with this country/world.

Throughout the 70s, Britain was a basket case, skinhead fascists on the one hand, and out of control, self-centred trade unionists on the other, and, from 1974, a Labour Government which seemed to have not a clue as what to do about anything and which, eventually, fell out with its own supporters in 1978/9. The result, the 'Winter of Discontent' which handed control of the country to Tory extremists for the next eighteen years. The whole centre of gravity of British politics shifted inexorably to the right. The drift has since continued. Even accelerated since 2015.

Philip Castle's[i] artwork, based on an idea by Ian, reinforced that mood: paranoia, conspiracy, fear, manipulation. The mid-1970s did that to you.

---

[i] Philip Castle was born in 1942. He studied at the *Royal College of Art* and worked for *Vogue* and the *Daily Express*. He later specialised in airbrush techniques and was responsible for numerous film and record posters and album covers, e.g. Kubrick's *A Clockwork Orange* and *Full Metal Jacket*, Ken Russell's *The Boyfriend*, Tim Burton's *Mars Attacks*, and Jack Nicholson's *Goin' South*, and for Paul McCartney's *Wings* tour; and album sleeves for David Bowie (*Aladdin Sane*), Rolling Stones (*It's only Rock 'n' Roll*), Mott the Hoople, *The Cars*, Elkie Brooks, and *Pulp* (*His 'n' Hers*). He also designed the cover for the computer game *Elite*. There is a series of four interviews with Philip concerning his work conducted in 2011 by Steve Mepsted on *YouTube*: *https://www.youtube.com/@stevemepsted1/videos*

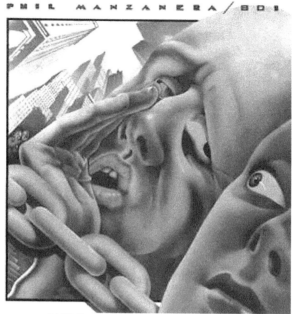

81 Philip Castle's artwork for Listen Now

The title track, *Listen Now*, with lyrics written by Ian, set a grim tone.

But, first, a little about the recording process. The basic track, Phil, rhythm guitar (on the far right of the final stereo mix), Billy Livsey[i], *Fender Rhodes*, Dave Mattacks[ii], drums and me, was recorded in the main studio at *Basing Street*. Both Billy and Dave were key to the feel and mood of the piece, playing sparingly but with ornamentations at just the right place. Progressively, over many months, extras were added. Some extra, often multi-tracked, guitars and Phil's blistering solo elements. Over the final chorus's (4:35) an extra floor tom-tom was added on beats 2 and 4 (to the

---

[i] Billy Livsey is an American keyboard player and composer originally from St Louis and now living in Nashville but who, in 1976-7, was based in London. He has played with an impressive roster of major artists such as Tina Turner (he played keyboards on her hit *What's Love Got to Do with It*), Ronnie Lane, Leo Sayer, Gallagher & Lyle, Cliff Richard, Kevin Ayers, and Pete Townshend. [see: *https://www.billylivseymusic.com*].

[ii] David James Mattacks, born 1948, is, perhaps, best known for his work with various British folk-rock bands, most especially *Fairport Convention* which he joined after the tragic death of drummer Martin Lamble in a road accident on the M1 on 12th May 1969. He has also worked with the *Albion Country Band, Steeleye Span, Camel*, Nick Drake, Richard Thompson and John Martyn to name but a very few. A consummate professional and lovely guy, and the heartbeat of too many albums and bands to list here [see: *https://www.davemattacks.com*].

left in the stereo mix). At around 5:56 I added a *Wurlitzer* piano run to smooth the transition from the main four-square rhythm to the 'swing' part where the lightly phased bass part then briefly took up the same line. Lastly, the great Mel Collins[i] was given the track, and he went away to write and arrange the 'big band' section at the end, as well as the other earlier brass parts and the lovely soprano sax solo (there's another beautifully lyrical one on *Initial Speed*).

Simon's vocal parts were mainly doubled, except for the 'talking' intro ('Sometimes dawns that day…'). In parts, especially the chorus's and the 'You've gotta listen now' intro, Ian and I also sang. The ethereal voices, multiple vocal overlays first heard on *10cc's* fabulous *I'm Not in Love*, which come and go throughout the track (and the album) were painstakingly laid down by *10cc's* Kevn Godley and Lol Creme, and are first heard deep in the mix at 2:31.

Now the lyrics:

You've gotta listen now and recognise the circle
You've gotta listen now, get wise before they lift your eyes
You've gotta listen now and hold your children closer
You've gotta listen now, get down or you won't be around
Now, now listen, now listen

Sometimes dawns that day when the man calls for his pay
And you gotta go through that, yes you've gotta live through that
And when you've paid what you owe you might have to travel slow
But you gotta go through that, so you've gotta live through that
But when the masters of the tame require to repossess your name
You don't have to go through that, you don't have to live through that

Thunder rolling down out of dried-up skies
Every inch of earth crying out for water
Television man spelling out the price
Everywhere the sheep creeping to the slaughter
Cold weather coming, people feel the fire
Living on Dead End Street with no desire
Is it any wonder you've got no power
When you pay a thief to keep it for you?

---

[i] Melvyn Desmond Collins was born in 1947 on the Isle of Man. His father, Derek, was a sax player who played with such stars as Shirley Bassey and Judy Garland. Mel has played with a huge range of the best in British music and a much-abbreviated list contains: *King Crimson, Camel, 10cc*, Eric Clapton, *Bad Company, Dire Straits*, Bryan Ferry, *The Rolling Stones* and Joan Armatrading. A brilliant player and all-round good guy, for more go here: *https://www.dgmlive.com/biographies/mel-collins*.

Is it a surprise that your wine is sour
When you let a liar choose the brew he pours you?
Talk on the wire about force and choice
It's uncomfortable to raise your voice

Everybody whispering behind their hand
Selling their despair to any stronger man
Don't have to listen now

We taught ourselves to trust our heads
It's getting us nowhere
If fifty-five million hearts can't feel it
We'll never know where

Polish up your silver and hide your gold
Send the lookout man down to every corner
Gather in the place where it's bought and sold
Next to where you once used to be a learner
Cold weather coming, people feel the fire
Living on Dead End Street with no desire
You gotta listen now

Now listen, now now listen

© Phil Manzanera, Ian and Bill MacCormick

These lyrics, and mine on the song *Law and Order*, were the result of a distillation of several ongoing political themes in both the UK and USA. Mix in a heavy dose of the dystopian paranoia of Philip K Dick, whose books both Ian and I devoured. Start with *The Man in the High Castle*, then *The Three Stigmata of Palmer Eldritch*, *The Game Players of Titan* and *Do Androids Dream of Electric Sheep?* and the results were never going to be pretty.

The first strand was the rise of the *National Front* an organisation which, in the '70s, marched to the dismal chant: 'The *National Front* is a racist front, join the *National Front*'.

The *National Front* was formed on 7th February 1967 from a motley collection of tiny ultra-right wing organisations: the *British National Party*, the *League of Empire Loyalists*, the *Racial Preservation Society*, the *Greater Britain Movement*, and elements of the *Anglo-Rhodesian Society*. The members were basically a bunch of neo-Nazi, anti-Semitic, anti-immigrant, white supremacists many of whom had their political roots in Mosley's pre-war *British Union of Fascists* which, of course, was inspired by Hitler and the Brown Shirts, and Mussolini's Fascists.

The total membership of the new party was just 2,500 but then, many extreme right-wingers must have wondered what the point of such an organisation was when, a few years before in the 1964 General Election, Tory activists campaigning in the West Midlands constituency of Smethwick felt able to push leaflets through doors with the headline:

'If you want a nigger for a neighbour vote Labour'.[i]

Whilst, nationally, the Labour enjoyed a 3.5% swing from the Conservatives, in Smethwick[ii], a Labour-held seat which had elected Patrick Gordon Walker since a by-election in 1945, the Tory candidate and local councillor, Peter Griffiths, generated a swing of 7.2% to the Tories. An unrepentant Griffiths, who later advocated 'apartheid (as) an alternative to integration'[2] was elected with a majority of 1,774. His supporters yelled 'Where are your niggers now, Walker?' when the Labour candidate left the count.

In the House of Commons, the Labour leader, Harold Wilson, described Griffiths[iii] as a 'Parliamentary leper', but he was not disowned by the Tory leader Alec Douglas-Home[iv]. So, what need of a racist party of the extreme right if this was acceptable within the Conservative Party?

Then there was Enoch Powell. On 20th April 1968, he gave his infamous 'rivers of blood' speech in an attack on black immigration from the Commonwealth in general, and on Labour's 1968 *Race Relations Bill* in particular. At the time, Powell was a member of the Tory Shadow Cabinet under Ted Heath. Again, what need of a racist party of the extreme right if such ideas were acceptable within the Conservative Party? OK, Powell was sacked from the Shadow Cabinet, but he stood as an official candidate for the Tories in his Wolverhampton South-West seat in 1970 and more than doubled his majority.

---

[i] I apologise for the use of the horribly derogatory word but it needs to be there to give proper context. I hope you feel as appalled as I do at seeing it in print.

[ii] In 1918, suffragette Christabel Pankhurst stood in Smethwick for the *Women's Party*. She lost to the Labour candidate by 775 votes, or 4.4%.

Oswald Mosley, previously a Tory MP but by then representing Labour, won the seat in a by-election in 1926, holding it in 1929. He left the Labour Party to form the *New Party* but lost the seat in 1931. He then formed the *British Union of Fascists* in 1932, taking inspiration from Mussolini's Italian Fascists. Mosley was interned in 1940 and the *BUF* proscribed. He died in 1980.

[iii] He lost to Labour's Andrew Faulds, a well-known TV actor, in 1966. Perhaps surprisingly, he was selected to fight Portsmouth North for the Tories in February 1974 but lost. Selected again in 1979, he won the seat and held it in three General Elections before losing in 1997. He died in 2013.

[iv] To be fair, the local Labour Party, too, was institutionally racist. The Labour-controlled *Sandwell Youth Club* and the local *Labour Club* both operated a ban on 'coloured' people joining [Jeffries, S, *Britain's most racist election: the story of Smethwick, 50 years on*, The Guardian, 15th October 2014].

201

The background to Powell's speech was the expulsion of Asians from Kenya in 1968, many of whom fled to Britain. These included Christie Fernandes. Fernandes, with Uma Mootien-Pillay from Mauritius, are the parents of a certain Sue-Ellen[i] Cassiana Braverman, *aka* Suella Braverman, the virulently anti-immigrant Home Secretary in office, if not in touch with reality, between 25th October 2022 and 13th November 2023. Then, in 1972, Idi Amin, followed the same path in Uganda and he expelled its Asian residents, of whom c. 27,000 came to Britain. These included Sushil and Anjana Patel who ran a convenience store in the capital, Kampala. They are the parents of one Priti Sushil Patel, previously the virulently anti-immigrant Home Secretary between 2019 and 2022. And, of course, the virulently anti-immigrant Prime Minister Rishi Sunak's parents both also came to Britain from East Africa in the 60s. His father, Yashveer, left Nairobi in 1966, settling in Liverpool. His mother, Usha, was the daughter of two Punjabis living in Tanzania who moved to Britain in 1966[ii].

There is nothing quite like pulling up the drawbridge against the rest of humanity once you are safe and sound. Appalling hypocrites of the first order the lot of them.

Idi Amin's actions were seized upon by the NF which organised demonstrations and rallies opposing the admittance of Ugandan Asians to the country. Membership increased and, on 7th December 1972, the NF candidate polled 7% in a Parliamentary by-election in Uxbridge. On 24th May 1973, one of its leading figures, Martin Webster, took 16% of the vote in another by-election in West Bromwich (this seat shared a border with Smethwick). Though subsequent elections were disappointing, they fielded enough candidates in both 1974 General Elections, 54 in February and 90 in October, to qualify for a free TV broadcast. Even so, every candidate lost their deposit. In 1976, on the back of the expulsion of Asians from Malawi, the NF enjoyed a resurgence, but it was short-lived. As tends to be the case with the extremes of politics on both right and left, factionalism was never far below the surface and arguments, personal attacks and divisions split the party over and over again.

One of their targets for recruitment, however, became football crowds at places like Millwall (see page 213). It was on this subject that I wrote an article for the *New Musical Express* at my late brother's suggestion. It was this that attracted the 'death threat' from some idiot in Manchester and my one and only contact (that I know of) with a representative of Special Branch, a rather nice detective sergeant sent to investigate and reassure.

---

[i] Named after the rather wayward and unstable character played by Linda Grey in the TV soap opera *Dallas*. Seems about right.
[ii] Tanzania expelled its remaining Asian population in 1972.

Throughout 1976, the *NF* fielded candidates in numerous London council by-elections, especially in areas with large black, Asian or Jewish communities[i], sometimes gaining 10-12% of the vote. But, on 1st July, two competing right-wing factions, the *National Party* with 26%, and the *National Front* with 18%, combined to take more votes, 975, than the *Labour* candidate, 968, in the Deptford, Lewisham, council by-election. The subsequent growth of the *National Front* in that London borough would eventually lead to the Battle of Lewisham on 13th August 1977 in which 2,000 NF supporters were confronted by 5,000 counter demonstrators organised under the banner of the *Lewisham Campaign Against Racism and Fascism*.[ii] I used to keep up to speed with the activities of the *NF* and other similar organisations with a subscription to the monthly magazine *Searchlight* which started to publish *exposés* of their goings-on in February 1975. Its founders, Gerry Gable and Maurice Ludmer, helped set up the *Anti-Nazi League* in 1977.

Such was the British political and personal background to the writing of some of the lyrics on *Listen Now*.

But there was a lot more.

THE SUDDEN DEMISE of *Street Life* in June 1976, with its suggestion of phone tapping and other interference from interested parties in the security services, came as something of a revelation. The involvement of organisations like MI5 and Special Branch in undermining freedom of speech and thought, however, was underpinned by revelations made in a seminal article in the weekly magazine *Time Out* on 21st May 1976, three weeks before *Street Life's* final edition. It was written by a British investigative journalist, Duncan Campbell, and an American, Mark Jeffrey Hosenball[iii].

---

[i] Barnet 3 by-elections out 4, Bexley 5 out of 5, Brent 4 out of 5, Croydon 3 out of 6, Enfield 6 out 6, Greenwich 6 out of 7, Hackney 2 out of 2 (and 20% of the vote in Kingsmead, 15th July), Haringey 5 out of 5, Harrow 2 out of 2, Hillingdon 3 out of 5, Hounslow 5 out of 7, Lewisham 2 out of 3, Newham 2 out 3 (19% of the vote in Canning Town and Grange and second place, 14th July), Southwark 4 out of 4 (two National Party), Tower Hamlets 3 out of 3, Waltham Forest 3 out of 3, Wandsworth 3 out of 5.

[ii] For more read Special Branch's report on the day's activities here:
https://www.ucpi.org.uk/wp-content/uploads/2021/04/MPS-0733367.pdf

[iii] Hosenball was born in Cleveland, Ohio, in 1951 but came to Britain in 1969, attending a school in Reading for a year. He went to the University of Pennsylvania before getting a degree at Trinity College, Dublin. After his deportation to the USA he worked for *Dateline NBC*, *Newsweek* and *Reuters*. He has won several awards for his journalism which focuses on the War on Terror, US politics and air safety issues. He lives in Washington, DC.

Campbell was a brilliant student whose mother worked at Bletchley Park during the war alongside Alan Turing. Graduating from Brasenose College, Oxford with a 1st Class degree in physics, Campbell then gained an MSc at Sussex University going on to write for the *Brighton Voice*, a radical newspaper founded in 1973[i]. He was an early expert in computing and programming. He then started to do research into a secretive government organisation which, ironically, was the offspring of Bletchley Park, itself previously known as the *Government Code and Cypher School* (*GC&CS*). The *GC&CS* was formed as the result of a merger of two intelligence gathering organisations from the First World War: *MI1* (*British Military Intelligence, Section 1*) and the Royal Navy's *Room 40* (later *NID25*). Both contained codebreaking and cryptanalysis sections, and these were merged in 1919 to form *GC&CS*.

82 The Eavesdroppers, Time Out, 21st May 1976

The bulk of these operations moved to Bletchley Park near Milton Keynes during the Second World War where they focussed on breaking the codes generated by the German *Enigma* and *Lorenz* cipher machines. The programme was known as *Ultra*, and contributed mightily to Allied successes against the Axis, not least helping to win the prolonged Battle of the Atlantic against the U-Boat wolfpacks. As part of the process, engineers, many from the Post Office, designed and built *Colossus*, the world's first properly programmable computer (destroyed after the war).

---

[i] For more about Campbell see: *https://www.duncancampbell.org/content/biography*

Bletchley Park closed down in 1946 and *GC&CS* moved temporarily to RAF Eastcote[i], at the northern end of what is now the London Borough of Hillingdon. It was renamed the *Government Communications Headquarters* (*GCHQ*) in June 1946. In 1954 it moved to the vicinity of Cheltenham to take advantage of a telecommunications infrastructure set up by the US Army during the war. Since then, *GCHQ* and the American *National Security Agency* (*NSA*) have shared information as part of the *United Kingdom – United States of America Agreement* (now part of the *Five Eyes* multilateral intelligence agreement including Canada, Australia and New Zealand).

In 1975, Senator Frank Church (Democrat, Idaho) was chair of the *Senate Select Committee to Study Governmental Operations with Respect to Intelligence Activities* which started to investigate the activities of both the *NSA* and the *CIA*[ii]. Unknown to him, he was already under electronic surveillance by the *NSA* as part of *Project Minaret*. *Minaret* monitored the activities of people and organisations inside and outside the USA and Church, an opponent of the Vietnam War, was but one of some 1,650 US citizens investigated. Others included Martin Luther King, Muhammad Ali, Tom Hayden and Jane Fonda, and, for some reason, Howard Baker, Republican Senator for Tennessee, later Senate Majority Leader, and Ronald Reagan's White House Chief of Staff, 1978-8. *GCHQ* co-operated in this programme, handing over any intercepted communications to the *NSA*.

The existence of *GCHQ* was a state secret, as were its *SIGINT* (*Signals Intelligence*) activities. *SIGINT* involved, amongst other things, telephone tapping, the interception of wireless communications, and has since been

---

[i] Now a housing estate, Pembroke Park.
[ii] Church's work led to the *Foreign Intelligence Surveillance Act*, 1978. In early 1976, Church entered the race for the Democratic Presidential nomination. Although he won the primaries in Nebraska, Idaho, Oregon, and Montana, he was too late to stop Jimmy Carter who had locked up the nomination. He expected to be offered the role as Vice President, but it is believed the *CIA* passed false information to Carter suggesting Church's committee had been infiltrated by the *KGB*. Walter Mondale was selected instead. In 1980, James Jesus Angleton, chief of counterintelligence for CIA from 1954 to 1975, a fellow Idahoan, persuaded Republican congressman Steve Symms (1st District, Idaho) to run against Church. An *'Anybody but Church'* (*ABC*) committee was set up, financed by the right-wing *National Conservative Political Action Committee* (*NCPAC*). Under existing campaign finance rules, the *ABC* and *NCPAC* committees could spend what they liked, and they did. Then, on polling day, the major networks declared Reagan had won the Presidency with a huge majority before the polls closed in Idaho. It is thought this depressed turnout in one of Church's best areas. Church lost by 4,262 votes, or 0.9%. He died from pancreatic cancer on 12th January 1984.
[See: *https://theintercept.com/2023/05/09/cia-frank-church-richard-welch-book/*]

extended to all forms of internet communication. Until 21st May 1976, the acronym *GCHQ* had never been published in a British newspaper.

Campbell and Hosenball's article, *The Eavesdroppers*, smashed through this barrier of secrecy. State retribution was delayed but definitive. Hosenball, who was now working for the *Evening Standard*, had permission to stay in Britain until at least 11th December 1976 when his current work permit expired. On 15th November, Hosenball received a letter from the newly appointed *Labour* Home Secretary, Merlyn Rees[i]. In it, Rees wrote:

"The Secretary of State has considered information that Mr. Hosenball has, while resident in the United Kingdom, in consort with others, sought to obtain and has obtained for publication, information harmful to the security of the United Kingdom and that this information has included information prejudicial to the safety of the servants of the Crown ... In the light of the foregoing, the Secretary of State has decided that Mr. Hosenball's departure from the United Kingdom would be conducive to the public good as being in the interests of national security and he has accordingly decided to make a deportation order against him."[3]

Hosenball appealed twice against the decision, the final appeal being heard in front of the Master of the Rolls Alfred Thompson Denning, Baron Denning, Lord Justice of Appeal Geoffrey Dawson Lane[ii], Baron Lane, and Lord Justice of Appeal Sir James Roualeyn Hovell-Thurlow-Cumming-Bruce[iii]. The establishment with a capital 'E'.

Whilst admitting Hosenball never saw the details of the allegations against him, all three judges found in favour of the Home Secretary and Hosenball was deported. Indeed, Denning admitted that:

"Now I would like to say at once that if this were a case in which the ordinary rules of natural justice were to be observed, some criticism could be directed on it. For one thing, the Home Secretary himself, and I expect the advisory panel also, had a good deal of confidential information before them of which Mr Hosenball knew nothing and was told nothing; and which he had no opportunity of correcting or contradicting; or of testing by cross-examination. In addition, he was not given sufficient information of the charges against him so as to be able effectively to deal with them or answer them..."[4]

But he went on:

---

[i] He succeeded Roy Jenkins on 10th September 1976. Jenkins resigned his seat to become the first British President of the European Commission in January 1977.
[ii] Later Lord Chief Justice of England, 1980-1992.
[iii] Son of the 6th Baron Thurlow.

"But this is no ordinary case. It is a case in which national security is involved, and our history shows that, when the state itself is endangered, our cherished freedoms may have to take second place. Even natural justice itself may suffer a set-back."[5]

This case, heard in the Court of Appeal, needs to be considered against the backdrop of what was to become known as the *ABC Trial*, a farcical event which culminated in the prosecution, but with either no or minimal punishment, of the three accused: Crispin Aubrey, John Berry and Duncan Campbell. And this, after the first trial was abandoned when the jury foreman was exposed as a former officer in the *Special Air Service*.[i]

83 L-R: Duncan Campbell, the late Crispin Aubrey, and John Berry

John Berry was a former corporal involved in the previously mentioned *SIGINT* activities of the British security apparatus when based in Cyprus in 1970. On 18th February 1977, he was interviewed in his home by Duncan Campbell and another *Time Out* writer, Crispin Aubrey. Having determined that most of what they were told was out of date, Campbell and Aubrey left the house and were promptly arrested by Special Branch, as was Berry. Special Branch knew about the meeting because, after the publication of *The Eavesdroppers*, Campbell's phones had been tapped. By *GCHQ*. All three were charged with breaches of Section 2 of the *Official Secrets Act, 1911*, i.e. either communicating or receiving 'classified

---

i For a lot more about the *ABC Trial* and its ramifications see:
https://www.duncancampbell.org/content/abc-case

information to unauthorised persons'. Campbell was later additionally charged with 'collecting classified information'.

The resulting trial in November 1978 was laughable and wholly counter-productive. The 'collecting classified information' charge against Campbell was dropped before a trial notable for the lamentable performance of a *SIGINT* officer, a 'Colonel B' later identified as Colonel Hugh Anthony Johnstone, the administrative head of *SIGINT* in the Army. Throughout the trial it was shown most of the information 'collected' was freely available, much of it in the USA. Though convicted, Campbell later wrote:

> "It ended in convictions under Section 2 for each of us, but with negligible penalty – in the case of myself and fellow journalist Aubrey, no penalty at all."[6]

The prosecution was also counter-productive in that it triggered repeated attempts to introduce *Freedom of Information Bills* to the House of Commons. Later in 1978, the Liberal MP for the Isle of Ely, Clement Freud, came top in the ballot for Private Member's Bills and he introduced a *Freedom of Information Bill*. Though lost because of the 1979 General Election, Labour MP Frank Hooley introduced another in 1981 which fell when opposed by the Thatcher government. In 1984, Liberal MP and party leader David Steel introduced another bill, the first in a series of similar bills many of which became law[i].

The depressing aspect of this heavy-handed suppression of information and dissent was that it was being done under the auspices of a Labour Government which seemed content to accept whatever the vested interests of the security services told them. Radical they were not.

In 1976, journalist Tony Bunyan published a book entitled: *The History and Practice of the Political Police in Britain*. A second edition, published in 1980, was reviewed in the periodical *Crime and Social Justice* by Rob Reiner. He wrote:

> "What Bunyan clearly establishes is that the British state has developed a formidable battery of repressive agencies for the detection and suppression of political dissent. Dissent, moreover, is given a wide interpretation by these agencies, encompassing anything outside a narrow frame of political activity, especially if it is on the left… In practice all these agencies (then Special Branch, MI5 and MI6) operate with almost complete independence, as the

---

[i] *Data Protection Act* (1984), *Local Government (Access to Information) Act* (1984), *Access to Personal Files Act* (1987), *Access to Medical Reports Act* (1988), *Environment and Safety Information Act* (1988), Section 2, *Official Secrets Act* repealed 1989, *Access to Health Records Act* (1990), *Freedom of Information Act* (2000).

records of scandals concerning the revelation that Sir Anthny Blunt was a Russian spy have emphasized once more. Detailed Parliamentary questioning on these agencies has usually been fobbed off by arguments that they are not constitutionally responsible to Parliament …"[7]

As all of this was happening under a so-called socialist government, we wondered at the time what might happen if an administration more sympathetic to repression and committed to the power of the state was elected. One led, for example, by Margaret Thatcher, leader of the Tory Party since 1975. Thatcher, after all, was a considerable fan of Gen. Augusto José Ramón Pinochet Ugarte (she described him as a 'staunch, true friend' in a speech at a fringe meeting at the 1999 Conservative Party Conference). Pinochet, if you need reminding, was the Chilean Army general who led the bloody CIA-assisted coup against the democratically elected left-wing government of President Salvador Allende in September 1973. Allende was amongst the first of some 1,213 killed in the coup. Subsequently, the Pinochet regime unleashed a campaign of murder, torture, rape and assassination[i] against the Chilean people and, unabashed, in 1978 gave an amnesty to all those involved in its prosecution. In 1991, the Chilean *National Commission for Truth and Reconciliation*[ii] gave an official total for deaths and 'disappearances' of as many as 2,279.[8] In addition, it was estimated 27,255 had been tortured, as many as 80,000 interned, and approximately 200,000 forced into exile.

It was facts like this, and the totalitarian fears it generated, which led me to write *Law and Order*.

Saw your face on TV
You said it's alright have no fear
I'm here,
Panics ended,
Your rights defended
From those who tried to tell you
About the other side of life
The strife that's going on
Go to sleep now
Count the sheep now
With us the dream will never end
It's easy to take what you are told

---

[i] Pinochet's agents organised the car-bomb assassination of Chilean *Socialist Party* leader, Orlando Letelier, in Washington, DC, in 1976.
[ii] The full, and relentlessly harrowing, report can be read here:
https://www.usip.org/sites/default/files/resources/collections/truth_commissions/Chile90-Report/Chile90-Report.pdf

They said we need law and order,
But now all your lives are bought and sold
And just for some law and order

Now the days grow colder
The plans they've got for you are clear
So clear
You're not so sure
You want that cure
And those who tried to tell you
About the shit that's going down
Are found out on the moor
But just don't ask how
Curfew starts now
Get off the streets and bolt the door

We'll get away from here one day
I'll take you across the border
There's gotta be somewhere we can stay
Where they don't need law and order

© Phil Manzanera/Bill MacCormick

I can only assume that US-based reviewer Pshawn Cassidy failed to understand the background when he criticised the words as:

"...painfully clichéd, sort of a *Dragnet* cast reunion." (see page 414)

Dragnet was a TV series about the Los Angeles Police Department which first saw the light of day in 1951, and, therefore, has little relevance to the actual subject matter, but there you go.

Not all of the songs were 'political'. *Postcard Love* is about love unrequited (see page 132). And I sing this along with Simon, but with me a bit forward in the mix. *City of Light* concerns the desperate plight of women, young and old, trapped in prostitution by exploitative men, both pimps and punters. Ian's *Flight 19* features star-crossed lovers Suzie and Johnny, though the track's title is taken from a strange event which took place on 5th December 1945 over the Bermuda Triangle when Flight 19, four US Navy *Grumman Avenger* Torpedo Bombers, disappeared without trace on a training mission. All fourteen men were believed to have died. In addition, a *Martin PBM Mariner* flying boat sent out to look for them disappeared and another thirteen men were lost. No-one has ever satisfactorily explained what happened. The 'discovery' of the untouched aircraft, parked in the Sonoran Desert but minus their crews, features at the beginning of the classic Spielberg film of 1977, *Close Encounters of the Third Kind*. Lastly, I have always felt *That Falling Feeling* was a peculiarly personal song to Ian who had experienced three relationship failures in quick succession, and which materially impacted on his life and happiness.

The album was scheduled for an autumn release. Towards the end of July, *Flight 19* was selected as a single and this was cut at *Trident* on 25th July. In the meantime, at a place called *Ezee Hire* in North London, we started to rehearse for a UK tour to promote the album. The nucleus of the band was to be Phil, Simon and me and to this trio were added The Great Paul Thompson on drums and Dave Skinner on keyboards and vocals.

Dave, born in 1946, was the oldest member of the band and, alongside Andrew Rose, was part of a duo called *Twice as Much* who recorded two albums in the 60s when they were managed by Andrew Loog Oldham, manager of the *Stones*. In 1972 he joined the band *Uncle Dog* whose lead singer was Carol Grimes (see page 63). The bass player at the time was John Porter who, in 1973, played on the second *Roxy Music* album and toured with the band. When Bryan Ferry recorded his first solo album, *These Foolish Things*, Porter recommended Dave to play keyboards. He would also later play piano on Ferry's fourth solo album, *In Your Mind*, in early 1977. It was during these sessions that Phil got to know him and recruited him for the tour[i].

After some final studio work at *Basing Street*, the *Listen Now* album was cut at *Trident* on 1st August. Rehearsals ran through early August during which time demos were recorded of material, some of which appeared on *K-Scope* (*Slow Motion TV* and *Remote Control* plus another track called *Blue Gray Uniform*, written by Paul Wheeler, which didn't [see page 134]). On Friday, 12th August, Phil flew to the Algarve for a two-week holiday, and so did I. We stayed about 40 kms apart, him in Carvoiero and me in Vale de Lobo, meeting up a couple of times for a glass of Vinho Verde or six.

Flight 19 was released on either 2nd or 9th September (diary a little confused here) and did little. The band continued to rehearse and, on Sunday, 18th September, I played my last cricket match of the season for the OA 1st XI against Orpington, finishing the season with bowling figures of 156 overs, 29 maidens, 456 runs and 31 wickets, or a bowling average of 14.7 at 2.9 runs per over. Pretty decent. Makes you wonder why I wasn't called up for international duty. But then, I was never appointed Prime Minister either. Odd, that.

The album was scheduled for release on 23rd September and, the following Monday, we repaired to a sound studio at Shepperton where we spent two weeks rehearsing, the final sessions being production rehearsals with the PA and lights.

---

[i] He also played keyboards on the 1978/9 *Roxy Music Manifesto* tour.

The set list was made up of a mix of material drawn from *Diamond Head*, *Roxy's Country Life* album, the *801 Live* set and *Listen Now* plus another, *Remote Control*, which ended up on the *K-Scope* album in 1978. The main set included *Out of the Blue* with *Remote Control* and *Miss Shapiro/You Really Got Me* as encores (if required). In total, it ran for about 80 minutes. The songs played were:

TNK (Tomorrow Never Knows)
Flight 19
Listen Now
Law and Order
Que?
City of Light
Initial Speed
That Falling Feeling
Diamond Head
Out of the Blue
Remote Control
Miss Shapiro
You Really Got Me

The tour started on Tuesday, 11th October, apparently at Lady Margaret Hall in Cambridge. I say 'apparently' as I have absolutely no recollection of this gig. Anyway, we drove there in two brand spanking new *Ford Granadas*, and we drove back. Next night was Southampton, where my cousin Ewan was in the audience. Decent enough performance. Again, we drove down, and we drove back. If it's Thursday it must be Surrey University in Guildford and, maintaining the academic theme, East Anglia Uni on Friday, and Leicester Uni on Saturday.

I, however, had noted that my football team was playing at home that Saturday. For the reason that I found their nickname vaguely romantic, and because they were the best team in the country when I was aged about 7 or 8, I supported Wolverhampton Wanderers[i]. They were due to take on West Ham on 15th October 1977. West Ham had been a horror show for the opening months of the season and were later relegated for the first time in a quarter of a century. Having been promoted the previous season, Wolves were now bumbling around the lower reaches of the First Division (as it was then called) and were on the brink of a calamitous decade when building a new stand in 1979 nearly bankrupted the club. It went into receivership in 1982 and dropped into the Fourth Division (currently the Second Division. Somewhere it makes sense).

---

[i] First Division: 53-54 Champions, 54-55 Runners-up, 57-58 Champions, 58-59 Champions, 59-60 Runners-up. FA Cup winners 59-60.

So, now that I could drive, I decided to borrow one of the *Granadas* and drive the 170 miles from Norwich to Wolverhampton, take in the game, and then drive the c. 60 miles east to Leicester in time for the show. Seemed like a good idea at the time. Mr Manzanera, hearing of my plans, and never having previously attended a professional football match, decided to tag along.

We get to *Molineux* which is not exactly crammed, a crowd of c. 19,300, and I buy two tickets for the *North Bank*. Ideally, I would have got us some seats, but Phil fancied experiencing a proper football crowd which meant standing, as one was then allowed to do. I chose the *North Bank* because, in those days, the 'nutters' who preferred a punch up (or 'ruck' as they liked to call it) occupied half of the very large *South Bank* so that they could lob food, and empty and, sometimes, full bottles into the neighbouring enclosure in which cowered the away fans (I once went into the 'away' end with a friend who supported Liverpool and can vouch for the torrent of abuse and missiles, some of it concrete blocks, which emanated from the headcases the other side of the double fence which was all that separated us. Didn't help that Liverpool won easily).

Hooliganism was going through one of its more aggressive phases about this time, probably not helped by the general economic malaise affecting the country and which would soon spawn Thatcherism and all of its attendant ills.

The previous season I had taken my life in my hands to watch Wolves play at Millwall ('Nobody likes us, we don't care') in their old and decrepit stadium, *The Den* in Cold Blow Lane[i]. It was a bright crisp New Year's Day as the two teams tried, and failed, to play decent football on a rutted, grassless pitch. One down, Wolves equalised late on. As they celebrated, a lone individual emerged from the crowd behind the Wolves goal, ran the length of the pitch and tried to assault the goal scorer. It got the biggest cheer of the day.

In those days Millwall had 'fan' groups called *F Troop* (later known as the *Millwall Bushwackers*), *Treatment*, and the *Half-Way Line*. The latter name is fairly self-explanatory as that was where they congregated. They were basically the younger, trainee yobs. The hoped to graduate to *Treatment*, who used to wear surgical masks on their heads to reflect what opposition fans would require should they run into them, something almost impossible to avoid in those days as there was but a single road out of the ground and up towards New Cross Station. The senior thugs were in *F Troop*, the heavy mob – or 'firm' as such gangs liked to call themselves as a reference to organised criminal gangs.

---

[i] Demolished in 1993, they now play at the *New Den* in Bermondsey.

Millwall fans had an appalling reputation for violence. So bad, indeed, that *Panorama* made a documentary about them, broadcast on 14th November 1977[i]. I went to the New Year's Day game incognito, stood with some older Millwall fans, cheered when they scored, and groaned when Wolves equalised. It's called self-preservation.

Back to *Molineux*. The *North Bank* was not exactly genteel, but I guessed it might be less dangerous for a tall, well-spoken lad from South London, i.e. Phil.

Now, Phil does not sound 'posh' but he certainly sounds 'Home Counties'. And Wolves were playing a London team. He was intrigued by the entire process and, rather than maintain a close-lipped silence throughout the game, he repeatedly asked me questions about players, tactics, the stadium… As he was several inches taller than the average attendee, his voice carried. I soon became aware that a group of ashen-faced and tight-lipped Wolves fans (ashen-faced and tight-lipped because West Ham were 1-2 ahead) was beginning to surround us.

"Who's that player? He's very good," chirped Phil brightly, pointing to Trevor Brooking, resplendent in the claret and blue of the Hammers. "Oh well tackled," he exclaimed as Billy Bonds gently deposited a Wolves player into the crowd with a tackle guaranteed to attract a 15-minute intervention from VAR and several red cards nowadays.

Really? I mean, Phil, shut the fuck up!

My only recourse was loudly to recite the name of every Wolves player on the pitch whilst stating, in no uncertain terms, I had no idea who any of the West Ham players were and, also, that they were rubbish whoever they were. So, starting from the back I pronounced:

> "In goal Paul Bradshaw, fullbacks Geoff Palmer and Derek Parkin, the blonde one, centre halves Maurice Daly[ii] and Colin Brazier, midfield Martin Patching, Kenny Hibbitt, Willie Carr with the red hair, and Alan Sunderland, he's good[iii], up front the great John Richards and the tall guy is Norman Bell."

Credentials accepted, the surrounding group dispersed, perhaps feeling better as Wolves had equalised and the final score was 2-2.

Having explained to Phil that we had come close to a tour-finishing hammering by disgruntled Wolves fans, we hot-footed it to the car, got out of town pronto, and high-tailed it towards the East Midlands.

---

[i] You can watch it here if you can stomach it:
https://www.youtube.com/watch?v=ighcTmfAfr4

[ii] Or it could have been Parkin in central defence and Daly at fullback. Neither were proper centre backs which might explain the score line.

[iii] Too good for Wolves as it turned out as he moved to Arsenal two weeks later.

I'm sure we were wonderful at Leicester Uni, and can see no reason not to suggest the same about Birmingham Town Hall the next night. We were given Monday night off for good behaviour, enabling us to briefly renew acquaintances with our nearest and dearest before heading west.

Plymouth, like Rotterdam and numerous other ports, had fallen victim to the close attention of the Luftwaffe in 1940/1 and large parts of the old city were flattened. The existence of the large naval base at Devonport on its western edge made the place a particular target. From here, Royal Navy warships departed in their efforts to combat the German U-Boat menace in what became the Battle of the Atlantic. The first bombs fell on 6th July 1940, but it was not until the spring of 1941 that the Germans decided to give it a good going over. According to Crispin Gill, in his book *Plymouth: A New History*, 22,000 houses were damaged or destroyed, along with the main shopping areas, 26 schools, eight cinemas and 41 churches. Some 1,174 residents were killed and 4½ thousand wounded. Its reconstruction, between 1946 and 1962, was not, in this writer's estimation, a success, with the centre of the city a rather windswept, soulless landscape of concrete and glass.

One building which escaped was, in 1977, called the *Berni Grand Hotel*, an 1870s edifice on the Promenade which we graced with our presence. Though now an apartment block called *The Grand*,[i] it was, and is, a fine-looking cream-coloured building which overlooks The Hoe and Plymouth Sound. The 'Bernis' in the title were ex-pat Italians Frank (interned during the war) and Aldo (who sensibly held a British passport) who'd run cafes in Plymouth and Exeter during the war (both destroyed by German bombs). In the mid-1950s they started to open restaurants, the first in Bristol, which then proceeded to proliferate at an alarming rate across the country. *Berni Inns* popped up everywhere and were hugely popular, not least because you could get steak (well done, none of that French 'rare' nonsense) and chips, a roll and butter, and ice cream for the knock-down price of just 7/6d (or 37p in modern money. Somewhere between a tenner and score nowadays, John). For a starter, it had to be the prawn cocktail with a violently coloured Marie Rose sauce and, pushing the boat out here, you could always replace the ice cream with a Black Forest gateau. T'was the height of 'sophistication' and helped cement Britain's place in the culinary and gastronomic relegation zone for decades to come. Places like the ubiquitous *Wimpy Bar* no doubt helped reinforce this unwanted reputation.

---

[i] So grand is *The Grand* that the road to its rear is called Grand Hotel Road.

Frank and Aldo bought *The Grand* in 1963[i], installed four restaurants, and hosted *The Beatles* in the *Steak and Duck Bar* when they stopped off *en route* to Cornwall for the filming of *Magical Mystery Tour*. 17/6d (88p) for half a duck. They could afford it.

Anyway, we played a club called *Castaways* on Union Street near the centre of Plymouth. I believe it later became *JFK's*, then *Club 103*. Derelict for many years, it was recently renovated but nearly burnt down in October 2023 in an arson attack.

Quite why I have told you all of this I have no idea. Must be the nerd in me. We played. Plymouth loved us/tolerated us/bottled us off the stage...your guess is as good as mine. Next day we pottered off to Oxford to play the Poly, then, apparently, what is now Hereford College of Arts, before sprinting across country to Essex University and then north to Nottingham where we played the Portland Building in the University.

This I do remember mainly for the incredible heat generated, the place being absolutely rammed, and because someone stole my shirt. When I say 'shirt' I am not talking about any old *M&S* polo shirt the likes of which currently fill my (ever diminishing) side of the wardrobe, but one Mr Manzanera had specially created for the tour, possibly by Wendy Dagworthy or some other friendly fashion luminary of the time. We were all provided with white jackets, fetchingly tight shirts, and tight white trousers. In a nod to punk, various zips were involved, some in useful, and others in inexplicable, locations. And they came with large *801* badges with the numbers cut out of silvery metal.

As I recall, we did both encores that night and, prior to embarking on the final song, it was so hot I stripped off my shirt to give the good students of Nottingham a rarely seen view of my perfectly toned torso. In those days I was still under twelve stone (less than 170lbs for our American readers, or 76 Kg for residents of the continent) and my stomach was flat. If I looked down, I could see my toes without having to lean forward. Happy days, long since gone. Anyway, said shirt was placed for safe keeping on top of my amp, a rather large *Ampeg* as I recall. I was later told that, as we finally bid the rapturous crowd farewell, a male student clambered onto the stage, grabbed the shirt, and legged it before he could be rugby tackled by any members of the road crew.

I hope he feels proud of himself. I hope he still has it, though preferably washed by now. If he contacts me and returns it, I will not prosecute. There's probably a statute of limitations on stolen shirts anyway.

---

[i] It was sold in 1985. The restaurant chain was sold to *Grand Metropolitan* in 1970. In 1995, *Whitbread* bought them and they were renamed *Beefeater*.

216

84 The 1977 801 Tour: the stolen shirt

On Saturday, 23rd October we played the *Victoria Palace Theatre*. Wasn't great to be honest. Place lacked atmosphere, especially compared to the raucous, ebullient crowd at Nottingham. On stage, though, we were joined by the ever-wonderful Andy Mackay for his oboe work on *Out of the Blue*. The gig also gave family and friends the chance to see us in action and to get together after the show for drinks and… a piece of *801* cake. The pile of plates to the left of it in the photo above suggests servings were rather on the small side.

The tour then headed north, though with a day extra off as the gig in Southport was cancelled for some reason. So, on Wednesday, 26th October, we set off up the M1/M6: destination Liverpool. We stayed in the fairly plush *Atlantic Tower* overlooking the Prince's Dock and played the Mountford Hall at Liverpool University where, back in 72, *Mole* and *Roxy* had shared the bill. Next was Huddersfield Poly plus a stay up the road at the *Dragonara* (now *Hilton*), Leeds, followed, before Paul Thompson enjoyed a triumphant return to Newcastle where we played the famous *Mayfair Ballroom*. It had been in use as rock venue for many years since its opening in 1961. Back then, it was a proper ballroom with a Canadian

Maple wood dance floor, a revolving stage, an all-round balcony, and fixtures, fittings and furnishings in ludicrously bad, OTT, taste. Brilliant. You name them, they played there: *The Animals, The Small Faces, Led Zeppelin* when they were the *New Yardbirds* and again when they were *Led Zeppelin*, Bowie, *The Who...*

85 The 801, Victoria Palace Theatre
L-R: Andy Mackay, PM, Simon Ainley, Dave Skinner, BM and TGPT

That night the place was packed with high-spirited Geordies and the person they really wanted to see was The Very Great Paul Thompson, one of their own, rock drummer *par excellence* and one of the nicest people you are ever likely to meet. What a drummer. The place was buzzing, the crowd enthused, both by the presence of TGPT but also, no doubt, by copious quantities of *Newcastle Brown* (other drinks were available). It was a very good night and we returned to the distinctly upmarket *Gosforth Park Hotel* on something of a 'natural' high. The unnatural, and personally embarrassing, ones were yet to come.

86 The Mayfair Ballroom, Newcastle.
As it looked in 1961

Frankly, it would have made better sense to play Newcastle on the Saturday instead of Hull University but, no, we had to flog 100 miles up the A1(M) on Friday and then 145 miles back down the same road on Saturday. The high spot of the journey on a bright sunny day was when I spotted a police car on a bridge over the M62 somewhere near Goole in time to give driver Chris Kettle time to reduce speed from 120 mph to 70 mph without causing a multi-car pile-up.

87 Eddie Jobson onstage at Hull University.

Hull was special because we were joined on stage by another *Roxy alumni* – violinist and keyboard player Eddie Jobson. Eddie came to *Roxy* via *Curved Air* and Bryan Ferry's *These Foolish Things* album. Over the next three years he played and recorded with *Roxy* on three of their best and most successful albums *Stranded, Country Life* and *Siren,* all 'top three' albums in the UK. Later, of course, he played alongside John Wetton, Bill Bruford and Alan Holdsworth in the 'supergroup' *UK*, and with the late Frank Zappa, appearing on half a dozen albums. A consummate musician, seemingly capable of turning his hand to almost any instrument at a moment's notice, he joined us on stage for a rousing performance of *Roxy's Out of the Blue.* I recorded the performance on cassette and Phil released a tidied-up version in 2001.

For reasons to which I was not privy, dates in Canterbury and Swansea were cancelled, giving us three days off before we, again, dragged ourselves up the M1 and M6 towards Manchester. The gig was at the University so was something of a hero's return for recent graduate Simon. As an impecunious student I doubt he had previously seen the plush, ornate interior of the *Midland Hotel,* an enormous Victorian/Edwardian red brick edifice built by the *Midland Railway Company* next to the former Manchester Central railway station[i]. With hair his length he might not have been let in.

According to some, Hitler rather took a fancy to the building and, it is suggested, the Luftwaffe avoided bombing the immediate area although, as from 22nd December 1940, Manchester was badly bombed for two days[ii]. The Hitler story seems somewhat unlikely as the *Free Trade Hall,* 110 metres to the west, was hit and, let's be honest, aerial bombing in World War Two was never *that* accurate. It is true, however, that the worst damage was away to the north of the city.

This date was to be special not just because of Simon's homecoming but because we were to be joined on stage not only by Andy Mackay but also by two local lads (well, Prestwich to be precise) *10cc's* Kevin Godley and Lol Creme. Kevin lived just down the road from Phil's Chertsey pad, living in a house previously owned by *The Who's* Keith Moon and he and Lol had added vocal support on various parts of the *Listen Now* album. Now they were to lurk towards the left rear of the stage where they joined in enthusiastically on backing vocals and, at the same time, made free with various bits of percussion. To add ever more spice, Phil had ordered up a mobile recording studio which meant, in an ideal world (which never occurred) we should be error free, in tune and on time.

---

[i] Now a convention and exhibition centre.
[ii] 684 civilians died and more than 2,000 were injured.

The hall was not even standing room only. I suspect there may have been some of the lighter weight young ladies whose feet did not touch the ground such was the crush. Fire regulations? Who needs them?

Simon was introduced to the crowd as 'one of their own' to great acclaim and the band steamed along. We were about two-thirds of the way through the main set when we arrived at Phil's showpiece, and often show-stopper, the instrumental *Diamond Head*. After a lovely keyboard intro by Dave Skinner, the rest of the band joined in before Phil's searing guitar took the lead. Or not.

I was facing Paul, as we jointly thudded our way through the opening bars, and was only dimly aware that something odd was going on. This feeling was reinforced when, out of the corner of my eye, I saw one of the road crew dive across the stage in the general direction of Phil's feet. Phil, perplexed, was staring down at his guitar, no doubt wondering why absolutely no noise was coming out of it. Someone, between songs, had trodden on his lead (all well before radio mics, etc.). It was thus unplugged. Not guilty, your honour. The rest of us blundered on whilst frantic efforts were made to get Mr Manzanera back in the game. Then, surprisingly, given that he was the man who'd spent the entirety of *Pooh and the Ostrich Feather's* first gig with his back to the audience, and who was not known for his verbal interactions with an audience, Phil waved his hands indicating we should stop. We did. The crowd looked confused. Phil commandeered a mic and said something along the lines of:

"Sorry about that. Technical malfunction. But we are going to stay here until we get it right."

Cue audience laughter and widespread cheering. Two encores after a fairly rousing *Out of the Blue* and we were done. Could have played more. For some reason, it was another 24 years before the live recording saw the light of day. It has its moments.

I cannot let this book pass without saying something about Phil Manzanera, my oldest musical colleague and friend. I think it fair to say that Phil has never been the most technical of lead guitarists. Obviously, there are numerous guitarists who can play quicker, cram more notes into a bar than Glaswegians in a pub at closing time, are flashier, pose better, display grander flourishes. And, then, when they have finished you find you cannot remember an idea, a melody, an exploration of the tune or the technology which makes you shake your head and smile.

There are too many guitar players who think of nothing but speed. I remember watching a video of a well-known Scandinavian 'speed king' held in awe by rather too many budding guitarists. What became very clear, very quickly, was that all he was doing was playing scales at various places on the fretboard. Up, and down, and up and down. At extreme

221

speed. Clever, perhaps. Profound? Moving? Creative? No. In fact, quite the most tedious thing imaginable. Phil has never indulged in such time-wasting self-indulgence. If a note is not necessary, don't play it, might be his motto. His guitar parts are designed to enhance the whole, sometimes with melodic contributions, sometimes with explorations of sound/noise, sometimes with drama, always thoughtful, to the point. Musical, not simply technical.

One early influence was the great and lately lamented Randy California from the LA band *Spirit*. *Spirit* was one of the bands brought to our attention by Robert when he in the USA on the Hendrix tour in 1968. Their first album has some great material but, for most of us at the time, it was the song *Uncle Jack* and California's solo which made us go weak at the knees. A guitar part you could sing along with, clever, creative and with a still inexplicable doubling of the part which, somehow, he reproduced live, as we all saw at still the best gig I have ever seen: the *Lyceum Ballroom* in 1970. California continued with such contributions over the band's first four albums, none of which sold or gained the recognition they so clearly deserved. Another excellent example might be his fluid, dramatic, sublime solo on the opening track of their third album, *Clear*. The track is *Dark Eyed Woman* and, OK, I am a nerd, but I can still sing that solo note for note. And laugh at the end of it all. It is that damned good. Tragically lost to a rip tide off Hawaii saving his son from drowning in 1997, California was one of the greatest West Coast guitarists, god (if such a thing exists) rest him.

Phil then extended this approach to his song writing from *Quiet Sun* onwards. His ideas were always different, original, from the dramatic solo guitar theme *Lagrima* which became a feature on four albums in varying forms – *Diamond Head, Quiet Sun, 801 Live* and *801 at Manchester* – through the Terry Riley influenced *Trot* and on through his *Roxy* contributions and beyond to the series of solo albums he has released in the 21st Century.

The next night we apparently played the *Maniqui* nightclub in Falkirk, 230 miles, and more than four hours' drive, away from Manchester. I know we stayed overnight some 23 miles to the east at what was then the *Esso Motor Hotel*, Craigleith (later a *Crest Hotel* and now a *Holiday Inn Express* in case you wish to follow in our footsteps) but about the gig – nothing. I'm sure Falkirk is a lovely place and Falkirkians or, as I am informed by *Google*, the Bairns of Falkirk as they are known, are wonderful people. I see their football team, *aka* The Bairns, is, as of late November 2023, top of Scottish League One and are hoping to regain their place in the Championship lost in 2019. Good luck to them. You will probably know whether they succeeded by the time you read this nonsense. Sadly, Falkirk was also the scene of the decisive defeat by Edward I of a Scots army led by William Wallace on 22nd July 1298. Wallace, before he was hung, drawn,

222

emasculated and quartered at Smithfield on 23rd August 1303, was a decent guerilla leader but a useless General, as the Battle of Falkirk proved. Unfortunately, however, the film *Braveheart* means that Wallace is forever associated with Mel Gibson. One would not wish that on most people.

Our next stop was 60 miles to the north. Dundee, without wishing to offend the local Dundonians, was not the most fabulous of places back in 1977. I am sure it has changed for the better in the intervening years. According to *Wikipedia*, back in 2015 *GQ Magazine* even described it as the 'Coolest Little City in Britain'.

Previously, it was known for 'jute, jam and journalism' and was a place famous for the eponymous cake, for marmalade, newspapers, and was made wealthy on the back of the jute trade back in the Victorian era. To expand: every supermarket shop will have a Dundee Cake on its shelves; a certain James Keiller was responsible for the first commercial marmalade in 1797; and D C Thomson, formed in 1905, was a highly conservative publisher of numerous regional newspapers and the kids' comics *The Beano* and *The Dandy*. The jute was imported from parts of the Empire in South-East Asia and this necessarily led to the growth of port facilities in Dundee alongside shipbuilding and whaling, the whale oil being used to lubricate the fibres of the jute before it was milled into textiles of various types. Victorian Dundee, therefore, must have smelt a bit back in the day.

The city lies on the north bank of the Firth of Tay over which, in 1878, a poorly designed and not very robust railway bridge was built. On Sunday, 28th November 1879, the middle part collapsed during a huge storm and a train from the *North British Railway Company*, coming from the town of Burntisland on the north side of the Firth of Forth opposite Edinburgh, disappeared into the raging waters of the Tay. All 75 people on board perished. The disaster was commemorated by various works of 'literature', the most infamous being William McGonagall's *The Tay Bridge Disaster*, later described as one of the worst poems in the English language. Its opening verse sets the tone:

Beautiful railway bridge of the silv'ry Tay
Alas! I am very sorry to say
That ninety lives have been taken away
On the last sabbath day of 1879
Which will be remember'd for a very long time.'

All of which makes some of my lyrics seem worthy of the Nobel Prize for Literature.

One of its other claims to fame is that the stadiums of its two professional football clubs – *Dundee* (based at Dens Park), and *Dundee United* (Tannadice) – are closer together than any two other major football stadiums in the United Kingdom. Just 111 metres separates the two grounds. Liverpool and Everton, on the other hand, are 730 metres away from another, kept apart by the green space of Stanley Park[i].

Dundee was also the political home of Winston Churchill from 1908 to 1922, i.e. the days when he was a Liberal MP and not a Conservative one. Churchill had 'crossed the floor' in 1904 in response to a nasty piece of Tory legislation called *The Aliens Bill*, designed to limit Jewish immigration into Britain. His expressed opinion, that he believed in 'the old tolerant and generous practice of free entry and asylum to which this country has so long adhered and from which it has so greatly gained', would surely rule him out of membership of the current racist bunch of Tory MPs which constitute bulk of the parliamentary party nowadays and for some time since.

In 1908 he was appointed to the Cabinet as President of the Board of Trade. In those days, joining the Cabinet required the MP to submit himself to a by-election which election Churchill duly lost by over 400 votes (4%). Dundee, in those days, was a two-seat constituency. One MP was Labour's Alexander Wilkie, who won the seat in the 1906 General Election. The other was the Liberal Edmund Robertson, first elected in 1885. Robertson was 'kicked upstairs', being made Baron Lochee, of Gowrie in the County of Perth, and Churchill won the by-election with a handy 2,709 majority. He retained the seat until 1922 when, extraordinarily, he was beaten into a poor fourth place by one Edwin Scrymgeour, the first, and only, MP for the *Scottish Prohibition Party*, who went on to hold the seat until 1931.

Pursuing the political theme (you really want to know this guff. You know you do) in February 1974, the Dundee East constituency was won by Gordon Wilson of the *Scottish National Party*. Though the seat returned to Labour in 1987, the SNP regained it in 2005 and have held it since.

Who cares? you might well ask. The answer being because the *SNP* is all our family's fault. Well, vaguely. A relative, John MacDonald MacCormick, formed the *Glasgow University Scottish Nationalist Association* in 1927 which morphed into the *National Party of Scotland* the following year. In 1934 it merged with the *Scottish Party* to form the *Scottish National Party*. John MacCormick was its National Secretary for eight years. Later becoming more of a devolutionist, he joined the *Liberal Party* and was elected Rector of the University of Glasgow in 1950. He died in 1961. In February 1974, his older son, Iain, was elected *SNP* MP for Argyll, which constituency contains the island of Iona on which my father was born. He held the seat until 1979. John's second son, Neil, the regius professor of

---

[i] Everton's new stadium at Bramley Moor Dock will, assuming it is finished, be 2.6 kms west of Anfield.

Public Law and Vice-Principal of the University of Edinburgh, was an *SNP* member of the European Parliament for ten years.

So, it is clearly, all our fault Scotland is being run by the incompetent bunch of nationalist numpties currently in power (as of 2023). I've always believed the *SNP* would dissolve pretty much overnight if independence was ever achieved, fracturing into its various conservative, liberal, socialist, regionalist, etc., components. The 70's war cry of 'It's Scotland's oil!' is no longer the effective rallying point of old. And, with some suggesting Japan now makes better whiskey, that basically leaves haggis and the bagpipes and neither of them are going to be the foundation of a robust independent economy.

Which digression is all very well, you say (and quite rightly) but what else happened in Dundee on the night of Friday, 4th November 1977?

Well, now that I have abandoned all aspirations to be Prime Minister of this benighted country, though, to be blunt, my elderly cat Twiglet could make a better job of running UK Plc than the current mob, I can, at last, come clean. As you will know, if you have been paying attention and doing anything other than just looking at the pretty pictures, my experience with modern drug culture was minimal. This was, perhaps, untypical of the average rock musician. Indeed, the only element of the triad of 'sex and drugs and rock 'n roll' of which I partook was the latter third.

Except in Dundee. And it didn't involve sex.

Someone, no names, no pack drill, suggested that I might 'enjoy' the rather dull, grey and drab surroundings of Dundee, and the *University Student Association* in which we were to play, rather more if I snorted some white powder. And not *Eno's Liver Salts* either. A £10 note[i] was duly rolled up. A white line was laid out. I hoovered it up my nostrils.

And waited.

And waited.

Absolutely bugger all.

Went on stage. Nothing.

Came off stage and fraternised with some students in the bar. Nothing.

Went back to the hotel (which I have down as the *Centre Grand* but I can find no record such a place). Nothing.

Well, nothing except not feeling remotely sleepy. Having tried and failed to get some shut eye I went down to the bar where there was, on the wall, a large TV. There was a game of sorts which involved shooting ducks as they flew across the screen. I was still there, massacring the poor, defenceless waterfowl, when the restaurant opened for breakfast. Some porridge, a fry-up, and plenty of coffee seemed a good idea. And toast, plenty of toast and the local marmalade.

---

[i] Worth £66 nowadays as I am sure you are desperate to know.

In walked Chris Kettle, tour manager *extraordinaire*. Eyebrows were raised. Musos were supposed to be tucked up in bed at 7.30 a.m., not chowing down on the final crumbs of their eighth piece of toast. He was leaving fairly soon for the next show in Glasgow, 80 odd miles away. Did I want to come? Why the hell not?

I sat in the back of the *Granada*, all bright and perky. Until somewhere near Stirling. Total collapso. I simply could not stay awake.

We duly arrived at Glasgow's premier hotel, *The Albany* on Bothwell Street. This hotel opened in 1973 and was the first luxury hotel in the city. One of its main claims to fame was that there was a TV in every bedroom. So, 'luxury' is obviously very relative. This was now the place stars stayed when visiting Glasgow. Soon after its opening, it was besieged by a horde of weeping, semi-hysterical teenage girls desperate to see any one of the *Osmonds* (but, preferably, Donnie) briefly staying there. Earlier in 1977, Rod Stewart and his girlfriend Britt Ekland occupied the penthouse suite which, apparently, they let him have for just £48 (£317 now) for bed and breakfast, a discount of £15 on the normal room rate. Bargain.

88 The Four Seasons Restaurant in The Albany.
Where I fell asleep in my dinner

My room, to which I was helped, was decent. Large bed, bathroom, mini bar. The usual. I just went to sleep, fully clothed. That night we were due to play *Strathclyde University*. My presence at the sound check had already been discounted so one of the roadies took my place. Probably made a better job of it. About 6 p.m. Mr Kettle came to rouse me. Apparently still borderline comatose, he ran a hot bath in which I fell asleep, slipping gently beneath the surface to emerge coughing and spluttering.

Food, Chris decided was the answer. We wandered downstairs and were guided to a discreet table in the *Four Seasons Restaurant* – one of *the* places to be seen in central Glasgow. A meal of some sort was ordered, and a plate placed in front of me. Aghast, Chris watched as I rested my face on the plate and started to snore.

There seemed only one solution. I was taken back to my room and another line of white powder was set out before me by someone unknown. This time a rolled up £20 note was proffered. Woefully co-ordinated, I attempted to inhale said illegal substance. Some of it stuck to the inside of my nose. This caused an immediate heavy nosebleed which obliterated the face of William Shakespeare[i] before the note was snatched out of my hand. The rest of the stuff lodged in my throat, immediately freezing my vocal cords. I now could not speak, let alone sing as was expected later that night.

But it was now time to go to the gig about a mile away to the east. On the way, we stopped at a small supermarket. A bottle of whiskey and a bag of sugar was purchased. At the gig, a kettle was found. I was fed hot toddies of whiskey, water, and sugar in the hope it might de-frost my larynx. Then we went on stage. I was propped up against my speaker cabinet and, for the entire show, two of the road crew crouched behind me ready to catch me should I fall over backwards. No need! Some of the white powder had, indeed, got into the blood stream and I was reviving.

The gig finished, I was now garrulous and wanted nothing more than to talk the hind leg off the nearest donkey – or human, should one become available. And one did. Propping up the bar in *The Albany* was a certain John Martyn, great, but sadly late, songwriter and guitarist. We had never met, though my late brother had given his albums good reviews in the *NME*, but, nonetheless, I plonked myself down next to him and asked what he was drinking. 'Rusty Nails' was the answer, which was something completely new to me, but I watched as the barman poured *Drambuie* and Scotch into the same glass. OK, then, Rusty Nails it was. We sat. We drank. We chatted. Sometime in the middle of the night we went our separate ways. I went back to the room where I would have watched TV for the rest of the night as the brain was more than frazzled. I would have done, but TV stopped about midnight in those days.

---

[i] The Series D £20 note was introduced in 1970 with the Queen on one side and Mr Shakespeare on t'other. These were phased out in 1991 and Shakespeare replaced by Michael Faraday. In 1999, Faraday was replaced by Edward Elgar. Subsequently, economist Adam Smith and painter J M W Turner have featured on this note. A new series, G II, with Charles III on it, is due in 2024.

I never saw Mr Martyn again. Sadly, after a life lived rather too hard, John died on 29th January 2009 aged just sixty. An amazingly innovative and creative musician, if you don't know his stuff, really, give it a listen. *Solid Air*, released in 1973 is brilliant.

89 The Albany bar where John Martyn and I supped Rusty Nails.
No idea how many. We sat at the far end.

The next day we drove 200 miles to Redcar. Didn't know Teesside. All I knew was we were to play the Coatham Bowl[i]. Being a soppy, soft southerner, I imagined some large circular venue with tiered seats though without wondering why a place like Coatham/Redcar would want/need such an establishment. But it was clearly a well-recognised venue, advertising gigs in the back pages of the *Melody Maker* on a weekly basis. In fact, *Van der Graaf Generator* played there the week before us, and the *Pat Travers Band* was due the week after.

I was thus somewhat surprised when we arrived at the gig to find the place was a less-than-glamorous bowling alley. The stage was barely a stage, and the ceiling height barely accommodated our lighting rig. When we played, the heat from the lights was so great I could feel my hair shrivelling. As I was already displaying the first signs of male pattern baldness and valued every hair which deigned to remain on my head, this was not good news. It was not quite the finale the tour deserved.

---

[i] Later renamed the Redcar Bowl, it was demolished in 2014. A rather swish new leisure centre has since been built on the site.

90 The re-named Coatham Bowl
Shortly before its demolition in 2014

Our hotel that night was the *Royal York* in Coatham Road, just along from the gig. Seven years earlier, on 22nd December 1970, and as the *York Hotel*, it had burnt down with the loss of four lives. Re-named the *Royal York*, after it was re-opened by the Duchess of Gloucester, it was owned by the then Chairman of Middlesbrough FC. Just so you know.

Thus ended the *801 Listen Now Tour*, though, on 14th November, the band reconvened for a John Peel session recorded at their Delaware Studios[i]. There was a vague intention to add some European dates in early 1978, but then other things got in the way. A new Manzanera solo album and, far more significantly, a group reunion.

---

[i] This was released in 2001 with some other tracks on the *Manzanera Archives: Rare One* CD and can be heard at a variety of locations on *YouTube*.

ENDNOTES:

[1] Interview with Douglas Keay, *Women's Own*, 23rd September 1987.

[2] Griffiths, P, *A Question of Colour?*, 1966.

[3] Court Of Appeal, Civil Division, R *v Secretary of State for the Home Department, ex parte Hosenball*, 25th, 28th and 29th March 1977.

[4] Ibid.

[5] Ibid.

[6] Campbell, D, *Official Secrecy and British Libertarianism*, The Socialist Register, 1979.

[7] Tony Bunyan: *The History and Practice of the Political Police in Britain*, 1976. Review by Rob Reiner of 2nd edition 1980 in *Crime and Social Justice*, No. 13, Summer 1980, pages 55-8.

[8] *The Guardian*, Chile under Pinochet – a chronology, 24th March 1999.

K-SCOPE

L ET'S BE HONEST, *K-Scope* was done in an increasing rush as the imminent *Roxy* reunion loomed. It might have benefited from some of the time and attention to detail bestowed on *Listen Now*. Well, that's what I used to think. I will admit that, for a long time, I regarded the album as perhaps the weakest of Phil's three solo albums (to that point), thinking it a less internally coherent piece, with some high points, but rather more lows. But, listening to it for the first time in many a long year, I have changed my opinion. In fact, I am more than pleasantly surprised.

There is, perhaps because of the fast-approaching deadline, an urgency about some of the playing not present on *Diamond Head* and *Listen Now*. Some of the lyric themes and imagery carry forward from that latter album in things like *Remote Control* and *Slow Motion TV*, and *Walking Through Heaven's Door* has clear links to the content of *City of Light*, but the two Manzanera band instrumentals have a drive not present on previous albums. The album's coda, *You Are Here*, has a lyricism and melancholy all its own. And, throughout, Simon Phillips and *Split Enz's* Eddie Rayner are immense!

Writing for the album started in 1977 once the final vocal tracks had been added to *Listen Now*. At this time, Phil had no plans other than to make another solo album and, as it turned out, put together a band to promote *Listen Now*. In the meantime, the same basic trio which had written the previous album repaired to St Ann's Hill Court to kick ideas around. The only difference was that, on 26th May, I passed my driving test (first time!) and could now drive down rather than get a train from Waterloo.

The album would eventually consist of ten tracks:

two group instrumentals, *K-Scope* and *N-Shift*, written by Phil;
a solo instrumental by Phil – *You Are Here*;
a proto-punk anthem called *Remote Control* written by Ian;
one track written by Phil and John Wetton, i.e. *Numbers*;
one PM/I Mac track entitled *Hot Spot*;
three PM/B Mac songs: *Cuban Crisis*, *Gone Flying* and *Walking Through Heaven's Door*; and
one on which Phil, Simon and I collaborated: *Slow Motion TV*

The Manzanera/MacCormick collaborations were all spawned from sessions in Phil's Chertsey abode. Again, Phil came forward with ideas which were then kicked around, rough demos recorded and distributed so that top lines and lyrics might be found. One of Phil's ideas we could not find a way forward on ended up as the track *Manifesto* on *Roxy Music's* eponymous album.

From late 1977 through to the spring of 1978 recording sessions were fitted in, some at *Basing Street*, but the bulk of the album was recorded between March and May at *Yes* bass player Chris Squire's *Sun Park Studios*.

Two of the tracks recorded there, *Remote Control* and *Slow Motion TV*, utilised the 1977 touring band. Written by Ian before the *801* Tour, *Remote Control* was more than a nod to the burgeoning punk scene. It was something the audience could pogo to, as was proved when it was included in the set list for the tour. Two demos were recorded of the song pre-tour, one pretty much as appears on *K-Scope* and another, since released on *Rare One*, a jokey, laid-back, West Coast, 'psychedelic' version, the veritable antithesis of punk. Fun, but silly. *Slow Motion TV* was another track worked up before the tour and to which Simon contributed both in its composition and its final recording.

The remaining Manzanera/MacCormick songs, and Phil's two instrumentals, reunited the original *801 Live* rhythm section. Yes, Simon Phillips was back. We would play on six of the backing tracks with Simon joining Phil and John Wetton on the track *Numbers*. This was recorded at a separate session by Phil and John and, I believe, Simon's drums added later. This always seemed to me somewhat of an outlier on the album. It didn't quite 'fit'. A purely personal opinion obviously but, whilst I love John's bass playing on almost everything he did, especially the two *Family* albums, *Fearless* and *Bandstand*, and with *King Crimson*, this was missing from this piece. To be honest, I don't really 'get' it.

Phil had the structure of the two band instrumentals, *K-Scope* and *N-Shift*, pretty much down and for Simon and me it was simply a case of providing the foundations and a few flourishes. The intro to *K-Scope*, of course, was later sampled for *No Church in the Wild* by Kanye West (or Ye, or St, or whatever the bloated ego calls itself nowadays) and Jay-Z in 2011. The resulting royalties contributed considerably more than loose change to the Manzanera pension fund[i].

After the backing track was recorded, the sound was enhanced by a typical sax 'Big Band' courtesy of Mel Collins, with a brief flourish of the *Gizmo* with the help of Lol Creme (to be heard about 1:30-1:50) and, at the end, a typical Manzanera non-standard guitar solo played on his *Rickenbacker* 12-string and reminiscent of another outing of the *Ricky* on the *Quiet Sun* track *Trot*.

The other group instrumental was *N-Shift* which was the last time I got to play with the late Francis Monkman. Perhaps not as immediately urgent as *K-Scope* it, too, features, Señor Manzanera on 12-string on a track which chugs along nicely.

---

[i] See *https://www.independent.co.uk/arts-entertainment/music/features/phil-manzanera-on-jay-z-kanye-west-and-the-riff-that-changed-his-life-10128766.html*

The other songs had seen a rather longer gestation period as Ian and I came up with vocal parts and lyrics. Their subject matter would in some cases carry forward from *Listen Now*. In running order they were:

Cuban Crisis, a track kept afloat by Eddie Rayner's keyboard work and Simon's playful drums. The bass part confirmed, if there was ever any doubt, that I was no Aston 'Family Man' Barrett or Robbie Shakespeare;

Hot Spot on which, at Phil's absolute insistence, I had to reproduce the bass part from the demo recorded down in Chertsey note for note. Then, in a series of role reversals, I played the snare/bass drum over the guitar solo outro, whilst Eddie Rayner on a *Moog* took over from the bass guitar for the riff at the end. The backing track was then notable for the opening frenetic soprano sax solo by Mel Collins who also contributed an alto sax improv and his trade-mark one-man brass section;

Gone Flying which was propelled by Simon's nimble, driving drums; and

Walking through Heaven's Door on which, very sensibly, Phil replaced my rather pedestrian bass part on the second half of the song with John Wetton's infinitely better playing. Earlier in the piece, the extremely simple single-note bass part was played on a heavily compressed *Kramer* bass with an unusual aluminium neck. One for the technical nerds amongst us.

The last track is also notable for some lovely soprano sax playing by the inimitable Mel Collins. Listening back to his work on *Listen Now* and *K-Scope* it surprises me that Mel wasn't a far bigger 'name' in the music scene. Yes, he was a hugely in demand session player who worked with the best in the business for decades. Take a look at his *Wikipedia* page[i]. The list of bands and artists he has played with are as long as my arms and those of several others. But he never truly stepped into the limelight. He is a lovely man and, I assume, has been content to add his imaginative and lyrical playing to the work of whoever asked. If you look at the section on the page entitled 'Band by years' he was continuously employed pretty much every year from 1965 to the present day. It must be one of the most distinguished careers in popular music.

WITH THE BACKING TRACKS DOWN we now moved to vocals. Phil and I expected a continuation of the *Listen Now* sessions with Simon taking the lead. It was not to be, as Simon Ainley was hit by the first serious shock to anyone's preconceptions. Confidently expecting to carry on as the Manzanera lead singer, he turned up at the vocal overdub sessions with a heavy cold and a wonky voice. For once his timing was seriously bad. Phil

---

[i] https://en.wikipedia.org/wiki/Mel_Collins

was a man in a hurry. Bryan Ferry had finalised the recording of his fifth solo album, *The Bride Stripped Bare*, and word was received that the three-year long *Roxy* sabbatical was coming to an end. Everyone needed some serious injections of dosh or, rather, the creative juices were flowing. A new album and a world tour beckoned. Phil's timescale for recording and mixing the album was suddenly and dramatically curtailed. Thus, a replacement vocalist was required, like, *now*, man and, unfortunately for Simon, one was available in the shape of *Split Enz* singer and crazed All Black Tim Finn.

Phil knew Tim and his brother Neil (later to form the hugely successful *Crowded House*) from his time producing the New Zealand band's second studio album, *Second Thoughts*. Phil had seen the band when on tour with Australia and their eccentric and eclectic sound appealed. Neil joined the band in April 1977 when they recorded their third album, *Dizrythmia* (they liked a good pun), but the band then hit something of a dead-end. Thus, three of them, the brothers Finn and brilliant keyboard player Eddie Rayner, were at a loose end. Good for them, not so for Simon. His contribution was ruthlessly reduced to a few rhythm guitar chops and a third of a publishing royalty on one track. Then, he was history. And soon to fall into the clutches of two guys called Dave at a *Young's* pub, *The Railway Bell*, in Gipsy Hill, South London. Alcohol. Dangerous stuff.

Tim now took his place on every song bar two, with Neil adding extra backing vocals as required.

My lyric to *Cuban Crisis* tested Tim Finn's lung capacity to its limits, especially the lines which seem have baffled almost all of the lyric web sites (which clearly just copy one another as they all reproduce the same errors) as they needed to be sung in one breath:

Disposable tunes
That's when 'moon' rhymes with 'June'
Seems to ruffle her conscience
And give her the pique
How else could I pay
For those long months away
With those so special people
Who live in Mustique?

An inconsequential little number, one is amused by its pretension.

Hot Spot was much a more serious affair. One might describe it as Armageddon rock or Post-Nuclear catastrophe disco. Take your pick. Ian managed to pack in references to all sorts of armaments in a post-apocalyptic lyric, the second verse of which reads (again mis-translated everywhere on the web):

My pickup told me I'm a lazy dog coz I dig to go cruisin'
And I was riding high on the hog until I saw what she was using
I said "hey Baby what you need a needle for?"
She said, "it used to be illegal Now it's the law
We all shooting atropine To make damn sure
Every day since they started up the third world war"
Let's go where the night sky breaks
With red flames and your bare skin rots
Where the melting girders make the building quake
And everybody's burning, burning at the Hot Spot
It's a hellfire creation
Nobody wants to know
The neutron radiation
Makes your body glow

So, let's get to the cheerful references:

Lazy Dog, a cheap kinetic energy weapon used by the US in Vietnam[i];
Cruisin', Cruise missiles like those deployed in Britain under Thatcher[ii];
Hog: a reference to the *Fairchild Republic A-10 Thunderbolt II* a US military aircraft *aka* the *Warthog* or simply *Hog*[iii]; and

---

[i] According to *Wikipedia*, the *Lazy Dog* is a small, unguided kinetic projectile used by the U.S. Air Force. 1.75 inches (44 mm) long and 0.5 inches (13 mm) in diameter, weighing about 0.7 ounces (20 g), they were designed to be dropped from aircraft. They contained no explosive charge but, as they fell, they developed significant kinetic energy making them lethal. Able to easily penetrate soft cover such as the jungle canopy, several inches of sand, or light armour. *Lazy Dog* munitions were simple and relatively cheap ... Used primarily during the Korean and the Vietnam Wars. [*https://en.wikipedia.org/wiki/Lazy_Dog_(bomb)*].

[ii] The German *V1 Flying Bomb*, the Doodlebug as it was known colloquially, was the first operational cruise missile. Since then, subsonic, supersonic and hypersonic variants have been developed world-wide. It was the *BGM-109G Ground Launched Cruise Missile* which was deployed from July 1982 at both RAF Greenham Common and RAF Molesworth under the command of the *501st Tactical Missile Wing*. They were eventually removed in 1991. I remember being stopped by the police one night at a roundabout on the A303 near Andover only to see a convoy of cruise missile equipped transporters out on exercises. Though based at Greenham Common, if ever used in anger, they were to be sent out into the countryside to fire from remote and undetectable locations. This would have made the UK a prime target for Soviet retaliation or pre-emptive strikes. The deployment of such weaponry added Britain to the list of the USA's 'Unsinkable aircraft carriers' which it had created around the world, most notably in Taiwan.

[iii] This was a heavily-armoured, single-seat, twin-turbofan, straight-wing, subsonic attack aircraft developed during the 1970s after the US found its existing close support aircraft inadequate during the Vietnam conflict. Its main armament was a

Atropine, an antidote to chemical weapons poisoning.

So, all in all, a bouncy little number about the end of the world. Which leaves:

Gone Flying' and *Walking Through Heaven's Door* the lyrics of which share a theme of people taking a refuge in drugs or, being fed a convenient diet of unhealthy shit – political, pharmaceutical, dietary – to make them compliant. *Big Brother* rides again.

Gone Flying was a track worked up *chez* Manzanera and was one of two tracks on which I sing lead vocals, partly because of Simon's dodgy larynx and partly because Tim Finn was not around. The other track on which I take up the lead singer's mantle in the absence of anyone more suitable was *Walking Through Heaven's Door*. Seems to me to work quite well, but then I would say that wouldn't I.

Finally *You Are Here was* recorded solo by Phil and was a precursor to his 1982 album *Primitive Guitars*. It provides a wistful and melancholy ending to the album. I really like it.

So, *K-Scope*. A lot better than I remember.

On 14th, 15th and 27th June, the album was cut at *Strawberry Mastering* in Strutton Ground, Westminster, a recently opened facility of which Rick Dickson, previously manager of *10cc*, was a director. The cutting engineer was a guy called Melvyn Abrahams who certainly knew what he was about. Behind an unassuming door in the street which was basically a market *Strawberry* was plush and well-equipped and was later used by *Roxy* and *The Bee Gees* amongst many others.

The album was released that autumn but, by September, other events overtook everything else. *Roxy* announced their reunion and plans to record a new album. And I, too, had fallen into the clutches of the 'two guys named Dave'.

Against my better judgement, I became a *Random*.

General Electric GAU-8/A Avenger seven-barrel 20 mm autocannon. It first came into service with the *354th Tactical Fighter Wing* in October 1977. It served in both Gulf Wars, in Afghanistan and against Islamic State. It is still in service.

RANDOM HOLD

D ULWICH COLLEGE IS, as you all now know, a large public school in South East London. About 1,400 boys go there. It sprawls across acres of prime suburban turf, surrounded playing fields and the nearby golf course. It's one of the wealthiest schools in the country. It 'owns' Dulwich Village. It controls the look and the feel of the area surrounding even down to the colour of your front door.

In the 60s and 70s, the school was renowned for its academic excellence, it's sport... and, for a period of about six years either side of 1970, for producing a rash of more, and often, less successful rock and roll musicians.

First up came three young gentlemen, resplendent in their school blazers and caps. Their names: Philip Targett-Adams, Charles Hayward and William MacCormick. Philip, a boarder in Blew House, was in the school swimming and water polo teams and played Number 8 for the Second XV rugby team. Bill was carving out a name for himself as a part-time 'school rebel'. Also a member of the 2nd XV, he was in the school 1st XI at cricket where he and a colleague caused consternation by refusing to have their hair cut the regulation length above the ears. Dangerous! Then came Charlie. He didn't play sport unless absolutely forced. He got his exercise smashing the living daylights out of a large, red glitter, double bass drum, *Premier* drum kit.

This bunch were to become the core of the justly renowned school psychedelic rock band *Pooh and the Ostrich Feather*. But you know all of this.

Unknown to them, several youngsters of varying ages attended their regular performances in the School's Baths Hall. Each of them harboured some, as yet, unformed desire to be up there performing, posing and generally larking about. They were, in age order, David Ferguson, Simon Ainley and David Rhodes.

DF was serious, non-sporty, heavily into Labour Party politics and interested in the theatre and drinking large quantities of *Holsten Pils* (or whatever its equivalent was in those days).

Simon was not so serious, a bit sporty in a light-hearted fashion and interested in ladies, rock 'n' roll, ladies, beer and ladies (or whatever their equivalent was in those days).

DR was *very* serious for one so young, played guitar, spent his time intimidating his opposite number in school rugby matches (he played hooker for the school 1st XV. For our American cousins that's a position not a profession) and was planning to become very interested in *Courage Special Bitter* when he could convince the barman at 'The Dog', the local pub in Dulwich Village, *aka The Crown and Greyhound*, he was old enough.

Little did they know that, several years later, they would all become professional rock musicians (with varying degrees of success) and that four of them would, in 1978, become part of the same eccentric and hugely unsuccessful rock combo: *Random Hold*.

But then, that's not their fault. Dulwich didn't teach Precognition at A-Level in those days.

RANDOM HOLD WAS THE BRAINCHILD of David Rhodes and David Ferguson. The sonic, musical and visual personality of the band, throughout all its incarnations, was theirs. No-one else impacted significantly on the band's character. Theirs was the vision and the music. Variously described as 'gloom rock' and 'songs for swinging suicides', the band's music tended towards bleakness and darkness with an underlying air of threat and malevolence. And that was on a good night.

The initial drive to make music or, perhaps more accurately, create sounds, was spawned by the two David's disappointment and disillusion with the Manzanera/Eno *801* concert at the *Queen Elizabeth Hall* on Friday, 3rd September 1976 (*Ed.* although I quite enjoyed it). The two found themselves sitting next to one another and, after the performance, decided – either over a curry (Rhodes), or in the pub (Ferguson), whichever a few beers were bound to be involved – that the concert lacked 'danger', was too mainstream and was a waste of the assembled musicians' talents. They could do better, they concluded.

The two knew one another in a distant way. Three years separated them at Dulwich and, for a time, Rhodes messed about musically with Ferguson's younger brother. After leaving Dulwich, Ferguson went to the *London School of Slavonic and East European Studies* to study Serbo-Croat (as one does, although we never heard him utter word one in that particular Balkan tongue). On becoming the only Serbo-Croat graduate in the UK, he embarked on a variety of jobs, many involving forays into the theatre where he sound engineered, stage managed and made noises 'stage left' in productions from Edinburgh to London via Stoke.

All the while, he maintained the close family interest in the 'about to self-destruct' British Labour Party. This led to numerous acrimonious political arguments with me as, in 1973, I had joined that equally hopeless cause, the Liberal Party. We drank in the same pub, *The Railway Bell*, in Gipsy Hill, South London, and we could often be seen shouting at one another in a reasoned and rational way late on Friday nights, a pint of *Young's Bitter* in each hand.

David Rhodes, meanwhile, having survived his final year at Dulwich (playing, for one not too large, a peculiarly and riskily aggressive season for the school's rugby 1st XV), went on the classic path for the budding rock musician. He studied 'Fine Art', first at Leeds and then London.

Their co-incident arrival in adjoining seats on the South Bank can be viewed, therefore, as serendipitous (unless, of course, you were employed by one of the record companies that went on to lose thousands signing them in later years).

Having been badgered into pursuing the decision to turn round modern music by Rhodes' then girlfriend, the two Davids set to work with a will. The fact that Mr Ferguson had no particular musical skills and that Mr Rhodes had successfully forgotten most of the guitar licks learned at school was not, at least initially, a problem. This was going to be experimental music with a capital X!

Armed with Rhodes' guitar, a *stylophone*, and an old bass guitar, the two perfected reproducing the sounds of thousands of insects in a mating frenzy until, by accident, DF played a note on the bass, bottom E probably, by mistake. Suddenly, the whole world of tonality was laid before them. Playing to people, rather than teasing mosquitoes, became the objective.

91 Manscheinen - their PR pitch

A series of small musical *soirées* was arranged in the wholly inappropriate surroundings of working-class Rotherhithe. Four nights, the 16th-19th December 1976, were taken up with performances at the *Warehouse Theatre* at 99, Rotherhithe Street, SE16 in front of a total of 24 friends and more or less bemused punters. Quite what the locals made of it is not recorded but, in a later interview, Ferguson recalls:

> "One gig was so bad we took the audience down to the pub for a drink instead."

I was always unavoidably detained whenever it came to an invitation to these shows. He even went to the lengths of visiting the Black Country to see his team Wolves beat Bolton 1-0 as an excuse for his absence.

1976 slid inevitably into 1977. The Rhodes/Ferguson axis developed a new sound and adopted a new identity – *Manscheinen*. The Teutonic overtones reflected their interest in bands like *Can* and *Kraftwerk*.

They tried becoming marginally more accessible. They even composed a press release. *Manscheinen's* publicity was a little rough and ready in those days. A single sheet of A4, one side comprised some rather murky black logos of indeterminate species, and the other some erratically typed red text. This piece of prose gives an illuminating insight into the mindset of the two Davids at the time:

> "*Manscheinen* are a performing duo currently working in the field of electric instruments. In no way, however, do they wish to be classified as simply another heartless electronic noise producing outfit. Their music is not synthesised but rather it consists of processed natural sounds. The music evolves from improvisation which is later codified and structured to retain as far as possible the spontaneity of the original idea when in performance.
>
> *Manscheinen* are David Ferguson and David Rhodes.
>
> David Rhodes is a sculptor who has worked both in Leeds and London. Educated primarily at Dulwich College and then at *St Martin's School of Art*, David plays guitar and was involved in the nascent Dulwich music school which was to produce *Quiet Sun* amongst other more peculiar offshoots.
>
> David Ferguson was also educated at Dulwich College and then went on to read Slavonic Studies at *London University*. This was then followed by a two-year period working in repertory theatres in Stoke, London and Edinburgh. David plays a bass and stylophone (*à la* Rolf[i]), and has written various scores for the theatre, notably the *Liverpool Playhouse* production of *Equus*.
>
> Both David's ambitions when they grow up are to be swimming pools.
>
> *Manscheinen* are available to play at either your coming-out or coming-in party. We also have a tape of short tunes to smell your wet buds, should you feel so inclined.
>
> For further information contact: David Rhodes/David Ferguson.
> Ask for David."

It does not appear that our two partially excavated swimming pools were immediately inundated with numerous offers of work. Or, indeed, *any* offers of work. Looking back from a distance of years, one is not remotely surprised.

---

[i] I.e, the late and completely unlamented convicted paedophile Rolf Harris.

Meanwhile, two soon, or eventually, to become *Randoms* were at work together, as you will know if you bothered to read the previous chapter. So, whilst the two Davids pursued popular success and critical acclaim with *Manscheinen*, the 1977 version of the *801* – Ainley, MacCormick, Manzanera, Thompson and Skinner (along with a veritable host of guest stars) – swept all before them with a rollicking tour of Great Britain.

Rather less 'rollicking' was the *Manscheinen* demo tape then in swift circulation around the music business. It was later described by one recipient, Allan Jones of the *Melody Maker*, as:

> "… extended, largely abstract, formless pieces; tape loops and dislocated melodic fragments that spend an inordinate amount of time running slowly on the spot."

Allan is always a nice, polite man. In this case, excessively so.

The tape did not unlock untold riches for the 2 Ds. No, they were to continue suffering for their art, whilst Simon and I were getting legless for ours in places as widespread as Dundee, Redcar and Plymouth.

1977 ended with us working expectantly towards the next Manzanera album (*K-Scope*) whilst Rhodes and Ferguson concluded that playing something that the listener could sing along to might well be the answer to commercial success after all. They also decided a new name was in order. Regular frequenters of the odd Public House, a phrase from a fruit machine seemed eminently appropriate. *Random Hold* it was.

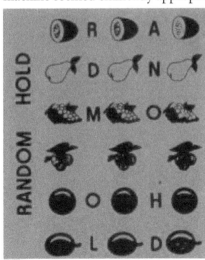

92 The first Random Hold demo. Imagine the background is orange.

A new demo tape was recorded, a rather fetching little electronic number clad in an orange cover. One side was cunningly recorded to sound like the music was being played at the bottom of a deep well through several layers of thick mud, and the other *was* recorded at the bottom of a deep well through several layers of thick mud in an establishment in Covent Garden called *The Basement Club*. An appropriate venue given the band's position in the musical pecking order.

But all was not lost. The earliest known coverage generated by *Random Hold* was the piece below (accompanied by the photo even further below) in a local newspaper, the *South East London Mercury*. It appeared on 29th September 1977:

SELECTRIC

It makes a change to come across a band that doesn't depend on ripping guitar licks and screaming vocals to put its music across.

Random Hold are such a select band. This two-piece was formed a year ago by Dave Ferguson and Dave Rhodes, who between them play various keyboards, bass, electric chordaphone and guitar.

They achieve their distinctive sound by utilizing a series of process systems involving tape delay, noise filter units, de-synchronised sound, rhythm generators and many other 'little black boxes'.

Crammed into Ferguson's Camberwell home's front room, amid £5,500-worth of fancy-looking equipment and miles and miles of wire, the duo has been laying down tracks for a demo tape.

But what happens if the recognised companies don't like their music?

Ferguson replied without hesitation: "We believe in our music enough to bring out a recording on a private pressing. Nothing has happened to rock music in the past six years. It's vitally important to move forward all the time. We want to change the basis of music. We realise that we could struggle doing it, but we like to think of ourselves as the Second New Wave – or at least the lasting result of the new wave. Our music is 'body music' – it excites. A strong rhythm is an essential part of all our songs. We want to expand and are forming a theatrical roadshow for live gigs."

They gave me a sneak preview of the demo tape. It has exceptional sound quality. The numbers have a solid, rhythmic, almost hypnotic beat running through them. There seems to be a heavy *Pink Floyd* influence in their writing, though both Davids dislike the band.

You can sample *Random Hold's* music at the *Basement Club*, Covent Garden, tomorrow night.

Rob Hope

All I can say is that I am not sure to which demo tape Mr Hope was listening.

As we know, a combination of a virus and terribly bad timing did for Simon's prospects of continuing with Mr Manzanera, who was now back with *Roxy* working on the *Manifesto* album. But, as ever, one man's cloud was another's mixed blessing. The 2 Ds were experimenting with song formats, though, as you might expect, they were not of the standard verse/chorus/verse/chorus/bridge/middle-eight/verse/chorus variety. They even tried working with other musicians! One such was an extremely tall, good-looking drummer called Pete Phipps, of whom more later.

One night, propped up by the bar of the *Railway Bell*, they sensed Simon's crushing disappointment at missing out on a promising musical career. Thinking that a second guitarist and another voice might be useful in their pursuit of musical acceptance they pounced with all the ruthlessness of a pair of beer-drinking piranhas. In his weakened state, Ainley put up little resistance and, before he knew it, he was a full-time *Random*.

93 Dave Ferguson's front room.
The two Davids looking typically cheerful

A drummer was found but then they came up against the same problem experienced by *Quiet Sun* seven years earlier – a dearth of suitable bass players. Then the drummer disappeared too. Their solution to this problem was not, as in 1970, to employ someone who had never before touched the bass. Rather, they put the bass and drum parts on tape and then played along to it. An ingenious solution, and one soon emulated by musicians with far less talent and creativity than the two Davids, though, with these others, it was a way of covering up their own gross inadequacies. However innovative this move was, it was one which failed to impress some audiences who thought they were miming. As we shall soon discover.

Anyway, looking like 80% of a normal band, contact was made with several agencies with a view to widening their limited gigging experience. One such, *Albion*, controlled two well-known small venues in London, *The Nashville* and *The Hope and Anchor*. They were also trying to set up a record label and were on the look-out for new bands with innovative musical ideas and a sound to match. Step forward *Random Hold*.

94 *Random Hold*
(clockwise from the top left):
Dave F, David R, Michael (soon to disappear), Simon

A few gigs were organised and invitations sent out to friends and others to attend. By this time, with the *K-Scope* sessions at an end (cutting was completed at *Strawberry* in Strutton Ground on 27th May), I was at something of a loose end. I spent most of his time playing cricket (with several mean sessions of swing bowling for the Old Alleynian 1st XI[i]), a bit of footie and the odd energetic set of squash. So, as ever, I was fit. Otherwise, though, I was a bit perplexed about what the future held. Manzanera was going to be occupied for some time to come with *Roxy Music*, five years as it turned out, and I was running out of friends with whom to play. Nevertheless, of one thing I was certain, no way was I going to see that bunch of lunatics called *Random Hold. No Way*!

The trouble was, there was simply no getting away from them. Every Friday, and quite a few Saturdays, I met up with one or all of the band in the pub. Simon cajoled. DF grunted. DR muttered obliquely. Eventually, a mid-week cricket match in Epsom was cancelled and, in a moment of serious weakness, I was eventually persuaded to go and see the band play on Thursday, 20th July at the *Nashville*. To my horror I was pleasantly surprised, even excited. Something was seriously wrong.

The next gig I attended was at the *Rock Garden* on Thursday, 10th August 1978. The *Randoms* were to support *Adam and the Ants*. The *Rock Garden* was never the most attractive of venues. Okay, let's not beat around the bush, it was a filthy little hole in the ground. Entered by a set of stairs akin to a rather dubious Gents' loo in a seedy part of Soho, the stage was

---

[i] The season's bowling figures were, as I am sure you are desperate to know: 305 overs, 64 maidens, 926 runs and 39 wickets. Not quite as good as the year before.

tiny, the ceiling low, the walls damp, the floor slippery and the lighting dim. The only things smaller than the stage were the two tiny and dingy dressing rooms which were, if anything, even dirtier and more decrepit than the main room. A dump with no redeeming features.

By this time, *Adam and the Ants* had a couple of Peel sessions under the belts and, a few days before, signed a recording contract with *Decca*, but they were a year away from their first even minor hit single[i]. For reasons not quite clear, a bunch of neo-Nazi hooligans masquerading as a rock music crowd attached themselves to *Adam and the Ants* (themselves a pleasant enough group of lads) and, when not pogoing and gobbing in unison to the seriously unsubtle *Ant* rhythms, they liked to spend their time intimidating, assaulting and generally aggravating anyone who did not accept their peculiarly aggressive, low-brow view of life.

Tonight, it would be the turn of the *Randoms* to suffer. To make matters worse, the *Ants'* nest in front of them could not understand the absence of a real, live drummer and the presence, instead, of a whirring tape machine. Jumping to the conclusion that the whole band was miming, they were subjected to a torrent of verbal abuse, phlegm and beer, some of it still in the glass, within a few moments of arriving on stage. Retreat was the only option in face of such animal aggression and the band recoiled off stage pursued by a final volley of swear words, spit and venom. They were best off out of it. Later, one of the bouncers was beaten up, and attending police found a variety of weapons both about the person and discarded around the room and the road outside. It was an exciting night.

Despite the mini-riot, I was still intrigued. And the two Davids sensed vulnerability.

Six days later, on Wednesday, 16th August, Dave Ferguson and Simon Ainley visited me at the small house in Penge I shared with my then girlfriend (now wife) Helen. Over cups of tea and idle chit chat, the cunning couple slipped a quick, sly question into the conversation. Before I knew it, I said 'yes'. Grinning hugely, Ferguson and Ainley made good their escape with a cheery 'see you on Monday, then'.

It was only a while later that I realised I had:

1. agreed to join *Random Hold*; and
2. undertaken to pay all overheads for the foreseeable future.

We started rehearsing the following Monday. Whilst rehearsals carried on in a desultory fashion at a variety of rooms known variously as *Fair Deal*, *Silversound* and *Access*, I started to contact useful people in *The Business* to see what sort of interest I could rustle up. High on the list were *Albion*

---

[i] *Kings of the Wild Frontier* released on *CBS* which reached No. 48.

and my acquaintances at *Roxy's EG Management*. In addition, the princely sum of £8.90 was spent on an advert for the *Melody Maker's Musicians Wanted* columns. It read:

Wanted: drummer for modern band. Immediate rehearsals. Deals pending. Phone.....

As with the music, the advert was taut, spare, (muscular?) and to the point. Of course, the use of the word 'modern' was a well-known code amongst musos. It meant 'so far ahead of its time no record company in its right mind will touch this with a barge pole' but the band weren't to know that. And 'deals pending', well, that was an out and out lie, equivalent to saying 'National Lottery jackpot win pending' nowadays.

The band continued its tour of the rehearsal rooms of South London. One day it was *Visual Earth Studios* then it was back to *Fair Deal*. By mid-September a few unemployed drummers had been in touch, much against their better judgement. Many were auditioned but one was called. For a few brief days, Richard Marcangelo became a *Random*.

95 L-R: Ainley, Rhodes, MacCormick, Ferguson, Marcangelo
Ainley and Rhode's trousers caught in an early 70s time loop

A tape with three songs was now available, having been recorded at my expense on the 21ˢᵗ August, and it was dutifully hawked around a cosmopolitan bunch of journalists, record executives, DJs and others. Amongst the seriously underwhelmed recipients were: John Gill and Angus McKinnon of *Sounds*, Ian Birch at the *NME*, John Peel, *WEA, Polydor, Island, EMI, Virgin, CBS, Arista, Sire, Radar, MCA, Phonogram, Charisma, Chrysalis, RCA* and *Bronze*.

We were nothing if not thorough.

By now, Marcangelo sensing which way the wind was blowing, and, being offered a gig that paid (an albeit very small amount), was off into the sunset. Another *MM* ad was placed and, whilst we awaited the inevitable tidal wave of interest, the band headed off into the country in classic 'getting their heads together' mode. David Ferguson's parents, sensibly abandoning their son, were living in the pleasant Oxfordshire countryside. Rather less sensibly they said 'yes' when asked if he could bring a few friends round for a few days. The attractive village of Stanton St John was more than just a decent place to hang out, make strange noises and breath fresh air. It also possessed a wonderful pub serving *Wadsworth's 6X* and a publican who described the then pound notes as 'little green drinking vouchers'. Heaven.

After a refreshing break, and with many of Ferguson seniors' neighbours now calling for them to be expelled from the village and, preferably, the county, the boys returned to London and, oh happy day, within a few days met, heard, then hired a new drummer. David Leach, tall, blonde, tousle haired and bespectacled seemed just what the doctor ordered. Rehearsals took on greater energy and urgency.

To celebrate this fact, I was now spending money like water. September saw a first instalment of £150 for rehearsals and adverts (£1,000+ in modern dosh). October was altogether heavier with expenses mounting to £600 (£4,000 nowadays) including equipment hire, more rehearsals, press handouts and subsidies to various members of the band who otherwise might have starved. In spite of persistent attempts to generate some interest, the only return on this investment came with the line-up's first two paid gigs - £25 (£150) at the *Corn Dolly*, a pub in Oxford, on 24th October, and the 'don't spend it all at once' sum of £10 for a performance at the aforementioned *Basement Club* in Covent Garden three days later.

Early November saw several more appearances:

Wednesday, 1st November - *Rock Garden*, Covent Garden (£15)
Friday, 10th November - *The Music Machine* (£15)
Sunday, 12th November - *Rock Garden* (£15)

In the meantime, a small piece in *Sounds* by John Gill raised morale somewhat. Entitled *Dr Caligari's Greatest Hits* it gave short write ups to *Ten Bands Who Are... Different*. Amongst the bands mentioned were the *Art Bears*, Charlie Hayward's *This Heat*, the extraordinary *Throbbing Gristle* as well as the *Randoms*. It was a short piece, but welcome nonetheless:

"*Random Hold* were (surely 'was', John) formed a couple of years ago as what apparently was an experimental music group, heavily involved in improvisation and electronics. They have undergone considerable line-up changes since their inception (one line-up included bassist Duncan Lane, brother of Malcolm from *Metabolist*). By all accounts are well-connected in the new music scene, as their acquisition of ex-*801* bassist Bill MacCormick would suggest.

Each line-up change seems to have brought them closer to the rock mainstream and they might be brutally categorised as a less arty/more rocky version of *Quiet Sun* (*Ed.* You what?) – or *The Pop Group* minus the 'primitivism'. Present incarnation is strongly into harmonies but they lay these against cryptic arrangements of keyboards, guitar, bass and drums. Rhythms and melodies travel a parallel course to the likes of *XTC*. Hit the newsprint a while back when they were viciously attacked by an *Adam and the Ants* audience. They seem to have had more success in dealings with the machine (*Ed.* WtF?!) – of whom they are not afraid – than the rest of the groups mentioned herein. They have had brief, but invariably fraught, relationships with various booking agencies, and have also attracted the interest of a few labels. Are currently working in studios on demo tapes with no particular label in sight (*Ed.* That's more like it) and are frequent giggers around London and environs."

On Friday, 24th November, the boys set off back up the A40 towards Oxford where we were due to play *Pembroke College Students Union* for the unprecedented sum of £60 + 50% of the door money. We played, pretty well so it seemed, wandered up the road in search of food, and returned to find that some student pranksters had let down all four tyres on the van. We eventually made it back to London in the early hours of the morning. In an effort to forget, I took myself off to White Hart Lane to see Wolves lose to Spurs. In spite of this, we still generated a small but enthusiastic mention in an Oxford Student magazine. The author, masquerading under the title of *Our IBM Computer Correspondent*, stated:

Machine Men Demolish Pembroke College Shock Horror
Seeing *RANDOM HOLD* stuck in a list of 'different music' groups in the latest *Sounds* (next to *Throbbing Gristle* and *The Normal*) I went down to catch the second half of their set at *Pembroke College* Friday Night. Verily, they were more normal than *The Normal*, but produced a lovely tight sound, economically restraining their innovative style.

The bassist was (I think) with Phil Manzanera, and gives out some good undulating, sometimes jazzy, basslines and the rest of the band seem to build on this, with the effective lead guitar drones bordering at times on the *Buzzcockish* (though not boring).

Imagewise, it was short hair and ties, and they seemed confident enough (even if they didn't talk to the audience much). Mankind meets the Machine it certainly wasn't, and keyboards player David Ferguson asserted after that their music is 'very, human and personal'. On this I noted one song – *With People (not in love)*.

I liked it a lot (i.e. very pleasantly surprised) and so did the audience, though dancing was in little evidence (and the music was quite danceable). Mr Ferguson, on the dancing: 'I don't care so long as they get off on it in their own way'.

See them next time possible with an open mind (that's for the *Ants* fans, who gave them a hard time at the *Nashville* (*sic*). P.S. the fact that he said *P. Image* was brilliant is not why they get a good review!!!!"

Monday, 27th November was to be an important day. Sometime before, Alan Black and Alec Byrn from *Polydor* promised faithfully, i.e. cross my heart, etc., to visit. After several disappointments, it seemed the band would have the chance to impress some A&R men at long last. We booked *Wharf Studios* for the day. The 'studios' were located at the *New Concordia Wharf* on the Thames just east of Tower Bridge. It was part of a Dickensian rabbit warren of Victorian docks on the Bermondsey shore, next to an evil smelling sugar refinery. It consisted of a series of low-roofed rooms, some of which were sound-proofed and turned into rehearsal rooms. In a cost-cutting exercise to make George Osborne proud, the *Randoms* booked the smallest, and for several hours we practised earnestly, wearing overcoats and gloves against the damp cold that seeped into the building from the river. By 5 p.m. it was clear something was amiss. Then a phone call from the *Polydor* offices told the same old story. Something more important/enticing/interesting had come up and the two ABs weren't coming.

The general desire was to pack up, go to the pub and try to get warm but there was a problem. I had also invited journalist Allan Jones from the *Melody Maker*. We knew one another from times past and my involvement in the Manzanera projects, *801 Live* and *Listen Now*. Allan, being a decent sort, said he would come down so we would have to wait for him. With only a few minutes of our booked time left, a shivering and somewhat disorientated Jones appeared. He'd gone astray in the dimly lit back streets of Bermondsey, possibly had his pockets picked by the Artful Dodger, and only stumbled across this out-of-the-way establishment by chance.

Grudgingly, we agreed to make his journey worthwhile. As he stood on one side of the small studio we took up position on the other. After forty minutes it was mutually agreed enough was enough and all parties retired gratefully to the local pub for a long and increasingly hysterical chat. Then Jones disappeared into the night and we set off for our various homes.

Nothing appeared in the next edition of *Melody Maker* and, with nothing to do until 11th December, when we were due to re-appear at the *Music Machine*, the band spent a disconsolate ten days twiddling thumbs and wondering where the next week's rent would come from.

Thursday, 7th December, was to be another day's rehearsal at *Wharf.* Before he left, I wandered down the road to the local Indian grocery shop where I bought his daily newspaper and, today, the new edition of the *Melody Maker.* I idly flicked through it. On reaching page 19 I nearly walked under a car sitting innocently by the side of the road. Then, laughing maniacally, I sprinted up the road to the house and rushed to the phone.

Allan Jones had come up trumps. Big time.

96 RH looking our normal cheerful selves.
L-R: Ferguson, Ainley, Leach, Rhodes, MacCormick

THE MIDDLE CLASS ANSWERS BACK was the title. It was, perhaps, the, longest article ever carried by the *Melody Maker* (or any other music rag) about a band with no label, no manager, no publisher, and few prospects. It filled both centre pages and ran onto a third. Several fetching photographs adorned the piece. For those of you with time on your hands, the entire article is now to be found as *Appendix 13* (see page 420).

The impact of Allan's article was immediate. Although its timing, just before Christmas, meant that nothing definite was settled, suddenly I was in the strange position of A&R men phoning me, of A&R men being in when I called, of A&R men asking to meet at my convenience.

Allan followed up the interview with a rather more downbeat review of our December 11th gig at the dreaded *Music Machine* at King's Cross[i]. He was, shall we say, 'constructively critical':

---

[i] Previously the *King's Cross Theatre* at which *Mole* were unfortunate enough to play several times.

Music Machine
Allan Jones, *Melody Maker*, 23rd December 1978

The Music Machine in Camden Town is very possibly the least salubrious rock music venue in the capital, perhaps the entire country. At its best it resembles some especially grotesque, gothic chamber; at its most desperate it looks like the *Lyceum* transferred to hell and condemned to an eternity of slow decay. It was *Random Hold's* severe misfortune last Monday to appear on one of the venue's really bad nights.

The audience – a smattering of bondage punks, a few student nurses and their escorts and a clutch of A&R men lined up against the bar looking like plain clothes cops – could without any considerable difficulty have been forced into a small biscuit tin. The very atmosphere seemed to be suffering from some kind of terminal cancer.

It was not, then, the most celebrated location for one of this group's infrequent performances (they were actually supporting an Irish folk-rock group, of uncertain worth, called *Spud*). The sterile, lethargic atmosphere, the absence of an involved or interested audience and, a capricious sound system successfully conspired to undermine the band's potential. It wasn't so much that the circumstances defeated the subtleties of their music, rather that its intensity was entirely lost in the abject void of the *Music Machine*.

Simultaneously, the evening exposed their weaknesses and the vulnerability of their repertoire. Thus far in their brief career they have gigged only sporadically and they have yet to really test the strength and durability of several of their compositions; they need do extended run of gigs to isolate and define their strengths, as it were, and to either dispose of those items whose deficiencies detract from the impact of their better songs, or invest them with a more genuine force.

They suffer, too, at present from a lack of personality; their collective diffidence, and the absence of an individual whose identity (ego, even) is virile enough to create some kind of focus, lends to their appearance an unfortunate anonymity. They will have to learn – quickly – how best to communicate an empathy with their prospective audience: currently there is just too much shuffling of feet and muttering of incoherent asides whenever there is a pause of more than a minute between numbers.

These, perhaps, will be identified as minor points of criticism, but they are points which will have to be faced and considered if *Random Hold* are to fulfil their commercial aspirations. (And, I must just say, they need to sort out the visuals: coming on dressed in an assortment of second-hand suits and kipper ties is hardly an arresting image with which to confront the populace.) The news isn't all blue, however.

The were moments when *Random Hold*, most boldly overcame the manifold difficulties of the evening, most notably during *We Are People Out Of Love*, which featured a vocal of suspended menace from David Rhodes, which built to an explosive climax. *The Ballad*, too, possessed a sense of adventure and purpose which elsewhere seemed missing, with David Ferguson's keyboards creating dense atmospherics beneath the guitar interplay between Rhodes and Simon Ainley (their vocal interplay – chopping and swapping strategic lines – here and during *The Heart of a Crowd* was similarly charged with interest).

The most effective piece, though, was the already celebrated *Montgomery Clift*, its climax featuring the two guitarists alternating violent phrases that seemed to mount one upon the other in a. fierce conclusion that put one briefly in mind of the kind of virulent exchanges between Verlaine and Richard Lloyd on *Television's Marquee Moon*.

Random Hold now, need nothing more than to work. They should not be rushed into a recording studio to produce a debut album before they've really sharpened and defined their material. They should now be dumped in the back of a Transit; if that's what's needed, and made to confront a variety of audiences. Then they will find their own voice and record an album worthy of their promise."

There was little or nothing set up for January, except for another round of rehearsals. And a gig on Saturday 20th supporting, of all people, *The Troggs*. And, yes, they played *Wild Thing* along with obligatory Ocarina[i] solo courtesy of Reg Presley). Then, on the 24th, it was back to Oxford's *Corn Dolly* (DF knew the publican) with a third appearance on the 30th at the infamous *Rock Garden*.

But rehearsals took on a new urgency when *Polydor* offered us demo time in their studios off Oxford Street. We were given three days, Monday 15th to Wednesday 17th, in which to self-produce something impressive.

We did. Probably our best ever versions of *Second Nature* and *With People Out of Love* were put on tape and copies ferreted away for other ears to hear. Because the *MM* article hadn't just gingered up the foot-dragging *Polydor* A&R department. Just along the road from *Polydor's* offices were

---

[i] An ancient wind instrument popular amongst the Aztecs and Mayans. Brought to Europe whilst, back home, Cortes and his mates merrily slaughtered the local natives. I doubt any god, European or Central American, could work out quite how *The Troggs* of all people got hold of one.

those of *Chrysalis*. And, down Oxford Street to the east, was the home of newly formed *Genetic Records*, brainchild of Martin Rushent the producer of the recently successful *Stranglers*. All three were now courting the band, as were a variety of publishing companies and agencies.

97 The chat which changed our lives - briefly.
Enthusiastically about to talk to Allan Jones

On the night of Tuesday, 30ᵗʰ January the *Rock Garden* was unusually full. The slowly growing band of *Random Hold* supporters was almost outnumbered by teams of A&R men, music publishers and other music business hangers. They eyed one another suspiciously through the gloomy, foetid atmosphere. It was turning into a cattle auction, highest bid wins!

Such unwarranted attention was in danger of turning the boys' heads. Serious discussions about the nature of any record deal (low advances, good royalty rates, play the long game) were rapidly undermined by an ever-growing list of increasingly exotic and expensive equipment the band 'just had to have'. But, that night, the band played well. Be-suited businessmen pressed their way into the tiny dressing room offering congratulations, doling out cards, writing down phone numbers, whilst the sticky, grimy musicians knocked back pints of watery lager.

February became one long business meeting. Armed now with Ian Adams, a lawyer knowledgeable about such matters, I sprinted from meeting to meeting. I gave *EG Management* one last shot, playing Mark Fenwick (who went on to run the family department store, *Fenwick's* in Bond Street) the demo of *With People out of Love*. In a typical ferment of manic energy, Mark described the song enthusiastically as 'savage' before coming down to earth with a bang. *Killing Joke* had just joined the *EG* roster, and one bunch of psychologically disturbed musos was enough for any management company.

Disappointed, but not distraught, Ian and I trekked around central London. One day it was *Polydor* and the *Cowbell Agency*, next it was *Genetic* and *Song Music Publishers*, then *Chrysalis* and *Chappells* then back to *Polydor*. At each meeting the amount of the advance increased, creeping steadily up: £20,000, £25,000, £35,000. It was like a silly game of poker with everyone in the band wondering when someone would call our bluff.

In between business meetings, we tried to carry on rehearsing at *Wharf Studios*, where even the guys who ran the place got caught up in the near hysteria of the situation. Every few hours, they would call me out of rehearsals to field calls from A&R men increasingly desperate to sign the band. Two real live gigs were arranged, both on almost 'home turf' in Oxford, with the band due to play again at *Pembroke College* on Saturday, 24th, and then at *Oxford Polytechnic* on Monday, 26th.

For the first time, the band's out-of-town guest list was more than just friends. Music executives who couldn't find the time to cross the River Thames before Christmas were now fighting with one another to flog up the A40 to see us in Oxford. The field was now narrowing down to three main contenders: *Polydor*, *Chrysalis* and *Genetic* and all three sent multiple representatives to *Pembroke*. In addition, *Chappell's Publishing* turned up. Something else changed. Instead of kipping on Dave Ferguson's parents' floor, the band stayed two nights in a hotel. Things were definitely looking up.

Again, the gig went well. Again, the men in suits swarmed round offering best wishes and inviting calls.

The next fortnight was frantic:

Tuesday, 27th February
11 a.m. meet Ian Adam
12 p.m. *Chrysalis*
2 p.m. *Polydor*
Phone Martin Rushent/*Genetic*
Wednesday, 28th February
Polydor
Thursday, 1st March
Phone *Polydor*
11 a.m. *Genetic*
Friday, 2nd March
12 p.m. *Warner Bros Music Publishers*
2 p.m. *Chrysalis*

Monday, 5th March
5 p.m. *Chrysalis*
Tuesday, 6th March
3 p.m. *Polydor*
5 p.m. *Chrysalis*
Wednesday, 7th March
12 p.m. *Polydor*
1 p.m. *Lupus Music Publishers*
3.30 p.m. *Chrysalis*
6 p.m. Martin Rushent/*Genetic*
Thursday, 8th March
Group Meeting
Friday, 9th March
9.30 a.m. *Genetic*
12 p.m. *Warner Bros Music Publishers*
4 p.m. *Lupus Music Publishers*
Monday, 12th March
10.30 a.m. *Polydor*
12.30 p.m. *Chappells*
3.00 p.m. *Bright Music Publishing*
Tuesday, 13th March
10.30 a.m. *Genetic*

On Wednesday, 14th March, we went back into *Polydor's* demo studios for a second session. This time we recorded *Precarious Timbers, The Ballad* and *Verona Rolls*. Again, more companies than just *Polydor* got to hear us, helping to generate even more interest.

By the end of the third week in March the game was complete. Ian and I had cranked up the price of signing *Random Hold* to something like £70,000. The figure was an unprecedented amount for a band few had ever heard of and who, three months before, couldn't have given our music away. A publishing deal would allow yet more cash to be harvested.

On Monday, 19th March, I picked up the phone and, as the rest of the group toured the music equipment shops of Charing Cross Road and the West End, for the last time called Stuart Slater at *Chrysalis* and Martin Rushent at *Genetic*. *Random Hold* had signed for *Polydor Records*.

Our advance was the equivalent of £½ million nowadays.

WITH THE BAND SITTING ON A FAT CHEQUE from *Polydor*, the first thing the lads embarked on was a spending spree, with new equipment the main priority. It was a case of new guitars, synthesisers, drums and keyboards all round – and no expense was spared. Everyone spent between £1,000 and £2,000 on new kit. For Dave Rhodes it was a *Fender Jazzmaster* and a *Dan Armstrong Plexiglass Guitar* through a *Roland JC120 amp*. David Ferguson accumulated a collection of *Korg* and *Moog* keyboards and *Roland* special effects through a special heavy duty *Yamaha* amp and speaker. For me it was an *Aria* and a *Wal* bass through a huge *Ampeg V4B*. Dave Leach collected a bright, sparkling chrome finish *Premier* drumkit with a mixture of *Zildjian* and *Avedis* cymbals. And we're buggered if we can remember what Simon bought other than a *Lab Series L7 amp*. Boy, was it fun.

Then, heavy duty flight cases, in a rather fetching shade of muddy green, were specially designed, built and stamped *Random Hold* in red. The band went round in something of a daze, with unprovoked outbursts of hysterical giggling a not uncommon occurrence.

As everyone fondled their new instruments, the business of screwing yet more cash out of unwary music companies continued apace. Management and publishing were still up for grabs and a number of new players were sniffing around. Meetings were arranged with *Panache Music* and *Intersong* as deals were sought for the band's publishing rights.

Rehearsals resumed at a less than pre-possessing place called *Base Studio* in Tooley Street on Thursday, 29th March and ran until the 6th April when we discovered that the less than scrupulous manager of the studio was happily loaning out our brand new equipment to bands without their knowledge.

On Monday, 16th April, rehearsals resumed back with our chums at *Wharf*. But *Wharf* was not standing still either. Moving into an old church off the Borough Road, they built three or four much larger and better equipped rehearsal rooms as well as a recording studio out the back. The new, rather clean and comfortable surroundings fitted the band's new image of itself. No more roughing it for us!

Only two days' rehearsal were available before we were due to play, yet again, at our favourite haunt – *The Rock Garden*. Wednesday, 18th April dawned bright and clear (OK, it could have been pissing with rain but 'bright and clear' fits in better with the general mood of the moment) and we headed off to the gig. The main problem for us this night wasn't a bunch of beer throwing neo-Nazis but the fact that we had so much equipment we could barely get it on the stage. But no matter, we played – to a noticeably bigger audience than before – and retired to the dressing room only to be invited back outside to meet and greet some 'important people'. These important people turned out to be a large, affable character with a large, mid-Victorian style beard, a talkative and enthusiastic red-haired lady and a slightly built, quiet, almost shy, man who looked somewhat familiar.

It later emerged an artist, a certain Graham Dean, and a friend of the 'somewhat familiar' one, saw the band at an earlier gig and alerted his mate to *Random Hold's* existence. Interested, the friend dragged his managers down to see us that night. Now they all stood and chatted with the band in the beer-soaked debris of a post-gig *Rock Garden*.

The bearded one, it turned out, was Tony Smith, manager of *Genesis*, *Brand X* and others. He ran *Hit and Run Management* as well as publishers *Hit and Run Music*. He was inordinately wealthy, surprisingly down to earth, and a good laugh. The talkative lady was one Gail Colson. Gail, previously very senior at *Charisma Records*, *Genesis's* first label, then left to manage, amongst others, the quiet, shy man who accompanied her. He, it turned out, was Peter Gabriel.

Whilst general disappointment was expressed by all three when they discovered we had signed a recording contract, this was tempered more than somewhat when Tony and Gail found out the size of the advance. They were encouraged still further when they realised the band were neither managed nor published. With very little prodding from Mr Gabriel, the band were invited down to the *Hit and Run* offices in Shaftesbury Avenue to discuss both.

Within a few days, it became clear the heavens had, for once, aligned, and that this was the right combination of forces. Things moved swiftly along, with the band signing a publishing deal with *Hit and Run Music* (and collecting another few grand on the way) and a management agreement with Gail's company, *Gailforce*, which operated under the general *Hit and Run* umbrella. *Polydor*, too, were delighted at this outcome assuming that, with the power of *Genesis/Gailforce* management behind us, the band would sweep to multi-million pound sales within months.

Rehearsals resumed at *Wharf* and continued in a somewhat haphazard way through May. With the band now able to pay itself, and with some of my investment returned, the financial pressure eased. Things seemed set fair for the future. Little did I know that matters were afoot that were to transform the band in the short term and limit its lifespan in the future. The two Davids had been busy to thinking about the direction of *RH* and, as plans for recording an album were put in place, the urgency of their ruminations intensified.

Towards the end of May, a meeting was arranged by the two Davids to which only I was invited. There, they dropped something of a bombshell. Two issues were raised. First, concern about a medical problem being experienced by David Leach which prevented him from rehearsing as often as planned. There was a solution, admittedly a radical, and brutal, one. They would replace David with Pete Phipps – the tall, good-looking drummer who briefly played with them twelve months before. Pete's background was intriguing. Part of the original two drummer band that backed Gary Glitter on his '70s hits, he was available and the two Davids wanted him. Now seemed a good time. Pete was in.

Then they raised the position of Simon. Their view was he no longer fitted their musical vision. His contribution was too 'poppy' for a band with a very serious world view. Simon's bluesy licks no longer dovetailed with the image and ethos of the band. He must go if the band was to remain true to its ideals. This put me in a tricky position. I got on well with Simon – he's an easy guy to like (but there were no real 'personality' clashes at this time). His rock guitar counterpoint and vocal style seemed to balance the austere playing and declamatory singing of Rhodes. Certainly the feel and sound of the music had changed out of all recognition from the quasi-Krautrock monotony I had done my best to avoid. Who drove the change I cannot say. I was not there. But then, I also suspected *Polydor Records* might find this move rather alarming. They clearly viewed Simon as the understandable and presentable front man of a band they had signed in spite of having absolutely no idea what the music was about. On the other hand, this was the two Davids' band. The writing was 95% theirs, and to my mind they dominated and directed the sound and style. Apart from the bass parts, my significant contribution was to allow the group to get a deal by financing them through some tricky months, but it was *their* band which others then joined. Somewhat reluctantly I agreed.

Simon was invited for a drink at the *Dulwich Wood House*, a pub on Sydenham Hill. There, tucked away in a corner, the news was broken to the crest-fallen guitarist. Most of the talking was done by the Davids with Simon protesting his ability to change and his total commitment to the band. It was an unhappy and uncomfortable afternoon for all concerned. Simon's chance of rock stardom was snatched away from him for the second time. He certainly did not see it coming and was understandably devastated. The news was broken to David Leach in an even less pleasant and certainly less personal way. Having not been 100% for a while, he was at home when I, who drew the short straw for this duty, called. The telephone conversation was tense, fraught. *Polydor* were told of the changes after the event so they could not intervene. There was, however, an immediate and detectable change of attitude amongst the A&R men who signed us. A very substantial sum was invested in our success and yet, within weeks, changes *Polydor* didn't like and failed to understand seemed set to reduce the commercial value of our new 'product'.

Gail Colson also entertained ideas for the band not on our planned agenda. Her involvement with Peter Gabriel was one of long standing, and Peter was now scheduled to produce a new album. As before, he planned to ship over from the States the hugely talented (but also hugely expensive) bunch of musicians who habitually played on his albums: Tony Levin, Larry Fast and Jerry Marotta. Gail had other ideas. To the *Random's* immense surprise, on the last day in May, the three of us were shipped off down to Peter's house in Bath to help him work out some of the numbers written for the planned album. After a hugely enjoyable three days or so, in which time we also got to play *Solsbury Hill* with the great man, we returned to London both amused and bemused.

Quite what the point of the exercise was we were not sure. Was Gail seriously hoping to persuade Peter to cut his overheads by employing low grade British musicians as opposed to the far higher quality, though far higher maintenance, USA version? Or were we just being used to stimulate the Gabriel creative juices in order that he might fulfil his contractual obligation to *Charisma*? More likely this a subtle way of allowing Peter to run his eye over David Rhodes with a view to him appearing on the said album? An informed guess would suggest the latter.

June wandered along in a summer haze. Gail told Peter Gabriel that any hopes he might have harboured of producing the *Random Hold* album must be given up. His commitment must be to his new album. Instead, as producer, Gail proposed another experienced musician from the same *Charisma/Hit and Run* stable: ex-*Van Der Graaf Generator* front man, Peter Hammill. A provisional date was set for the start of recording – end of July.

On Monday, 25th June, the band resumed rehearsals at *Wharf*, only now we were a four piece.

AS WE WERE MORE OR LESS STARTING FROM SCRATCH, a lengthy period of rehearsals was in order. Not only did Pete Phipps have to learn the songs, he and I needed to build a rapport within the rhythm section. Furthermore, David Rhodes was now to take on the weight of being the band's only lead vocalist and the stage front man.

Eleven days' worth of rehearsals took place between the 25th June and the inauspicious Friday, 13th July. The band played one gig, at the *Nashville* on Monday 16th July, before another three days' rehearsing. Then, the equipment was shipped off to the chosen recording studio – *Startling Studios aka* Tittenhurst Park, Ascot.

Startling was built by Ringo Starr in the house previously owned by John Lennon. Tittenhurst Park was a large Georgian country house built in the early 1830s by Thomas Holloway, the man who also founded the previously mentioned *Royal Holloway College*. Bought by the horticulturalist, Thomas Lowinsky, in 1898, the park was filled with exotic trees and rhododendrons which we were too late to see in full display. John Lennon bought the place in 1969 for £150,000 (c. £3 to 4 million) and he and Yoko Ono lived there until they sold it, in turn, to Ringo Starr in 1973. The house, its spacious grounds and, most especially, the large, empty white living room, featured in Lennon's *Imagine* video. Tucked away in a hallway was an old upright piano to which was attached a brass plaque. On it was written 'John Lennon wrote *Lucy in the Sky with Diamonds* on this piano 1967'. Outside the huge French windows was a series of wide, grassed terraces on which the band members could be seen playing enthusiastic games of frisbee from time to time. The central steps down the terraces led to the guitar-shaped lake Lennon constructed before his departure for New York. The grounds themselves were huge and reputed to contain more varieties of tree than any other park in the country.

98 Tittenhurst Park, home of Startling Studios.

Now, the house was a residential 24-track recording studio, with live-in cook/housekeeper, a huge kitchen, palatial bedrooms, and a general air of luxury. The band, plus Peter Hammill, took up residence. The studio was booked for three weeks, and, from the sessions, *Polydor* expected a single and an album. The band had other ideas, however. Over a period of some time, a concept had been sketched out which allowed for the inclusion of all of the band's material, with the exception of one or two tracks not rehearsed with Peter Phipps (e.g. *Littlewoods Jeans* and *Verona Rolls*). There were sixteen songs in all and, together, they would comprise a double album. The virtue of this, as the band saw it, was that the first release of *Random Hold* would truly make a mark, almost a large dent, when it was released. Secondly, we would have got shot of all the songs written over the previous eighteen months and could then happily look towards composing a completely new batch for 'next time'. Nothing like a good bit of forward planning.

The sixteen tracks comprised nearly eighty minutes of music and this would take some sort of recording in the time available. Some tracks went down more easily than others.

Meat, the set opening, punk-like thrash over which David Ferguson intoned the threatening lyric caused problems. Not with the backing track but with the vocal. DF's delivery was of a malevolence that, though perfectly suitable for the piece, proved too threatening, bordering on evil, for Peter Hammill. The vocals were dropped.

The soon-to-be single *Etceteraville* suffered from a low frequency sympathetic resonance from the bass on certain parts. A problem never truly solved in spite of all attempts by me and others to identify and dampen the vibration.

With People out of Love was recorded, mixed, and released without anyone appearing to notice that a bass string was out of tune (nastily flat).

Numerous attempts to re-create the original feeling and exuberance of the first semi-impromptu performance of *The View from Here* continuously failed and Peter was forced to resort to edits and cross-fades to achieve, as near as possible, the required musical objective.

Finally, it was decided to substitute my voice for some of Simon's vocal parts. Never the happiest of lead singers, I found standing alone in the huge dining room, singing to a control room the other side of the wide hall and enormous kitchen a daunting experience. My singing lacked the necessary conviction and the songs involved sagged accordingly.

All was not gloom and despondency. A visit by brother, Ian, led to the production of the humorously entitled *Fear (Eats the Soul)*, some of which was recorded during a long, alcohol-fuelled dinner. Certain pieces, like *Dolphin Logic*, *Avalanche* and *Tunnel Vision* captured the cataclysmic thunder that was at the heart of a decent *Random Hold* performance.

By Friday, 10th August the recording was more or less complete and so I popped back home in Penge. I got dressed up in a white Italian suit and, looking like a member of the mafia on his summer vacation, trotted off to *Bromley Registry Office* to marry long-time girlfriend, Helen. The honeymoon was over by about 5 p.m. on Saturday when I jumped back in the car and headed back to Ascot for the final tidying up at the studio.

The album was not to be mixed there, however, as Peter chose to use another studio for this purpose, *The Farmyard* in Little Chalfont. Everyone arrived there on Monday 13th August expecting a continuation of the same co-operative spirit that more or less permeated the *Startling* sessions. For one member, at least, the coming days were a shock. Mixing was scheduled to run for seven days (from the 13th to the 19th). Again, this was a 'live in' facility and, for the first few days, the group duly congregated each morning on the row of sofas and armchairs lined up behind the desk. At the desk were Peter and engineer. Neil Kernon. Physically, therefore, their

261

backs were turned on the group members and, to me at least, it soon became clear that these backs were turned more than just physically.

Peter Hammill's ideas about the sound he wanted became clear. Suggestions seemed unwelcome. The band appeared excluded from this part of the process. For me, this was a deeply frustrating experience. Although I may not have recorded anything like Peter's volume of music, I had been in studios regularly since 1972 and was used to being able to make suggestions and put forward ideas. Working with Robert Wyatt, Phil Manzanera and Brian Eno was always a co-operative venture where everyone's ideas and comments were, at least, seriously considered. This was not, however, Peter's view of how mixing worked. After two or three days, I decided enough was enough and went home. The mixing was completed in my absence.

From time to time, different members of the *Polydor* A&R department visited the studios. Alec Byrn (who later went on to work for *EG*) was their main point of contact along with Alan Black. It was they who allowed the 'asking price' for the signing of the band to be cranked up to the £70,000 mark and it was they who were being looked at by their bosses to get a quick return on the investment. What was needed was a single and, to be frank, nothing stood out. No particular track shrieked 'hit'. But, needs must when the devil drives, as they say (quite who says this we're not sure and anyone who did say it would be regarded as a distinctly odd fellow). The track *Etceteraville* was selected as the *Random's* first foray onto vinyl. A release date in late October was agreed.

In the meantime, mixing over, the band returned to *Wharf* for a couple of days to continue the familiarisation programme that would have best been done *before* recording took place. Then, on Thursday, 23rd August, we set off to watch Peter Gabriel play a 'one-off' gig at the *Bath Pavilion* prior to starting his own recording sessions. We visited Peter Hammill at his house near Westbury on the way. The following day, we played at *Friars* in Aylesbury before the band entered a strangely quiet period throughout the whole of September, punctuated only by a three-day re-mix session at *Trident Studios* over the 8th-10th. One of the main reasons for the inactivity was that David Rhodes was playing on the new Peter Gabriel album being recorded in Bath on the *Manor Mobile*. There was little we could do in the absence of our lead guitarist/vocalist.

Rehearsals resumed on October 1st, again at *Wharf*, for a week. *Polydor* were gearing themselves up for the release of the single, now scheduled for the third week of the month. The band was lined up for a series of dates at the famous *Marquee* in Wardour Street, Soho, playing every second Sunday there from 14th October, finishing on 13th November. In addition, we would play the *Nashville* on the 9th November, before starting a tour as support to *XTC* on the 23rd. It was hardly a hectic schedule for a band with a single to promote and an album due for release.

Etceteraville received a distinctly cool critical reaction. The first review came from Ian Birch in the *Melody Maker* on 20th October:

> "Gulp, another disappointment. Taking a cue in part from Phil Manzanera's solo work (which is hardly surprising, as *Holder* Bill MacCormick was intimately involved in at least *Diamond Head, 801 Live, Listen Now* and *K-Scope*), it stays within a rock format while experimenting gently round the edges. Perhaps producer Peter Hammill is most at fault. Instead of offsetting the band's bedrock base with a lightness of detail which would have helped focus the words, he's kept the sound, er, earth bound, almost as if he had kitted everyone out in diver's suits before they entered the studio. A shame."

For reasons known only to the *Melody Maker* the single was reviewed again two weeks later, on 3rd November by Chris Bohn:

> "RANDOM HOLD: *Etceteraville* (*Polydor* POSP85) The combination of these men's earnestness and Peter Hammill's hefty production makes this a good album track plainly wasted in single form, though their penchant for melodrama ('Hang on tight, Johnny') unexpectedly catches you by the throat once or twice."

Released six weeks before the band started any serious gigging, with no noticeable air play push (itself an indication of the dramatic collapse of faith being displayed by *Polydor*), and hardly any press coverage, the single was dead in the water. *Etceteraville* sank without trace.

EARLY NOVEMBER SLIPPED SOMBRELY PAST. The complete failure of *Etceteraville* to generate any excitement, interest, or airplay, still further eroded *Polydor's* faith in the band. On the other hand, as *Polydor* had done precious little to help the single, its failure was something of a self-fulfilling prophesy.

The 'season' at the *Marquee* helped cheer spirits. First up, Paul Suter of *Sounds* penned a decent review, although he missed half the set:

PAUL SUTER, *Sounds*, 10th November 1979

In which the *Marquee* plumbs new depths: well would you expect the headliners to go on at 8.45? So yours truly's decision to watch assorted cinematographic faux-pas on the TV ('For those of you watching in black and white, the yellow ball is behind the blue . . .') before shifting his butt resulted in a mere 50 per cent dose of *Random Hold* and a firm resolve to see the whole set next time; 'cos they were magnificent.

Any band containing a drummer from the *Glitter Band* (Peter Phipps), a bassist from *Matching Mole* (Bill MacCormick) and a guitarist (David Rhodes) who's been working on a Peter Gabriel album is likely to have an interesting approach, and *Random Hold* don't disappoint on that score.

The assorted synthesisers of David Ferguson are the major element of the sound, couching everything in an eerie air of unreality, which is built upon with a sparse rhythmic approach from the rest of the band, tending to fill out as the number progresses The effect is hypnotic and incredibly powerful, particularly on one song which builds a doomy drone into a shattering climax with a deliberately, discordant guitar break: My notebook simply says 'gasp' at this point . . . 'breathtaking' is a feeble understatement, but the best I can manage.

If parallels have to be drawn, *Japan* are probably the closest comparison. Both bands rely on creating a surreal atmosphere with their keyboards and then playing briskly but mysteriously on a percussive base, raising the tension.

They tread between the realms of absolute garbage and stirring hard rock, and securing an image and an audience is not going to be easy whilst pursuing this act of brinkmanship. Hopefully they won't be put off though, because the tension and excitement that they generate should by rights be their key to success.

And, on 1st December, Allan Jones again rode to the rescue with a half-decent review of the third gig:

RANDOM HOLD, *Marquee*, Allan Jones, *Melody Maker*, 1st December 1979

We always seem to meet in the most inauspicious circumstances, *Random Hold* and I. Last December I saw them in Bermondsey: an audience of one in a derelict rehearsal studio. Later that month *Random Hold* were threatening to outnumber the audience at the *Music Machine*. I was relieved last Tuesday to find that they'd invited along a few more friends to the *Marquee*. Fortunately, there was no evidence of the uncomfortable self-consciousness that has so far afflicted their studio work.

Tuesday night found a band in control of its (quite considerable) resources, sure of its direction without being predictable. Since the departure of Simon Ainley (gtr/vcl) much of the audience's attention is now directed at David Rhodes. Rhodes responds admirably to the demands of new responsibilities. He seemed not to miss Ainley, and the second guitar was missed noticeably by these ears only on *The Ballad*. Rhodes was constantly busy, but his contributions were adroitly placed and newer cluttered. Solos were infrequent, sometimes reluctantly offered, but memorable throughout when they occurred.

The diffidence at their early gigs has been replaced by a cautious confidence. Both Rhodes and David Ferguson (keyboards and vocals) are now more extrovert, though MacCormick still looks nervous and uncomfortable, teeth clenched, eyes glazed, on the far right of the stage. Crucially, they've learned to communicate the intensity of their music without resorting to crass effects or excessive volume. They've invested shrewdly in a modest, but cleverly effective lighting rig.

The bulk of their repertoire is still drawn from the early demo tapes, but some of the newer material – *Dolphin Logic*, *The View From Here*, especially is shaping nicely. Ferguson's synthesizer back drops are becoming increasingly more assured and varied – especially so on *Precarious Timbers* and *Avalanche*. Peter Phipps, who has replaced David Leach behind the drums is a good rock drummer, but perhaps a little too stolid.

The evening's highlight was undoubtedly *With People Out of Love*. Ferguson's repetitive synthesizer motif and the insinuating pulse of the syndrum tape loop created a cool, menacing atmosphere. Rhodes was caught in a pale spotlight, his voice fraught with anxiety and an increasing malevolence. The piece built to a final outburst reminiscent of *Roxy's In Every Dream Home A Heartache*, with Rhodes unleashing a scything solo that ran itself blind.

Random Hold aren't quite there yet, but they're on the way. Now if they'd only show Hammill the door.

On the 23rd, the *XTC* tour started. *XTC* were going through one of their more popular phases and their current single, *Making Plans for Nigel*,[i] was doing well. This bunch of intelligent west-country lads were a pleasure to play with, and certainly deserved the modest success they gained over the years and probably a whole lot more. Both bands played a peculiarly English-style of rock music though there was far more humour in an *XTC* performance than in a typical *RH* one! The tour started at *Nottingham University* in The Portland Building, a venue that I knew, having played there in 1977 with Phil Manzanera on the *Listen Now* tour.

| Friday, 23rd November | Portland Building, *Nottingham University* |
| Saturday, 24th November | *Birmingham University* |

---

[i] Taken from the 1979 Steve Lillywhite-produced *Drums and Wires* (Virgin), it reached No. 17 on the Singles Charts, staying there for eleven weeks. Lillywhite then produced Peter Gabriel's third solo album on which David Rhodes played.

Sunday, 25th November   *Hexagon Theatre*, Reading
Monday, 26th November   *The Odeon*, Canterbury

RANDOM HOLD, Canterbury Odeon, Chris Welch, *Musicians Only*, 8th December 1979

Art has been known to imitate nature. In the challenging world of *Random Hold*, art sometimes appears to imitate science. Are they the first DOR band? (That's Disco Orientated Rock to you). Do they have a future? These and other significant, questions taxed my concentration during an intriguing performance by the band at *Canterbury Odeon* on Monday last week.

It never ceases to amaze me how by a subtle blend of herbs, spices, talent and influences, musicians can keep coming up with new directions within the format of modern rock. *Random Hold* are succeeding in creating a new sound and approach by melding together various factors that affected their individual pasts.

For example, their drummer Peter Phipps, with pop star looks, was once a driving force in the *G Band* which backed Gary Glitter. Hardly promising material for a band which consists mainly of ex-Dulwich College chaps? Not at all. His muscular drive and metronomic beat is the perfect foil for the more cerebral approach adopted by synthesiser operative and founder member David Ferguson. The unswerving drum-machine beat produces a maniacal, almost Teutonic thunder, and indeed one of their themes is set to a spirited march tempo. Occasionally they use a *Roland* rhythm box, but most of the solid slog comes from the flesh and blood machine.

But one should not gain the impression that *Random Hold* are producing music for mindless automatons. There is a refreshing intelligence to their lyrics which deal with subjects like the terrors of motorway driving, modern architecture and patriotism, and they have a flair for melody as in the appealing item from their *Polydor* EP, *Montgomery Clift*. On this piece guitarist David Rhodes comes to the fore, although none of the band are into displays of technique and scarcely solo at all in the accepted sense.

Ferguson freely admits he is not a keyboard player of any great skill. Nevertheless, the sound and concept of the band is strong. Rhodes has a great voice – very clear, very British, and exerts the most effective stage presence. As the band develops and wins a bigger fan following, they would be well advised to smarten up their visuals, although they confide that they don't want to fall into the Gary Numan trap.

Bassist Bill MacCormick was previously a member of *Quiet Sun*, *Matching Mole*, *Gong*, *This Heat* and *801* and indeed it was exposure to Phil Manzanera and Eno's *801* that provided initial inspiration to form *Random Hold*.

Some of the music has a frantic, Mediterranean feel about it that reminded me curiously of Cat Stevens. *Central Reservation* had that disco beat behind simple keyboard chords and clear, white light vocals, and *Dolphin Logic* featured heavy, sustained chords alternating with Morse code-like repetition, like a tape loop left in an abandoned, remote-controlled radio shack. *Flag* marched with terrifying determination, and reached a groaning climax.

The audience, despite a vociferous lobby for the main group *XTC*, were moved to applaud in a manner that was both heartening and encouraging for a new group and with a more vigorous stage act they will soon win their own brand of loyalty.

The Gear: David Rhodes (guitar): *Fender Stratocaster, Fender Jazzmaster, Dan-Armstrong See-Thru., Roland JC 120, Roland 201 reverb/echo, Boss 10 band Graphic Equaliser, Black Box Fuzz*.

Bill MacCormick (bass): *Wal Pro II* bass guitar, *Aria SB 1000, Fender Precision, Peter Cornish pedal board* (fuzz, phase, envelope), *Ampeg V4B, Ampeg SVT* cabinet.

Peter Phipps (drums): *Sonor Silver Pearl* kit, comprising, 22in bass drum, *Premier 51/2in* snare drum, *Sonor* tom toms including 14, 15, 16 and 18in. *Paiste* 15in hi-hats, 18in 2002 crash and 22in 2002 crash, *Zildjian* 20in crash and all *Premier* stands.

David Ferguson (keyboards): *Korg 800 DV, Micro Korg, Mini Korg, Logan String Melody, Wasp synthesiser, Roland 101 Echo, Stylophone, Yamaha 100W* amp, *Roland rhythm box, Coloursound fuzz, MXR blue box, Boss 6-channel mixer* and many tapes and tape loops.

On Tuesday, 27th November, *XTC* flew to Munich for a German TV broadcast. The tour resumed the next day at Manchester University, then:

Thursday, 29th November	*Leicester Polytechnic*
Friday, 30th November	*Langley College of Further Education*
Saturday, 1st December	*Plymouth Polytechnic*
Sunday, 2nd December	*Poole Arts Centre*

There was then a fortnight's gap before

Thursday, 20th December	*Music Machine* (not with *XTC*)
Saturday, 22nd December	*Friars*, Aylesbury
Sunday, 23rd December	*Brunell Room*, Swindon

So, hardly the most strenuous of tours. Along the way, in the first week of December, phase two of *Random Hold's* cunning plan for world domination was allowed to escape by a less than enthusiastic *Polydor*.

Avalanche was part of the strategy to use up as much as possible of the material so expensively recorded over the summer. It was an EP (Extended Play for those of you too young to remember such things, and a strange hybrid, half single and half album) and it fell again to the *Melody Maker's* Ian Birch to give it a quick mauling on 8th December:

> RANDOM HOLD: *Avalanche* (*Polydor* RHX 1). A five-tracker that really promises more than it delivers. The *Hold* are clearly four gifted musicians with a bundle of ideas, but their post *Diamond Head/801* line of attack needs a lot more pruning and consolidation before it'll achieve the desired effect. The songs, mainly written by David Ferguson and David Rhodes, aim to build separate, forceful moods with their gradual layering on of effects and impressionistic lyrics – but they never quite make it. The blame must go in large part to producer Peter Hammill who has kept the overall sound dull and sodden rather than emphasizing the cut-and-thrust of the songs. Still, it's early days."

It came as no great shock when *Avalanche* repeated the singular lack of success achieved by *Etceteraville*. Again, media presence was minimal, a problem that was to beset the band throughout its life. It is, for example, extraordinary that, with the potential power of *Polydor* and *Hit & Run* behind us, the band never played a session for any radio station in the UK. Advertising and in-store promotion were also noticeable only by their absence. It would seem, in retrospect, that *Polydor* had made an early decision not to throw good money after bad. They certainly did their level best to ensure a negative return on their investment throughout the year the band were signed to them.

As Christmas loomed, Chris Welch of *Musicians Only*, followed up his approving review of the Canterbury concert with a lengthy interview with the two Davids (see page 431). It rounded off a difficult year with a morale raising boost.

AFTER THE *XTC* TOUR, we faced another lengthy lay-off until a resumption of rehearsals on Monday, 28th January. In the intervening period, I went into the *Hit and Run* offices to discuss the planned Gabriel tour of the UK. Peter wanted the band to be his support act for the tour which was due to start in mid-February. There was now an essential issue on his mind: where to stay *en route*. Peter was not an enthusiastic tourer and long ago concluded such taxing exercises were best done in as civilised a manner as possible. This meant the best hotels in the most attractive locations and so he and I sat down for a few hours with an AA road map, the *Good Hotel Guide* and we planned *Gabriel's Gourmet Guide to British Rock 'n' Roll Tours*.

In the meantime, Gail Colson was busily calling in favours from friends, and two brief pieces appeared in the national press, predicting great things for the band in 1980:

Nina Myskow, *The Sun*, 4th January 1980
This year watch for British band *Random Hold*. Their music shows talent, menace, originality and brains. A dynamic combination.

Anne Nightingale, *Daily Express*, 4th January 1980
Hot 10 for the Eighties
Random Hold is a four-piece band from Oxford, started by ex-stage manager David Ferguson and guitarist David Rhodes. 'We don't class ourselves as musicians' said Ferguson. 'We wanted to do the sort of show that all kinds of people will come to. There are too many cliques in rock music'.

A couple of days before the rehearsals were due to resume, I got a call from Robert Wyatt who asked me to play bass on a single he was recording for *Rough Trade* (*Caimanera/Arauco*). *Caimanera* featured some lovely playing by Harry Beckett on flugelhorn. It was the last time I played with my long-time friend and musical colleague. It was very nearly a neat bookend for the musical period of my life which started with meeting Robert in 1966 and was to conclude in a few months' time.

On the 28th, it was down to work. All the while, the two Davids were being driven to distraction by the antics of the *Polydor* design department. They were set the task of coming up with suitable cover artwork for the forthcoming album, an issue which previously proved beyond them on the previous releases. Every few days, we would meet up and DF would regale us with ever more hilarious descriptions of new and exotic designs, none of which seemed to have the remotest connection to the music or the band. One cover which remains in the memory consisted of a fish hanging by a hook which was attached to the big toe of a human foot. The band did briefly consider naming the album *ToeHookFish* in an attempt to confuse the unwary, but then we got bored and someone bought another round of drinks to take our minds off things.

Rehearsals went on for eight days before we played a couple of pre-tour warm up gigs. The first was at *Queen Elizabeth College* in Kensington on 8th February. This was remarkable mainly for the seeming lack of damage incurred when David Rhodes vigorously head-butted a parking meter which tried to mug him in a nearby road. Three days later, we played at *Darwen College*, part of Kent University. On the 14th we schlepped off down to *Shepperton Film Studios* to do some run throughs with the Gabriel sound team on one of the big sound stages (a facility not often offered to support acts). A few days later we picked up the large *Peugeot Estate* that was to be our transport for the tour and, early on Wednesday, 20th

February, we piled into the car and headed off down the M4 towards Exeter.

The Gabriel tour was on.

THE COMPLETE ENTOURAGE for the Gabriel/*Random* tour of the UK consisted of twenty-six people. Fifteen of them were the sound, lighting and trucking crew led by Albert Lawrence, and included the *Random's* roadie, Pete Donovan, a tall, imperturbable gent who seemed temperamentally well suited to the somewhat volatile nature of certain band members. In addition, there were the five members of the Gabriel band, Peter himself, ace drummer Jerry Marotta, synth specialist Larry Fast, the extraordinary Tony Levin on bass and *Chapman Stick*, and John Ellis, brought in to play the guitar parts, many of which David Rhodes played on the album *Peter Gabriel III*. Tour Manager was Rick French and Gail Colson, manager of both acts, was also present throughout the tour.

Unlike most headliners, Peter took the view there would no 'them' and 'us' when it came to touring. He insisted his band and the *Randoms* stay in the same hotels and, in most respects, the tour operated as if everyone was part of the same organisation. The Gabriel crew helped Pete Donovan out whenever required and *vice versa*. We were always given a decent length of time for our sound checks (which other support act could say that?). The bands ate together and socialised. They took photographs of one another during performances and popped in and out of one another's dressing rooms for a chat or a beer. Regularly, members of the *Randoms* would go one stage to join in on the moving and rousing choruses to *Biko* at the end of Peter's set. Gee, it was just like one big family!

And most significantly, before each concert started, Peter went on stage and introduced the *Randoms* as: 'one of my favourite bands and one of the best bands around at the moment'. For anyone who has been part of a support band the significance of this last element cannot be overstated. Most support bands are mainly viewed an as unnecessary inconvenience by the audience of hardcore fans there to see their favourites perform. Consequently, they either play to an empty auditorium or to one filled with people whose only interest is to see them leave the stage as soon as possible. Peter's intervention meant, at least, that those people there would feel duty bound to give the *Randoms* some sort of hearing. It helped immeasurably and made the tour even more of a pleasure than it would anyway have been.

The tour started on Wednesday 20th February, and lasted four weeks:

Wednesday 20th February	*Exeter University*
Thursday, 21st February	Taunton *Odeon*
Saturday, 23rd February	Birmingham *Odeon*
Sunday, 24th February	Leicester *De Monfort Hall*

Monday, 25th February	Sheffield *City Hall*
Wednesday, 27th February	*Dundee University*
Thursday, 28th February	Aberdeen *Capitol Theatre*
Friday, 29th February	Glasgow *Apollo*
Saturday, 1st March	Edinburgh *Odeon*
Monday, 3rd March	Newcastle *City Hall*
Tuesday, 4th March	Liverpool *Empire*
Wednesday, 5th March	Manchester *Apollo*
Friday, 7th March	Cardiff *Sophia Gardens*
Saturday, 8th March	Southampton *Gaumont*
Tuesday, 11th March	Hammersmith *Odeon*
Wednesday, 12th March	Hammersmith *Odeon*
Thursday, 13th March	Hammersmith *Odeon*
Saturday, 15th March	Brighton *Centre*
Sunday, 16th March	*Bath University*

Whenever possible, days off were spent in attractive hotels deep in the countryside where both bands would relax and get to know one another. And days off were frequent, every three or four days, and some of the hotels selected by Peter and me proved spectacular for both location, food, and accommodation. On the 26th, for example, the bands stayed at the *Dryburgh Abbey Hotel*, an impressive mansion set overlooking the River Tweed. The previous night was Sheffield and the next night would be Dundee. Despite the penetrating cold of a February night deep in the Scottish Borders, David Rhodes and Peter decided a hike across the nearby moorland was in order. It was only after several hours that the rest of us, who'd spent a highly civilised time warming our toes in front of a huge log fire and our insides with the odd dram or two of singularly fine malt whiskey, realised the two of them had failed to return. Some anxiety was caused until they crept in, very cold and dripping wet. One or other of them had decided that fording the Tweed and having a look at the Abbey from the other bank seemed like a jolly good idea. Then, of course, they had to re-cross the river, dodging the odd flying salmon on the way.

At the beginning of the tour, the *Random Hold* album was released. It was titled *The View From Here* and reviews were awaited with some trepidation after the initial critical reaction to the first two releases. The first in the field was the *Melody Maker* on 23rd February. This time neither Allan Jones nor Ian Birch were the reviewers. This may have been useful because John Orme came without any preconceptions and reviewed it as he heard it. There was a distinct sense of shock, and relief, when the review was read. Orme described it as 'a work of promise and reward'. Blimey, he quite liked it! (see page 439).

Buoyed by the first signs of a critical upswing, we played decently at Exeter and Taunton before enjoying a day off in London in advance of the journey up the M1 to Birmingham. Beginning to work as a more formidable unit, playing was proving, at last, a pretty pleasant experience. Even notoriously partisan crowds like Glasgow and Liverpool were taken on, and whilst not exactly battered into submission, some casualties were caused. Almost every gig we played, Tony Levin (one of *the* best bass players and nicest people it's been my pleasure to see/hear/know) would lurk at the side of the stage snapping away relentlessly. Every time we came off stage we were greeted warmly by Peter and his band and, most nights, the *Randoms* would either sneak into the hall to watch, or would stand at the side of the stage to enjoy, Gabriel's riveting performances.

During this period an anonymous but encouraging note appeared in an unknown magazine (and we only publish it here because they were nice about the band):

> If you've got tickets for the current Peter Gabriel tour, you're advised to go along early to catch the opening act. The band is called *Random Hold* and if you haven't heard of them before you should check them out. They play what they call 'highly emotional dance music', but not just for cliques like mods or ska fans: If there's a comparison, it's with *Talking Heads* – but in their aims, rather than their style.
>
> The band started when two students, David Ferguson and David Rhodes, went to see Phil Manzanera and Eno's temporary band *801*. They became angry at how uninventive that band was and decided they could do better themselves which is ironic because *801's* bass player Bill MacCormick is now with *Random Hold*.
>
> To start with, the two Daves were an experimental duo doing workshops, using backing tapes and rhythm boxes and playing for things like puppet theatres. But they decided that they weren't getting through to the audiences so, after various comings and goings, Bill joined on bass and Pete Phipps came in on drums. Those two had different musical experiences; MacCormick had played with almost every experimental British jazz-fusion band going, and Phipps had been with Gary Glitter's *G Band*. The new band came under the wing of Tony Smith (manager of Peter Gabriel), and *Random Hold* were born.
>
> The band went out to *Startling Studios* (once the home of John Lennon and now residence of Ringo Starr) and in a mere three weeks they had recorded enough material for a double album. They decided to release everything they had recorded – but in different ways and at different times. First came a single, *Etceteraville*, and then

last November came the impressive EP containing songs like *Film Music* and *Montgomery Clift*. Now the rest has just been released as an album called *The View From Here*.

In Edinburgh we met up with Hugh Fielder from *Sounds* for a quick interview over breakfast in the huge old railway station hotel, the *North British*, that stands above *Waverley Station*. He seemed genuinely interested and the article reflected this when it was published three weeks later even if the description of the band's history, and the 'managerial' activities of yours truly, were more than a little bit wide of the mark.

99 On tour and on Arthur's Seat, Edinburgh

He also gave the band a good mention when he reviewed the concert:

Gabriel/*Random Hold*, Edinburgh Odeon Hugh Fielder, *Sounds*, 8th March 1980

No-one qualifies as a cult hero the way Peter Gabriel does. Chucking up *Genesis* just before they made the super league, coming up with just two solo albums in the space of four years that required a dedicated and sympathetic disposition to compete with the torrent of frantic activity on almost every street corner, and infrequent appearances in strange and often unaccommodating places. But Gabriel is trying hard.

In a medium which, despite its rebellious facade is fast becoming institutionalised, predictable and even moribund, he is playing with the ground rules. This goes as far as questioning the whole star/fan-worship syndrome and constantly trying to break new ground in presenting himself and his songs on stage. He's doing it from a position of some strength but that doesn't alter the fact that he's stuck to his guns for longer than most of the New Wave has done. His following has stayed fiercely loyal over the years, a factor which both helps and hinders him: it must be a comfort to know that you can always find an audience whenever you want but riding roughshod over their expectations can tax their affections.

Most of them missed his first appearance on stage, however. He walked on at the very beginning of the concert to give support group *Random Hold* his personal sponsorship. He managed to do it without making it a big deal, condescending or patronising. He simply introduced them said that they were one of best bands he'd heard in the last year and walked quickly away.

Random Hold proved worthy of Gabriel's endorsement with a committed and convincing set that took its inspiration from several illustrious sources of the Seventies: *Roxy Music*, Bowie, *Pink Floyd* etc. – and placed them firmly in a current context.

They're not afraid of a good melody and when they got away from the Teutonic stomp that characterised too many of the songs, they revealed a sharp sense of texture and dynamics. What they need is a hit to help them stand out in the crowd and with a little perseverance they should get one.

At the same time, new-found convert Paul Suter came out with a mixed review of the album. A curate's egg of an album got a curate's egg of a review: good in parts (see page 440).

Less useful was the almost total lack of coverage that the band's performances received in the music press whose focus was, understandably, almost entirely on Gabriel and his new material. So, although the band were playing to bigger audiences than ever, and receiving reasonably decent reactions, this fact was not being relayed any further. Again, radio play of the album was insignificant, a reflection of *Polydor's* soon-to-be-made decision to drop the act.

On the 15th March, as the tour drew to a close, the *NME*, in the shape of Graham Lock, reviewed the album. Again, the review was favourable (see page 440).

The same day, however, the *Record Mirror* reinforced its position as the pre-eminent teeny-bop, brain-dead British music weekly when it slagged off the band viciously, comparing it in derogatory fashion to *Talking Heads* (a comparison with which the band was actually quietly pleased):

RANDOM HOLD, The View From Here, Robin Smith, *Record Mirror*,

OH GOD, this is *Polydor's* attempt at signing something approaching an ART band. You know the sort of thing – a bleak photo of a building on the album cover and meaningful songs like *Dolphin Logic* and *Etceteraville* delivered in the post punk grand spiky style.

Doubtless much of this album is way above the head of a dummy like me. It sounds like an overdriven machine with oil shortage. The aforementioned *Dolphin Logic* is quite the most tedious and boring thing I've heard since I foolishly listened to a *Talking Heads* album all the way through without a tea break.

Silver Spoons, Golden Tongues and *Central Reservation* are real classics in unreserved pretension and have zombie like choruses. *Central Reservation* features much robotic vocals and an uncomfortable theme that has the same effect as stroking a porcupine. *Etceteraville* has a zappy little intro but once again the lads settle back comfortably into dark passages and stark images. Yawn.

People Out Of Love is absolutely hellish. It goes on and on with guitars grating steadily and vocals quickly solidifying over a repetitive drum beat. *The View From Here* boasts a *Steely Dan* type intro before it breaks, into a tune that sounds like the worst excesses of Bill Nelson after *Be Bop Deluxe* split. Listen to this dross at your peril. I'm off to watch the *Muppet Show*.

Seven days later, Chris Bohn in the *Melody Maker* presented himself as a lone voice of dissent with a critical review of Peter's set at the *Hammersmith Odeon*. He did, however, mutter some slightly positive comments about the *Randoms* on the way:

Random Hold at the *Hammersmith Odeon* (supporting Peter Gabriel) Chris Bohn, *Melody Maker*, March 22nd 1980

Nothing compromising, though, about *Random Hold*, an incessantly dark despairing band, whose set is like sitting through an Ingmar Bergman movie – one knows it's good, but that doesn't necessarily imply immediate acceptance. At least they confront, even if they don't excite. Sombrely austere guitar and keyboards provide the severest of colourings to the hollow thud of Bill MacCormick's dominant bass. The resulting angst isn't so much alleviated by the band recognising it – as opposed to the psyche searching of the younger *Joy Division* – as increased by their knowing there's no way out. Oh me!

The tour finished on the 16th March at a hastily convened extra gig in Peter's hometown of Bath where Kate Bush was spotted in the audience. That night, my wife, Peter and I headed east along the M4 towards London. Somewhere in Berkshire, the car unexpectedly slowed to a halt with the petrol gauge on empty. Thankfully, the AA were not long in coming and we were soon on our way. Then, as we entered the Earls Court area, the car engine started to scream in a most unattractive fashion before, literally, grinding to a halt. Peter cheerfully hailed taxis for all concerned and we headed home leaving the car sitting sadly by the side of the road.

It seemed an appropriate event for the end of the tour. Soon, everything would lurch to a halt for the band. Ten days later, just as the album received some decent reviews, *Polydor* confirmed they were dropping us. The A&R men who had signed us were also consigned to the dustbin of history. The timing was perfect.

With the end of the tour and the release of the album, now should have been the time for the band to get into some heavy gigging to promote the album. Some radio sessions, too, would have been useful. But all that fell by the wayside when *Polydor* dropped the band. Of particular frustration was the fact that a scheduled BBC *In Concert*, due to be recorded on March 24th, was dropped. Throughout the twelve months with the label not one British radio session or interview was arranged. A triumph for all concerned.

Thankfully, and prudently, we kept back some of the *Polydor* and *Hit and Run* advances for emergencies – and this was certainly one. Matters were not entirely bleak. Tony Smith and Gail Colson made it clear there were no plans to drop the band, and Peter asked us support him on his forthcoming tour of the USA. So, while Gail and Tony tried to find an outlet for the *Random Hold* material in the US, we decided it was time to record some more tracks as demos for a potential second album. Several new songs such as *Camouflage* and *Passive Camera* had already been aired during the Gabriel UK tour and these, together with four or five others, would be the basis for the projected *Random Hold* album number 2.

Rehearsals and recording were all done at *Wharf Studios* and in their newly completed *Black Wing* 24-track studio. The sessions were scattered across late April and for a couple of tracks the band was augmented by Vic Martin who played additional keyboards. The sessions went well, and the self-produced demos admirably reflected the musical evolution of the band, in particular a move away from some of the more ponderous songs to a lighter and more rhythmically complex and confident style.

But this burst of productive and creative energy was again dissipated during another period of enforced inactivity. Though we did not know it, the band's last UK gig had been and gone, and, between the end of mixing the demos and the start of pre-USA rehearsals on Monday 9th June, we did nothing. Quite how the two Davids filled their time is not clear. Pete Phipps undoubtedly played lots of tennis (he was rarely seen out of tennis shorts and shoes during the summer months). I, on the other hand, became increasingly involved in something that would come to dominate his life throughout the 80s and 90s – politics.

Our managers, meanwhile, found a company prepared to release an album to coincide with the US tour. *Passport Records* was part of *Jem Records Inc.* based in South Plainfield, New Jersey. They were not large, but they seemed enthusiastic and were prepared to cough up some much-needed dollars to help with the tour expenses. They also undertook to generate some media interest and, in the space of four short weeks, produced more radio and press interviews than *Polydor* managed in a year.

The band rehearsed for five days before Pete Donovan turned up and the equipment was loaded up and sent off to Gatwick. With all the necessary work permits and visas, we followed early the following morning. One thing which helped reduce the costs was that my dad still worked in the airline charter business. He persuaded a colleague to give us free tickets out and back to the USA. In addition, they arranged for the band's ¾ of a ton of equipment to clear customs at both ends with the minimum of fuss, and to be treated as excess baggage and not expensive freight.

At noon, *Flight TV401* took off heading for Los Angeles. Accompanying the band were Peter Gabriel and guitarist John Ellis. The *747* landed at LA at 3 p.m. local time and we were swept almost regally through both customs and immigration. Picking up our car from *Budget*, we headed off to our hotel, the *Sunset Beverley*, just along from the large *Tower Records* on Sunset Strip. Continuing with the tradition of such events, the tour started for the *Randoms* with three days off. But, hey, that's rock 'n' roll. Somewhat jet-lagged, the lads took to their beds early, but one, at least, could not sleep and, as a result, was given an interesting introduction to big city life, American-style.

David Ferguson was awake and curious, and seemed to think a walk along Sunset Boulevard in the early morning was the same as a stroll around suburban south London. He had not gone far before the air was punctuated by a series of frantic shrieks. Suddenly, a partially clothed woman sprinted out from a side turning and, screaming all the while, ran past a rooted Ferguson, before disappearing from view a block ahead. As our English hero stood transfixed by this apparition, a man, brandishing a large knife, charged furiously past, chasing her around the same corner a hundred yards ahead. Somewhat nervously, David decided he could not leave the lady to a bloody fate and, concerned at the sudden silence, did the daft thing and started to jog after them. As he turned the corner, the reason for the silence was explained. Thankfully, the man was not standing over a bloodied corpse, instead he was spread-eagled across the bonnet of an LAPD black and white and held down by two burly cops, with the woman cowering in the back seat. Welcome to the good ole USofA, David!

The other days off were rather less frantic. One day we headed off down the Santa Ana Freeway and did *Disneyland* (which we all loved! How politically incorrect can you get). Another day we drove the length of Sunset Boulevard until we hit the Pacific. There we dabbled our toes in the ocean, observed Los Angelenos at play on the beach, and found a bar which served warm British beer. One evening we headed east to *Graumann's Chinese Theatre* where we saw *The Shining* (as if David hadn't seen enough women being terrorised by knife wielding madmen). The other highlight was when I emptied a loosely capped bottle of tomato ketchup over the head of a neighbouring diner at a *Howard Johnson's*. Thankfully, the person concerned was neither armed nor dangerous, this being the days before the insane move towards concealed gun carrying. We certainly knew how to enjoy ourselves!

The first concert was on Wednesday, 19th June at the *Arlington Theatre* in Santa Barbara but this did not involve us. We went anyway, keen to see Peter's show and to have a look around the town. The following night was our first performance. The venue was the open-air amphitheatre of the *Greek Theatre* in Griffith Park. The first shock to the system came when we made the acquaintance of the *Teamsters* who worked the stage at the theatre. Any attempt to lift or carry anything was inadvisable as such actions were bound to bring about the immediate intervention of a 'union' man whose job it was to lift that flight case, move that amplifier, or open that guitar case. About the only thing they didn't do was play the instruments. Roadie Pete Donovan was reduced to standing and pointing, and the group retired to the dressing room where we started to work our way through the massive supply of beer, cold cuts, fruit, and salads which occupied a large section of the band room.

As in the UK, Peter introduced the band. The sound was good, we performed OK if briefly (*Teamster* overtime cost $100 a minute!) and the tour started off well. The next night everyone headed for the *Forum* where *The Who* were playing and, with Peter to the fore, we were introduced to them. In our room back at the *Sunset Beverley* it was decided that touring the US might not be too bad a thing.

The following day, everyone struggled aboard *Flight UA887* to San Francisco. We were to play three consecutive nights, one at the *Civic Auditorium*, San Jose, and two at the *Fox Warfield Theatre* in the heart of San Francisco. Here, we did our first interviews, one with a lady journalist from the *San Jose Mercury* (see page 442), another with a guy from the *Oakland Tribune* (see page 444), and a third with a radio station in San Rafael. As with several UK interviews, history and timelines got somewhat jumbled but, in general, it was positive stuff, a reaction which continued throughout the tour as you, patient reader, will discover. As it quickly becomes boring (and to save space), the repeated recital of how the band was formed has been excised from the interviews. You are not missing much except, perhaps, that either the two David's recollections of what happened were deliberately vague or, and perish the thought, their memories somewhat alcohol influenced. Alternatively, the various reporters failed in their basic task of writing down or recording accurately what the interviewees said.

100 On stage in the Gabriel Tour
[Photos: Tony Levin]

Peter had slotted in another day-off at the end of the Bay area gigs, and both bands abandoned their hotel in San Mateo and headed across the Golden Gate Bridge to find an ocean-side hotel somewhere near Point Reyes. A day resting one's tootsies in the Humboldt Current ensued. It was sunny. It was chilled. Result: some fell asleep and OD'ed on the rays. They went on stage with severely burnt feet. One crew member ended up in hospital with sun stroke. Otherwise, the Bay area was a reasonable success and Peter was happy, he'd found time to indulge his liking for roller coasters with a ride on a particularly stomach churning one at San Jose's *Great America Parkway*.

On Wednesday, 25th June, the tour moved to the heat and humidity of Chicago in mid-summer. Here, spending even a few minutes out of the air-conditioned hotel, reduced the unwary to a dripping puddle of sweat. Here we were interviewed by Joan Tortorici Ruppert of the *Illinois Entertainer* (see page 445) before heading off to the elderly and decrepit *Uptown Theatre*. So decrepit, indeed, the balcony was closed on safety grounds. It was, perhaps, as dangerous as some of the neighbourhoods the band drove through on a more exotic than usual scenic route to the gig. The Chicago audience was kind and the band was pretty well received. The low points of the tour were to come.

For the road crew, life was now getting tough. After dismantling the stage after Chicago they were on the road for the 850 mile drive to Cleveland. Life for the musicians was rather more civilised and, at 11.30 a.m., *UA304* took to the skies for the two-hour flight to the city known fondly as *The Mistake on the Lake*. Cleveland was a 'rust belt' berg and the *Holiday Inn Lakeside* looked out over the foetid waters of Lake Erie. The venue tonight was the *Music Hall*, a modern and soulless auditorium. For the first time, our performance was lacklustre and the audience reaction muted. It was with no great sadness, therefore, that the *Randoms* boarded *Flight AL266* for Buffalo in upstate New York. We did get a decent album review in a magazine from nearby Detroit though (see page 446).

Although we were staying in yet another *Holiday Inn* in Buffalo, that night we were due to play at the *Auditorium* in Rochester, a short drive to the east along *Interstate 90*. Rochester was like Cleveland, only smaller, scruffier, and on a different lake (Lake Ontario). The audience was similar too, and we played another downbeat and ragged set which led to a few words being exchanged backstage. The following day, after an interview at a local Buffalo radio station, we set off to play Buffalo's *Kleinhans Music Hall* at the poetically named *Symphony Circle*. There followed the low point of the tour. The band played poorly, the audience was cool, and David Ferguson and I tried replicating one of our regular alcohol-fuelled political arguments at the top of our voices in front of the complete Gabriel entourage and a large number of guests.

Monday, 30th June was a much-needed day of rest and we, accompanied by Peter, headed off to gasp at Niagara Falls and visit another theme park, this one reputed to have the steepest roller coaster in North America. Whilst everyone was scared shitless, Peter insisted on several rides and finished the day with numerous descents of a steep and wild water chute. He is completely barking. But lovely for all that.

On the 1st July, the tour moved on to Toronto where we picked up a car and drove, via the northern shore of Lake Ontario, the 450 kms to Ottawa. Not consulting a map and completely misjudging the time it takes to drive between cities in North America would become a recurring theme on what was left of the tour. We did, however, get an interesting glimpse of rural eastern Canada. The sensible people flew.

With the arguments, and poor performances, looming over us, the Ottawa gig could have been another disastrous night. But, as is the way of these things, the venting of pent-up anger seemed to have done everyone some good. The performance was awesome (*Ed.* Really? *BM.* Yes) and the crowd reacted accordingly. Against our better judgement, the band was called back on stage for an encore, an unlikely occurrence for a support band, and we could easily have done more. Amusingly, this was the last night Peter introduced the band on stage until the last gig of the tour at the *Tower Theatre*, Philadelphia. The local press liked it too:

The Ottawa Journal, 3rd July 1980

There appeared to be some thought put into the choice of opening act. *Random Hold* was not merely a band to fill in time before the major attraction appeared. It complemented Gabriel's vision by adding its own dimension to it.

The band created an atmosphere of danger and fear; slowly building a thick mood of dark sobriety, then puncturing it with spontaneous madness. If people of the 50s wondered what the music of the '80s might be like, this is what they might have imagined. Perhaps the music of the '80s is the way it is because this is how many imagined it should be. Whatever the case, *Random Hold* brings you a step further down the cosmic evolutionary path but its intentions are not campily calculated.

The words *Random Hold* that make the band's name suggests the set of contradictions that are their musical work print. At times they seem so coldly calculated, but at any given moment it could lose control and lurch into tribal chaos. Opposites.

Random Hold seems to have a fascination for those notions which are not nailed down in the ordered realm of scientific knowledge. This is evident by the name of their soon-to-be released, LP, *Etceteraville*, but this preoccupation is particularly defined by the song *Passive Camera* about taking photos of everything that moves.

At the end of their set the crowd applauded madly, even though it is unlikely many had even heard of the group before last night. It was overall an audience that were as adventurous as the music they had come to hear.

The next venue was the huge *Maple Leaf Gardens* in Toronto, an enormous ice hockey rink filled to capacity with some 18,000 dedicated Gabriel fans. No matter, we took the place by storm. This time, though, we resisted the temptation – and the voluble requests – to do an encore. To set the seal on our performance, a few minutes after we came off stage, various attractive young ladies found their way into the dressing room where they were eyed nervously by the band before they retired, confused by the absence of reaction. Strange people these English musicians.

The band then made it three in a row with another storming performance at the *Forum Concert Bowl* in Montreal. After the gig, we decided to go out to celebrate, got lost and spent a couple of hours driving around greater Montreal looking for *Loews La Cité Hotel* where everyone was staying. Getting out of the hotel the following day was also something of a problem. The many tennis fans in the team, Phipps, Colson, Gabriel and most of his band, had their eyes glued to the television as one of the epic Bjorn Borg/John McEnroe Wimbledon finals was played out[i]. It was with considerable reluctance that we set off for the airport and the forty-minute flight to Quebec.

Any hopes the band would make it four triumphs out of four were shattered at the *Pavillion de la Jeunesse* in Quebec. A moderately sized, concrete basketball stadium, the acoustics were awful, the heat and humidity unbearable, and the audience tepid. Everyone, including the Gabriel band, were more than happy to leave and head for New York, which we reached in the late afternoon of Sunday, 6th July.

It was about this time *Passport Records* came up with a suggestion to extend *Random Hold's* stay in the States. The plan was this: *Passport* would cover the expenses of a tour of small clubs which would last for a month or two. They sounded out several West Coast venues and the response was promising. The work would be tough, relentless even, but, if we wanted to capitalise on the impact so far made, it was a sensible plan. We discussed it and were initially favourable to the scheme to the extent that I phoned my wife, Helen, to tell her we might not be returning as planned. Went down well. But, a few days later, the decision was made to return home first before coming back in the early autumn.

On the Monday, the two bands were due to play Central Park in daylight as part of a *Doctor Pepper* music festival. For the only time on the tour a sound check was impossible. The on-stage monitoring was awful, the acoustics worse, and the audience, a typical bunch of cynical New Yorkers, not interested. We reciprocated with a performance which reflected our complete dismay at the conditions. We were later trashed in a

---

[i] Won by Borg 1–6, 7–5, 6–3, 6–7 (16–18), 8–6 in one of the greatest tennis matches ever.

vitriolic review by the appropriately named Philip Bashe in a magazine called *Good Times*. Good times they definitely were not.

The next day we set off for Boston. Whilst everyone else flew on the New York-Boston shuttle, the *Randoms*, again without consulting a map, decided to drive. With the then prevailing speed limits of 55 mph, the journey took over 5 hours with stops. We checked into the hotel and then drove to the *Orpheum Theater* where we left the car. Both performance and reaction were reasonable and we, tired from the journey, decided to head off back to the hotel without watching Gabriel. Finding only a space where the car had been, we hailed a taxi and returned to the hotel before calling the police to report the theft of our vehicle. By the time, two heavily armed Boston policemen arrived, the team was somewhat 'tired and emotional' after having gained intimate acquaintance with numerous bottles of *Millers, Coors, Bud* and the like. It is not thought that the Boston constabulary were desperately amused by the performance of these four extremely inebriated English musicians, and they departed advising us that the chances of finding the car were zero... or less.

Every cloud having a silver lining, we could now board the shuttle and fly back to Newark but then, again, seriously misjudged times and distances. Rather than taking the relatively short trip (70 kms) down the *Garden State Parkway* to the *Convention Hall*, Asbury Park, where we were due to play that night, we drove, instead, along the *New Jersey Turnpike* to Philadelphia, where the hotel was, checked in, and then drove the back to Asbury Park, a distance more than twice as far. Arriving in time to do a bare five-minute sound check, the gig was pretty shambolic and the audience reaction vague.

The last night of the tour was at the famous *Tower Theatre* in Philadelphia and was trailed in a local magazine called *The Aquarian*.

Random Hold takes a Musical Stand
The Aquarian, 23rd July 1980
Following *Random Hold's* Central Park concert, synthesizer player David Ferguson noted that most Americans are totally unfamiliar with the meanings of the group's song titles and even with its name, for that matter. The group (bassist Bill MacCormick, drummer Pete Phipps, guitarist David Rhodes and Ferguson), making its first tour of the U.S., opened for Peter Gabriel.

Central Reservation a song from the British band's American debut LP, *Etceteraville (Passport)*, 'doesn't have any meaning over here; it's not a clear term', explained Ferguson. 'In England, it's the grass verge on a motorway. The song', he continued, 'was originally conceived as a song about driving cars down motorways and about certain emotional expectations of doing that at night – the excitement of not knowing what's in front of you. Over here, some people have taken it to be about a love affair that had gone wrong'.

Ferguson suggested that the group's vagueness was perhaps intentional, designed to allow the listener to draw his or her own interpretation...

... Two years later, they decided to branch out by writing rock tunes, still employing the same 'feeling for noise'. Does Ferguson feel that *Random Hold's* music might be too esoteric for most listeners?

'In England', he stated, matter-of-factly, 'we don't fit very comfortably into radio programming, and I don't think we fit very comfortably here either. The airwaves, both here and there, are dominated by history lessons. I work on the general principle that it's a good idea to turn radios off. What I think we're doing', he added, 'is taking a stand with the music and our viewpoints as well, a stand which disapproves of a lot of the stuff we see around us. Instantaneous acceptance, in a way, would be a harmful thing'. Ferguson decided that if *Random Hold's* music were accepted on a grand scale, most people would choose to employ it as 'coffee table music', which would be equally unnerving.

Both performance and reaction at *The Tower* were OK and, as a historic audio document, I recorded the gigs, but what surprised the band most was the immediate and hurried dispersal of the audience. Normally, a few dozen at least hung around trying to grab a word with Peter but, tonight, the kids legged it within minutes of the show ending. It was only on the return journey through West Phillie that the band realised why. At every traffic light, this bunch of white boys were given hard stares by any number of heavy looking (and possibly heavily armed) black guys. We were certainly not in the right 'hood' and it was with some relief the *Holiday Inn* was spotted.

Everyone was given two days off in New York before catching the plane home from JFK. The people at *Passport* expressed their enthusiasm at what they took to be the imminent return of the band and, at 7.30 p.m., we settled back into our seats aboard *Flight GK40* as the *747* climbed steeply, turned on an easterly heading to run south of Long Island before turning northeast towards Newfoundland, home... and oblivion.

WHETHER RANDOM HOLD WOULD HAVE SURVIVED if we had moved seamlessly on to the US dates after the Gabriel tour finished is debatable. Whether the time after the return gave the two Davids the chance to consider the future of the band, or whether they had already considered it and had returned home purely to find a new bass player I cannot say.

What he can say is that after a short break, I was invited to a meeting at David Ferguson's flat in West Dulwich. The atmosphere was bleak and the message uncompromising. They had decided that I was no longer suitable for the band. Was it 'musical differences' or a 'personality clash'? Afterwards I was not entirely clear. What I did know was that I was bloody angry and bitter. Having risked a lot of money, and spent a lot of time getting the band into a position where we were wanted back in the USA by a record company that wanted to invest in us, was the ultimate in frustration.

Returning home to the house in Penge, I spent the rest of the day ranting and raving and generally giving Helen and the cats a seriously hard time. The next morning, I phoned Gail Colson and was rather surprised to discover that neither she, nor Tony Smith, knew anything about the events of the previous day. She suggested we meet, and I headed off to Shaftesbury Avenue to talk matters over. With me went the band's books.

Both Tony and Gail seemed genuinely perplexed at the turn of events. I then dropped a bombshell of my own. The band still owed me several thousand pounds from the pre-*Polydor* period I had not yet recovered. The figures were checked and agreed, and, without quibble, Gail signed a cheque for the balance owed. The payment effectively emptied the *Random Hold* bank account.

The two Davids now had a band without a bass player (a problem that could be rectified) but also without any cash (a problem not so easily resolved). Faced with this predicament, and with the only recourse being a long dragged out, poorly financed tour of tiny US clubs, the two Davids chucked it in. Rhodes, of course, had an outlet, as it was clear that Peter Gabriel would like him to play live as well as on record in the near future. Ferguson decided on forming a *Random Hold* Mk 2 and set to recruiting new musicians for the project.

Given the abruptness and acrimony of the break-up it was inevitable the two Davids and I would not speak for some long time. Or, indeed, ever. Well, you'd think so wouldn't you. But these guys are/were pretty weird. Within a few weeks of breaking up the band that was to make and sell millions, I was managing (albeit briefly) the re-incarnated *Random Hold* and was helping to produce some demo tapes for David Rhodes at a little studio near Clapham Common.

Random Hold, however, was dead, the briefest of footnotes in the history of rock 'n' roll. The band's break-up was, perhaps fittingly, reported in the *Melody Maker*, the one music paper that consistently reported our actions and who, by printing the Allan Jones article in its entirety, allowed at least some of our music to see the light of day:

RANDOM HOLD: picture flickers
Melody Maker, 16th August 1980

In last week's issue, *Random Hold* were looking for a new bass player. This week, they're also looking for a new keyboardist, drummer and guitarist. In other words, *Random Hold* have split up.

The band began with guitarist David Rhodes and keyboardist David Ferguson's disillusionment with the state of rock 'n' roll in September 1976 which led to their forming the experimental duo *Manscheinen* who went under the curious statement that 'All art is halitosis; *Manscheinen* are toothpaste!'

The *Random Hold* that split featured the two Davids, bass player Bill MacCormick, formerly of *Quiet Sun* and Robert Wyatt's *Matching Mole*, and drummer Pete Phipps, who'd previously spent five years smashing the skins for the *Glitter Band* (no comment). In between the band incorporated drummer David Leach and guitarist/vocalist Simon Ainley (ex-*Eric Smith Explosion* and *801*).

Random Hold signed to *Polydor* under the aegis of *Hit and Run Management* (who also handle *Genesis*, Peter Hammill and Peter Gabriel) and released one album, two singles and an EP, all produced by Hammill before knocking it on the head. They toured with *XTC* and supported Peter Gabriel on his recent English and American tours. Gabriel introduced them as 'one of the most exciting young bands I've heard'.

The split came about on the band's return from the States (their last gig being at the *Tower Theatre*, Philadelphia) when Bill MacCormick was sacked. Surprised, Bill?

'You could say that'. MacCormick was initially stunned, as the reaction to the band in the States was excellent. He cites the reason for the eventual split as the incompatibility between the two Davids. Also, having dumped both Ainley and himself, *Random Hold* ran out of scapegoats. Five days after MacCormick was sacked, *Random Hold* split up. 'It lasted about five weeks less than I thought'.

Founder member Ferguson didn't believe MacCormick was 'right for the sort of music *Random Hold* should be doing. It was a question of not having the faith to carry on, David and I knew there was something missing'.

It was Rhodes, the band's focal point on stage and writer of 90% of their material, who axed MacCormick, and it was between he and Ferguson that the decision to break up was made. To have carried on would have meant renegotiating a new record deal and touring round the small clubs and colleges which neither Rhodes nor Ferguson felt like attempting again.

WITHIN A FEW MONTHS, DAVID RHODES joined up with Peter Gabriel to form a partnership that endures to this day. His distinctive and original guitar style would soon be in demand, and he has played with some of the finest artists and bands around. If I harbour a sense of disappointment with David's career it is only that he did not actively pursue his own writing until relatively recently, i.e. 2009, when he released a solo album, *Bittersweet*, and again in 2013, with *Rhodes*. The material he was producing towards the end of *Random Hold's* short life and the songs he recorded on those demo tapes in 1980 were outstanding and deserved to be heard by a wider audience.

David Ferguson signed a deal with *RCA* and recorded another *Random Hold* album, *Burn the Buildings*, and then did a deal with *Atlantic* with a band called *Nine Ways to Win* (another fruit machine reference) before turning to a lucrative and artistically successful career in soundtrack music. His breakthrough was with the soundtrack to a *Granada* documentary *The Sword of Islam*. Later, his scores appeared on a large number of TV programmes: two BBC children's dramas, *Moondial* and *A Country Boy*, BBC adaptations of Ruth Rendell's *A Fatal Inversion* and *A Dark Adapted Eye*, and the second series of Granada's thriller *Cracker*, starring Robbie Coltrane. He was nominated for an *Ivor Novello Award* for the Carlton/BBC thriller *The Woman in White*. I can remember hearing some theme music, I think it was for *Moondial*, and telling my wife that it had to be by Ferguson, his sound was so distinctive. He later became Chairman of the *British Academy of Songwriters, Composers and Authors* (*BASCA* and now the *Ivor's Academy*) and, making use of his political skills, campaigned vigorously, and internationally, for improved royalty rates and intellectual rights for composers. David tragically died from cancer on 5th July 2009, aged 56. *BASCA* organised a memorial get together at which I spoke. Peter Gabriel was there, too, and, nearly thirty years after we last saw one another, he greeted me like a long-lost friend.

Looking back, I think I knew I had reached my limitations as a bass player. That is not a difficult decision to come to when, every night for almost a month, one witnessed at close quarters displays of bass-playing wizardry by Tony Levin to which one could never aspire. My time was up. I had a good run for my money. It was time to move on.

I briefly flirted with the idea of going into management. Indeed, Tony Smith, suggested setting up a new company with him as joint owner. I would manage the re-vamped *Random Hold* and search for other new talent. But, within weeks of having to deal with the numpties who inhabited various A&R departments (I have a particularly negative recollection of the people at *MCA*), I decided I'd had enough of the music business. By early 1981 I had severed most of my links with the industry. Instead, I turned to politics. As you do.

FOR A COUPLE OF YEARS after the band broke up, I was intermittently amused by the *Polydor* royalty statements which showed an outstanding balance of something like £69,000 on the advance. But the advance was 'recoupable not returnable'. An essential clause in any recording contract.

Then, despite its singular lack of success, David Ferguson somehow persuaded a small, independent label to press up a few hundred vinyl copies of the original double album. It was entitled *Avalanche*. In 2001, I organised the release of two *Random Hold* CD boxed sets: *The View from Here*, the originally conceived album, plus live recordings of the band's last gig at the *Tower Theatre* in 1980; and *Over View*, an archive collection of everything else from before I joined through to the last demo tapes recorded before the Gabriel US Tour. They may well still be out there somewhere for all I know. If they are, who's getting the royalties???

Apart from that, the rest is silence.

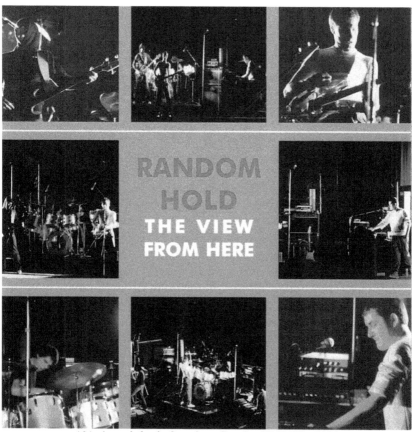

101 Artwork for the first of two Random Hold CDs, 2001.
Amazingly, it has twelve reviews on Amazon. They are all 5-Stars!
The second CD was entitled Over View and contained all of the band's demos.

WHERE ARE SOME OF THEM NOW?

PHIL MANZANERA

Phil continued to be prolific both as a player and producer after *Roxy Music* re-formed to record *Manifesto*. Two more *Roxy* albums followed: *Flesh and Blood*, partly recorded as his *Gallery Studio* at St Ann's Hill Court, and *Avalon*. He then produced his fourth solo album, *Primitive Guitars*, in 1982. In the mid-80s he briefly formed *The Explorers* with Andy Mackay, releasing two albums. In 1991, he was musical director of the extraordinary *Guitar Legends* festival in Seville. Since then, he has produced numerous albums, including many featuring artists from Latin America and Spain; David Gilmour's solo album *On an Island*; and produced a series of solo albums: *Vozero, 6 PM, 50 Minutes Later, Firebird VII, The Sound of Blue* and, most recently, *Caught by the Heart* with singer Tim Finn.

In 2001 he joined the re-formed *Roxy Music* on a 52-date world tour, Further gigs followed in 2003/4, again in 2011 and finally in 2022 when the band wrapped up its career at the O2.

His autobiography, *Revolucion to Roxy*, was published in 2024.

CHARLES HAYWARD

Charles has remained an active, some might say hyperactive, presence on the British experimental music scene ever since *Quiet Sun* first broke up in 1971. After a brief stint with *Gong* and the recording of *Mainstream*, Charles formed *This Heat* with Charles Bullen and Gareth Williams. I helped with the recording of some demos in late 1975 but their eponymous album did not emerge until 1979, with a second album, *Deceit*, released in 1981. He later formed *Camberwell Now* with bass player Trefor Goronwy which released two EPs before breaking up in 1987. He then embarked on a solo career, building up a cult following in Japan of all places. He has collaborated with too many musicians to mention over an extended career in which his energy, creativity, and desire to explore the outer reaches of music have never flagged. In early 2024, he went on tour with his most recent band: *Abstract Concrete*.

ROBERT WYATT

After *Ruth is Stranger than Richard* Robert did not record another solo album until 1985 when *Old Rottenhat* was released. That is not to say he was inactive but, during that interval, he chose to work with other musicians: *Henry Cow*, Carla Bley, Mike Mantler, and Brian Eno amongst them. In 1983 he had a hit single with the Elvis Costello/Clive Langer song *Shipbuilding*, an acid commentary on the recent Falklands War. It reached No. 35 in the UK singles charts. Although he continued to collaborate with other artists, it was a series of widely spaced solo albums which cemented his place in the pantheon of great British musicians/composers: *Dondestan* (1991), *Shleep* (1997), *Cuckooland* (2003) and *Comicopera* (2007). The last three were wholly or partly recorded at Phil's new *Gallery Studio* in Kilburn which he partly designed to accommodate Robert and Alfie when they took up residence during the sessions.

He announced he had stopped making music in 2014, and he and Alfie live quietly in Louth in Lincolnshire.

DAVID RHODES

Soon after the demise of *Random Hold*, David took up the role he has fulfilled ever since: guitarist with Peter Gabriel. He has appeared on every Gabriel album of new material since 1980: *Peter Gabriel 3* aka *Melt*, *So* (1986), *Us* (1992, *Up* (2002), and *I/O* (2023), as well as the soundtrack albums *Birdy* (1985), *Passion* (1989) and *Long Walk Home* (2002). In between, David worked with *Japan*, *Talk Talk*, Joan Armatrading, Paul McCartney, Tori Amos, and Kate Bush amongst many others.

He, very belatedly, released his first solo album in 2009, *Bittersweet*. This was followed up in 2013 by *Rhodes*. He has occasionally toured with a trio playing this material but, with the drip-fed release of Gabriels' *I/O*, a new track every full moon from January 2022 and the full album on 1st December 2023, he was again back with Peter and a large scale world tour.

A unique, thoughtful, and creative guitarist and musician, he is a man who would never play multiple notes when one would suffice.

ME

The least interesting of the lot. Left the music business in 1980 and sold most of my guitars, etc. Stood as Liberal candidate for Beckenham in the 1983 Greater London Council elections. Was one of three candidates short-listed to fight the Bermondsey By-Election in 1983, won by Liberal Simon Hughes. Appointed the Liberal Party's London Area Agent, 1984. Ran computerised campaigns from the Brecon and Radnor by-election of 1985 (won by Liberal Richard Livsey) through to Kincardine and Deeside in 1991 (won by Liberal Democrat Nicol Stephen). Elected to Bromley Brough Council for the Anerley ward, 1990 (Re-elected 1994 and 1998. Retired 2002). Set up a polling organisation which did the Liberal Democrats' market research up to the 1997 General Election.

Forced to retire on health grounds, 1998.

Written a few books since then.

This is one of them.

Sorry.

POSTSCRIPT - 2003

102 Ian MacDonald MacCormick. Big bro'. 1948-2003
[Photo: Ritva Saarriko]

ON THE EVENING OF 20TH AUGUST 2003, Ian MacCormick pinned a terse note on the front door of his little house in Wotton under Edge. It read: 'Call the Police'. The next morning, officers from the Gloucestershire Constabulary found him lying dead on the sofa. It was the final, and successful, attempt to take his own life.

It was tragic waste of a brilliant mind even if, for him, it might have been relief from the turmoil and anguish of his last few years.

At Dulwich College he was recognised as 'the outstanding poet of his generation'. He won the Alleynian Prize for creative writing in successive years, 1965/6 and 1966/7. And, after he had gone up to King's College, Cambridge, a place given without needing to know his A-Level results, a special section devoted to his poetry was included in the Winter 1968 edition of the school magazine, *The Alleynian*. One was called *Dead Cold*:

> *The estuary is icy; I have a cold.*
> *When one is ill, one is five points*
> *Nearer death. The fisher fleet files out*
> *To colden shallow cod with complex*
> *Cures. Deed me a deadtime Dory.*
> *The river is death-breath, burst*
> *And whistling from cold lungs.*
>
> *The siren has a haemorrhage of sound*
> *All over the fog. Heave deeply.*
> *Cold flows the travelling tide*
> *Into baleful oceans. In the same way*
> *Tides of grass heave over tumuli,*
> *And sirens haemorrhage cold fish*
> *All over my face on the fog barrows.*

Ian won his place at King's College ostensibly to read English, in 1968. He spent most of the year dropping acid and, to quote an early *Mothers of Invention* song, 'smoking an awful lot of dope'. He changed courses to, and from, Archaeology and Anthropology in order to successfully avoid the end of year exams. And then he left.

The use of marijuana became something of a constant in his life. Even as he descended into a series of bouts of severe depression, it was his view that smoking dope was what got him through the day. In my, admittedly belated, opinion it was what killed him.

His first, and serious, suicide attempt was in the mid-70s and the bottle of paracetamol he consumed only failed because the added bottle of vodka made him throw up the pills. A second attempt in the 90s was clearly a call for help as he sought the assistance of his neighbours who called an ambulance.

In between all of this, he had been the Assistant Editor of the *New Musical Express*, helping editor Nick Logan take it from its 60s teeny-bop market to being the biggest-selling serious music weekly in Britain. At the same time he helped to recruit such major literary and journalistic figures as Charles Shaar Murray, Nick Kent and Tony Tyler.

In the late 80s, and under the name *Sub Rosa*, he composed and recorded an entire album of his own songs at Phil's new state-of-the-art recording studio in the Stables at St Ann's Hill Court.

Then he wrote his seminal books: *Revolution in the Head* and *The New Shostakovich*. After the success of the former book he was given a large advance by *Random House* to write a similar work on the songs of David Bowie. I have read what little of it exists. It would have been equally brilliant and revelatory. He was also working on a major reference work on the myths and legends associated with the world's wildlife. Again, the 200 or so pages he completed were outstanding.

In the 90s and beyond he wrote for *Mojo* and *Uncut*[i] and, with the *Random House* advance, bought the house in Wootton under Edge, moving out of our parent's house in Cirencester where he had lived for some fifteen years.

There, though, he became increasingly isolated and uncommunicative. We spoke less and less frequently and conversations tended to be brief. I later discovered that he had been diagnosed with schizophrenia to add to his depressive periods.

Some years after his death, I read an article in *The Times* about the effect use of marijuana could have on certain susceptible people, people who went on to develop schizophrenia. It listed ten personality characteristics of such people. I could associate nine of them directly with Ian, not least his inability to maintain relationships. This led to break-ups with two lovely girlfriends and a falling-out with an increasing number of long term friends and colleagues. Sadly, one of these was Brian Eno whom he had come to know well both through the *NME* and from working in the studio with Phil and me.

He became lonely, found work increasingly difficult to finish, and started to worry about money. In his head, he developed fantastical relationships with people he had never met. All the while, his only 'relief' was the dope sent by friends who did not realise they were only helping to cause more problems than they solved. In truth, all they did was what he asked by sending him the drugs.

By August 2003 it was all too much to bear.

His final note asked us to think of him getting 'closer to the light'. He was not religious but had a belief in something spiritual beyond the material world. This is not an idea I share, but I hope this belief brought him some comfort in his last moments.

APART FROM RUNNING PHIL'S WEB SITE and, a bit later, the official *Genesis* and Phil Collins' web sites, my involvement in the music business ceased in 1980. My last recorded bass part, however, appears on a song Phil wrote

---

[i] Many of his articles were later republished as *The People's Music*. Updated and revised versions of *Revolution in the Head* and *The New Shostakovich* were published posthumously.

after Ian committed suicide. Entitled *Wish You Well*, it appeared on his 2004 album *6 PM*. It is a lovely, *Beatle*-like, song which Phil sings himself, but which also features a harmonica part in remembrance of Ian's playing of the instrument way back.

Phil asked me to add a bass solo, an instrument I had not touched for 23 years. After some effort and blisters I managed it. I think the whole piece is a fitting tribute to a brilliant, creative and analytical mind, and a presence I miss every day.

I hope Phil won't mind if I reproduce the lyrics here. They mean a lot to me.

Goodbye old friend
Out on Flight 19
Off with Saint Serene
I wish you well

If there's another state
If what you said is true
We'll meet again some day
As we wander through

You found a way
To make yourself be heard
Seems like the time had come
To leave the people's world

Goodbye old friend
Out on Flight 19
Off with Saint Serene
I wish you well

And somewhere
Far on a red horizon
Your flame
Lightens a darkened mind
And somehow
It doesn't seem so surprising
'Cos the truth
Was right there before your eyes

I wish you well, I wish you well
I wish you well, I wish you well

© Phil Manzanera 2004

PPS - 2020

IN 2015 MY WIFE AND I were on a cruise in the Mediterranean. We started out from Malta, visiting Sicily and Naples and were cruising towards Corfu overnight. I don't sleep well anyway but, in a foreign bed, rather poorly. So, lying there, staring at the ceiling of the suite for hours on end for some reason I started going over some *Quiet Sun* music in my head. Before long, I was creating a new, expanded, version of the album with added extras, in particular a brass section. It sounded pretty damn good.

Some months later I jokingly mentioned it to Phil. He stores these things away. Just in case.

At the end of 2019 he called me. About a *Quiet Sun* reunion. Apparently, a Japanese promoter with whom Phil had previously worked wanted the band to play a variety of jazz clubs in Tokyo and some other Japanese cities. All expenses, including those of our partners, would be covered. All to take place in late 2020 or early 2021.

I pointed out I had not touched a bass guitar in nearly 40 years. No, problem, was Phil's view. Work at it for three months or so and see how it feels. What about Charles Hayward, I ventured? We'll get Charles over, see what he thinks. And Dave Jarrett, of whose whereabouts we were both ignorant? If necessary we can get someone in to play those parts, Phil replied. And a brass section? There are plenty of great young Japanese players. The promoter will organise that.

So, no way out.

In January 2020, I drove up to Phil's place in Kilburn where we were to meet Charles and see what he felt about the idea. Initially sceptical, he was won round. We would do this and, should anyone else be interested in paying us to play at festivals and the like, we would look at each offer on its merits. Brass Section? I offered to pay to get some charts made up.

We would film and record everything, rehearsals, performances, life in Japan, etc., so there was some end product to flog to unsuspecting punters at the end of it in a boost to the pension funds.

I toddled off home, dusted down the *Peavey* bass which had been quietly snoozing in the corner of the office. I bought a tiny little *Vox* bass amp which plugged directly into the guitar and which would allow me to play along with the tracks. I even bought a little gizmo with which to strengthen up my somewhat arthritic fingers. All seemed set fair. I would, at long last, get to play the bass solo on *Rongwrong*. Live.

And then Covid.

So near and yet so far. It would have been a nice way of bookending the career. Shame.

WE ARE ALL JUST PASSING THROUGH

AVE ATQUE VALE

103 Philip Paul Brisco Miller104

Phil Miller, grimacing, singular and meticulous prog rock guitarist and stalwart of the
'Canterbury scene' in the 1970s who enjoyed boating
Obituary, *The Times,* 2nd November 2017

PHIL MILLER'S FELLOW MUSICIANS liked to tease him that he
terrified audiences into submission with the fearsome grimaces that
accompanied his gut-twisting guitar solos. On stage his agonised
expressions resembled 'a professor grappling with an inordinately complex
equation' according to one critic.

In reality, it was his meticulous and technically precise playing that held
audiences spellbound over more than 40 years as a member of several of
the most adventurous and outré exponents of brain-scrambling prog rock,
including *Matching Mole, Hatfield & The North* and *National Health.*

A stalwart of the extended musical family known as the 'Canterbury
Scene', Miller hailed from the backwaters of Hertfordshire rather than the
cathedral city in Kent, but the branding became synonymous with a
distinctive fusion of rock, jazz and Anglo-Saxon whimsy after seminal
prog acts *Soft Machine* and *Caravan* emerged from Canterbury in the mid-
1960s. The groups went on to spawn a complicated family tree of interrelated bands in which Miller played.

Yet Miller was not a musician who could be easily pigeon-holed, for he
developed a unique, cliché-free style of guitar playing so singular that it
was hard to detect any obvious influences. He would 'rather play a wrong
note than a note somebody else had played', according to Robert Wyatt,
the former *Soft Machine* drummer with whom he formed *Matching Mole* in
1971.

His compositions were sometimes so cerebral and complex that they
were sometimes impossible to play. Some pieces had 'so many notes you

couldn't ask somebody to do it live, so I got a machine to do it' he confessed.

Off stage he was warm, mild mannered and self-effacing. John Greaves, a close friend who played bass with him, described him as 'a gentle, taciturn man whose shy demeanour belied an unerring instinct for what's right and what isn't'. Another friend was Jonathan Coe who named his novel *The Rotters' Club* after a 1975 album Miller made with the band *Hatfield & The North*.

He was born Philip Paul Brisco Miller in Barnet in 1949, the son of a coffee broker, and grew up in Sawbridgeworth, Hertfordshire, where he lived next door to Pip Pyle, the group's drummer, who died in 2006. Educated at a Catholic boarding school and then at *Cambridge Technical College* he took up the guitar at the age of 15.

He formed his first professional group, *Delivery*, in 1968 with Pyle and his older brother Steve Miller on keyboards. A popular fixture on the university circuit, *Delivery* broke up in 1971, when Miller joined Wyatt in *Matching Mole*, a band noted for their fiendishly complex time signatures. When the group had run their course after recording two albums, he teamed up again with Pyle, his brother Steve and Richard Sinclair of Caravan to form *Hatfield & The North*.

Named after a sign on the A1 in north London, the group was promptly signed by Richard Branson to *Virgin Records*, which at the time was awash with cash from the unexpected success of Mike Oldfield's *Tubular Bells* and was boldly spending the windfall on the most experimental and uncommercial acts it could find. When the group broke up in 1975, he formed *National Health* before taking the plunge to become a band leader by forming the *Phil Miller Quartet*, later renamed *In Cahoots*.

Uniting jazz and rock musicians, Miller led the band through twelve albums, although he was not always enamoured with every aspect of the leader's role. 'It's what you have to do if you want to hear your music played, but you have to do the chores – get the gigs, book the rehearsal room and incur the phone bill,' he noted.

He was married to Herm, a painter who did some of the artwork for his albums. He supported Tottenham Hotspur FC and enjoyed boating on the Thames in a *Fleetwind* 12-foot sailing dinghy built by his father for his 14th birthday. His dedication for his music, however, left little time for much else. 'He played the guitar from the moment he got out of bed until the moment he went to sleep and never stopped working on his music until his illness prevented him.' said Benj Lefevre, a lifelong friend. 'He was just one of those rare individuals who never got bent out of shape.'

Phil Miller, musician, was born on 22nd January 1949.
He died from cancer on 18th October 2017, aged 68.
© *The Times Newspapers*, 2017

105 *HUGH COLIN HOPPER106*
Obituary, *The Guardian*, 10th June 2009
Adam Sweeting

THE COMPOSER AND BASS PLAYER Hugh Hopper, who has died aged 64 of leukaemia, achieved his highest public profile through his work with *Soft Machine* between 1968 and 1972, though mass-market acceptance was never high on his list of priorities. Hopper will be remembered by connoisseurs of British experimental art-rock for his instrumental gifts and his idiosyncratic composing style, with *Soft Machine* as well as on a long string of solo albums, the most recent of which was *Dune* (2008).

Born in Kent, Hopper found himself in at the ground floor of what would become known as the 'Canterbury scene', a musical and philosophical network encompassing *Kevin Ayers & The Whole World, Gong, Caravan* and *Henry Cow*, when he became a member of the *Wilde Flowers*. This was a fairly conventional pop and soul band that nonetheless served as a seed bed for the late-1960s flowering of progressive music in the cathedral city. Future *Soft Machinists* Robert Wyatt and Kevin Ayers also passed though the *Wilde Flowers*, as did the future members of *Caravan*.

Hopper joined *Soft Machine* at the end of 1968, after they had toured with Jimi Hendrix in the US, recorded a debut album in New York that was released solely in America, and had briefly featured the future *Police* guitarist Andy Summers. Hopper, having been the group's tour manager, replaced bassist/vocalist Ayers, completing the three-piece *Soft Machine* alongside the drummer Wyatt (with whom Hopper had briefly played, with the Australian guitarist/composer Daevid Allen) and the organist Mike Ratledge.

It was this line-up that recorded the second album, *Volume Two*, an early experiment in jazz fusion, and that also appeared uncredited on a couple of tracks on the first solo album by *Pink Floyd's* Syd Barrett, *The Madcap Laughs*. *Soft Machine* experimented by adding a quartet of horn players, then shed three of them and kept the fourth, the saxophonist Elton Dean, as their new full-time member. They recorded the albums *Third* and *Fourth*, exhibiting ever greater instrumental finesse, and established a milestone in the history of progressive rock when they played at the BBC Proms at the Royal Albert Hall in London, in 1970.

The quartet's hyperactive musical intelligence led to friction, and for many onlookers Wyatt's departure in 1971 marked the end of the 'real' *Soft Machine*. Hopper left in 1973 after recording *Six*, leaving the band to beat a path towards more conventional jazz-rock.

He said afterwards that towards the end of his time with the group he was beginning to feel like a civil servant: "I knew exactly where I was going to be a year ahead and I didn't like that. Also I didn't like the musical direction the band was heading in, and I wasn't personal friends with the rest of the band."

Just before leaving the group, Hopper had struck out towards independence by recording his first solo album, *1984*, an arresting mix of avant-garde musicality and multitrack sleight of hand. Once free of the *Softs*, he put in stints with some of the most inventive musicians of the era, including the *Carla Bley Band*, *Isotope* and *Gilgamesh*. He maintained his *Soft Machine* connection via regular collaborations with Dean. They appeared together in a quartet completed by the pianist Keith Tippett and the drummer Joe Gallivan, and hooked up with the drummer Pip Pyle (from *Gong*, and *Hatfield and the North*) and Alan Gowen in the Canterbury-based 'supergroup' *Soft Heap*, who recorded an album in 1978.

Hopper temporarily retreated from music at the start of the 1980s, but, feeling refreshed, bounced back to collaborate with Phil Miller's band *In Cahoots*, and appeared on Pyle's solo album *Equipe Out* with Dean and other Canterbury alumni (both Dean and Pyle died in 2006). The 1990s saw a string of intriguing Hopper solo albums including *Meccano Pelorus*, *Carousel* and *Hooligan Romantics*. In 2002, he banded together with Dean and fellow ex-*Soft Machine* guitarist Allan Holdsworth and drummer John

Marshall to form *Soft Works*. This later transformed itself into *Soft Machine Legacy*, mixing new compositions with extracts from the *Soft Machine* catalogue.

In June 2008, Hopper underwent chemotherapy after being diagnosed with leukaemia. A benefit concert was held for him at London's *100 Club* last December, featuring friends and collaborators from all phases of his career.

"The musicians and writers who give me most pleasure are those who know instinctively when to use the sledgehammer and when to use the delicate paintbrush," he told the *Glasgow Herald* in 1995. "I hope I am also one of them."

He married his partner Christine two days before his death.

Hugh Colin Hopper, musician, born 29th April 1945;
died 7th June 2009.
© *The Guardian*, 2009

107 *GARY WINDO108*
Aymeric Leroy, Calyx website
(*http://www.calyx-canterbury.fr/mus/windo_gary.html*)

A HIGHLY ORIGINAL MUSICIAN with an instantly recognizable style, Gary Windo was marginally involved with the Canterbury scene in the Seventies. Most notable was his work with Robert Wyatt on the albums *Rock Bottom* (1974) and *Ruth Is Stranger Than Richard* (1975), and Hugh Hopper on *1984* (1973) and *Hoppertunity Box* (1976). He was also a member of the Carla Bley band for three years.

Windo was born in England in a musical family, and began playing music at a very early age. He took up drums and accordion at six, then guitar at 12 and finally saxophone at 17. He settled in the USA in 1960, studying tenor sax and music theory with Wayne Marsh and Lennie Tristano. A long period of apprenticeship, both on- and off-stage, followed during the Sixties, until he finally decided to move back to England in 1969.

After jamming in London jazz clubs with musicians like Johnny Griffin, Chick Corea and Jimmy Ruffin, Windo rapidly became a fixture of the scene. In March 1970, he took part in an all-star jam session with Jack Bruce, Mitch Mitchell, Brian Auger and Graham Bond. And later that year he joined several jazz ensembles: Chris McGregor's *Brotherhood of Breath*,

Keith Tippett's 50-piece orchestra *Centipede*, and *Symbiosis*, a jamming band featuring Mongezi Feza, Roy Babbington and Robert Wyatt.

Having played pub gigs with guitarist Ray Russell's heavy-rock trio *The Running Man*, Windo recruited Russell for his own *Gary Windo Quartet*, which also featured Mongezi Feza on trumpet and Alan Rushton on drums. In the Summer of 1972, he played on Hugh Hopper's first solo album, *1984*, and the following year formed the jazz quartet *WMWM* with Robert Wyatt, pianist Dave MacRae and bassist Ron Matthewson. He almost became a member of the new line-up of Wyatt's *Matching Mole*, before Wyatt had his accident and the project was shelved. However, Windo appeared on his subsequent albums *Rock Bottom* and *Ruth Is Stranger Than Richard*.

Meanwhile, Windo kept touring with *Brotherhood of Breath* and *Centipede*, and formed *Gary Windo & Friends*, with his wife Pam Windo on piano, guitarist Richard Brunton and the rhythm section of Bill MacCormick and Nick Mason. This line-up played its sole gig at Maidstone College of Arts in November 1975, but was the precursor to Windo's *Steam Radio Tapes* project, recorded between 1976 and 1978 but never completed. Among the participants were, along with the aforementioned, Julie Tippetts, Robert Wyatt, Steve Hillage and Hugh Hopper.

In May 1976, Windo played on Hopper's album *Hoppertunity Box*, and followed him into Carla Bley's band, in time for the European Tour 1977 album. But while Hopper left to return to England, Windo followed Bley in America, playing on *Musique Mécanique* as well as various related projects – Michael Mantler's *More Movies*, Nick Mason's *Fictitious Sports*... While in New York he also recorded the album *Loaded Vinyl*, with Pam Windo and CBB members Steve Swallow and D. Sharpe, but again it remained unreleased; and he appeared on Daevid Allen's New York *Gong* album, *About Time*.

Windo spent subsequent years in America, doing copious session work as well as incidental music for TV shows such as *Saturday Night Live*, touring as special guest with *NRBQ* and the *Psychedelic Furs*. He also played with Pam Windo & *The Shades*, and recorded his first released solo album, *Dogface* (1982). Between 1984-88 he led his own rock quartet, the *Gary Windo Band*, with Knox Chandler (guitar), Jack Robinson (bass) and Steve Moses (drums). The album *Deep Water* (1987), released on *Island Records*, resulted.

From the late Eighties onwards, Windo resumed teaching and kept gigging with various bands. Having met writer Michael King while the latter was doing research for his book *Wrong Movements – A Robert Wyatt Discography*, he started dusting off old tapes and assembling a compilation album of unreleased material recorded with various line-ups, both as sideman and leader. The title *His Master's Bones* had been chosen when

Windo died of a heart failure triggered by an asthma attack, in 1992. The project was finally completed by King and released in 1996 by *Cuneiform Records*. A second volume of archive recordings appeared in 2004 on the same label, under the title *Anglo-American*.

109 LLOYD WATSON
Eulogy given by his sister, Norma Watson-Palmer, at his funeral in Peterborough Cathedral

A LETTER TO MY BROTHER

Dear Lloyd,

To use your favourite greeting to me – "Now then"!

So, big brother, you were very disappointed when Mum came home from hospital in August 1955 with a baby girl and not the Alsatian dog you wanted, but I hope you loved me as much as I loved you.

I remember you taking me to see *The Beatles* film *Help* at the Embassy? You held my hand and walked slowly as I had my leg in a cast yet again. You were so attentive and kind, but it took ages to get out of the cinema as you kept stopping to talk to everyone you knew and we nearly missed the 301 bus home.

You loved tormenting and teasing me. Your tormenting could get so bad at times that Mum and Dad separated us at meal times – you in the kitchen and me in the dining room!

Mum always called our family "Us Four". We were often four against the world as we faced up to prejudice but, Mum's motto of "Look up as it's harder to cry" saw us through and, I hope will see me through today, especially when I look up at this beautiful ceiling.

You were the first mixed-race boy to go to *Deacons Grammar School* where our cousins Trevor and Stuart were already studying. Whenever the cry went up "Someone's picking on Lloyd again" they both dived in to rescue you.

Not only were you blessed with the musical gene, but you had a phenomenal memory for facts, figures and trivia. From you I learnt that the word "Caribbean" came from the original tribe called The Caribs who were almost wiped out in the 15th century. They never taught that in schools! I'd watch in awe as you whizzed through a crossword puzzle or speed read your school textbooks and retain everything... and I mean everything!

Maths was never my strong subject like it was yours, so you set the times tables to soul music songs for me. How you laughed when I said the teacher had asked me a question about the 12 times table and I asked her to wait while I sang *You Don't Know Like I Know* by Sam & Dave so I could recall what 8 x 12 was. I can't remember what that total would be now! Your mind was such that I often joked that if you'd been at Bletchley Park in WW2, you'd have broken Enigma before the Germans had even invented it!

Music has always been part of both sides of the family. NanNan Gilbert used to play the organ at Ely Cathedral and later Coates Church, Mum could play the piano, and Grandma Suzette and Grandad Edwin in Jamaica lived their lives in the gentle laid back but firm style of the Caribbean... apart from the fact that each of their six children would sing in Church EVERY Sunday and know how to dance before they could walk. So it was no surprise that Mum spotted your musical talent and scrimped to find 2/6 for weekly piano lessons which went swimmingly until the teacher told Mum to save her money and find another instrument for you to learn as you could play better than she could. Mum took you to the pantomime and you needed no encouragement to get on stage with the harmonica player Ronald Chesney, leaving with a gift of a real miniature harmonica. Mum was petrified and knotted string through it so you could play it without swallowing it. The other year in one of our numerous text exchanges you told me about Mum taking you to see the pantomime Cinderella at *The Embassy Theatre*, and you described the scene where an old white-haired cobbler was sitting making the glass slipper, with pink and blue spotlights shining down on him and "Morning" from Pier Gynt by Grieg as the background music. That was your first encounter with music, theatre and atmosphere that you later recalled while watching David Bowie from the side of the stage in London.

Cousins Stuart Smith (RIP) and Alan Laud both played guitars and, realising you were interested when Stuart and Alan showed you some basic chords, Dad bought you an acoustic guitar for the princely sum of £6 and that, along with a Robert Johnson album that Mum bought you at Leicester Market started your love of soul and blues that continued right up to the end. Mum watched fascinated as you cobbled together a harmonica neck stand from a wire coat hanger... then promptly went to *Treutlin's* music shop to buy the real thing.

I remember sitting in the car with Mum while Dad went in to watch you and Ian Hatch at your first ever paid gig on 28th September 1963 at *The Cock Inn*, Werrington, Peterborough. I so wanted to go in and watch but was far too young so had to be satisfied with a bottle of pop and a packet of crisps while listening through the open window! That became the story of my life until I was old enough.

Then came *The Pathfinders* with Eddie Cavanagh, Ian Hatch and Dave Horton. The band were so named because Eddie's Dad, Vic, was with The Pathfinders in WW2. The band were booked most weekends but you still handed in your homework on time.

In 1966 came *The Soulmates* with Ian Bowen, Les Hill and assorted other musicians, and people began to take notice of your talent. Tickets for dances sold out instantly. I vividly remember Friday 10th March 1967 when you came back from a gig at USAF Alconbury, jumped out of the van, shouted goodnight to the others, slammed the front door and flew up the stairs in two bounds, burst into Mum & Dad's bedroom shouting "Dad! Dad! Three black guys asked if they could sing with the band tonight. They sang *For Your Precious Love* by Jerry Butler. It was real soul Dad; you'll love it. Oh, Mum, I forgot, they're coming for Sunday dinner tomorrow before we go to *The Harrow* at Deeping for a gig. I think they're going to join us"... and they did. Those airmen were Al Chisholm and Pee Wee Frye and, when his rota as a military policeman allowed, by Ray Gates.

Those were the days when girls brought YOU home under the umbrella so you wouldn't get your hair wet, then Mum and Dad had to take the girls home!

What about the Saturday afternoon when you threw me out of the front room when Al arrived clutching a single under his right arm? You needed the room to play the record so my history homework and I decamped to the back room while Al learnt the words and phrasing and you learnt the chords and that night the good people of Thorney Toll at the dance in the village hall were the first audience to hear *Sweet Soul Music* by Arthur Conley that Al had received from America that very morning. Now THAT'S history right there.

On 26th June 1966 *The Soulmates* opened for blues legend John Lee Hooker at *The Gaeity Club*, Ramsey. The band watched his show in awe, and you drank in every second.

The Soulmates won the Beat Competition at the Elwes Hall which, considering the musical talent of the band and the enthusiasm of the audience wasn't surprising. Mum & Dad beamed with pride and their faces are etched into my memory. When Al, PeeWee and Ray had to leave the UK, Mum was convinced that they would be sent to Vietnam and she fretted about them. Such a shame that she died before I found Al on *Facebook* and learnt he is singing with *The Contours*, and Pee Wee, who really is Stevie Wonder's cousin, sings with the *Motown Legends Gospel Choir*. Sadly, no trace of Ray has been found.

Pee Wee took you to meet Stevie when he was over on tour. You said you were still in two minds as to whether he was making it up... until you both walked into his hotel room and watched the two men hug and play fight. You and Pee Wee watched from the side of the stage and sneaked on to do a little back-up vocals. You hated computers and smart phones but was overjoyed when I showed you Al singing *Just A Little Misunderstanding* with *The Contours*. I spoke with Al the day after you left us and he sends his love to you, his friend.

On Saturday 6th January 1968 Paul Read who was *The Soulmates'* Manager took you and Pee Wee to *The Tin Hat Club* in Kettering to see *Fleetwood Mac*, got chatting to the band and asked if you and Pee Wee could jam on stage with them. Pee Wee sang *Stormy Monday* while you played the great Peter Green's guitar. Do you remember how astonished you were when I told you that years later while I was working at the BBC, I "legalled" a documentary about Peter. He declined to take part but rang from a public phone box the following day to say he was pleased with the broadcast. We chatted for a while and I mentioned you jamming with the band. Peter immediately recalled the night and asked me to pass on his best wishes. I did, and your expression was pure delight.

In 1969 in Cambridge, John Mayall invited you to join the band for a few numbers. You were so excited when you told us the following day.

There then came Lloyd Watson's *Pocket Edition* playing a mixture of soul and blues. Most weekends saw the band playing somewhere.

You joined *Ma Grinder's Blues Mission* backing visiting blues musicians every Monday night at *The Halcyon pub*. There were so many touring bands who played there, – Champion Jack Dupree, Duster Bennett and *Chicken Shack* are just three of the names that spring to mind. I'd often hear Mum counting as she went downstairs on a Tuesday morning – she was counting the number of touring musicians you'd brought home who had nowhere to sleep so she knew how many cooked breakfasts to make! Nobody was turned away. Her rationale was "Well I hope some other mother would do that for my boy if the need arose". You signed with *Blue Horizon*, cut tracks with Top Topham and worked with the talented Duster Bennet.

Moving on, there was *In The Beginning* with Rex Gates and Adrian Titman and it was with them that you initially entered the *Melody Maker Folk/Rock Competition*. Rex and Adrian took up the chance to play on the *QE2* so you changed your entry from the band to the solo section, and did just three solo gigs – the regionals, the semi-final and the final. The first Mum, Dad and I knew about it was when you returned from *The Roundhouse* in London in the early hours brandishing your trophy. When Dad asked why you hadn't told them before, you replied "I didn't want to let you down if I came nowhere". You never did let us down. Part of your prize was an appearance on the *BBC2* music show *The Old Grey Whistle Test*. Dad was on nights that Tuesday so he got a pass out, drove home, had a cup of tea, sat with Mum and I while we watched you, calmly put his coat on and drove back to *Perkins* to finish his shift. That appearance was spotted by David Bowie and led to you being offered the chance to open for him and *Roxy Music* at the famous *Rainbow* in Finsbury Park. During my time at the *BBC* I learnt that your performance of *Death Letter Blues* by Son House was played on the exact spot that the great man did his own performance; a fact that you found astounding. During the intervening time you opened for *Vinegar Joe*, *Procul Harum*, *King Crimson*, *Status Quo* and so many more. *Status Quo's* hit *Down Down* features the open tuning you showed Francis Rossi and Rick Parfitt how to do pre-gig at Croydon I believe.

Mum, Dad and I travelled down to the Sunday show at *The Rainbow* and met up with our cousin Shelia from Jamaica who was a nurse at Kings College Hospital and, most importantly, knew the way to Finsbury Park by car. We watched nervously as you strode on stage, strapped on your guitar and off you went. That night David Bowie had lent you his acoustic guitar as someone had broken into your dressing room the previous night and stolen yours. You put us on the guest list for the after-show party where David Bowie came over and introduced himself to us. When he'd moved on, Mum, bless her, uttered the words that only a mother can "A strange looking young man but impeccable manners"!

You were the opening act for *Roxy Music* on their UK and European tours. The reports in the music press of you climbing out of the window of a posh restaurant after a show, staggering along the ledge then re-entering from another window all the while juggling a wine glass and shouting "It's all part of the act chaps" are not exaggerated. Neither are the reports of you losing your glasses while staring out of the bus window with Brian Eno to stare at a passing pretty girl, only for the car travelling behind you to run over them! Hasty calls were made and Dad and I shot down to *EG Management* offices with one of your old pairs. That plan worked perfectly… at least until one of the lenses fell out and smashed! Undeterred, you cut a picture of an eye out of a magazine, sellotaped it over the frame and played on! What jolly japes eh?! You were so chuffed in October 2018 when you receive a text from Phil Manzanera calling you "The Bestest" but you were still modest about your talent, saying "What an honour from a fellow musician of his standing". It's also an honour for us to have Phil and Bill MacCormick here with us today.

In May 1976 your determination and talent was tested when you were electrocuted at a gig in the long gone but fondly remembered *Golden Fleece* in Peterborough. Only the quick reaction of fellow musician Mick Davison saved your fingers and your life, helped by the fact that you had one foot on the darts mat and were wearing an old pair of desert boots you rescued from the dustbin every time Mum threw them out. Paramedics took you to A&E where my friend Elizabeth was Sister on duty, recognised you and pleaded with the doctors to do all they could to save your hands. You were bandaged up, returned to the pub and strode in waving your hands and doing a passable Al Jolson impersonation. You were back at *The Falcon* the next night playing with Colin Hodgkinson and Rex Gates, with lollipop sticks bandaged onto your right hand and a much larger slide stuck to one of the fingers of your left and played the entire night, much to the astonishment of the two A&E doctors who came to watch. Long, painful skin grafts were undertaken at Addenbrookes Hospital in Cambridge. To lighten the mood on the ward, you somehow managed to climb on a chair (no mean feat with the fingers of your left hand sewn into your right upper arm), peer over the panel dividing the men from the women and shout "Hey up ladies! My rounds will start shortly so clean nighties on please"!

Do you remember the night we had to come over to find you after they'd called to say you'd disappeared? Nobody had seen you since tea time. Visiting Hours were over by the time we got to Cambridge but no porter was on duty so we rushed to the ward as fast as Dad's speeds of slow and stop would allow. I told Matron there was nobody on duty and before she finished her sentence of "No it's Peter's night off and he plays with his band" than I asked "Which pub?" There you were in your slippers and pyjamas playing tambourine with the band and resting it on your head between songs so you could partake of a sneaky alcoholic beverage! Your explanation to Matron of "Well, I only came here because some bright spark has decided to put a lock on the door of the room where the piano is kept" resulted in the offending lock being swiftly removed so you could continue your rehabilitation in the hospital!

Phil Manzanera from *Roxy Music* rang while you were in hospital and said he was putting a project together to do some gigs over the summer and wanted you to join the band. Back we went to Cambridge to pass the message on and I was immediately despatched to find the surgeon so you could bellow at him "Fire up the scalpel young man, I've got a tour and album to make"! You joined *801* and had the time of your life with Phil, Brian Eno, Simon Phillips. Bill MacCormick and Frances Monkman. The project was a short tour, an appearance at the *Reading Festival* and culminating in the final show at the Queen Elizabeth Hall, London being recorded. That amazing album has gone down in music history as one of the best live albums of all time.

When Bob and I got married we booked *The One Eyed Cats* to play at the reception. You, of course, knew all the guys and asked if you could sit in with them to play a song you'd written for me. The band learnt the song on the hoof, I stood spellbound and you stayed on stage all night! No surprise there eh?!

After Mum died in 2009, Dad wore her wedding and engagement rings on a chain around his neck. You inherited those rings from Dad after his death in 2014 and would kiss them each time you launched into another blistering solo so… as this is my solo… KISS RINGS.

On my 60th birthday after a few too many G&T's, I got up to sing with you, Rob and Mark when you played Tom Petty's *Won't Back Down*. Your look of disdain was priceless and when I asked later if I was in key you replied "Not really. I couldn't work out if you were singing in the key of Yale or Chubb".

You continued to play locally whenever you could and was overjoyed when your children displayed musical talents. Elliot took to the guitar like the proverbial duck to water, Aynsley became an accomplished drummer, Lauren is a wonderful singer, and Lauren's baby, Rudy, has already been to music festivals… so your heritage continues.

Aynsley died on 22nd August 2017 and, coming so soon after the deaths of Mum and Dad, knocked you sideways and you never really recovered your zest for life. Your solitude was always important to you, but it then became your prison but also your safe place. You shut yourself away and I watched the light go out of your eyes. Occasionally, there was a quick glimpse of the old Lloyd – the brother who was so popular about Peterborough that I had to check the coast was clear before I ventured onto "your territory" usually with my best friend Claire Trowell in tow.

The late Phil Lynott from *Thin Lizzy* was a good friend when I lived in London. He always wanted a photograph of you and him standing back-to-back with me peeping between you and he wanted to call it "Book

Ends". Sadly, the only night you came in the *Black Lion* in West Hampstead was the very night when Phil wasn't there… so the photograph never happened although it probably has now. A chat with Phil Lynott's mother, Philomena two years ago led to her sending you a message. She said "Tell Lloyd he will never get over the grief of losing a child but, God willing, he'll learn to hold the hand of that grief and walk beside it". Sadly, that did not happen for you but you still sent me a text at 10.40 every Friday night which was the time that Dad died as we nursed him and you'd say "Time to strap the geetar on and play a bit of blues for Dad. Have to keep the old fingers supple". I miss those texts.

On a particularly low day after Aynsley died you said "I miss my boy. All I ever wanted to do was play my geetar and make people happy. Hard to do when I don't feel happy". Well, let me tell you, that going by the outpouring of love and tributes from all over the world, you DID make people happy so, as far as I am concerned, it's JOB DONE!

I can imagine how humbled you'd be to learn that US blues legend Travis Haddix dedicated his 80th birthday gig in Tennessee last month to you, and that your old mate Top Topham sent me a message yesterday saying "I give blessings to Lloyd".

You controlled your arrival into this world and you controlled your exit to the big gig in the sky.

Elliot, Nikki, Bob and I were with you as you quietly slipped away to the sound of *Many Rivers To Cross* and *801* playing *Diamond Head*. I truly believe that Mum and Dad were waiting for you with their gentle rebuke of "And what time do you call this", Aynsley was on drums alongside cousin Stuart, David Bowie, Rick Parfitt, and your heroes Robert Johnson and Son House, for the first of many jam sessions and with your old mate Gunner, whose death just a few weeks ago upset you so much, looking on saying "You don't need a key here Lloyd, and you can go anywhere in your slippers"!

Before I sign off, I can say that you were right; that little book you lent me about Delta Country Blues is magnificent. I'd promised to give it back to you. Obviously I can't now, but rest assured, it's safe with me and I'll treasure it.

This is your Last Gig. You've earnt your rest but I know you will watch over us all.

See you on the other side matey.

Love, Nonzy

Ladies and gentlemen, I give you Lloyd Watson………………..

· © *https://theyplayedpeterborough.com/lloyd-watson/*

Obituary, *The Guardian*, 31ˢᵗ July 2023
Adam Sweeting

Francis Monkman, who has died of cancer aged 73, was a gifted classically trained musician who brought his technical skills and eclectic tastes to a rich variety of projects. These included stints with *Curved Air* and with the guitarist John Williams's classical-crossover band *Sky*, as well as collaborations with artists including *Renaissance*, Kate Bush, Brian Eno and the *Roxy Music* guitarist Phil Manzanera. Monkman's much-admired soundtrack for John Mackenzie's *The Long Good Friday* (1980) was an integral part of the film's success, and prompted him to leave *Sky* to concentrate on other soundtracks. His playing also featured on numerous film scores, including *Raiders of the Lost Ark* (1981) and the James Bond films *The Spy Who Loved Me* (1977) and *Live and Let Die* (1973).

Part of Britain's late-1960s progressive rock boom, *Curved Air* mixed rock music with various classical influences, and gave Monkman his first taste of popular success. When the band started, he was still in the middle of his classical music degree. However, he was beginning to feel the lure of rock music, and while his main instrument was keyboards, he also learned to play guitar, partly inspired by the fretboard pyrotechnics of Jimi Hendrix.

"*Curved Air* started in about 1969," he recalled. "That dovetailed with the end of studies at the *Royal College of Music*. I had to decide between the second half of my [Bachelor of Music] and going on the road. It wasn't a very hard decision."

Curved Air evolved out of *Sisyphus*, which had been formed by Monkman and the violinist Darryl Way, who had studied at the *Royal*

College of Music. The line-up was completed by the drummer Florian Pilkington-Miksa, the bass player Rob Martin and the pianist Nick Simon. They were subsequently joined by the vocalist Sonja Kristina, while Simon quit. At Monkman's instigation they adopted their new name, derived from the American minimalist composer Terry Riley's composition *A Rainbow in Curved Air.* Monkman had become a Riley fan when he played in the first London performance of the composer's piece, *In C.*

In 1970 *Curved Air* became the first British group signed to *Warner Bros.* Their debut album, *Air Conditioning,* was released in November that year. Its accomplished and novel mix of rock songs and classically influenced pieces, notably the rock-baroque hybrid *Vivaldi,* helped it reach No 8 on the UK album chart.

It accrued extra publicity by being one of the earliest picture discs, though was subsequently reissued on conventional vinyl. The group's defining *Second Album* (1971) reached No 11 on the chart, and contained their best-remembered song, *Back Street Luv,* a No 4 UK single, providing them with an appearance on *Top of the Pops.*

Their third album, *Phantasmagoria* (1972), was praised in many quarters as their finest hour, though it only made it to No 20, and it marked the end of Monkman's stint with the group, not least because his enthusiasm for extended musical improvisations jarred badly against Way's fastidious perfectionism. "Darryl and I respect each other's work, but we don't really see eye to eye on most things," he said. Also, despite their success, the group was struggling financially. In 1974 Monkman rejoined them temporarily for a tour, with the objective of paying off *Curved Air's* tax liabilities, which was recorded for the album *Live* (1975).

Monkman was born in Hampstead, north London, the son of the BBC producer and scriptwriter Kenneth Monkman and his wife, Vita (nee Duncombe Mann). Both parents were music lovers, and they had a harpsichord made for their son.

After attending *Hill House Prep School* in Knightsbridge (where Prince Charles was a contemporary), Monkman went to *Westminster School,* where he studied harpsichord and organ. While still there he would sometimes play the organ at morning services in Westminster Abbey. Then he went to the *Royal College of Music,* where his expertise on the harpsichord won him the Raymond Russell prize. He also joined Neville Marriner's *Academy of St Martin in the Fields chamber ensemble.*

After he left *Curved Air,* Monkman exercised his talents in a variety of directions. He played on *Renaissance's* album *Prologue* (1972), and worked with Lynsey de Paul and Al Stewart. In 1976 he teamed up with Eno and Manzanera to form *801.* The band only played three shows, but the resulting album, *801 Live,* became a cult success internationally.

He played organ and harpsichord on Kate Bush's album *Lionheart*, with *The Shadows* on their 20 Golden Greats tour in 1977, and played keyboards on *Voyage*, the solo album by *The Shadows'* drummer Brian Bennett. In between, he found time to give classical harpsichord recitals.

Monkman was recruited to *Sky* after he had played on Williams's solo album *Travelling* (1978), and he stayed with the group long enough to feature on their albums *Sky* and *Sky 2* (1979 and 1980). His musical expertise and wide-ranging tastes dovetailed perfectly with the group's adventures in rock, classical and jazz styles, and their debut album reached No 9 in the UK, while *Sky 2* made it to No 1, also selling strongly around the world. Monkman was one of the band's main composers, contributing, among other pieces, the four-part, 17-minute suite *Fifo* to *Sky 2*. He appeared on *Top of the Pops* again when *Sky's* single *Toccata* – an arrangement of Bach prominently featuring Monkman's harpsichord – reached No 5 in the UK.

In his later years Monkman released albums including *Dweller on the Threshold* (1981) and *21st Century Blues* (2001). In 2021 he revisited his long-standing passion for organ and harpsichord by releasing *The Bach Family*, a collection of organ pieces by J S Bach and other members of the Bach musical dynasty.

In the 70s he married Uiko Chida, but they subsequently divorced. Their daughter, Maya, died in a road accident. Monkman is survived by his partner, Christine.

Anthony Francis Keigwin Monkman, composer and musician,
born 9th June 1949; died 12th May 2023.

© The Guardian, 2023

111 DAVID FERGUSON
Obituary, *The Guardian*, 28th July 2009
Mark Fishlock

MY FRIEND AND COLLEAGUE David Ferguson, who has died of pancreatic cancer aged 56, drew on a deeply ingrained sense of justice and fair play to spend the last decade of his life campaigning tirelessly for the rights of composers and songwriters.

One of Britain's most successful television composers, with credits including *Cracker*, *Rebus*, *Bravo Two Zero*, and *Auf Wiedersehen Pet*, he became increasingly drawn into the politics of the music world, serving for six years as chairman of *BASCA* (the *British Academy of Songwriters, Composers and Authors*), the organisation representing the UK's music writers. He was also a director of the collection societies *PRS* and *MCPS*, the lobbying body UK Music and was founding chairman of the cross-genre freelancers' organisation, the *Creators' Rights Alliance*.

He saw that the future battles over many of the fundamental issues facing composers were going to be fought in Europe, and it was largely his vision that brought about the creation of a pan-European grouping of writers, with the *European Composers and Songwriters Alliance (ECSA)* at its head.

David grew into a skilled and forceful political operator, an uneasy role for many creative people. He was passionate and uncompromising, winning the respect and even the affection of his fiercest adversaries.

Born in London, he had grown up in a politically aware family, where talk around the dinner table often turned to political philosophy and issues such as social justice. After *Dulwich College* and a degree in Slavonic studies from the *School of Slavonic and East European Studies, London University*, he worked as a teacher and in the theatre before turning to music full time.

In 1976, with a schoolfriend, David Rhodes, he formed the band *Manscheinen*, which became *Random Hold*, who were signed to *Polydor*, toured with Peter Gabriel and continue to have a cult following. When the band eventually broke up in 1980, David moved into composing soundtrack music.

While working on one high-profile commission, he received a call from an American lawyer, who threatened he would 'never work in this industry again' if he didn't sign the publishing rights in his music to the TV production company. That incident became the catalyst for the next stage in David's life, a stage that would see him making his considerable presence felt in the corridors of power of Westminster and Brussels.

When it became clear that time was short, he became the committed family man, marrying Silvina, whom he had met and fallen in love with some two years before, and making an album with his son Sam, which was recorded at Peter Gabriel's *Real World* studios near his home in Bath.

David's last public appearance was at the *Ivor Novello Awards* in May, where he received *BASCA's* highest accolade, the Academy fellowship.

He is survived by Sam, the son of an earlier relationship, and Silvina.

© *The Guardian*, 2009

112 IAN MACDONALD MACCORMICK
Obituary, *The Guardian*, 8th September 2003
Richard Williams
An outstanding writer on the music of the Beatles - and a scrupulous
defender of Shostakovich

PROBABLY NO OTHER CRITIC – not even the late William Mann of *The Times*, with his famous mention of pandiatonic clusters – contributed more to an enlightened enjoyment of the work of *The Beatles* than Ian MacDonald, who has died aged 54. In his book *Revolution In The Head*, first published in 1994, MacDonald carefully anatomised every record *The Beatles* made, drawing attention to broad themes, particular examples of inspiration and moments of human frailty alike.

What could have been a dry task instead produced a volume so engagingly readable, so fresh in its perceptions and so enjoyable to argue with that, in an already overcrowded field, it became an immediate hit. Without a hint of sycophancy, MacDonald had managed to describe the magic created by John Lennon, Paul McCartney, George Harrison and Ringo Starr in such a way as to reacquaint those who were around at the time with their own original enthusiasm, while alerting listeners of later generations to the precise qualities that had made *The Beatles* so exceptional. Its introduction alone provides something close to a definitive evocation of the factors that turned the 1960s into 'the sixties'.

It came out of the blue, in the sense that MacDonald had been virtually silent on the subject of popular music for several years before its publication. But its clarity and conviction were wholly characteristic of his critical approach, which had been formed in the mid-1970s while he was a member of the collection of talented writers and editors whose weekly outpourings made the *New Musical Express* the most compelling music paper of its era.

Four years before the appearance of *Revolution In The Head* he had attracted similar levels of acclaim from a very different quarter when he published *The New Shostakovich*, a biographical re-evaluation in which he attacked the *KGB's* attempts to discredit the composer's own memoirs. MacDonald's scrupulous analysis was illuminated as much by his own deep study of the Soviet system as by his ability to immerse himself totally in whatever music he was thinking about at the time[i].

Born in London, with the surname MacCormick, he attended Dulwich College, where, at the beginning of the 1960s, he fell under the spell of the kinds of music – the blues, folk music and jazz – that became the dominant influence on those musicians of his own generation who were to create the decade's soundtrack.

At King's College, Cambridge, where he switched from English literature to archaeology and anthropology, he fell among kindred spirits. There may never be a better concise description of that evidently charmed time and place than MacDonald's wry paragraph, with its gathering rhythm and subtle alliteration: "During the academic year of 1968-69, Cambridge University felt an alien influence from beyond its sober curtain walls. Solemn flagstones frowned up at kaftans, wooden beads and waist-length hair. Staid courtyards winced to the sounds of *Beggars Banquet*, *The White Album*, *Big Pink* and *Dr John The Night Tripper* drifting through leaded windows. The stately air was fragrant with marijuana and no one seemed to be doing a stroke of work."

Despite the obvious attractions of such a world, he dropped out at the end of his first year and for a time involved himself in producing lyrics for *Quiet Sun*, an experimental rock band which included his brother, Bill MacCormick, and the future guitarist of *Roxy Music*, Phil Manzanera. In 1972 he joined the staff of the *NME*, where he remained for several years as an assistant editor. While not as widely celebrated as Nick Kent, Charles Shaar Murray, Mick Farren, Tony Parsons or Julie Burchill, MacDonald was nevertheless one of the most significant figures in the *NME's* revival under the editorship of Nick Logan.

---

[i] Ian's web site *Music under Soviet Rule* has been maintained by the *Southern Illinois University* at Edwardsville since his death, and can be found here: *https://www.siue.edu/~aho/musov/contents.html*

His own editing skills were a vital element of the formula. This was a time when an *NME* headline could enter the lexicon, and 'Sten Guns in Knightsbridge', attached to a famous early piece on *The Clash*, was his. So, in a different register, was the decision to hire the brilliant stylist Brian Case to write about jazz.

MacDonald's own byline was a guarantee of a thoughtful, usually provocative piece; his interests ranged from Laura Nyro and Neil Young through Miles Davis and *Steely Dan* to Terry Riley and John Tavener. By the time he left the paper, its circulation had more than doubled, overtaking its chief rival, the *Melody Maker*, on the way to selling 220,000 copies a week.

As he lamented in his later writings, in those days music and the values it represented mattered to audience and commentators alike in a way that might seem preposterous to a generation raised amid a marketing-led culture. He and I once met for lunch in a Holland Park bistro for the sole purpose of continuing an argument, begun in print, over the authenticity of Barry White's music.

By 1975 the success of *Roxy Music* had enabled Phil Manzanera to undertake solo projects, including an occasional band known as the *801*. He and MacDonald resumed their collaboration, the latter contributing Orwellian lyrics to a fine album titled *Listen Now*. Twenty-five years later, Brian Eno, another member of the original *Roxy Music*, would help MacDonald produce a solo album of his own songs, *Sub Rosa*, released on Manzanera's label.

Revolution In The Head was the product of a lengthy period spent living away from London, and its success encouraged him to write for a new generation of music magazines. His exacting, trenchant and sometimes very funny essays appeared first in *Mojo* and then in *Uncut*; a collection of them was published earlier this year under the title *The People's Music*.

The climax of the anthology is a lengthy meditation on the life and work of Nick Drake, the precociously gifted singer-songwriter whom MacDonald had encountered at Cambridge and who committed suicide in 1974, when still in his mid-twenties. Written with an intensity that at times overwhelms its ostensible subject, it can now be seen to have provided clues to MacDonald's own lengthy struggle with profound depression. "Can it be", he asks, apropos of Drake's preoccupation with spiritual transcendence, "that the materialist worldview, in which there is no intrinsic meaning, is slowly murdering our souls?" The decision to commit suicide, at his home in Wotton-under-Edge, Gloucestershire, indicates that he had drawn his own conclusion.

Ian MacDonald (MacCormick), author and critic, born October 3rd 1948; died August 20th 2003.
©*The Guardian*, 2003

IAN MACDONALD
Obituary, *The Times*, 25th August 2003
Author of a magnificent book about *The Beatles*

ONE OF THE LEADERS IN MODERN ROCK CRITICISM, Ian MacDonald had an impressively broad appreciation of different kinds of music. He wrote books about musicians as diverse as Stockhausen and *The Beatles* and his writing was acclaimed in the classical and rock worlds.

Like many others, from Mick Jagger to Eric Clapton, who grew up in the English suburbs in the 1950s and early 1960s, he developed a youthful fascination with blues music and such black American performers as Big Bill Broonzy and Sonny Terry and Brownie McGhee. Then one day in 1963, he heard Bob Dylan's first album. He later wrote eloquently of how the experience changed his life and of the 'awe' in which he came to regard Dylan.

He left school in 1967 and went up to Cambridge two years later to read English. After a term, he switched to archaeology and anthropology but dropped out after his first year. His brother Bill MacCormick was at the time playing in an avant-garde band called *Quiet Sun* with the future *Roxy Music* guitarist Phil Manzanera. MacDonald helped to write several pieces of music for the group, which subsequently appeared many years later on an archive release.

By 1971 he had turned to writing about music and was contributing regularly to *New Musical Express*, and in 1972 he joined the full-time staff. His thoughtful and authoritative criticism made him one of the paper's most respected figures, always prepared to challenge the received wisdom of the day and to argue his case with passion and erudition.

One example will suffice. When Neil Young's *On the Beach* was released in 1974, it was met by an overwhelmingly negative critical reaction. There the album's reputation might have rested. But a few weeks later, MacDonald reassessed the record in *NME* and stuck out his neck to proclaim all the other critics wrong and to insist that it was a masterpiece. The MacDonald view eventually came to prevail and *On the Beach* is now widely regarded as a classic.

In 1975 MacDonald left *NME* and became a freelance, writing for classical music titles as much as rock magazines. He never married and often appeared a troubled individual, the uncertainty of his personal life contrasting starkly with the assured authority of his prose. In the 1980s he returned to his parents' home in Cirencester, where he lived for the next decade. He also returned to making music and in the mid-1980s recorded the album *Sub Rosa*, released on a small independent label run by Manzanera.

321

In 1990 he published *The New Shostakovitch*, a study of the Russian composer which caused considerable controversy among classical critics. However, the book won the endorsement of the composer's son Maxim Shostakovitch, who called it 'one of the best books' ever written about his father.

Then, in 1994 MacDonald published the hugely influential *Revolution In the Head: The Beatles Records and the Sixties*. Its detailed intellectual analysis of the group's songs stands head and shoulders above the routine of most rock writing, and even Paul McCartney, who took issue with some of MacDonald's conclusions, called it a 'brilliant' piece of work.

During the 1990s MacDonald became more active in rock journalism once again, writing for the two heavyweight music monthlies, *Mojo* and *Uncut*. When he switched his allegiance to the latter on its appearance in 1997, his monthly reviews and articles became a highlight of the magazine. He was just as likely to tell the reviews editor that he wanted to write about jazz re-releases or obscure Brazilian records as he was to cover the latest rock blockbusters. By that stage, he had a readership that would devour anything he wrote, regardless of what kind of music it was about

In 2003 he published *The People's Music*, a collection of his rock journalism that included chapters on artists as diverse as Dylan, Nick Drake, Marvin Gaye, *Steely Dan* and Miles Davis. As heretical as ever, in it he also argued that punk had destroyed the 'skills base' of British pop and criticised the emergence of sequenced music, which he felt had destroyed individuality. At the time of his death he was working on a revised edition of *Revolution in the Head*, in which he planned to take greater account of George Harrison's contribution to the band. Over the past two years, he had fallen into a deep depression over the state of the world and he died by his own hand.

Ian MacDonald, music writer, was born on October 3,1948.
He died on August 21, 2003, aged 54.

© *The Times*, 25th August 2003

APPENDICES

Appendix 1: The *Quiet Sun* Press Pack 1970

The first *Quiet Sun* press release which so offended Muff Winwood at *Island Records*.

Quiet Sun

QUIET SUN began as a group co-founded by Bill MacCormick, Philip Manzanera, and Charles Hayward in early 1966. It has gone through many changes of style and personnel over the years, but the present line-up is the only one with which the original trio has felt satisfied.

Bill's meeting and subsequent friendship with *Soft Machine's* Robert Wyatt in 1965 has had a formative influence on the group. *Quiet Sun's* material is extended, unusually structured and predominantly instrumental in nature. Since the saxophonist left at Christmas the overall sound has developed an aggressive confidence and an increased awareness of the possibilities of electronic instruments.

The members of *Quiet Sun* are as follows:

David Jarrett
Keyboards

David was born in London in 1946 and educated at Dulwich College and Sussex University where he obtained a First in Mathematics. Winding up a period of research at Oxford, he joined the group eight months ago to handle piano and organ. He has been playing keyboards for sixteen years and his chief influences are Bud Powell, Cecil Taylor, and Larry Young. He wants to bring the solo improvisational techniques of avant-garde jazz to rock, and in this respect finds the work of *Soft Machine* and *Lifetime* particularly interesting.

Charles Hayward
Drums, Percussion

Youngest of the group at 19, he has been a drummer for half his life, also winning two prizes for his piano playing. He indicates Andrew Cyrille and Terry Riley as direct influences, declaring objective approval of the music of Erik Satie and Cecil Taylor. He is, in addition, an admirer of the modern art of Marcel Duchamp and is personally involved in the theatre, having had one of his plays, *The Dance of the Teletape*, produced at the Royal Court in 1967. He would like the group to become the platform for a variety of mixed media events when it achieves a final maturity and uniformity of approach.

PHILIP MANZANERA.
GUITAR
Although born in England at Westminster, he was brought up in Cuba during the revolution and speaks fluent Spanish. Later he moved to Venezuela where he developed his interests in guitar and Afro-Cuban percussion, also learning piano and tiplé, a Colombian stringed instrument. Returning to England to complete his education at Dulwich, he met Bill and Charles and formed the first of many groups with them. Subsequently, his guitar style was liberated by exposure to the range and freedom of Frank Zappa, the technique and feeling of Jimi Hendrix, and the tonal control of Randy California (*Spirit*), whilst still retaining its original South American inflection. At present engaged on developing a style of 'pure sound' he wishes to be instrumental in refining rock in anticipation of future audience demand for more subtlety – and, in this connection, he admires the work of *Soft Machine*, Keith Tippet, and *Yes*.

BILL MACCORMICK
BASS, VOCALS
Born in 1951 in Westminster, he formed the prototype of the current group with Philip and Charles at Dulwich College in 1966. At the same time, he got to know Robert Wyatt and other members of the *Soft Machine*, *The Whole World*, and *Caravan*, subsequently being extensively influenced by their music and attitudes. Within the context of the groups music he admires the work in composition and instrumental work of Pharoah Sander and Hugh Hopper, and less directly Chris Squires of *Yes* and Phil Lesh (*Grateful Dead*).

Appendix 2: The *Quiet Sun* Press Pack 1975

N.B. Written by Ian Macdonald (MacCormick), it takes some liberties with facts. But, hey, who cares anymore?

Ever seen the inside of a 24-track studio? Or Mission Control, Houston, for that matter? Relatively speaking, they're much the same. If you don't concentrate, the technology certainly won't – and, your average musician being what he is, you'll be working well if you can cut your album – from backing-tracks to final mix – in under a month.

Diamond Head, the recently released and much-lauded solo debut by *Roxy Music's* toreador of the *Telecaster* PHIL MANZANERA, took 26 days between January and February of this year. Which means it was 'on time' – a rare occurrence in this present era. Slightly more remarkable is the fact that Manzanera managed to record a second album at the same sessions: *Mainstream* – a complex and intense performance by a group called QUIET SUN. Thus, the work-o-meter swung up to 'very fast' and a lot of the environmental hysteria suppressed and channelled so cunningly by Señor Manzanera in the majestic *Diamond Head* burst out during the urgent, clock-watching, early-hours takes for *Mainstream*.

Hot, dark, manic, and electrifying, *Mainstream* stands smouldering in the debris of a multiple collision between elements of *Lifetime*, *The Soft Machine*, *The Velvet Underground*, and a stray nuclear warhead. Beyond a shared use of vivid colour and high-voltage execution, *Mainstream* seems to have little in common with its sister album, *Diamond Head* herself. But look closer (and roll credits…):

PHIL MANZANERA, Guitars.

To those listeners unfamiliar with the freedom and ferocity of Phil's playing on *Alma* and *Miss Shapiro* (*Diamond Head*), his work on *Mainstream* will come as a shock. It ought not to. QUIET SUN is where Manzanera came from and his notable guitar contributions to *Roxy* favourites like *Ladytron*, *The Bogus Man*, *Serenade*, *Mother of Pearl*, and *Prairie Rose* distil and concentrate a lyricism and power evolved in quite different musical circumstances.

Back in 1966 our boy was at school at Dulwich College, a large and fairly conventional public school in South London. Dreaming spires, green swards... and rock 'n' roll. *The Beatles*, *Dylan* and *The Beach Boys* were at their heights. The American West Coast was beginning to open up. The 'alternative society' was beginning to make itself felt. Phil Manzanera was beginning to practise on an old *Hofner Galaxie*.

1967 was nice if you liked that sort of thing. At Dulwich College if you didn't like that sort of thing, you were either very boring or one of the teachers. With this premise in mind and a stack of import stuff by Zappa, *Beefheart*, *Spirit* and *The Velvet Underground* under his arm, Phil approached a chum of his, hereafter referred to as:

BILL MACCORMICK, Bass.
Later to play scintillating runs on a *Fender Precision* for the likes of *Gong* and *Matching Mole*, MacCormick at this time believed himself to be either a drummer or a vocalist. The group he formed with Manzanera – the long forgotten *Pooh And The Ostrich Feather* – believed him to be a vocalist too, and so he was. However, the drums were to be played by a volatile lad from the year below these two:

CHARLES HAYWARD, Percussion.
Charlie did a lot of screaming and playing his bizarre kit in a manner roughly equidistant between Andrew Cyrille and Keith Moon. He joined Manzanera and MacCormick in writing the band's earliest material, collaborating with Phil on a paean to famed surrealist Marcel Duchamps entitled *Marcel My Dada*, the theme of which can be heard menacing the genial levity of *Frontera* on *Diamond Head*.

For three years and with a constantly evolving line-up, *Pooh and the Ostrich Feather* were *The Grateful Dead* of Dulwich – a thankless task, as you can imagine. But inspiration was just around the corner in Dalmore Road, where lived Robert Wyatt and most of the contemporary *Soft Machine*. MacCormick became friends with Wyatt and stole all his licks. But in order to incorporate elements of *The Soft Machine* into a band which encored with Paul Butterfield's *Born in Chicago*, certain members had to be liquidated. This was affected without mercy.

Manzanera, MacCormick, and Hayward conferred over a possible fourth recruitment in the wake of the 1970 *putsch*, and resolved that what they needed most desperately was somebody with a PhD in Mathematics. Consequently, they ran through a list of Old Boys of the school and came up with:

DAVE JARRETT, Keyboards.

The coincidence was too good to be true. With a will, the quartet got down to rehearsals – only to discover that they had no bass-player. Vocalist and drummer (failed) MacCormick conducted a series of auditions with bassists on leave from Victor Sylvester until losing his patience at 11.06 a.m. on March 3rd 1970 and taking up the troublesome instrument himself. Within three hours he had tuned the bottom E.

Within two years, QUIET SUN had accumulated the mass of complex and distinctive material which serves as source for both *Mainstream* and approximately half of *Diamond Head*. At this point, it was decided to call a halt. Phil was spending a lot of time round at Bryan Ferry's house, pretending to operate a mixing console and tuning David O'List's guitars. Bill, having not recovered from the Portsmouth Poly jam between QUIET SUN and Robert Wyatt's *Symbiosis*, was hot for more and suggested to Wyatt that the bass-player he needed for *Matching Mole* need not necessarily be Charlie Mingus. Charles was flitting back and forth between Mal Dean's *Amazing Band* and David Allen's *Gong*, in the meantime writing songs that nobody could play – like *Rongwrong* on *Mainstream*. Dave, moreover, had a yen to lecture on quantum physics.

QUIET SUN ceased in 1972… to resurface, three years later, on the HELP label with an album of material selected from their original set. Recording *Mainstream* was hell, although a good time was had by one and all in strict accordance with studio etiquette. The group had time for only two brief rehearsals and most of the basic tracks on the finished album are first takes. It sounds hectic, and it was.

But worse than this was the fact that *Diamond Head* was being recorded in the same place at the same time. Special observers were brought in to make sure that parts of one album did not defect to the other – a task made more herculean by the fact that not only were *Diamond Head* and *Mainstream* the first twins born in a London studio, but they also shared many musical features. For example: *Mainstream* opens with Engineer Rhett Davies's live cue-in, followed by *Sol Caliente*. The tune being played on echoplexed fuzz guitar might strike fans of *Diamond Head's Lagrima* as familiar. In fact, *Lagrima*, *Frontera*, *East Of Echo*, and *Alma* all derive from one extended QUIET SUN composition – Phil Manzanera's *Corazon Y Alma (Heart And Soul)* – written in early 1971. Less obvious is the similarity of the 5/4 bass riff from *Same Time Next Week* and what's happening behind Manzanera's savage outburst on Track Two, Side Two of *Mainstream* – *Trot*, vintage 1970. Indeed, if you listen to *East Of Echo*, you encounter three or four QUIET SUN references now placed in their original context by *Mainstream*. The two records co-relate, in other words. In their duality they illuminate each other. Quick – buy both. You know it makes sense.

328

APPENDIX 3: *QUIET SUN* – PRESS 1975

113 Nigel Soper's design for the front cover of Mainstream

The album was released as *Island Records' HELP 19* in the summer of 1975. It was accompanied by one of Ian's usually erudite press releases but, unlike the typed version in 1970, this was nicely printed and inserted into a plush back and gold folder along with a group photo taken in the back garden of Phil's house in Acton. How things change.

Press alerted, a round of interviews took place and articles started to appear in the music press in August.

Reviews came soon after, and reactions were a little different to Mr Winwood's back in 1970. 'Lacking bite'? Not any more.

329

114 Quiet Sun 1975. Phil's back garden, Acton

QUIET SIDE OF THE SUN
Allan Jones, *Melody Maker*, 16.8.75

IT ALL BEGAN WITH *POOH AND THE OSTRICH FEATHER*. Laugh if you must, but that band have just produced the most brain-searing convincingly malevolent album to stagger out of a recording studio since the *Velvet Underground*. The album is released this week and it's called *Mainstream*.

The band who have unleashed this monster are known no longer as *Pooh And The Ostrich Feather*. Sometime around 1970, they must have realised that they sounded a shade too much like the title of a *Temperance Seven* album, and changed it to *Quiet Sun*. *Quiet Sun* were (and are on *Mainstream*), Bill MacCormick (electric bass, treated bass, back-up voices), Charles Hayward (drums, percussion, keyboards, voice), Dave Jarrett (*Fender Rhodes* & *Steinway* grand pianos, *Farfisa* & *Hammond* organs, *VCS 3*), and Phillip Targett-Adams Manzanera. Thats right; *Roxy Music's* Phil Manzanera.

Back in 1967, Manzanera was at school in Dulwich, along with MacCormick and Hayward. This enterprising trio set out, with no lack of ambition, to establish Dulwich as a hotbed of radical musical activity. Armed with an insubstantial arsenal of equipment and the obligatory light show, the trio – backed by a constantly changing group of teenage instrumentalists – proceeded to devastate Dulwich and all points south. They were, apparently very big in Sydenham.

Psychedelic to the last, *Quiet Sun* concentrated on acid-tinged arrangements of *Crossroads* and *Rollin' 'n' Tumblin'*, with Manzanera already well into his primitive, but effective, echoplexed fuzz-guitar routines, generally coming on like the Home Counties' very own Randy California. Set against these surrogate West Coast vamps were rather more zappy compositions like Charles Hayward's homage to the celebrated surrealist Marcel Duchamp enticingly titled *Marcel My Dada*.

The *Soft Machine* established themselves as an important influence on the emerging *Quiet Sun*, and if it hadn't been for the group's own inherent intelligence and Bill MacCormick's friendship with Robert Wyatt, it's not inconceivable that the band would have been counted out as another of those Sons Of Canterbury outfits specialising in tricky time signatures who were thrown up in the surf of the *Softs'* pioneering assault on contemporary English music. Fortunately, *Quiet Sun* decided they wanted to be neither Dulwich's reply to the *Grateful Dead* nor the new *Caravan*.

"When we were thinking in commercial terms, I suppose we wanted to become the new *Led Zeppelin* or the new *Yes*," comments Bill MacCormick, flicking fine beads of sweat from his forehead. "The rest of the time we wanted to become the new *Lifetime*".

As early as 1966, Bill had become friendly with Robert Wyatt. The *Softs* had rented a house in Dulwich near the school at which he, Manzanera and Hayward were laying down their operational plans for a massive attack on English rock. Bill was a regular house-guest *Chez Soft Machine* and was taken with Robert's expansive taste in music. By the time *Quiet Sun* reached its final form as a quartet with the inclusion of Jarrett on keyboards (there was a sax player, Dave Monaghan, involved for a short time, too), they were well involved in composing and performing extremely complex pieces. In fact, the material which is featured on *Mainstream* and several of the themes which appear on Manzanera's excellent solo album, *Diamond Head*, were composed by *Quiet Sun* between 1970 and 1972, which was the life span of the original band.

"That period, generally, opened up a lot of musical horizons," reflects Manzanera. "Just listening to all those different groups like the *Soft Machine*, and the groups which came out of America at the time like Zappa, who was using the techniques of jazz in a rock context, that combination and Bill being turned onto jazz by Robert really changed the direction of our music. That whole period for me was like a musical university."

Quiet Sun's premature fusion of complex styles didn't exactly line the band up for immediate success. They secured a committed following around Dulwich, where they played at any available venue: everything from youth clubs, church halls, school halls, basements and front rooms. "It was the height of that acoustic, singer/songwriter period. Everyone wanted to be Crosby, Stills and Nash," says Manzanera. "*Quiet Sun*, of course, was the complete antithesis of all that."

If *Quiet Sun's* audience displayed an encouraging tolerance in the band's increasingly adventurous performances, record companies were a little less forthcoming in support of their idealistic experimentation. "There really wasn't a company which was willing to sign us up," continues Manzanera, "although the guy at *Warner Brothers*, who in the same three months turned down *Roxy*, gave us the chance to go down to a recording studio they had in Dorset to record some demos."

Quiet Sun split up in 1972 because of the economic pressures, and resulting conflicts within the band which were precipitated. *Mainstream* then, an album which would have shaken the foundations of rock had it been recorded three years ago, has had to exist as a vague idea ever since. Until Phil decided to record his solo debut, and revive *Quiet Sun* at the same time.

But, following the disintegration of *Quiet Sun*, Manzanera replaced a guitarist called David O'List in a band called *Roxy Music*. The rest of that story is – as they say – history.

Hayward's first move was to join Mal Dean's *Amazing Band*, which set him off in another direction as a drummer. He'd already been interested by people like Frank Perry and Tony Oxley, but this was the first chance for him to gain any practical experience of this kind of music. Then he joined *Gong*. "I was with them for two months, and I just couldn't take it. It was all too much for me. There were some ridiculous emotional scenes, which I couldn't handle So I left. Then I started working with *High Tide*. I left them, told them some story about how I wanted to go and tour Europe, and split. It was about that time that I tried to get the original *Radar Favourites* together." As you might have heard, *Radar Favourites* have recently decided to dissolve through financial problems. Charles isn't quite as pessimistic as Geoff Leigh about the future of *Radar Favourites*: "I have a certain emotional affiliation with the name – it's my rock project name – and I feel rather sad that someone has said that *Radar Favourites* is finished without them consulting me first."

Bill MacCormick's name might be more familiar. It should be, since he's amongst the best bass players around. Should you require any evidence just check out Eno's *Here Come The Warm Jets*, Manzanera's *Diamond Head*, *Mainstream*, particularly his own composition *Mummy Was An Asteroid, Daddy Was A Small Non-stick Kitchen Utensil* and his work with Robert Wyatt's *Matching Mole* (two albums, both deleted) and on Robert's *Ruth Is Stranger Than Richard*.

When *Matching Mole* collapsed in disarray, MacCormick received a telephone call from Wyatt who informed him that *Gong* were looking for a bass player: "I thought, 'Whoopee . . .' (he does not sound enthusiastic at the memory). This van met me somewhere in London, the door opened and I got in, and there were half a dozen other bass players who'd got the same message. That was all I needed – an audition for *Gong*." He got the job and crossed the Channel to join *Gong* in France. Like Charles, his association with Daevid Allen's pothead pixies was brief: "About ten days.

It took me that long to convince myself that being in *Gong* wasn't quite what I was looking for."

On his return to England Bill met Robert again, and with Francis Monkman and Gary Windo they decided to form a new band. In June of 1973 they began rehearsing some songs which Robert had written in Venice (which would eventually form the first side of Robert's *Rock Bottom* album). "At the end of the first week of rehearsals Gary phoned me in hysteria on a Saturday morning and said that Robert had fallen out of a window. At the time, Robert was living in a flat on the top floor of a 15-storey block of flats. So I thought that was that . . . Then Gary explained what had actually happened. Two days later I went into hospital, in sympathy, with appendicitis. Anyway for a long time the doctors didn't know how badly Robert was injured. So we vaguely kept the idea together and thought that we might get another drummer in, and Robert would play keyboards. But as it turned out, Robert was in hospital for nearly seven months, and wasn't really fit when he came out. So that was all knocked on the head."

"In the September of that year I did a few things on Eno's first album, and then I didn't do anything musical at all for quite some time. I just didn't feel like it, and I had no energy for music. Until about last October when Phil said that he was doing his album and that he'd also like to get the *Quiet Sun* thing done as well."

Phil: "I listened to some of the live tapes we'd made of *Quiet Sun*, and it seemed such a pity that we'd never put it down on record, because there was so much good music there. I thought it would be valid, and I fitted it into the 26-day schedule I'd arranged for recording *Diamond Head*. In a way, I'm glad that it was recorded now and not four years ago. Because at that time we would never have had the conviction to record the album as we have, with all the roughness left intact. Whereas, now we can say that's just how it's meant to be."

Charles: "We were always an extremely aggressive band, possibly more aggressive than the record suggests. And I couldn't have imagined the album being produced in any other way. It had to be almost live, with all the irregularities left, to capture the way we played. I think we managed to capture that energy."

THE QUIET SUN EVOLVES
Angus Mackinnon, *Sounds*, 23.8.75
QUIET SUN EVOLVED out a of a stream of Dulwich College, London, bands, emerging between 1967 and 1970, and masquerading under the general cognomen of, er, *Pooh And The Ostrich Feather*. Bill MacCormick (basses - but only after a period of aspiring vocalist and drummer), Charles Hayward (drums and percussion, various) and Phil Manzanera

(guitars and devices, latterly of *Roxy Music*) formed the nucleus of these embryonic line-ups. However, attempts (premature) to take the South-East of England by aggressively electronic strategy met with limited success. Later Dave Jarrett was added on keyboards and, formalising the band's instrumentation, MacCormick decided to take over the bass vacancy himself, after an interminable run of auditions.

Quiet Sun weren't exactly welcomed by the business with open arms. At one stage they were sent down to Dorset by *Warner Brothers* to record some demo tapes. Vocals had to be recorded in the hall, stone-walled and resonant, as there was no appropriate booth. Nonetheless, *Warners* were not overly enamoured of the venture's results, and neither were *Harvest*, another company expressing a modicum of vague interest. Gigs remained hard to come by and were mostly situated in, as MacCormick recalls, "church halls that were later pulled down". But, after two years or more spent mostly rehearsing and not performing, Manzanera and MacCormick decided that what the world really needed was a Mk. 2 *Yes*. Hayward and Jarrett thought otherwise. End of band in early 1972. Before their time.

Manzanera earned himself a place in *Roxy*, replacing Dave O'List, Jarrett lectured on quantum physics, whilst Hayward and MacCormick involved themselves in a bewildering number of alternative projects. MacCormick joined Robert Wyatt, David Sinclair and Phil Miller in *Matching Mole Mk. I*, and enjoyed the dubious privilege of being among the last musicians to record in *CBS's* old Bond Street studios, where the 16-track contrived to run at unpredictably varying speeds and there was an unhealthy amount of interference from pneumatic drills and hydraulic excavators working in the road outside. Still, *Mole's Little Red Record* does sound surprisingly resilient, in spite of these various hindrances. A short spell in *Gong* followed, and then the formation of *Mole Mk. 2*, this time with Francis Monkman and Gary Windo, abruptly and very sadly halted by Wyatt's horrifying accident. MacCormick took time off to stand for his local council.

Meanwhile Hayward had also played in *Gong*, after a short spell with Mal Dean's *Amazing Band*. His stay in *Gong* itself was even shorter. It was apparent right from the start that Hayward's world-view and that of Daevid Allen's didn't entirely coincide. At this stage *Gong* were entering one of their periodic 'terminal' phases, with, in this instance, Christian Tritsch about to leave, and a certain amount of re-assessment going on. Both Hayward and MacCormick talk enthusiastically of the potentials they believed *Gong* could have realised, had there not been such a drastic discrepancy between what the band envisaged and achieved.

Anyway, Hayward had by now joined the remnants of *High Tide*: Peter Pavli (bass), Tony Hill (guitar) and Simon House (violin). This line-up endured for about three months before Hayward decided to form a band of his own. "It was the first time I'd actually organised anything like that, which is probably why it didn't do too well," he adds self-deprecatingly. He remembers one particularly strange date at Bishop's Stortford, where the stage was razor thin, players thrust into the audience's bellies, and the venue's back wall held up by a hydraulic arm. This venture operated under two names, either *Short Back and Sides* or *All Wet And Dripping*, whichever you prefer. Next up, Hayward involved himself in a duet, *Dolphin Logic*, just himself and a guitarist; "a kind of living room duet, totally improvised, not jazz, ethnic rather and very beautiful to listen to. I'm very proud of the tapes we made." *Radar Favourites* followed, along with Geoff Leigh and *Logic's* other member, guitarist Charles Bullock. *Favourites* have, it seems, recently folded.

All of which brings us up to late 1974, when Manzanera approached the rest of *Quiet Sun* with the idea of recording an album of their material, as he'd booked in himself to record his solo album, *Diamond Head*. So, after only two proper rehearsals and a maelstrom of frantic sessions *Mainstream* emerged, sounding something like an electric commentary on Armageddon and aftermath, startlingly tense.

Mainstream is an extraordinary record and should be procured without delay – the kind of offering that, at one stroke, justifies the existence of a popular music network. It's supremely accessible, uncompromising and adventurous. What more could you ask for indeed? There is, unfortunately, no possibility of *Quiet Sun* performing again, due to Manzanera's commitment to *Roxy*, and other complications. MacCormick has since played on Wyatt's *Ruth Is Stranger Than Richard* and is now pondering as to "how I can write my *Average White Band* single". He views the album as "essentially something that's been very good to do. I mean, I can play it when I'm forty and remember..." *Island* are planning an American release, as one of the leaders of a new Stateside label, which is certainly a welcome move. When asked what expectations he had for *Mainstream's* success in this country, Hayward replies. "Well, it might get bought or it might not I suppose, it might even jump up and bite the listener." Try it then and see.

MANZANERA - BLAZING QUIETLY
David Fudger, *Disc*, 23.8.75
PHIL MANZANERA had some explaining to do. I mean, he's going to give *Roxy Music* fans a big surprise with his latest extra-curricular Venture. The man who plays the death-ray guitar has re-formed *Quiet Sun*, a band from his pre-*Roxy* public schooldays and with them he has produced an intensely complex, instrumental album. The other members of *Quiet Sun* are bassist Bill MacCormick, keyboard man Dave Jarrett and drummer Charles Hayward. Between them they can lay claim to a devious musical history embracing such names as *Matching Mole*, *Soft Machine*, Mal Dean's

Amazing Band, Gong, High Tide and *Radar Favourites*. Yep, a bunch of esoteric, musical bizzarroids who deal in time signatures that turn toe-tapping pop fans into epileptics.

Manzanera's contribution to *Mainstream* – the album's title – is still as devastating as a nose diving Jumbo jet but his guitar playing set against the intricate jazz/rock structure of the music, reveals a dexterity and control unexpressed on *Roxy* albums. Is Phil tired of the limitations of the *Roxy* framework? Is this the end of a beautiful relationship? Can Chelsea make a comeback this season? Over to the man himself who is currently in the recording studio with his *Roxy* teammates working on the next *R. Music* release. What's the deal Phil? What's with this *Quiet Sun* mob. "Why ja do it?"

"Basically it's an album of music by a group that existed four or five years ago," was the cool Manzanera reply, "before it was commercially possible for a group like that to exist. It was the year before *Roxy Music* and as far as the record companies were concerned there was no commercial potential at all for a group playing quite complicated instrumentals. The advent of people like *King Crimson* and the *Mahavishnu Orchestra* has changed that. I was listening to some tapes of *Quiet Sun* last year and I thought that it would be a worthwhile project to record the songs. It's part of my personal musical background. It's music I enjoy listening to and playing as well as the rock group stuff."

Manzanera is personally pleased with the fruits of this musical reunion. Is it going to produce more? "We certainly wrote a lot of material around that time. There's enough material to do two or three albums, but we'll see how this one goes, whether there are enough people interested." What about performing? "Obviously the commitments which I have make it pretty impossible to do any performing with *Quiet Sun*, but if there was a demand for it we might be able to fit some in. At the moment I've got the *Roxy* album and then the tours that we're going to be doing in-the autumn."

Phil feels that *Mainstream* has given him a chance to develop his playing away from the confines of rock. "It's much more abstract type of playing for me. A style which I haven't had an opportunity to exhibit on many of the records I've done, except for possibly stuff outside *Roxy*. It's more like some of the stuff I played on John Cale's records like *Gun* on his *Fear* album. That is the nearest I've come to *Mainstream* in a rock context. It's really one extreme of my playing I suppose which is much more abstract than the melodic, possibly more conventional 'rock' style that I had to do to fit in with *Roxy Music*. Apart from that," he added, "the actual songs, I mean the pieces of music really, are quite complicated. I think people will like it if they give it a chance. If they make an effort."

The initial response to *Mainstream* has been good, and for Phil that's very good. "I'm always underestimating people's tastes – things have obviously changed so much since we first started playing that kind of music. It was so different at the time, people found it very difficult. Maybe by now people have been conditioned, er . . . prepared by all the other groups. They might not find it so inaccessible."

What about the other members of *Roxy Music*? How accessible did they find *Quiet Sun*. Phil was unsure. "Well, I don't think any of them have heard it yet," Manzanera chuckled, "I suspect that they probably wouldn't like it, though I obviously can't say until they have heard it. If they don't say anything to me, I'll assume that they don't like it. Obviously, I don't discount the fact that they might like it." Phil is obviously very sensitive to the views of the others.

On the subject of *Roxy Music* Manzanera was a little cagey when asked about the band's plans for the immediate future. "I think," Manzanera began, "it's quite possible to say that there will be quite," then hesitantly, "a change – obviously I can't give any details – not in personnel, but in stage act. I think it's about time for us to come up with something new and I think we have got . . er . . . the music's certainly changed and the whole stage show will be quite different. I'm really looking forward to this tour – I'm very excited about it. Everybody, I think, is really looking forward to this tour. Now we're integrating all the members of the band more fully, so that it's really becoming a 'group'. Johnny Gustafson will be playing bass with the band which will be great as he hasn't actually played on an English tour before. He did the Australian/New Zealand leg of our touring last year and it was very successful. As far as I know he's going to be doing it with us and he plays bass on the album." So, things look very rosy for *Roxy Music* and even rosier for Phil Manzanera, with two irons in the fire. It must be very comforting to have another little combo to fall back on should the glitz-rock kings take a tumble.

APPENDIX 4: *QUIET SUN* – ALBUM REVIEWS

Angus MacKinnon, *Sounds*

CURRENTLY BEING ADVERTISED very unassumingly and available at a modest price, *Mainstream* is probably the most invigorating record you're likely to hear this Summer. Rush-recorded – most of the basic tracks are first takes – alongside Phil Manzanera's self-effacingly generous *Diamond Head*, *Mainstream* possesses in abundance qualities all too rarely expressed, let alone combined: inspired musicianship, total lack of compromise and, most importantly, a sense of feverish excitement and utter dedication.

Quiet Sun, who folded in early 1972 after two years spent struggling against complete indifference shown them by record and management companies alike, were Bill MacCormick (basses), Dave Jarrett (keyboards), Charles Hayward (drums, keyboards, vocals) and Phil Manzanera (guitars). For the purposes of *Mainstream* itself, Eno helps out with assorted treatments and synthesisers.

There are seven cuts here, with everybody composing. There are those who have offhandedly suggested that this kind of music is 'obsolete'; I'd reply that they're mistaken on several counts, mostly concerned with the aforementioned dynamism and essential freshness of this record, achievements a great deal more vital (and valid) than vacuous attempts at Musico-temporality. But, those who've wished to hear Manzanera in a more open, expansive context than *Roxy Music* will not be disappointed, his playing is throughout forceful and provocatively abrasive.

Group sound is co-operative, intricately meshed. *Sol Caliente*, *Trot* and *Mummy Was An Asteroid, Daddy Was A Small Non-Stick Kitchen Utensil* are perhaps the most immediate cuts, whilst *Bargain Classics* and *R.F.D.* rely on Jarrett's lush, electronic textures. *Trumpets With Motherhood* and *Rongwrong* spotlight Hayward, being, respectively, a percussive interlude and an ingenuous vocal outing for him.

I think the only occasion I've been fortunate enough to hear music of comparable intensity and excellence was when seeing *Lifetime* in concert at Croydon some years back. However, you've the added bonus of being able to hear *Mainstream* as often as you like. All in all, it's an offer you can't and shouldn't refuse.

NOT FOR THE NERVOUS
Allan Jones, *Melody Maker*

THIS ALBUM IS NOT to be approached casually. Neither is it to be recommended to those suffering from any kind of nervous disposition. *Quiet Sun* have waited five years to record this album, and the energy which has for so long been restrained is here unleashed in the most manic and passionate rush of music that has been committed to vinyl so far this year.

Recorded at the same time as Phil Manzanera's *Diamond Head* album, *Mainstream* offers a selection of *Quiet Sun* material – they have enough for at least two more albums – which is positively lethal in its uncompromising intensity. The album presents a facet of Manzanera which has previously been merely suggested through his work with John Cale, principally his lacerating solo on *Gun*, and on certain *Roxy Music* compositions, like the opening guitar volley which introduced *Mother of Pearl*.

His contributions to *Mainstream* see his ability for producing the most virulent guitar statements in contemporary rock taken to a frightening, and at times awesome, extreme. In the opening track, Manzanera's own *Sol Caliente*, he contrives to defy most existing notions of guitar playing and comes on like a blazing Messerschmitt, twitching neurotically in spasms of barely controlled vehemence. Listen to this track a dozen times in succession and I guarantee you'll be crawling on the carpet searching for fragments of your brain.

It would, however, be totally unpardonable to even suggest that Manzanera dominates *Mainstream*. Such are the talents of Bill MacCormick (bass), Dave Jarrett (keyboards), and Charles Hayward (drums and keyboards), that one would venture the opinion that were *Quiet Sun* ever to develop outside the context of what appears to be a one off reunion album, they would probably be the most formidable line-up in the country. They have packed more force into the five minutes and 37 seconds of Jarrett's *Bargain Classics* than *Led Zeppelin* mustered over four sides of *Physical Graffiti*.

Really, there hasn't been much music like this (apart from some of *Can's* aural violence) since the *Velvet's White Light/White Heat*. There's that same sense of urgency and intelligence on the point of collapse which characterised, say, *I Heard Her Call My Name* and *Sister Ray*. But where the *Velvets* would sometimes charge straight through into the most completely nihilistic zones of sound *Quiet Sun* achieve and maintain a more tolerable balance. This is best exemplified by the inclusion of Jarrett's beautiful keyboard piece, *R.F.D.*, which closes the first side with a welcome release of tension, and Charles Hayward's two compositions, *Trumpets With Motherhood* and *Rongwrong*. The former is a brief and hilarious piece for percussion and kazoos, a swanee whistle and harmonica which prefaces *Classics*, and the latter is the only 'song' on the album. It features Hayward singing the most off-the-wall lyrics this side of Syd Barrett's *The Madcap Laughs* in a voice not a million miles removed from Captain Lunacy's own.

Elsewhere we have Manzanera's glorious *Trot*, with the guitarist in stunning form on all manner of guitars and a dazzling solo from Jarrett on a *Steinway* grand piano. But perhaps the most outstanding track is Bill MacCormick's fearsome *Mummy Was An Asteroid Daddy Was A Small Non-*

Stick Kitchen Utensil. With Eno on *VCS 3* synthesiser (he's deployed elsewhere on all manner of electronic effects), and Jarrett and Manzanera combing straight through the atmosphere on *Farfisa* organ and meat cleaver guitar, and with MacCormick placing himself head and fretboard above almost every other bass guitarist in the neighbourhood (particularly on the final passage, which could literally melt a sensitive record player), the final effect is something which has to be heard to be believed. But don't stand too close to the speakers. I really don't know how even a drummer of Hayward's capabilities held it all together.

I can think of no more than a handful of albums released this year which demand your attention as much as *Mainstream*, and since it's being issued on *Island's* bargain label, *HELP*, at under £2 you can't afford to miss it. This one will molest your brain . . . at least you've been warned. -

QUIET FIRE!
Dave Fudger, *Disc*
BIG PHIL STRIKES AGAIN! Mr Manzanera has got himself another band (*Roxy* watch out!) dredged up from his dark and murky public school days and they have turned out a dazzling piece of post 60s *Soft*-ish instrumental complexorama. The name of the ensemble is *Quiet Sun* and aptly dubbed they be. Their music is intriguing, intense and at times extremely volatile.

With executive and consultant assistance from none other than the phantom of the recording studio – Eno tunes with titles like *Trumpets With Motherhood, Mummy Was An Asteroid, Daddy Was A Small Non-Stick Kitchen Utensil* and *RFD (Ri-F***ing-Diculous)* accommodate the blazing guitar abstractions of our Phil.

'Twixt him and t'other *Sunners* – Charles Hayward (drums), Dave Jarrett (keyboards) and Bill MacCormick (bass) – an album that proudly exhibits its influences has been produced. The mention of a *Soft Machine* influence might make you think that regular *Roxy* fans will find this record a little hard to pick up on. Well, not at all gang. The presentation of the music, albeit complex, is subtle and infectious. Mr Manzanera's own belief is that although in 1969/70 when the band was originally conceived, their kind of music was not commercially acceptable, many bands have since prepared the way for an album such as this today.

Although this is a big departure from his role with *Roxy Music*, for Phil Manzanera, deathray guitarist, this is your life – and you're going to get a whole new load of respect y'all.

FROM THE REALMS OF TIME...
Pete Erskine, *NME*
FOR A LARGELY un-promoted debut of five-year-old off-the-wall electric jazz acrobatics performed by a defunct band, *Mainstream* ain't doing at all bad. *Island* reckon it's their fourth or fifth biggest seller at the moment –

hot on the heels of *Bad Company* and *Cat Stevens*. The fact that *Roxy's* Phil Manzanera and former *Matching Mole* bassist Bill MacCormick are involved might have something to do with it. So might the fact that *Mainstream* is released as part of *Island's Help* budget series.

Basically though, in spite of the superficial incongruity of certain sections of the album, it does exude considerable quantities of intense manic energy – itself something of a sales point in these universally bland times. And, better still, it's totally unpredictable and instrumentally rather skilfully executed.

Quiet Sun originated from a 1967 Dulwich College consortium vending a crossbreed of early *Velvets*, *G. Dead* and *Airplane*-fashioned material. Known as *Pooh and The Ostrich Feather* the band comprised Manzanera, drummer Charles Hayward, MacCormick and his brother Ian (better known to you as I. Mac). Their approach contained a large element of self-effacing humour and diverse musical absurdities until – with the advent of the *Soft Machine* – they decided to get a bit serious, trying for something in a similar vein, but with a little more youthful verve; I. Mac describes it as "a young enthusiastic boys' version of the Soft Machine."

Quiet Sun were born, lasted two years, were almost signed to *Warners* and *Harvest* (prior to the *Harvest* auditions they had no name; *Harvest* demanded they think one up in an hour whilst the tapes were running – the final choice has been a source of embarrassment ever since). During this period they worked up a fair scrapbook of material but broke up before having a chance to commit any of it to plastic – MacCormick to Robert Wyatt's *Softs* offshoot *Matching Mole*, Hayward to *Gong* and Manzanera to the embryonic *Roxy*.

Five years later Manzanera found himself in the studios cutting his solo album, *Diamond Head*. Pondering over the fact that some of the material he was working on had originated from the old *Quiet Sun* repertoire he booked a few extra days, persuaded their former pianist Dave Jarrett to take a break from his mathematics lecturing and reassembled the band (augmenting it with Eno) for their debut album. Of five-year-old material.

The more ardent observers among you will now therefore be able to complete the links between cuts like *Frontera* on *Diamond Head*, *Team Spirit* on Wyatt's *Ruth Is Stranger Than Richard* and the bass figure employed in Manzanera's *Trot* here (which also vaguely correlates with his *Same Time Last Week* on *Diamond Head*). So, in context, the album has to have some relevance as a point of reference. Another selling point?

I only wonder because aside from these rather obvious points I'm still trying to divine why such an apparently uncommercial, superficially indigestible and even dated collection of material is so viable; even more so than the universally appealing melodic qualities of *Diamond Head*. Personally, the nearest I can get to it is on Jarrett's gentle, relatively straightforward piece *R.F.D.*, the closing third of Manzanera's *Sol Caliente* which gels into a beautiful elusive guitar solo of considerable imagination, and brother Bill's six minute *Mummy Was An Asteroid Daddy Was A Small Non-stick Kitchen Utensil.* Illogical.

David Platt, *HiFi for Pleasure*
QUIET SUN were together from 1970 to 1972, and consisted of Phil Manzanera on guitars, Bill MacCormick on bass, Charles Hayward on percussion and Dave Jarrett on keyboards. Manzanera then left to find fame and (presumably) fortune with *Roxy Music*, MacCormick to find less fame and no fortune but a superb partnership with Robert Wyatt in *Matching Mole*; Hayward joined *Gong*, intermittently, and Jarrett went to teach mathematics.

Early this year Manzanera brought them together again, during the sessions for his excellent *Diamond Head* and, augmented by Eno, they cut this set of material composed before they split. The result is exhilaratingly energetic, fresh and inventive; Jarrett's keyboard work is particularly noteworthy and. the band coheres in a way which belies their lack of rehearsal and the speed at which the record was cut. There are echoes of early *Soft Machine*, the *Nice* and *Gong* and, as a bonus, a Syd Barrett vocal by Hayward on *Rongwrong*.

This is one of the year's best records, and a giveaway at £1.75. Why sit at home and listen to Schoenberg in the bath? Buy this and influence people.

Ron Gott, *Trouser Press*
THIS RECORD may not be every Anglophile's dream, but for some it will be sheer Nirvana. *Mainstream* marks the reincarnation of a band which dates back to 1970 and includes one Phil Manzanera of *Roxy Music*, as well as ex-*Matching Mole* bassist Bill MacCormick, Dave Jarrett, keyboards, and Charles Hayward, drums. Not to mention another cameo appearance by everyone's favourite, Eno, on synthesizers, treatments, and oblique strategies.

Whatever preconceived ideas you may have about this album sounding like *Roxy* or even Phil's *Diamond Head*, erase them right now. What's on this vinyl is a ferocious combination of the ideas on the first two *Velvet Underground* albums coupled with the musical inventiveness of *King Crimson* or *Soft Machine*.

The album was rehearsed and recorded in the same 26-day period in which *Diamond Head* was done. When listening to the two, a similarity in melodies is evident in many tunes. An example being the acoustic track, *Lagrima*, from *Diamond Head* is played note for note on *Sol Caliente*, the opening track from *Mainstream*. In fact, *Lagrima*, *Frontera*, *East of Echo*, and

Alma are all taken from a song Manzanera composed with the band in 1971 called *Corazon y Alma*.

Manzanera's guitar technique is truly one of the most interesting to be heard in years. His virtuosity is not derived from how many notes a second he can play or how far he can stretch a string; instead he concentrates on constructing leads from short, lyrical phrases. This with the combination of his unique guitar sound makes for a breathtaking presentation and should help to distinguish him as one of the most original guitarists in rock.

Trying to give descriptions and compare the tracks would be hopeless. This album must be heard to be believed. The musicians are superb, the production flawless. Hopefully the band won't wait as long to do a second album as it took to get this one.

Forbes Magilligan, *Liquorice*

FIRST THE FACTS. This is a very good record. It only costs £1.75p (a nugget in the sludge these days), and is the best release on *Island's Help* label since Robin Williamson's *Myrrh*.

The material performed on *Mainstream* is around five years old; *Quiet Sun* are Dave Jarrett/keyboards, Phil Manzanera/guitars, Bill MacCormick/bass, Richard (*sic*) Hayward/drums, Eno and Ian MacCormick appear on the record too. The album sleeve is a goodie, and a Stateside release is being planned too.

It is eminently more preferable to have *Mainstream* than countless puerile figures such as *Yes/Joe Walsh* et al. Everyone in *Quiet Sun* composes; there are two Manzanera pieces two each from Jarrett and Hayward and one from Bill MacCormick. The overall sound is very strong and attacking, blistering maybe.

You need to play *Mainstream* a good few times before getting to grips to it. I find the seven pieces on the album more preferable than the pieces on *Diamond Head*. They have more of continuity and a feel. Personal favourites are Jarrett's *Bargain Classics* and *R.F.D.*, Hayward's *Rongwrong* and Manzanera's *Trot*. It's all mighty good, fervent stuff, bursting with energy and tottering between tranquillity and pandemonium.

ECHOES OF DULWICH COLLEGE IN NOT SO MAINSTREAM MUSIC
Cedric Porter, *South London Press*

THE HALCYON days when Dulwich was a hotbed of progressive pop are recalled with the issue of an LP deceptively titled *Mainstream* by a group called *Quiet Sun*. In 1967, *Quiet Sun* called themselves *Pooh and the Ostrich Feather* with a quick turnover of musicians – with all of them pupils at Dulwich College. Getting under way round the corner in Dalmore Rd., Dulwich, were Robert Wyatt and most of the original line-up of *Soft Machine* – about to become the darlings of the underground and even to get bouquets from the straight world by becoming the first pop group to play at a Promenade Concert.

Phil Manzanera, (now with *Roxy Music*) on guitars, Bill MacCormick on bass and Charles Hayward on percussion were making some pretty weirdo noises in SE21. The line-up was completed by a Dulwich College old boy, Dave Jarrett, on keyboards. But their ideas of electronic musical wizardry turned out to be too ahead of their time. For two years the group now renamed spent more time playing to themselves than to people.

They split up in 1971 and went their separate ways, Jarrett deserting music altogether. But last year, Manzanera, booked himself in to a studio to record a solo album and came up with the idea of getting together with the rest of the group to record an LP of *Quiet Sun* material as well.

Mainstream is heady stuff ranging from potent musical ideas to pointless meandering. Although suffering from a lack of rehearsal time, it also gains from a peculiar sense of intensity.

Appendix 5: *Matching Mole* – Press

MOLE IN A HOLE
Richard Williams, *Melody Maker*, 29th April 1972.
Robert Wyatt talks to Richard Williams

ON A CLEAR DAY, you can see the South Downs. Robert Wyatt looks out of the 21st floor window, down at the traffic speeding along Westway, and right over London to the chalky hills beyond.

At the moment, all he can actually see is trouble. Which is ridiculous, I'm sure you'll agree, for a man acclaimed as one of rock's most intelligent drummers and most inventive vocalists, with a solid background in one of our most respected bands.

But his child, *Matching Mole*, is up to the neck in it. A little earlier, he and his manager were forced to cancel two gigs, in Plymouth, and Penzance, for the craziest of reasons.

"My manager rang me up," he says, "and told me that it would cost us £180 to do the gigs. And we were only going to be paid £160 for them. So we couldn't afford it, and we've had to cancel."

He admits that it goes against his personal motto – "When in doubt, play" – but there it is, and he's sorry for the people who genuinely wanted to hear the *Mole*.

The band was formed last year, after a period of emotional turmoil for the small, flaxen-haired drummer. "I wanted to use the kind of electronic, sounds you hear in rock and roll, but for improvising. I suppose it doesn't sound like a very extensive philosophical dream. But I was happiest in the *Soft Machine* when it was an all-electric trio, first with Kevin and then with Hugh and after that it wasn't quite my dream band any more."

So he put together guitarist Phil Miller from *Delivery*, organist Dave Sinclair from *Caravan*, and bass guitarist Bill MacCormick from *Quiet Sun*. Since then despite an outward appearance of calm and certainty, it's been mostly trouble – at least on the business level.

To begin with. they were severely undercapitalised, unable to buy the equipment they wanted. They're in trouble now, for instance, because the *Soft Machine* have gone off to Italy for six weeks with most of the gear that the *Mole* was using.

Their equipment was either inadequate, unreliable, or late being delivered, and that's why they had a string of bad gigs at the beginning. Robert stopped singing for a while, even, because neither he nor the band could hear what he was doing.

They've never had their own van, which makes it harder, because hiring stuff is more expensive than owning it, and that's why they had to blow out those two West Country gigs. While I was there, Robert and Bill were discussing the possibility of buying a van which their manager had heard was for sale, for £50. It's not all limousines and expensive dope in the rock and roll world.

Their album, which has just come out, was a chapter of near-disasters. They were told to record it at *CBS's* old studios (unlike the *Softs*, who can pick their own independent studio), and little went right. They had to junk a lot of the stuff when it was discovered that two of the 16-tracks weren't working, and Bill reckons that the equipment as a whole was functioning properly on only three of their 16 sessions. The tape machines, for instance, were found to be revolving at varying speeds, which isn't exactly a help. They went to *CBS* to master it, and the machine broke down, so the company did it while the band was in Holland, and cut it with too much bass. That had to be rectified, and the record was weeks late coming out.

Other problems: someone nicked the *Softs'* mixer while it was in the Mole's care, and it cost them £180 to replace. Bill then had to spend £190 on a new *Fender* (*sic*) after another light-fingered gent had lifted his instrument. They're so low on equipment, that two of the special amps they bought for the monitor are being used to amplify the PA.

On the credit side, there's been the tour with John Mayall, which has got better and better for them. A few weeks ago, Sinclair left the band and was replaced by New Zealander Dave MacRae, from *Nucleus*.

"Dave Sinclair left because the band wasn't playing as many songs as we'd originally intended, and he's a songs man really. He likes to know whether a piece has got a four-bar intro or an eight-bar intro, and not just a 'sort of intro.'"

"Actually, his departure reflects me finding a balance. Late last summer, I felt a very strong need to do songs – but maybe I was over-reacting, I tried to get Dave Sinclair to freak out a trifle, and he does it beautifully, but he feels uncomfortable while he's doing it because he likes to know what note the bass is going to do next."

"I'd been very impressed by Dave MacRae, even when he was tuning up, because he's one of those musicians who can play anything and make it sound beautiful. I thought it was amazing that such a great musician wasn't unavailably committed to some exclusive project."

"He's my very favourite keyboard player now, and I think we all feel that – one of the great musicians. Every band should have Dave MacRae in it!"

The present situation gives Robert a severe sense of *deja-vu*, because it's obvious that the only way they're going to make it is by working heavily on the Continent – just as the *Soft Machine* did, in the late Sixties.

"We've thought of buying a house there, and just corning over for gigs. But don't like it, because I'm a Londoner really, and I want to live here."

346

"It's worse than it was in the early days of the *Softs*, because then we could live with my Mum and practice in the front room, with no panic about rent or food."

"The Continent could be our salvation, because there's a general all-round interest in new music as soon as you cross the Channel. We've got three gigs in France in May with Mayall, for which we're getting 4,500 dollars. Here, we've been going out for £65. Of course, if the bands I've been in had relied on Britain, I'd never have made a living out of music. It's not the same situation, but it's freakily reminiscent."

"Musicians tend to get a bit poncey, expecting the world to fall at their feet more than other people, but this isn't like that."

Musically, though, the band is going from strength to strength, with vast improvements weekly over the music represented on the album.

"Because of the *Soft Machine*, people expected polished results – from the shifty studios and broken-down equipment that we were using. But the second *Festival Hall* gig with Mayall was definitely a turning-point – it pulled things together."

The most exciting thing recently is that Dave MacRae's tentatively pushed a couple of his tunes in front of us, and they're just ecstatic to play. You can't wait for the next note to come along.

"Phil and Bill are also writing. Bill's first composition is very clever – it's too hard to play. So he's trying something slower."

There are just nine gigs in the book. "We'd like people to come and hear us, while we're still around."

MOLE: A SPIRIT OF TOGETHERNESS
Steve Peacock, *Sounds*, 29th April 1972
WHEN YOU GO TO A GIG, the Matching Mole you see before you is quite unlike the Matching Mole you hear on their first album; it's not unusual for bands to change a lot in the three months it often takes between recording an album and getting it out, but in the case of Matching Mole, there's rather more to it than usual.

"The first time Robert phoned me up he said he wanted to do an album of love songs", says bass guitarist Bill MacCormick. It didn't turn out quite like that, but there are two songs on the first side of the album, songs that represent a kind of release of frustration for Robert Wyatt that needed to happen before he shed his Soft Machine skin and started to get fully involved with the new group.

"Apart from wanting to get into a new band I'd also built up a certain amount of frustration whilst sitting about in various potential homes, writing letters to people that turned into lyrics and writing lyrics that turned into letters and getting all confused. A certain amount of frustration had built up that I hadn't put off my chest before".

347

Sitting around in keyboard player Dave MacRae's flat, talking to the band, you notice that the hesitancy and confusion of our last interview (*Sounds* 11/12/71) has given way to a much stronger feeling of confidence and optimism. I've never actually seen Robert brimming with self-confidence but this time he's a lot closer. The period of change is over, and now it's a question of the group as it is now (David Sinclair, the original organist, has left and Dave MacRae has joined full time after working on most of the sessions) growing together.

"When I'm not playing", says Robert, "I forget that I'm meant to be a drummer, so I sit in places with pianos singing songs and I think 'oh yes, that's what I do'. Then of course when I'm actually working again I find that I'm actually a drummer, so quite a different set of preoccupations and interests start coming up in your head. I've never quite resolved the difference between the two, so I'll probably spend the rest of my life tossing between them..."

"It's not the technical difficulty, it's the emotional difficulty of it being a totally different role in a group – to be singing songs and playing drums is a totally different relationship to be having with everybody. I find it more natural when I'm actually working to work from the point of view of a drummer".

Though when he was with the *Soft Machine* he once said he was an out of work singer who just happened to be playing drums.

"I only really started drumming because nobody else could. There were people around with pianos and guitars and things and they needed a drummer. I tried singing with other drummers but they never did it right, and the way to make sure the drummer was doing it right is to play the drums yourself".

So did he feel he'd basically resolved the dilemma? "No, I've decided that I'm really an organist. I'm at my happiest when very, very pissed and playing the *Mellotron*, or something like that. But it has nothing to do with proficiency and I'd have to be very pissed to get on stage and touch a keyboard".

So now, with *Matching Mole* a few months into its life, they were evolving through finding out about each other and what they can do together.

Dave: "It's more or less like that but with any band it's not an immediate process where you can walk in and do it. There's always the start which makes everyone want to walk in and play together, but once you get past that point it's a matter of finding out just how much you can do together, which we're still doing. Hopefully the lifeline won't run out on us – we're still improving, there's no doubt about that".

"It's important to have that spirit in what you're doing, it's important to want to get it on – and not in the way that you know you can to affect an

348

audience so they go 'rah, rah, rah'. Everyone doesn't consciously avoid that, but tries to create an original-sounding music, which I think is about where it's at really. Otherwise you might as well take the route where the money is – and everyone knows where it is".

Phil Miller: "We're playing for an audience, but primarily to give them something that's ours not what they think we can do. We want to give them something that's our identity, not what they could superimpose on us".

Though they're all pretty pleased with the album as it is – although the sound could have been a lot better if they'd been allowed to use a modern studio with the right equipment and it is history. The night before I spoke to them they'd been recording a session at the *BBC* for John Walters which'll be broadcast on *Top Gear* soon. This, they felt, caught the present band pretty well.

Robert: "The thing to remember overall is that this *Matching Mole* hasn't made a record yet. I'm amazed I feel I can say this but anyone who wants to who's interested in hearing this band and can't hear us live, please listen to the thing we did with John Walters when it comes out. Either I was more drunk than I thought I was or we really got off last night... radio's usually an anaemic medium for musicians, it's so hard for musicians to get off in a studio, but I'd be happy for anyone who wanted to know what we were doing who couldn't go to a gig, to hear that session".

"People say 'why make the album before you'd formed the group?', but the reason was that I wanted to. My preoccupation before I left the group I was in before was that there were a few little things I wanted to do, get off my chest. But that was only a quarter of an hour's worth of work, and from then on I wanted to get back into the real business of music making, which is in fact co-operative".

THE MOLE IN HIS HOLE
Ian MacDonald, *Cream*, Vol. 2, No. 2, June 1972
Robert Wyatt on how the *Soft Machine* broke down

WHY DID YOU LEAVE THE SOFTS and what are you up to in Matching Mole?
Lots of reasons - and my decisions about doing new things are so varied that they must be rationalisations of some basic thing that I really cannot pin down at all. I needed a complete change of life. At the time, it must have looked like from the outside that I had it made. In fact I was miserable. Absolutely miserable. So everything had to change on every level.

What were the main problems?
Well, I can justify or get pissed off with characteristics of people I'm working with according to whether I'm getting certain musical things I want from them and whether I'm giving the necessary in return. If they

are and I am, I see our personal relationship as satisfactory. But if I feel they're not doing what they should be doing or I'm not able to give them what a musician should, then this tends to manifest itself in personality difficulties and I start to dislike the person intensely. And the scapegoat in this case became Elton Dean.

I was jealous and proud of being in it with Mike and Hugh and that their thinking had, as I'd thought it would, finally manifested itself in some amazingly original music – and I felt that Elton didn't appreciate it. The thing is, when we decided to expand the line-up, we thought in terms almost of an artisan to play the ideas already coming from the group as it stood. We needed a wider range of noises more than fresh ideas and also we wanted to try out being a rhythm section behind a soloist for a while. But either we weren't a good enough rhythm section or Elton wasn't interesting enough in that context to carry off those kind of responsibilities – and I don't think he gave a shit anyway. I don't think he was interested in what *Soft Machine* was. It was a better-paid, more secure gig than his previous ones, and... I don't want to sound vicious about him, I mean we had good and bad gigs, he rightly liked Mike's writing a lot, and he and I liked very much playing together, blowing freely, and loosening up the prepared things. It balanced out very well sometimes. But it was essentially a false relationship. Not merely strained – relations in the *Soft Machine* had always been a bit bizarre.

How?

Everyone had very different contributions to make to the band and we couldn't really agree; it could only be paths crossing, because we started out in different places and were going in different directions – and what would be satisfactory to one person simply wouldn't be to another. It'd be baffling. Like, someone would write a composition which you'd think beautiful and then arrange it and give the solo to just the wrong person, by which time it'd be too inextricably embarrassing to rearrange it. You know, it's his tune, leave him alone. We got so we didn't really know what each other was on about.

When did that start?

The time the seven-piece went to France. Autumn, 1969. There were amazing difficulties on all levels, not excluding the practical one of not having the equipment or the money for seven people. Eventually it cracked completely. Poor old Nick got really screwed up. You know, there was a lot of happiness, a lot of new things, a lot of problems, a lot of neuroses, added to which it was incredibly cold in the van and we were all a bit disorientated. The cracks just started to appear. The identity of the group became like a memory after that... for me.

How did it actually happen then?

Well… you get other people in to play Mike and Hugh's stuff, but to get in they have to be musically ambitious which means after a while they want to play some of their own material, and they play it to you, and you don't like it, right? And then it comes out in the open, let's face it, he's meant to be there for you, not you for him, and a hierarchy emerges which freaks out those people who consider they're wrongly placed in that hierarchy. The natural tendency then is to withdraw – cos no-one wants to think of himself as a shit or a schmuck. Then everybody starts getting formal with each other and by then it's turned into another job. From then on it's just a matter of time, really. Just a matter of time.

But, obviously my memories of that time with the *Soft Machine* are – well, like anyone's memories, like…

Where do those four records come into your memories? Is it documentary?

I never considered the *Soft Machine* recorded in any kind of intelligent relationship to our progress, what we actually sounded like. We'd take new compositions into the studio, record them, two months later learn how to play them, six months later discard them, and then a month after that go back into the studio again with more new things we hadn't learned to play properly. The *Soft Machine* at its best is hardly on record. At best, those records are only an indication of what the group was all about.

Are you going to keep a sharper eye on the way Matching Mole is recorded?

No, it'll probably be just as… I mean, all I've done is choose people with potential for excellence in themselves, not their similarity or me-worship or anything like that, so there'll be just as many difficulties – except there was no condescension in the original choice of people. No more Eltoning, in other words. Inasmuch as I ought to have owned up to him what I was asking him to do. Won't make that mistake again. In fact, I've avoided any quick, easy way to get a slick band together and it's yet to emerge what the new group will naturally be – if someone'll be on top of their music enough to turn into a leading-light, for example.

So what about the album?

Making that record and forming the group were two separate things. I'd have made it whether I'd formed a group or not. It's me. I had total control over it, said I'd choose the material, do the editing, litter the whole thing with fiddling about on the *Mellotron* – with or without anybody's approval. It seemed years since I'd done a record. At the same time, I wanted to form a group because my ideas are more intense than numerous, I'm not a great fountain of ideas and I need to be in a group. I need other people around me to use their ideas and imaginations to pull the best out of me. Besides, I had to say I was forming a group etcetera or they wouldn't have let me do the record. Obviously they only like to record people who are out on the road with an act or something to promote it.

Is that pressure on you now?

Don't know really. I refuse to be pressured anyway.

So what comes next? Are you the leader or what?

Inasmuch as I chose the people in the band. But I see myself more as someone who pulls people together who might otherwise not have thought of it. Giving them opportunities. Like, Dave McRae is in no sense out of work – he's in constant demand as a session-musician – but *Matching Mole* is giving him an opportunity to play his music in a way that all the rest – Mike Gibbs, Ian Carr and so on – doesn't. I make space, is what I'm saying. I know what I'm good at and let other people get on and do what they're good at.

I feel what I'm doing, however much I enjoy doing it, doesn't cover enough ground to make me think I'm living a complete creative life. There are a few people who write – Hugh, Mike, Dave McRae, Kevin – with whom I like to fit in. I'm not capable of setting up situations by myself alone. I need other people, but only a very few special people and it's fucking hard to find them.

So what were those two solo albums you made in Los Angeles?

Well, the *Soft Machine* in its first version had broken up, we'd done the last gig with Hendrix, at the *Hollywood Bowl*, Mike went back to London, Kevin went on to Majorca. The record company didn't know we'd broken up – the first album wasn't released yet, though it was six months since we'd recorded it – and there seemed no obligation to carry on; and I'd got various things I'd been wanting to do that I couldn't do with the group as it then was. It was a great relief to get into the studio and play all the instruments myself and do it along without having to be democratic about it. That's all.

What did you record?

There were two sets. See, I went to the record company and said 'Look, Mike's gone back to London', I dunno… I mean, it was winter, 1968, and I'd just got back to New York and I'd been approached to do some film music and I was quite happy. But they said 'No, listen, this record's amazing, we want to put it out, the group should go on the road'. So I said 'Is it? Should it?' And phoned up Mike in London and said 'Do you want to start up a new version of the group?' And he said 'No, yes, no, yes, Yes'. And I came back and he did his first writing for the group – bits of *Esther's Nose Job* which was pinched off a bass-line of Kevin's, actually – and we did these tunes I'd been doing which turned out to be the first side of Volume Two – arrangements of bits and pieces of half-forgotten stuff Hugh had done years ago for the *Wilde Flowers* that I'd worked into a whole in L.A. – plus *Moon in June*. Which didn't turn up till *Third* because I

was terrified it'd be played wrong. Even then, I did all of it by myself –
except the organ solo of course. That was Mike.
Might you ever do another solo album?

Not foreseeably, no. I feel so much closer to the people in *Matching
Mole* in terms of melody, feeling, and the rest. I'm not scared of doing my
stuff with them. They've all been in groups that've done songs, for
example, and I haven't been in one of them since I was with Kevin.
Does that mean more songs in your set?

I'm dubious about it, because they'd be more complicated than the
kind I've done before, and I might find it hard singing and playing at the
same time. Bill might do some, but he'd probably have to write it himself.
My stuff's written for my voice or is too specifically about me. And the
others would find it hard to write for someone like me who can't read
music and has a range of about three notes and you mustn't write a
semitone on either side of them if you expect it to be remotely in tune.
So what are you up to live at the moment?

Rehearsing, mostly. Or we have been. Up until the second gig at the
Festival Hall we were rehearsing in public; since then, with the exception of
a disaster at Canterbury, we've to a great extent sorted ourselves out. I say
this chiefly because most people would naturally think a group like this is
pretty well-off, 'contract with *CBS*, album out, etc.' In fact we're very poor
and can't actually afford to rehearse properly even. We've had a lot of
equipment nicked and the promoters in Britain aren't paying us a living
wage. I'm not carping – we're paying our dues, like any other band –it's
just that I want people to know that we don't use mikes that stop working
every five minutes because we like them; we can't afford better. And when
the PA blows, it's not... bravura, or something. It's poverty.
How do you see the roles of the other three in Matching Mole?

Phil is the only guitarist who doesn't conceptually piss me off a bit. I
agree with him about how to play guitar and I really don't with anyone
else. I admire lots of names – same ones everyone else does – and I don't
want to start putting down other guitarists that aren't working in *Matching
Mole*, but...

Well, the theory's like this: the technical side of 'I'm-a-guitarist'
guitarists is based on imitation bebop horn lines. But the sound's weak
compared to what's come out of less technical music like urban blues and
rock and roll. So the idea these days is to get the two going together, the
facility and the sound. And everybody's saying a lot of guys are doing it,
but I don't think they are. Like, someone for whom I have great overall
admiration and who isn't going to give a shit what I say anyway, which is
John McLaughlin. He's the answer to my dream of an acoustic guitarist
who does what John Williams claims to be doing, which is total control of
the guitar, understanding of it harmonically, understanding of bebop,

understanding of Hendrix, and using the lot. But, as an electric guitarist, I find he does amateurish parodies of rock guitarists, but in a sort of tasteful, speedy way. If you analyse the solos on *The Inner Mounting Flame*, they're... they piss me off, frankly. As opposed to the Miroslav Vitous album where he's very good, or as an acoustic player on *My Goal's Beyond*. He's undoubtedly the most on-top-of-his-instrument guitarist around, but, in the end, frustrating – in a way that I don't think Phil will be. Because, though he lacks that facility, he really understands sound and harmony in a way that other guitarists don't. They just don't.

Dave... he's very simply the best musician I've ever worked with in my life. That's about all I can say.

Bill's a bass-guitarist, not a bass-player or a guitarist turned bass-guitarist. I just trust his taste and intelligence, besides which he's amazingly ambitious for his own music. He's actually an idealist and it's not just a job for him – it's important to him that what we're doing has a potential for being very good and satisfying. I knew him before I thought of him as a musician and I never thought he'd turn out to be capable of playing like he does; I'm pre-disposed to believe that anybody who could be that clear and objective in discussion could actually turn out to have that egotistical madness, that... silliness that most good players have. Sloppy thinking on my part, really. I saw him with his group and I was surprised what a natural performer he was – in fact I think of him as quite showbizzy really. So few people, in any case, outside of Jack Bruce and maybe Steve Swallow, have really used the bass-guitar. Not functionally; there are some fantastic functional players around, like Sly Stone's and the guy with Edgar Winter. Bill pushes all aspects of the instrument and he's sometimes very demanding to play with.

Do you ever think you and/or the band are taking yourselves a bit too seriously?

Sure. But it's a piece of self-deception that's as necessary as a raincoat in the rain. In performance or in any process like that, you arrive at a strange kind of elated insanity. You feel like God. And it's hard to feel like God and not take yourself a bit seriously. Or something. Know what I mean?

Perhaps I meant self-involvement when two or three thousand people are watching you.

People used to say this about the other group I was in – which shall be nameless, and which I won't name, but can only be described as the *Soft Machine* – that we didn't acknowledge or play for people who'd come to see something else, that's true, but eventually the people who got to know and like us were incredibly relieved to have their intelligence and their sensitivity flattered enough to follow us in whatever way our fancy was taking us. In an inverted way, that's just a flash, avant-garde version of showbusiness, really. How many people you lose in the process God only knows but, if I can make a living at it, I'm happy.

354

Any gripes about that show business in general?

What an opportunity! God. Yeah, okay. See, in the good old days, back when the Teds used to beat me up and take off me Dizzy Gillespie records and stick on Elvis, there was even so a thing about values in music. One knew where the real worth was. The barriers were very rigid, sure, but it wasn't confused like it is now. Today, the pop press is always telling me, the barriers are down and someone who used to get off on *Marmalade* celebrates his coming-of-age or whatever by going over to the Other Chart or whatever it's called in *Time Out* and thinks he's digging jazz or classical music when he's listening to his new Keith Emerson album. He's not. It's just pop in another form.

And I think the general smugness of music-listening today – I see it in people's record collections – is regrettable. If half the guys digging Keith Emerson because they thought he was jazz actually put themselves out and listened to, say Keith Jarrett playing the real thing... well! I just dislike the air of easiness about it today, as if good music is now miraculously disseminated to all via *ELP* or whatever. The really good musicians are, as ever, out of work – and the barriers are not down at all, it's an illusion.

When a fifteen year old chick is digging Marc Bolan is she having the illusion that she's hearing great music or is she hearing great music?

Is it an illusion you're asking me that question? No, look. You've got to be honest with yourself. When I was fifteen, I'd be looking around in a record-shop and I'd come across an album-sleeve saying Charlie Parker is the Guvnor. None of my friends had even heard of him. The Bird? Who? But I bought one of his records to find out. And I didn't like it at all – just seemed a lot of fast noises. But I went on with it, trusting opinion of sources I respected, kept listening, and found out that Parker was, in fact, the Guvnor. And I took it from there.

That sort of experience is available for anyone, but I don't care whether or not they take it. Elvis Presley may also be the Guvnor, I dunno. But he's not pretending to be more than he is, nor are his fans. But fans of 'progressive' or 'underground' music are. It's both a pity and a downright shame. It's a pity that Keith Jarrett has so little recognition he has to play in a group he doesn't really fit into, or even like, but the leader is lazy enough to let other people play in his time. And it's a downright shame that he can't form his own group because virtually no-one has bothered to find out about him. Because it's easy and okay and progressive to dig Keith Emerson. Right? That's all.

MATCHING MOLE: THE BEGINNING OF ANOTHER EAR
Al Clark, *Time Out*, 16th-22nd June 1972 (part of a far longer piece)
FEW BANDS HAVE FACED such a discrepancy between the enthusiasm of their welcome and the uncertainty of their economics as *Matching Mole*.

Multiply an average musicbiz melodrama by the number of holes it'd take to fill the Wembley Empire Pool and you'll come up with some semblance of the equipment, transport and pocket-money problems that have continually confronted this merry and determined little combo of *Foster's Lager* addicts. This, together with a considerable affection for Robert Wyatt's drumming and voicing, Phil Miller's guitaring, Bill MacCormick's bassing and Dave MacRae's keyboarding (and the now-departed Dave Sinclair's keyboarding on their record, the excellent CBS 64850) prompted Al Clark to wander along to a rehearsal in Dave's front room, and afterwards talk with Robert across the kitchen table...

THE EVOLVING MOLE

And then there was *Matching Mole*, or Machine Molle as some prophetic bilingual punsters would insist. Bill MacCormick was a civil servant at the time of joining but before that was in a group called *Quiet Sun* who did unusual time signature things. Phil Miller was in *Delivery* but also worked with people like Roy Babbington, and spent long amounts of time learning his way around his instrument. Or, as Robert put it: 'His main background is sitting around playing guitar without any money'. Robert met Dave MacRae through *Nucleus* who were looking for a new drummer after John Marshall went to join Jack Bruce and, ultimately and ironically, the *Soft Machine*. Dave still plays piano for them as well as making his considerable contribution to the Mole.

'Dave MacRae is an antipodean from another planet, and my life started out with them. He's such a total musician – equally happy in Australian jazz groups, knowing his Cecil Taylor, doing a Coca Cola ad or grooving behind Buddy Rich or Sarah Vaughan. The most important contribution he made to the record was being there, tuning up his piano and talking and putting on little odd plinking noises through all the instrumental things, and just creating the atmosphere of being in a room with all he can do but not doing it. It's not so much what he plays but of how different the record would've been if he hadn't been there'.

The man who did play most of the keyboard parts on the record, David Sinclair, is now late of *Caravan*, late of *Matching Mole* and currently working on some songs with a friend, and drummer Pip Pyle. Why late of *Matching Mole*?

'Well, although he joined to play and rave as well as do the songs, the only thing that really worked compatibly was the song playing. He's a great freaker-outer on organ. A keyboard man with a sense of madness is very rare, keyboard people are usually very schooled and can wreck musical madness with their knowledge of what should be happening. Dave can lose himself in wonderful ways, but when you're trying to build your tune that you're going to play night after night, it's not enough to have a few things in common. You've really got to have so much in common. You can afford casual relationships on a record you can't afford in a working group'.

Was there any track on the record particularly representative of the further-evolved *Mole*?

'Hopefully I'm now becoming a quarter of whatever gets said or played. So for me *Part of the Dance* is the most useful pointer to the group because it was written by Phil and I'm just doing my quarter on it, like I'm doing now and like I hope to be doing on the next album'.

Does that necessarily exclude any more *O Carolines* or *Signed Curtains*?

'Those things are like cutting off malignant parts of a diseased body. I really don't need them anymore. To be able to write and sing those, without sounding too precious I hope, relieves some of the things that got… However, there's no way of making plans about that. I suppose I shall sit around pianos and sing and think up word games at certain times for the resto of my life. And. if I'm in the studio, I'll do it'.

AFTERPIECE

A few days later, with the group having one off to France on the Gallic leg of their John Mayall tour, I put my brain cells in a small cardboard box and take them down to an armchair in front of a television screen in South London's ETV studios. Resting in the certain knowledge that the Mole won't be bothering with any of the right on and rock 'n' roll medleys that might make them rich tax exiles before they get to Avignon, I settle back and watch the playback of a broadcast they taped a few days earlier.

Dave, like an electronic Gandalf with impossibly long fingers, guides the smoky, shifting rhythms over Bill's obsessive Focal Timekeeper bass line and curls elegantly up and down whatever part of the keyboard he fancies. Phil, hunched and Grecian-God-Curled, is the ideal group guitarist, waiting for the moment to contribute effectively and knowing what an effective contribution amounts to. Bill and Phil, like Bill and Ben, have a special binding language and don't even have to say anything. Robert doing his voice bits isn't a pretty sight but makes a remarkable sound, like a man sobbing his heart out inside an echo chamber. *Matching Mole* seems to be the sum total of all their lives so far.

It really is a quartet now. And I only talked to Robert. Aw shucks. See them soon. Nice boys every one of them, even if they don't go for smart casuals and fast cars. They're probably the most coherent and adventurous British band that's still accessible these days, equally balancing strong themes and inspired deviations. And they're not doing much, apart from rehearsing. Music-Music never did go down all that well. Still, it's always a new pigeon-hole and there's plenty of money and support in them. In *Mole*-holes there's only music…

MATCHING MOLE/QEH
Ian MacDonald, *NME*

MATCHING MOLE'S LAST British appearance before a month's tour of the Continent was witnessed by a surprisingly large audience, in view of the fact that the event received virtually no publicity at all.

They played with conviction and sometimes rather alarming volume through a continuous hour-long selection from their forthcoming album *The Little Red Record*, demonstrating that their music can encompass a wider emotional range than practically any band you can think of.

Instrumental high spots included some delicate impressionism on Dave MacRae's *Smoke Signal* and an impassioned *Lything and Gracing* with a wound-up Phil Miller guitar break liberating itself finally in free atonality. However, the best performances were of a batch of songs full of serpentine melodies and minor changes and all vehicles for Robert Wyatt's firework display of a voice, reaching into the stratosphere on Bill MacCormick's *Gloria Gloom* and turning on a mock operatic tenor for MacRae's *Drinking my politics away*. Perversely, the best moment came right at the beginning with a tragically beautiful Miller-Wyatt collaboration, *God Song*; it'll be the stand-out track on *The Little Red Record* as *O Caroline* was on the first album – but only just because everything *Matching Mole* are playing these days is of world class.

APPENDIX 6: *MATCHING MOLE* ALBUM REVIEWS

Hervé Miller[i], *Best,* June 1972
Matching Mole
WHEN ROBERT WYATT left the *Soft Machine*, where he was already *only* a drummer, it definitely became a very esoteric avant-garde music group, more or less akin to jazz. The extroverted and crazy tendency, which still makes *Softs'* first LP the best record of true pop music ever recorded, disappeared with its last representative. An inevitable rupture, I suppose, so that the other tendency, fascinating, but very narcissistic, that of Monsieurs Ratledge, Hopper & Dean, can express themselves fully. But the magic of the old *Softs*, this magic which rested precisely on an explosive balance between the two trends, it was up to Robert to perpetuate it, he who had always been the link, through a double musical orientation which borders on schizophrenia.

Hence *Matching Mole*, an ironic response to the Molle Machine: from the outset, the name of the group sets the tone. With Robert, two very young musicians, Bill MacCormick (bass) and Phil Miller (guitar), and then a long-time musical friend, David Sinclair (organ and piano), another member of the *Softs* family since he was a member of *Caravan*. This album is already no longer so much a reflection of the music of the group, which has evolved all the more as Sinclair has already left and been replaced by Dave MacRae, discreetly present on this disc on electric piano. But it will satisfy all those nostalgic for the old *Soft Machine*, all those who sorely missed the particular timbre of Robert Wyatt's voice. And the latter also takes advantage of the opportunity to express himself on the piano (remarkable on *Signed Curtain*) and even on the *Mellotron*, of which he makes much more inventive use than the *Moodies* or *Crimson* (*Dedicated to Hugh, but you weren't listening*). The disc has uneven moments which must be attributed to the fact that the group was very new at the time of recording, but the whole is largely up to what one could expect from Father Wyatt. *Instant Pussy* and *Instant Kitten*, it's all the magic of *Save yourself* rediscovered.

In fact, I refer you to these titles because they are written on the cover, but it is a little arbitrary, because, according to good *Softs'* practice, each side is of course uninterrupted.

David Sinclair, if he is not Ratledge, is far from being without interest (*O Caroline*), the young Bill MacCormick acquits himself very well of his task, in the company of such a drummer. But it is Phil Miller who especially impresses. We're always waiting around the corner for a guitarist who ventures into this kind of musical context, but Phil easily convinces.

---

[i] Hervé Miller sadly died in March 2021.

We find in his playing the influence of his masters, Coryell and McLaughlin, but he proves himself worthy of it while developing his own style, served by a boundless imagination. There are people like that who never disappoint...

MOLE SEE RED
Matching Mole - Little Red Record
Richard Williams, *Melody Maker*
FROM WHAT I HEAR ON THE GRAPEVINE, *Matching Mole's* second album was conceived in an atmosphere not entirely consisting of sweetness and light. Personality clashes apparently marred the sessions, which may mean that the group will have a different configuration next time we see it in public.

While these difficulties will no doubt work themselves out with the passing of time, they make the fact of this record's excellence even more remarkable. To say that I enjoy it is to say that Russians like vodka; after only a few days, it's already part of the furniture. Robert is such a warm, likeable person, and I've yet to hear any music in which he's been involved which hasn't possessed these qualities, in some measure. John Peel has described this group as 'a *Mahavishnu Orchestra* with a sense of humour', and if there's anything I've felt lacking from the Mahavishnu mob, it's wit.

So what do we have here? We have some great playing, for a start, from Dave MacRae, who may well be the best electric pianist in the whole world. Having modified his instrument himself, he produces sounds which need hearing to be believed, and his facility is astonishing – but he never lets it get in the way of his innate lyricism. He's a monster. Robert, too, plays the best I've heard him, attacking furiously and swinging like mad all over the place. Phil Miller's guitar and Bill MacCormick's bass are rather more than adequate through choons like MacRae's *Smoke Signal, March Ides* and *Brandy as in Benj* and Bill's *Flora Fidgit*. They're constantly achieving the unexpected, retaining warmth in their improvisations. But although these may be the meat of the record, it's the spice which interest me most: there's *Nan True's Hole* on which guest speaker Ruby Crystal (a Darling girl) recites a dialogue between prostitute and inexperienced customer, backed by a dark, forbidding Hammer-like theme; there's *Gloria Gloom* featuring the throbbing electronic synths of Captain Eno; and there's *God Song,* Robert's statement on religion. In the artless style of the first album's *O Caroline* he sings: 'What on earth are you doing, God? Next time you send your boy down here, give him a wife and a sexy daughter…'. Here's hoping this band stays together, one way or another; if they do, they'll produce something even better than this very friendly record.

This article courtesy of Phil Howitt's archive

Dee Jay - Sound of the Month - December 1972
Matching Mole - *Little Red Record*
John Peel

CONTRARY TO WHAT you may believe, a great deal of the best and most creative rock music comes from without the Anglo-American axis. Bands like *Can*, *Amon Duul II*, *Faust* and *Neu* from Germany, *Komintern* from France, *Supersister* and *Focus* from Holland are experimenting to a greater or lesser degree with a whole new range of sounds and experiences.

Because of their experiments they seldom achieve much popular stature in their own countries and the same fate may well befall *Matching Mole* in this country — and for the same reasons. As with nearly all experimental records this LP is not without flaws, but the successes that there are are remarkable — and they are not academic and unapproachable successes either. There's power, wit and skill involved throughout and drummer Robert Wyatt, keyboards man Dave MacRae, guitarist Phil Miller and bass player Bill MacCormick have, with producer Robert Fripp of *King Crimson* and synthesizer star Eno, of *Roxy Music*, made an LP which is more accessible than a lot of the fashionable nonsense that makes the album charts.

APPENDIX 7: *RUTH/RICHARD* PRESS/REVIEWS

ROBERT WYATT: *Ruth Is Stranger Than Richard* (Virgin)
Pete Erskine, *NME*

INITIALLY, IT'S REALLY HARD to take an overview on this one. *Rock Bottom* (*Ruth's* extraordinarily beautiful autobiographical predecessor) had a more directly tangible continuity to it (whether accidental or otherwise) but *Ruth*, as Overall Concept, feels very much like a collection of snapshots, of which *Team Spirit* is the only really potent standout.

There are reasons for this, Al Clark, *Virgin Records'* press office Oberleutnant and a few other things besides, told me. Like, instead of just wrapping up the promotion T-shirts and mailing off the fibreglass brief case stickers, he actually has something like a 100 per cent personal involvement with the label's artists – not the least of which is R. Wyatt (He is credited on the sleeve – with Ivor Cutler – 'for Mental Health').

So I called Al up and asked him why I was finding it impossible to review *Ruth Is Stranger Than Richard* and he drew my attention to the lyrics of *Team Spirit* and furnished me with a brief but detailed dossier of background information.

Or at least confirmed a few, hazy half-guesses.

Post *Rock Bottom* and around the time of the Great Unreleased Wyatt Single, *Yesterday Man* (the follow-up to *I'm A Believer* which subsequently saw light of day on the *Virgin V* sampler), Robert found himself labouring under considerable duress. From a slightly more esoteric musical grounding in the *Softs* etc, he suddenly found himself (a) the object of universal admiration, winner of the *Victor Ludorum* for *Rock Bottom* (artistically the most successful unintentioned concept album ever), and (b) a mass media personality with *I'm A Believer*.

He worked himself hard, too hard. Did interviews with everybody. Allowed himself to become immersed in the whole top twenty push-me-pull-you, and initially quite enjoyed it – to the extent of adapting his musical philosophies to the outlook that showbiz was actually Where It Was At and that Things Arty were to be regarded with a healthy suspicion.

But in fact, it wasn't that clear-cut. All Wyatt was trying to say was that perhaps Noddy Holder and Albert Ayler should both be accorded proportionate respect.

So he appeared on *Top Of The Pops* in his wheelchair. He appeared on the cover of *NME* in his wheelchair – with the rest of the folk involved in his first solo concert also in wheelchairs. Maybe, in the philanthropic way he had investigated the effects of his accident through *Rock Bottom*, to get people to laugh, almost; altruistically, to help exorcise any potential discomfort which those who came into contact with him might feel. By bringing it out into the open. By stating it. Almost by making a mockery of it – like Lenny Bruce exhorting folks to call a nigger a Nigger because after a while the term will become meaningless.

Then two things happened: *Virgin* refused to release *Yesterday Man* as a follow up single; and Robert Wyatt rowed with *Top Of The Pops* producer Robin Nash. Nash – a sensitive gentleman – claimed that Robert's appearing on *TOTP* in his wheelchair was 'distasteful'. Robert retorted that if being a wheelchair didn't hang him up so why should it upset anybody else?

The incident – combined with *Virgin's* apparent lack of faith in the commerciality of the single and the fact that Wyatt had simply depleted his already-curtailed energy reserves – affected him deeply.

Ruth Is Stranger Than Richard may therefore be seen as the product of this disillusion ... and of the impending fear of a creative impasse (that often actually creates that which it is trying to avoid) always brought about with the pressures of the requirements to do the same thing twice – i.e. make a musical statement as stunning (preferably even more so) than *Rock Bottom*.

Wyatt could've done either of two things: could've retired, sat back and mulled it over – and risked being overwhelmed by his own creative inertia in the process. Or he could have pushed ahead and forced himself out of his situation – tortuously, piece by piece.

With *Ruth Is Stranger Than Richard* he's taken the latter course, owned up (again) by admitting that initially he has no great co-ordinated theme to lay upon us, no mind-blitzing core – but a collection of odds and ends. Which he has determined to make good odds and ends.

But, more important, perhaps catalysed by the aforementioned incidents, he has admitted to the agony that thus far he has managed to be appearing to shrug off.

So *Team Spirit*, credited to Wyatt, bass player Bill MacCormick and Phil Manzanera, is a melodic adaptation of *Frontera* on Manzanera's *Diamond Head* LP. Manzanera had written the tune for it, Wyatt had written the lyrics in Spanish. He apparently liked the tune so much that he decided upon an elongated adaptation of it here.

It's slower. Where *Frontera* was free and airy, *Team Spirit* is more cloying and compacted. Bill MacCormick's bass accompaniment in the opening bars is beautiful and agile – almost a string bass feel. Mongezi Feza pulls out a strange rotating trumpet figure.

Wyatt delivers the lyrics: he seems to be despairing a little, at his physical semi-helplessness, and – as revealed further into the song – the vulnerability he feels at being dependent.

Returning to the effects of that interim period – and in the light of Wyatt's recent declaration that his singles' days are over – it also seems fairly obvious that the *Ruth* side of the album (which is divided into two sides – *Ruth* and *Richard*) is a deliberate return to his jazz days. Hence the inclusion of Charlie Haden's *Song For Che* and Feza's *Sonia*.

Soup Song (which opens *Ruth*), written in collaboration with old *Wilde Flowers'* colleague Brian Hopper, is the reflection of one of Wyatt's culinary phases (soupçon) – enunciated musically and lyrically in Dadaist early-*Softs* fashion.

The majority of the other side – *Richard* – is taken up with subsections of *Muddy Mouse* opening with fifty seconds of Wyatt (voice) and Fred Frith (piano) free-forming, culminating in *Muddy Mouth* with superb chord changes

Solar Flares – Wyatt's only solo self-composed tune here – comes closest to anything here to the kind of overall feel represented by *Rock Bottom* – that high breathy organ-pipe backdrop over a gentle repetitive rhythm section.

Still very fragmented, though. But an essential record, if only for *Team Spirit*. I must allow it a little more time.

RUTH, RICHARD AND ROBERT
Allan Jones, *Melody Maker*
Robert Wyatt's new album Ruth Is Stranger Than Richard *seems certain to get a favourable reception— yet its creator seems unwilling to talk about it.*
ALLAN JONES tries to pin him down...
ROBERT WYATT is reclining comfortably against a generous supply of pillows and cushions like a bearded Buddha, surrounded by evidence of domestic tranquillity and convenience.

His lady, Alfie, makes tea. Florence Mutt dozes peacefully at the foot of the bed, and Mr Wyatt, with considerable skill, evades questions about his most recent artistic endeavour, *Ruth Is Stranger Than Richard*

It seems, initially, that Robert is suffering from some kind of post-natal depression after delivering this, his second album, in under a year, and he's using the conversation to excise some personal doubts which have been undermining his confidence in both himself and, by implication, the new work.

'I just don't seem to function as a professional musician'. he begins. 'I haven't seemed to establish any kind of working procedure or recording procedure or writing procedure'.

'It seems to me that I know less and less what it is I'm actually attempting to do as I get older... You know, I watch lots of singers turn out album after album, and I marvel at their continued interest in their own voice.

364

'They seem to sustain a remarkable interest which is really quite sensible, I suppose... It's just that the more my interests in music develop, the more they seem to develop away from my own personal potential'.

His own voice, he says, horrifies him. He'll try treating it in various ways to extend its possibilities ('it's one of my favourite ways of keeping myself awake'), but it's still a personal relief whenever the focus is directed away from his voice to another instrument.

'It is strange, really, because in theory it is my favourite instrument, because it's the only one that everybody's got. You use it all day in conversation and it's a very interesting instrument We've all got our own version of it'.

Of the way he's manipulated his voice on say, *Solar Flares* (on the new album), he says, yes it was encouraging to discover he could create something satisfactory without relying entirely upon the assistance of other musicians.

It's at about this point in the conversation, when one is being lulled into a false sense of security, that one suddenly realises that all this is something, of a diversionary tactic.

One wouldn't, perhaps, have imagined Wyatt to be unduly apprehensive about the impending reaction to *Ruth Is...* even though it does come as successor to the brilliant *Rock Bottom*.

THERE MAY BE SOMETHING of that in Wyatt, but it would be closer to the truth and no exaggeration to suggest that he would rather talk about anything (from Andre Breton to Barry White as he does later) than about his own work.

Phil Manzanera described him as being in a particularly anti-guitar mood at the time of recording *Ruth Is...* (not that *Rock Bottom* could be described as paradise for a Robin Trower freak). Even as casual a remark as this sets Robert off at another tangent.

'I look at the pop polls, you know, and I see awards for top guitarists and singers . . . and then I see trombones, trumpets, oboes, flutes, ocarinas, and they're all listed under Miscellaneous Instruments... And I think to meself, in me own quiet way, 'Oh, really? That's interesting. So much for the last few hundred years of music.'

Robert scratches his head. lights another cigarette and settles back. 'It was', he begins squinting through the smoke, 'harder to cope with this album psychologically because I was almost convinced that I'd never record another one. There was no immediate motivation.

'Then I thought, well, it really is time to start another album. It seemed my job in a sense. I'm a fake Communist, you see, and I believe that everybody has a job in the community, on whatever level they're working'.

He looks as if he'd rather be someplace other than this as he explains.

'And I think my, er, job is to record tunes... sometimes. Unfortunately, I can go a year or more without feeling any compulsion to commit myself to a particular bunch of tunes or any particular set of treatments...'

'Before *Rock Bottom* I hadn't had a chance for a long time to record, or do anything at all, so a great deal of frustration accumulated and with that album it was like turning on a tap and letting it all run out.

'Since doing that I've resumed my inhibited self- conscious state of mind, whereby I find it difficult to do anything at all'. A disarming smile does nothing alleviate the seriousness that pronouncement.

STILL, WE CAN'T LINGER. *Rock Bottom*, he concedes was – in that it was a most private selection of songs and insights of a particularly autobiographical nature – the least self-conscious of his records.

'The thing is that *Rock Bottom* relied more on my voice than anything I'd done before, and anything which relies on the voice is communicated very directly to other people, and they react to it very personally'.

'An idea played on the voice, therefore, automatically becomes, or seems, more personal than the same idea played on another instrument...'

'The idea, basically, was just to make a nice record, not to explain to the world what a terrible time I was having. For me, the words and the ideas ... there's simply no possible excuse for making them public unless there are some nice tunes to go with them. So, the 'meaning' is actually less important to me than making something pleasant to listen to'.

Long silence. But, Robert; isn't that *really* only your old self-consciousness coming back after the act?

'Yes. But even so, I've always thought that the whole bit about self-expression is a little misleading. I don't hold any particular faith in the notion of expressing yourself and thinking that you can actually communicate to other people something which is private and personal'.

'I think that you can make objects which other people can respond to and appreciate. And that might be quite closely related to what you had in mind when you made the actual object'.

"But I still don't really have much faith in the idea, or even the necessity, of really expressing yourself, of saying 'fuck it, I'm all bottled up. I must tell the world how I feel'.

Surely, though, the songs on *Rock Bottom* particularly aren't moving merely because the author has a facility for writing an attractive tune and having the taste and perception to choose musicians sympathetic to interpreting those compositions? The act of creation, after all, isn't that facile.

'No, it isn't. You're right. It's a question of vanity, really. Something I don't like to admit. I suppose it's a question of vanity. If you have the opportunity to use words, and make them more than just noises, it's an ability which you have to attempt to use as widely as possible …'

'I try to make my songs work on every possible level, quite consciously. Most of the songs on *Rock Bottom* were written while we were thinking of ideas for the third *Matching Mole* album'.

WE SEEM TO HAVE REACHED something of an intermediate conclusion here. And having accepted *Rock Bottom* as the important statement that it is, or was to Wyatt as an artist (as important as was, *Plastic Ono Band*, even *In My Life* to Lennon, *The Man who sold the World* to Bowie, *Blonde On Blonde* as a loose example, to Dylan), the way is open to broaden the conversation.

Let's take, to begin with, Wyatt's lyrics, which have always, at their best, revealed a quality out of the mainstream of rock writing, In one sense parts of *Rock Bottom*, indeed, owe something to the Surrealist precept of automatic writing, hut go one stage further than surrendering personal autonomy to the dream flow and exercise a finely-developed sense of poetry within his writing.

He agrees his writing owes little to the rock mainstream, and that he's quite consciously avoided this.

'Like, I've never thought of myself as being a mouthpiece for the, er, 'Youth Culture', I've always been on the fringe of what's happened in rock. I'm basically no more worried about identifying with the problems of a street punk than I am with the problems of old-age pensioners. I feel no allegiance to any of those gangs out there'.

Robert has previously expressed his disappointment at the lack of widespread creative energy within rock at the moment.

While new directions and possibilities are being explored and investigated by individuals and groups outside the rock mainstream (*Henry Cow/Slapp Happy* in one context; Cale, Harper and, say, Eno in another), the majority of people concerned with music are still waiting eager anticipation for the arrival of a new rock messiah (the new Dylan/*Stones*/*Beatles*).

This situation leads, via a thought provoked by Eno, to the suggestion that any further developments of significance will evolve from the cooperative efforts of a group of artists sharing a common responsibility.

A situation which would have as its antecedents the Zurich-based Dadaists or the Paris-based Surrealists, movements which Wyatt regards with affection and admiration.

He considers this thesis with some enthusiasm, but remains a little reluctant to draw a comparison between the group of artists in English rock who share similar ambitions and perspectives and the Dadaists and

Surrealists, whose strength and velocity was derived from the interaction of individuals operating within a common identity.

That rock develops at a pedestrian pace is not unrelated to the fact that 'music is a more unwieldy business', he thinks.

'Conceptually, it moves that much slower. Music, perhaps, as a form, has a much more functional job'.

'In order to work on any large scale, music has to overwhelm or titillate the senses. And, in other words, someone could come along with an incredible way of manipulating your ears, like Sly Stone, and there's no way you can discuss, in the same terms, the conceptual basis of something like *Stand*, which is a great record'.

'You know, this is all very interesting, but there are other things going on at the moment which we haven't taken into account, which are basically political'.

'In other words the avant-garde we're talking about still belong to a quite cogent tradition of an elite of academic artists in an affluent society, But the general growth of Socialism in various forms around the world has probably made the existence of those elitist power groups more impossible'.

'They're unwanted in a way. I've discussed this with *Henry Cow*, who consider themselves to be very politically motivated'.

'The whole idea of small groups of iconoclastic artists were based on the idea of groups of establishment artists reacting against them. We're in a situation now where we're unlikely to have either'.

'We're at a point where the dams have burst, and the mutual invasion of popular culture and academic culture are so interswamped, and there's something going on that is really too big for any of us individuals to see or put in any context'.

THE ADVENT OF RECORDING PROCEDURES, the availability of tape recorders of reasonable sophistication is, to a significant extent, precipitating a growing momentum, he feels. The recording idiom is changing to the extent where there are opportunities for artists to involve themselves in music.

'People can see possibilities of developing music which has not been suggested by other forms of music at all, but ideas from completely different persuasions'.

It's a process which he finds is undermining the monopoly of 'the monster bands' (i.e. *ELP* and their cohorts). From his comparative isolation he can allow himself a freedom of perspective on that situation.

'My ideal state of life of would be one total inactivity, I suppose. I don't approve of these people charging about all the time'.

'I mean, I suppose Elton John feels he has to be seen everywhere ... It concerns me that people view with impatience anybody when they're not actually coming out with New Product.'

'There are periods in every one's creative life which aren't productive in themselves but which are part of a continual creative process ...'

'I don't think musicians have been singled out for special treatment on that point ... It can be alarming, though. It gives a strange impression that people disappear when they haven't got a new album out.

'There again, I don't feel it's a problem special to musicians ... I mean, I don't feel particularly that no one understands me. The bloke next door to me here, he's not a musician and no one understands him either'.

"He doesn't seem worried about it, so why should I?'

ROBERT WYATT: *Ruth Is Stranger Than Richard*
Allan Jones, *Melody Maker*

IT HAS COME AS NO SURPRISE to discover I am not altogether alone in experiencing some difficulty in coming to terms with *Ruth is Stranger Than Richard*. It is a most disturbing record. There are moments here which appear to be the product of a vision so bleak that even the more optimistic perceptions persist as terminal daydreams streaked with the most profound depression.

Initially, moreover, there seems no centre to the emotional and physical structure of the album. However, although *Ruth* may lack the overall clarity of sound which characterised *Rock Bottom*, this album's superficial untidiness shouldn't be mistaken for any lack of concentration. The seemingly casual selection of the compositions, emphasised by the devious tactics of separating the album into two distinct entities – side *Ruth*, and side *Richard* – is deceptive in that it disguises the vital integration of Robert's themes, an integration which becomes more evident with repeated listening and the source from which much of his material was derived. The lyrical stance adopted by Robert on this album owes more to Samuel Beckett than Chuck Berry. The direct inspiration for *Ruth* seems to have been Beckett's horrific novel, *How It Is*. Heavier than that you cannot get. *Ruth* explores a reality which is as harrowing in its reflection of helplessness as *How It Is*, but the experience is made tolerable because even at his most desperate (*Team Spirit*, which alludes most forcefully to Beckett's strange landscapes) Robert is not given to emotional firework displays and hangs tenaciously to a facade of humour. So we have *Soup Song* – which opens side *Richard* – and is full of dada irreverence for logic, and *Sonia*, which follows is less the arbitrary choice than it seems at first, being fired by an enthusiasm for Mongezi Feza's exuberant and joyous composition. I've mentioned these tracks as appearing on side *Richard*, but increasingly as one is drawn into the album one ceases to distinguish between such distinctions. In a way which recalls Beckett's novel *Ruth Is Stranger Than Richard* unfolds not as a narrative, nor does it exist as a continuous and developing mood, but as a series of interrelated episodes, each with an individual strength, and its impact finally is in its subtle orchestration of disparate but not unconnected emotions. There's a disconcerting sense of defenceless isolation evident in the opening lines of *Muddy Mouse* (a) – the first of three brief extracts which appear on side *Richard* – which indicates the ominous despair manifested more directly on *Team Spirit* and, less vehemently, on the six-minute *Muddy Mouth*. The forlorn, childlike apprehension of *Muddy Mouse* and *Muddy Mouth* is continued through the fragile beauty of *Solar Flares*, but gives way to a starker, more sombre atmosphere on *Five Black Notes and One White Note* and the interpretation of Charlie Haden's *Song For Che*. But it's with the eight-minute *Team Spirit* that all the themes which colour the album are brought into the open. It reveals the same grim determination which characterises *Song For Che*, but here the quick run of Robert's humour is abruptly terminated in a swirling maelstrom of saxes and Laurie Allan's drums. It begins calmly enough with Bill MacCormick's exceptionally executed bass line before rising to a furious pitch with Gary Windo and Steve (*sic* George) Khan's chilling solos. The song staggers to a disintegrating and inconclusive climax which recalls those final moments of panic in a dream, just before waking. *Ruth Is Stranger Than Richard* is an album which sabotages any conventional approach. One has to be drawn into it slowly, picking out familiar points of reference at first, then with growing confidence begin to assimilate some of the finer details in its design. It's an important and essential album.

That's all.

ROBERT WYATT: *Ruth Is Stranger Than Richard*
Steve Peacock, *Sounds*

IN A WAY, Robert Wyatt's 'comeback' with *Rock Bottom* was misleading. Quite naturally, both the album and the man found themselves sitting firmly in the spotlight when it came out, first because the album was excellent and second it was Robert. It was also fairly natural for people to conclude that with his first album since his accident and year in hospital, this was Robert Wyatt's New Direction – that he'd found a new system of working. So you're ready for *Rock Bottom* Part Two'? Robert Wyatt isn't – the New Direction was your idea and mine not his. Robert has always been hesitant about committing his songs, ideas, himself to tape: especially when people are expecting a follow up. Apparently, the decision to go in and record *Ruth* was almost spur of the moment; a conglomerate of musicians was quickly assembled and the album done in just over a week. In essence, it is a small group album — piano, bass and drums, with horns prominent. The bulk of the *Ruth* features Laurie Allan drums, Bill MacCormick bass and Robert on voice and keyboards, with Gary Windo and Nisar Ahmad (George) Khan on horns, Eno joins in on 'direct inject anti-jazz ray gun' on the side's longest cut *Team Spirit*. The line up (with Eno on synthesiser and guitar) also invades Richard for five minutes or so to perform *Five black notes and one white note* a sleazy waltz with horns drawing out the theme. Bill MacCormick's lead bass lines are magnificent. But there are deviations, naturally, Richard has that piece plus *Solar Flares* with just Robert MacCormick and Windo, threaded *onto Muddy Mouse* — a duet between Robert's voice and Fred Frith at piano — fragments of which appear at the beginning of the side between *Flares* and *Notes* and then extend into *Muddy Mouth* to close the side. Perhaps the muddy mice and mouth are the closest the album delivers to a link with *Rock Bottom*. Certainly the way Fred Frith combines Robert's feel for piano and empathy with his voice with a more schooled technique is remarkable. The deviation on *Ruth* is Mongezi Feza's *Sonia*, recorded around the time Robert did *Yesterday Man* with Nick Mason producing and featuring the many trumpets of M. Feza, John Greaves on bass, Gary Windo, and Robert on drums and piano; it originally appeared on *Spear's Townships* album and Robert says he did it as he'd have recorded it had he produced the Spear album. See? *Soup Song* starts with fairly straight forward stride/boogie piano and ends in disarray, and Charlie Haden's *Song For Che* drifts with purpose. But the key to the album is *Team Spirit*, a new version of the song Robert sang in Spanish on Phil Manzanera's *Diamond Head* album — *Frontera*. I can't find the words to define what I mean but if you listen too, back to back, you'll see what I hope I mean. Er ...

These press cuttings courtesy of Phil Howitt's archive to whom much thanks.

APPENDIX 8: *801* MK I – PRESS 1976

FOUR DAY WONDER
John Ingham, *Sounds*
Featuring Phil Manzanera, Eno, Francis Monkman, Simon Phillips,
Bill MacCormick and Lloyd Watson

'THIS ONE WON'T RUN AND RUN'
AS WE FINISHED THE INTERVIEW, Phil's face assumed an anxious expression. 'You're going to mention the others in the band aren't you?' he asked earnestly. 'It's not going to be just me?'

But of course I'm going to mention the others, Phil old bean. Like so: In the hard white light of the sauna-like video room at *Island Records*, the Phil Manzanera Band are engaged in that musical discussion and argument humorously called a rehearsal. They are ranged in a rough ellipse, Francis Monkman's electric piano and Simon Phillips' Babel like tower of drums at either end. Between them stand the guitarists. Facing them, like a conductor behind his synthesiser and *Farfisa* organ podium, Eno – directs the shape of *Baby's on Fire*. Periodically his slim, dark brown cigar goes out.

''This will be the third time it's been on record', he says as they attempt different ways of improving it. 'I want it to still retain some interest'. He is quickly clarified; there is only a chance that *Baby's on Fire* will see the light of record. Francis begins with an almost random beep. Eno's fingers dance a Morse code from the *Farfisa*. Then the rest of the ensemble crash into life. The rhythm is slower, Bill MacCormick's bass dirty and greasy, Phillips holding down a funk strewn rhythm. Manzanera sticks to a tight rhythm while Lloyd Watson makes loud whoops. Eno sings with one hand on his hip, the other lazily running over the keys. Phil takes the first solo, precise and clean, overtaken by Watson's stinging slide. Falling back into the song the band build to an impossible din, Eno's burbling *Farfisa* insistently crunches to a somewhat ungainly halt.

They discuss the imperfect sections, play it again. MacCormick studies the ceiling in deep concentration as he vigorously fingers a one note bass run. 'When I stop', Eno demonstrates a sequence, 'it sounds like 1/2 time. I'm on 16'.

'Or 15', ripostes Francis quietly. There are a few chuckles at this musical *bon mot*. 'Yeah', smiles Phil, 'We should all play 10/16 for a bit just there'.

Although it's billed as the Phil Manzanera Band 'that's quite erroneous', asserts Phil. 'It's much more of a group, even though it's only for four concerts. So when I put it together I bore that in mind. I wanted to have the feel side of music and the ideas side, which is basically Eno and Lloyd as an axis on one side and then Francis and Simon, who are super technical, and then Bill and me, who have a bit of both. So I wanted to combine these two extremes in a group, rather than these guys standing up there playing *Diamond Head*. That's why it's *Phil Manzanera Featuring All These People*. Everybody has been involved with the arrangements and all the material is from *Quiet Sun* albums, Eno albums, *Diamond Head* and they're all joined together and chopped around and changed around. It's almost like new music'.

The reward of all this conceptualisation and preparation is four concerts. The original plan had been to only play Continental festivals this being the Year of The Festival in Europe. 'I thought it would be interesting to play my music live, and also to play festivals. I haven't played a lot of festivals... yet. I thought it would be nice in summer to get outside, play outdoors. It's a totally different feel'. The imagery of the *Roxy Music* guitarist fronting his own ensemble was so enticing that two festivals advertised his imminent presence on their respective stages in the French rock magazine *Rock et Folk* when neither had contacted the artiste, and still haven't. There is also the legendary Continental efficiency; festivals were cancelled or were unsatisfactory, until finally Phil was reduced to a paltry five gigs, three of them – Reading, the *Queen Elizabeth Hall*, and a warm-up somewhere in Norfolk in Britain. Then another festival collapsed, leaving him with only one European appearance at Corbieres.

And afterwards, pfoot. Finished. Business as usual. Phillips and Monkman are much in demand for sessions, it's been hard to get Phillips just for rehearsals. 'We're lucky to have Lloyd Watson at all. He was badly electrocuted on stage a month ago. He was stuck to this hot microphone, jerking, and because he always leaps about everybody thought he was doing Elvis impersonations! It's miraculous he's as unhurt as he is'. Veterans of the *Roxy For Your Pleasure* tour may remember the energetic Watson's blitzkrieg solo guitar opening sets, which invariably brought the house down. There are those of you who may also remember Mr. Watson's antics in Italy where he lost his glasses hanging out of the car on the autostrada, and Paris, where he climaxed a drunken dinner by dancing down the length of the table and out the window. His sole contribution to recorded music an exquisite multi-tracked solo on Eno's *Here Come The Warm Jets*, Lloyd now spends Sundays playing in a local Peterborough pub with *Back Door* bassist Tim Hodgkinson.

And the timely appearance of Brian Eno, just as it seemed he was going to vanish from the modern world. A move on Manzanera's part to return The Refreshing Experience to his rightful prominence? 'Yeah... To a certain extent I think he's gotten too highbrow, though he would never admit to that'.

In keeping with his attitude of a group, all involved are acting as investors. I put the venture to them and they said alright. Everybody gets an equal share of any profits and everyone pays an equal share of the cost. It's only fair. Otherwise, the two people who always have sessions would be paid as session musicians. I can't afford that, so it's either get into it or forget it'. At this juncture the tour manager enters. 'I've got some good news for you', he says to Phil. 'Corbieres has been cancelled'. *The Phil Manzanera Band Featuring All These People* is reduced to three appearances. The accounts take on a reddish hue.

But even without other commitments or financial juggling, there is the appeal of planned obsolescence, of a group whose short existence turns each appearance into an Event. 'I never went to the *ACNE* June 1 thing, but the people who did must have enjoyed it, and they'll never see that again, ever. It's an event and it's over and that's that. I like that'. But what's an Event if it can't be recalled in future times? Ergo, record the *Royal Festival Hall* (*sic*) appearance for a live album. If only because . . . 'The songs are now in collages and medleys, things like that. We've been quite ruthless with the songs. Anything that wasn't good or didn't fit in we've just chucked out, so some of them are barely recognisable'.

And all this feverish activity is but one facet of Phil Manzanera, musician. 'This period that *Roxy* is supposed to be having off is, as far as I'm concerned, a time for doing as many different projects as possible. When I finished doing the live *Roxy* album I went straight into producing the *Split Enz* album, and now this, and when this is finished I have another solo album. I just want to utilise all the time. Also, last year I decided, having done a lot of work in the studio, to concentrate on live performing. And this year, with all the *Roxy* tours and two tours of America, which is a hell of a lot of live playing, and then *GO*, and now this. I enjoyed some of *GO*; I enjoyed working with Stevie Winwood... It was just very badly organised. But it was worth it to meet the people involved'.

Split Enz are a quirky, complex, highly original New Zealand group Manzanera discovered on television in Australia. 'I didn't expect to really hear any of the music that interests me at all while I was out there. They didn't mention their name at all, so I didn't know who they were, but I was very interested. Then we did a gig in Sydney, arrived halfway through the opening act, and it was *Split Enz*. I mentioned to their manager that I wouldn't mind getting involved and helping in any way. The group came over in March, we made the album and then sold it. They're so entertaining. The record doesn't really make sense until you've seen them'.

Manzanera is quite interested in producing other bands, providing of course that he likes the music. In any case, there is his solo album. Two solo albums, actually. 'The first part will come out in the new year and will have nine songs on it, mostly singing, perhaps no instrumentals at all. Part two will come out about six months later, and be all instrumental. I'm not going to be singing, obviously. My first idea was to build up a sound using

374

three or four voices and doing it throughout the album, or else use just one singer. At the moment it's in the balance. The songs are much more 'feel' songs than the last album. Songs with strange structures to them. Hopefully, there will be much more unity to them'. All in all, a busy schedule any way you slice it.

'You see, whereas people like Eno or Bryan (Ferry) or most of the people I know who work in a similar direction, music isn't the only thing they can do. They can go off and become graphic designers or artists or painters or whatever. I've got only one alternative, which is music'. How important is it, then to establish the Manzanera monicker as an entity in its own right? 'Not that important, because I like working with people. I like to be in a group but I wouldn't really like to be in the Phil Manzanera Band full time. I like being in *Roxy*, I like being in a group, but I like doing these other things as well. I want the best of everything. As it turned out the *Roxy* sabbatical was a natural thing. We discussed not making an album this summer because we've made an album every summer for the past four years. Apart from missing all the good weather', he laughs, 'You get into a sterile routine. For us, at this stage, I it's not very productive for us. You take a risk, a terrible risk really, in taking all this I time off. I've always been struck by John Entwistle saying two years off the road and *The Who* almost didn't get back together again. That's obviously a risk you take, but you have to take them, otherwise you stop coming up with ideas that are fresh. It's a way of carrying on longer… if it works'.

And if it doesn't work? 'I'd probably join a band, if someone offered me a gig'. You wouldn't assemble one yourself? 'I might, if I had the right people. But I don't know, it depends, I'd have to see at the time. I hope it doesn't happen because I like playing with Bryan and I like playing with Paul, and I hope that Eddie doesn't decide that he likes playing with Zappa full time, because I enjoy playing onstage with them and I respect their capabilities. Because I've played with quite a lot of different people in the past few years and I really do like playing with *Roxy*, otherwise I wouldn't carry on playing with them. I'm going to do my best to make sure it doesn't, you know… But what the other people decide is an entirely different matter. The last time I spoke to Bryan we were still carrying on with our Master Plan'.

PRODUCTIVE TENSION VITAL NEW RESEARCH
Angus Mackinnon, *NME*

RELAX, IT'S JUST MANZANERA, Eno and Co. furthering the boundaries of rock and roll again.
THE VIDEO ROOM, *Island Records*, Hammersmith.
MIDNIGHT (US NAVY) BLUE carpets and seating, pale lime green walls, all available floor space cluttered with musical machinery. A soundproof

ocean bed chamber where Poseidon submarines come home to die. The Phil Manzanera Band are in rehearsal.

'Can't we do something with this section in 13/8? I don't like counting it in. Maybe a tap on the cowbell as a call sign? All right, let's try it again. One, two, three...' Take eight. Democracy in action. The laborious minutiae of refinement. Five musicians involved in a Chinese box game. Taking apart, piecing together again. Manzanera and Brian Eno need no introduction. Their accomplices include bassist Bill MacCormick who played with Manzanera in *Quiet Sun*, joined Robert Wyatt's *Matching Mole*, then *Gong* (for a hectic ten days). Simon Phillips is a young session drummer, a refugee from Ann Odell's shortlived *Chopyn* he combines the exactitude of a Bill Bruford with the versatility of a Dave Mattacks. Guitarist (sometimes slide) Lloyd Watson supported *Roxy Music* and *King Crimson* on various tours, nearly electrocuted himself earlier this year, but survived to tell the unpleasant tale. Francis Monkman, who contributed electric keyboards, is absent; his credits embrace *Curved Air* and a short stay alongside MacCormick in *Matching Mole II*.

Sol Caliente began life as a *Quiet Sun* piece, a heady exercise in armour-plated manoeuvrability. It's been combined with *East Of Echo* and the snappily titled *Mummy Was An Asteroid, Daddy Was A Small Non-stick Kitchen Utensil* two other compositions from a similar period when *Quiet Sun*, who had everything going for them except interested promoters and record companies, finally resorting to playing village fetes for charity. When fully rehearsed and re-run one final time, *Sol* plays like unrepentant, arcane *Starless and Bible Black Crimso* – only without any of Fripp's predilection for wilful claustrophobics. Manzanera allows himself a short, ferrous solo over Watson's vital chording, Eno chip-chops his synthesiser keyboard and it's all up in six minutes. And you want more. Commendable concentration.

Manzanera's original intention had been to form a band and play open air festivals through the summer, in France mostly. However a riot at one such event in Arles – Christian Vander's cosmi-mythological *Magma* were due to appear – persuaded Giscard D'Estaing that all similar events should be cancelled for the duration. So no expense-paying festivals.

Meanwhile the unplanned but welcome addition of Eno has widened the already extensive amount of material (from *Quiet Sun's Mainstream* and Manzanera's *Diamond Head*) still further. Eno's conscientiously oblique, 'non-musical' approach in rehearsal has brought about interesting developments. After an impromptu rendition of *The Crystals' Then He Kissed Me*, the band place *Sombre Reptiles* under close scrutiny. There's a simple rhythm track on drum box with Phillips embellishing here and there, and Eno joins Watson and Manzanera on guitar. 'This', Manzanera suggests, 'is primarily an opportunity for tone control'. 'The only problem being', comments Eno, 'that my guitar won't oblige. What can one expect from a £9 instrument? I suspect the controls don't work at all'. A compromise is reached. Eno has to rest the machine heads of his guitar against an amplifier to maintain any feedback, then switches everything off for a precise fade out. The extemporisation seems to work, *Reptiles* ends up sounding as malevolent as anything off *Can's* autumnal *Ege Bamyasi*.

Three weeks later the band's *Queen Elizabeth Hall* concert is recorded for a live album. The set is consistently enjoyable, occasionally stunning. *Diamond Head* itself has been overhauled, dominated by Manzanera's orbital guitar bled hazily through Eno's switchboard. *Fat Lady Of Limbourg* is mesmeric – Eno and *Warm Jets*-style apparel trapped in a single spot beam the coda is braced by an (intentionally?) brazen riff. *Third Uncle* and *Baby's on Fire* shudder and swirl as the guitars of Manzanera and Watson flail like the appendages of a mine-clearing tank.

Various moments make me wish that this, the band's first London date, wasn't also their last. For instance, MacCormick and Philips pace some outrageous rhythmic athletics as the lengthy intro to *Tomorrow Never Knows* swarms in; the two players attain a pulsing, *Magic Band*-like freefloat. Manzanera's own vitriolic solos seem so much better placed in this material than in post-*Stranded Roxy*. All six musicians evidently thrive in the environment despite the inevitable technical problems and the Hall's curiously 'live' acoustics. Nonetheless I suspect that the resultant album, however interesting, will relegate itself to the status of a comparatively innocuous souvenir of the evening's music and will also become, in many ways a mildly infuriating document.

Why infuriating? Because it will represent something of an underachievement. In a matter of weeks this band had mutated into an extremely sophisticated, adventurous unit – and this largely on the strength of rehearsing a preponderance of old material. But impressive though this process of 'reconstruction' has been all the evidence indicates that the sextet could (and would) achieve immeasurably more if awarded a longer lease of life and especially if let loose on new compositions, possibly in the shape of a group studio album. Apparently neither *Island* nor *E.G.* initially placed much confidence in the project – well, I hope they've found good reason to have a little more faith in the light of the *QE Hall* performance and the fact that it was sold out.

Manzanera of course, has his second solo album underway, but it remains in a state of semi-completion. Most of the backing tracks are finished and he's considering releasing it in two parts, one compromising songs, the other instrumentals, rather than alternate the two aspects as he did (albeit successfully) on *Diamond Head*. But that album didn't sell as well as it might have done – and I doubt very much whether either the live record or his next solo will reach the audience they merit unless their release is supported by further live appearances.

But that's as may be. More important – in purely aesthetic terms – is the nature of the group beast. The Manzanera Band deal in a currency that tries and tests unorthodox structures without becoming so idiosyncratic as to be completely impenetrable. Since the demise of *King Crimson* there's been a noticeable dearth of experimental (rock) music in the UK that still remains helpfully accessible that may perhaps tax the listener but never antagonise. Manzanera and Eno themselves approach the theory and practice of making music in ways that are often diametrically opposed, but to find both these methods combined in a group context seems to make for a purposeful, productive tension, empiricism can and does fulfil a vital function; it becomes a blood plasma for other musicians, in Eno's own phrase 'musical Research and Development' – an infusion that's always needed. If the Manzanera Band do curtail their activities now, then the outlook could be euphemistically described as bleak.

PHIL AND ENO'S ADVENTURE
Allan Jones, *Melody Maker*

PHIL MANZANERA featuring… the title of a new musical project by the *Roxy Music* guitarist in collaboration with Brian Eno, will make its official debut at the *Reading Festival* on Saturday, August 28. Manzanera's name alone appears on the advertisements for the event, and it has been popularly assumed that his appearance at the festival is confirmation of a decision to pursue a solo career. Similarly, the announcement that Manzanera was to play at Reading was seen as further evidence of the demise of *Roxy*.

The situation, though, is rather more complex, however according to Manzanera. *Roxy Music*, for instance, have not split up in any conventional sense. It was decided, explains Manzanera, after the completion of *Viva!*, the *Roxy Music* live album that the band should temporarily suspend all collective activity. There was, Manzanera emphasises, no internal dissension or personal incompatibility. *Roxy*, he says, could, with no great difficulty, have produced their annual album and toured in the autumn, but, independently, the members of the group all thought some kind of sabbatical was required. So, rather than conform to the expectations of their audience and deliver another album, the group decided to follow individual pursuits for at least nine months and re-form in the Spring of 1976.

Manzanera, at Christmas, had, started work on his second solo album and was preparing an album with *Split Enz* a New Zealand band who supported *Roxy* on their Australian tour last year, whose record he has recently produced for *Chrysalis*. Manzanera had been working on his solo album with bassist Bill MacCormick and drummer Simon Phillips and, during the sessions for that project – which also involved Brian Eno – began to consider the possibility of using these musicians as the nucleus of a group which would perform at several of this summer's open air events. His original concept was quite simple: the group would select their repertoire from material already recorded and featured on either his solo album, *Diamond Head, Quiet Sun's Mainstream* or on Eno's solo albums. The project was to be considered as a collaboration rather than a solo venture, he insists, and admits to being horrified by press reports of the Reading appearance, which described the event as his solo debut.

Inevitably, Eno's involvement has, as Manzanera remarks, changed his initial concept, which has now assumed a more ambitious outlook. Manzanera's original idea, Eno offers, was slightly more innocent than his own. He had, he explains, been thinking for some time of establishing some kind of framework which would allow a band to accommodate the experimental and unexpected in their performance. He had, in fact, explored this concept during the recording of *Another Green World* when he assembled a group of disparate individuals and encouraged them to exploit their own ideas without restraint and without any preconceived ambition.

'For me', Eno explains, 'projects aren't really interesting if you can predict their outcome. One of the most encouraging things, actually, about our recent rehearsals has been that something has been happening, that none of us anticipated. You see, I think the moment something becomes really exciting is the moment you start to lose grip of an idea and the idea takes on an identity of its own. Some very exciting things have been happening, particularly during the last rehearsal'.

Manzanera's approach to the project is, he admits, rather less cerebral. Instinctively though, he realised, after protracted and occasionally heated discussions with Eno prior to the group's current rehearsals that their ideas were entirely compatible. They reached, then, a compromise: the group's repertoire would be chosen from the aforementioned albums, but the songs selected would be used to provide a base from which the musicians could develop individual ideas.

'We've taken', says Eno, 'a lot of liberties with the original songs and their arrangements. Sometimes, we've taken a fragment of a song and isolated it and developed it, and discovered possibilities in that fragment and the way we've treated it which weren't at all apparent at the time the original song was recorded. In that sense the project is something of an adventure. We are making a conscious attempt to create something new from the original songs. Phil and I both agree that we must break away from the idea that you tour or play concerts merely to promote a new album, so you give concert which are really no more than fairly faithful replicas of recorded music. I'm much more interested in creating a flexible musical situation where the musicians are required to experiment and innovate'.

Manzanera, of course, is a musician of sufficient intelligence and imagination to accommodate and appreciate Eno's theories and notions and has, furthermore, established an exciting musical partnership, represented on *Diamond Head* and *Taking Tiger Mountain* particularly (to consider only Eno's post-*Roxy Music* recordings). One wonders, though, how the other musicians involved in the project have reacted to Eno's radical approach. Bill MacCormick has, of course, recorded with Eno on several occasions previously, but Simon Phillips, Francis Monkman, the former *Curved Air* keyboard player, and Lloyd Watson, who completes the line-up on slide guitar, have no previous experience of working with Eno. Eno admits he found it initially difficult to communicate his ideas to the group, and found their unwillingness to enter into any dialogue disconcerting.

'No-one actually wanted to rationalise the ideas which were being thrown up. Everyone wanted to play rather than talk. I maintain, you see, that there is a difference between doing something and knowing you're doing it and doing something and not knowing you're doing it. I believe that it's very important to be conscious of being in an experimental situation. I can't play ideas for the musicians or indicate note sequences. So I did have some difficulty in getting certain ideas across. We'd rehearse and everyone would play quite furiously and then shut up completely'.

'This', Manzanera adds, 'is always a problem when you assemble a group of musicians who've never played together before. There's a feeling that you have to prove yourself. So there's an incredible amount of virtuoso playing, with everyone out to play as fast and as impressively as possible. It's really a form of ritual which happens all the time.' Eno, he elaborates, does relish the prospect of unsettling musicians and provoking them to attempt things they would not, in more conventional situations, even consider. I recall from an earlier conversation with Manzanera, that he had, occasionally, found it rather difficult to tolerate the various ways Eno used, in the early days of *Roxy*, to treat his guitar. 'Oh, certainly', he replies 'Sometimes what I was playing bore no resemblance to what was coming out of the P.A. I often couldn't believe what was happening. I know that during a solo the spotlight was upon me, and I would go through all the motions of playing the solo and reacting to what I was playing but often what the audience heard was not something I was playing'.

'At that time', Eno continues, 'I had an echo delay system that was rather complicated. Phil's guitar was being fed through two *Revoxs* that I was operating, and I was splitting the signal two ways on two separate recorders and then playing them back at two different delays, and changing the delay all the time'. 'I remember once', says Manzanera, 'taking my hands off the guitar and still hearing myself playing. That's why he had to leave. I said either he leaves or I give up playing the guitar'.

'That's not quite true', counters Eno, 'I said that I wouldn't stay in *Roxy* unless I could do the same thing with Bryan's voice'. Both Manzanera and Eno emphasise the point that the current project is in no way a permanent collaboration They will be playing only a few concerts this summer, including Reading, of course, and the Corbiere Festival in the South of France, with the possibility of further concerts later in the year. 'One of the most exciting things about this group', says Eno, 'is the knowledge that it is going to be a brief collaboration. You see, there's a certain transitional period in the history of most groups which, usually, can be associated with the period when the group is most interesting. It's that period when the people involved are no longer uncomfortable with one another, but not so comfortable they become complacent. I really think that's why groups in their early stages are very interesting. You find that a group in its early stages is full of contradictions and paradoxes, and the musicians are excited by that and have enough mutual trust to exploit all the possibilities open to them. This group will, hopefully, achieve that kind of flexibility'.

No-one could possibly accuse Eno of excluding the unprecedented and the unpredictable from his career since he left *Roxy*. Three solo albums two albums with Robert Fripp, collaborations with *Genesis*, John Cale, and Robert Wyatt, the formation of *Obscure Records*, the composition of a score for the recent *Sparrowfall*, can all be catalogued as evidence of his diverse and impressive achievements over the last three years. Most bizarre and intriguing of the projects with which he has been involved, however, is the collaboration with David Bowie, Robert Fripp and Iggy Stooge, which was announced some weeks ago. Bowie, apparently, had heard and liked Eno's first solo albums and had been very impressed by *Another Green World*. They met, originally, at Wembley during Bowie's concert series there and Eno was invited to participate in the recording of a forthcoming Iggy album. Nothing definite was planned but Bowie was determined, it seems, that he and Eno should work together. Weeks later Eno received an urgent telephone call from Bowie. 'He said he was in Paris and Robert Fripp and I should fly over immediately. Fripp was still in Sherborne (where he is involved in some religious study), and I knew he wouldn't be able to go, but I was interested in the idea of working with Bowie. I then got another call and was told that there were all kinds of disruptions in the Bowie camp so everything's been cancelled for the moment. I've no real idea about the nature of the project or what role I was expected to fulfil all I know is that it was for Iggy's album."

THE CENTRE SPREAD or PHIL MANZANERA ON TOAST
Simon Husbands, *Way Ahead*
'THE NAME COMES from that of a newly burgeoning alliance of creative artist and scientists which hopes to unveil endeavours in a variety of forms over the next few years.

'What?? Oh! What??'

801, that is.

Oh!

Look dumbo, and listen well, Phil Manzanera (*Roxy* – remember) and Brian Eno (uhh... remember) formed this band see. Just for a few gigs and an album and that's all really. O.K? Good.

What do you mean, what for? I dunno, ask him, you know that geezer Manzanera, go on I dare you! 'Ere, Phil mate, what's with this *801* business?

'*801* seemed like a good name or number, because it's so abstract. It was meant to encompass lots of other things as well – I don't know if they'll all come off. It was just a name as a vehicle for lots of different projects, like the *801* Art Show, or something'. Or something.

Cut to Phil Manzanera's house in darkest Acton, where our hero sits musing about life in general and especially the aforesaid *801* project. Three gigs and one album recorded at one of the three, is all there is in the offing, at least at the present time, but beggars can't be choosers, as they say, and we all of us, should be glad we have that much. Now the album is out, don't delay, and buy today, if you have any interest in good music at all. Incidentally the idea was formed when... oh, well, Phil can probably tell you better than. Tell us, Phil.

'We went away to the country with Eno, and Bill MacCormick and his brother Ian and talked about the whole project and we realised we probably weren't going to get to do many gigs, so we decided to make the most of these concerts by recording the set and constructing it so it was an album. So, when we came to rehearsing the set we did it in terms of Side One and Side Two'.

The material, as found on the album of the third gig at the *Queen Elizabeth Hall*, was taken off five albums – Eno's three solo albums, Phil's solo, *Diamond Head*, and the *Quiet Sun* album *Mainstream* (as Phil used to play with them pre-*Roxy*). Simply called *801 Live* the album covers a wide range of styles and sounds, probably due to the assortment of musicians in the band. Roll credits please – Phil Manzanera and Lloyd Watson on guitars, Bill MacCormick on bass, Francis Monkman (*Curved Air's* instigator) on keyboards, Simon Phillips on drums, and Brian Eno on vocals, synthesisers and odd swirly noises. Six musicians from a very wide background joining together for a common aim to produce the best music they can. The next voice you hear is Phil's.

'When I thought about the project, those were the musicians I thought of immediately because I wanted to have, on the one hand, two people who are technically brilliant, who are Simon and Francis and who are session musicians, and technically very excellent and on the other hand you have Eno, who isn't technically deficient, but doesn't make any pretensions to technique, but is like an idea's man, and Lloyd Watson who is a bluesy-type person. In the middle you have me and Bill, somewhere between technique and deficient!'

Modest kind of chap, isn't he? Oh, sorry, I interrupted.

'I thought this combination would work well together although we did have teething troubles and at one stage it almost fell through because of the differences between Eno and Francis. They had a long talk and sorted everything out and it was really worth it in the end. There was this tension created, which made for a better set'. He's telling the truth you know, you've only got to listen to numbers like *Baby's on Fire*, *Third Uncle* and the excellent version of the *Kink's You Really Got Me*. I'll repeat that, *You Really Got Me* – how many bands do you see playing that kind of music as well as a totally atmospheric piece (sort of) such as *Sombre Reptiles* off *Another Green World*, and doing the two styles really well, making the change effortlessly? Not the *Bay City Rollers* probably!

John Peel, that famous (or is it infamous?) person liked the band so much at Reading, that he said they were the best band throughout the Festival: Gasp! 'John Peel was fantastic – he was really kind – and that was only the second gig! I've been on lots of tours, *Roxy* obviously, when it takes at least five gigs before you begin to learn any new material! Also, you aren't allowed sound checks at Reading so we just went on not knowing whether anything was working, and Francis was driving down from Yorkshire and literally arrived one minute before we went on. We'd re-arranged the set to do it without keyboards, so we were relieved when Francis turned up that it didn't really matter what it was like on stage'. Real professionals, these boys, you know?

The band doesn't come across as Manzanera playing his greatest hits, but as a six-man band putting everything they've got into the performance. MacCormick's playing throughout the album is excellent, working superbly with Phillips' effortless drums. Monkman and Eno combine (!) perfectly (as on *Baby's on Fire*) and both Manzanera and Watson combine their guitars well, especially on a superbly executed *Diamond Head* with Phil's guitar being treated by Eno's synthesisers very nicely. Eno's vocals, too, sound perfectly in context (refer back to the *Quiet Sun* track – *Rongwrong*). In short, to have captured this band for posterity on record is a stroke of genius. It doesn't look as if we're going to get any more for a long time though, as all the musicians have now dispersed to do their own individual projects. Phillips and Monkman return to their sessions, Eno's working with Bowie etc. So grab it whilst it's hot, folks!

Phil doesn't know who's going to buy his album though. 'I really don't know who will buy the album, presumably it will be people who are vaguely interested in Eno or myself, or Bill, who was in Robert Wyatt's *Matching Mole*, I really don't know!' People have said that your best work has been outside *Roxy* – what do you say to that? 'Well... I don't know what to say really'. Come on Phil we want a bit of scandal show us all you can get bitchy too: 'One man's meat is another man's poison'. Better. 'Just because one person says that, doesn't mean it's true. There have been things I've really been proud of – ideas I've contributed to Roxy, or arrangements I've thought of, or things I've done outside which I've been proud of – so for me it's really all the same thing. There are things in each which are great and others which are terrible!'

Over the past two or three years Phil has done quite a bit of work with Mr. Brian Eno, on his own albums, on John Cale's etc. 'We're sort of friends. You go through periods where you get sick of your friends and you don't see them, then you see them a lot in a short period and it's been like that with Eno. As long as we remain friendly we'll probably carry on working together. Maybe every year for the past three years we've worked together for about a month every year. That's probably about the limit we can stand each other'. Well!

He's started to talk quite frankly now so perhaps we can get a bit of scandal concerning B. Ferry Esq and his jolly bunch of men, *Roxy Music*. Let's see shall we? Ferry has said that if he enjoys playing with the band he's formed for his solo efforts better than *Roxy*, he'll call it a day with the aforesaid *Roxy*. What do you say to that? 'Uhmmmmmm, it's difficult to say anything without being bitchy. John Wetton has joined a band with Rick Wakeman, Chris Spedding has his own group now – that leaves Paul Thompson and Bryan, who've always worked together. You see, what we've always done in *Roxy* is experiment in different areas – we started out as a band with a lot of ideas which was relatively 'bitty' in that you get a lot of ideas in a very short space of time, whereas now we have fewer ideas in a longer space. Over the last two albums we've been trying to get into things to do with feel, which is much more difficult, and something that only comes with time'.

What he's saying is that *Roxy* have still achieved a lot, which is my personal belief as well, so although the words did not actually come, we can assume that 'Roxy To Stay Together' will be the headline when they all meet for a board meeting in the Spring. Pay attention now chaps, a short history lesson ensues. *Roxy Music* started around 1972, the brainchild of Bryan Ferry and it was obvious, through the stage act and Ferry's press statements that he was in charge. However, over the following four years, the group seems to be now more of a group of musicians rather than a lead singer with a backing band. On the last tour, for example, Phil played *Diamond Head*, and Andy Mackay played *Wild Weekend*, whilst Big Bry slunk off backstage.

'I think you probably underestimate everybody if you think it was Bryan's brainchild, but right from the beginning there were lots of people with strong personalities and strong ideas. It's always been a group collaboration, then at a certain point in our career, after the first album, we decided that we needed to have somebody right in the middle of the stage for people to catch onto. (Excuse me, Phil – er Eno used to play stage right and Bryan stage left thank you). So it sort of layered over the years and been encouraged by the press, but it never has been, it's just the way it's been put over'.

Mmmm. Well, pressing on with all the dignity of a drugged elephant, we move onto Phil's new solo album which is 60% finished. *Diamond Head*, his first, came out over a year ago and was unusual in that it was more like a bunch of musicians taking it in turns to play all each other's material, rather than a solo album. Guest list included Robert Wyatt, Eno, John Wetton, all of *Quiet Sun*, plus many others, the total effect being an album of many different styles. One muses whether the second in the series will be of a similar nature, doesn't one?

'No'. Oh. 'It's not like *Diamond Head* at all. It's taking shape now, and I keep changing it every week as there's a lot of material recorded. There's over 67 minutes of material and I don't want to do a double album, so it will be a single album. It's a question of chucking out the stuff you don't want. There will be one vocal sound all the way through and there will be much more unity about it. There have been lots of musicians playing so I don't know who will end up on the album. Bill MacCormick will probably end up doing all the bass, drummers will probably be Bill Bruford (gasp), Simon Phillips and Dave Mattacks, and maybe Kevin Godley of *10cc* There'll be one long sunny-type instrumental, with five songs on one side so in that sense there will be a lot of different styles, as on the last album'.

When Phil was a short-trousered non-shaver, he was mixed up with Bill the Mac in a band called *Quiet Sun* (as I've said before, if you'd been listening) who wrote fairly complex music, and practised for a year perfecting their music, till they split up. However seven years later *Quiet Sun* released an album entitled *Mainstream*. Why? Who? And even 'How could this be so?' 'It was really a thing I had to get off my chest, as it were, for it was material we'd written in 1969 and it seemed a pity that we'd spent a year rehearsing and getting a set together that it had never gone down on record. At the time no record company was interested in that kind of music, but because of people like *Mahavishnu* and *King Crimson*, record companies took that kind of music to a wider audience so it was possible to record that last year, and for it to do reasonably well which we were all surprised at. We could do another album – we've got the material but it is a question of whether it's worth it – it will require a bit of thought really'.

Phil, I'm sure loads of budding musicians out there would like to know whether it's easy to write music, like wot you do? 'Some things come easily, others take longer but I write in different ways with different people. I always like to write with someone else – the instrumentals are a different matter – but all the songs with *Roxy* like *Out of the Blue* and *Prairie Rose*, have been written in the *Roxy* way of writing'. So, children, in detail everything you wanted to know about the 'Roxy Way Of Writing':

'What happened in the past is:- the week before recording an album we've got together and played through a series of chord sequences and then gone into the studio and laid down those sequences and put on solos and everything, the whole feel of the piece in fact. Then Bryan would go away and write, or tried to write, a lyric for it. Most people throw ideas around till the song builds in shape. It's hit-or-miss, some songs have turned out like classics, others have disappeared into oblivion. I want to get into the normal way of writing'.

If you cast a discerning eye over a lot of new bands coming up you'll find that many seem to be returning to their roots so to speak. Prime examples being *Dr Feelgood* and *Eddie and The Hot Rods*, music turning full circle and getting down to basics. Will Manzanera follow this trend? 'I think it's fine going back to the roots providing you are writing your own material, and not just playing old numbers. If you take the essence of rock music, which is excitement and enthusiasm and apply it to your own material, it's fine and from that point of view I probably will be going in that direction, but I won't be playing *Johnny B. Goode*! It's nice to do it once or twice, but to base your whole style on that is leading you up a blind alley'.

Elsewhere in this fine magazine can be found an article on a New Zealand band *Split Enz*, who have just had their first album in this country produced by Phil. They have to be seen to be believed, and the music is quite abnormal too but refer back to my colleague's article, else I'll infringe copyright. Parts of the album remind me of early *Roxy* – is this why Phil produced them do you think? 'I saw them briefly on T.V. in Australia and I couldn't believe it! I turned up at a gig and they were our support band. The first thing I liked about them was the music, and I liked the floating-like mood they had afterwards. I found out there was this other side to them, their stage performance, being entertaining on stage, which is a different thing. I enjoy watching them. They're all very intelligent and the writers in the band are capable of writing tiny very interesting melodies

386

and there are elements in the music which remind me of early *Soft Machine*, and psychedelia. It all makes sense to see them perform, whereas if you see a picture or listen to the album it all seems very bizarre – that's what really appealed to me'.

Remember *Rock Follies*? You do? I am sorry. When it was being slagged off at all counts I wondered what the other members of *Roxy* thought to Andy MacKay's excursion into the more seedy side of rock, so when this interview came up I decided to ask a few probing questions in the right quarters. 'Andy played me a tape on the American tour and I thought 'I don't really like this', but then I came back and saw the series and thought the music fitted the series. I couldn't listen to the music on its own, For the whole sickly *Thames T.V.* type plays the music fitted perfectly so it was successful, but I personally don't like the music as songs on their own'. Tactful of you Phil – I'm sure Andy wouldn't have it any other way, even if the vast majority of the people would.

As far as future plans go, Phil has a project in mind with Lol Creme and Kevin Godley of *10cc* based around the *Gizmo*, a gadget invented by said gentlemen, which enables a guitarist to get many different sounds out of a guitar. 'I was up in Manchester last week learning how to play the *Gizmo* and I really do think it's going to have a big influence on what I will be playing over the next few years, because you can do so many things with it – you just play chords and it sounds like whole string sections. It will be on the market next June, and it will have a great influence on a lot of guitarists over the next five years, it opens up so many new areas in music'. Phil's a very busy man, as you have probably gathered – his solo album will be out early next year, hopefully *Roxy* will be back soon after that and with this other project with *10cc* he should have a very busy year. As I walked off into the sunset I found myself reflecting on all I had just heard and filled with a warm glow, thought casually to myself, 'Nice chap, that Manzanera bloke, if he tried hard he could make quite a name for himself. Or something'.

Stephen Lavers, *National Rockstar*

MANZANERA HIMSELF has been working on a number of solo projects. He masterminded the formation of *801*, a temporary band designed to fill in the time left by his holiday from *Roxy*. Their album *801 Live* was released last Friday on *Island*.

The music consists of new arrangements of tracks from albums by Manzanera, Eno and the former's pre-<u>Roxy</u> group *Quiet Sun*. Also, Lennon and McCartney's *Tomorrow Never Knows* and the Kinks' *You Really Got Me*. Line-up: Manzanera (lead guitar), Brian Eno (keyboards, synthesiser, guitar and vocals), Lloyd Watson (slide guitar and vocals), Francis Monkman

(*Fender Rhodes* and *clavinet*), Bill MacCormick (bass and vocals) and Simon Phillips (drums and rhythm generator).

The album was recorded on September 3 at *801's* third and last gig at the *Queen Elizabeth Hall*, London. A warm-up at Cromer in Norfolk and an appearance at the *Reading Festival* complete the list. But why so few gigs:

'We didn't intend it that way. I put the band together to play at festivals. We had booked a lot of European dates, but they kept getting cancelled. Then, the week before we were going to France, their government banned all festivals because of a Hells Angel's riot in Marseilles. Then the others fell through for different reasons, and it ended up with just these three concerts'.

'The idea was to put a band together to play some past album material that had never been played before live. Then things changed. I went away into the country with Eno and Bill MacCormick and started having a dialogue about the purpose of this venture. We wanted to do concerts that weren't just to be throwaway copies of the music on the albums. We wanted to form a band that would rearrange numbers and integrate them into a set. I wanted the group to have different elements in it. On the one hand, you'd have accomplished technicians like Francis Monkman and Simon Phillips, and at the other extreme you'd have Eno and Lloyd Watson, both more for feel. In the middle there'd be Bill MacCormick and me. Because we had these different approaches yes, it did create tension. We had arguments in working out the arrangements. But they were productive'.

His relationship with Eno provides a good example: 'There are certain fundamental differences between us. I like variety, for some reason he doesn't – we often argue about that. He's heavily into systems music which is the same thing repeated... No, that's a superficial statement to make, it's much more complicated than that. Even I don't understand half of it. I've always felt uncomfortable about Eno's lyrics for *Miss Shapiro*, which is on the album. They are unconventional. I always have to fight against my yearning for the conventional. I've always thought that's one of my biggest hang-ups. We end up working together for about a month a year, then we just naturally drift apart. He gets fed up with me, I get fed up with him'.

MANZANERA'S MUSIC itself is hardly conventional. His first band, formed in the sixth form, *Pooh and the Ostrich Feathers*, looked to the *Velvet Underground*, *Soft Machine*, *The Doors* and Zappa as mentors. After leaving school in 1969 the band renamed itself *Quiet Sun*.

'We rehearsed for about a year and did three gigs. We approached record companies but not many were interested in instrumental rock and roll played in funny time signatures. If we had been doing it two years later then probably we would have signed with a company like *Virgin*'.

'I went through a great crisis between the age of 15, when my father died, and 20. I desperately wanted to get involved in the rock business. I had a burning ambition, but I wasn't progressing at the speed I thought necessary to get in. It was depressing getting rejected by the record companies. It was a make or break situation – I had to do something. It caused me a lot of traumas, but it made me determined'.

When *Quiet Sun* broke up Manzanera replied to an ad for a lead guitarist with *Roxy Music*. He was interested because *Roxy* had received a better write up from Richard Williams than his old band in a newspaper column intended to expose new talent.

'I went to see Bryan Ferry and Andy Mackay, who were living in Battersea, with a tape of *Quiet Sun* material. They didn't particularly like it but they picked up on a few aspects of my primitive guitar playing. I didn't join them then, because they wanted a name in the band to help them and they got Dave O'List. He only stayed two or three months because there was a personality clash. I went to see the audition they did (for what's now our management company) and O'List and Paul Thompson had a fight over some petty little detail in front of everyone'. A few months later Manzanera finally joined Roxy Music.

APPENDIX 9: *801* MK. I – CONCERT REVIEWS

Harry Doherty, *Melody Maker*
IF WE WERE SURE of what to expect from Rory Gallagher, then the opposite was the case for Phil Manzanera's band, a motley crew that included Phil's old *Roxy* bosom buddy Brian Eno, on keyboards, guitar, and vocals. The band, surprisingly tight, played material that spanned the solo projects of both Manzanera and Eno who thrived in his apparent role as director of the whole operation. There was nothing ethereal about their set, a fine performance that mixed the spontaneity of straight rock with the undeniable virtuosity in the ranks (Manzanera and Eno's skills are acknowledged but bass player Bill MacCormick deserves more attention). They charmed us all at the conclusion with their raunchy version of *You Really Got Me*. Check 'em out.

Simon Kinnersley, *Bath & West Evening Chronicle*
THE MOST EXHILARATING and challenging performance of the festival came from the newly formed Brian Eno, Phil Manzanera unnamed band. With a line-up that included such accomplished performers as Francis Monkman (keyboards), Simon Phillips (drums) and Bill MacCormick on bass, they delivered some music of stunning proportions... ...Featuring material from Eno's *Taking Tiger Mountain By Strategy* and *Here Come The Warm Jets*, and Manzanera's more recent *Diamond Head*, the set was chequered with fearsome guitar runs and powerful and melodic rhythms, while Eno added his fascinating and unique treatments. One hopes this project is to be developed.

Mo Geller, *NME*
BILLED AS SPECIAL GUESTS, Phil Manzanera with Eno, Francis Monkman, Lloyd Watson, Bill MacCormick and Simon Phillips – under the collective tag *801* – took the stage for the most interesting and adventurous music for the day. For a too, too short three quarters of an hour they hit peak after peak. Bright jazzy guitar runs, jaggedly staccato or sweetly mellifluous, powerhouse drumming, dazzling individual work, overwhelming unison and really rocking harder than anyone else the whole day. A couple of numbers from *Diamond Head* and from Eno's *Taking Tiger Mountain By Strategy*, *You Really Got Me* and they were gone.

John Peel, *Sounds*
FROM HERE WE MOVED on to what was, for me the musical highpoint of the weekend, the set played by Phil Manzanera, Eno et al. In these days, when predictability is prized above all other things, these musicians are a rare breed indeed. One looks forward doesn't one, to the LP which is

rumoured to have been recorded by the same team at a London concert last Friday.

Hugh Fielder, *Sounds*
Queen Elizabeth Hall

WATCH OUT, here they come. Just a minute… Oh hell, they've gone. You've just missed the Phil Manzanera Band unless you caught them at the *Reading Festival* or at their 'farewell' performance at the *Queen Elizabeth Hall* last Friday. Which is a pity because the combination of Phil and his old *Roxy* playmate Eno together with Lloyd Watson on slide guitar, Francis Monkman on keyboards, Bill MacCormick on bass and Simon Phillips on drums, gave an object lesson on just how refreshing rock and roll can be when you haven't got image or status to live up to.

Any suspicions that this was just going to be a jolly jam session were dispelled right from the start. You don't get as musically tight as they were without a lot of hard work. And the obvious enjoyment the band got from playing together was soon reciprocated by the audience. After the introduction, *Lagrima* (from Phil's *Diamond Head* album), the band moved into a roaring adaptation of Lennon and McCartney's *Tomorrow Never Knows* which gave band and crowd alike something to chew on.

It was with the instrumental *Sol Caliente* that the individual characteristics of the band started to come through. MacCormick and Phillips drove the piece forward just inside the speed limit as Manzanera eased into overdrive above them. Eno pottered around his keyboards in relaxed fashion and occasionally added some wordless vocals. Real lyrics were forthcoming in the next number, *Rongwrong* (from the *Quiet Sun* album) where Eno's naked-sounding voice (with no echo or resonance on the microphone) contrasted with some flowing slide work from Lloyd Watson.

Audience appreciation was growing steadily and reached a peak on Manzanera's own *Diamond Head* where the simple descending theme, with Phil merging the notes to an almost continuous wail, was pursued relentlessly to a powerful climax. Distortion problems prevented Phil's solo on Eno's *Baby's on Fire* from coming through distinctly but Eno's voice had by now lost all its early reticence and the rest of the band bubbled away enthusiastically.

Clarity returned with the distinctive riff of *Miss Shapiro* which later gave way to the even more distinctive strains of the Kinks' *You Really Got Me* and despite some appallingly distracting lighting effects the band showed most punk groups exactly where they should get off. They'd only been on stage an hour and the hall management wanted everyone out by 10 p.m. so they just had time for one encore – *Third Uncle* which Eno introduced as 'the fastest song ever written'.

Much of the evening's success stemmed from the fact that the band stuck to playing rock music (albeit of a somewhat sophisticated variety) and were never tempted to delve into other areas. The concert was recorded and hopefully the ensuing live album may prompt Manzanera to give the band another run during *Roxy's* sabbatical. It would be a shame if such natural ebullient went to waste.

APPENDIX 10: *801* MK. I – ALBUM REVIEWS

SERIOUS MUSICAL ACCEPTANCE BY LATE 1976
Angus MacKinnon, *NME*
MOST LIVE albums are of no more than token value. The promotional guff will claim that we should have been there but since we weren't we can grab this instead. It's an accommodating consumer service, I suppose, but all the bluster rarely justifies the release of material that's only documenting the minutiae of studio-to-stage transfer. *801 Live* is, like Bowie's *David Live* or Dylan's *Before The Flood*, one of the exceptions that prove the rule. It's a properly creative live recording, on which songs differ radically from their blueprints.

801 were conceived by *Roxy's* Phil Manzanera & Co. as a summer of '76 spree and this is a useful summary of their operations. The set is a mixture of *Quiet Sun* material, Manzanera/Eno collaborations and a pair of gold-plated oldies thrown in for sheer enjoyment purposes. It's all been sensibly reshuffled and tightly edited to make an untroubled run onto record.

The selections almost obliterate their studio counterparts in terms of tension and spontaneity. Although most amenable, Manzanera's solo album maintained a hedge-hopping low profile; potential excitement was often exchanged for painstaking exactitude. Play these versions of *Diamond Head* and *Miss Shapiro* and you'll get the picture. *Diamond Head* began life as a prettily florid melody; here it's unsanctioned purpose and power. Manzanera's guitar feeds greedily off Eno's treatments until he severs the connection for a final break, all metal and mobility. *Miss Shapiro* has *801* wrenching themselves into a ritual frenzy as Eno snaps off chains of image-associated lyrics.

In fact, Eno's singing is a real surprise. I've often found it strangely extraneous on his own records, whereas here it's completely attuned to the band's performance. His neo-nasal delivery of *Baby's on Fire*, deadpan intonation on the humorously motorik version of The Kinks' *You Really Got Me* and philosophical balladeering on the restrained *Rongwrong* are all telling.

Manzanera's *Lagrima* opens, its rarefied melody quartering back and forth like an Andean condor, just guitar and electronics. Whereupon *801* take their breathless arrangement of Lennon-McCartney's *Tomorrow Never Knows* right up into Cloud Nine. A cirrus sweep of keyboards from Francis Monkman and Eno clears the way for Bill MacCormick's exuberant bass, Manzanera and Lloyd Watson's snickering guitars and Simon Phillips' splattered drums and hi-hat. On your feet or out of your head for zero-gravity nostalgia as Eno's vocals are tape slowed into the mix. The initial momentum is maintained until closedown. *T.N.K.* is stoned and immaculate, a peak of psychedelic revivalism.

The name of the *801* game is energy, and an energy undiluted through all the complex changes of *East Of Asteroid* or slipways of *Sombre Reptiles*. Watson's slide is a satisfying foil for Manzanera's more acrimonious playing. MacCormick (whose bass is at once intricate and warm-blooded) and Phillips are the kind of rhythm section most bands can only dream about having aboard. Monkman's electric piano and clavinet balance out against Eno's more wayward contributions. The recording quality is excellent, even with both sides well over the 20 minute mark.

It would be great to see *801* become a more permanent live fixture. I almost hope Roxy's sabbatical is extended indefinitely. Who need *Roxy Music*, now anyway? They simply haven't cut it on album since the cataclysmic *Stranded*. In addition, Ferry's solo work has improved noticeably since last autumn. His next record of original songs could well take on from where *Stranded* left off. *Roxy* have become an ineffectual exercise in self-parody whilst *801* do what they do with unbridled enthusiasm. Admittedly, the two units place their emphasis on very different aspects, but it seems pointless for *Roxy* to continue firing on less than one cylinder (and I doubt very much whether things will change even after a year's break) – thus ensuring that *801* effectively cease trading as a band right now. In *801* Manzanera has a really strong base on which to build. It's altogether far too good am offer for him to refuse.

PHIL MANZANERA AND *801* SOAR
Michael Bloom, Rolling Stone

PHIL MANZANERA IS one of the world's last psychedelic guitarists. His electric hippie asides spiced Bryan Ferry's romantic histrionics in *Roxy Music*, while his practicality often anchored Brian Eno's ballooning aesthetics. Now, with his own floating *801* entourage, Manzanera has created one of the last – and best – psychedelic bands in the world.

Manzanera as bandleader is a sensitive collaborator, sort of a Frank Zappa with humility. Deciding from the start that *801* was to be a communal project, he found players whose contributions would complement his own and who could expand to fill any available space. He's organized his maverick musicians into a smoking performance unit in much the same way that his cohort, Eno, juggles quixotic hooks and phrases into delectable pop songs. That Manzanera has chosen splendid players helps, of course – drummer Simon Phillips (Jack Bruce), bassist Bill MacCormick (*Matching Mole*), pianist Francis Monkman (*Curved Air*) and the unfathomable Eno – but most of *801's* firepower stems from his own concise direction.

The first record, *801 Live,* surfaced in England almost two years ago, as if by accident. *801* was then an ad hoc group Manzanera and Eno formed in order to play a few concerts together. This set, recorded at their third and final show, may well be the most vital live album of the decade. There are no egotistical displays or star wars – even Manzanera's longest solo is a whirlwind two-dozen bars in the intro to *Miss Shapiro.* Instead, he teases the performers through momentous changes and tricky offbeats, uniting everyone by ordeal. The band emerges not only tight but spontaneous, and the ensemble texture is rich and explosive, like the finest from the Sixties groups.

Kevin Martin, *The Lamb*, Texas

AFTER WEEKS of anticipatory hysteria I finally acquired my copy of *801/Live.* Almost destroying my turntable in the process, I played the album and listened intently. It is a record that is filled with many sounds. Strangely enough, the one sound I recall most vividly is a sharp rapping, like a hammer striking nails. And the nails were being driven into the coffin of *Roxy Music.*

Perhaps I should back up a bit. The members of *Roxy Music* have taken a year off for ventures outside the band. Phil Manzanera (quite possibly the best thing that's ever happened to the electric guitar) and former *Roxy* strategist Eno (profiled in last month's issue) formed a band called *801* and played three concerts this fall. *801* is rounded out by bassist Bill MacCormick (*Matching Mole* and *Quiet Sun*), drummer Simon Phillips, Lloyd Watson on slide guitar and vocals, and Francis Monkman (ex-*Curved Air*) on *Fender Rhodes* and *clavinet.* Their performance at the *Queen Elizabeth Hall* was recorded on *Island's* mobile unit.

It is, in my opinion, one of the best live albums ever made. The selections include two cuts from the *Quiet Sun* LP, three from Eno's solo albums, and three from Manzanera's solo effort, *Diamond Head.* The remaining two cuts are Anglo classics. *The Beatles' Tomorrow Never Knows* and *The Kinks You Really Got Me* are given tasteful yet offbeat treatments.

Lagrima, which appears on *Diamond Head* and as the beginning of *Sol Caliente* on the aforementioned *Quiet Sun* album, opens with its most beautiful rendition yet. *Lagrima* slowly merges into *TNK* with Eno's vocals sounding stronger than ever before. This is one of the very few times anyone has done justice to the Fab Four and this cut alone is worth the price of this disc. Following with *East of Asteroid* and *Rongwrong, Quiet Sun* again (it should be mentioned that *Quiet Sun* was Manzanera's pre-*Roxy* band that he reformed to record an extraordinary album, *Mainstream*), *801* wins the *Soft Machine* sound alike contest hands down. Playing with aggression and subtlety simultaneously, if you can believe that, these guys actually improve on the original versions.

The last cut on side one is perhaps the most incredible of all (I hate to compare). *Sombre Reptiles* should cease forever any doubts concerning Eno's compositional brilliance. Taken from his masterpiece *Another Green World*, *Reptiles* is the quintessential Eno composition. One of Eno's favourite strategies is laying down a simple progression of notes which becomes complex to the human ear with repetition. This technique is used with tremendous success here. Considering the 'vertical complexity' (a favourite Eno descriptive phrase) of *Reptiles*, the fact that it is performed with such skill and emotion is almost unbelievable. Phew! All of this and I haven't even mentioned side two.

Not that side two isn't worth mentioning. *Baby's on Fire*, from Eno's *Here Come the Warm Jets* LP, is given a less frantic treatment, and is a vast improvement over the June 1, 1974 version. On *Diamond Head*, the title cut from PM's solo album, Manzanera displays his guitar virtuosity. The beauty and power of this piece is showcased dramatically. Manzanera's international background provides many influences and flavourings for his compositional and is a direct contributor lo his truly original style. Eno's heavy vocals dominate a high energy version of *Miss Shapiro*, another gem from *Diamond Head*. This points to the strength of the Manzanera/Eno songwriting team. Just the hint of these two men forming any sort of permanent alliance is enough to cause irrational behaviour on my part. The possibilities would be limitless.

A very sophisticated version of *You Really Got Me* follows with Eno's monotone vocal giving the song a mood quite unlike any it has known before. Closing with a reprise of *Miss Shapiro* that has the audience clapping in unison, *801* attempts to end a concert that should achieve legendary status with little difficulty. Not yet satisfied (greedy twits), the crowd demands an encore. And what an encore. An incredible version of Eno's *Third Uncle* follows with Eno apathetically mumbling the lyrics while Manzanera goes absolutely berserk on his guitar.

This brings us back to the question of *Roxy Music's* future, if it exists. With all of its members displaying the ability to succeed outside the band it seems unlikely we will ever see Roxy Music together again. To quote one who knows:

I remember all those moments lost in wonder
that we'll never find again
There's no more time for us
Nothing is there for us to share but yesterday
Bryan Ferry, *Song for Europe*

If this is true it is sad indeed. The pop music world will never again see the likes of *Roxy Music*. But we can remember and we can look forward to many years of incredible music from everyone involved. *801 Live* is the beginning of a great new tradition.

AT LAST, INNOVATIVE, IMMACULATE, DYNAMIC TECHNO-ROCK
Stephen Lavers, *National Rockstar*
RECORDED LIVE at their third and final performance this summer, the band was masterminded by *Roxy's* Phil Manzanera and former comrade Brian Eno. With the exception of a *Beatles'* and a *Kinks'* number, all the material is drawn from their solo albums and Manzanera's pre-*Roxy Quiet Sun*. Every trick is rearranged and sparkling fresh! They perform with more feeling and cohesion than bands that have been together for years.
Lagrima, the first track, is a wall of cascading pulsating sound, built up by Manzanera on lead guitar that soon develops into a ripping, spaced-out, flowing adaptation of the *Beatles' Tomorrow Never Knows*. Each track is different. There are unusually structured *Soft Machine-ish* instrumentals like *East Of Asteroid*. Repeated riffs on guitar backed by an undercurrent of synthesisers combine with a shattering bass rhythm by Bill MacCormick. *Sombre Reptiles* is a slithering sand dance led by an introspective Eno on snakey synthesizers.

Favourite tracks are Eno's surreal *Baby's on Fire* and *Miss Shapiro*. The first opens with funky abstract keyboards contrasting with strange ambiguous lyrics delivered by Eno in detached fake shock horror tones, that is transformed by glinting slide guitar from Lloyd Watson. *Miss Shapiro* is constructed on an incredible bouncing rhythm laid down by bass, synthesisers and lead guitar interposed by absurd alliterated lyrics that keep you amused as well as becoming part of the total sound. Rock climax is a skull rattling gutsy adaptation of *Kinks' You Really Got Me* underpinned by one blinking electronic ping.
At last, music for the mind and body.

Richard Williams, *Melody Maker*
A FEW WEEKS AGO, while writing in this column about the prevailing ghastly organisation of contemporary rock concerts I mentioned that I hoped one day to leave such an event feeling happy, fulfilled, and not the least bit irritated. Conveniently, and to fit the theory, I'd expunged the memory of one concert which gave me exactly those feelings, in abundance: the appearance of a pick-up group called *801* at London's *Queen Elizabeth Hall* in September.

801 was, of course, the outfit created by Phil Manzanera to fill some of his time during *Roxy Music's* alleged Sabbatical. Against all the odds, the affair was enchanting and profound in equal measure, an absolute paragon of what can be achieved in this context, given musicians with intelligence, imagination, and sensitivity. Also, in a way, it sums up an era: the one which began, perhaps, with the *Soft Machine's* first gig and has now peaked as a commercial force. But, hearteningly, the concert never came on like an epitaph; rather, it suggested that there may be much more ground still ripe for exploration than has yet been covered. At the concert's close, I felt that these musicians had successfully proposed their own future, and laid the groundwork for a rewarding, creative longevity stretching far beyond the limits of their status, as an early Seventies commercial phenomenon.

Now, I'm pleased to report, that concert is available, almost in its entirety on an album called *801 Live*. Along with *Songs In The Key Of Life*, it's this winter's essential purchase. As a live album, it avoids the obvious polarities of function: it's neither a staggeringly 'perfect' monument to past glories (like *Viva Roxy Music* or *Rock Of Ages*), nor an impressionistic, journalistic document of a one-off happening (like *Hard Rain* or *June 1, 1974*). This is no dead statement, no oddball jotting. It is valuable simply in its own right, as music pure and simple, with a scope and density of content, virtually unparalleled in its field.

The musicians are Manzanera and Lloyd Watson (guitars), Brian Eno (synthesizer, tapes, guitar, and chief voice), Francis Monkman (electric piano and clavinet), Bill MacCormick (bass guitar), and Simon Phillips (drums). Not, you'll admit, a line-up noted for its homogeneity, beyond the obvious link-ups. Yet somehow they coalesce perfectly for the occasion: you might expect Phillips' schooled and session-honed drumming to be too full of current licks, for instance, but he responds to his colleagues' musical demands with a thoroughly sympathetic and supportive display. The same goes for Monkman, another fearsome musician whose role here is mainly the addition of colour and texture (remember, though, that he was rehearsing a new band with Robert Wyatt before the drummer had his accident a few years ago).

For once, to convey the full value of the record, it's necessary to describe it from beginning to end. The proceedings open with a train whistle (an amusing reference to the cover of Phil's solo album, *Diamond Head*) before the leader performs a short version of his solo piece *Lagrima*, his instrument treated by Eno's synthesizer. It's been edited from the full concert length, and it makes you want to hear more of such collaborations between these two, after the manner of the Eno/Fripp recordings. *Lagrima* dissolves into a churning band section composed of contrasting overlaid rifts which, after a couple of minutes, turns out to be John Lennon's *Tomorrow Never Knows*.

The choice of this song is the first indication that here is something special: how many other groups would attempt it? Certainly there are none who could an interpretation so faithful to the spirit of the original, yet so full of its own character. The spirits are strangely stirred when Eno's flat, mournful vocal reaches the words '...and love is all, and love Is everything/It is knowing. It Is knowing...' and I was even more moved to

398

discover that this performance took place ten years and one month, almost to the day, after the release of *Revolver*, the song's parent album. There is careful evocation of that period: bubbling keyboards imitating speeded-up tapes underline altered vocal sounds (notably one whooshing entry, presumably the result of echo added during the mixing stage). I hope Lennon hears it: he'll be pleased and proud. (I almost added 'of his children'.)

East Of Asteroid and *Rongwrong* focus on a later period in British rock, when Zappa and the *Softs* were the twin deities and *Quiet Sun* were among their lesser-known disciples. Both are in a sense abstract pieces, typical of their time in that they concentrate on solving musical equations, tickling a certain 1970 undergraduate sensibility, yet *801's* collective wit is acute enough to transform them, superficially, into thoroughly contemporary artefacts. The wandering bass ending to the second song is, though, a real period piece, an example of the kind of technique that Bryan Ferry would annex in the early days of *Roxy*, in order to broaden the effect of his songs and to give the band its 'experimental' edge.

The side ends with what I remember as being a particularly moving treatment of Eno's *Sombre Reptiles*, a highlight of his unjustly neglected *Another Green World* LP. It's a serpentine melodic loop, and I'm sorry it's faded on the album after three minutes, because you wish it to go on forever. Monkman's chattering *Fender Rhodes* and *clavinet* add a subtle and apposite extra dimension, and on this kind of composition you can hear Eno growing into something more than a mere purveyor of novelties. (If you don't have *Another Green World*, please check it out. It's far beyond *Warm Jets* and *Tiger Mountain* in every sense.)

Side Two opens up with the third recorded version of the same composer's *Baby's on Fire*. In place of the *Rainbow* recording's blistering fire there's a lighter, more contemporary feel, and the piece is worthwhile for the twin guitar solos. Manzanera's typical soaring excursion, and Watson's furious steel scrabblings. Amusingly enough, it grinds to a halt on the *Black Is Black/I'm On Fire* riff.

For the first time, and after an admirable display of reticence, Manzanera takes command for a six-minute reading of his *Diamond Head* theme. Again, it's wholly characteristic: full-blown widescreen romance, the sweet guitar leaping out of the frame in full Todd-AO colour. He's a funny player, some nights sounding like an angel and others unable to hit an E-major chord straight, but here he's consistently workmanlike, and more.

The terse, tough *Miss Shapiro* comes next, from the same source, its eccentricity pinned down by the rhythm section's devotion and work-rate. The guitars snarl, struggling to free themselves during a torrid introduction. Now they loosen up, and the fun begins. A familiar chopped guitar pattern prefaces *You Really Got Me*, played with deadpan brilliance and sung in a curious but winning close harmony by Eno, Watson, and MacCormick. Underneath it all, someone hammers out unvarying one-note quavers on a keyboard, and the mind races back through the original *Re-make/Re-model*, past *All Tomorrow's Parties*, and comes to rest with Terry Riley's *In C*. Ray Davies meets the Systems Minimalists! When such confluence can take place, we must realise that we've been living through a period of unusual artistic freedom.

There's an encore: Eno's *Third Uncle* with the three rhythm guitarists all flicking out the bludgeoning key pattern. Phillips noodles impatiently during the solo, gathers himself and launches the sextet into a final bloody assault. If the funk bands try very hard, this is how they'll sound one day. It's vicious, and the point is driven home when the record ends with the fast chord of the song, applause deleted.

During the concert, these people collectively reached a point where virtually anything is possible. The music seemed to me to embody all the virtues of the very early *Roxy Music*, with the freedom to try and the freedom to fail. Except that now they're more confident, more able, more eloquent. Manzanera, Eno, and the rest of the 'school' to which they belong have, if they wish, a lengthy and increasingly fascinating creative life ahead of them. As the words of *Tomorrow Never Knows* suggest, *801 Live* may well be simply the end of the beginning.

Ray Dellar, *HiFi News*

AS IT SEEMS that I'm destined never to review Stevie Wonder's *Songs in the Key of Life* – last month my copy got lost somewhere in Geepeeohland, this month I've received a replacement that's pressed more like corned beef – I feel the next best thing to do is to recommend an album that is, in its own way, of equal importance.

Can it be by Bowie, Stewart or Lennon, you ask? Well no – it's actually by a band known as *801*, the album being titled *801 Live*. Now I suppose I'd better explain that *801* is really a kind of a *Roxy* offshoot, conceived by Eno and Phil Manzanera. And on the evidence of this recording, made at the *Queen Elizabeth Hall*, last September, the band – Eno (vocals/synthesiser etc.), Manzanera (guitar), Bill MacCormick (bass/vocals), Francis Monkman (keyboards), Simon Phillips (drums) and Lloyd Watson (slide guitar/vocals) – would appear to be somewhat more interesting than *Roxy* itself at this point in time.

M & E's *Miss Shapiro* is, for instance, a beaut of a track, throwing up lyrical images faster than a well-executed Hindu shuffle. Then, just when you're set and mentally motoring along with the band, a familiar riff is thrown up like a detour sign and you're off down 'deja-vu' alley, via a surformed version of the *Kinks' You really got me* that works amazingly well. *801* is a band that really likes to stick its head out.

Not content to zoom through originals like *Third Uncle* and *Baby's on Fire* in a manner that leaves the listener hung up with jet lag, they even have the audacity to present a version of the *Beatles' Tomorrow Never Knows* that somehow retains the mystic charm of the original yet has that additional something that is very much a part of *801*. And any band that pulls off something of that nature – as *801* successfully do – goes immediately to the top of my 'bands to look out for in '77' listing. I suggest you put them on yours.

Ashley Franklin, *Liquorice*
801 WAS BORN OUT of Phil Manzanera's desire 'to play a few summer festivals', something which he never had the chance to do as a member of *Roxy Music*. Similarly, *801* is a product of what Manzanera has never had enough elbow-room to produce under Ferry. Come next Spring, *Roxy* will be needing Manzanera, but does Manzanera need *Roxy*?

Siren pales in comparison with *801 Live*, an album brimming with ideas and inspiration – all the more shame that this group isn't going to be allowed to develop any further. One doubts the necessity and validity of so many live albums nowadays, but *801 Live* passes the test – a perfectly balanced melange of fresh compositions, classic oldies and radically reworked studio material. Eno doodles on the synth, treats the guitars and gives off a surprisingly more than passable voice; Bill MacCormick plays his typically flourishing bass lines; Lloyd Watson does *Melody Maker* proud as he strikes, slides and slurps his guitar to great effect; drummer Simon Phillips hammers away most assuredly; Francis Monkman, who painted rainbows in *Curved Air*, soars and scans on the keyboards (good to see him in action – he's understated his talent for too long).

Album highlights are *Lagrima* which receives the phased swirling Manzaguitar treatment, and which segues into *TNK* (*Tomorrow Never Knows*), a bold version of Lennon's neglected *Revolver* classic. The meshing of the instruments is quite masterful, and Monkman's contribution dazzling. *Diamond Head* shows the lush, floating magic of Manzanera's guitar of the studio version transformed here to one of raw, stirring power. *You Really Got Me* receives a neat, novel treatment, and Eno even sings in tune.

We need more bands like *801* – bands with a wide, cross-sectional approach, unafraid to experiment, and committed more to innovation than income. You know, bands like *801* ought to be given arts council grants.

ROCKSY MUSIC
Vivien Goldman, *Sounds*
THURSDAY SEPTEMBER 2, 1976. British Left-Fielders' night out at the *Queen Elizabeth Hall* in London. It was *801's* second and last gig (the other was *Reading Festival*). Phil Manzanera put together the six musicians, some of them from his former band *Quiet Sun*, specially for those two dates. Just for kicks.

As you might expect from musicians of Eno's and Phil's imagination and dedication, *801* were in no way a jamming band. Although the musicians don't play together on any regular formal basis, *801* are tight, responsive and as mutually sympathetic as any established gigging/recording band. Their music's a fruitful meeting-ground between *Quiet Sun's* experimental free form jazz, *Roxy's* snazzy commercial bite, and Eno's highly personal games/adventures with words and music. The tracks are from Phil's solo *Diamond Head* album, Eno's three *Island* solo albums, and *Q.S's Mainstream*.

Drummer Simon Phillips dominates, free as jazz but militant (i.e. brisk, stirring, aggressive) as the best Jamaican drummers. Eno's vocals are always exciting. His delivery's polished and stylised, like Ferry's. Meanwhile Manzanera, notably on his instrumental showcase, *Diamond Head*, reels off shimmering silken ribbons of guitar lines with Allmanesque fluid grace, or rocks ferociously. Three cheers for the *Island Mobile's* crystalline recording they don't miss a lick. *801* produced, at *Basing Street*, and the sound's so immaculate that if it wasn't for tumultuous waves of applause phasing in and out, *Live* could pass for a studio album. The unmistakably live quality is due to the exuberance and spontaneous energy in the music, not, as in most live albums, the roughness of the sound.

Miss Shapiro judders with excitement. Phil's eloquence is pure soul, Phillips' drums are frighteningly intense. Eno implodes into the song – first biting off words like bullets, then opening sensually in the middle break. His enunciation is clipped and English, as always, clear and tough as a diamond; then Phil's angry guitar slams the band forward into a menacing attack on the *Kinks' You Really Got Me*. Eno sounds psychotic, as his keyboards bleep with infuriating deliberation; like an Oriental water torture, each note drips inexorably into the nerve centres.

All this, and rock 'n' roll too.

PHIL MANZANERA AND 801 SOAR
One of the last and best psychedelic bands in the world
Michael Bloom, *Rolling Stone*
801 Live, Phil Manzaneray/*801* Polydor
PHIL MANZANERA IS one of the world's last psychedelic guitarists. His electric hippie asides spiced Bryan Ferry's romantic histrionics in *Roxy*

Music, while his practicality often anchored Brian Eno's ballooning aesthetics. Now, with his own floating *801* entourage, Manzanera has created one of the last – and best – psychedelic bands in the world.

Manzanera as bandleader is a sensitive collaborator, sort of a Frank Zappa with humility. Deciding from the start that *801* was to be a communal project, he found players whose contributions would complement his own and who could expand to fill any available space. He's organized his maverick musicians into a smoking performance unit in much the same way that his cohort, Eno, juggles quixotic hooks and phrases into delectable pop songs.

That Manzanera has chosen splendid players helps, of course – drummer Simon Phillips (Jack Bruce), bassist Bill MacCormick (*Matching Mole*), pianist Francis Monkman (*Curved Air*), harmonists Lol Creme and Kevin Godley (*10cc*) and the unfathomable Eno – but most of *801's* firepower stems from his own concise direction.

The first record, *801 Live*, surfaced in England almost two years ago, as if by accident. *801* was then an ad hoc group Manzanera and Eno formed in order to play a few concerts together. This set, recorded at their third and final show, may well be the most vital live album of the decade. There are no egotistical displays or star wars – even Manzanera's longest solo is a whirlwind two-dozen bars in the intro to *Miss Shapiro*. Instead, he teases the performers through momentous changes and tricky offbeats, uniting everyone by ordeal. The band emerges not only tight but spontaneous, and the ensemble texture is rich and explosive, like the finest from the Sixties groups.

APPENDIX 11: THE *801 LIVE* PRESS PACK

O N THURSDAY, SEPTEMBER 3rd 1976 a group called *The 801* played their third and last gig at London's *Queen Elizabeth Hall* to a packed house. One warm-up gig at in Norfolk and a Saturday evening appearance at the *Reading Festival* completed the band's performing pedigree – and although some of the material they played on those three occasions may have sounded familiar to fans of the *Roxy* fringe, to most it was totally new.

The 801, a project master-minded by *Roxy's* Phil Manzanera to fill the vacation that group is currently taking, began rehearsing at *Island Studios*, Hammersmith, about three weeks before their first gig. The musicians included Eno (on keyboards, synthesise, guitar, and vocals), Lloyd Watson (slide-guitar and vocals), Francis Monkman (*Fender Rhodes* and *clavinet*), Bill MacCormick (bass and vocals), and Simon Phillips (drums and rhythm generator). The music consisted of more or less mutated selections from albums by Manzanera, Eno, and Phil's pre-*Roxy* group *Quiet Sun*, plus a full-scale rearrangement of Lennon-McCartney's *Tomorrow Never Knows* and an off-the-wall excursion into *The Kinks'* 1964 hit *You Really Got Me*.

At the *Reading Festival* the band's atmospheric spaciousness and power surprised and impressed many of the press who, reasonably enough, had been expecting something more informal and self-indulgent. A mobile recording studio was present at the *Queen Elizabeth Hall* concert to capture THE *801's* resounding confirmation of their promise – not to mention the audience's enthusiastic response.

801 Live is the record of that appearance.

THE MUSICIANS

PHIL MANZANERA... aside from his regular work in *Roxy Music*, Phil has recorded one solo-album *Diamond Head* (1975) and a group-album with *Quiet Sun*, his pre-*Roxy* outfit, called *Mainstream* (1975). Recently he appeared at the Albert Hall with Steve Winwood and Mike Shrieve for the world premiere of Stomu Yamashta's *Go* and this summer, produced the debut album of *Split Enz*, a new group from New Zealand. He is currently completing work on an as-yet-untitled studio album.

BRIAN ENO... since leaving *Roxy* in 1973, Eno has recorded three solo-albums – *Here Come The Warm Jets* (1974), *Taking Tiger Mountain (By Strategy)* (1975), and *Another Green World* (1976). In addition he has collaborated with ex-*King Crimson* guitarist Robert Fripp on two experimental albums – *No Pussyfooting* (1974) and *Evening Star* (1976) – and founded the *Obscure Records* label, an outlet for what the music business would hold to be uncommercial sounds and through which he has also released his own

404

Discreet Music (1976). Appearing also on *Diamond Head*, *Mainstream*, and *June 1st 1974* (with John Cale, Kevin Ayers, and Nico), he spends the rest of his time writing and lecturing on Fine Arts and Systems Theory, composing music for stage and cinema, and collaborating on such special projects as the *Oblique Strategies* system (1975) with artist Peter Schmidt. Currently working with David Bowie, he will go into the studio to begin his fourth solo album in November.

LLOYD WATSON... winner of the 1972 *Melody Maker* newcomer's award, Lloyd toured with *Roxy* in 1973 and has appeared on Andy Mackay's *In Search of Eddie Riff* (1974) and Eno's *Here Come The Warm Jets*. Currently he plays informally in a band with *Back Door's* Colin Hodgkinson in his hometown of Peterborough.

FRANCIS MONKMAN... studied at the *Royal Academy of Music* between 1967 and 1970, thereafter recording three albums as co-leader of *Curved Air*, before leaving that band in 1972 to concentrate on session-work and classical harpsichord. He is also an expert in kendo and tai ch'i.

BILL MACCORMICK... played with Phil Manzanera in *Quiet Sun* 1970-71, recorded two albums as a member of Robert Wyatt's *Matching Mole* in 1972, and briefly joined *Gong* in 1973. He has appeared on Wyatt's *Ruth Is Stranger Than Richard*, Eno's *Here Come The Warm Jets*, and Manzanera's *Diamond Head* – together with Phil, drummer Charles Hayward, and keyboard-player Dave Jarrett, recording *Quiet Sun's Mainstream* last year. A writer on American politics, he has just returned from the United States where he covered the Presidential primaries, and is currently working with Phil on the follow-up to *Diamond Head* and with Gary Windo and Hugh Hopper on yet another album.

SIMON PHILLIPS... is a session-drummer of growing repute, having so far contributed to albums by Roger Glover, *Greenslade*, Veronique Sanson, and Albert Hammond. He is currently working with Jack Bruce. He will be among those featured on Phil Manzanera's next studio recording.

APPENDIX 12: *LISTEN NOW* - REVIEWS

MUSIC FOR BAD DREAMS
Ian Birch, *Melody Maker*, October 29th 1977

'NEVER FORGET, that Revenger and Reporter begin with the same letter'. So announces Lemmy Caution in *Alphaville*, one of the most stunning fantasy films ever made. Caution, an American detective, is sent to Alphaville, city of the future, to destroy its heartless computer-controlled civilisation. It's a place where 'inhabitants have become slaves of electronic probabilities, tranquilisers come with very hotel room and the eternal present reign'. The movie is an amazingly elegant combination of documentary, modern myth and pop art.

Now I'm not claiming that *Listen Now* tries to vinylise Alphaville (the ever-fashionable compass point of Orwell's *1984* is probably more appropriate) but it does have a similar effect. Beautifully refined, intricate and deceptively distanced with a unified concept (to use a now debased word in its best sense) underlying the whole. Don't turn off because you've not so far encountered terms like 'aggressive' or 'raw' or 'high energy' or 'buzzsaw': *Listen Now* is a superb album, and its subtleties emerge with every listen.

The cover artwork bears this out. Based on an idea by Ian MacCormick, who co-wrote three of the songs with Manzanera, it depicts a stylised inner-city nightmare of the future – or is it present? In the foreground, one dehumanised figure whispers behind a cupped hand to an incredulous second. To their left another couple, shadowing, the first, act similarly. All four are corralled by chain links and a New York-like skyline.

The music just makes the implications even more unnerving, Manzanera has recruited Bill (also bassist/vocalist) and Ian MacCormick to supply the lyrics and the brothers explore the idea of – dare I say – the Totalitarian State. *City Of Light* subtitled *42nd Street Blues*, describes urban collapse, the stage immediately prior to an Alphaville situation. 'Blinds are drawn cross windows facing nowhere / In the day the darkness is complete / Close your eyes and try to cry away your nightmares / You just know the downtown city street / Where darkness reigns'. Curfew is just a shot away.

The media is ruthlessly supervised for the sake of *Law And Order*. A face on the TV falsely assures that everything is all right. 'It's easy to take what you are told'. The title track goes beyond depicting the callous repression and, in almost biblical imagery, admonishes: 'Is it any wonder you've got no power / When you pay a thief to keep it for you? / Is it a surprise that your wine is sour / When you let a liar choose the brew he ours you?'. In the face of such manipulation, personal loves and beliefs become a wilderness of confusion. *That Falling, Feeling* (a great name for a song) starts: 'Yesterday you knew what to say / To keep them sweet / But just one fall and it's all you can do / To keep your feet'. The tale of Suzie and Johnny in *Flight 19* – (which I, to my shame, slagged-off as a single – sackcloth and ashes for a week) charts the anguish that misunderstanding entails.

By now you probably think I'm a contender for *Pseuds Corner* or just plain mad. All I can do is refer you to the 12-incher in question. Ah yes, the music. For once the cast list of session luminaries works democratically and with total conviction. It's impossible not to draw a parallel with *10cc* in their early vintage period; in fact, *Gizmo* pioneers Lol Creme and Kevin Godley appear on several cuts, and nowhere is their influence stronger than on *Flight 19*, with those high-pitched harmonies. Manzanera has yoked the finely wrought song structures of *10cc* to both his own understated style and the type of saw-toothed menace he added, for instance, to *Roxy Music* at their best, the reactivated *Quiet Sun* project, and John Cale on the epic *Slow Dazzle*. The parts never gel. They weave in and out of a main theme with consummate brooding ease.

City Of Light opens on a staccato piano reminiscent of *A Day In The Life* (remember the *Beatles*?) to be joined by Bill MacCormick's heartbeat bass-line and Simon Ainley's vocals, which sound like a sandpapered version of Eno's. Their meticulous smoothness reinforces the chill, just as much as Manzanera's harsh and splintered chords. *Listen Now* builds gradually but purposively around another sturdy foundation (MacCormick's bass and Dave Mattacks' drums) with some surprising twists and turns. The harmonies ebb and flow, while Mel Collins overdubs 'saxes and big band'. As well as the six bona fide songs, there are three instrumentals written solely by Manzanera. *Island* is a beautifully sensual piece evoking every cyborg's daydream of a palm tree haven *Que?*, on the other hand, is a quick fire burst of white heat, while *Initial Speed* makes amphetamine seem like a depressant. Manzanera's guitars snap against Monkman's sprung coiled synthesiser.

A final request: don't let this one slip by unnoticed.

HERE'S LOOKING AT YOU WINSTON SMITH
PHIL PULLS A CREEPY ONE
Angus MacKinnon, *NME*, 24th September 1977
WE MAY PARANOID but that doesn't mean they're not out to get us. The cover of *Listen Now* pictures two furtive exchanges of news and views. The four faces are grotesquely airbrushed, in bruise blue and vein purple; chain links angle across the scene as skyscrapers lean out of a drab sky. Roll on *1984* and the regiments of Thought Police. Philip Castle's artwork mirrors the Orwellian tenor of *Listen Now* all too well.

Of course, former *Roxy Music* guitarist Phil Manzanera commissioned song lyrics from the likes of Eno, John Wetton and Robert Wyatt for *Diamond Head*, his first solo album, but these weren't thematically unified. Here bassist Bill MacCormick and his brother Ian have supplied six sets of words; their preoccupations are closely linked with the cover theme. To wit, *Listen Now* ('Talk on the wire about force and choice / It's uncomfortable to raise your voice') and *Law and Order* ('It's easy to take what you are told / They said we need law and order') consider media manipulation and the strong state as actual/imminent. *City of Light* ('Blinds are drawn across windows facing nowhere / In the day, the darkness is complete') sets a scene of inner city scarescaping,; *Flight 19*, *Postcard Love* and *That Falling Feeling* describe the concomitant breakdown of personal relationships.

I'm not reading too much into it am I, chaps? No, I don't think so. But you get the drift, and a bleak, apprehensive one it is too. Apprehensive? Unsettled, unsettling? On reflection, that quality's not new to Manzanera's output. I'm thinking of the harshly ferrous edge to his work with John Cale (*Gun* and *Heartbreak Hotel*) and Nico (*The End*) – to say nothing of the barely screened hysteria of some of *Mainstream*, the belated offering by *Quiet Sun*, his pre-*Roxy* concern. As it is, *Listen Now* provides a more explicit framework for these aspects of Manzanera's musicianship.

And despite the fact that Manzanera is obsessively attentive to detail in the studio, that the album was recorded at intervals over some eighteen months and that it involves 15 or more players *Listen Now* is – almost surprisingly – a coherent composite. It would be pointless to reiterate every initiative taken by Manzanera and *801* on this showing. Nonetheless *Sheet Music* – to my mind, the apogee of *10cc's* achievement – serves as a useful point of comparison. *Listen Now* shares a similar outward urge.

Flight 19 is sophisticated rock craftsmanship of the highest order. Savour its structure (verse, chorus, middle eight, solo, repeat) and adventurous use of same. Although for the most part typically reticent, Manzanera fronts three instrumentals, *Island* (as in refuge and sense of calm) reveals his catholic tastes; it's *Diamond Head* rephrased, a heady turn of melody interspersed with vaguely Hawaiian lead parts. *Que?* is a terse funnel of serrated sound and *Initial Speed* exactly what its title implies: a spiral synthesiser motif alternating with Manzanera on guitars, various.

Songwise, *Listen Now*, and *Law And Order* open and close side one, both pieces sidestepping around a rhythm reminiscent of Andy Mackay's *Love Is The Drug* but with twice the snazz thanks to Bill MacCormick and drummer Dave Mattacks. *Listen Now* bridges unexpectedly through a Mel Collins sax solo into a military big band coda – sound for thought. *City of Light* treats Simon Ainley's vocals (Eno and Robert Wyatt crossed) over brutal staccato piano; the ominous atmospherics are reinforced by

Manzanera's chilling chord fractures. I haven't been this intimidated by studio sound since *Can's Tago Mago*. *Postcard Love* and *That Falling Feeling* round off; a pair of wryly arranged but profoundly depressing ballads: the, er, human catchment.

Just for the book, among those contributing to *Listen Now* are Brian Eno, Eddie Jobson, Francis Monkman and *Split Enz* Eddie Rayner (keyboards), Simon Phillips (drums), Kevin Godley (voices) and Lol Creme (*Gizmo*). *Listen Now* bears out its conceptual premise.

George Orwell's legacy has already inspired some remarkable music in Hugh Hopper's *1984* and Bowie's *Diamond Dogs*. Here's more of the same.

MAINSTREAM AVANT-GARDE TURNS POP/MoR
...AND CRITIC RETIRES CONFUSED
Jon Savage, *Sounds*, October 15th 1977
I DON'T KNOW what I expected but I thought it would be good (I mean credentials: *Roxy Music*/ Eno/*Diamond Head*/*Tomorrow Never Knows*/Nico/etc.) but this wasn't it... It would be very easy to write this album off as hip MoR. Whatever that means. Actually it's a very good pop album. Aaaaah, fragmentation! Paradoxically, the number of categories restricts you even more within them... This album doesn't fall outside them but cuts through enough to make the idea look silly. I suppose I'm trying to say that there are hidden strengths here which aren't immediately apparent and which take time to seep through. Like water dripping, or subtle muzak encroachment...

So what we have here is *Love Is The Drug Roxy*/*Diamond Head* style music, or music with enough of both in them to make it recognisable, mixed with other elements (disco bass/*CSNY-Beatles* harmonies/ritzy 'total package'' cover, i.e. down to the label centre) to make it an attractive product. In fact, at times the album reeks of *Beatles* through *10cc* – it's no accident that Kevin Godley and Lol Creme appear – tempered with Manzanera quirkiness.

Well so far it sounds like a mainstream avantgarde turns pop/MoR eventually style move, but wait... Look at the lyrics. Without exception/redemption, the songs are bitter, down. Communication breakdown/big city paranoia/Big Brother/synthetic media distance moving to total Isolation... 'Is it any wonder when you've got no power/When you pay a thief to keep it from you?'... 'And though they say that home is where the heart is/They don't know that this damned city's heart is dead...' Or: 'Saw your face on TV/You said it's alright have no fear/I'm here/Panic's ended/Your rights defended/From those who tried to tell you /About the other side of life...' sung oh so sweet, lilting.

Ooooh, how do you match the two? Do you need to? Like reggae maybe: analogous heavy message in sweet medium, except little kickback.

Bearing in mind its creators considerable pedigree, it wouldn't be too much to surmise that the record is fighting fire with fire: using the established commercial medium to get over message, mirroring bland synthetic control with cool, production distanced music... with taped airport ambience (ersatz synthetic through synthetic...). Mmmmmm.

Now: care is needed here because I'm not habituated to this stuff recently: but this doesn't inspire me like *Diamond Head* did. That seemed an album of joyous risks, like the riotous punning of *Miss Shapiro* – this is, after all, *801* and is more calculating, consistent, and cold-blooded. Objectively, this album is too excellent not to be rewarded starwise, but personally... A lack of vitality, a certain coldness at the centre worries me. What they want, I don't know... money? Cultural subversion? But some parts I really do like. What the hell: fire usually gets assimilated by fire and I have to feeling this'll happen here. But listen: it's fine... (retreats in confusion...).

Tim Lott, *Record Mirror*, 22nd October 1977

AN INTERESTING bastard. Not Manzanera, *801*. At the head, Manzanera with his borderline rock-jazz guitar. Avant-garde supremo, Eno. The kitsch bizarre Tim Finn of *Split Enz* and the hyperpop, Lol Creme and Kevin Godley. Drummer from the folk wave Dave Mattacks. The list goes on... on Eddie Jobson, Mel Collins, Francis Monkman; the result is, in a sense, inevitable, an unavoidable fusion of elemental, far-removed styles.

So you expect it to be fragmented, directionless, ego-tripping. You're wrong. It's a smart merger, the commercial formula of popjazz, highly technical but melodic instrumentals over perfect Crosby, Stills and Nash-brand harmonies. Unlike the *801 Live* album there are no long, difficult improvisations, no heavyweight techno wizard indigestibles. Only pop crafting and simple economy. There's a lot more accent on the lyrics than you might expect and though they ain't exactly sheer poetry, they're not embarrassing, which is unusual coming from a band who are primarily musicians. The main pitfall avoided, it's not too clever-clever, it's 'accessible'.

Listen now and you're going to like it without thinking.

VIVID TIME LEAP BY MANZANERA
Nottingham Evening Post, 25th November 1977

THE ALL-PERVADING thinkspeak dictatorship of George Orwell's *1984* has inspired many a rock musician over the years from Hugh Hopper's explicit *1984* to David Bowie's more oblique *Diamond Dogs* venture. Phil Manzanera's nightmare *Listen Now* (*Polydor*) makes the same time-jump to paint a more perceptively chilling and creepily vivid portrait than most before him, thanks to the underplayed power of the lyrics, dreamily hypnotic vocal delivery of Simon Ainley and the clean limbed dynamism of Manzanera's arrangement coupled with his own stylish guitar playing.

The bruisy-faced, whispering paranoiacs on the cover, trapped between heavy chains and the austere intimidating city sky-scape, pitch the mood perfectly for the ex-*Roxy Music* guitarist and the explorations of *801*. *City of Light* subtitled *42nd Street Blues* indicates the horrors of no escaping into the dark anonymous corners – the oppressive swirl-echo vocals, deep-jabbing piano and menacing guitar riffs leaving you two feet tall. But *Flight 19* is a well-crafted piece of quality rock with the same vivacity as *10cc's* seminal *Sheet Music* set. In fact, Kevin Godley turns up here on chorus lines and Lol Creme cranks up the lush effects of their *gizmo* gadgetry.

The opener *Listen Now* steals a stealthy hook and sets the uncomfortable tenor of claustrophobic futurism while Mel Collins injects incursive sax and big band effects. *Law and Order*, about media-manipulation, is wrapped around a similarly purposeful Bill MacCormick-Dave Mattacks bass-drums assemblage. And two black-lined ballads of ghostly despair *Postcard Love* and *That Falling Feeling* come between you and wipe-out, but only just. The set also includes three instrumentals: *Island* with Manzanera's guitars set in relaxed counterpoint to Brian Eno's synth pastelwash; *Que* a jazzy tunnel of energy and *Initial Speed* a synth cascade by Francis Monkman brushed against the guitarist's response and Collins' soprano sax slide.

Less gregarious than *Diamond Head* it carries a sting in the tail. As Big Brother would tell Winston Smith: cut out the thoughtcrime and *Listen Now*.

TUNE IN TO PHIL'S NEW SOUND
Prescot and Huyton Reporter, 11th November 1977
SOPHISTICATED rock craftsmanship of the highest class – that's the latest album from former *Roxy Music* guitarist Phil Manzanera and his band *801*. Title *Listen Now (Island)*; it sees Phil and his impressive crew treading a distinctly Orwellian path in almost every sense. This excursion into *1984* comprises nine tracks, all but three featuring vocals from Manzanera's co-writers Bill and Ian MacCormick backed by a fluid line-up of other musicians. The album also provides the first showcase for Lol Creme and Kevin Godley's fabled *Gizmo*, the amazing gadget which bows instead of plucks a guitar, outside their ambitious new *Consequence* triple-set.

Listen Now kicks-off with its title track, which gets the listener right into the apprehensive, unsettling atmosphere of the LP. The track is haunting and whispery, Simon Ainley's lead vocal rasping out the depressingly sinister lyrics ('Everywhere the sheep creeping to the slaughter / Cold weather coming people feel the fire / Living on Dead End Street ,with no desire'). Then comes the fine single *Flight 19* with a classical construction and adventurous use by Manzanera of guitars. Eno throws in a few treatments here and there, and the *Gizmo* apparently pops its head up, though I've no idea where.

A note calmness is struck by *Island*. It's a fine instrumental with contributions from Simon Phillips (drums), Bill (bass), Eddie Jobson (*Fender* piano). Eno (synthesiser) and, of course, the man himself on guitars. *Law and Order* closes the side complete with a catchy *Love is the Drug* style rhythm. It also continues deathly theme with lines like: 'Curfew starts now / Get off the streets and bolt the door'.

The other side begins with *Que?* another Manzanera instrumental, closely followed by *City of Light*. A perfectly produced slice of sheer studio intimidation the track stands as a highlight of the set. The man's icy guitar javelins boost the whole thing superbly. *Initial Speed* follows, and the instrumental beauty chatters along, weaving in and out of a synthesiser whirlwind with a fetching saxophone line from Mel Collins. Ballads *Postcard Love* and *That Falling Feeling* round things off with more depression and doom.

And the George Orwell legacy which inspired works like Bowie's *Diamond Dogs* has struck once more. This kind of thing is not all that new to Phil Manzanera though, as his work with Nico, John Cale and his pre-Roxy outfit *Quiet Sun* proves. But, after witnessing and savouring the magnificence of the recent *801 Live* album, I must admit I was surprised by the contents and overall theme and concept of *Listen Now* though by no means disappointed. It's a creepy one, but I think you'll like it! Rating: 8½

Manchester Evening News, 18th October 1977
ONCE POLL WINNING GUITARIST with *Roxy Music*, Phil Manzanera is back on the album scene with the second LP from the band *The 801*. The band plays Manchester University on November 2. In some respects it's a disappointing disc after what was a great debut disc. The music has strayed into being MOR rock but for all that it is admittedly catchy and melodic for night adventures. Title of the LP is *Listen Now*. The single is *Flight 19*.

Chris West, *Western Mail*, 27th October 1977
MORE IMMEDIATELY ACCESSIBLE is a collection from ex-*Roxy Music* guitarist Phil Manzanera. A series of tracks recorded over an 18-month period, which accounts for the ups and downs. *Listen Now* (Polydor 2302 074) sneaks up stealthily and insinuates itself coyly into one's memory bank, to be hummed at random moments. Echoes of *Roxy*, naturally, but that's no bad thing.

Penny Valentine, *Time Out*, 18th November 1977
Phil Manzanera/*801: Listen Now* (Polydor).

HIP EASY LISTENING doesn't have to be a derogatory term, as Manzanera proves with this latest delivery by a re-assembled *801*. Two years in the making, while the ex-*Roxy* guitarist flitted between other projects, *Listen Now* is an amalgam of influences from *10cc* to *Weather Report*. The music has an immediacy and impact rare in such loose-knit combines and although you find yourself singing *Flight 19* in the bath and the whole album takes on a cosy familiarity after a few plays, this is not necessarily a problem.

What is? The extraordinary discrepancy between intent and result. While the Manzanera/MacCormick lyrics reflect the album cover's paranoia and angst, they become subservient to a music dedicated to shifting the mood in the opposite direction. The result detracts from the hardly original but well-crafted nightmares of urban alienation and despair, leaving a pleasant but ultimately confusing set.

Pshawn Cassidy, *Trouser Press*, January 1978
Phil Manzanera/*801 Listen Now*, Polydor 2302 074

BRYAN FERRY LOOKS LIKE A CHAMELEON and Phil Manzanera acts like one. Perhaps that's why they still get along. *Diamond Head*, Phil's first solo album (released over two years ago), was a warm and charming patchwork of contributions from Eno, John Wetton and Bill MacCormick; aurally disparate but all first-rate material. *801 Live* was sort of an Odd Ditties Phil/Eno style. And now, I suppose due to the unspoken-but-apparently-so end of *Roxy Music*, he has put together a real band and graced us with *Listen Now*, an obsessively Enoid, cold concept album – the pragmatic cynic's guide to today and tomorrow.

The primary musicians are Manzanera on guitar, vocalist Simon Ainley, lyricist Bill MacCormick on bass, and drummer Simon Phillips. Appearances are also made by Mel Collins, Lol Creme, Eno, Tim Finn, Kevin Godley, Eddie Jobson, Billy Livsey, Ian MacCormick, Dave Mattacks, Francis Monkman, Eddie Raynor and John White.

As a whole, the magnificently packaged *Listen Now* is a baffling record; philosophically it leaves much to be desired and musically is rather standoffish. Yet I keep listening to it over and over again and suspect I will shortly become addicted. The opening title cut is a tremendous pastiche with a *Wall Street Shuffle* back-beat provided by Godley and Mattacks, the ambience of *Diamond Head's Alma*, a big-band break courtesy of Mel Collins, and chanting refrain of 'now listen, now now listen' identical to the 'shop steward' chorus in Manzanera/Eno's *Miss Shapiro*.

Flight 19 (the single), which I had written off as bland pop, sounds much better in the context of the LP but is still primarily a vehicle for

Ainley's creepy cloned Eno voice. *Island* is a beautiful instrumental reminiscent of *Another Green World*, with darkly lyrical guitar and bass interweavings. *Law and Order*, while a nice song, verbally is painfully cliched, sort of a *Dragnet* cast reunion in 1984.

Que?, a brief instrumental, opens the second side and segues into *City of Light*, which begins by strangely but successfully pairing the percussion of Eno's *Sombre Reptiles* and the middle break in *A Day in the Life*. *Initial Speed*, a weak instrumental, reveals the Godley/Creme gizmo; in this case truth is surely better than consequences. *Postcard Love* is a beautiful bittersweet song of unrequited love: 'You bared your heart/She trumped it every time'. *That Falling Feeling* closes the album with some fine guitar and a perfect description of the mental state of Manzanera/MacCormick et al. on *Listen Now*. I hope they cheer up.

Western Evening Mail, October 1977
Phil Manzanera - *801* - *Listen Now* (Polydor):
THE FRONT COVER reveals austere, imposing, faceless skyscrapers embracing bleak-shot heavens. In the dank shadows lie a couple of dazed yet defiant packages of humanity. The scene is completed by an indestructible chain running through the images, while the couple's hunted faces twist up out of the corner. An alarming document, a sort of visual account of the totalitarianism conceived in Orwell's 1984.

Actually no such affiliations are mentioned either on the sleeve or during the album. But that's the kind of mood it pursues. I hesitate to say 'concept' but I suggest that it's featured here in its best and most effective form. Through his solo ventures *Diamond Head* and *801 Live*, Manzanera has followed a challenging course. The music has been mainly striking and vigorous and is in many respects as contemporary as much of the material currently being produced by David Bowie. But while Bowie is apparently prepared to operate in a series of bleak and often disturbing scenarios, Manzanera's *801* seems to strike a more optimistic note amid a string of striking and intricately constructed musical collages. The depressing theme implied by the cover is pursued by the magnificent title track. Its fierce chords gradually eroding the attractive opening themes. *City of Light*, placing greater accent on its lyrical content is no less disturbing.

As a whole *Listen Now* is an ambitious attempt by linking these themes to achieve what many would say is impossible. Through its sheer effrontery not to mention outstanding material and musicianship, it's one of the outstanding works of the year. It defies categorisation and for that reason should be investigated by one and all.

Mike Mills, *What's On in London*, 4th November 1977
Phil Manzanera, *801: Listen Now* (Polydor 2302 074).
GUITARIST WITH THE NOW DORMANT *Roxy Music*, Manzanera has always dazzled with his individual and inventive playing. Coming to *Roxy* from his own *Quiet Sun* group he reformed the band for the album *Mainstream* and has always kept his hand in with adventurous work outside the hit-making ensemble and made the notable solo set *Diamond Head*.

With *801*, already acclaimed for their live album in 1976 (with different personnel) Phil has produced what must be his best work to date. This album is a classic, instant and appealing, yet rewarding to repeated careful listening. The line-up of musicians varies from track to track, and there are guest appearances by Lol Creme and Kevin Godley (with Gizmo) among many others. Three tracks are instrumentals: *Initial Speed, Island*, and *Que?* are splendid, but the main strength of the album for me is the surprising success of the songs as songs. They are beautifully constructed with strong lyrics which generally escape pretentiousness.

Phil Manzanera. your time is now.

Michael Bloom, *Rolling Stone*
Listen Now, Phil Manzanera/*801*, Polydor
LISTEN NOW, A STUDIO LP recorded last year, deals less with group fibre and more with subtler sonic alchemy. Texture is still of paramount importance, but Manzanera achieves it here by carefully manipulating a smorgasbord of sound effects (again with Eno as his lieutenant) into a dark, moody canvas reminiscent of *Pink Floyd*. Lyrics which might otherwise have seemed simple-minded instead provide a bitter paranoiac focus. A few reminders of virtuosity, like *Initial Speed*, brighten the doomy landscape and round out the record. Throughout, Phil Manzanera proves he's got a singular and profound understanding of rock dynamics. Now all he has to do is gather a permanent touring band and take the world by storm.

Appendix 13: The *Listen Now* Tour Press Pack

IN 1975 PHIL MANZANERA, until then known to the rock audience chiefly as poll-winning guitarist with the enormously successful *Roxy Music*, emerged from a brief bout of frenetic activity in the recording studio with two albums of disturbing originality – *Diamond Head*, a solo-venture of self-penned instrumentals and songs (the latter in collaboration with such luminaries as Robert Wyatt and Eno), and *Mainstream*, a *Melody Maker* 'Album Of The Month' nomination, featuring Phil's pre-*Roxy* unit *Quiet Sun*.

Such was the critical and commercial enthusiasm for both records that Phil was back in the studio before the end of the year, working on backing tracks for the follow-up to *Diamond Head*. However, events were to conspire against a repeat of the rapidity with which that album and its companion-piece had been produced. Always ready to lend aid when asked – in 1974 alone he appeared either as guitarist, co-composer, or producer on *Roxy's Country Life*, Eno's *Here Come The Warm Jets* and *Taking Tiger Mountain (By Strategy)*, Bryan Ferry's *Another Time, Another Place*, John Cale's *Fear*, and Nico's *The End* – he found himself constantly interrupted by invitations to play elsewhere.

First there was *Slow Dazzle*, another album with Cale, then *Siren*, *Roxy's* fifth album, and a huge quantity of touring with the band – eventually to result in the 'live' album *Viva!*, for which Phil personally went through the tapes of every gig Roxy had recorded. Then there was producing *Split Enz*, a New Zealand band he'd caught during *Roxy's* 1974 tour of the Antipodes, followed by his part in the presentation at the Albert Hall of Stomu Yamashta's *Go* in partnership with Stevie Winwood.

Despite the pace and fullness of his career, Phil had managed to put sufficient work in on his own album when yet another project intervened, cancelling the sessions set for final mixing. This was *The 801*, an apparently random collection of 'star' instrumentalists who – and this must surely be a 'first' in this field – belied all expectation by appearing at the 1976 *Reading Festival* as a genuine *group*, not only avoiding all the usual pitfalls of competitive self-indulgence and token audience pleasing, but producing music with a coherence and scope of its own.

'The musical highpoint of the weekend', said John Peel. 'The most interesting and adventurous music of the day', said *New Musical Express*. Later, when *801 Live* (a recording of the band's third and final gig at London's *Queen Elizabeth Hall*) was released, the superlatives flew thicker and Richard Williams devoted his *M.M.* column to a rave review of the band which he astutely praised for their controlled eclecticism, singling out

416

in particular the visionary reinterpretation of *The Beatles'* '66 classic *Tomorrow Never Knows*.

But *801*, at least in its initial guise, was regarded by the participants merely as a testing-ground and no attempt was made to hold the original line-up together. Slide-guitarist Lloyd Watson returned to his semi-professional life in Peterborough, drummer Simon Phillips joined the Jack Bruce Band, keyboard-player Francis Monkman went back to sessions and harpsichord recitals, and Eno headed for Berlin to join David Bowie. At this point Bryan Ferry asked Phil to come with him on his world tour. He agreed – and the final sessions for the solo album were put back until July 1977, at which time *Listen Now* was at long last completed.

Released in September, it will be credited to Phil in collaboration with *The 801* and, for the occasion, a new line-up has been organised to handle 'live' performances. Of the originals only two remain – Phil and his long-time colleague from *Quiet Sun* Bill MacCormick (bass, vocals). Together, on and off, for ten years, they met at Dulwich College in South London, playing in several groups before leaving school to form *Quiet Sun* in 1970. Phil was from Colombia via Cuba where, as a child, he'd witnessed the entry into Havana of the triumphant freedom fighters of Fidel Castro. He was a thoughtful guitarist, onto the serpentine double-tracking of Randy California, a form-conscious player with a brand of mingled spontaneity and deliberation reminiscent of George Harrison.

The college equivalent of a university activist, Bill progressed from disaffection to vocals to drums to bass which he took up at the inauguration of *Quiet Sun*, once it was realized that nobody else could play the bass-lines he had written. Living close to the legendary Dalmore Road home of the *Soft Machine*, they played several dates with Robert Wyatt's *Symbiosis* and, when 1972 saw the departure of Phil to *Roxy Music* and the big-time, Bill was Robert Wyatt's choice for a bass-player in his new band *Matching Mole*. While Phil toured and recorded with *Roxy* and wrote *Amazona*, Bill toured and recorded with *Matching Mole* and wrote *Gloria Gloom* with Robert.

Matching Mole folded, shortly after their second album (*Little Red Record*) when Robert Wyatt suffered an incapacitating accident. Meanwhile, *Roxy Music* went from stride to stride. Bill played on Eno's *Here Come the Warm Jets* and got into local politics; Phil toured the world and co-wrote with Bryan *Out of the Blue* and *Prairie Rose*. As soon as the original tension had relaxed and he had some time to himself, Phil invited Bill, along with Robert and Eno, to guest on his solo album *Diamond Head* and join in a specially reformed *Quiet Sun* to record the compositions that were to become known as *Mainstream*. The material – with the exception of *The Flex*, *Big Day*, *Miss Shapiro*, and *Diamond Head* itself – was all derived from

Quiet Sun, one song, *Frontera*, gaining a new Spanish lyric from Robert Wyatt.

Returning to the post-*Siren Roxy*, Phil recorded backing-tracks for *Listen Now* whenever he could. Bill did some studio work with Gary Windo, who he'd known since the days of *Symbiosis* and had worked with on Robert Wyatt's *Ruth is Stranger than Richard*. While Phil awaited the expected break-up of *Roxy Music*, Bill went to America and interviewed Senator George McGovern for *Streetlife*, not knowing that the paper had already gone bankrupt.

Finally, *The 801* found Phil and Bill back in the same group. When it disbanded, it was only a matter of time before it would be reformed. This time Eno won't be there (once again he's collaborating with Bowie) and Simon Phillips too is absent (contracted to Jack Bruce). Replacing Francis Monkman on keyboards and singing will be Dave Skinner (ex-*Uncle Dog*, ex-*Clancy*), whilst another Dulwich rocker, Simon Ainley (lead vocals, guitar) was included in the *801* line-up. Finalising the line-up, on drums will be none other than The Great Paul Thompson, powerhouse of *Roxy Music*.

Listen Now itself consists of nine tracks – all but three featuring vocals from Simon and Bill backed by a more or less fluid line-up of other musicians. *Initial Speed*, *Island*, and *Que?* are instrumentals during which the omnipresence of Phil Manzanera on composition, production, and guitar comes into its own. (NB at certain points, one can witness the first use outside *10cc* of Godley and Creme's synthetic secret, the fabled *Gizmo*). Of the remaining songs, three, *Postcard Love*, *Law and Order* and *City of Light* were written by Manzanera and MacCormick and three *Flight 19*, *That Falling Feeling*, and *Listen Now* itself by Phil with Bill's brother, Ian.

AUTUMN TOUR
Date   Town & Venues
October
11th Cambridge University (Lady Mitchell Hall)
12th Southampton University (Old Refectory)
13th Guildford, Surrey University
14th Norwich, University of East Anglia
15th Leicester University
16th Birmingham Town Hall
18th Plymouth, Castaways' Leisure Centre
20th Oxford Polytechnic
21st Colchester, University of Essex
22nd Nottingham University (Portland Building)
23rd London, Victoria Palace
25th Southport, Floral Hall

26th Liverpool University (Mountford Hall)
27th Huddersfield Polytechnic
28th Newcastle, Mayfair Ballroom
29th Hull University

November
1st Swansea, Brangwyn Hall
2nd Manchester University
3rd Falkirk, Maniqui Ballroom
4th Dundee Student Association
5th Glasgow, Strathclyde University
6th Redcar, Coatham Bowl

PHIL MANZANERA DISCOGRAPHY:

Diamond Head
Quiet Sun - Mainstream
801 Live
Listen Now - 23rd Sept. 1977
Flight 19 - 9th Sept. Single

APPENDIX 14: *RANDOM HOLD* – THE ALLAN JONES ARTICLE

THE MIDDLE CLASS ANSWERS BACK
'We're all as mercenary as the next man. It's not impossible that we'll end up like every other rock band in the world' – Random Hold.
ALLAN JONES thinks otherwise, Pictures by BARRY PLUMMER
Melody Maker, 9th December 1978

MONDAY NIGHT, somewhere in Bermondsey. Lost of course. Wandering bewildered and frozen through the utterly confusing warren of backstreets, alleys and dockside dead-ends crushed between the river and the Jamaica Road. Collar up, hands so deep in pockets that your shoulders are pulled right down around your knees. Just a maze, down here, of darkness and the occasional reassurance of the sodium glare. Derelict factories lurk in the shadows. Rusted curls of barbed wire and broken bottles defy intruders along the tops of the shattered walls flanking the narrow backtracks. Hope on a slow wane.

And just about to surrender to the misery of the adventure and retreat to the nearest pub when you stumble frostbitten upon the *New Concordia Wharf.* The heart rises in quiet celebration. Contact made. At last. You stumble with a distinct lack of nimble athleticism past the abandoned autos, fall into a concrete passage violently lit by naked overhead bulbs. Flight cases litter the long hallway. Tattered posters and graffiti on the walls. Push open heavy fire-door, into soundproofed rehearsal studio. Say hi to *Random Hold*.

Group looks disenchanted: not in the most optimistic of moods. They have been waiting through a long, cold afternoon for an A&R chap from *Polydor*. He called an hour ago to cancel the meeting. *Random Hold* are disappointed and angry. They are reluctant to play. The reporter feels uncomfortable. The group decide to throw caution and reticence out the window. They will play.

A left-to-right (*Ed.* Actually, right-to-left but hell, who cares) picture caption (with brief biographical details) would read:

David Ferguson – Age 25. Synthesizers and voice. Previously member of experimental music group, *Manscheinen*. Founder member of *Random Hold*. Studied Serbo-Croat at the *London School of Slavonic and East European Studies*. Worked as sound engineer and wrote scores for theatre productions in Edinburgh, London and Stoke.

David Rhodes – Age 22. Guitar and vocals. Previously member of experimental group *Manscheinen*. Founder member of *Random Hold*. Studied Fine Art in Leeds and London.

Simon Ainley – Age 24. Guitar and vocal. Previously member of Phil Manzanera's *801*. Performed on *Listen Now* and *K-Scope*. Studied architecture in Manchester. Joined *Random Hold* in April, 1978.

Bill MacCormick – Age 27. Bass and vocal. Previously member of *Quiet Sun*, *Matching Mole*, *Gong* and *801*. Performed and composed for/on: *Matching Mole*, *Matching Mole's Little Red Record*, *Quiet Sun's Mainstream*, Eno's *Here Come The Warm Jets*, *Before And After Science* and *Music For Films*, Robert Wyatt's *Ruth Is Stranger Than Richard*, Phil Manzanera's *Diamond Head*, *801 Live*, *Listen Now* and *K-Scope*.

David Leach – Age 23. Drums. Previously member of the *Lesser Known Tunisians*. Studied Philosophy and Politics in Southampton. Joined *Random Hold* in October 1978.

115 L to R: Leach, MacCormick, Ainley, Rhodes, Ferguson

I TAKE A SEAT against the wall of the studio. The band tune up across the room, about a yard in front of me: the group looks self-conscious. 'A captive audience, at last'. says Ainley, nervously. 'The largest audience we've ever played to', says MacCormick. 'It would be very embarrassing if he started throwing things', says Rhodes. 'This is the first number', says Ferguson. 'Sorry', says Leach, dropping a drum stick.

RANDOM HOLD'S music successfully eludes any convenient classification, which is not to suggest that it is at all esoteric or even

421

overtly experimental. They have recently been ranked alongside new, ostensibly alternative bands like *The Pop Group*, *This Heat*, *Cabaret Voltaire*, *The Art Bears*, *The Human League*, *Metabolist* and (gulp) *Throbbing Gristle*, a desperate bunch whose predecessors are supposed to include the likes of *Can*, *Faust*, *Henry Cow* and others who pioneered the links between rock and the electronic avant-garde. *Random Hold* are not satisfied with the categorisation, for reasons they will later explain.

They play, maybe seven or eight pieces on Monday at the *Wharf Music* studios, and it is difficult from such a brief introduction (in conspicuously curious circumstances) to either coherently describe, or fully assess, the immediate impact of their music. It is instantly arresting; not at all remote or intimidating in any self-consciously experimental fashion. They are clearly not reluctant to make full use of the more orthodox, musical vocabulary of rock: several songs are built around the kind of nagging, almost dogged, riffs of conventional heavy rock. There are harmonies! Melodic songs with beginnings, middles and ends (though not necessarily in that order)! The lyrics are oblique, cryptic, maybe, but not obscure. But any recognisable device is filtered through an intriguing process of reconstruction. They are predictable only in their eclecticism, and their determination to eschew familiar constructions.

Ferguson's synthesizers and pre-recorded tape loops create an impressionistic backdrop which, though limited, is used to precise effect. MacCormick is a bass player of consistent invention and Leach anchors the music solidly in the here and now. No effete meanderings here, mate. Ainley and Rhodes (a very interesting young guitarist) mount zigzag guitar assaults and the principal vocal leads (the only number they did which failed to impress conclusively featured Ferguson on lead vocal – it was, I think, something called *Littlewoods Jeans* – and he sounded, unfortunately, like a BBC announcer on the edge of a nervous breakdown commentating on a royal parade).

There were moments – as they veered more toward conventional rock – when I thought that maybe eight years ago they would probably have been described by Chris Welch as a progressive group. I imagined the band with a light show and psychedelic slides, playing solos with their backs to their audience. Then David Rhodes would throw in a fractured guitar line and it would somehow be echoed by MacCormick, and the music would take off on another tangent and the image would be dispelled.

The songs that most firmly lodged themselves in the memory were I think, *We Are People Out of Love* and *Montgomery Clift* (with *The Ballad* coming in a close third). *People Out Of Love*, like most of *Random Hold's* material, is fiercely emotional – though it's given to no tortured histrionics – with an underbelly of black humour. It opens with a synthetic drum tape-loop and a repetitive synthesizer *motif*, over which David Rhodes, in a

422

taut vocal performance, delivers the sly, ominous lyric. The atmosphere is close to that created by *Roxy Music* on *Strictly Confidential*: the melody set against an almost neurotic confessional from the singer (shades, too of *In Every Dream Home A Heartache*, perhaps). Rhode's monologue continues, with the narrator expressing his emotional disaffection in increasingly violent terms, as the other instruments overwhelm the backing tapes. Rhodes begins to thrash out a rhythm part, which Ainley counterpoints with discreet blues guitar – the effect is ingenious and mesmerising. The piece concludes with a frenetic crescendo, with Rhodes almost purple in the face with anxiety, urging himself into a disconcerting frenzy.

Montgomery Clift an earlier song, I think (at least it appears on a tape made by *Random Hold* last April), is constructed around a similar musical premise. It takes as its theme Clift's curious neurotic habit of hanging himself from windows whenever he was struck by one of his frequent depressions. A great idea for a song. *Random Hold* invest the disturbing scenario with a characteristic intensity, full of creeping menace which again reaches a crazed climax. Listening to the April tape, there are echoes in Ainley's vocal of Howard Devoto's declamatory style of brooding narration: an affectation that has now been usurped by a more individual reading. The piece ends. I'm impressed. The group don't know quite what to do. I wonder whether I should applaud. I think it might be a little ostentatious in the circumstances. 'Well', says MacCormick. 'He's still here'.

I HAD MEANT, originally, to travel with *Random Hold* to Oxford last Friday. They were playing a rare gig at *Pembroke College*. The group's gig sheet, at the moment, is as blank as a sheet of ice, a predicament they don't anticipate will be rectified before Christmas. The New Year, they hope, will introduce a change in their fortunes. The Oxford gig – for which they were thankful and think was a success – was typical of the ill-luck that has persistently afflicted them. They returned to their van after a meal to find that someone had let down all the tyres. 'And they've probably pissed in the petrol tank', a college porter casually informed them. They were still trying to repair the damage at 4 a.m. on Saturday. Oy vey!

This was a minor incident, however, compared to some of the difficulties they've faced this year. 'We're in a difficult, irritating situation', MacCormick explains later on Monday, in a pub around the corner from the rehearsal studio. 'We're not short of interest. Seven or eight record companies have already expressed interest in us. Four or five have been down to see us. We've got a publishing company interested. So were not short of that kind of interest from, shall we say; the business. But were caught in this vicious circle, whereby we can't get gigs because nobody knows who we are. And until we do some gigs, of course, nobody's going to have the chance to find out anything about us. Nobody's going to give us any publicity. Nobody's going to write about us. And until we break out of that, things simply won't move fast enough'.

The problem, he feels, is not peculiar to *Random Hold*. It's typical, he thinks, of the indifference most new bands encounter and have quickly to overcome if they are to survive and prosper. The difficulties are perhaps more emphasised and critical though in their case because they are without a manager, and without finance to subsidise them through this crucial period. At present, MacCormick is actually financing the group himself. I hope he has an understanding bank manager.

They have further been plagued by differences of opinion with various agencies, principally *Albion*, who control the *Nashville* – an influential showcase still for an emerging band – and also the *Hope & Anchor*. 'They're vastly overburdened with acts, of course, but for various reasons they're not fantastically keen about booking us'. This has less to do with *Albion's* reluctance to involve themselves with a band like *Random Hold* with a reputation for playing experimental music than with the band's refusal to sign a contract with *Albion Records* and *Albion's* publishing company. *Albion*, then, wanted, the whole *Random Hold* package:

'They wanted everything, and we weren't prepared to sign ourselves to a publishing deal with a company which has no track record, no international tie-up or anything. Nothing, really, in Europe or America. It would have been ludicrous. Anyway, as soon as we refused to sign that deal, the agency lost interest in us immediately. As it is, we fortunately have one of the major publishing companies interested and they're now trying to negotiate a recording deal for us. So we have that interest, which is encouraging. But the frustrating thing is that we need to play, to take that interest one step further. To persuade somebody to actually sign us'.

MACCORMICK accepts gracefully that the kind of music being pursued by *Random Hold* fits uneasily into most fashionably accepted styles at the moment. He is, nevertheless, convinced that, given the opportunity, audiences will react favourably to their music. So far, they have experienced no considerable antipathy, although they were received recently with considerable hostility by an *Adam & The Ants* audience at the *Rock Garden*. This, they feel, was an isolated incident, provoked less by their music than the impatience of the audience who had ears only for the *Ants* (unfortunate buggers).

'If it had been a Beatles re-union', says Ferguson, 'they would've been gobbed off stage. *The Ants* have a very, very fanatical audience. They don't want to hear anybody else. And they certainly didn't want to hear us. There were other contributory factors. It was before Bill joined, and at that time we were using pre-recorded bass parts. And they thought we were miming everything. And they didn't like that'.

'As soon as I got to the microphone', Ainley adds drolly, 'someone in the audience shouted 'Fuck off! Go away!' Charming, I thought'.

'I was in the audience', adds MacCormick, 'and it was very unpleasant. *Adam and the Ants'* audience was just a bunch of little fascists. That was the problem. The nastiest audience I've ever seen'.

'One of the bouncers was bottled', says David Rhodes, contributing to the catalogue of disaster. 'We found a knife under the coach we'd turned up in. Two guys were evicted for carrying meat cleavers'. My God, this never happened to the *Joystrings*.

'I should say', comments Ainley, 'that Adam did apologise later. He's rather a decent chap, really. His audience are murder, though'.

I ASK, IN AN ATTEMPT to chart the genesis of *Random Hold*, the extent to which the basic concept of the group has changed in emphasis and direction since the addition of MacCormick and Leach to the original trio of Ferguson and Rhodes and Ainley. Ferguson and Rhodes, the two founder members, are initially reluctant to retrace the group's entire history. MacCormick persuades them that it would be informative.

'Well', Rhodes begins, 'we went along to the *801* gig at the *Queen Elizabeth Hall* (this would be in the late summer of 1976) and we didn't like it at all. And we met in the pub afterwards and said, 'Right, tomorrow we'll start on something of our own. We've decided that we don't like that. Let's do something ourselves'. I'm not sure what we didn't like. It wasn't quite working properly. It looked as if there was a lot of talent going to waste. It wasn't exciting. It was playing very safe'.

Ferguson: 'It wasn't dangerous'. Rhodes: 'It seemed very easy. We wanted to try to set up something that maybe wasn't quite so easy'. Ferguson, at this time, had never played an instrument. Rhodes had not played guitar for several years, since quitting a band called *Mad Wog and Englishman*. 'They had one, too', chips in MacCormick. 'And I don't mean an Englishman'.

'The feeling then', says Ferguson, recalling the impulse to form some kind of group, 'was similar to what became the great punk adage – you know, the feeling that anybody can play'.

Rhodes: 'That was a very important part of it. I suppose our desire to do something different was as much a reaction to the mainstream of music, and the way it was going down. The desire to do something different was something we shared with punk, in that respect'.

Ferguson: 'Except that we didn't at that time intend to become professional, as it were. We just wanted originally to do little arty workshop things. It was originally very vague, I suppose. The original intention, when we first got together, was just to have one instrument – the guitar and lots of tape effects, prerecorded tapes and things. To experiment with textures. Because I'd never played an instrument in my life. I had an old bass guitar, and the second week we were together I bought a stylophone and a wah-wah pedal. And that's basically what we used'.

'My God', says MacCormick. 'What am I doing with these people?'

FOR THEIR FIRST VENTURE, Rhodes and Ferguson assumed the name *Manscheinen*, and they recorded a tape of their improvisations which was, as they put it, 'scattered amongst the press and disc-jockey fraternity'. No one took much notice. I recall, now, actually receiving a copy. Listening to it now is an amusing experience: clearly influenced by the Eno-Fripp experiments heard on *No Pussyfooting* and *Evening Star*, it consists of extended, largely abstract, formless pieces; tape loops and dislocated melodic fragments that spend an inordinate amount of time running slowly on the spot. Ferguson admits that these experiments were useful as a kind of apprenticeship, little more.

They soon realised the limitations of their ideas in this context, and began to write more considered and concise songs. At which point Simon Ainley first became involved – They kept asking me, and I eventually ran out of excuses'. Ainley alludes vaguely, to his involvements prior to his work with Manzanera, and *801* on *Listen Now*. 'I was at university... played in a few stand-up Chuck Berry rock 'n' roll bands...'.

And', says MacCormick, cheerfully blowing the gaff: 'he was at the same boarding school as Phil'. It later emerges that both Ferguson and Rhodes were there, too an incestuous little bunch, *non*? Ainley having graduated from university, began writing songs – 'I decided I wanted to become a rock 'n' roll star' – which he later sent to Manzanera asking for the guitarist's opinion and advice: 'Phil didn't like the songs at all, but thought he could use my voice. And a star was born'.

Ainley joined *Random Hold* shortly after the original duo suffered an apparently horrendous time with a drummer called Peter Phipps, a former member of the *Glitter Band*, no less. Ferguson: 'He had an enormous, gigantic kit. It would've taken up half the stage of the *Rainbow*. Deafeningly loud. We were able to lose him, fortunately'.

Rhodes: 'So there was the three of us... David, myself and Simon. And then Bill decided we were in need of salvation and came in and sacked our managers for us, took us into an eight-track studio to record the demo, and generally made himself so indispensable that we asked him to join a day later'.

'I must admit', says MacCormick, continuing a story which is beginning to assume epic proportions, 'that invitations to go and see these two (FR) had been many. And I'd always managed to find a reason for not going

Then when Simon joined they did a gig at the *Nashville*. I was, inevitably, invited. I couldn't find an excuse to refuse. So I turned up expecting, if not the worst, at least not being able to tap my foot or even nod my head to the music. And, actually, in the middle of the set I did find myself tapping my foot to it. And, I had to admit, I was rather impressed by it. They were obviously going around in ever-increasing circles at the time, though, with their management and other people. So I offered my assistance in whatever way they thought might be useful. So they immediately took all my money. And now I'm broke.'

THE CONVERSATION, at about this point begins to veer into a general debate about the attitudes of the record companies to music that defied various established conventions, and the influence of punk in forcing a reassessment of the traditional views of the music establishment which need not in any detail detain us here. The thought strikes me, though, that *Random Hold* might be seen by many recent converts to punk and its perspectives as just a bunch of academics wanking around on the fringes of rock 'n' roll, affecting experimental attitudes.

MacCormick: 'It's one of the great fallacies of modern culture that rock music is a working-class music. The great explosion of pop music in the Sixties came from the art schools. And I reckon, at least, that rock music is a middle-class music'.

Ferguson: 'To criticise us for our educational backgrounds is nonsense. It's like saying we can't feel any emotion or passion. Passion is not to do with things like *Urry Up 'Arry We're Goin' Down The Pub*... That's pathetic. That's just drivel. A pathetic fallacy. A really spurious working-class statement. You can't ask us to be as simple as that. You can't take simplistic stances if you don't think simplistically. If you go around saying 'All politicians are cheats, all politicians are liars', then you are just patently, obviously, ignorant'.

MacCormick: 'One of the things that was said about the new wave was that it was all about returning rock 'n' roll to its working-class roots. In reality, it didn't really have any working-class roots to return to. If you look at, Jagger, say, or Lennon and McCartney, you see it's not true. Lennon and McCartney might have come from Liverpool, which certainly has a fairly large working-class population, but they both came from essentially middle-class families. And even if they were working-class it, proves nothing. Think of Bryan Ferry, fair enough, his father was a miner in County Durham. But you look at the path Bryan took on his career – he's an art school man. And there has probably been a greater middle-class influence on his approach to his life and work then any working-class influence, I'm sure that he'd admit that. The influence of him being the son of a County Durham miner is minimal. And it was from the very start. He's obviously developed further away from that the more he's mixed in sophisticated society, but its influence was minimal from the start. I'm afraid the true influence of the working-class in rock music is very small. And I suppose there are very simple reasons for it. The simple reason is that it's a very expensive kind of career. There's an enormous expense involved in putting together a group…'

Ferguson: 'If my parents weren't prepared to support me to a certain extent, I wouldn't be able to do this. I don't see why I shouldn't admit that'.

MacCormick: 'I think it applies to all of us here. If it wasn't for the indulgence of our parents over the years then we would have succumbed to ordinary jobs or topped ourselves. And I think that's true of most musicians. I think when you get something like that *Sham 69* single, it's very much like the attitude of your average TV programmer – 'This is what you want, this is what you get, because you're the working class'. They're supposed to want the *Sun* and the *Daily Mirror*. They're supposed to want rubbish. It's talking down to people. It's assuming all sorts of things about people: And it's outrageous.'

MACCORMICK HAS NOT YET been prominently featured as a writer in *Random Hold* – though, they might introduce to their current repertoire *Walking Through Heaven's Door* and *Gone Flying* both of which appeared on *K-Scope* but his songs, especially, those he contributed to *Listen Now* (he and his brother, Ian, wrote all the lyrics for that album) revealed a definite pre-occupation with political concerns. I wondered, since he'd brought up the very subject, whether his writing for *Random Hold* would continue to reflect these concerns. It would seem inevitable, I suggest. The lyrics for *Listen Now* were too pertinent and forceful to imply that they were written to comply with any concept of Manzanera's design.

'The thing about that album', he says, 'is that without Ian and myself, without our ideas and lyrics behind it, that album would not have come out the way it did at all. Phil doesn't have any contact, any relationship with what's really going on in this area. I'm not suggesting that Phil – or anybody else for that matter – should have any definite political views. I happen to have definite views. So does Ian, and to a certain extent our ideas overlap. Phil is really the typical good-time, easy-going nice fellow, whose worries about what goes on in the rest of the world are absolutely minimal. Fair enough. The problem is that he doesn't, have any particular urge, therefore, to say anything. I do. That's why those songs on *Listen Now* were the way they were. That's why the lyrics on the songs we wrote for *K-Scope* are the way they are'.

Personally – and I know we're going to have some Godalmighty rows in *Random Hold* about this – I don't see any reason to change that emphasis. There are enough good love songs in the world for me not to have to write any more. If somebody wants to write a love song for the group, fair enough. I know what I want to write about. And that is maybe going to feel uncomfortable for people to sing and play. Simon admitted last year when he had to sing the lyrics we'd written for *Listen Now* that he didn't know why they were the way they were. But the two songs on *Listen Now*, which were the most overtly political – the title track and *Law and Order* – were written out of very personal concern for what was happening. Ian wrote the lyric for *Listen Now* in a very depressed state. As a general sort of warning. It was written when the *National Front*, in particular, were beginning to make some headway. And the general feeling was pretty desperate'.

I MENTIONED EARLIER that *Random Hold* had recently been written about as part of a vague movement that included the likes of *The Pop Group*, *This Heat* and *Cabaret Voltaire*, and that they were unhappy with the comparison. 'We might have come from the same starting points', MacCormick explains. 'And there are some personal connections, but I don't think we are in any way remotely connected to any of them'.

'We're simply not as esoteric as them', says David Rhodes. 'I can't see any of those groups really selling many records. And we want to sell thousands and thousands of records and become very successful'.

'Most of those bands, I think', observes Ferguson, 'with some possible exceptions like *The Pop Group*, would probably be happy being fringe theatre companies or the musical equivalents'.

'There's no point', MacCormick elaborates, 'in getting involved in the record business, with management companies and record companies and the whole lot, unless you want to make money. It's a business that thrives on turnover and sales. And you have to accept a certain complicity in the business machinery. Otherwise you have to be satisfied with doing things on a very small scale with rotten equipment. If you want to achieve something more ambitious, you have to get involved where the big money is. With the major companies. It's as simple as that. And you are prepared to make the concessions and the compromises that signing a deal with a major company will probably involve?'

'I don't think there's any danger in making a compromise if you can benefit from it', Rhodes argues. 'I think the danger to a group always comes after they're successful. It's a question of whether you're able to remain as true to your ideals as you were when you started out. There are so few bands that have made it in a big way who've been able to keep up their original impetus, to retain those qualities that originally gave them that genesis of interest. There are very few who have managed to stay true to their original ideals once they've become successful'.

'That's when the pressure is brought to bear on a band by the record companies', adds MacCormick. 'You've had a successful album, and they want you to stick to the same magic formula. And you do the tour and the audience only wants to hear what they already know...'

'Yes', says Ferguson. 'That might be the case. But I really can't see *Random Hold* doing a 12th anniversary album, you know. The possibility is too remote. At the same time I'm not putting a time limit on it. It's all a question of what actually opens up for us. But I don't intend carrying on something once I've become bored with it'.

'It's all very well saying that now', MacCormick reminds them (your reporter has taken a back seat in the discussion by this stage leaving the lads to get on with their group therapy session). 'It'll be much more difficult to act upon that when there's guaranteed money coming in, and you've got your flat, and your television games . . . the pressure will be on us if we become only half as successful as we hope we'll be. It's not impossible that we'll end up like every other rock band in the world. We'll think it's so great to be successful that the temptations will probably be too great to resist . . .'

'Yes', says Rhodes, a little peeved, 'But we're fairly bloody-minded . . .'

'Ahhhh', scorns MacCormick, 'you come across other bands who've been fairly bloody-minded. Look what's happened to them. It's a matter of knowing that you've got money coming in . . you know that you can afford certain things. You want a new car? You want a new guitar? Off you go to the management company and there you'll find the money for it. And you try to get out of that. And don't tell me that you won't be a problem. You won't give up all that easily just for your ideals'.

'Yeah', Ferguson says, as miffed as Rhodes (but humorously, you understand), 'But we're not asking for an incredible, unbelievable amount of money. Just enough to function on. I mean, if anybody came along and offered us a quarter of a million quid, it would be very nice .. but...'

'Come on, David', laughs MacCormick. 'Let's face it, if anybody offered us that kind of money, nobody in this band would turn it down. We'd all be thinking – 'Ah, my own pinball machine. A jukebox. My own *Seawolf* television game! Let's face it, when it comes down to it, we're all as mercenary as the next man. We'd just find ways of justifying it, that's all'.

'I'd like a red sports car', says David Leach. We all look at him.

'Bloody 'ell', says Ainley. 'You don't say, much, but when you do, you really come out with some gems'.

I ask if anyone would like a drink and turn off the tape recorder.

APPENDIX 15: *RANDOM HOLD* UK PRESS

RANDOM HOLD... 1983 NEW WAVE... MOVED FROM TAPE TO LIVE MUSIC... AGAINST THE MASTURBATORY DISCO EXPERIENCE
The Chris Welch Interview, *Musicians Only*, 22nd December 1979
IS THERE STILL room for experimentation with rock music, or is it doomed to be held tightly in the grip of dictates of fashion? There is nothing intrinsically wrong with fashion as a form of entertainment and light relief from daily pressures and responsibilities. But if rock becomes too bound up in ephemera and froth, then it does so at its peril. For trends tend to die very suddenly and without warning, leaving many a chief advocate stranded and gasping for air. Ideas are seized upon like deposits of uranium and get exploited in a mad scramble.

What rock and all forms of popular music urgently require are prospectors, bold individuals who are-prepared for isolation and hardship as they explore unknown territory. Without the prospectors, then reserves of ideas and energy can sink to dangerously low levels.

Among the most hopeful explorers to surface in recent months have been the studious but reasonably merry men of *Random Hold*.

While they tinker with synthesisers, and use guitars as sound machines rather than solo instruments, they are also known to play a mean game of pool. *Random Hold* have just completed their first major tour, supporting *XTC* where they got a fair hearing from partisan audiences and sympathetic reviews. They are still crystallising their direction and attempting to hone their stage act, which they admit falls somewhat short in the superspectacular department. But the essence is that *Random Hold* have put together an interesting and intelligent combination of sounds and influences. The beat is solid (but don't call it disco).

The vocals from cropped-haired David Rhodes are precise and very British, while the drums, synthesisers, bass and keyboards form a powerful, attacking raft of sound. The founder members of the band are Rhodes and another Dave – Ferguson, whose keyboards, include *Mini* and *Micro Korgs*, *Logan String Melody*, *Wasp synthesiser* and various stylophones. Rhodes plays *Fender Stratocaster*, *Fender Jazzmaster* and *Dan Armstrong* see-through guitars.

Was the XTC tour a useful exercise for the band?

'We learnt a lot of simple things most pop musicians know about anyway', said Ferguson. 'We learned what it's like to play in a different place every night, which we've never done before. And we learnt an enormous amount about how to present ourselves on stage. By the end of the tour we were a lot looser and there were more attempts to project'.

Did they regard themselves as rock musicians?

'We'd never considered it before the tour, although Peter and Bill did because they'd done a lot of it before in different groups', said Rhodes. 'We had naive views that you just went along and played and people would naturally get involved very quickly. And, of course, they don't. They go to see a show a performance. You have to be careful not to be too self-indulgent. Through your actions, you should be handing over, giving the music'.

I remembered them saying once before that they wanted people to dance to their music. Did this still apply?

'We say that people should feel the music. Body movement is an essential part of rock. We want to disturb people's emotions', said Rhodes.

Did they think they had managed to do that on the XTC tour.

'Well, it wasn't strictly our audience. We were there as guests. Paying guests! Sss, ssssh!'

There was much hearty laughter at this musician's joke. Ferguson felt that it was good experience to play to an audience that wasn't strictly prepared to see them. They had received some critical praise along with somewhat paternal suggestions about how they could improve. I wondered how they reacted to people telling them what they should and should not do.

'The reviews have been quite fair', thought Rhodes. 'They've said we've got a lot of work to do and that's true. We've got to make the thing – an act. Having got involved in rock music we have to accept the gradings, the criteria. But it would be nice to start breaking down the categories and cubby-holes they put you in, so that people aren't always just going to see guitar and keyboard soloists'.

Said Ferguson: 'It's a shame people don't judge each individual piece of work put out on its merits. I can say there is a recent Cliff Richard single which was great, and so was the first Specials' single. You should be able to pick and choose from any area and judge them individually. But people find it a lot easier to associate with groups or cliques. We'd like to appeal to a very large cross-section'.

What was the basis of the Random Hold sound?

Said Rhodes: 'It's rather pompous to talk about our 'sound'. But we use all four instruments working towards one end, in a democratic way. The four sounds are supposed to meld together. We're not keyboard or guitar based as such. Our ideas haven't changed about that, but they've been damaged slightly by involvement with The Biz. But that is to be expected. We get people telling us what to do all the time. They say we are 'old-hat' and that we've got nothing to offer'.

I was astonished to hear this as I was under the impression that Random Hold represented the New Wave of 1983, at least until August of that year.

432

'Because we don't fit into any of the current trends, they don't know what to call us. We're not on any bandwagon', said Ferguson firmly. 'It's an incredible thing. As soon as you use synthesisers, people start saying you sound like *Pink Floyd*, or *Genesis* or Gary Numan or *Kraftwerk*. I don't think we sound like any of those. Neither are we mechanical nor flashy. What we are doing musically is very crude, and we're trying not to be dry about it. We're not playing *Mekanik* music. It's emotional music. Some nights things go better than others.

'I used to get very upset if things went wrong at just one gig', said Rhodes. 'I'd brood over it. But you learn to accept that while you'd love each show to be complete, it doesn't always happen!' Rhodes burst into highly emotional, unmechanical roars of laughter. 'That's why we go out every night and play. We're searching for that one magical gig when everything goes right'.

Originally the band were going to release a double album as they felt every track was so important, but eventually they put out their EP Avalanche on Polydor which sold for a mere £1.49. The tracks included Meat, The Ballad, Avalanche, Film Music and the popular Montgomery Clift. The EP was produced by Peter Hammill.

'The album, when we do it, will be called *The View From Here* said Rhodes, 'and that will be out in February. Working with Peter was good, although some people don't think it was the best production in the world. But it isn't flashy and it was true to the way we were. We've actually changed quite a lot in our approach since. But in no way are we ashamed of the EP. It was the first time we'd ever put anything on record'.

David Ferguson (26) does not claim to be a gifted synthesiser player but uses the keyboards as a tonal colour machine. He was previously a member of the experimental group Manscheinen, and at one time studied Serbo-Croat at the London School of Slavonic Studies. He also taught Drama at my old school, Catford Secondary. David Rhodes (23) was also a member of Manscheinen and studied Fine Arts in Leeds for a while before being lured to the glitter of stardom in rock 'n' roll.

'I like to think I approach the guitar in the same way as Dave', said Rhodes. 'Just making sounds. I don't know any licks or standards'.

Did this mean he couldn't play Johnny B Goode?

'No way. I once spent a long time learning *Storm In A Teacup*…. do you remember that pop song?'

'Vaguely', I lied. This was a cue for Rhodes to start singing.

'Pitter, patter, pitter, patter', he warbled blithely. It seemed unlikely that *Random Hold* would fare too well in the Eurovision Song Contest.

Once David had been restrained from singing any further, I asked them how these two unlikely experimentalists had come together.

"Originally, we did experimental things with tapes', explained Rhodes. 'David played stylophone and an old bass guitar which was barely in tune. We were just making noises, and the idea was to do workshop things. We had the idea the audience should be able to switch on and off various elements in the music. We never got that together. The idea was they could control what we were playing through switching or by giving them buzzers and bells for instructions. The concept came from film, where a movie goes to a certain point in the story line and then the audience can choose its ending'.

It struck me this could lead to anarchy and chaos.

'When it came to playing the workshops, the music went quite strongly and in fact we didn't want to leave it up to the audience to decide', admitted Rhodes. 'We wanted control. We ended up doing backing for a couple of small theatre shows. We also did our own show with slides, but decided that just playing to twenty people a night wasn't much fun for them or us, because everybody felt very self-conscious. We wanted to do some songs and that's how we got involved in rock music. But neither of us had really done anything before that. Initially the songs were very stilted. We used a rhythm box and would play and sing along to our tapes for a few months'.

Rhodes and Ferguson got in a guitarist and singer who worked with them for nine months, and a drummer was added. Then, after some changes, they ended up with Bill MacCormick on bass guitar who had previously worked with Quiet Sun, Matching Mole, Gong, This Heat and 801. They went through a couple of drummers and the original guitarist, and finally brought in Peter Phipps, who had previously worked with the legendary G Band.

'It was only when Bill joined that we stopped using backing tapes', said Rhodes. 'We realised that with an audience, we needed flexibility of tempos, depending on the vibe. That's why we moved from taped to live music. We still use them for linkage, but not for effects because with voltage supplies varying you never know if you are going to be in tune with them. That was a problem we used to have. We'd be miles out. And to use a rhythm box you need incredibly close monitoring. We used to give our old drummer headphones when we were using tapes, just to keep him in time. None of our previous drummers could keep in time with rhythm boxes or tapes, except for Pete. Trouble is rhythm boxes don't swing!" said Rhodes.

A lot of their songs seemed to be concerned with the environment and put in a social context. Was this correct?

'We try not to be specific', explained Rhodes. 'We're in an urban environment, and we try to recognise the emotions that occur within that. We don't say these buildings are wrong, or cars are bad. Our songs suggest the idea of people surviving in these circumstances, trying to cope. It's dodgy territory, you see. We might end up saying people ought to be doing something else, which is not true. Things are as they are. We are not preaching revolution. All you get from revolution is a state of affairs

434

equally bad if not worse because the equilibrium has gone. We recognise these things and hope other people will lock on to it'.

Said Ferguson: 'Our piece called *Central Reservation*, however, is very objective. It is about speed, rush and collapse. Motorways can be dreadful places, but they can be so exhilarating. You should be able to enjoy your surroundings. Even industrial buildings can be beautiful. There is a bridge on the M40 that seems to hang suspended over the road, and every time I look at it, I think, 'that is marvellous!' Music is the same as building. You have an idea then go out and construct it. Our writing is structured. The only reason some building is awful is because they have not been thought out. The great thing about working in the music environment is it does afford you extra time to think about what's going on around you. I had to catch the Tube in the rush hour recently, and I'd never had to experience it before because of my job. But you can see what society has constructed which takes over from the individual. Nobody seems to take any responsibility. But when you are on a stage, you are in a way, responsible towards the audience and you're trying to share an experience. You've got to work at pulling that together'.

Did the rest of the band share their convictions:

'Oh yes', choruses the two Daves. 'They certainly aren't doing it for the money! Their input is huge', added Rhodes.

'The great thing is playing to audiences who really care', insisted Ferguson. 'Playing those kind of gigs like Friars Aylesbury is really good for us and Peter's audience are very fair. They will get into the support act'.

I had described Random Hold's music as being somewhat disco-oriented, at least as far as the rhythm section was concerned.

'Disco is maybe a bit too specialised', thought Rhodes. 'We're more into the body feeling, and rock is body music'.

Ferguson was more emphatic. 'We definitely do not have anything in common with disco. People treat something that is very ordinary and try to make something special out of it. I find it pretty weird that we should devote large periods of time to dancing to type music, when you are not getting any emotional feedback. You are just performing, and if you are into performing, then for God's sake go out and do something real'.

I wasn't suggesting that Random Hold were a disco band, but that they used the disco licks as a pulse.

Once again Rhodes was more acquiescent. 'We don't actually change rhythms during songs. But I don't see that as restrictive'.

Weren't they making intelligent use of a fashionable rhythm? This seemed to cause Dave Ferguson's hackles to rise perceptibly.

'Only one song that we do has got a disco rhythm and that's *Central Reservation*. On the EP some of the songs are waltzes. So? That's not particularly fashionable. And they're much slower than disco tunes'.

It seemed I had caused a certain amount of chagrin within the ranks by harping on this aspect and apologised. But it was no use. Dave Ferguson aimed a punch at my head, and Rhodes began turning over the office furniture. We fought steadily for some ten minutes and then decided to continue the conversation on a more rational level.

'I just thought it was an interesting aspect of the music', I panted, wiping blood from my eyes and rearranging the desks and chairs. 'We do want to groove', said Rhodes conceding my point, 'although that is a very old-fashioned term'.

'You see', said Ferguson, breathing heavily, 'The discotheque is not a shared experience, it's a masturbatory experience, if you'll excuse the term. All they are concerned with is their own dance routines and they don't give a (expletive deleted) what the music is like as long as it has the regulation beats per minute. It's gone up to 132 now. A couple of years ago it was all 126'.

So they were experts in disco. In fact, Random Hold are bringing back the fresh winds of experimentation to rock that has been in the stranglehold of formalised amateurism and bland machine-tooled pop. There are no categories for Random Hold's music, and I refuse to invent one. Go and see them, and find out for yourselves in a shared experience at your nearest human communications centre.

RANDOM NOISE
How Random Hold learnt to live without tonal experimentation.
Hugh Fielder, *Sounds*, 22nd March 1980

MOST BANDS can point to a positive influence that propelled them out of the closet to face the world as a rock and roll band – years ago it used to be Chuck Berry but these days it's more likely to be David Bowie... or maybe the *Jags*(!): But *Random Hold's* formative influence was a negative one. David Ferguson and David Rhodes went along to see *801* featuring Phil Manzanera and Brian Eno at the *Queen Elizabeth Hall* in September 1976 with high expectations. 'I was looking forward to some musical experimentation but I found it a very staid affair', remembers Rhodes. 'There didn't seem to be an element of risk involved', adds Ferguson.

I remember the gig as an enjoyable one and certainly in the light of Manzanera's retreat to the bland security of *Roxy Music* it seems a positively adventurous step. But then I didn't go out and form a band the following day. The two Daves did. 'That gig was the catalyst we needed', says Rhodes. 'The two of us got together and started making noises immediately afterwards'.

They're starting to get somewhere with their noises now. *Random Hold* have been supporting Peter Gabriel on his tour and I met them over breakfast in the austere grandeur of the *North British Hotel* in Edinburgh, feeling a lot less paranoid about the length of my hair than I was the night before. But these skinheads are of the Mensa variety rather than the Mensi variety, thanks to the clean Dulwich College education that's shaped the vowels and minds of three quarters of them, and given them expectations.

The early expectations of the two Daves were of the tonal variety and the initial name they gave to their group, *Manscheinen*, is probably sufficient musical description in itself. They played four gigs in Rotherhithe to a total of 24 people. 'One gig was so bad we took the audience down to the pub for a drink instead', remembers Ferguson.

The name *Random Hold* was born soon after guitarist and vocalist Simon Ainley joined them – the two Daves were playing whatever they could lay their hands on around this time – but after another series of gigs they made the big decision to stop their tonal experimentation and see if they could write songs instead.

It was around this time that bassist Bill MacCormick, who'd played with *801* that fateful day and had also done time with *Quiet Sun*, *Matching Mole*, *Gong* and *This Heat* was induced to join up. He'd also shared the two Daves' Dulwich education (although their ages are such that the connection is more tenuous than you might imagine). Because of his seniority and his experience of the R&R system Bill was also appointed manager. He repaid the compliment by firing a succession of drummers and talking to bigger labels rather than the small independents they'd been in contact with before. 'But we still weren't smiling as yet', he says.

Nevertheless, the music was starting to take a more positive direction. Bowie's *Low* had given them all heart and after just one gig with a new line-up they found themselves signed to *Polydor*, aided by a magazine article that implied that *Polydor* were very interested in the band – they weren't that interested but they were after they read the article. Such is the power of the press. They recorded a single which they promptly rejected and then Bill fired another drummer and the second guitarist.

If that bemused *Polydor* a little the new drummer must have astonished them. He was Pete Phipps from the *Glitter Band!* A surreptitious look under the breakfast table reveals that Pete is wearing plimsolls and not 15-inch heels and silver lame trousers. And the story is already getting complicated enough without getting sidetracked, so I say little and keep scribbling between bites of toast and marmalade.

But by this time we've reached 1979 and there are no more line-up changes to come. Instead, there's a single called *Etceteraville* which the band didn't reject and which came out last October to the infinite delight of the 700 people who bought it. 'We wanted to record a double album to clear all the material we'd written and start afresh', says Dave Ferguson. 'But it didn't work out that way. We had only played one gig with Pete drumming and we'd signed to *Hit and Run* management who also manage Peter Hammill. So we started recording with him producing and he felt we should use some new songs as well'.

What eventually emerged was a five-track EP at the beginning of the year and their album, *The View From Here*, a few weeks ago. I'd advise new listeners to start with the EP as it's more adventurous than the album which is harder to assimilate. But better still go and see them live first. They've played only a handful of gigs so far but they are planning to do a lot over the coming months. And I suspect that that, more than all the other changes they've been through, will refine their sound and direction. Already they sound more accessible than they do on record.

'We want to get played on the radio now', says Dave Rhodes. 'Once you're playing you want to be heard. Dave Rhodes is starting to get into the lyrical side of things and we're getting more melodic'.

But Bill sums up the band's intentions best. 'It's about taking chances and risks. If there ever became a *Random Hold* formula it would fall apart quickly'.

APPENDIX 16: *RANDOM HOLD* - ALBUM REVIEWS

RANDOM HOLD, *The View From Here*, John Orme,
Melody Maker, 23rd February 1980

RANDOM HOLD can claim the rare and satisfying distinction that their music matches and fulfils their name and all its resonances: a concern with the mechanisms and components of rock, a bleak lyrical aspect and instrumental bias leaning towards synthesiser disturbance and guitar distortion, and the occupation of a musical quarter once populated by bands like *Matching Mole* and Phil Manzanera's *801*. Bill MacCormick, resolute bassman with both those bands, provides the direct link with such a past, but (with only minor grumbles) the band and producer Peter Hammill have produced a work of promise and reward in an area often skirted but rarely entered with conviction.

The album, the band's first, has a compact thematic feel, from David Ferguson's beguiling synth jitter which opens *What Happened* to the stark, conclusive siren warning that halts *The View From Here*. Hammill's production gives the band a thick, gutsy feel, tucking fat chunks of David Rhodes' guitar on either side of the stereo balance and characteristically isolating the strained, pained vocals within the body of the mix. The band keep a rough vocal edge, varying in feel from dislocated Brian Eno to same of John Lydon's more measured work on the *PIL Metal Box* outing. 'We are caught between discipline and desire', runs the vocal turbulence on *Dolphin Logic*, a track that works admirably, the vocal agonies offset by an instrumental track that is just too solid, adding an uneasy, jarring dimension in the song's neurosis.

Random Hold's themes are not new – they concern themselves with the future prospect of mind-control states (*Etceteraville*), and the current problems of individuals hiding and seeking in increasingly alienating societies. But the band's considered, highly intelligent use of the musical hardware at their disposal to counterpoint and embellish the lyrical themes of the songs is a major strength. The band's principal quality is the achievement of maintaining a progressive instrumental stance without turning to traditional solos or lengthy 'work-out' sections, and communicating the message of their choice, a largely dour and doomy view, with a variety of music that sparks with a crisp intelligence.

A track like *Etceteraville* covers the band's main strength and weakness – the lyric is trite and superficial, but the balance of words and music succeeds far better than the vision of, say, Bill Nelson's *Red Noise* album which achieved a result as foreign and distracted as the future fears of the composer. The three extended tracks that make up side two, headed by

Etceteraville, represent the album's most complete achievement, allowing an unhurried development of the band's concerns and fears.

I find their message one-dimensionally pessimistic and fashionably future imperfect (after-alienate mints, anyone?) but I'm a sucker for the way they tell it.

OUT OF LOVE
Paul Suter, *Sounds*, 8th March 1980
I'VE BEEN LOOKING FORWARD to this album for a long time, so it's particularly saddening that the deed has failed to live up to the promise. The introductory *Etceteraville* single (also included here) was blessed with the excellent *Precarious Timbers* on its B side, and the ensuing five track *Avalanche* EP was simply stunning from beginning to end, a frightening blend of power and mesmeric intensity.

So what went wrong? Well, not exactly wrong, but awry. The single, EP and album all come from the same sessions, so maybe it's just a case of miscalculation stripping the album of *Random Hold's* peaks.

The music is stark and eerie, couched in David Ferguson's distant synth, an insistent presence akin to a suspense thriller soundtrack. Bill MacCormick's grumbling bass adds further texture whilst Pete Phipps cracks out the rhythm that intensifies the effectiveness of their moodmaking. David Rhodes' guitar is the primary weapon, its assault capacity best captured in the blistering violence that terminates *With People (Out Of Love)*.

The opening *What Happened* brings early *Roxy Music* to mind with its bubbling, insistent synth and strange vocals, whilst the ensuing *Dolphin Logic* states *Random Hold's* own case rather better. It's sinister and intense, building from doomy synth chords into a swirling storm of riffing and voices, only rivalled by side two's *With People (Out Of Love)* a mystic and distant piece that's simultaneously poignant and menacing. Elsewhere though, nothing really happens. *Central Reservation* and the title track are both intermittently impressive, but not sufficiently so, and the overall result is disappointing.

Random Hold are a stunning band, they will scare the living daylights out of Peter Gabriel on his current tour, but this album is not the masterstroke it should have been. For a mere £1.49 the five track *Avalanche* EP is the manifesto you should be examining, because *Random Hold* deserve your support and *The View from Here* isn't the way to win it.

RANDOM HOLD, The View From Here, Graham Lock, *NME*,
15th March 1980
RANDOM HOLD, YOU MIGHT SAY, are red-blooded artisans where *Magazine* are anaemic artists. Practitioners of a sturdily dramatic music that pulses in

fine robust fashion even while the lyrics make an ineffectual nod towards the same bleak todays and tomorrows that trouble Devoto's devotions.

The vocals – wrenching white soulful – impress too, but the strengths of this album are primarily instrumental. Through the ornate crescendoes of *Silver Spoons, Golden Tongues* and moody atmospherics of *With People (Out of Love)* to the title track's swiftly shifting rhythmic flow, the music retains its ominous edge.

The staunch basis for this authority comes from Peter Phipps (ex-*Glitter Band* – sussed you Pete!) flaying the drums like a manic carpet beater, and ex-*Matching Mole* and *801*-er Bill MacCormick, whose bass growls and prowls with customary aplomb.

Complementing them are David Rhodes, whose dark chunky guitar occasionally flares with aggression, and David Ferguson on keyboards that flit and swoop, coax and grumble. And knitting all together with consummate skill is the subtle hand of producer Peter Hammill.

Random Hold do falter at times. *What Happened* builds well only to sag at the weak chorus, a fault that also afflicts the generally inane *Etceteraville*.

The odd lapse aside, *The View from Here* attacks with force and vitality. No new visions, but it runs full-pelt through that grey area where rock traditionally gets bogged down in orchestrations or ersatz jazziness, and emerges with most flags flying.

APPENDIX 17: RANDOM *HOLD* – NORTH AMERICAN PRESS

RANDOM HOLD TO OPEN SHOW FOR OLD FRIEND
Gail S Tagashira, *San Jose Mercury*, 20th June 1980

BOTH PETER GABRIEL'S BAND and *Random Hold* arrived from England five days ago, but after that, it's been each band for itself. Gabriel's the headliner on this concert tour, so he has two hours of stage cues, lighting effects and even a try-out performance near Los Angeles before his official opening here in San Jose, Saturday night. As the opening act, *Random Hold* has only 45 minutes onstage, almost nothing in the way of special effects.

The band finished a similar tour of England last week. So, to pass the time, all four musicians have been typical Los Angeles tourists for several days, enjoying the corniest sightseeing trips around Southern California.

'Isn't this great?' synthesizer and singer David Ferguson bubbled in his British accent, watching an *Ironside* rerun in his hotel room. 'The other night, we saw *The Shining*, then last night, we went to *Graumann's Chinese (Theater)* to look at footprints in the cement and today we're off to Disneyland. I hope they let us in. If we're not careful, suppose they don't admit us?'

Outside, the sun was shining and Ferguson said he missed the English rain. He's spent a fortune on tanning lotions. When *Random Hold* opens Peter Gabriel's show in the *Civic Auditorium*, it won't be just the band's Bay area visit. 'It'll be our first gig in the States – ever', Ferguson said.

Nothing has been handed to the band or been easy despite the impressive track record of its members. When Brian Eno's temporary band, *801*, made its final performance, with Phil Manzanera sitting in as guest performer (*Ed.* WtF? Let us not even go there), Ferguson and guitarist David Rhodes decided something was missing at the final concert. The next day, on September 4th, 1976, the two set out to discover the missing element.

Rhodes had studied fine arts in Leeds and London. It seemed logical for him to sing and play guitar. Ferguson had studied Serbo-Croat at the *London School of Slavonic and East European Studies*, worked as a sound engineer and written scores for theater productions in Edinburgh, London and Stoke. Long determined to remain a non-musician, he broke down and bought an old bass guitar and a stylophone. Together, Ferguson and Rhodes formed *Manscheinen*, a group devoted to experimental music. Tapes were recorded, mailed to record companies and ignored. They wrote the soundtrack for a puppet theater production titled *The Long and Lonely*

Voyage of the Sole Spermatozoa. When *Manscheinein* quietly faded into the London fog, hardly a soul noticed.

Early in 1978, former *801* singer arid guitarist Simon Ainley was recruited, along with a drummer – the first of several – and *Random Hold* was formed, to underwhelming corporate response. 'In England', Ferguson recalled, 'with the punk thing, so popular at the time, if you weren't punk, it took forever to get the labels to hear you. Now it's ska'.

Forced to take action to survive, bassist and financier Bill MacCormick allowed himself to be drafted in a moment of weakness. A cabinet shuffle followed, complete with dismissals of managers and drummers. To add an element of new technology, former *Plessey Electronics* drummer David Leach was introduced. After more tapes, a few performances and word of mouth, *Random Hold* finally signed a recording contract. Then Ainley and Leach left. The new manager decided that what the band needed was a good looker, some glamor. Enter Pete Phipps, the tall drummer formerly with Gary Glitter and the *G Band*.

Through Gabriel, the band connected with Peter Hammill, who produced record after record – albums, singles, extended-plays, 12-inch mini-albums, in the rural setting of *Startling Studios*. Gabriel was an early supporter of the band and is now regarded as a true friend. On the recent Gabriel-*Random Hold* tour in England, he called them 'one of the best bands he'd heard in the last year'. Without hoopla, the once-charismatic performer with *Genesis* quickly scooted on and offstage minus regalia, costumes and disguises before anyone realized who he was.

'Fashion's really boring', Ferguson said, thinking about *Random Hold's* stage personae. 'It's always last year's thing anyway. David and I wear parachute trousers because they're the most comfortable to move in. Bill's always got a hood on and Pete wears tennis gear because he prefers playing tennis to playing drums'.

Random Hold's been compared to *Pink Floyd*, David Bowie and *Roxy Music*.

'Different people read different things into different songs. We like to think we're fairly eclectic rockers. Except for knowing Peter quite well, we're not influenced by *Genesis*'. Both bands play 'rock with a slightly new angle to it', the synthesizer specialist said. 'It's not get down and boogie. It's fairly real'.

Shows are Saturday at 8 p.m. in San Jose *Civic Auditorium*, Sunday, and Monday at 8 p.m. in *Fox Warfield Theater*, Market and Sixth Streets in San Francisco. Tickets are $8.50 and $9.50.

FLEDGLING RANDOM HOLD DARES TO TRY SOME ORIGINAL SOUNDS
By Larry Kelp, *Oakland Tribune*, 27th June 1980

THE BAND IS *RANDOM HOLD*, and it plays modern tribal music for the new suburbs. 'We weren't musicians, really', David Ferguson said. 'We started with pre-recorded tapes of insects and vacuum cleaners slowed down, that sort of thing'. Instead of joining the rest of the new wave crowd, English avant-rock band *Random Hold* attracted the attention of the art and classical-rock intelligentsia of Europe.

Random Hold seems to have all the credentials needed to score big. All except one: it refuses to make pop songs. Instead, the quartet has plunged into the nether reaches of sound, playing quirky games with instrumental textures and shifting exotic rhythms, and only a hint of new wave straightforwardness.

'If we'd gone out to be a hit, we'd have done more blues licks and disco beats, a few guitar, solos and grown our hair longer', electronic keyboardist Ferguson quipped while in San Francisco for the group's first local concert earlier this week. The band had been the opening act for cult hero Peter Gabriel. That English star had heard *Random Hold*, liked the musicians' attitude, and hired them to open his English tour, rehired them for his present American tour, and will probably drag them across Europe later in the summer. Gabriel cares enough to show up early at each concert and introduce *Random Hold* to the audience: 'They're one of the best bands I've seen in a long time'. Not bad for a group founded by two total amateurs.

The debut album, just released in the United States, *Etceteraville* (on *Passport Records*), is not the most comfortable listening matter to drop onto the stereo after a hard day at the steel mill. The sounds are quite reminiscent of the Bowie Eno-*Roxy Music-Tuxedomoon* brands of dark, compelling sounds that take a lot of patience to appreciate. This is not the finished product of a mature band. It's a first step, with some lapses and loose ends. But it's also fresh. As with the band's concert here, the music is exciting because it does pursue a newer direction. Listen to the instrumental track on *Montgomery Clift*. At first it is irritating, but within moments it draws you into its heavily rhythmic web…

… 'We got into our style for the same reason the new wave people were into theirs', Ferguson explained. 'We didn't like what was available in music, the tired old men trotting out the same old recycled classical riffs. You know – *Yes, Emerson, Lake and Palmer*. But unlike new wave, we weren't trying to push social causes while going backwards to the old styles of early rock, the rockabilly, ska and punk. For me, the *Sex Pistols'* album was great, and everything else since then has been copies. It's hard trying to come up with something new, but it's far more interesting. We've been listening to folk music of other cultures from Albania to Africa, with rhythm-based songs'.

WEIRD ENGLISH
Random Hold by Joan Tortorici Ruppert, *Illinois Entertainer*, August 1980

EERIE BUT ORDINARY, *Random Hold's* pre-show soundcheck is running smoothly enough. Songs are started, abruptly stopped as problems are pinpointed and hopefully corrected within the sizeable limitations of the *Uptown Theater*. 'Oh, what happened to you?' sings David Rhodes, *Random Hold's* guitarist/vocalist who can remind your ears of a young Bryan Ferry. His lyrics reverberate through the empty balconies while behind the stage curtain Peter Gabriel and his drummer break into impromptu time steps.

Later in the evening Gabriel will introduce *Random Hold* as one of his favorite bands. A back-up spot on a Gabriel tour can be quite an opportunity for a new group, so *Random Hold* is working hard to make the best of good situation.

'During this tour I suppose we expect to meet the beginnings of our American audience', says *Random Hold* keyboard man David Ferguson. 'I think we'd like to lay the groundwork so we can come back in the fall and do a small tour of clubs, preferably with a new album to promote'...

... While this was a positive move for the band, other deals were not working out as well. They had already signed with *Polydor Records* in England, hoping to press a double album 'to get everything we'd written out of the way', but *Polydor* flatly refused.

'So, when it came time for an 'official' U. S. release *Polydor* used a mixture of previous English releases and one track that was never released anywhere', explains Ferguson. The end result was *Etceteraville*, a single album and their only U.S. vinyl thus far. Not at all what you'd call easy listening, *Etceteraville* mingles steady heartbeat rhythms with a slightly twisted vocal viewpoint throughout. Lyrics lean toward the dark side, satirically so on their memorable title track.

'Yes, it is kind of depressing', agrees Ferguson with nothing short of a grin. 'We're trying to depopulate the world through suicide. You should hear the English releases, they were more depressing!' Taking their mental health into their own hands, *Passport Records* bought the arty *Etceteraville* from *Polydor U.K.*

'But we don't know who our next album will be with', admits Ferguson. 'We think *Passport* wants us to stay, but these things can be very complicated'. He takes a rare pause for breath. 'What's not complicated is our music. Neither David (Rhodes) nor I classify ourselves as immensely competent. I can't play whizzy solos and I never want to. I don't think rock 'n' roll deserves that. The last thing the world needs is another Rick Wakeman. So we tried to get the best, most flexible rhythm section we could, which we found in Bill and Pete (Phipps, ex-Gary Glitter drummer) to play very skillfully under what David and I were doing mechanically and straight. If we had a rhythm section playing as badly as David and I, we'd end up sounding like Gary Numan. We don't want to sound like robots because our songs are about feelings, emotions'.

MacCormick adds that the U.S. is a great place to be different and still be heard. 'And in England, most bands just wind up playing ska music', says Ferguson disdainfully. 'That's what's expected of you. It's really very boring, just reviving what people did better twenty years ago. I admire the *Two-Tone* politics of blacks and whites together, but the music is ho-hum'.

Instead, *Random Hold* finds more inspiration in ethnic folk music, picking up on the 'rhythmic ideas, droning tones' found there. In this respect they are traveling on the same wavelength as Peter Gabriel's latest offerings, which might partially account for Gabriel's embracing them as a back-up band during his current tour. As a matter of fact, David Rhodes added guitar tracks to many cuts on Gabriel's newest album and even David Ferguson, the 'non-musician' got a liner credit for his screeches on *Biko*.

'Working with Peter is fine', says Ferguson, 'but sometimes it gets a bit frustrating when interviewers talk with us and ask us questions about Gabriel's set'. Such are the thorns on the paths of new groups – especially for groups that are virtually unknown. And in the case of *Random Hold*, a lot of people just don't know what to make of this strange quartet that doesn't give a hoot about convention.

Sure, they've been called 'new wave maturing" by *Record World*, but just how vague can you get? Predictably, Ferguson goes it one better. 'Of course we're trying to avoid all stereotypes. After this tour I suppose if there's one stereotype, it will be that we're weird and very English. And I don't mind that at all'.

RANDOM HOLD Etceteraville
by Gary Kahn, *City Magazine*, August 1980

RANDOM HOLD WAS FORMED in concept in early 1978 at which time the band's personnel included ex-*801* guitarist/vocalist Simon Ainley along with Dave Rhodes and Dave Ferguson from the short-lived experimental band *Manscheinen*. Since that time *Random Hold* has undergone various comings and goings (Ainley left '78, and drummer Peter Phipps from Gary Glitter's band was added). The present line-up includes founding members Rhodes and Ferguson, drummer Phipps and bassist Bill MacCormick who, at age 28, has been a member of *Quiet Sun, Matching Mole, Gong, This Heat* and *801*, and has also performed and/or composed on three Brian Eno albums (*Ed.* Eh?) as well as Phil Manzanera's *Diamond Head, 801 Live* and *K-Scope*, to name a few.

The band's eclectic sound reflects its members' diverse musical backgrounds. The songs on *Etceteraville* (what a great name) are at times peaceful and serene (as on *Precarious Timbers*) and at other times they are intensely urgent and forceful as on *What Happened, Montgomery Clift* or *Silver Spoons* where the music takes on an ominous bodeful aspect.

It's stirring mood music that has a way of putting the listener's head into some unusually interesting places. *Random Hold* traverses some truly exciting musical terrain here. *Film Music* is one of the most moving cuts with its shadowy surreal disposition and pensive lyrics:

'No future anymore,
He's working to forget,
She lives with someone else,
Unable to remember what they felt'

On songs like these an atmosphere of sullen resignation pervades and the effect is overpowering. Keyboard man David Ferguson obviously knows his craft well and is quite adept at creating emotionally charged imagery through his masterful use of the synthesizer which almost seems calculated to induce altered mental states.

Etceteraville straddles the middle ground between pop and experimental music and balances Brian Ferry-like vocals and David Rhodes churning guitar against the ever-present background of Ferguson's haunting synthesizer.

APPENDIX 18: HUGH HOPPER'S BASS EXERCISES
(See page 138)

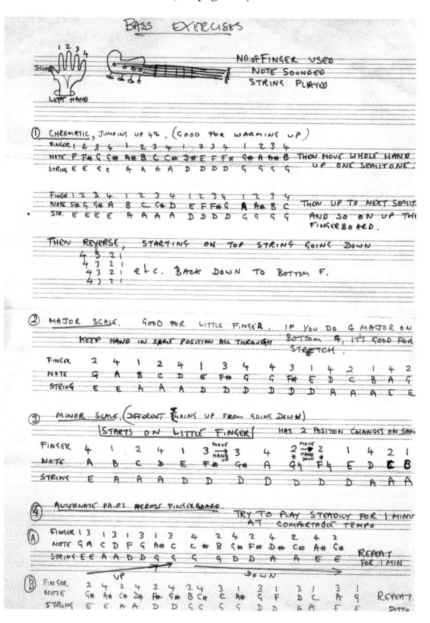

448

(5) THIRD & FOURTH FINGER ONLY.   PLAYED SLOWLY FOR 1 MINUTE

FINGER	3	4	3	4	3	4	3	4
NOTE	G#	A	G#	D	F#	G	8	C
STRING	E	E	E	A	A	D	D	G	G

REPEAT 1 MIN.

(6) 6/8 EX   LEADS WITH LITTLE FINGER

(A)

FINGER	4	2	3	1	3	2
NOTE	D	G	G#	B	G#	G
STRINGS	A	E	E	A	E	E

REPEAT 1 MINUTE

THEN DO ON OTHER STRINGS

(B) INVERTED

FINGER	4	2	3	1	3	2
NOTE	A	C	C#	F#	C#	C
STRINS.	E	A	A	E	A	A

DITTO

(7) DIAGONALS

FINGER	4	3	2	1	2	3	4	1	2	3	4	3	2	1
NOTE	C	F#	C	F#	C	F#	C	A	F	C#	A	C#	F	A
STRING	G	D	A	E	A	D	G	G	D	A	E	A	D	G

REPEAT FOR 1 MINUTE

DISCOGRAPHY

Matching Mole (*CBS*), April 1972

O Caroline [D. Sinclair/R. Wyatt]
Instant Pussy [R. Wyatt]
Signed Curtain [R. Wyatt]
Part of the Dance [P. Miller]
Instant Kitten [R. Wyatt]
Dedicated to Hugh, but you weren't Listening [R. Wyatt]
Beer as in Braindeer [R. Wyatt]
Immediate Curtain [R. Wyatt]

Robert Wyatt - drums, voice, piano, *Mellotron*
Phil Miller - guitar
Bill MacCormick - bass
David Sinclair - piano, organ
Guest Super Star: Dave MacRae - electric piano

Little Red Record (*CBS*), November 1972

Starting in the middle of the day we can drink our politics away [D. MacRae/R. Wyatt]
March Ides [D. MacRae]
Nan True's Hole [P. Miller/R. Wyatt]
Righteous Rhumba [P. Miller/R. Wyatt]
Brandy as in Benj [D. MacRae]
Gloria Gloom [B. MacCormick/R. Wyatt]
God Song [P. Miller/R. Wyatt]
Flora Fidgit [B. MacCormick]
Smoke Signal [D. MacRae]

Robert Wyatt - drums, voice
Phil Miller - guitar
Dave MacRae - electric piano, organ
Bill MacCormick - bass
Brian Eno - VCS3 (on *Gloria Gloom*)
Der Mutter Korus: Alfreda Benge, Julie Christie, Dave Gale

BBC RADIO 1 LIVE IN CONCERT

BBC Radio 1 Live in Concert (*Windsong*), 1994
Paris Theatre, 27th July 1972

Instant Pussy [R. Wyatt]
Lything and Gracing [P/ Miller]
March Ides [D. MacRae]
Part of the Dance [P. Miller]
Brandy as in Benj [D. MacRae]

Robert Wyatt - drums, voice
Phil Miller - guitar
Dave MacRae - electric piano
Bill MacCormick - bass

Smoke Signals (*Cuneiform*), 2001

Intro
March Ides I [D. MacRae]
Smoke Rings [D. MacRae]
Nan True's Hole [P. Miller]
Brandy as in Benji [D. MacRae]
Electric Piano solo [D. MacRae]
March Ides II [D. MacRae]
Instant Pussy [R. Wyatt]
Smoke Signal [D. MacRae]
Lything & Gracing [P. Miller]

Robert Wyatt - drums, voice
Phil Miller - guitar
Dave MacRae - electric piano
Bill MacCormick - bass

March (*Cuneiform*), 2002

March Ides I [D. MacRae]
Instant Pussy [R. Wyatt]
Smoke Signal [D. MacRae]
Part of the Dance [P. Miller]
No 'Alf measures [R. Wyatt/K Ayers]
Lything & Gracing [P. Miller]
Waterloo Lily [D Sinclair]

Robert Wyatt - drums, voice
Phil Miller - guitar
Dave MacRae - electric piano
Bill MacCormick - bass

On the Radio (*Hux*), 2007

Various BBC studio recordings, Jan-July, 1972
March Ides I [D. MacRae]
Instant Pussy [R. Wyatt]
Smoke Signal [D. MacRae]
Part of the Dance [P. Miller]
No 'Alf measures [R. Wyatt/K Ayers]
Lything & Gracing [P. Miller]
Immediate Kitten [R. Wyatt]
Instant Pussy [R. Wyatt]
Lything & Gracing [P. Miller]
March Ides I [D. MacRae]
Part of the Dance [P. Miller]
Matching Mole:MacRae]

Robert Wyatt - drums, voice (all)
Phil Miller – guitar (all)
Bill MacCormick - bass (all)
David Sinclair - organ (2 & 5)
Dave MacRae - electric piano (all)

Matching Mole – Boxed Set (*Esoteric*), 2012

CD 1
Original album remastered plus
O Caroline/Signed Curtain (single)
Part of the Dance (extended version)
CD 2
Signed Curtain (Take 2)
Memories Membrane [H Hopper]
Part of the Dance (Take 1)
Horse [D Sinclair]
BBC John Peel recordings:
Immediate Kitten
March Ides/Instant Pussy/Smoke Signal

Robert Wyatt - drums, voice, piano, *Mellotron*
Phil Miller – guitar
Bill MacCormick - bass
David Sinclair - organ
Dave MacRae - electric piano

MATCHING MOLE'S
LITTLE RED RECORD

Little Red Records – Boxed set (*Esoteric*), 2012

CD 1
Original album re-mastered
CD 2
BBC In Concert
Instant Pussy/Lything and Gracing
March Ides
Part Of The Dance/Brandy As In Benj
Unreleased studio sessions:
Smoke Signal (Take Four)
Flora Fidget (Take Eight)
Mutter Korus

Robert Wyatt - drums, voice
Phil Miller - guitar
Dave MacRae - electric piano
Bill MacCormick – bass
Brian Eno - VCS3 (on *Gloria Gloom*)
Der Mutter Korus: Alfreda Benge, Julie
    Christie, Dave Gale

Mainstream (Island. also later re-releases), 1975

Sol Caliente [Manzanera]
Trumpets with Motherhood [Hayward]
Bargain Classics [Jarrett]
R.F.D. [Jarrett]
*Mummy was an Asteroid, Daddy was a Small
    Non-Stick Kitchen Utensil* [MacCormick]
Trot [Manzanera]
Rongwrong [Hayward]

Phil Manzanera – electric & treated 6 & 12
    string guitars, *Fender Rhodes* piano
Dave Jarrett – *Fender Rhodes* and *Steinway
    Grand* pianos, *Farfisa* and *Hammond* organs,
    VCS3
Bill MacCormick – electric & treated basses,
    backing vocals
Charles Hayward – drums, lead vocals,
    percussion, keyboards
Brian Eno – synthesizer, treatments &
    Oblique Strategies
Ian MacCormick – backing vocals

Diamond Head (Island also later re-releases), 1975

Frontera [Manzanera, & & W MacCormick, Wyatt]
Diamond Head [Manzanera]
Big Day [Manzanera, Eno]
The Flex [Manzanera]
Same Time Next Week [Manzanera, Wetton]
Miss Shapiro [Manzanera, Eno]
East of Echo [Manzanera]
Lagrima [Manzanera]
Alma [Manzanera, W. MacCormick]

Ruth is Stranger than Richard (Virgin), 1975

Soup Song [Brian Hopper, Wyatt]
Sonia [Mongezi Feza]
Team Spirit [W & I MacCormick, Manzanera, Wyatt]
Song for Che [Charlie Haden]
Muddy Mouse (a) [Fred Frith, Wyatt]
Solar Flares [Wyatt]
Muddy Mouse (b) [Frith, Wyatt]
5 Black Notes and 1 White Note [Jacques Offenbach; arr. Wyatt]
Muddy Mouse (c)/Muddy Mouth [Frith, Wyatt]

801 Live (Island, also later re-releases), 1976

Lagrima [Manzanera]
TNK (Tomorrow Never Knows) [Lennon, McCartney]
East of Asteroid [Manzanera, W MacCormick]
Rongwrong [Hayward, Eno]
Sombre Reptiles [Eno]
Baby's on Fire [Eno]
Diamond Head [Manzanera]
Miss Shapiro [Manzanera, Eno]
You Really Got Me [Ray Davies]
Third Uncle [Eno]

Phil Manzanera – guitar
Lloyd Watson – slide guitar, vocals
Francis Monkman – *Fender Rhodes* piano, *Clavinet*
Brian Eno – keyboards, vocals, synthesizers, guitar
Bill MacCormick – bass, vocals
Simon Phillips – drums, rhythm generator

Listen Now (Island, also later re-releases), 1976

Listen Now [I & W MacCormick, Manzanera]
Flight 19 [I MacCormick, Manzanera]
Island [Manzanera]
Law and Order [W MacCormick, Manzanera]
¿Que? [Manzanera]
City of Light [W MacCormick, Manzanera]
Initial Speed [Manzanera]
Postcard Love [W MacCormick, Manzanera]
That Falling Feeling (I MacCormick,
    Manzanera]

K-Scope (Polydor, also later re-releases), 1978

K-Scope [Manzanera]
Remote Control [I MacCormick]
Cuban Crisis [Manzanera, W MacCormick]
Hot Spot [Manzanera, I MacCormick]
Numbers [Manzanera, John Wetton]
Slow Motion TV [Manzanera, W
    MacCormick, Simon Ainley]
Gone Flying [Manzanera, W MacCormick]
N-Shift [Manzanera]
Walking Through Heaven's Door [Manzanera, W
    MacCormick]
You Are Here [Manzanera]

The View from Here (Polydor then Voiceprint)

1980/2001
14-track studio album
10-track final live performance Tower
Theatre, Philadelphia, July 10th, 1980

Over View (Voiceprint), 2001

17-tracks of unreleased demos

801 Live at Manchester (Expression), 2001

TNK (Tomorrow Never Knows)
Flight 19 [Manzanera, I MacCormick]
Listen Now [Manzanera, I & W MacCormick]
Law And Order [Manzanera, W MacCormick]
Diamond Head [Manzanera]
Out Of The Blue [Manzanera, B Ferry]
Remote Control [I MacCormick]
Miss Shapiro [Manzanera, E Eno]
You Really Got Me [Ray Davies]

Phil Manzanera – Guitars
Simon Ainley – Guitars & vocals
Bill MacCormick – Bass & vocals
Dave Skinner – Keyboards & vocals
Paul Thompson – Drums
Guests:
Andy Mackay – Saxes and oboe
Kevon Godley, Lol Crème – Backing vocals

INDEX

Milton Keynes UK
Ingram Content Group UK Ltd.
UKHW050206230824
447187UK00014B/150